Occult Arcana

Occult Arcana

A study of Mythology, Philosophy,
Theology, Theurgy, Symbolism, Science,
Western and Eastern Magic(k)

&

Parahistory, Parapsychology, Holidays,
Talismans, Spells, Curses, Psychic Abilities,
Demonology, and Alchemy

RYAN DANIEL GABLE

(c) 2024

Table of Contents

12) The Way of Living Resurrection

The Civilizing Way of Japan
The Civilizing Way of Egypt
The Civilizing Way of South & Central America
Levitating Stones
Mysteries of Xibalba & the Grand Medicine Society (*Midewiwin*)
Magdalin of West & East: *Vastu Shastra* & *Feng Shui*
The Oracle of Delphi
The Civilizing Way of Plant Spirits
Necromancy
General *Divination* & *Superstition*
Sacred Groves & Wise Trees

13) The Creation of Man, Earth & Natural Law AND Ancient Maps

The Dark Father & Triumphant Son
Pandora's Box & the Wooden Chest
Deluges of Water, Ice & Fire
Earth Crust Displacement & Ancient Maps
Biblical Science
Hopi Creationism
Maya Creationism
Norse Creationism
Egyptian Creationism
Codes, Commandments & Correlations
Commandments of Ancient India, Buddhism & Taoism
The Seven Esoteric Stages of Creation
The Seven Rosicrucian Aphorisms of Creation
The Seven Hermetic Principles as expressed in *The Kybalion*
Returning to the Garden
The Five Weights

14) Conquering the *Celestial Fire*

The *Middle Path* of *uraeus* and *bindi*
The *Samothracian Mysteries* & Electric Head
Controlling the Elements
Lycanthropy & Lilith
Wendigos, the Sandman & Night-Mares
Orpheus & the Muses
Dat Rosa Mel Apibus: The Rosy Apple

20) Temple of the Spirit & Keys to the Heavenly Kingdom

The *Three Fates* & *Platonopolis*
The Revelation of St. John
The Kingdom of Heaven
The Eternal Predator
Original Sin
Made Alive in Christ
Eschatology, Tribulation & the Triune Sun
Judgement Day
False Idols & the *Tower of Babel*
The Manitou

21) Goëtia, White Magic & Sex Magic

The Dark Arts
Origins of Goëtia & the Magus
Other forms of Magic: Black, White, Grey, Yellow, Placebo
Magical Blessings
Exorcising Demons & Driving out the Scapegoat
Sex Magic
Kama Sutra

22) Elementals & Spirit Conjuration

The Golden Dawn System
The Science & Psychology of Magic & Mythology
The Four Elements & Threefold World
Elementals & Vampires
Dictionary of the Infernal & The Magus
Magical Images
Be Mindful of Your Thoughts
Of Superior Spirits, their Offices & Subordinates
Table of Planetary Hours
The 72 Solomonic Spirits & Seals
The Seven Olympic Spirits
The Demons from Collin de Plancy's, *Dictionnaire Infernal,* 1863

23) Witchcraft, the Art of Conjuration & the Afterlife Trinity

The Pagan & Christian Witch
Witchcraft Lore: Familiars, Wandering Dames & the *Black Mass*
Persecuting Witches with a Hammer
Suppositions of Witchcraft
The Afterlife Trinity: Heaven, Purgatory & Hell
Making Pacts

A Golden Saying of Epictetus

CLXXV

Never call yourself a Philosopher nor talk much among the unlearned about Principles, but do that which follows from them. Thus at a banquet, do not discuss how people ought to eat; but eat as you ought. Remember that Socrates thus entirely avoided ostentation. Men would come to him desiring to be recommended to philosophers, and he would conduct them thither himself--so well did he bear being overlooked. Accordingly if any talk concerning principles should arise among the unlearned, be you for the most part silent. For you run great risk of spewing up what you have ill digested. And when a man tells you that you know nothing and you are not nettled at it, then you may be sure that you have begun the work.

*Epictetus was a Greek philosopher. He expressed a philosophy of brotherhood and Stoicism, the lifestyle of a person who can endure hardship without showing their feelings or complaining.

The Essence of Shinto

Motohisa Yamakage

It is not good if people become attached to the experiences in the other worlds or seek this kind of experience too much. This annuls the whole purpose of the exercise, because it introduces a new attachment, which can arouse negative feeling of arrogance and pride. You should neither boast of yourself by talking about your own experience nor discuss whose experience is inferior or superior.

Preface

There is power in science; there is power in thought; there is power in myth; there is power in magic; there is power in spoken word; there is power in written form.

A book does not need to contain specific magical formulae or secret codes to assist in the discovery supernatural treasures. If correctly written the text itself acts as magic formulae that, if it plays strongly enough on the imagination, can have the same desired outcome: discovery of the *Philosopher's Stone*. For a neophyte the information contained herein is greatly beneficial for spiritual growth, while hopefully for an adept it provides a new perspective or better clarification on certain occult subjects.

The intention of this text is not to mimic the great philosophers, alchemists, physicians, and authors from time immemorial, nor is it meant to deceptively steal their works and pass them off as new. This author has great respect for these men and the few women who have worked so tirelessly to pass along information to future generations in symbolic form. Beyond the famous names are also the timeless fairy tales, legends, folklores, and myths that greatly influence society and still permeate throughout our modern world. Many contain occult concepts or are themselves founded on the same.

There are perhaps few if any able to write with the elegance or passion of past generations and we are not attempting to do so with such inspirations that now seem to rarely influence man. But no matter how great a thinker, no single man, women, or any text, contains or maintains the *absolute truth*. Therefore, it is important to remember that what follows in these pages is merely a dissertation of occult studies and not a final guide. Nevertheless, it is indeed an alchemical work capable of causing a transmutation of body-mind-soul-spirit for all readers. These topics have had the same outcome on this author, who is, it should be noted, under the influence of no substances or spirits, with exception to what we may call *truth*.

We strive to revitalize the new world with the same life found in the philosophies, symbols, and myths of the old world. Let it be considered that "I," and this is the only time a reference to the ego and self will be used, am not a part of any secret society, mystery school, nor the student of what some may precariously call a master. I am not a part of any group, organization, institution, or identification, including those of a religious or political affiliation, nor am I an atheist or an anarchist. To define is to place limits, and therefore, true comprehension comes about through the intangible means of silent communication. My philosophy is *truth*, as the word implies a love thereof. My intention is objectivity and enlightenment. My aim is to inform, not convince. And yet, we must apply some manner of definition to understand things otherwise beyond our comprehension. Without definition there is chaos.

Although esoteric and occult studies remain vast, they are rooted within a universal philosophy that is difficult, if not impossible by finite terms, to explain in words. Language places restriction and erects barriers to understandings. By this it is to be understood that there are some things man should consider far too sacred to profane with definition. For these concepts and the manner by which we live our lives, we shall take a note from the Greek philosopher Pythagoras: *"Silence is better than unmeaning words."*

This text is meant to be a lantern of truth that will assist in illuminating the darkness of ignorance and misinformation as we examine the subjects of philosophy, theology, science, metaphor, allegory, myth, alchemy, talismans, stones, diabolism, mysticism, psychic abilities, western and eastern magic, psychology, and the art of *resurrection*.

What we call "reality" or "existence" is both a state of *matter* and a state of *mind*. According to mainline scientists in the 20th and 21st centuries, though these concepts are ancient, much of what we believe "exists" is simply a matter of decoding a tiny fraction of the "visible" world. The electromagnetic spectrum is estimated to be between 0.005% and 0.5% of all that "exists" in the "universe." *Visible Light* is only a fraction of that small percentage. All that we "know" and "experience" occurs within this tiny frequency range: our brain and five accepted senses decoding what we call "reality." The brain is a decoder of information, taking sensations of taste, touch, smell, sound, and sight, which are transmitted through electrical impulse, and processing them into interpreted "reality." But even within this process we are only decoding a few dozen out of millions of sensations experienced every second or moment.

What does this tell us? *Reality* is far more than physical and largely occurring inside our skull rather than outside our body. This means the *paranormal* is not so ab-normal and that *magic* and *occult* studies are just as rooted in *science* and psychology as they are in the *arcana*. This is where we speculate on the forces of nature operating behind the *body* of *matter*.

Ryan Daniel Gable,
writing in Arizona, 2024

~

"In this book, Ryan Gable has done extraordinary work on behalf of the forces of light. I am astonished by the colossal amount of lore he has gathered from different traditions around the world as well as by his penetrating analysis, much of which is quite cutting edge. I don't agree with all of it, but nor would I want to, because this is a book which intends to push the boundaries. It reminds me of the great baggy monsters of books that Victorian scholars used to write – except that much of the fascination lies in the way he traces ancient esoteric lore in modern culture."

Mark Booth, author of <u>The Secret History of the World,</u>
<u>The Secret History of Dante</u> and <u>The Sacred History.</u>

Microcosmus Hypochondriacus by Malachias Geiger, Munich, 1651.

The Philosophy of Theology & Science

"Technological progress has merely provided us with more efficient means for going backwards."

~ Aldous Huxley ~

Makroprosopos & Mikroprosopos

Is it possible to obtain immortality, thus defined as "the ability to live forever; eternal life?" What shall we consider *eternal* besides that which in some manner is "lasting or existing forever; without end or beginning?" To be unaware of an existence confined not to the destitute conditions of mortal man and society, but to some phantom realm where events do not transpire in a linear fashion is to have no understanding of beginning or end.

In the Beginning there was no *time* because there was no *matter* or *form* - or *observer* to define such - and thus no way to measure the changing positions of objects in space. Without form there was no matter and without the measurements of objects in space there was no time. When GOD acted to *create the heavens and the earth,* HE was reflecting upon himself, as depicted by the *White & Black God*(s); God was staring into a mirror and seeing his upside-down reflection. The Hebrew Zohar describes the reflecting God as *The Great Face* (Makroprosopos) and *The Little Face* (Mikroprosopos). The former has a long *white beard* and the latter a *black beard*. As the kabbalistic text details: *"The Age of the Aged, the Unknown of the Unknown, has a form and yet has no form…"* This was the philosophical discourse of Plato, too, that truth was not bound by fact and could only be known by analogy, i.e., to not know.

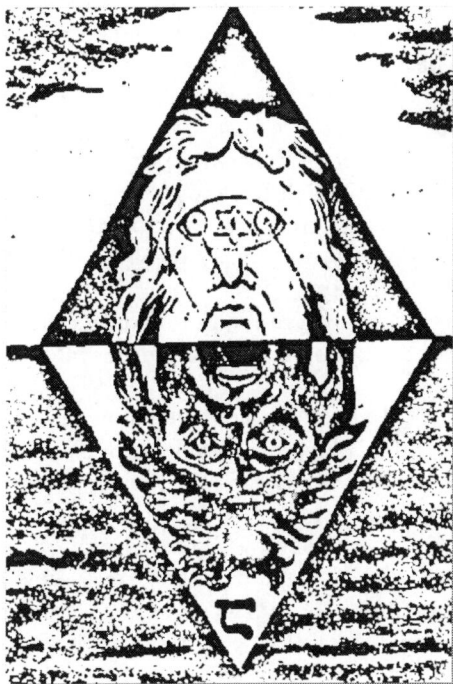

A Kabbalistic depiction of God reflecting upon himself.

When GOD is viewed in a mirror or reflecting pool, he also becomes DOG, which may relate to the Dog Star Sirius, *dogma,* and the Dog Days of Summer.

Modern *science* says that *matter* was formed first and was followed by a cosmic accident known as *mind* or consciousness. *Esoteric science* says that the *mind* was no mistake of *matter* and that instead consciousness created the former. There is therefore nothing that happens anywhere in *creation* that is not influenced by the human mind – a reflection of the *mind of God* (*So God created man in his own image, in the image of God he created him*).

Esoteric tradition further teaches that emotions affect both our bodies and the material world outside these vessels. Emotions, and more importantly how we respond to such conditions, determine whether we grow or remain stagnant in our existence.

We shall define *existence* as, "the fact or state of living or having objective reality," an obscure definition in opposition to our immortal sense of the words, *existence, reality*, or what is considered *real* as opposed to the *unreal*. In short of summarizing definitions with a restricted language, we must recognize that our understanding of the word "real" is simply defined as "actually existing as a thing or occurring in fact; not imagined or supposed." So, to be *real* is to exist; and to exist is to be alive in a particular place dictated by the constraints of the material world, along with mankind's perception of the construct of linear time.

Esoteric traditions suggest the opposite, that *real* is defined not by *matter* and *objects*, but instead by *mind* and *thought*. The *real* is thus what we *imagine* – in terms of *creating our own reality* – instead of what we *see, taste, touch, hear*, and *smell*. This does not mean, however, there is no purpose behind our senses and that all physical reality is purposeless. On the contrary, *material reality* is an emanation of *cosmic forces*, of spirits, gods, etc., interacting through humans and nature. Author of The Secret History of the World, Mark Booth, writes how these *"Thought-Beings expressed themselves through people."* He provides the thought experiment: *"If today we naturally think of people thinking, in ancient times they thought of Thoughts peopling."*

These human *Thought-Beings* or *forms of thought* are forged from imagination and concentration. They are known throughout the world as Tulpa (Tibetan), Golem (Hebrew) Egregore (general occult sciences), and Aquastor (Paracelsus).

The esoteric tradition holds that what we call God is *pure mind* reflecting on itself. From this *source* emanates *divine rays of light* which work to *create* and *influence*, by way of hierarchy, ever lower forms until reaching the crystalized matter of our mundane world. Kabbalists call this world *malkuth*. Booth goes on to describe these emanations of *pure thought* as such:

> *"Pure mind to begin with, these thought-emanations later became a sort of proto-matter, energy that became increasingly dense, then became matter so ethereal that it was finer than gas, without particles of any kind. Eventually the emanations became gas, then liquid and finally solids."*

Emanations from *source* work their way downward into stricter and more specific levels, acting to create and organize each new *dimension* or *world*. Traditionally the symbol of *morning dew* on plants was seen as proof of a *Cosmic Mind* reflecting on *that which is below*. Dew is a symbol of the cosmic forces that work spiritually on our conscience while we sleep. If we are living with a weighty conscience, it may be difficult to rest. From this *mind*, or from *God the Father*, falls *divine graces*, rays of light, and all creation. In Hebrew it is called Makroprosopos, or *The Great Face*, and as mythologist Joseph Campbell writes, *"from the strands of its white beard the entire world proceeds."*

Each *emanation* or *ray* has also been ascribed some characteristic and personality, some classifiable intelligence. Working with these intelligences was at the core of *Mystery Schools* in the ancient world, preserving a *sacred wisdom* we still find embedded in the works of some of the most iconic stories, movies, television shows, etc., today. Since the *mind* was, and is, considered more powerful as a progenitor of matter, it was, and still is, considered dangerous for any person to simply establish direct communion with the spirt world. We may say today that this danger is *opening yourself up for possession*. In a sense, this is true, but more to the point such danger lies in not being sufficiently mentally and physically prepared to deal with higher intelligences. This is why, as Booth points out, *"In the ancient world controlled communion with the gods and spirits was preserve of the Mystery schools."*

These gods and goddesses are both intelligences beyond and above, and a part of, human consciousness. Booth says that explaining the physical universe was the *great miracle* of science and that for esoteric philosophy the same miracle was an explanation of human consciousness. This is certainly true, but we can say even more about such fact. The ancient accounts of history as they pertain to such things were truly, with every supernatural occurrence, an account of both the unfolding of human consciousness and measures by which to scientifically understand the world. Modern science is thus a reductionist field which has separated natural from supernatural, astronomy from astrology, and chemistry from alchemy. Science itself is merely observational inquiry, making mythology and occult philosophy its earliest form.

We find the same understanding in observing the underworld in mythology as both a contemporary, for the time, *hell*, but an early form of psychology which links that domain with the unconscious mind. In both symbols we find the cave or skull by which this *underworld* may be entered. And in both symbols, we find a timeless link that truly has no past, present, or future, outside our perceptions of time. These ideas are eternal. If there was no time or matter *in the Beginning*, then how can one describe today an event that occurred in this ancient past? If there was no time, then how can there truly be a proper understanding of birth or death? In this truth it is evidence that there was no beginning and there is no end, that what we perceive as such exists always in the *now*, and in our concept of God, the *Alpha & Omega*.

There is only the eternal NOW - *the present moment*. All concepts of a past and future are expressed or remembered in the NOW. All actions and reactions occur in the NOW. The past is *now*, and the future is *now*.

Alchemical engraving from the *Mutus Liber*, published in 1677 anonymously and republished in Jonathan Black's The Secret History of the World. Precipitation of the morning dew is a symbol of emanations from the Cosmic Mind into the realm of matter. Dew brings new life, a symbol of spiritual forces that work on the conscience during rest or night. The two characters in the image are collecting dew, which is symbolic of reaping the benefits of spiritual exercises performed the night before. When Jacob awakens from a dream wherein God promises that he would inherent the land in which he sleeps, he brushes off the morning dew and realizes his resting place was the sacred land all along, i.e., the Kingdom of God dwelled within Jacob from the beginning.

In superstition, ignorance, and fear (*three great evils*), especially of death, man has attempted to understand the world by erecting edifices of higher learning. These compartmentalized institutions today rely on subjective authority, rather than objective investigations, to decipher the complex nature of existence by flawed means. By this separation of the different fields of study man has not only segregated himself from others, but erected barriers to understanding by restricting information with conclusions often derived before fact, and often with a dogmatic demand to believe. Here we can see that both *science* and *religion* as they stand are fields of investigation into body and mind, and fields furthermore that have been influenced by dogmatic and reckless *faith*. Philosopher Manly Palmer Hall writes of these various divisions and subdivisions that leave man so helpless:

> "*That which man believes he knows he has divided into a host of subdivisions, each of which is served by intellects naturally segregative and separative... Never will knowledge be possible, however, until we realize that each party is helpless without all the others; that all branches of learning are useless until merged into a single science representing the sum of human thoughts, feelings, and belief.*"

To be rich, young, and to never taste death, are a few of the aspiring elements lusted after throughout history, and in the modern day. To the commoner these are literalities, and therefore, the *spiritually dead* search for a literal fountain of youth and for literal gold. For the alchemist these are metaphors concealed by allegories; their lead is the corporeal and their gold is the spiritual.

The transformation of self by the conquering of instinctual desires elevates man to above that of the animal. In this symbol can be understood the true meaning of *slaying a great dragon to acquire its gold*, or the misconceptions of "human" or "animal" sacrifices. The *burn offering* is a *sacrifice* of the reptile brain, or *red dragon*, which gave the beast (animal self) *his power, and his seat, and great authority* (Revelation 13).

The human and animal sacrifices are an overcoming of basic desires so that attention may be focused on more than generative instinct. To this, the magician Eliphas Levi writes:

> "*To change lead, mercury, and all other metals into gold, to possess the universal medicine and the elixir of life such is the problem which must be solved to accomplish this desire and to realize this dream.*"

By transcending the reality of animal instincts and the reptile brain, a philosopher may find meaning beyond that which is concerned with reproductive processes. In alchemy the *elixir of life* is *truth* in visible nature, i.e., the sun, and in the subterranean and mineral worlds, it is perfect gold. This is the philosophical gold of religion; that absolute and supreme *reason* often referred to as the *Great Work* or *Search for the Absolute*.

Gold is the metal of the sun and thus signifies the warmth and light of heaven, as opposed to the darkness and cold of hell. Most of our holidays – *holy days* – are founded with this symbolism. The *Great Work* is the ultimate goal of theurgists, and all those on an esoteric journey with intention to invoke an illuminating awareness of Divinity. In alchemy, this work is also referred to as *god-working*, *ceremonial magic*, and *Divine action*.

One Japanese tradition holds that the hare, which finds refuge on the moon, works with pestle and mortar to make the *elixir of life*. Since the moon is *the great reflector* of the sun, itself a lens for the spiritual influences of God to penetrate the earth and man, it acts as a mirror for reflecting God's *will*. Booth points out what many Christians themselves have in common with esoteric science: "*the heart is the portal through which Sun god enters our lives.*" The moon is also the overseer of night and thus has authority over our unconscious, where the symbols of occult tradition work their greatest influence. From this underworld, one is transformed and eventually resurrected from a mundane mental state by realizing their *true* form. This transformation was acted out in dramas within the *Mystery Schools* of the ancient world, preserving sacred wisdom that man has always in some capacity strived to obtain – aligning himself with the *forces of nature* and *mind of God*.

What we classify as the physical world is but an inversion of the spiritual domain, and vice versa. Such a concept is known by the famous hermetic philosophy: *As Above, So Below*. Our world is really *"humanity turned inside out."* Science today accepts that *biorhythms* are real; these are observable facts like our Circadian Rhythms and the changing season. Few realize the relationship our bodies otherwise share with nature below and above. For example, we breathe on average 25,920 times per day, which more than coincidentally is the number of years it takes the sun to complete a full cycle of the zodiac - great Platonic Year. Our organs and bones and blood and nervous system and limbs all correspond and feel affects from the world immediately around us and directly above. This is why we associate colors, plants, animals, planets, etc., with the human body. In magical practice, which is really a form of psychology, we call these *sympathies*. Modern *color therapy* employs such ideas, as some colors are calming and healing while others are provoking of more heated conditions.

Theological Dogma

Of the edifices for understanding the world grew three great systems of thought: theology, science, and philosophy.

Theology sprouted because of the realization of man's immortality. With the lack of proper medical care, food, and necessary information relating to the natural world, along with willful ignorance, theology brought about salvation through the following of God's *divine plan*. It was based on the idea of *original sin* and attempted to explain events as the scheme of an all-powerful deity or controlling mind.

Esoteric tradition teaches that the *divine plan* is followed when one works in unison with the laws of nature.

The concept of a monotheistic God was the result of the unification of polytheistic pagan deities, which ultimately were already expressions of one central *source*. Various individual elements of nature were personified as having their own deity and these elements were then combined into one God. Polytheism is really a more simplistic monotheism, which, in turn, is a more complex polytheism.

Modern monotheists have accepted that any such principles of polytheism are simply too archaic and therefore must be converted in order to save any semblance of the divine left in the world. The polytheist, however, still sees God in all things rather than in certain selective instances of existence.

One of the most ancient beliefs, *animism*, professes that all natural phenomena - plants, rocks, metals, etc., were able to express some element of a soul. When ancient man walked in a forest he heard the wisdom of the trees by listening to their conscious whispers through the rustling of branches and leaves, which were, of course, initiated by the elemental spirits. These creatures were separated into four groups representing the further divinity of the number four, as in the four winds, seasons, corners, etc. These spirits, of course, took on their associated characteristics and could rightfully control their associated elements.

Gnomes, Undines, Sylphs, and Salamanders collectively made up the elements of the earth, water, air or ether, and fire.

It is from the *Gnomes*, those elementals of the earth, rock, dirt, wood, etc., for which we get stories of goblins and their leader Gob.

The *Undines* occupy water and invoke imagines of mermaids and serpentine creatures like Melusine.

Sylphs were considered entirely intangible and invisible but provide us with the idea of the great eastern wind, as this was their creative domain.

Salamanders were elementals of fire similarly related to the fire-gods known as the *Djinn* for which we derive the idea of *genies*.

These concepts primarily are traced to the Persian cults of Mithraism and Zoroastrianism, and they further led to the foundations of many Judeo-Christian and Islamic beliefs in beings of fire. We find their source in the Greek *Daemon*, a name referring to a divine spirit. There were seven similar horrible demons of Babylon called *maskim*. The parallel Arab *ghul* were more akin to tricksters. Manly Hall explains how, *"The Christian Church gathered all the elemental entities together under the title of 'Demon,'"* inverting simplistic Polytheism into a sophisticated monotheism with mandates that all but the true God be seen as his oppressors and false idols. Hall adds:

> *"This information is a misnomer with far-reaching consequences because to the ordinary mind, the word demon means an evil thing, and the Nature spirits are essentially no more malevolent than are the minerals, plants, and animals."*

Demons were once considered mortals of impressive quality, claimed by the gods after death. In Neo-Platonism these demons were transformed into divinities. All other heroes and gods of ancient polytheism became *"servants of the one God,"* as Kurt Seligmann wrote.

While God and each elemental spirit represents a part of the divine, the modern conception of God in any monotheistic theology thus became a finite being. Instead of God being depicted as manifesting in all that exists, and maintaining power over this creation, He was confined to a singular, all-powerful, all-knowing, omnipresent deity only contacted by the priestly class.

God would no longer be found in nature, or within our *divine self*, and instead was only to be communed with in an institution of theological and scientific oppression. Whereas the *Mystery Schools* certainly restricted access to their inner sanctum due to the dangers of the unprepared in taking journeys *out of the body*, they never *killed God* outside their walls.

Theological dogma removed the realization to look within oneself without being labeled a heretic, witch, or devil worshiper. Hall adds of these restraints:

> *"Theology is the emotional, changeable, violent, and at periodic intervals bursts forth in many forms of irrational excess. Theology occupies a middle ground between materiality and truly illuminated spirituality which, transcending theology, becomes a comprehension, in part at least, of divine concerns."*

We know the reaction of Muslims when one depicts Mohammed or Allah. Although grossly misunderstood by the literalist, there are philosophical doctrines to explain these reactions. It is the same reason that man is not to look upon the face of God, for the true light is blinding. By depicting a prophet or God it is believed by both Muslims and Jews that their *true nature* is being insulted and distorted. If one depicts the *infinite* by *finite* expression, it is considered sacrilegious.

By altering simplistic polytheism and replacing it with a complex monotheism, those accusing the profane of idol worship, or even less understood devil worship, are truly creating a complex polytheism under the worship of the *mono*. Through the opposing concepts of good and evil, God and the devil, and light and dark, there is equilibrium. Balances between memory and forgetfulness, action and inaction, desire and non-desire, etc., are the metrics that balance excitement and stagnation. As Booth writes:

> *"if the most fundamental conditions of human consciousness were not characterized by this set of exceptionally fine balances, it would not be possible for us to exercise free thought or free will."* Likewise, *"In coincidences we sometimes feel we catch a hint, albeit an elusive one, of a deep pattern of meaning hidden behind the muddle of every day experience."*

What Booth is saying, in Layman's terms, is that *free will* has always been our innate ability to decide if we will follow the *divine plan*. In other words, we have a *choice*, and although there are consequences to our actions, making that choice is our *free will* even if the universe seems indifferent to our suffering or pleasure. Of coincidences we are to understand that there is perhaps some force acting on *matter*, i.e., the *mind of God* and the hierarchies of spirits acting through humans – *Thoughts peopling*.

Of the numerations or attributes of God there are many, from the *First Cause* to *all that is graced below*. Hinduism, for example, embraces a single deity known as Brahman, while still recognizing other gods and goddesses. Hindus typically believe that there are various paths to reaching the *true God*. They strive to achieve *dharma*, a code of living emphasizing good conduct and morality.

The so-called *false idols* have today become the very edifices constructed to find that which always exists internally and exteranly. False idols also include those perverting the sacred for personal gains, be them financial or otherwise. The committing of *idolatry* is not always with use of graven images, but also in confusing images with what they actually represent, and, arguably, depicting God in any concrete way.

It is considered perversion for some to take the magnificence of God and apply personality or human characteristics. Providing God with a personality degrades His nature and limits it to the lower spheres of man. Perversion has further resulted by providing God with a name and extending His (referring to the androgynous qualities of God) likeness to a physical son, and not just an emissary of the above – this mistranslates the trinity and corrupts the essence of *divinity*. The *true trinity* is *mind, body, spirit (soul)*. When we are resurrected from the unconscious underworld then we find ourselves *born again* as a *son of God* rather than a *son of Man*.

Complex polytheism could thus be seen as perverted monotheism and is essentially a philosophic atheism; for the SOURCE of all – God or Supreme Deity – is neither a principle nor personality to be explained or depicted. Manly Hall expands on this concept:

> *"Impersonality is the divine attribute; it is a state inherent in the nature of God, and a condition to which man must obtain in the quest of his own divinity... If the personality – yes, even the individuality – of God is discarded as an illusion of the human mind, Deity is thereby elevated to its true philosophic estate, namely, and all-pervading, universalize essence. It naturally follows that this essence is without either footstool or throne; it does not hover over either communities or individuals but is distributed without partiality throughout the entire substance space."*

To divert man from the very substance of God is to rob man of his ability to realize his own divine attributes – as told in *Beauty and the Beast*, wherein the latter is a prince named Adam, cursed to live as an animal. Does this remind anyone of the *fall of man* from the *Garden*?

Theological-institutional dogma has professed almost nothing but heresy out of fear and ignorance. In this way, one may call theologians *false prophets* and their institutional edifices of worship a mockery to the temples and caves utilized by the ancient *Mystery Schools* for the development of internal divinity. And yet, they still preserve the *secret teachings of all ages* between the pages of their *holy books*.

Their materiality binds and constricts to hold steady their ever-decreasing will to actually become free from the bondage of this world, offering salvation vicariously through soulless hymns, misunderstood rituals, a confession booth, or another form of penance. And yet, one may see the hymns, rituals, confessions, etc., as symbols that act on the imaginations and trigger unconscious transformations beyond the physical church, mosque, temple, and so on. After all, one must simply have *faith*.

These men and women, in their base literal interpretations, are materialists, and their precepts only exist due to vulgar sciences trying to understand the material sphere and explain it as *everything* and *nothing* simultaneously. Perhaps this is why there seems to be so much lethargy in such intuitions. Thus, as Hall explains:

> "*Materiality does not attack the body or the conscious functioning of the mind; it assails the will power and destroys the morale.*"

These men and women, void of the literal or symbolic interpretation of such a deity, could be called Satanists in their seeming worship of the material world. Unlike the Devil, a character inverting the living with death –LIVE inverts to EVIL - Satan is merely a spiritual consciousness and adversarial force, one that certainly would seek to focus attention on material matters further illuminated by Lucifers *false light*.

Satan comes from the Roman and Greek gods of agriculture, debauchery, chaos, and time, known as Saturn and Cronus respectively. In Hebrew, śāṭān is simply a generic term for accuser.

Saturn's image has been painted differently in many cultures but remains the foundation for *Father Time* and *The Grim Reaper*. Saturn is the god of time and is said to speed and then reverse this material perception, often watching flowers die for amusement only to bring them back to life. This spirit of destruction is also one allowing for creation, as by death there is availability for new life to sprout. He is the *Grim Reaper* because he is *death*, the oppositional and balancing force of life or birth. Although Saturn brings chaos and destruction, what some may term evil, he represents an evil that is necessary. Saturn is required to bring about fundamental change and new life. He carries a scythe as the agricultural god whose body is consumed during the year-end harvest festival. When our time comes, or *death comes for us*, he uses the scythe to cut us down like the stalk of a plant.

In Egypt he is known as Osiris and painted green for which the Celts know him as the *Green Man*. It is said that Saturn/Satan "plants" (an agricultural analogy) into each of his children the seeds of their own destruction, and this is why you commonly see the grossly misunderstood images of Satan eating humans – his children.

Satan is not the Devil, and neither is Lucifer, who is the light bearer and Morning Star for which the planet Venus rises every four years. The Morning Star is Lucifer, the "bearer of light," known by the Greek word "Phosphorus," which is broken down into "phos" (light) and "phoros" (bringing). Venus rises in the western hemisphere, home of the water elementals, for four years as the *Evening Star*, and then rises in the eastern hemisphere, home of the air elementals, for four years as the *Morning Star*. Satan provides us with opposition and Lucifer with hardships to overcome. The differences between these characters are summed up in the detailed writings of Mark Booth (also Jonathan Black) in his book <u>The Sacred History</u>:

> *"The Saturn snake – Saturn – attacks from the outside, while the Venus snake – Lucifer – insinuates itself inside us. Because of Satan, the spirit of opposition, life is often hard to bear. Because of Satan, we are attacked. Because of Satan, we – like Mother Earth – are tested to our very limits, to the point where we want to give up. Lucifer attacks us in different ways. Lucifer makes us liable to make mistakes. He endowed matter with a glamor that would dazzle people and blind them to higher truths."*

(Left) Saturn Devouring His Child by the Flemish painter Peter Paul Rubens

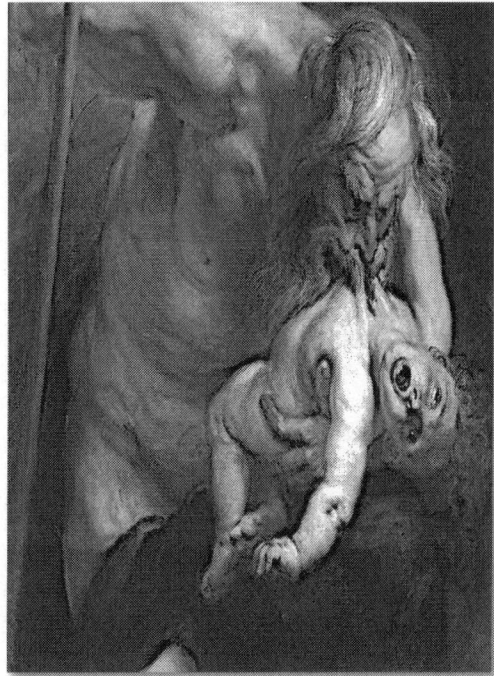

(Right) Devouring His Son by the Spanish painter Francisco Goya

The astrological house of Saturn is the goat Capricorn, commonly depicted in symbolic mythology as the Greek God Pan or the Celtic God Cernunnos. These characters share attributes also given to the Egyptian goddess Isis. Their horns or antlers come from similar places, which include the astrological houses of *Capricorn the Goat, Aries the Ram*, and *Taurus the Bull*. These images are likewise the origin for "Devil Horns" and relate through characters of fertility and animal sexuality like Pan to one being "horny."

Pan, son of the nymph Dryope, is the author of sacred dances and the sender of nightmares like the *mare* from Germanic and Slavic folklore. Some see the *mare* itself as a *demon*. The goat is furthermore a symbol of "evil" since these animals are notoriously difficult to manage, and as Sarah Iles Johnston writes, *"for a culture in which herding is important, therefore, the goat is a potent symbol of trouble and possible loss of livelihood."* In this capacity, we see why Satan is seen as the *opposition*.

These anthropomorphized images represent a sophisticated system of esoteric symbolism. The symbols are seen in the hands of the Egyptian Pharaohs holding a crook and flail, objects to herd the bull (Taurus) and ram (Aries). Author and forensic geologist Scott Wolter writes of the Egyptian King Akhenaten, who is often depicted with the crook and flail:

> *"Akhenaten's new religion essentially changed the old religion of veneration of the setting sun to the veneration of the rising sun…Akhenaten's attempt to unite the followers of both religions is one of the multiple meanings symbolized by the crook and flail. The flail herds the bulls or the followers of Taurus, and the crook was used to herd the sheep or the followers of Aries."*

Akhenaten's attempts to unify polytheism under monotheism resulted in his eventual murder by theological mob.

This variation of worshiping the rising sun, although possibly as a portal for divine influences to enter our world, rather than the setting sun is a profound reversal of beliefs that once abound in the civilized world. It relates to the worship of Venus as both a morning and evening star. It relates to the symbolism of initiation ceremonies in the *Mystery Schools* beginning with the entrance of a candidate into a temple through the west and their emergence after resurrection to the east. The west represented the land of shadow, the setting sun and evening star, while the east signified the rising sun and morning star. The dead must pass the western horizon and descend through Atum's adobe into Amenti, or the Nether World.

The entire process involved a series of preparations including probation that could last half a decade, a cleansing or baptismal process, hallucinatory substances, sensory deprivation and, finally, a living resurrection. Be these rites in Egypt, Greece, India, Asia, or the Americas, they were all similar. Candidates had to experience feelings and emotions similar to death, just as they had to perform tasks representing the trials of life.

As Booth points out:

> *"At different times the techniques used by these 'schools' involved sensory deprivation, breathing exercises, sacred dance, drama, hallucinogenic drugs and different ways of redirecting sexual energies."*

> *"In mystery schools candidates wishing to join were made to fall down a well, undergo trial by water, squeeze through a very small door and hold logic-chopping discussions with anthropomorphic animals."*

Theology overall combines elements of mythology, occult science, astrology and astronomy, superstition, fear, and ignorance, theurgy, etc., into a one-size-fits-all dogma we call religion. Of the many religions, the latter is true for all, only slightly varying in focus and intensity.

True enlightenment comes about when we recognize and accept our individual and non-physical self as a hypothetical expression of one *source*, while maintaining a foot in our five-sense world; when we conquer the fear of death and recognize that resurrection of spirit or soul occurs while still living.

Scientific Dogma

Of the second great edifice was erected *science*. Through theology, we are made to want what the mind of God wants. Man has, however, largely rejected these *natural laws* and replaced them with more direct forms of control. Science allows for this control through experimental processes and the perception of progress made through technological mechanisms of the tangible sort. Manly Hall explains of this technological materialism how *"the scientist has no comprehension of an activity independent of and disassociated from matter; hence his sphere of usefulness is limited to the lower world and its phenomena."*

Far from debasing science there are great allowances granted to man to develop medicine, mechanical conveniences, and additional systems for observing and learning. Although scientists tend to mock the paranormal or unseen worlds, some of the most recognized and progressive discoveries were found through occult research. These include Robert Boyle, a practicing Alchemist – Law of Thermodynamics; Robert Hooke, a practicing Alchemist – Inventor of the Microscope; William Harvey, a practicing Alchemist – Discovered circulation of the blood; Francis Crick, experimented with altered states of consciousness and LSD – Discovered double helix DNA and won the Nobel Prize with James Watson; Sir Robert Moray, Rosicrucian Philosopher – published first scientific journal, *Philosophical Transactions*.

The radio and television were both invented as the result of attempts to contact the spirit worlds and capture psychic influences.

One of the gods of material science, Charles Darwin, also attended séances and was a close friend of Max Müller, who translated Sanskrit texts. His idea involving a certain "evolution" of fish, amphibians, land animals, and humans is distinctively like the occult writings of Theosophist Frank Baum. In the <u>Wonderful Wizard of Oz</u> there are different human natures represented by the lion, tin man, and scarecrow, which comprise the animal, mineral and vegetable bodies respectively. Similar are these to the seven known storylines, which are the seven original planetary gods and their consciousnesses, and the more commonly known *seven dwarfs* from *Snow White*, a character depicted resting in a glass coffin. This is latter detail is a custom of the Order of the Rose Cross - Rosicrucians – to bring one closer to death, much like the usage of skeletal images by the Freemasonic Orders. These are all *memento mori*. They are reminders that all mortal beings will parish, and although death is ever at hand there are methods by which to free oneself so that death becomes a form of birth. In order to find God, we were led blindfolded into the temple of theological dogma and directed to never search outside those walls. Now we are being led by science blindfolded into the temple of scientific dogma and further directed to never search beyond those walls. In both cases, *slavation* is to be found with man and his idea of God, rather than with God Himself. Likewise, in our search for evidence of otherworldly life, we are led blind into a section of the temple of science by searching externally for what might already exist before us in ways we cannot imagine.

Just as theology has promised us everlasting life through vicarious atonement, scientists now exclaim they have found the great elixir for which the establishment has otherwise ridiculed, mocked and excommunicated the alchemists. Yet scientists promise us equated salvation through vicarious atonement of technological materialism – *the technological elixir*. Manly Hall adds of this profane science:

> *"Physical immortality, therefore, may be regarded as the ultimate goal of science, which can conceive of no other form of immortality."*

It seems the goal of science is to only extend life for the few while systematically developing new methods by which to, even if accidentally, exterminate the many. Anyone asking questions of the moral variety are considered heretics to scientific dogma. They are portrayed as standing in the way of biased progress. Is this not philosophically congruent with the dogmas of a misunderstood heaven and hell, where many are rewarded or punished infinitely for finite transgressions?

We have been blinded by the *false light* of the mythological trickster to believe that a God so powerful and loving can only be found within institutions of weakness and hatred, even if such temples are otherwise filled with images of light and impressions of love. The false light of that same trickster deceives us to believe we are merely a form of insignificant life on an insignificant planet, in an insignificant solar system, orbiting an insignificant star. To this degree, scientific dogmas often tell us that we will eventually be able to understand *everything* with unified theories but that we should remember it is all really an expression of *nothing*.

Philosophical Truth

Philosophically it is true, for what truth may be, that we are insignificant and inferior, but we ARE also significant and superior. Thus, the truth of mankind's liberation can be found in exploring the abandoned halls of magnificent philosophic temples. You will conclude that God and everlasting life are already integrated into the very essence of existence. If *mind* preceded *matter*, then we really are *made in his own image*.

There is no need for vicarious attornment by any materialism or technology. Those of us relying on material means for external salvation are wasting time, and those squandering time are surrendering opportunity for growth. However, materiality is God's creation, and it can be used just as well to honor the divine, as is the case for the indigenous Japanese practice of Shintō.

The *philosophical truth* is that, objectively, theology and science are dogs barking up the correct *tree of life*. And although a serpent often tempts them to some branch with a convincing argument that this part represents the entire tree, the true *fruit of wisdom* is guarded by a tempter for its own protection against profanity.

In conclusion of this section, Manly Hall says:

"The physical body of what man calls knowledge is science; the emotional body, theology; and the mental and supramental bodies, natural and mystical philosophy respectively."

Secret Mysteries of all Ages

"Unless men increase in wisdom as much as in knowledge, an increase in knowledge will be an increase in sorrow."

~ Bertrand Russell ~

Birth & Death

    Man is a *spirit* with a *soul* and *body*; in fact, several bodies, which are vehicles to experience both the tangible and intangible.

    When we are *born*, our parents typically celebrate our birth having had their intellectual capacity for philosophical thought stolen from them by the gods of the phantom world. We move through life in a linear fashion celebrating each birthday with the same excitement until many of us recognize the clever method by which death approaches. In sharp contrast, when someone we love dies, our ignorance dictates a sense of mourning, partly from fear of our own mortality. This mourning is not entirely of innate sadness for someone we cared for, but of a subconscious fear of our own mortality. It almost seems as if we know that death has liberated our loved one from the restraints of matter and we are jealous of their escape from this corporeal prison. Therefore, it is said one should celebrate death and mourn birth rather than the other way around.

    We are not saying that birth is sad, and death is exciting, but that in certain philosophical frames of mind this is essentially true. Far from being nihilistic, such a philosophy grapples with the death of the spirit at birth and the rebirth of the spirit at death. Symbols of death, or *memento mori*, are reminders not to worship death, but to live a full life as the Grim Reaper with his scythe could come to collect his crop at any time.

    Manly Hall writes here of the material womb in comparison with the worldly womb:

"Within the womb of matter fetal man is being prepared for birth into the greater universe of the realities… Buy physical birth we have nearly exchanged the amniotic fluids of the womb for the somewhat less dense atmospheric fluids of the world. We are still bound with to the earth by an umbilical cord of sense, interest, and desire, and not until through the development of our discerning faculties we acquire the power to sever this bondage to the inferior nature can it be said that we are really born."

    Our psychical *birth* may thus be seen as an abortion of spiritual essence in the womb of matter, and our *death* the releasing of spirit from its bondage, or a *true rebirth*. Mystical philosophy professes that everyone has the experience of two births and two deaths.

    The first, or *lesser birth*, is man's introduction into, or out of, the *irrational sphere* wherein he loses contact with the *spiritual spheres*. This is often referred to as a *deep spiritual sleep* and is told in the stories of *Sleeping Beauty* and *Beauty and the Beast*. The birth into *matter* is the *death* of the spiritual or higher self, which remains asleep in the tomb of material organisms until reawakening. To awaken this process while very much alive was the goal of alchemists and the ancient *Mystery Schools*. The second, or *greater birth,* indicates the *death* of *material*, or our lower self, which now liberated rises from the tomb and ascends into the heavens like Christ. The *lesser birth* is a *great death*, and the *greater birth* is a *lesser death*, and in fact a *rebirth*. In <u>Occult Science in India and Among the Ancients</u>, Louis Jacolliot confirms this: *"The first birth is merely the advent into material life, the second birth is the entrance to a spiritual life."*

Memento Mori in the *Mysteries*

The Roman goddess Ceres was known as Demeter in Greece. Her daughter's abduction into the underworld by Pluto, or Hades, was reenacted in a series of rituals known as the Lesser and Greater rites in the ancient Greek *Mystery Schools*. The rituals included three phases: descent, search, and ascent from the underworld. The drama was performed in the small town of Eleusis near Athens and relates or aligns with the triune cycle of existence: birth, life, and death. These three phases are further representations of the cycles of the moon, seasons on earth (including rebirth), or revolutions of the planets. They are cycles recalled and acted out in respect and veneration for nature, intended to awaken us from our *deep sleep*. The specifics of these rites were meant to evoke a higher understanding of Nature by allowing man to become more in tune with its qualities. What was taught in these sacred temples was not to be uttered outside their walls.

When Hades, transported by his chariot, abducts Persephone he also wears a magical helmet that renders him invisible. This story is like that of Creusa and Ion, the former just a youth, who was out one day collecting flowers on a cliff near a deep cave. Once she had her choice of flowers, she

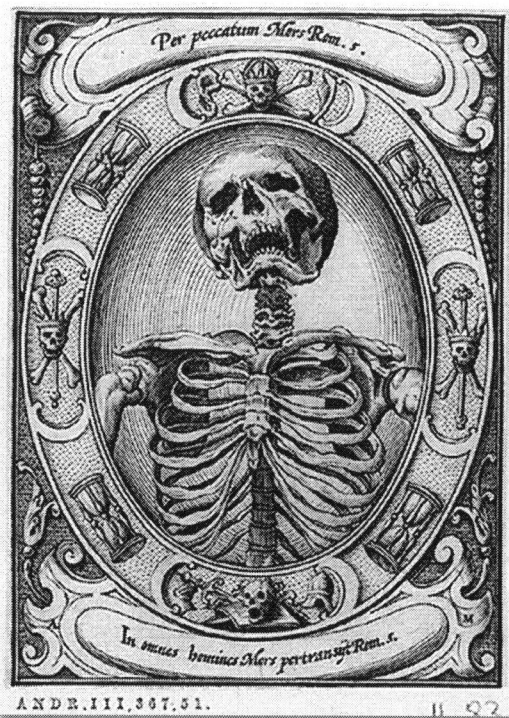

Memento Mori, a 1605 woodcut by Alexander Mair.

determines to go home before being caught up in the arms of a man who has appeared from nowhere, and as Edith Hamilton explains of this myth, *"as if the invisible had suddenly become visible."* This abductor was not Hades, but Apollo, and the son that Creusa bore from the union was Ion.

Persephone (Latin Proserpina) is the goddess or queen of the underworld because she is stolen away by Hades (Pluto) and forcibly taken to his Kingdom. Here upon the later arrival of Hermes upon orders from Zeus, she consumes 1/3 of a pomegranate – some say a single seed – which requires her to stay in the *Land of the Dead* for a comparable amount of time each year.

Some readers may recall the movie *Pan's Labyrinth* and how Ofelia is instructed to avoid eating anything in the *Pale Man's* (death) lair.

This beautiful myth was a way to preserve the scientific understanding of the changing of the seasons. Therefore, it was not merely myth, but also a philosophy, magic, and certainly the preservation of a sacred science.

Here is the full story: While wandering in fields looking for beautiful flowers, Zeus calls upon the narcissus, like a daffodil, to help distract young Persephone. When she reaches forth for the flower a chasm opens in the ground and a coal-black horse emerges drawing the chariot of Hades, who snatches the youth. After her daughter's abduction, Demeter (Ceres) is distraught, wandering the world searching for her beloved Persephone, like Isis searching for Osiris in Egyptian myth. She is so saddened by the abduction that she refuses even to taste the sweet nectar or *ambrosia* of the gods. Searching for nine days, she is then informed by the sun of Persephone's abduction into the world of shadows and death. Further distraught with this new information, Demeter enters Eleusis where she later demands a temple be built in her name to atone for the actions of a woman named Metaneira. Upon its completion, she takes to the temple. As the goddess of agriculture nothing was permitted to grow until she was appeased. Nearly a year passed, dreadful and cold, with no seed sprouting or crop growing due to Demeter's focus on the loss of her daughter.

Zeus then decided to intervene, fearing widespread death due to famine, and so he sends Hermes (Mercury) to the underworld to rescue Demeter's daughter. When Hermes arrives, Persephone joyfully leaves the side of Hades, who must obey Zeus, to return to the surface world. But Hades knows she would be forced to return if she eats of the fruit of mortality, and so he forces her to consume a pomegranate seed, just as Eve bit the poisoned apple of mortality in the Garden of Eden.

Persephone was therefore made to return to the palace of her husband for a third of each year. She was both divine and mortal, a parallel found in occult literature relating to the descent of soul into matter and its subsequent realization of its divine state and resurrection.

Hermes rescued Persephone from Hades, bringing her to the temple in Eleusis where Demeter was honored. With her daughter returned, they shared stories of their experiences, but Demeter soon feared losing her daughter upon learning of her eating the mortal fruit. To ward off famine Zeus once more sends a messenger, his own mother Rhea, to Demeter. She arrived at the temple speaking the following:

> *Come, my daughter, for Zeus, far-seeing, loud thundering, bids you.*
> *Come once again to the halls of the gods where you shall have honor.*
> *Where you will have your desire, your daughter, to comfort your sorrow.*
> *As each year is accomplished and bitter winter is ended*
> *For a third part only the kingdom of darkness shall hold her.*
> *For the rest you will keep her, you and the happy immortals.*
> *Peace now. Give men life which comes alone from your giving.*

Demeter did restore the fields once more with abundance and brought fresh flowers and green leaves back to a barren world. She then went to the princes of Eleusis, who had built her temple, and chose one named Triptolemus to be her ambassador to all men, to instruct them in the skill of growing corn. She also taught sacred rites; the *sacred mysteries* that no one was allowed to speak outside initiatory circles. Edith Hamilton explains in <u>Mythology: Timeless Tales of Gods and Heroes</u> of these rites:

> *"In the stories of both goddesses, Demeter and Persephone, the idea of sorrow was foremost. Demeter, goddess of the harvest wealth, was still more the divine sorrowing mother who saw her daughter die each year. Persephone was the radiant maiden of the spring and the summertime, whose light step upon the dry, brown hillside was enough to make it fresh and blooming…"*

In other words, Demeter represents darkness, like that experienced when Osiris tricked into a chest and sent into the underworld; it is a time when life on earth becomes harsh during the winter months, when food is not guaranteed.

Persephone represents the return of spring and summer, and in this capacity shares a likeness with Christ.

The charcoal horse of Hades is the "black horse" of Revelation 6:5 who carries "a pair of scales" to judge the dead during the *apocalypse*, or great unveiling, of the cycles of nature.

Likewise, Osiris in his reincarnation as Horus brought light and life back to the world. In the underworld Osiris is followed and assisted by the dog-jackal-headed god Anubis, who also weighs the dead by a scale. Saint Michael the Archangel carries the same scales as does the skeleton saint Santa Muerte (she has a scythe too).

The cycle of life and death continues as this radiant goddess Persephone, savior of mankind, ultimately descends back into the palace of Hades. Edith proceeds to describe *memento mori*:

"But all the while Persephone knew how brief that beauty was; fruits, flowers, leaves, all the fair growth of earth, must end with the coming of the cold and pass like herself into the power of death."

The time for which Persephone must spend in the underworld is a great detail in a story concealing a sophisticated understanding of natural seasonal cycles. Her return is prompted by the spring, when life returns to a barren world, days conquer nights in length, again the Wheel of the Year turns to Imbolc, Ostara, Beltane, and eventually Litha, the Summer Solstice.

Edith writes that Persephone *"did indeed rise from the dead every spring"* bringing with her *"the memory of where she had come from."* She was often referred to mysteriously as *"the maiden whose name may not be spoken."*

This interestingly associates her with both Isis and YHWH, a name never to be pronounced. To speak the name of God, as to depict, or even deny the image, constitutes blasphemy; it degrades and reduces as we have learned.

The underworld of Hades or Pluto has erratically been associated in some conceptions as a pit of fire and torment overseen in a hierarchy by the Devil and his demons. Philosophically the underworld is but the material sphere, and mor specifically unconsciousness.

Some say we come into this world as if we came from somewhere else. Logically we come out of this world just as the leaves come out of the branches of a tree, to relate a thought expressed by the philosopher Alan Watts.

The underworld, more commonly referred to as *hell*, has further been cultivated from mythology, as for example, the Norse goddess of the underworld was known as *Hel*.

These myths were meant to entertain the commoner, but to the initiate explained the changing of the seasons with complex, yet simple to understand, colorful stories of the natural world. They were entertaining still while maintaining an essential element of scientific understanding. Demeter's time of mourning and wandering was the time of winter, and her daughter's inevitable return signified the renewal of the earth in spring.

The abduction and rape of Persephone is symbolic of our divine nature, too, being assaulted by the animal soul and dragged downward into the darkness of Hades. The continual cycles of life and death, for humans and the seasons, was explained as an agreement made between the gods.

Lesser & Greater *Mysteries*

These stories were preserved in the ancient *Mysteries Schools*. Their symbolic and spiritual remnants are still found in institutional theology today. Only those considered worthy of being entrusted with the secrets of life, nature, and God, would be allowed entry into these sacred temples, and even then, upon strict probations and guidelines, and the fear of various forms of death should they ever teach these secrets publicly – perhaps this is what Jesus was truly accused of? Those without self-discipline and respect were never permitted in the school.

Manly Hall writes in <u>The Secret Destiny of America</u> of this sacred knowledge and its preservation from the *vulgar*, meaning those not mature or responsible enough to seek such wisdom:

Ceres (Demeter), patron of the Mystery Schools, from a mural painting in Pompeii.

> *"In ancient days all learning was regarded as sacred; wisdom was entrusted to the keeping of priest-philosophers, and they were permitted to communicate the choicest branches of the sciences only to duly initiated pupils. To bestow knowledge upon those who had not prepared their minds by years of discipline and self–purification profaned the mysteries, desecrated the sacred sciences."*

In Greece these rituals would be performed as part of an initiation that would entrust the neophyte with secrets of divine wisdom. Initiates into the inner sanctums were provided with new perspectives on the world, while undergoing a ritualistic living form of resurrection. The mysteries of birth, life, and death, which are evident in all things, from humans to the changing of the seasons, were taught in secret to prevent perversion and misuse.

Those reborn from the death of lower self and material ignorance are considered *born again* in the Christian sense, or as in the Buddhist ritual of *Kaidan Meguri*; the quality of overcoming lower animal nature to be reunited with the divine - *nous*. These rituals were known as the *Lesser* and *Greater* rites, which were carried out in Greece near the small town of Eleusis outside of Athens. The town name *Eleusis* means *"arrival at mystery or secrecy."*

The Pigmies of the Andaman Islands record a name for this resurrected person, *oko-jumu*, the *dreamer* who obtains new life after the trials and death.

The *Lesser Rites* of the Eleusinian *Mysteries* primarily focused on the abduction of Persephone by Hades or Pluto, and therefore the cult of Demeter (circa 1600 BC) falls under these Mysteries, named for the temple in which they were enacted. Initiations were performed in three stages that were broken into various rituals. The *Lesser Mystereis* were performed in the spring:

Katharsis: an instructional and purification rite

Sustasis: preparatory rite conducted by the seashore in salt water (according to Clement of Alexandria)

The *Greater Mysteries* were performed following the autumn equinox and lasted nine days, the time Demeter spent searching for her daughter. They were even more strictly prohibited except to high level initiates, who had undergone a period of moral observation and ritualistic requirements. As published in <u>Pagan Regeneration</u> by Harold R. Willoughby these requirements were required upon entrance to one of the temples:

> *"[Those can rightfully enter] who are pure and healthy in hand and heart and who have no evil conscience in themselves."*

In the final ritual, which commenced in the late hours, the initiate was locked inside the *Chamber of Mysteries*. It began with a reenactment of Persephone's (the soul) rape and her descent into the underworld, followed by her later ascent, whereupon the initiate was considered reborn.

Teleste: initiates were brought near the point of death so that they better experienced the line between the worlds of the living and dead.

Epopteia: conducted one year from the latter, this final stage was performed in the dark inside of a sacred chamber called "Telestron," meaning perfection.

A Roman relief from the first century, showing a candidate being led to an initiation ceremony. Reference can be found in Mark Booth's <u>The Secret History of the World.</u>

Manly Hall explains the relationship of the *Greater Mysteries* to seasonal cycles and Demeter: *"The Greater Mysteries (into which the candidate was admitted only after he had successfully passed through the ordeals of the Lesser, and not always then) were sacred to Ceres, the mother of Persephone, and represent her as wandering through the world in quest of her abducted daughter. Ceres carried two torches, intuition, and reason, to aid her in the search for her lost child (the soul). At last, she found Persephone not far from Eleusis, and out of gratitude taught the people there to cultivate corn, which is sacred to her. She also founded the Mysteries. Ceres appeared before Pluto, god of the souls of the dead, and pleaded with him to allow*

Persephone to return to her home. This the God at first refused to do because Persephone had eaten of the pomegranate, the fruit of mortality. At last, however, he compromised and agreed to permit Persephone to live in the upper world half of the year if she would stay with him in the darkness of Hades for the remaining half."

A similar account of Persephone's stay in Hades is preserved in the Indian *Katha Upanishad* whereby a human named Nachiketas visits the underworld realm of *Yama* - god of death. A strong parallel also exists here between the Japanese *Land of the Dead* or *World of Darkness*, known as *Yomi-no-kuni*, or just simply *Yomi*. This relationship between *Yama* and *Yomi* should not be ignored.

Nachiketas is warned that if he tastes any food while in Yama's mansion he will be confined there: *"Three nights within Yama's mansion stay… But taste not, though a guest, his food."*

In Japanese mythology we find Izanagi and Izanami involved in the same type of situation. These creator deities of Japan are the parents of Susanoo and Amaterasu, along with other children (islands), and the Shintō gods/spirits known as *Kami*. Their first-born son *Yebisu* is of particular interest here in regard to the Moses story, too, because he was also placed in a reed boat and set adrift on water after his birth.

More to the point, Izanagi was in mourning over the loss of his wife Izanami and therefore ventured to the land of *Yomi* to bring her back to the world of the living. Izanagi said to his wife, *"The lands that I and thouh made are not yet finished making; so come back!"* Although Izanami desires to return she has made the fatal mistake of eating food prepared in the underworld and thus cannot come back to the land of the living.

Metaphors, Allegories & Parables of the Soul

Much like the Masonic Order, there is another secret society operating today which still acts out these dramas. Known as the *National Grange of the Order of Patrons of Husbandry*, this organization – Grange – acts as a gathering organization for independent farmers. Degrees offered by the Grange are open to both men and women, though it is primarily the women taking up the names of the different goddesses of nature. When Persephone exits her subterranean palace to reunite with her mother on the surface, we find a relationship between the Greek Mysteries and the stories of Jesus and Lazarus rising from the dead. This resurrection is metaphoric, in that our divine essence, being dragged into matter, is freed to ascend into the higher spheres to realize, or reunite, with the *source*. The realization of the true self – soul - is accompanied by the release of fear from death. These and other similar stories are comprised of metaphors, allegories, and parables. They are metaphors wrapped in allegories and concealed by symbols and archetypes:

Metaphors: a figure of speech in which a word or phrase is applied to an object or action to which it is not literally applicable.

Allegory: a story, poem, or picture that can be interpreted to reveal a hidden meaning, typically a moral or political one.

Parables: a simple story used to illustrate a moral or spiritual lesson.

When asked by his disciples why he spoke in parables to the common people, Jesus replied in Matthew 13:11 saying, *"because the knowledge of the secrets of the kingdom of heaven has been given to you, but not to them."* Jesus is here explaining how to heal the sick, raise the dead, cast out demons, and preach the true gospel. His teachings are figurative and metaphoric. They are, as Hall writes on the question of to personal conversations had with a physical Jesus, *"symbolic references to the inner experiences of the spiritual life."*

In his book <u>How to Understand Your Bible</u>, Manly Hall explains what is meant by the incredible *teachings* and *miracles* of Jesus Christ:

Preach the Gospel: *"to teach or inform those who were prepared to receive instruction."*

Heal the Sick: *"to remedy not merely the infirmities of the flesh, but those of ignorance, fear, and superstition."*

Raise the Dead: *"to recover souls from materiality by the word of Truth."*

Cast out Demons: *"to modify the passions, emotions, and appetites"* of the individual.

Cleanse the Lepers: *"to purify those who were unclean of thought and deed."*

Although one may have *eyes to see* and *ears to hear*, our senses rarely extend beyond the material sphere. These *miracles* are alchemical in nature, much like the turning of water into wine:

"Though seeing, they do not see; though hearing,
they do not hear or understand."
"'You will be ever hearing but never understanding;
you will be ever seeing but never perceiving."

"For this people's heart has become calloused;
they hardly hear with their ears, and they have closed their eyes.

"Otherwise they might see with their eyes, hear with their ears,
understand with their hearts and turn, and I would heal them."

"But blessed are your eyes because they see, and your ears because they hear."

The resurrection of Jesus from the cave signifies the awakening of our higher self which otherwise would remain entombed in matter. The ascension of Jesus into heaven represents the rising of the higher self out of the tomb, or underworld, to reunite with *source*. In both cases, we are to understand the spiritual journey taken to awaken, learn, and realize our true nature as spirit.

A literal cave with a moist interior represents the maternal womb and was the location of many rituals of Living Resurrection. Such caves are also symbolic of the human skull and brain. Caves and mountains were naturally sacred locations, and the latter were often considered a home for the gods. Mountains were considered a place where man was in more direct contact with God and so those seeking divine assistance would travel to these locations. Mountains are where Moses, on Mt. Sinai (Jabal Mousa), received the Ten Commandments, and where the Ark of Noah came to rest at Mt. Ararat. An artificial pyramid is therefore a microcosm of the macrocosm that is a mountain. The internal chambers of such pyramidal temples are the microcosm of the macrocosm that is a natural cave. The same be said of burial mounds found from the Americas to Japan.

Initiates were entombed for three days in darkness where, using specially prepared drinks of a hallucinogenic nature, they would traverse the astral plane and have communion with spirits before returning to their body. This experience was meant to prepare the initiate for death with the realization that the body and daily life was merely one part of the vastness of existence. By overcoming the fear of uncertainty and awakening the Lower Self to the Higher Self, one could transfigure as described of Jesus in Matthew, Mark, and Luke. In Matthew 17:2 is described what occurred:

> "There he was transfigured before them. His face shone like the sun, and his clothes became as white as the light."

So powerful were these processes that a probationary period was erected preventing full initiation for up to three years. In the meantime, dedicated study to the sacred sciences was typically undertaken. Considering the physical and psychological dangers of these rites, in that of certain trials, and certainly of substances inducing altered states of consciousness, initiation was a limited enterprise.

To conquer death, as it is often perceived, is not to live forever in corporeal form; it is not to conquer life by extending the facilities of material existence. In this latter scientific endeavor, man is being subdued by materiality not conquering it. As life in the physical is death in the spiritual, and death in the physical is life in spiritual, to extend life in the physical is to extend death of the spiritual!

Conquering death is therefore overcoming bestial desires empowered by the great dragon, not living as a human for the extent of all time and cheating the Grim Reaper. Once the dragon of *desire* is killed, an initiate can reap the alchemical reward of the beast's gold. This is one mystery of alchemy and what is foretold in the book Revelation. From Genesis to Revelation, the Garden of Eden to Calvary, and from the *fall of man* to his *redemption*, the *Mystery Schools* taught how to transform lead into gold and water into wine. Otherwise, by concentrating on only material desires, the truth of our divine soul is further obscured and lost. Thus, the *fall* was caused by unkempt *desire* which resulted in the removal of man from paradise, in the Garden, to one of suffering in daily life.

These *desires* solidify our existence in the material sphere with superstition, fear, and ignorance. We are influenced and controlled by the expressions of material gods who, like Lucifer, endow matter with a glamor and dazzle, blinding the lower self to higher truths. Manly Hall explains of *desire* and its cultivation of suffering:

> "Desire breeds death, and he who has liberated himself from desire has liberated himself from death. Ignorance and death – which are synonymous in their inner nature – are indeed the last great adversary. He who vanquishes this twofold monster bypass power which is the inevitable product right-thinking has achieved conscious and enduring immortality."

Eliphas Levi writes in <u>Transcendental Magic: Its Doctrine and Ritual</u> of the knowledge of good and evil, the realization of *nakedness* experienced by the primordial parents - Adam and Eve, and the nature of suffering:

> "To know how to suffer, to forbear and to die – such are the first secrets which place us beyond the reach of affliction, the desires of the flesh and the fear of annihilation. The man who seeks and finds a glorious death has faith in immortality and universal humanity believes in it with him and for him, raising altars and statues to his memory in token of eternal life."

One need not experience physical death to be *dead*. Many proceed through life with a spiritual void for which they attempt to fill with *matter*. Those consumed by a finite world, entangled in tangible decaying elements, are thus consumed by *death* even in *life*. For what greater purpose in the experiences of *life* could there be but to contemplate one's own existence?

~

There are other forms of immortality beyond these *secret teachings*. Having one's name inscribed in history like Napoleon or having one's likeness recorded in myth or legend like that of the great King Arthur, means that one is certain to live forever. For who would say that any historical figure often discussed today is not immortal? Has Rome truly fallen or is it alive and well today in architecture, law, and religion?

The *Cosmic Mind*

Gods are not physical, per se, but instead anthropomorphized characteristics of nature and being. The Roman Venus or Greek Aphrodite may be said to incarnate and walk the earth when one falls in love or is struck with the arrow of Aphrodite's son Ero(s) - or the son of Venus known as Cupid. When man loves he is embodying the consciousness of Venus or Aphrodite. When man gives into conflict, he is embodying the consciousness of Mars, the husband of Venus. In this companionship of the gods, the love of Venus is balanced by the war god Mars (the Greek Ares), and vice versa. Hall explains: *"Being divine attributes; God thus becomes flesh in those mortal creatures who have unfolded and given expression within themselves to those godlike attributes."*

The gods and goddesses of antiquity, which are very much alive today, are the emanations of a *Great Cosmic Mind*.

"The reality of everyday experience," writes Mark Booth, *"is that thoughts are quite routinely introduced into what we like to think of as our private mental space from somewhere else. The ancients understood this 'somewhere else' as being some-one else, the someone being a god, an angel or a spirit."* When one witnessed a deer or owl, especially in the ancient world, they were seeing a manifestation of the Roman goddesses Diana (Greek, Artemis) and Minerva (Greek, Athena), or the Indian Lakshmi.

The polytheistic attributes of various gods were collectively emanations from the one true God, from which all *natural law* flows.

Nonetheless, Kings, Queens, Emperors, Empresses, Princes, Princesses, etc., have always taken on the mantle of these higher authorities to obtain their *sympathies* and claim a *divine right to rule*. Adhering to *Universal Laws* is to live in harmony with nature, which, void of human prejudice and discrimination, allows all men and women to live freely on earth. This is the *divine plan*. Any leader taking their people out of alignment with such laws is destined to lose any heavenly favor they may have otherwise had. The spirit is said to *leave them*. We can say the same about the institution of marriage between man and woman. When either party betrays the other and violates their vowels, they essentially are dissolving the wedding contract and are no longer beholden to each other. Therefore, to be obedient to a god was not to follow an earthly ruler, but simply to respect the laws of nature for which that god personified. And to be obedient and adhere to every law of nature was to worship the one true God, the *Cosmic Mind* that does not tolerate wickedness and deceit from a ruler or from a spouse.

Although the ocean can be deadly, its purpose is not to cause death. One must have respect for these powerful forces and not abuse them, which is why the *mysteries* of esoteric philosophy were concealed only to the dedicated and not to the derelict soul. By *dedicated* is meant to be understood the one in search of wisdom.

To reduce God to a variety of gods and goddesses is not degrading or vulgar, per se, because likewise it could be said that to restrict God to a singular and anthropomorphic character is just as sacrilegious and blasphemous.

Adherents to the doctrine of *eternal life* through *vicarious atonement* have often been tempted and seduced with *false doctrines*. Many have been tricked, largely unintentionally, by the *desire* for materiality in the descriptions of an *afterlife*: pearly gates and golden streets. Such things are merely symbols for the imagination to utilize in the process of self-development. They are not to be believed literally.

Golden streets represent the spiritual self that is transmuted from base matter, or animal consciousness, through a process of alchemy – lead and water turned into gold and wine.

Eternal life is not awarded, but the neophyte, after completing many trials, and refining the qualities of self to conquered personal demons, recognizes the eternal and immortal nature of the soul. Once the lost word of the Grand Master architect is recovered, we may find immortality in the *way, truth, life, light*, and *word* of the archetypical savior. Hell is merely an abstract idea for sorrow and suffering, whereby the ignorant and dead dwell, even those still very much alive; an underworld where the soul is swallowed by the beast of the temptation of material desires.

The truest depiction of *hell* is one of cold, darkness, and separation. The truest depiction of *heaven* is one of warmth, light, and unity. These are psychological conditions, too, when one considers the former feelings experienced by *betrayal* or *hatred* as opposed to the latter feelings of *love*. In fact, if you invert the word LOVE the result is EVOL, another variation of LIVE and EVIL, or LIFE and EFIL.

It is to be understood that by obeying the dictates of God is to live in harmony and balance with the fundamental elements and laws of nature. Students of the *secret teachings* are concerned with understanding the fundamental fabric of reality, or rather, the very lacking of such a fabric, and the advancement of society through philosophy in particular; the improvement of self through refining our thoughts, actions and emotions; the mastering of *desire*. Initiates of these schools of thought practiced discipline of intellect by repetition, and mastery of *desire* by going without. To live in harmony with God's *divine plan* is to be *made right with God*. According to Romans 3:21-24,

> *"But now apart from the law the righteousness of God has been made known, to which the Law and the Prophets testify. This righteousness is given through faith in Jesus Christ to all who believe. There is no different between Jew and Gentile, for all have sinned and fall short of the glory of God, and all are justified freely by his grace through the redemption that came by Christ Jesus."*

Louis Jacolliot explains in <u>Occult Science in India and Among the Ancients</u>, how initiates of the *mysteries* were careful *"during every moment of… public life never to covet the property or wife of another."* How similar does this Brahmanic code sound to the Egyptian *Confessions of Ma'at* (*"I have not envied or craved for that which belongs to another"*) or the *Ten Commandments* (*"thou shall not covet"*). In Exodus 20:17 we read the following full verse:

> *"You shall not covet your neighbour's house. You shall not covet your neighbour's wife, or his male or female servant, his ox or donkey, or anything that belongs to your neighbour."*

What we are reading here, and what is preserved in these sacred writings, is a prescription for both private property and personal development which rejects the lives and possessions of others. These are confessions and commandments to *live in harmony*, following the *divine plan* of the *Cosmic Mind,* by tending to your own business.

Celtic Mysteries

The rites of Greece and Egypt were also performed by the Celtic people and their priestly class called Druids, historically hailing from Britain, Ireland, and France. Their teachings were the prodigy of the *magi,* their *initiations* derived from Egypt, Chaldea, and Phoenician, being those primarily related to Kabbalah. They lived in abstinence, keeping secret the great mysteries in their possession; their rites were performed, not in temples, but in forest and *dolmens,* those megalithic tombs with large flat stones laid upon upright ones. Of Druidic myth, *Heol* or *Belen* was their sun god, *Hertha* or *Wertha* the eternal Isis, and *Camael* was their god of war. The Druidic *Holy Trinity* was thus: Heol, Hertha, and Camael. The highest divinity was *Esus,* whose symbol was a circle encompassing all within its circumference. Their goddess *Keridwen* personified wisdom like Minerva. The Druids studied natural science and only admitted adepts into higher ranks after lengthy discipline in like manner to the occult sciences of Egypt, Greece, and India. Those Druidic mysteries were concealed under the allegories, according to Hall, of the Blue Lodge of Masonry. Their education was superior to most of their colleagues on the continent, with Gallic youths sent to Druidic colleges in Britain for training in philosophy. Comprising three degrees, as the Blue Lodge of Masonry and occult sciences in India, amongst others, the lowest was that of *Ovate* (Ovydd). An honorary degree that required no special preparation, the Ovates dressed in green, the Druidic color of learning, and spent time learning medicine, astronomy, and music. Hall explains that an initiate of this level was admitted based on his *"general excellence and superior knowledge concerning the problems of life."* The green robes certainly related to the *green man* motif, or personified nature, found all throughout the world.

The second degree was that of a *Bard* (Beirdd), whose ranks wore blue robes to signify truth and harmony. They were to memorize thousands of the sacred Druidic poems, as with Hindu holy men, and were often chosen as teachers of the neophytes seeking entrance into the mysteries of their sect. These initiates wore the three sacred colors of the Order by striped robes composed of blue, green, and white.

The final division was that of the *Druid* (Derwyddon). Their job was to act as minister of the religious needs of the people, only after first obtaining the rank of *Bard Braint.* All Druids dressed in white, a symbol of purity equated to the pure Masonic gloves, and the sun, which is purifying and regenerating. Those Druids attempting exaltation to Arch-Druid, the spiritual head, were first required to pass six successive degrees. In his <u>Ten Great Religions</u>, James Freeman Clarke describes the beliefs of the Druids in greater detail: *"The Druids believed in three worlds and in transmigration from one to the other: In a world above this, in which happiness predominated; a world below, of misery; and this present state. This transmigration was to punish and reward and also to purify the soul. In the present world, said they, Good and Evil are so exactly balanced that man has the utmost freedom and is able to choose or reject either. The Welsh Triads tell us there are three objects of metempsychosis: to collect into the soul the properties of all being, to acquire a knowledge of all things, and to get power to conquer evil. There are also, they say, three kinds of knowledge: knowledge of the nature of each thing, of its cause, and its influence. There are three things which continually grow less: darkness, falsehood, and death. There are three which constantly increase: light, life, and truth."*

The Lion's Paw

If scientists believe they can reanimate bodies, perhaps they can, but any ancient notion of rising from the grave, or gaining immortality, is not one relating to vampires, zombies, or Frankenstein's monster. This is a moral battle and one typically lacking philosophical perspective, especially since the argument goes: *we should do it because we can.* These are stories that attract attention and intrigue, but do not explain the deeper meaning in the allegories or metaphors from whence they are extracted.

As we have seen, the resurrection of Jesus represents the rebirth of spirit from matter. In his association with the sun (son), and since as Booth put it, *"the heart is the portal through which Sun god enters our lives,"* Jesus is a wise man turned *son of God.* In fact, he is the *sun of god,* so far as the *SUN* itself is the *SON* of the *Grand Architect* and a portal for the *Ancient of Days* to influence life below. By this understanding, and the one of our own spirit, Jesus truly is the *son of God* too, as are we all sons and daughters of the Creator. Although first we are sons and daughters of man, it is only after initiation we become the sons and daughters of God.

Pythagoras, the Greek philosopher famous for his theorem, was also initiated into the *secret teachings* of Egypt within the Great Pyramid of Giza. He was placed in a coffin in the King's chamber for three days before being resurrected and offered the hand of an Egyptian hierophant speaking the words "come forth."

Pythagoras, from Hall's <u>The Secret Teachings of All Ages.</u>

The same story is told in John 11:43 where the King James Bible reads: *"And when he thus had spoken, he cried with a loud voice, Laz-a-rus, come forth."*

Lazarus was also dead, albeit symbolically, for three days in the tomb of materiality - the sacred maternal womb represented by the pyramid, cave, mountain, or mound - before being symbolically resurrected by the words "come forth." We learn from the Blackfoot people of Montana their myth about a character named Old Man, who created mankind from clay and then covered them up. Upon returning each day for a total of three, and on the forth morning, they were told to *"rise and walk; and they did so,"* as George Bird Grinnell writes in <u>Blackfoot Lodge Tales</u>. Lazarus, like Pythagoras, was initiated into the *mysteries* through a symbolic process of death and rebirth known as *Living Resurrection*, of which Jesus Christ was without doubt a master and thus a *son of God.*

In the *Pyramid Mysteries,* a priest, often wearing a lion's mask, would grip the hand of the initiate and pull them from the sarcophagus. This grip was known as the *Lion's Paw* and it pulled the initiate out of substance into life so that they could go forth as a great builder in the likeness of Chiram Abiff, the Masonic Grand Master.

Another well-known allegory is concealed by the Biblical story of Jonah, who is thrown into the ocean and swallowed by a great whale. The ocean is *maya,* or the *sea of illusion,* and the whale is the monster of *mortality.* In other familiar terms, the ocean is the underworld, the whale is Hades, and Jonah is Persephone. The Haida (Haidu) people of America's Pacific coast also tell of their hero-god, a Raven, being swallowed up by a great whale. Hall elucidates on this point:

> *"Jonah (the knower) is immersed in the sea of illusion (life) and swallowed by Cetus (the leviathan or monster of mortality)."*

Jonah remained in the whale's belly for three days, an allegory with parallels to various other dying–god myths. These stories also have very scientific meanings, derived from astronomy and astrology, relating to the death of the physical sun and its subsequent resurrection three days later during the winter solstice, along with all the various cycles of birth and death throughout the cosmos. They also contain a psychological basis, being that the great whale is actually our unconscious and the waters in which it swims the dark abyss. Many characters worldwide have been swallowed up in like manner to Jonah in the Bible: Finn MacCool was swallowed by a monstrous creature called *peist,* Maui was consumed by Hine-nui-te-po, Little Red Riding Hood by the wolf, Raven of the Bering Strait Eskimos by a whale-cow, Blood Clot Boy of the Blackfoot by a great fish, and the children of Saturn-Cronus are swallowed by time.

The Lion's Paw in the Pyramid Mysteries, from Hall's <u>The Lost Keys of Freemasonry.</u>

The Egyptian version is told by the story of Osiris and his resurrection through his sister-wife Isis. This union of the male and female is often referred to as the *Sacred Marriage* and it signifies the relationship between the generative principles of both sexes. It represents the redemption of the human soul from the tomb of matter. Osiris is the *Green Man*, the god of agriculture, who saves mankind from the darkness of night by sacrificing himself. Here we may also find the likeness of Jesus, Lazarus, Jonah, Prometheus, Maui, and even Persephone, for her return heralds the coming of new life. The idea of a soul immersed in a vessel is told in the Osiris story, too, when he is placed inside of a golden coffin with beautiful jewels. As god of agriculture, Osiris is the *seed* that needs sprouting. Therefore in the *mysteries* it is common to read of such analogies between the soul, the mystery of birth, and the magic of plant gorwth. The soul is watered and sprouts with wisdom; the harvest occurs nine months after the resurrected sun; the birth of a baby occurs nine months after conception. Much like Jesus, the body of Osiris was consumed symbolically as bread after the final harvest of the year, i.e., before the world was plunged into darkness. During this time Osiris was said to descend into the underworld to await resurrection. His descent is reminiscent of our soul becoming trapped in the illusion of matter, in need of a savior to bring us back from the dead.

The *Osirian bread* was made from the cultivation of Egyptian *kamut* (wheat), the stalks of which were said to be inhabited by the essence of Osiris. Upon the proper *cultivation* of our inner Osirian-seed, we all acquire the ability to rise from the dead. Those raised from this tomb by the strong grip of the *Lion's Paw* resurrect their master builder in perfecting their centers of thought, action, and emotion. With his resurrection through magic (natural law), Osiris brings life back to a barren land, while becoming the savior poised to free us from our seedling or egg. The symbolism of resurrection or rebirth is evident with the Bennu, Thunder, or Phoenix birds, which, after dying, rise renewed from their own ashes. They have undergone a transformative process, the essence of which is explained in the examples of Jesus *turning water into wine*, Masons transforming *rough ashlar into smooth cut stone*, and alchemists turning *lead into gold*.

Cinderella is Isis

The philosophy of a *lesser birth* and *greater birth*, or *spiritual death* and *spiritual rebirth*, can be found in **the story of *Sleeping Beauty***: in relation to our divine potentiality, our inner beauty remains in a state of deep sleep.

Aurora (Latin for *dawn*), or Briar Rose (more on the rose later), is born into a royal family. Her parents, the King and Queen, throw a party to celebrate her divine spiritual birth, as evidenced by the appearance of fairies and other spiritual creatures. Six fairies arrive to present her with blessings, and the seventh, the spirit of opposition, angry over not being invited, curses the baby to *death*. Before this permanent *death curse* could take effect, however, another fairy counters it with one of a powerful *sleep*, which was only to be broken by the kiss of a prince.

Later in her life, while wandering through the castle, she pricks her finger on a spindle of a spinning wheel and is cast into that death-like sleep. She thus experiences the *lesser physical birth* and the *great spiritual death*. We are all *Sleeping Beauty*, in a sense cursed to grow in physical beauty and grace, only to die later in life (or awaken from our sleep). Sine the word *aurora* in Latin means "goddess of the dawn," *Beauty* is like the rising sun or *Morning Star* of Venus.

There is a similar story called *Rapunzel*, in which we find the Baltic solar goddess *Saulė* held captive in a tower.

Aurora's birth to a royal family signifies her spiritually divine nature, as with prince Adam in *Beauty and the Beast*. The seven fairies represent the planetary spheres of consciousness, the seventh of which is the spirit of opposition known as Saturn. Aurora's death-like sleep signifies the soul submerged in matter and the kiss of a prince is symbolic of the *kiss of wisdom*.

The story of Cinderella is that of a girl working in the kitchen of a great palace. Her face is blackened by the soot of a stove and thus she acquires the name *Cinders*. She longs for a prince to unite with in sacred union, i.e., the *alchemical marriage*, so that she can overcome her lower instincts with higher purpose. We are all *Cinderella*, in a sense wandering a desolate landscape of mind and body (consider the Israelites) ever in search of our *true love* – wisdom or God – and the Promised Land. Famed mythologist Joseph Campbell explains that the divine soul is always searching in exile, even in the Holy Land:

> *"Exile, in fact, was anywhere, even in the Holy Land. Later the Kabbalah made it a central attribute of the divinity, for the Shekhinah (the divine spirit) is always in exile... Exile, therefore, was not a location away from the homeland, but a condition that is not salvation. The anticipated salvation would come when the messiah king of the seed of David arrived, and with this, a mass return to Jerusalem. Salvation would include the resurrection of the dead, who would also congregate en masse in Jerusalem."*

In Egypt the character we call Cinderella was known Isis who, in mourning the death of her husband, King Osiris, wanders the land in black veils. While searching, she begins working in the palace of the Syrian king where later it is discovered the coffin of her beloved is concealed within one of the palace's pillars. Using her magical powers (persuasion), Isis convinced the Syrian King to allow removal of the pillar so that she could revive her lover.

Upon resurrection, Osiris was once again taken from her and dismembered into fourteen pieces by his brother Set, who represents the pervasive animal nature always attempting to drag down the soul like Persephone into Hades. The fourteen pieces symbolize the separation of man from *source* and the scattering of perceived separateness throughout the corporeal sphere – thus we are always in exile searching for truth.

Isis once again embarks on a journey and finds thirteen, a number often associated with regeneration, of the fourteen pieces. The generative piece of Osiris, his penis, was not found and so Isis fashioned one from gold, or bee's wax. The penis was lost in the Nile River and, according to Plutarch, it was devoured by *lepidotus*, the *phagrus*, and the *oxyrynchus* (a form of pike).

Isis then proceeded to bind all remaining pieces in linen to create the first *mummy*. This binding also represented the submersion of soul in matter. Upon completion, she used the golden phallus to impregnate herself so that she may later give birth the savior Horus who, as god of the sun, avenges the death of his father. Horus is Osiris reborn in youthful form, and thus represents the various cycles of the sun that includes its yearly journey from birth to death. He is sometimes associated with *Sokar* or *Seker*, the Greek *Sokaris* or *Socharis*, the Memphite god of the dead. Horus is also very clearly the phoenix.

In another story, when the shade of Osiris is resurrected from the dead, he visits Isis as the *Holy Ghost* and impregnates her. She then gives birth to *Harpocrates*, another name for Horus, and a later incarnation of Osiris as the *God of Silence*, who is depicted holding his fingers to his mouth and warning all to keep the secrets of the *mysteries* from the profane.

Egyptian Madonna, depicting Isis suckling the infant Horus.

Her horns, like Hathor's, are derived from Ares and Taurus, the sheep/ram and bull herded by the crook and flail of Osiris.

Here we have a reference to the "Immaculate Conception" of Jesus in the Biblical story, when the angel Gabriel visited Mary. Classical images of Isis depict her suckling the infant Horus in like manner to Mary caring for the baby Jesus. The angel is a ray of light and Mary is the earth, the former penetrating the latter and impregnating her with seed.

In yet another version of the story, the chest containing Osiris washes up on the shore and by his consort Isis, and the god of wisdom *Djehuti*, or *Thoth*, he is resurrected. Therefore, by wisdom the dead are brought to life and the blind are made to see.

Images of Osiris often depict the resurrected king with a green face; for he is the *Green Man* with his body restricted by *matter*. His protruding head signifies intelligence lifted from ignorance, or light emanating from darkness. Both the Egyptian Ankh and the classic pentagram (*pentagrammaton* or *pentalpha*) further portray this esoteric truth. Of the *pentagram*, Eliphas Levi writes:

> *"The Pentagram signifies the domination of the mind over the elements, and the demons of air, the spirits of fire, the phantoms of water and ghosts of earth are enchained by this sign."*

Both the pentagram and a circle have influence over evil spirits, those still always subjected to higher intelligences. The *pentagram* or *pentangle* houses the four elements upon its four lower points, and upon the fifth, like that of the Ankh, is signified intelligence rising forth from the lower four corners of the infernal world. It has five obtuse angles (those within the open center), five acute (those within the points), and five double triangles (the surrounding triangles and points that are alike). In eastern tradition, the pentacle is known as *se-man* and is accompanied by the *do-man*, or grid, which acts as a protective agent.

Plutarch speaks to the symbolism of the holy Egyptian trinity of Osiris, Isis, and Horus, in the following manner. He says they represent Intelligence, Matter and Cosmos; that they are the most perfect triangle. Its base is Isis, or female essence, and equals four; the vertical parts are Osiris, the male essence, and equals three; the fifth point, like the pentagram and five wounds of Christ (stigmata), is their offspring Horus. J. G. Frazer, in The Golden Bough, wrote also of this myth:

> *"As Osiris died and rose again from the dead, so all men hoped to arise like him, from death to the life eternal."*

The circle hath neither beginning nor end; or has both simultaneously in every way. It is *infinite* and *perfect*. Therefore, the circle is used for bindings and conjurations. The magician stands within the circle to receive its protection from evil spirits - the *Magic Circle*. Some may conjure evil spirits in contrary manner by which they are called into the circle and remain there, while the magician remains on the outside likewise protected by the barrier.

Just as Osiris has a green face, Isis is covered in black veils as she mourns his loss. Upon reuniting with her beloved, the black veils become white in the wedding that follows.

The Osiris myth, like that of the "hero twins" of Guatemala, tells the tale of what has for centuries been referred to as *shamanism*: entering an altered state of consciousness, communing with therianthropes and spirits, being sacrificed in a spiritual body, and obtaining healing powers and knowledge before returning to the mundane world. Osiris does all these things alongside of Anubis (half jackal-half human) and many other characters.

The Isis myth, entwined with that of Osiris, is like that of Cinderella, as both are in search of their *prince charming*. This *prince* is the soul in exile. Reunited, Isis and Osiris are Christ and his Bride-Church, as described in:

Revelation 19:7-9

"Let us rejoice and be glad and give him glory! For the wedding of the Lamb has come, and his bride has made herself ready. Fine linen, bright and clean, was given to her to wear."

Ephesians 5:25-27

"Husbands, love your wives, just as Christ loved the church and gave himself up for her to make her holy, cleansing her by the washing with water through the word, and to present her to himself as a radiant church, without stain or wrinkle or any other blemish, but holy and blameless."

Similar fairy tales are not mere children's stories, but allegories of divine importance intended to convey a deeper meaning to those with *eyes to see* and *ears to hear*. Even if they are consumed subconsciously, the value of their imaginative qualities still penetrates our inner spiritual sanctum. They entertain while informing of divine matters in a metaphoric yet scientific manner. Ingeniously, the essences of these stories are passed along to each new generation without much contention, acting as a spiritual *Trojan Horse* infiltrating a world of chaos to implant seeds of order.

The Osiris (Asar) - Isis (Aset) Myth

The word *mythology* is derived from the Greek *mythos*, relating to words or stories that reflect the values and attitudes of a people. In antiquity, it was meant to convey a form of entertainment and education, along with promoting the very soul of a culture. The word has since been redefined to indicate something *imaginary*. Through this *perversion*, although not entirely intentional, the story of Osiris and Isis has been misunderstood as incestuous and perverse. The *profane* fail to understand that the relationship between this *cosmic couple* as both husband and wife, and brother and sister, is meant to relate to more than literalisms. Osiris is a King, and his wife Isis is his loyal Queen. Their companionship expresses the merging of passive and active principles displayed simply by a line and circle, or two lines comprising a Latin Cross. It is elsewhere known as the Chinese *Yin Yang*, Indian *Yab Yum*, or Japanese *In Yo*. Occultists know it as the *alchemical wedding* and Christians as the marriage of Christ and his Bride-Church.

The marriage of a candidate in the *mystery schools* was to take place metaphorically in a bridal chamber to a maternal bride. This unification of male and female was considered a sacred union that would allow for a *living resurrection* of the candidate whom, like the descended Osiris, reincarnates and rises from the tomb reborn as the *son and sun of God*.

Here is the full story: We begin with the Egyptian sky goddess *Nut*, daughter of *Shu* and *Tefnut*, the wife of *Seb* (Saturn), and mother of RA (Helios). Nut is unfaithful to RA and becomes pregnant with the children of Seb. Angered over her disloyalty, RA places a curse upon the woman that she may not give birth to her children during any month or year. Another of Nut's admirers, the god of wisdom and writing, Thoth, acts to help his love by playing at *tables* with Selene, the moon goddess. Thoth wins part of her illuminations for which he forms into five additional days to be added to the calendar of 360.

Now there are 365 days and more time for Nut to give birth. Through Thoth's assistance, Nut can give birth during these additional days and circumvent the curse of Ra. She brings forth the children known as Osiris (Child of Ra), Horus (Child of Ra), Typhon or Set (Child of Seb), Isis (Child of Thoth), and Nephthys (Child of Seb). The "child of" is to indicate the interpretations of the Greek philosopher Plutarch in this matter.

The duties of Osiris, the beast slayer, included traveling the world to educate mankind in *sacred sciences*, and those not as sacred, by the methods of persuasion and reason rather than violence or conflict. His endeavors are nearly identical to the civilizing gods of central and south America: Viracocha and Quetzalcoatl. By *beast slayer* we are to understand that Osiris is an externalized symbol of our own internal duty to slay the *great red dragon*.

The slaying of beasts also refers the spreading of knowledge sufficient to render man illuminated enough to rise from his death rest. Through wisdom, Osiris embodied the elements of Thoth from which he was born. By converting people with *reason* rather than *conflict* he was performing the miracle of turning *water into wine* or *lead into gold*. Violence and conflict are core elements of instinctual animal behavior, qualities held by Typhon, or Set, the brother and adversary of Osiris. According to the Plutarch the word *Typhon* means *insolence* and *pride*, two enemies of *understanding* and *truth*.

As a beacon of light, Osiris was thus a threat to Set who labored to usurp the kingly throne from his brother. In other words, Typhon-Set embodies the warning given to man in Proverbs 16:18, which says: *"Pride goeth before destruction, and an haughty spirit before a fall."*

Upon returning from his travels Osiris was welcomed by crowds of people rejoicing in triumph. In preparations set forth prior, Set invited his brother to a party in his honor and in celebration of those successful travels.

Some stories relate that Set was upset with Osiris for sleeping with his wife-sister Nephthys. Here we find that Nephthys is associated with the inferior sphere, i.e., death and decay, and that the travels of Osiris mingled the god with profane people (like Jesus with the downtrodden) in hopes of awakening their *sleeping beauty* and *sprouting the Osirian seed*. This what it means that Osiris slept with Nephthys. He mingled with his brother's wife in an attempt to enlighten man in like manner with Prometheus. This would be in strict contrast with Set or Typhon, the son of Seb (Saturn), lord of chaos and destruction. Osiris is composed of several elements, as are humans, his darker side personified by Set and his feminine by Isis. The traditional Egyptian trinity is Osiris, Isis, and Horus, but can also be held as Osiris, Set, and Isis, especially since Horus is simply Osiris reincarnated.

Once dinner concluded, Set announced a game he had devised as part of a devious scheme. A beautifully decorated chest made of cedar and lined with gold, ivory, silver, and lapis lazuli was offered as a gift to anyone able to fit inside, an interior that had specifically been designed to fit the body of Osiris. After many guests attempted with no success, Osiris lay in the coffin to exclaim the perfect nature of its design! Almost immediately Set

Osiris beguiled into the Chest, by Evelyn Paul.

Found in <u>Ancient Egyptian Myths and Legends</u> by Lewis Spence, 1915.

slammed the lid closed, hammered it with nails, and filled all cracks with molten lead, the metal of Satan. Chaotic Set, the adversary of *truth*, knew his brother (*truth* and *wisdom*) was a god and therefore could not be killed so he decided to have the chest buried or hidden. His fellow conspirators took the chest to the edge of the Nile under the watchful eye of children and flung it into the dark waters. After floating down the river to the Byblos coast of Syria, a young tamarisk tree halted the chest and grew roots around it, making the chest apart of its body.

The children that witnessed the accomplices of Typhon cast the chest into the Nile River assisted Isis in her search for her husband-brother, and thus is the reason Egyptians regarded the words of children with such high esteem. Set's scheme is the trick played upon the soul before its sinking into a deep deathful sleep. Manly Hall here discusses the idea of placing *truth* in the confines of an alluring *tomb*:

"With truth dead, or at least exiled to the invisible world, material facts were superseded by opinions;

opinions bred hatreds, and men finally fought and died over notions both senseless and soulless…Because the human mind demanded intellectual expression, Typhon sowed the seeds of intellectual confusion so that numerous orders of learning appeared which were convincingly plausible but untrue. These various orders of thought survived by catering to the weakness and limitations of the flesh."

In witnessing the magnificent tamarisk tree, which contained the chest and Osiris, in its grand splendor, the King of Syria had it removed and made into a pillar for his palace. Here is the reason why we say trees or pillars contain wisdom and a divine intelligence. The powerful and wise talking trees in Lord of the Rings (Saturn) is a great example of this archaic truth.

Moreover, Osiris is thus a prototype of Moses, who was placed in a basket and floated down the Nile to end his journey in an Egyptian palace. Moses was then "raised" in the palace just as the tree turned pillar had been "raised" in the Syrian palace. Considering that some believe Pharaoh Akhenaten to be Moses, of which there is serious evidence (*see* Did Moses Exist? by Acharya S), there is further evidence that both leaders (even if they are one) would certainly have been "raised" in the Egyptian *mystery dramas* and played the role of Osiris in their initiation.

The story of King Sargon of Akkad is also nearly identical, as he also placed in a basket and, as royalty, floated down a river. This was a common practice in the occult sciences of India as well and represents the emersion of the *divine soul* in a *bodily vessel* that is floated on the *river of souls*. Both Moses and Osiris were "raised" in a royal palace, one as a child and the other as a pillar. The tamarisk *tree* is therefore the *Tree of Life* whereby the soul ascends from Kabbalistic *Malkuth* to *Kether* and is upwardly inclined toward divinity or royalty.

Djed-pillar Amulet, from the Brooklyn Museum and Charles Edwin Wilbour Fund.

In one Greek story of *Dryope* and her sister *Iole* we find human intelligence enclosed inside a tree. Walking alongside Iole with her children alongside, Dryope made her way to a pool where she was to make garlands for nymphs. With her son she saw a lotus tree full of blossoms and plucked one for the baby. Suddenly blood began flowing down the stem and Dryope realized the tree was the nymph *Lotis*, who used its cover in fleeing an aggressive pursuer. Dryope herself tried to flee in horror but she quickly became rooted to the ground and covered in bark; she herself became like a tree. The ancient concept of pillars housing divine intelligences and wisdom is addressed in this myth, with similarities shared by the Masonic pillars of Solomon's Temple, *Boaz* and *Jachin*. These pillars are invariably known as *beauty* and *strength*, or *philosophy* and *science*. They represent the contrast between two extremes that must balance to maintain the structural integrity of the temple. In Egypt this pillar was *Djed*, representing the *backbone of Osiris*. It is a tree with no branches, or a pillar made of a bundle of reeds.

During the time of his abduction Isis mourns in sorrow for her lost companion in like manner to Demeter mourning the loss of her daughter Persephone. In searching for her husband, Isis cuts her hair and blackens her face with cinders from which we derive the story of *Cinderella*. Her black veils indicate mourning of the deceased, but also the distressing power of emotion. Her later white veils are those of the virginal bride in wedding.

When Isis becomes aware in her search that a tree holds the chest containing her husband, now a pillar in the royal palace of a king, she immediately travels to Byblos and takes a job as a servant, and nurse to the Queen's children. This is symbolic of the nurturing qualities of the maternal Isis. At night, when those in the palace are sleeping, she transforms into a swallow and soars around the pillar singing sad notes of discontent and sorrow.

Unveiling her divine nature, she later convinces the Syrian king to allow for the removal of the pillar and extraction of the chest contained therein. With the chest in her possession, she traveled to an island whereupon performing a series of magical rites, utilizing the superphysical nature of magic, she temporarily brings Osiris to life so that she may conceive Horus. This god is the son of the dead, a savior of all mankind, and one in the same - a *reincarnation* - of his father.

Isis eventually leaves the chest to travel to another sacred location, at which point Set discovers it in her absence. Some accounts report her traveling to meet or visit her son, likely meant to convey her giving birth to Horus in another location.

There are many accounts as to how Set was able to find Osiris. Some say that when Isis left, he merely stumbled across the chest while hunting by moonlight. Other versions suggest Set to have sensed where the chest was located, signifying the constant attempts of *darkness* or chaos in snuffing out any *light*. Whatever the case, he acted quickly to get rid of the body of his brother by dismembering him into fourteen pieces and scattering the remains.

These pieces are thought to represent the days it takes the Moon to move from *New* to *Full* in its monthly cycle. This dismemberment was one of the only ways Set found to vanquish Osiris more permanently, due to the fact a god cannot die. Neither can *truth*, it can only be oppressed. Set's inability to entirely defeat Osiris references the inner qualities of *truth* that lie dormant in each of us, suppressed and awaiting to be *resurrected* no matter how much chaos and death surround us in the world of the living.

The separating of pieces signifies the dispersal of various languages and people in like manner to the *Tower of Babel*. It also represents the separate individual components of humanity that ultimately emanate from one *source*, and the element of wisdom to be obtained in search by the Hermit. By cutting the body into fourteen pieces we are also reminded of Bacchus, the Roman god of wine, being ripped into seven pieces by the Titans. Orpheus was likewise torn limb from limb by the *Maenads* and just as Quetzalcoatl was crucified like Christ, his body was cut into pieces too.

Further interpretation may reveal that *truth* can be scattered in pieces, but through dedication (willpower) we may find and bandage those pieces once more, which will bind them in a *mummy of wisdom* with *Natural Magic*. And this is why Osiris "sets" in judgment of the dead in the underworld, assisted by Anubis and the *Eye of Horus,* which allows him to see. This *eyeball* was taken from Horus after he eventual defeated his uncle Set-Typhon. Thus, the sun **SET**S to usher in darkness, while the sun later awakens on the **HOR**IZON.

Osiris is seen here in the Hall of Judgement holding the crook and flail and judging the *dead.* The larger image that this segment is taken from can be seen below with Anubis, Thoth, and the *eater of the dead.*

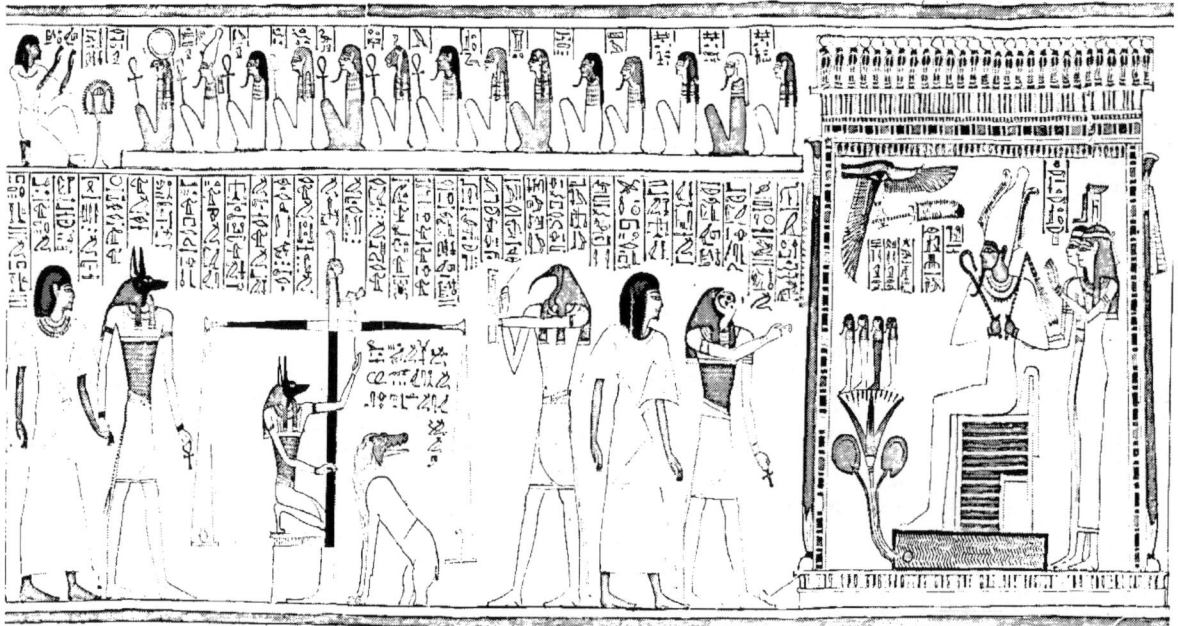

Upon returning from giving birth at a sacred place, or simply awakening the next morning in other stories, Isis discovers the missing body of Osiris. In some accounts, Set imprisons Isis and Horus upon the prophecy of Thoth that Horus will avenge his father's death and acquire his father's rule. Here we find a comparison with the Roman god Jupiter (Greek Zeus), who was to replace his father Saturn. Because of this prophecy Saturn sent his cohorts, the Titans, to kill the future king who was hidden away for protection by *Amalthea*, the Greek nymph and foster-mother of Zeus. When the Titans were defeated, they were imprisoned underground, and their sons were later depicted as red-eyed creatures with skin made of scales. Here we find a common depiction of demons that dwell in the underground lairs of a physical hell.

In a similar manner, Isis hides Horus in a papyrus swamp to ensure his safety just as Moses was placed in a basket and hidden in reeds by the riverbank. We find a similar motif in the story of how *Krishna* was born, when Devaki's brother *Kansa* (Kans) sent a red serpent to kill the child; he spoke, *"Thy enemy is born, they death is certain."* In Iran the King was persuaded to kill the infant Zarathustra. In Hebrew tradition the birth of Abraham threatened the rule of Nimrod, who acted to commit infanticide, itself an identical reaction of King Herod upon hearing of the birth of Jesus and his future kingship. Moses was being protected in his basket, of course, from the infanticide carried out in Egypt.

In collecting thirteen of the fourteen pieces, Isis, some say with the help of Nephthys, sewed them together with white linen into the first mummy. The number thirteen is important as it signifies *rebirth* or *regeneration* within the twelve houses of the zodiac (animal) wheel. After the sun passes through all twelve, the first house then becomes the number thirteen, and the cycle repeats. The letter "M" is also the thirteenth in the alphabet and signifies the maternal principle of MA relating to regeneration and procreation. The relationship to the zodiac is significant because the sun passes through various cycles represented by a wheel, and Osiris in his later incarnation as Horus, is synonymous with the sun.

Since the earth is tilted on its axis it wobbles slightly in its orbit. Therefore, the sun seems to move backward in an extended cycle throughout the houses of the zodiac. The sun occupies each house for roughly 2,160-years before moving to the next. To move through all twelve houses requires a period of roughly 25,000 years. This is known as the *Precession of the Equinoxes* and each of these ages were ruled over by a god, always to be usurped by his offspring. The real number of years is closer to 25,920, or the average number of times humans breathe each day.

The Age of Jesus is that of Pisces, the two fish, which is why fish symbolism is so prevalent in the Bible. This Age began roughly around 1 A.D., the birth of Jesus and the beginning of the Age of Pisces. At the end of this age begins the Age of Aquarius, the water bearer, and this what is meant in Matthew 28 about Jesus being with us *"to the very end of the age."* Author David Fideler explains how the god Mithras, or the sun, relates to the transition of *ages*:

> *"Mithras embodies the nature of Aeon by slaying the bull of Taurus and inaugurating the era of Aries, while Jesus is the sacrificial lamb of god who closes the Age of Aries, opens the Age of Pisces, and establishes the early Christian mysteries with their Piscean fish symbolism."*

The cult of Mithra, who killed the bull to end the age of Taurus and begin Pisces, is partly responsible for the current hat worn by the Papal in Rome. This headdress is referred to as the *Mitre* and is symbolic of a fish head, as it relates to Piscean Age fish symbolism, and water gods such as the Syrian Dagon, or the Mesopotamian Oannes, the fish god of the Philistines. Oannes was also like

Osiris, being that he was a god of grain and fertility, who brought universal wisdom to mankind. He further shared with Jesus the ability to multiply things, including food. When Jesus multiplied *"five loaves of bread and two fish"* in Matthew 14 we are again talking about Pisces. Hall describes each new *age* as a new personality of the sun:

> *"During these periods, or ages, religious worship takes the form of the appropriate celestial sign – that which the sun is said to assume as a personality in the same manner that a spirit assumes the body."*

The Greek goddess Aphrodite was also honored by the eating of fish on a Friday, which now bears the name of her Scandinavian counterpart Freya. Many cultures make *fish Friday* a tradition. The Hindu god Vishnu also incarnates as a fish avatar named Matsya.

Oannes

The Eye of Horus

As Osiris descends into the Underworld, his son Horus attempts to avenge his death by fighting with Typhon-Set. In combat, Horus loses his eye, which he then gives to his father so that he may see in the darkness of his new kingdom. This became known as the *Eye of RA*, the Chief god of Egypt (only overpowered by HEKA), or the *Eye of Horus*.

The *right eye* represents the sun, signifying the path of light followed by those knowledgeable of the *Pythagorean Y*. To cover this eye is the obscure the light and instead give advance to the *left eye* of the reflective moon. In Egyptian mythology, Horus loses the left eye, and it is this that allows Osiris to see in the land of shadows and reflections. Other stories say it was the right eye lost in battle. Either way, we have a very powerful myth here that spans the entire world.

Paul Carus explains in his <u>The History of the Devil and the Idea of Evil</u> that the left and right eyes represent the declining and rising sun, and their associated solstices: *"…the left or black eye of the decreasing sun, governing the year from the summer solstice to the winter solstice, which is contrasted with the right or bright eye of Hor, the increasing sun, which symbolizes growth of life and the spread of light from the winter solstice to the summer solstice."* He continues, in explaining the battle between Osiris and Set:

> *"Set was strong enough to slay Osiris, as night overcomes the light of the sun; but the sun is born again in the child-god Hor, who conquers Set and forces him to make the old serpent of death surrender the spoil. As the sun sets to rise again, so man dies to be reborn. The evil power is full of awe, but a righteous cause cannot be crushed, and, in spite of death, life is immortal."*

The Chief-god and sky-father in the Norse mythology, Odin, was a much different character than gods like Osiris, Zeus or Jupiter, but he shared commonalties with the same. Often depicted with two ravens perched on his shoulders, these birds would bring news from all around the world every day. Their names were *Hugin* (thought) and *Munin* (memory). Although Odin was supreme among gods and men, he constantly searched for wisdom. He visited the *Well of Wisdom*, guarded by *Mimir* the wise. In order that he was allowed to partake of the well, Mimir said Odin must first pay for the wisdom with his eye, for which he consented.

The Māori people of New Zealand preserve the myth of Tāwhirimātea, their weather god, who became so enraged when discovering his parents, Sky Father and Earth Mother, separated that he tore his eyes out. He then threw them into the sky where they became *Matariki* – the Pleiades.

The left eye was taken from *Izanagi-No-Mikoto*, creator god of Japan to whom the radiant solar goddess *Amaterasu* was born. In eastern tradition, another strange story from Japan informs us of the *Kazane no Enkon*. This is a woman killed by her husband with a farming sickle and turned into a vengeful spirit. She is usually portrayed with one open eye and one closed eye. According to The Dark Side of Japan by Antony Cummins:

"The closed eye has come to represent the moon, the open the sun."

In Arabic and Islamic lore there is al-Dajjāl, the *Deceiver*. In their eschatology, he is a false messianic figure prophesized to arrive in the end times before being destroyed by Christ, or *mahdī*, the *rightly guided one*. This antichrist is almost always described as a *"one-eyed man with a ruddy face and curling hair and the Arabic letter k-f-r ('unbelief') on his forehead,"* according to the Encyclopedia Britannica. The *Eye of Providence* or *All-Seeing Eye* is meant to represent, among other things, the omnipresence of deity. It indicates to the student of occult studies that no matter if he or she is in private or public, to always live virtuous; to follow the path of light; to control perverse will, desire, and to overcome ignorance. The presence of this "eye" is merely symbolic and is not to be taken as a literal and external creator – one beyond our world – constantly watching over our shoulder like a teacher in a classroom, or an architect overseeing construction. The eye is more relatable to *memento mori*, a reminder of our mortality and divine duties.

In later myths involving Typhon-Set and Horus, the pair symbolically wage a cyclical battle. Each evening Set is victorious in casting Osiris into the underworld and ruling by darkness. Every morning, though, Osiris is resurrected as Horus, the sun, who avenges the death of his father and brings light back to a dark world. We can again see the similarity to the Greek story of Demeter and Persephone. This battle occurs daily and nightly, and by seasonal changes throughout the year. Sunlight nurtures plants to grow while itself becoming very weak during the fall and winter months. It does not strengthen noticeably once more until near the end of winter and then during the spring equinox when days become longer than nights.

The archetypical battle between dark and light was personified in the conflict described by Persian Magi through the principles of good and evil, which were manifest like Osiris and Set under the names *Ormuzd*, or *Ahura Mazda* (creator god), and *Ahriman* (evil spirit). This epic battle between the progeny of darkness and the preservers of truth and wisdom is called *Armageddon*, "the last battle between good and evil before the Day of Judgment." We know it as *Ragnarök* from the Eddas and the *Kurukshetra* of the Mahabharata. D. M. Murdoch further explains in her book The Christ Conspiracy these dualistic concepts of good and evil, god and the devil, light and darkness:

"The dualistic concepts of absolute good and evil did not originate with Christianity but are found long before the Christian era, particularly within Zoroastrianism. Satan is an adaptation of the

Persian representative of evil 'Ahriman,' the twin brother of 'God,' the same as the Egyptian Set, Horus's twin and principal enemy, also known as 'Sata,' whence comes 'Satan.' Horus struggles with Set in the exact manner that Jesus battles with Satan, with 40 days in the wilderness, among other similarities, such as the revealing from the mount 'all the kingdoms of Earth.' This myth represents the triumph of light over dark or the sun's return to relieve the terror of the night. Horus/Set was the god of the two horizons; hence, Horus was the rising sun, and Set the time of the Sun-SET."

Meaning of the Osiris-Isis Myth

As a symbol of agriculture, Osiris was depicted literally as having green skin to signify foliage and fertility - the *Green Man* or wild man of the woods. He was conductor of law and teacher of all civilizing wisdom. Osiris can also be rightfully referred to as the *Great Hunter, Great Warrior, Beast Slayer, Orion the Hunter* in Greek mythology, and *Herne the Hunter* in Norse mythology. Some may recall a connection to the Biblical Nimrod, who was described in Genesis 10:9 as such: *"He was a mighty hunter before the Lord."*

Osiris is often referred to as the "universal master" – *neb tem* – or a *Lord of Beasts*. The great Hindu god Siva (Shiva or Rudra-Siva) is also known in one incarnation by the name *Pasupati*, a word meaning *lord of the animals* or *Beastmaster*. It may further be derived of Osiris his connection to Orion through the name *Ourien*, which, according to Mark Booth in <u>The Secret History of the World</u>, means semen:

> *"His [Osiris] name is connected with insemination, 'ourien' meaning semen, and what we call the belt of Orion is a euphemism. In ancient times it was a penis that became erect as the year progressed."*

The Mesopotamian stories of Nimrod, Ishtar, and Tammuz shares commonalities with the Osiris-Isis myth too. Ishtar is the morning star like Venus, the Queen of heaven, and her son is named Tammuz. He is also her lover, and the father of Nimrod, his father. Since Tammuz is a later incarnation Nimrod, he also becomes associated with the hunt and is given the appropriate tools to carry out this task. He is Horus and the Phoenix.

Our modern Cupid (Eros or Amor) is often depicted with a bow and arrow as well, symbolizing his connection to Tammuz, Nimrod, Horus, Osiris, Herne, Orion, and many other gods with similar attributes.

From the golden phallus of Osiris – the one Isis uses to impregnate herself - we may extract additional meanings of fertility in that of the golden-yellow sheaf of wheat held by the virgin of the zodiac. In gold, the metal of the sun, is a spiritual substance concealing the *first sperm* which impregnates the universal egg. In agricultural terms there is a spiritual light of wisdom which nurtures the Osirian seed to sprout just as the sun encourages the literal seed to sprout. In the ancient world the sun was personified as a newborn baby that grew into an old man throughout the year before dying in the winter. When the baby is reborn, we often refer to this as *Baby New Year*.

Similarly, so is the penis said to become erect throughout this yearly cycle, which obviously leads to ejaculation of *ourien*, impregnation of the earth, and the later birth of crops that are harvested for a last supper. An erect phallus also symbolizes, in Tantric Hinduism, mastery over bodily desires and matter.

The chest which entombs Osiris is adorned with earthly ornaments much like the dazzling matter that brings so many to their spiritual demise by the left-hand path of the *Pythagorean Y*. These tricks are *false lights* that deceive the soul. Therefore, the coffin or chest is the body of man, and when Osiris excitedly finds that it fits, only to have Set slam shut the lid and seal it with lead, it is reminiscent of Hades or Pluto grasping Persephone and pulling her into the darkness of his kingdom. When the chest is cast into the Nile River, we find reference to the casting of a soul into the River of Souls, the Milky Way, so that man becomes physically incarnate.

The fourteen pieces of the Osirian body represent the scattering of truth, which may be bandaged together in a reunion with the motherly Isis since it can never be destroyed. The magical actions performed on his body parts by Isis speak of watering the Osirian seed so that through the maternal may be brought forth a new incarnation, in this case Horus, while still alive – a *Living Resurrection*.

Some believe that the burial of Osiris is itself the death of seed, and his resurrection or rebirth is his appearance as Horus, the first green sprout of corn. Others believe Osiris himself to be the Nile River, while Isis is the land inundated and rendered fertile during its yearly inundation. Still others suggest the exact opposite, which may be more accurate considering Isis the patron of water.

The *Heliacal Rising* of Sirius signified this yearly inundation, typically occurring on July 23rd, when Sirius, Earth, and the Sun are aligned on the horizon. This is the origin for the *Dog Days of Summer*.

Another key to the myth says that Osiris was a mere 28 years of age at death, or that he reigned for 28 years. This then relates directly to the cycles and phases of our moon from whence we acquire the word *moonth* or *month*. The 12 months are based off the roughly 28-day cycles of the moon. There is also a strong connection to the female menstrual cycle with the word *menstrual* being derived from the Latin word *mensis,* meaning month.

These latter interpretations involving agriculture and celestial cycles may be well understood today, but it is difficult to imagine wise men from all over, often embarking on a perilous journey, traveling to distant lands, only to wait in patience to be admitted into the *mysteries* for which, if they were mundane, were so well known even to the uninitiated. Such myths were part of an ancient *esoteric science*, which is still today unknown to much of the public. Hall writes of these learned men and their travels to Egypt:

> *"The initiates of her Mysteries, returning to their own countries, not only felt themselves more than repaid for their hazardous journeys and long vigils but furthermore, they became founders of distinguished systems of thinking, disseminators of useful knowledge and in all cases bore witness to a broad and deep learning."*

We find encased in the myth of Osiris - inside the chest - an elaborate arcane story having survived conquest of land and truth. Depictions of Osiris often show a mummified body with uncovered head. This protruding part of the corporeal body represents the spirit, the living head, bound to matter (mummified), and imprisoned in the narrow binds of flesh. The early cross, or Ankh, with a circular top, preserves an important element of both the story of Osiris and the crucifixion of Christ. This cross is *physical matter,* representing the four corners of the world, that our soul is nailed to with *nails of illusion*. Also known as the *Crux Ansata*, or *Ansata Cross*, it symbolizes the head or spiritual nature of man protruding from the bindings of *matter*, again depicted in the partially mummified body of Osiris. The head of the Crux Ansata is the head of man, and the three additional protruding points are his arms and legs. The head rises upward much like the fifth point does from the other four points of a pentagram. These five points also represent the five wounds of Christ (stigmata) – feet, hands, and the crown of thorns. They are the five senses. In the philosophical language of the ancients, the Ankh was more accurately defined as *Life Bestowing*. It was worn always by Egyptian Adepts and carried by most of their pantheon of gods and goddesses.

The Osiris-Isis represents a hidden doctrine, and as the Church is called the Bride of Christ, we find in these *mysteries* a great Mother, the consort of heaven, who ensures nobility and inspires wisdom. She is the woman clothed in the sun with the moon at her feet and stars crowned upon her head. She flees to save her child from being consumed by the great dragon, just as *Amalthea* protected Jupiter from Saturn; as Jesus was protected from the infanticide of King Herod; or Moses was protected from infanticide in Egyptian.

This *great mother* is known in the far away land of Japan as Amaterasu, goddess of the sun, and Queen of Heaven. She, like Christ, spends three nights in an earthly tomb before being resurrected and bringing light and warmth back to the world.

As for the missing penis, devoured by the fish of the Nile, an interesting observation may be made. Mankind is the fish, and the phallus is the power of the *lost code* or *Word* of the Freemasonic Grand Master Hiram Abiff (the Widow's Son), which we have substituted with a golden replica or false idol. Manly Hall suggests that this golden phallus is also the three lettered word of Freemasonry concealed under the letters of A-U-M or OM.

This magical sound is the WORD of God, and when "God said" for there to "be light" in Genesis we are to understand both an occult and scientific principle known as *vibration*. It is something we experience each time we speak words comprised of individual symbols called letters. To *spell* them is to *cast a spell* and to write them in magical form, i.e., in *cursive*, is to *cast a curse*.

From the term *Widow's Son* is to be understand an initiate following in the footsteps of Horus, son of Isis. Freemasons are reborn through initiation to become *Sons of the Widow*, for which they are protected and guided under the wings of Isis. These initiates are all the embodiment of Horus, raised to form an army so that the death of Osiris (truth) may be avenged. Of the many initiates under the tutelage of Horus, Manly Hall writes:

> *"Out of the Hidden House, guarded by the silent god, must some day issue the glorious and illuminated Horus, the very incarnation of his own father, the personification of the lord of Abydos, the avenger of all evil and the just god in who there is no death."*

Typhon-Set in this story is the embodiment of perversion, comparable to the eternal betrayer Judas, the adversary, and he who undoes all selfless (good) things. He is the backbiter, or scorpion, who bestows the *kiss of death* upon Jesus. Typhon-Set represents ouroboros or Leviathan, the encircling of darkness around light, always present and ready to extinguish the fires of truth. He is the power of physical reality seeking to destroy the spiritual essence trapped in its substance. In this manner Typhon-Set also represents Cain and Osiris represents Abel. This character expresses the desire of the few over the needs of the many. He is the expression of selfish *want* rather than selfless *need*. Manly Hall explains this *desire* and how mankind is diverted from the truth, buried in the rubble of a collapsed temple:

> *"The desire for riches, pomp, power, and sovereignty by which this evil genius was obsessed, revealed the temptation by which humanity is deflected from its ultimate goal and led into the byways of sorrow and despair."*

A similar story is told about Hunahpu and Xbalanque, the "hero twins" from the ancient Quiche Maya book <u>Popul Vuh</u>. The pair of twins descend into an otherworld or underworld called

Xibalba after being abducted in their homes by messengers in the form of animals - usually owls. Once present in this alternate reality, or altered state of consciousness, Hunahpu and Xbalanque are transformed into therianthropes to approach and conquer the trials of the spiritual realm. After much pain, suffering, and transformation - at the hands of evil spirits - the couple return with supernatural powers of healing and wisdom. This is the quintessential shamanic journey.

Egyptians called this otherworld *Duat* and said it existed in the sky. The Maya referred to it as *Xibalba* and said it existed in an underworld. In either case, this *other* realm is one that can be reach above and within.

Secret Mysteries of the Shaman

The Egyptians and Mayans shared other similarities such as believing the Pharaoh or King would ascend into heaven upon death to be reborn as a star. The only trivial difference is that the *Duat* has twelve divisions and *Xibalba* has nine layers like *Dante's Inferno*.

Otherwise, in both Mesoamerica and Africa the afterlife voyage was made in a boat with beings that ferried the soul from one level to the next – these *beings* were comprised of a dog, bird, and monkey.

In Japan, coins were placed in purses around necks of the dead for them to pay the toll and cross the River of Three Roads (*Sanzu no Kawa*). In some places, the water was known as the River of Six Roads (*Rokudokawa*). Charon was the facilitator of this process for the Greek River Styx. In Japan, the *Shozuka Baba*, like the Slavic Baba Yaga, awaited payment.

Serpents featured prominently in not only these two seemingly different cultures but in virtually every mythology and spiritual experience preserved since ancient to modern times. Not only do we see therianthropes, or half-human/animal beings, but there are *"entoptic patterns of stars, zigzags, dots, and grids, flying discs… spirit beings, disembodied eyes, and an extraordinary menagerie of gigantic serpents, many of which are coiled around each other, or have multiple heads, or spit fire, or are elaborately winged and feathered,"* according to author Graham Hancock. Therianthropes are both a symbol of man's connection with nature and actual deities seen in altered states of consciousness.

Visions of such things are common throughout the world as described by those having properly prepared themselves to receive botanical and fungal hallucinogens such as *ayahuasca* or *psilocybin*.

Some may reach these altered states of consciousness through other means such as hyperventilation, starvation, dehydration, rhythmic dancing, drumming, bodily mutilation, etc., but these are dangerous and irrational. Others have the natural ability to slip into such states without drugs or ceremony. What is witnessed in these states, as described by Hancock in his book Supernatural, are paralleled through hunter-gatherer societies and their shamans, to Medieval European fairies and their abductions, all the way to contemporary UFO encounters.

The story is essentially the same: whether contacted at an early age or not to be a shaman or abductee, the individual will be floated into the sky, or climb there themselves, or be taken to an underworld, where they will interact with therianthropes, serpents, and spirits, experience what we may term medical experiments' have crystals or other objects implanted, be dismembered, be given special knowledge and then finally returned home having willfully sacrificed themselves like Jesus Christ, Odin, Maui, Prometheus, etc., for the betterment of their people. Anthropologist Felicitas Goodman explains how Osiris *"underwent a typical shamanic initiation in which his body was dismembered and then reassembled by his sister before he made his spirit journey to the Upper World."*

Initiates of the *mysteries* performed these dramas and induced altered states to experience the Osiris story firsthand.

It is documented, too, that many ancient Egyptian mummies were found to have psychoactive drugs still preserved, from nicotine to cocaine. Even for those dismissing such claims, the work of William Emboden, Professor of Biology at California State University, suggests that the *blue water lily* of the Nile River may have been used to induce hallucinatory states. He says they may have used opium and mandrake root as well.

The Middle East is home to *acacia* and *Syrian rue*, both when combined produce a biochemical mixture like that of the plants from which *ayahuasca* is derived in the Amazon. Poppy, the sacred plant of Demeter (Ceres), would certainly assist in producing such states too, as would purple *ergot* fungus which grows on the cereal grains – from *Ceres* we get the word *cereal*. A similar water lily also grows in Central America and was possibly used by the Maya much like their stone mushrooms express their interest in the more *magical* kind. The Aztecs were further known to have used *ololiuqui*, Morning Glory seeds with LSD-like qualities, as well as *teonanactl*, or mushrooms known as the "flesh of the gods."

To enter the unconscious, otherworld, underworld, and the like, was to experience, in a sense, the descent of the *soul* into *matter*. Shamans famously returned from these journeys, often having been dismembered like Osiris, or pierced by spears like Jesus or Odin, with sacred knowledge of botanicals. The spirits of these plants are thus the true *Green Man*.

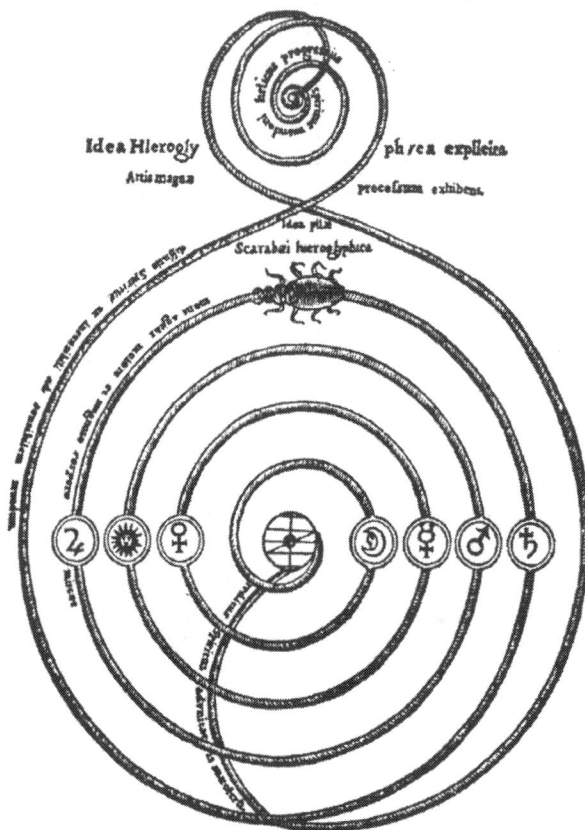

From Athanasius Kircher's Œdipus Ægyptiacus, this image represents the alchemical key according to the Egyptians. The scarab was a symbol of regeneration in Egypt and priests discovered in its habits and biology analogies by which base metals could be transmuted into gold. Here depicted is the path of the *seed* through each planetary body until, reaching the center, it is *perfected* for return once more to *source*. The path is symbolic of the transition of spirit/soul from the spiritual world into the physical world during the *lesser physical birth* – the *great spiritual death*. The second birth is symbolic of man's liberation from the material world, as he arises from the tomb into the heavens. The words in the small spiral at the top read: "*The spiral Progress of the mundane spirit.*" After the scarab has found its way around the spiral to the center of the lower part of the figure, it returns to the upper world along the path bearing the words: "*Return of the spirit to the center of unity.*"

Meaning of the Demeter-Persephone Myth

The story is a metaphor and an allegory. It is a symbolic tale concealing the wisdom of antiquity. Demeter-Ceres (Greek-Roman) is *agriculture personified* and her daughter Persephone-Proserpina is nature in all its beauty, personified as a young woman in the spring and summer months. Hades-Pluto is thus the *fall* and *winter* months personified, and his abduction and rape of Persephone-Proserpina is the same of the natural world, leaving it barren and naked.

In the *Mystery Schools*, this was *sacred wisdom* and the great *Secret of Mother Nature*, whose *veil* was never to be lifted by mortal man. When *ergot* was taken in Greece it would induce a state likened to *physical death* and allow one to commune with the dead. This substance, and those like it, including *blue water lily* in Egypt, would send one into the *underworld* by placing them into an internal slumber with barely detectable vitals.

The *mystery* dramas would thus place one into alignment with the forces of nature which are far superior to those of the individual self. Once properly aligned with, or in communion with, these forces, one could transcend the physical body and be *reborn*.

The entire process was physical but also psychological in that it triggered the *Dark Night of the Soul*, a phrase commonly used today, but stemming from a 16th-century Spanish mystic named St. John of the Cross.

In essence, one would enter the temple, representative of the underworld and body, and then descend into the *temple of self*, or unconsciousness, represented by the *underworld* and *Osirian chest*.

The Rape of Persephone (Proserpina), from *Thomassin's Recucil des Figures, Groupes, Themes, Fontaines, Vases etautres Ornements*

The Sorceress, by Jan van de Velde II, 1626.

The *anima*, or feminine unconscious side of man, and *animus*, the masculine unconscious side of woman, can be associated with the *active conscious mind* (masculine) and *passive unconscious mind* (feminine). The latter is further associated with the *underworld*, spirits, and demons. This is likely the reason many underworlds are run by a queen.

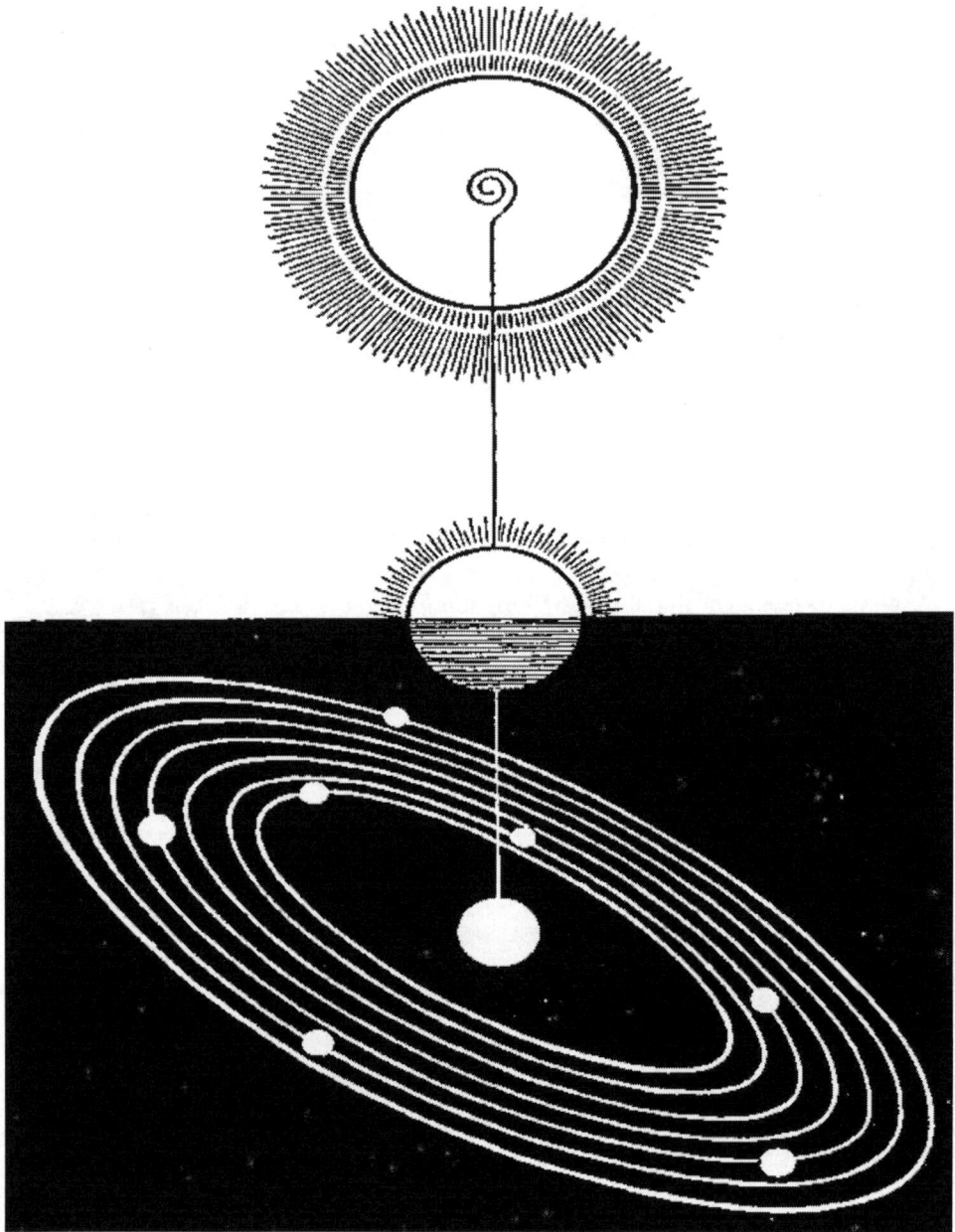

The Golden Thread, as published in Manly P. Hall's <u>Lectures on Ancient Philosophy.</u>

The upper portion of the diagram represents light from the superior sphere. Unwinding from *source*, a thread descends into the globular soul and then into the radiant center of the solar system. This image is like the alchemical key of Egypt represented by the scarab, which descends through the labyrinth of life, and upon death, ascends once more. The same is often depicted with a lotus flower, and sometimes with the Buddha offering divine assistance by a spider and its web.

The Phoenix from Lycosthenes' Prodigiorum, ac Ostentorum Chronicon.

The Phoenix is one of the most famous of all mystical creatures, utilized by the *Mystery Schools* as a symbol to conceal the truth behind esoteric philosophy and alchemy. Most consider the bird to be strictly a myth, but the Roman military commander Pliny describes the capture of one and its exhibition in the Roman Forum during Emperor Claudius' reign.

The Phoenix is related to the Bennu bird and Thunderbird, which all, dying and turning to ashes, rise anew from their own ashes. They have undergone a transformative process, the essence of which is explained in the story of Jesus *turning water into wine* or *bringing the dead back to life*. Just as masons *turn rough ashlar into smooth cut stone*, alchemists *turn lead into gold*. The bird's association with fire and the sun also preserve its association with gold.

An alchemical depiction of putrefaction & rebirth,
published in <u>Practical</u> by the German alchemist Basilius Valentinus.

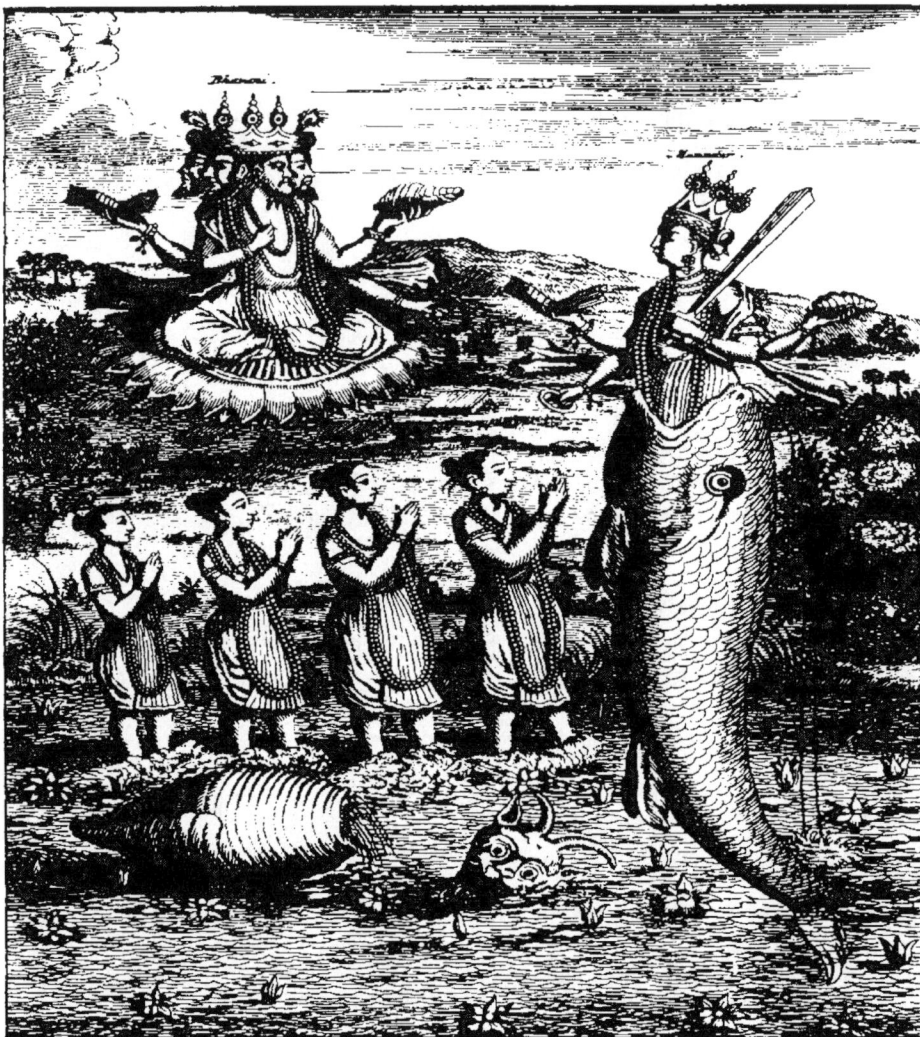

The First Incarnation of Vishnu, from Picart's <u>Religious Ceremonials</u>

The Bible is awash in symbols of the zodiac with common reference to bulls, lions and especially fish. The "five loaves of bread and two fish" were how Jesus fed thousands in the book of Matthew. The fish are symbols of Pisces, an age that began upon the birth of the Christian savior. Another savior named Oannes came in the form of a fish to the Chaldeans. Vishnu also incarnates as a fish avatar named Matsya, and Isis is often shown with one or more fish on her headdress. The Greek Aphrodite was herself honored by the eating of fish on a Friday as per her relationship to the Scandinavian Freya, who Friday was named after. Just as Oannes and Aphrodite came from the sea, so too did the Roman Venus.

Interestingly, the word *nun,* referring to a religious community of women dedicated to poverty, chastity, and obedience to God, still relates to "fish" and "growth" in similar standing to the Sumerian high priestesses, who presided over sacred ceremonies of *living resurrection.*

A History of the Macrocosm and Microcosm, published in 1617 by Robert Fludd.

This image represents the integration of *heavenly bodies* with *natural processes.* It is a symbolic diagram of the overall operations of nature. As explained in Mark Booth's book The Sacred History, Rupert *"Sheldrake asserts that the genetic code of living beings has not turned out to provide all the information needed for them to fully generate themselves, as its discoverers initially supposed, but only a small percentage of it. The rest must be 'out there' in the cosmos, and the plant or animal must be formed out of the interaction between the information described by the code and these external forces – perhaps the influence of the stars and planets as described by Boehme."*

Manly Hall explains the various inner and outer circles of this depiction in his book The Secret Teachings of All Ages:

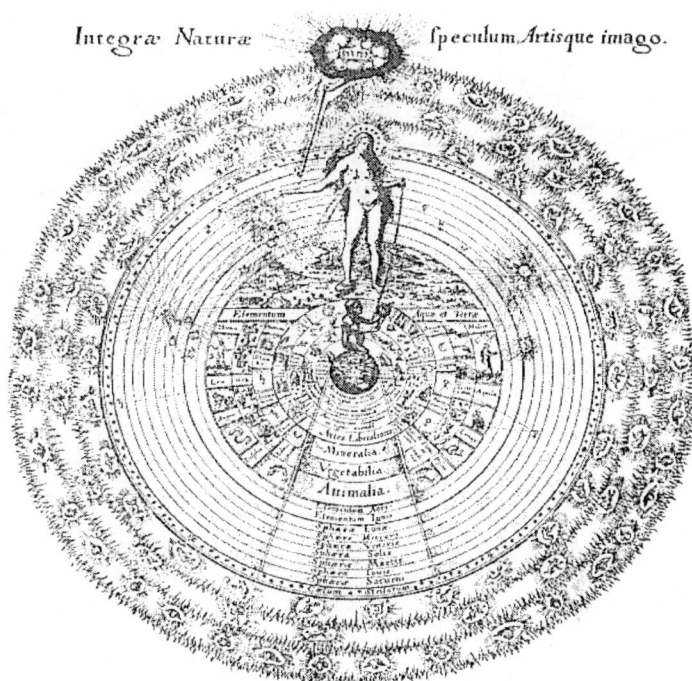

Integra Naturæ ⸳⸳⸳⸳ Speculum Artisque imago.

"Outside the circle of the starry heavens are the three fiery rings of the empyreum – the triple fire of the Supreme Creator – in which dwell the celestial creatures. Within he, of the stars are the circles of the planets and elements. After the element of air comes the circle of the world (earth). The circle of animals is followed by the circle of plants, which, in turn is followed by the circle of the minerals. Then come various industries and in the center is a terrestrial globe with an ape-man sitting upon it, measuring a sphere with a pair of compasses. This little figure represents the animal creation. In the outer ring of fire, above is the sacred name of Jehovah surrounded by clouds. From these clouds issues a hand holding a chain. Between the divine sphere and the lower world personified by the ape is the figure of a woman. It is to be specially noted that the female figure is merely holding the chain connecting her with the lower world, but the chain connecting her with the higher world ends in a shackle about her wrist. This female figure is capable of several interpretations: she may represent humanity suspended between divinity and the beast; she may represent Nature as the link between God and the lower world; or she may represent the human soul – the common denominator between the superior and the inferior."

Edward Waite considers Robert Fludd as a superior disciple of Paracelsus. He writes of his significance:

"The central figure of Rosicrucian literature, towering as an intellectual giant above the crowd of souffleurs, theosophists, and charlatanic Professors of the magnum opus, who, directly or otherwise, were connected with the mysterious Brotherhood, is Robertus de Fluctibus, the great English mystical philosopher of the seventeenth century, a man of immense erudition, of exalted mind, and, to judge by his writings, of extreme personal sanctity."

Esoteric Magic, Black Technology & Atlantis

"Everyone practices magic, whether they realize it or not, for magic, is the art of attracting particular influences, events, and situations within human life. Magic is a natural phenomenon because the universe is reflexive, responding to human thoughts, aspirations, and desires; students of cosmology, for example, realize that the universe will correspondingly provide evidence for any theory projected upon it."

~ David Fideler ~

Three Great Evils

In thinking of *magic* there is a tendency to attribute the concept to some sinister or supernatural force. We assume *magic* to be only the product of imagination and fantasy. Superficial thinkers often attribute to magic some physically manifested component accompanied by anthropomorphic deities erroneously characterizing those forces at play beyond visual sight. In an examination of nature, we find a *cause* for each *effect*, although many effects baffle or elude our understanding. Physical life depends upon *unseen forces*, and so it may be surmised that *magic* is merely representative of the qualities of the unseen and how they form the basis for life as we know it to unfold.

Magic is, as Richard Cavendish put it, a process used to tap into "mysterious forces" at work in the universe, *"moving beneath the external fabric of things like the invisible currents of the sea."*

Rarely is magic not categorized as supernatural, insinuating some less than legitimate quality. A belief or practice in magic is not supernatural, though, but superphysical. Understanding the invisible laws of nature, and an ability to bend them to your will, is to operate in the unseen, which is deemed impossible by the adherents of the strictly material. Ironically, this is what the hard sciences attempt to do daily.

Magic is super-physical and yet very physical, for the rustling of tree branches in the unseen wind is easily explained by both the occultist and scientists alike. Although such a *force* is mostly invisible, it is still operating in the physical world and not just supernatural, or *"some force beyond scientific understanding or the laws of nature."*

An unfounded belief in the *supernatural* ultimately leads to *superstition*, which is contrary to nature and distorts its values. Conversely, the superphysical qualities of the unseen are the basis for mysticism. Likewise, an unfounded belief in *scientific dogma* leads to the same *superstition* and distortions of nature.

Although magic is defined as, the "power of apparently influencing the course of events by using mysterious or supernatural forces," there must be an understanding that only in certain instances, wherein the observer is ignorant, can the laws of nature be passed off as supernatural phenomena or magic.

The word *magic* comes from the Greek *mageia*, which was both a science and religion of

Zoroastrian Priests out of Persia. Others suggest the word comes from *megas*, meaning the *great science*. From the Persian priests we acquire the word *magi* and what we know as *magician*.

Ancient civilizations are almost always considered inferior to the organized society conducting its study. Modern man infers his existence at any given moment in time – the NOW – to represent superiority over all others before. He rarely looks upon the past segments of even his own life from which any knowledge may be acquired for experiences yet to be had; thus, very often, he repeats his mistakes. The attitude of modern man is therefore rooted deeply in the superiority complex of *ego*, further fostered by the evils of *superstition* and *fear*, which are worsened by the evil of *ignorance*.

These are the *Three Great Evils* that aim to systematically vanquish *truth* and *wisdom*. They may be overcome by the opposite triune guides of love, hope, and faith. Through insufficient knowledge, mankind grows ever more superstitious and fearful of what is not understood. Through the preservation of self, we find that animal nature, or instinct, prompts the rejection of any superior knowledge based on dogmatic belief and comfort in the *current moment*.

If a past civilization was to have in its possession far greater wisdom and understanding of mathematics or science than modern man, then what does this information leave us with except with the instinct to deny their achievements for the lack of our own. Simply because a person has not had the opportunity of the present moment, we deem them to be ignorant. Such a dogmas is circularly ignorant because how we feel about *yesterday* is always trumped by *tomorrow*. No matter how great our achievements are today we act as if they are immediately obsolete the next day. There is a strong prejudice and patronizing attitude expressed by many so-called *experts* and *professionals* that any antiquated civilizations must not only be collectively ignorant, but wholly inferior to our own.

This bias classifies their art, writing, myth, and architecture to be barbarous attempts towards achieving what modern man deems the increasing height of accomplishment. This is generally true even though much of both western and eastern civilization bases its current entertainment and architecture on antiquity. We continue to perpetuate ideas built upon unstable foundations, knowing that one day they must collapse under the weight of their own ignorance. Manly Hall explains of this shallowness of learning:

> *"Although science has assumed the habiliments of erudition, there is a shallowness in our attitude towards learning that is disquieting to all but the superficially minded. We realize that the foundation of our present knowledge is inadequate of the structure that has been erected upon it…*
>
> *"Limited to the elements contained in modern materialism it is consequently difficult if not impossible, to adequately interpret any ancient civilization, for, with very few exceptions, these older races were steeped in abstractions. Hence their learning only provokes the ridicule of modern archeologists who have no vision beyond the cloud…*
>
> *"Our placid men of letters seemingly never suspect that they may be the self-deluded victims of a colossal hoax."*

Archaeologists and historians often enter their respected fields with preconceived conclusions that ignore any accumulated evidence to the contrary. Truth has been slain or exiled, and material facts are oppressed by opinions, which breed ignorance and conflict. Just as the ancient priests and black magicians of antiquity worked to keep the populace ignorantly in conflict, modern black magicians work the same sorcery. Their motivations are selfish and their means diabolic, while always portrayed in the garments of an angel or savior.

The proliferation of technology through the means of artificial intelligence, virtual reality, and augmented reality, are at the forefront of scientific atonement today. But the motivations behind such developments seem to be more opposed to human development than aligned with it; many technological advances promise us *immortality, superhuman abilities,* and other literalities.

Theological institutions promise *eternal life* through *faith* while often ignoring internal spiritual development. They have been all but replaced by a scientific establishment that now promises eternal life through mechanical technology and computers. The black priests of all ages pander to animal desires, being also entranced themselves, so that the great dragon finds no difficulty in fully consuming the spiritual nature of these men and women. Modern priests of science now pander to these same desires of flesh with conveniences that stagnate spiritual development. Logic is replaced with unreason, introspection by external authority, and even true intangible immortality with tangible mortality, albeit one that is prolonging the inevitable conclusion by promising infinite physical existence to finite physical material. Eliphas Levi writes in Transcendental Magic: Its Doctrine and Ritual of the temporary purpose of the human body:

> *"Bodies are only temporary shells, whence souls have to be liberated; but those who in this life obey the flesh build up an interior body or fluidic shell, which, after death, becomes their prison-house and torment, until the time arrives when they succeed in dissolving it in the warmth of the divine light, towards which, however, the burden of their grossness hinders them from ascending."*

Science has come to profess a form of *black magic* that aims to deceive and trick its loyal adherents with clever illusions relating to *everlasting life*. The superficial thinker is both entertained and entranced with the magical qualities of certain forms of technology. They seem to find solace in the promise of physical augmentation by mechanical means or are wholly unconcerned with the underlying implications; for to augment the body, or reality, is to "make greater by adding" to something, which implies that humans will be made "greater" through technological means. In the process it is believed that immortality may be achieved by these same means and that the infinite may be overcome by the finite. Such is the work of the *Dark Triade*: Lucifer, Satan, Devil.

Therefore, man labors for a future in which all needs are met instantaneously by means of instant gratification. Since the *fall of man* implies a time before *desire*, when all needs were met, any future world in which there is believed to be no *desire* will be certainly saturated in suffering if it is erected like the *Tower of Babel*. Metaphors and allegories such as this "tower" preserve essential wisdom from perversion. The tower, pyramid, ziggurat, etc., was a microcosm of the world representing the *Mountain of the Earth*. One should not try to be like God, a valuable lesson we can learn from the once great angel Lucifer in the book of Isaiah. Nothing here, however, should be misconstrued to suggest that technology is evil. The point we are laying out is that modern *black magicians* use technology as part of a *techno-death-cult* to further imprison the soul and cut man off from God.

The Golden Age & Atlantis

The Egyptians are given much credit for their magnificent achievements in civilization. It is evident that Egypt began as a magnificent civilization with no prior development, with later generations merely attempting to maintain what came before. All the most magnificent temples and pyramids far overshadow any built by later generations, which seem to poorly mimic the former. Many of the greatest structures are now dilapidated with meager attempts made towards their reconstruction or maintenance over the centuries. The newer structures show a distinct lack of attention to detail in building methods. This would indicate that the Egyptians were not the initiators, but inheritors of most of these monuments. Similarly, we find stories and myths that are baffling in their apparent complexity and indicate a superior knowledge of science, math, geometry, architecture, psychology, botany, and the like. Such preservations of antiquity can be found from the mounds of Japan to the megaliths of Malta, from the lost cities of India to the vast archeology treasures of Mesopotamia and Africa, to the forgotten monuments of found all over the Americas.

Many claim that beings from other worlds are responsible for the superior advancements of a previous civilizations. Others suggest that humans received this knowledge from a previous civilization existing on earth during some *Golden Age*, before recorded time. Without dismissing the former entirely, and as per the latter argument, it seems far more likely that a human dedicated to study, and personal development, would be able to achieve far more in the ancient world than is possible even today with all the so-called technological advancements, which often act as a deterrent to such advancements otherwise. Cataclysmic events, wars, the destruction of vast libraries, and the movement of time, have played critical roles in further obscuring the achievements of the past.

Both the mythology and architecture of Egypt has stood the greatest test of time to remain highly misunderstood by even the most learned scholars on the subject, primarily because these scholars usually study superficial literalisms as opposed to philosophical concepts and symbols. Others like E. A. Wallis Budge we are indebted to for his life's work as an Egyptologist.

It seems that as many of their tombs were rigged with booby traps to discourage grave robbers, so too are their myths rigged with traps to prevent the improper dissemination of their deeper meanings. As later generations were unable to maintain the grand monuments of a forgotten people, they were also unable to understand, even if they maintained, the great myths that preserved a lost wisdom.

The mimicking of great structures and myths resulted in the decline of civilization. As the progenitors of this earlier generation grew older, they passed along their knowledge in symbols, metaphors, allegories, and myths, to the *Mystery Schools* of antiquity, which ultimately led to some of the greatest thinkers in classical philosophy, mathematics, science, astronomy, music, and art.

Perhaps of all antediluvian civilizations, conceptual or with very scant evidence, the famed Atlantis itself was merely a metaphor loosely based on a single island, or a series of islands, that symbolized supreme truth sunken by the grossest ignorance. Perhaps the Atlanteans were overcome by the same, or similar, technological advancements that grow unabated today. There are striking similarities between the sinking of Atlantis, the Biblical story of the Tower of Babel, and the *fall of man* from the Garden. Each signifies spiritual involution and a *sinking* of the *soul-spirit* into *matter*.

According to the Egyptians, *Sekhet-Aaru* was a region of the world where the dead went to "live," in a manner like they had on earth. The Egyptians also told of an island paradise called *Ta-Neteru*, a land later destroyed by natural disasters. During *Zep Tepi*, the *First Time*, intermediaries between heaven and earth called *Urshu* were present among men. These *Watchers* were lesser deities to a group of gods called *Neteru*. Hence, *Ta-Neteru*, a land said to consist of islands with running waters and magnificent *gardens* where personal helpers of the gods were taken in the far, far south of Egypt.

A similar island paradise is preserved in eastern (Chinese) tradition too. They tell of a magical series of islands inhabited by people or gods kept immortal by a "drug which will prevent death," also called *pu ssu chih yao*.

In Japanese Shintō, the *soul-spirit* receives *eternal life* in the same place where all life is generated – the *Land of Mother*. This *land of the eternal* is found across the ocean. On Okinawa, the land of Kami is called *niraikanai* and it is also found across the ocean. In fact, the Japanese see the *other world* in general as existing beyond the ocean rather than above or below. This is like the mystical *Tokoyo*, a supposed fairyland east of Japan.

In the *Dhammapada*, Buddha tells a young man named Kappa (also a Japanese monster of water) about an island where all this suffering will be no more: *"for those struggling in midstream, in great fear of the flood, of growing old and of dying – for all those I say, an island exists where there is no place for impediments, no place for clinging: the island of no going beyond. I call it Nirvana, the complete destruction of old age and dying."* Nirvana is the extinguishing of the Threefold Fire of desire, hostility, and delusion. NIR means 'out' and VANA means 'blown' – to blow out the *threefold fire*.

Other names for this land include *Adamlanda, Adalandis, Atlan, Aztlan, Asgard, Shamballa*, and the *Garden of Alcinous*. All these titles have strong relationships with *wisdom*, which is often represented by the serpent, apple, and owl, among various other symbols. The serpent tempted man with knowledge of self and induced the *fall of man*. However, serpents are also the symbols of civilizing gods, as is the case from Australia to India to the Americas. A famous Greek legend also tells of a *paradise* land called *Hesperia* or *Hespera* that the Greeks called Poseid or Poseidon, the Roman Neptune, who was born possessing triune powers symbolized by his three-pronged trident.

In China the Eight Immortals knew the secrets of the nature like Poseidon-Neptune. In this eastern region of the world the immortal fruit is a peach, as told in the story of Han Hsiang.

In Avestic scripture this land is called *Airyana Vaejo*. Perhaps even the *Sea-King's Sanctuary*, or *The Palace of the Kami Great-Ocean-Possessor*, an underwater palace sitting amidst massive stones near Japan, fits into the same mythos.

On the famous island continent of Atlantis was supposedly a mountain where dwelled a primitive human named *Evenor*, ancestor of the ruling kings of Atlantis, with his wife *Leucipe*, and their only daughter *Cleito*. After the death of her parents, Poseidon seduced Cleito and she birthed him five pairs of male children. Each of them was given a piece of the islands, while the eldest son, Atlas, was made ruler of the others. Poseidon named the landmass *Atlantis* and the surrounding sea the *Atlantic* in honor of his elder son.

The lofty mountain that existed in the center of the Island(s) was essentially the home of the gods, like Mt. Olympus, the Japanese Mt. Fuji, Chinese Kun Lun Range, Hindu Mt. Meru (Sumeru) or Govardhan, or the Tibetan Mt. Kailash. The streets of this Atlantean mountaintop temple were paved with gold and its twelve gates were adorned with precious stones. Here we find similarity between *The City of the Golden Gate* - the capital of Atlantis - common descriptions of the Christian *Heaven* with golden streets and pearly gates, and also an archetype for the New Jerusalem. Author Ignatius Donnelly writes in <u>Atlantis</u> of its relationship to Greek history and mythology. He says that Atlantis *"is the key of the Greek mythology. There can be no question that these gods of Greece were human beings. The tendency to attach divine attributes to great earthly rulers is one deeply implanted in human nature."*

Plato famously writes in his *Timaeus* and *Critias* about this mythical and famed land, admitting that the tradition was simply passed to him through an ancestor named Solon, an Athenian lawmaker. Solon claims he learned of the story from an elderly priest in the land of Egypt, specifically at the Temple of Sais. The priest, in turn, had only learned of the story himself from written records in the Temple's archives. These *records* at the time were more than 8,000 years old. From what Plato, Solon, and this elderly priest from Egypt preserve for us is documentation of a land of prosperity and advancement during a *golden age*. This civilization was said to exist on a large island - not a metaphor - located opposite the Pillars of Hercules, presumed to be the modern Strait of Gibraltar. An immense global cataclysm essentially sunk the famous island nation beneath the sea in a single night and day. The timeframe of its sinking is dated to around 9,600 BC or 11,600 years ago.

Many civilizations later appeared seemingly out of nowhere with advancements beyond what common sense would allow for our limited and biased perceptions of primitive man. Similar societies were established from South and Central America to Africa and India. The idea is that the surviving inhabitants of Atlantis simply restarted civilization in various parts of the world, particularly in Egypt where Solon learned of Atlantis.

According to the *Edfu Building Texts*, the Egyptian lineage is a result of peoples who came from *"the Homeland of the Primeval Ones."* This land, as detailed in Underworld by author Graham Hancock, is *"said to have been destroyed suddenly in a great flood during which the majority of its 'divine inhabitants' were drowned."* Before Atlantis was submerged, it is believed the initiates of the *mysteries* carried with them their *secret doctrines* and immigrated to different parts of the world, including Egypt. From these immigrations they went on to establish centers of *esoteric wisdom* called *Mystery Schools*.

Atlantis, *from Manly P. Hall's* The Secret Teachings of All Ages

Despite much work on the subject, Atlantis is still ignored or mocked by most archeologists, geologists, scientists, historians, anthropologists, and the like. Ironically it is a malice for the truth, and pseudo-intellectual wickedness, that is said to have been the downfall of Atlantis. Much like the story of Atlantis, we today are threatened by the same ignorance. For our civilization to be regarded always in the present moment as superior to what came before, we enact aggressive displays of our technologies to demonstrate our dominance over nature. It seems man will unfortunately never collectively comprehend that in working with nature one may achieve much more physically and spiritually than is to ever be granted from working against nature, and certainly in working to distort nature.

Contrary to popular belief, Plato's Atlantis is not the only story of this sort, as we have seen. The Troano manuscript, which was written over 3,500 years ago by the Mayas of Yucatan, contains what many believe is an authentic account of the cataclysm which sank the famed continent. This document contains the following statement according to a translation by Le Plogeon:

> *"In the year 6 Kan, on the 11th Mulac in the month of Zac, there occurred terrible earthquakes, which continued without interruption until the 13th Chuen. The country of the hills of Mud, the land of Mu, was sacrificed; being twice upheaved it suddenly disappeared during one night, the basin being continually shaken by volcanic forces. Being confined, these caused the land to sink and to rise several times and in various places. At last the surface gave away and ten countries were torn asunder and scattered unable to stand the force of the convulsions, they sank with their 64,000,000 inhabitants."*

Prayers, Faith, Blessings, Fruit of Desire, The Crucifixion of Man, & Plant Intoxicants

"As it is said, those who do not remember the past are doomed to repeat it, and humans as a species are prone to amnesia. It is thus imperative that these all-important matters of religious ideology and doctrine be thoroughly explored and not left up to blind faith."

~ D. M, Murdoch ~

Prayers, Faith & Blessings

Miracles may be explained by better understanding the Laws of Nature for which there is action and reaction, attraction and repulsion. *Faith* is to be, or not to be, believed, but it is not a matter to be examined by science, for *"faith is belief in the reality of things unseen or veiled."* Despite this, many science-based academics hold their own version of *faith*.

Our reality is based on a limited number of data points out of millions processed by the body and senses every second. In physics the *observer effect* is described as a bias which occurs when we notice what we expect or behave in ways that influence others. As with *faith*, the power of the mind, or many minds, can, with intention, change reality ever so slightly. This is the purpose of holding *faith* and saying *prayers*. A *blessing* can be defined as *favor* and *protection* granted by God, usually invoked through spoken prayer. When someone sneezes and we say, *"God, bless you,"* this tradition harkens back to the Plague Pandemics of Europe, while the Romans would say, *"Jupiter, be with you."* With beautiful words we relate to the *Cosmic Mind* and with ugly words the *Infernal Realms.* The purpose of *prayers* and *hymns*, especially when performed in a grand ritual space like a cathedral, but particularly when uttered with *faith* and *intention*, is to *glorify God.* Manly Hall says that there is no need for any mystical effect, because the *"repeating of beautiful words which convey a gentle and loving thought has some effect."* This is the point of *prayer,* not to demand from creation all the things you *desire.* A great example of this fact is found in Matthew 6, verses 6 and 22:

> *"But you, when you pray, go into your room, and when you have shut your door, pray to your Father who is in the secret place; and your Father who sees in secret will reward you openly."*

> *"'The lamp of the body is the eye. If therefore your eye is good, your whole body will be full of light'."*

Prayers should thus be said within, by addressing internal consciousness, and not by making a spectacle. Our attention, assured by closing the door internally from the external, should then be directed not upward into the heavens but inward towards the heart, or *sanctum sanctorum.* The *lamp of the body* is the window in Noah's Ark, the *Third Eye, Inner Eye, Eye of Horus, Eye of Izanagi,* and the eye that Odin plucks out in his conversation with Mimir. For it is said that *he who watches over Israel neither slumbers nor sleeps.*

Crucified At The World Navel: The Hero's Journey

The cross is *physical matter,* representing the four corners of the world. The story of Jesus crucified is certainly metaphoric, even if it were also literal, because it represents our *soul-spirit* placed on the *matter-cross* with *nails of illusion* – the nails are the body's five senses, the *stigmata* of Christ.

Just as Jesus was crucified on a cross (made of *Paradise Plant*) and pierced by a spear of the Roman soldier Longinus, so too was Odin, in Norse mythology, crucified or hanged. Odin is the supreme god and creator, the god of victory and the dead. He was hanged on the *Yggdrasil* or *World Tree* with a spear thrust into his side. The reason for his suffering is likened to the suffering of Christ and Prometheus, who took fire from the gods and gave it to mankind. Maui of Polynesia steals the same from Mahu-ika and gives it to mankind. The following is said of Odin in the Icelandic <u>Edda</u>:

> *I ween that I hung of the windy tree,*
> *Hung there for nights full nine;*
> *With the spear I was wounded, and offered I was,*
> *To Othin, myself to myself,*
> *On the tree that none may ever know*
> *what root beneath it runs.*

Odin won the knowledge of Runes, too, by suffering for mankind. These are powerful magical inscriptions carved into metal, wood, stone, etc. Once their knowledge was obtained, Odin also gifted them to man like the promethean fire. Runes are thus the *Word of God.*

Christian Rätsch and Claudia Müller-Ebeling write of Odin and the runes in their book <u>Pagan Christmas</u>:

> *"Wotan is the god who is driven to amass knowledge. He was to know everything; he craves knowledge. For this, he travels all the lands over and - wounded by a spear - hangs himself upside down, for nine nights, on the shamanic world tree, to get to know all nine shamanic worlds and absorb all their knowledge. Then he breaks branches off of the world tree and throws them onto the Earth, where they arrange themselves into runes of beech slivers, forming letters that carry secret knowledge. Because of Wotan's self-sacrificial shedding of blood the runes become magic."*

Edith Hamilton writes of the same myth:

> *"The poets of the Norse mythology, who saw that victory was possible in death and that courage was never defeated, are the only spokesmen of rah belief of the whole great Teutonic race, of which England is a part, and ourselves through the first settlers in America."*

There are few texts pertaining to these myths - the <u>Younger Edda</u> and the <u>Elder Edda</u> - with the latter describing Odin's suffering:

> *Night whole nights on a wind-rocked tree,*
> *Wounded with a spear*

The Yggdrasil is also known as the *ash tree* in northern European mythology.

We find similar punishment incurred by Prometheus, who was tied to a rock and daily had a bird (usually an eagle) eat the liver from his side, which nightly regenerated. In other accounts the rock is a pole, or a cross, and Greek authors referred to this as "to be crucified."

Andromeda, daughter of Cepheus and Cassiopeia, was also bound to a rock as a sacrifice to a sea monster that could only be appeased by the same sacrifice. This was what her mother was required to suffer for arousing the anger of Neptune. The punishment of Prometheus for helping mankind was compounded since he actively *tricked* the gods, and thus he may be referred to as the "trickster," or false light, in association with Venus or Lucifer. Prometheus had arranged that as part of any animal sacrifice man would receive the best part of the animal and the gods would receive the worst. He deceived the gods by placing edible parts of an animal in a hide, then piling entrails on top. Beside the latter heap he placed the bones of an animal upon which he covered with shining fat. Zeus chose the fat, only to find bones beneath, and became furious over this deception and betrayal.

Jesus, Odin, and Prometheus felt compassion for mankind and paid the price by being pierced in their side. And also Adam in the Garden had a rib removed from his side, suffering for the creation of Eve, the mother of all mankind. In the Brhadaranyaka Upanishad it is described how the SELF was unhappy and alone, and so he *"divided this body, which was himself, in two parts… Therefore this human body (before one marries a wife) is like one of the halves of a split pea… He united with her; and from that were born men."* All creation and obtainment of wisdom comes by suffering, though pain only persists so long as one chooses to stay content in material pleasures, if they become an end.

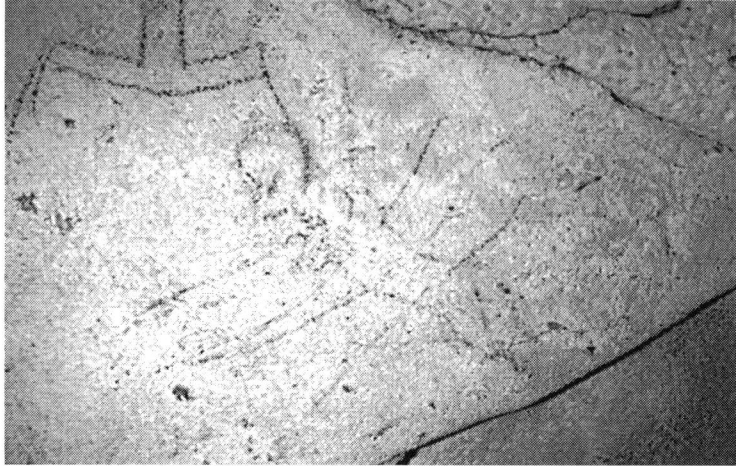

Wounded Man from Pech Merle cave in France.

Even Typhon-Set was crucified, having his hands tied behind his back to a post and knives driven into his body. The archangel Michael suffered for mankind in his battles against Lucifer, just like the Chinese ruler Fohi, who was born of a virgin, concurrently brought knowledge to his people by suffering. The same may be said of Saints, too, including St. Sabastian who is often depicted pierced with arrows and tied to a tree. Graham Hancock explains in <u>Supernatural</u> how the *wounded man* is much more than a metaphor, and that the motif is widespread:

> *"In the Amazon judge, when shamans of the Jivaro tribe enter trance under the influence of ayahuasca, they construe the same neurologically generated skin sensations as sharp little darts being fired at them by supernatural entities. Siberian Tungus shamans speak of initiatory trances, induced by ingestion of fly agaric mushrooms, in which they experience themselves to have been pierced with arrows, their flesh cut off, their bones torn out. Ju/'hoansi shamans in southern Africa often undergo great physical pain at certain stages of their trance and it is notable how frequently they… construe their neurologically generated somatic hallucinations as insect stings."*

The fundamental elements of what many perceive to be strictly Christian symbols are found all over the world and throughout time immemorial.

In Tibet (700 BC) the god *Indra,* king of the devas, was born of a virgin, walked on water as god of weather and rain, and was nailed to a cross before rising from the dead.

In Nepal (622 BC) the god *Iao* was nailed to a tree and raised from the grave. In Java (522 BC) the god *Wittoba* was nailed to a tree that was later symbolized by a crucifix.

Attis of Phrygia was born on December 25th of the virgin *Nana.* His body was eaten as bread by his followers. Attis was crucified partly, an event described as the god being tied to a tree. Death followed and after three days he was raised from a tomb. The blood of Attis ran down to redeem earth in similar fashion to the story of Adonis and Mithra(s), who ushered in a new age by slaying Taurus, the bull constellation. As Mithra(s) punctures the animal with a knife the bull transforms into the moon and his cloak becomes the night sky. Where the bull's blood falls upon the ground, flowers began blooming.

In Japan the female goddess of the sun, Amaterasu, hides in a cave for three days before the resurrection of her brilliant rays.

In Mesopotamia, when Inanna arrives nude before the judges of her sister Ereshkigal's underworld kingdom, she is turned into a corpse and placed on a stake. *"After three days and three nights had passed,"* she is resurrected.

Even the Central American civilizing god Quetzalcoatl was crucified to a cross, though one that resembled an X instead of a Latin T.

This was a story taken from the cult of Cybele dating back to at least 250 BC. Cybele was known as an even earlier sun goddess named Arinna (the Hittite sun goddess) or the Greek Rhea, from where we get MA (the mother - Nana), which became MA-Rhea or Mother Mary.

The same story is told of the Indian god Krishna (900 BC), whose father was in some accounts a carpenter like the earthly father of Jesus. Krishna was born of the virgin Devaki with a star signaling his arrival in flesh; he performed miracles and after dying was resurrected. Krishna was carried across water - or it is said he *walked on water* - by his father who hoped to switch the child out for a female baby due to the orders of King Kansa to *kill all male babies*. We also find this story similar to the *massacre of the innocents* in Matthew 2, with King Herod issuing *"orders to kill all the boys in Bethlehem and its vicinity who were two years old and under."* In another version of the Hindu account, as Joseph Campbell recounts, *"A tyrant-titan named Taraka had usurped the mastery of the world, and, according to the prophecy, only a son of the High God Siva could overthrow him."* The Biblical Nimrod likewise learned that a child would be born and rise up against him, and so he acted to confine all pregnant women and kill any male child born. A child was eventually born in exile, his mother birthing him in a cave. The child was the Hebrew father Abraham and his story is clearly yet another version of the Christ story – in actuality a common archetypical narrative all over the world because it speaks to the essence of human life and growth.

Then there is *Pyramus*, the most beautiful youth, and *Thisbe*, the fairest of maidens in Babylon. They loved each other deeply, but their parents forbade marriage. Living close to one another their homes shared a wall allowing them to communicate by way of a small crack. Eventually their yearning to be together was too overwhelming and so they hatched a plan to meet after dark. Their rendezvous was at the Tomb of Ninus, under a tall mulberry tree with white berries, next to a bubbling spring. Arriving earlier than her lover, Thisbe made her way to the tomb. As she approached, moonlight revealed a lioness coming out of the dark with bloody jaws from a fresh kill, searching for a drink from the bubbling spring. Fleeing the path of the lioness, Thisbe dropped her cloak, which was picked up torn apart by the animal. Pyramus arrived to find the bloody cloak torn to shreds next to lion tracks that seemed to confirm his lover was dead. He blamed himself for not being able to protect her, then he picked up the cloak while kissing it multiple times before carrying it to the mulberry tree. Holding the cloak firm, he drew his sword

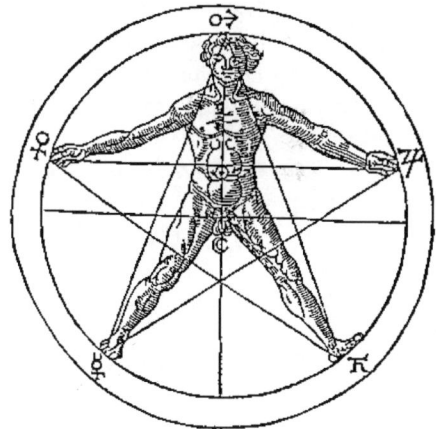

Man as Microcosm, from the work of Heinrich Cornelius Agrippa. Here we see man essentially crucified to the pentagram, tracing out the crucifixion of man in the cosmos.

and killed himself by plunging it into his side like Jesus and Odin upon the tree. The resulting flow of blood was said the reason why white mulberries were colored deep red. Edith Hamilton explains in <u>Mythology</u> the death of Pyramus: *"He drew his sword and plunged it into his side. The blood spurted up over the berries and dyes them dark red."* His blood stained the white berries dark red, providing us with an image of the ultimate sacrifice of the *self* for *love*. The death of Pyramus resulted from a piercing blow under a tree. Upon returning from hiding, Thisbe found her lover hanging on to life. He soon died. She then *"plunged into her heart the sword that was still wet with this life's blood."* We find in this story the archetype of Christ's unending love for his Bride, just as we find a reminder of *Romeo and Juliet*.

Upon the amulet of Orpheus there is a depiction of the poet crucified to a cross. We have already learned of the suffering of Osiris, locked in a chest by Typhon-Set for slaying beasts and teachings civilization to mankind. There is an interesting parallel here between Osiris and the Biblical Adam. As with many of the characters above, Adam has his side punctured so that God may remove a rib and make his consort Eve. In some stories it is the *penis bone* that was removed, immediately recalling the fourteenth piece of the body of Osiris, his penis, being eaten by fish in the Nile.

The Martyrdom of Saint Sebastian, by Giovanni Antonio Bazzi, 1525.

Both Adam and Eve tasted *desire* from the *forbidden fruit* offered by the *serpent* and were thus sent out of the Garden paradise. Although this story is rich in symbolism, there are many strict ways of interpreting the identities of the characters. Some believe the primordial couple simply disobeyed God and were rightfully punished. Others believe that God was a tyrant, and the serpent was freeing mankind from bondage. Some may look at the story as see it is something akin to an ayahuasca experience, considering the partially human serpent, beautiful Garden, and the wisdom granted to mankind.

These elements are like *mother ayahuasca*, beautiful gardens with serpents, and the wisdom granted to shamans on their trips. Occultists may see the story as metaphoric of the *esoteric evolution of man*, with the serpent on the tree essentially representing DNA and the tree itself representing the human spine.

Sitting upright under the *Tree of Enlightenment* (Bo Tree) we find the Buddha as a redeemer of the universe, the world savior incarnated as the principle of enlightenment. His upright posture and the tree itself, of which wooden planks for both (x) and (+) crosses are made, signify the crucifixion of the Prince, Siddhartha Gautama, and our soul crucified to matter.

Just as Jesus was tempted in the Wilderness (Matthew 4:1-11), Buddha was approached by Kama-Mara and his army, and after turning all their projectiles into flowers, Joseph Campbell explains how *"Mara then deployed his daughters, Desire, Pining, and Lust, surrounded by voluptuous attendants,"* in temptation, *"but the mind of the Great Being was not distracted."*

After doubting whether his message of enlightenment would be received, Brahma implores Buddha to become a "teacher of gods and men." Accepting his duty and responsibility, Buddha takes his wisdom to the people, *"bestowing the inestimable boon of the knowledge of the Way."* There is a parallel found here to Luke 23:34 when Jesus says, *"Father, forgive them, for they do not know what they are doing."*

In his classic book, The Hero With A Thousand Faces, Campbell explains the similarity between the western Christ and Eastern Buddha, and the relationship these stories share with Moses returning to his people with sacred commandments – essentially, also, the story of the Shaman:

> *"The Buddha beneath the Tree of Enlightenment (the Bo Tree) and Christ on Holy Rood (the Tree of Redemption) are analogous figures, incorporating an archetypal World Savior, World Tree motif, which is of immemorial antiquity."*

> *"The Old Testament records a comparable deed* [to the Buddha] *in its legend of Moses, who, in the third month of the departure of Israel out of the land of Egypt, came with his people into the wilderness of Sinai; and there Israel pitched their tents over against the mountain. And Moses went up to God, and the Lord called unto him from the mountain. The Lord gave to him the Tables of the Law and commanded Moses to return with these to Israel, the people of the Lord."*

The Grand Man of Zohar
by John Augustus Knapp, 1895

It is to be found at that immovable spot of Buddha the *axis mundi* or *world navel* around which all else revolves and springs forth. This is the central point of monad with its outer limiting ring which contains all creation and possibility within. That outer limit is the serpent, ouroboros, and also the rings which surround the bearded architect known as Saturn. Internally the center of monad is *self* and the serpent is an emissary of the unconscious, that dragon to be conquered. And indeed the dragon is killed, as Genesis 3:15 relates how the offspring of woman "will crush" the serpent's "head."

The motif of a virgin birth is also universal, signifying the protection of a Cosmic Mother who gives birth and then later often appears on the hero's journey as a companion, guide, and protector; in Christianity these roles are filled by Mother Mary and Mary Magdalene. A *Mary*, as goddess, shares a relationship with Kama-*Mara*, since he is the god of love (*kama-sutra*) and death. The *mother principle* is the bringer of death, only first being the provider of life and nurturing love. Generally speaking, Buddhism focuses on overcoming the inherent suffering of life, which, of course, is produced by birth. Buddha himself descended from heaven into his mother's womb, the giver of life contrasted to the teachings of her son, i.e., overcoming suffering and death. The awakening of self is the start of the hero's journey, leading to a spiritual journey that when completed amounts *"to a dying and a rebirth,"* writes Campbell. This is the story of Jesus crucified on the cross, Buddha gaining enlightenment under the Bo Tree, Attis crucified to a pine tree, Odin hanging from *Yggdrasil*, Yryn-ai-tojon tethered to the pillar of the world in Siberia, and the famous Greek Omphalos (meaning *navel*) stone associated with the center of the World. As Campbell writes of the *world axis*:

> *"Beneath this spot is the earth-supporting head of the cosmic serpent, the dragon, symbolical of the waters of the abyss, which are the divine life-creative energy and substance of the demiurge, the world-generative aspect of immortal being.' The tree of life, i.e., the universe itself, grows from this point. It is rooted in the supporting darkness; the golden sun bird perches on its peak; a spring, the inexhaustible well, bubbles at its foot."*

Encountered on the journey are guardians of the *threshold* that tempt or attempt to kill the hero. Campbell says that these regions, beyond threshold, be them "desert, jungle, deep sea, alien land, etc.," are essentially blank slates for the projecting of "unconscious content." One of the most famous monsters of these realms is Pan, also named Sylvanus or Faunus in Latin, a goat deity of *panic* and fear. Pan simply personifies the unknown and all the potential dangers of moving forward into that realm. Those without fear, however, who pay their way with offerings, are treated kindly by the goat of the woods. Advancing beyond the bounds of comfort into the unknown begins the adventure with a separation from the mundane, followed by trials, and finally a return to normal life with the hero being transfigured. Sometimes the threshold is external and other times *"the hero,"* Campbell says, *"goes inward, to be born again."* In Genesis 3:24 we learn of how God places a cherubim and flaming sword at the entrance of the Garden:

> *"After he drove the man out, he placed on the east side of the Garden of Eden cherubim and a flaming sword flashing back and forth to guard the way to the tree of life."*

Temples, shrines, altars, etc., are almost always defended by lions, dogs, foxes, gargoyles and the like. *"These are the threshold guardians to ward away all incapable of encountering the higher silence within,"* writes Campbell. Those seeing these protectors as demons misunderstand the imagery and are probably not ready to receive their wisdom.

Joseph Campbell summarizes here the journey of the hero, which is also the shamanic journey, the stories of Jesus and Buddha, and the *Dark Night of the Soul*:

> *"The mythological hero, setting forth from his common-day hut or castle, is lured, carried away, or else voluntarily proceeds, to the threshold of adventure. There he encounters a shadow presence that guards the passage. The hero may defeat or conciliate this power and go alive into the kingdom of the dark (brother-battle, dragon- battle; offering, charm), or be slain by the opponent and descend in death (dismemberment, crucifixion). Beyond the threshold, then, the hero journeys through a world of unfamiliar yet strangely intimate forces, some of which severely threaten him (tests), some of which give magical aid (helpers). When he arrives at the nadir of the mythological round, he undergoes a supreme ordeal and gains his reward. The triumph may be represented as the hero's sexual union with the goddess-mother of the world (sacred marriage), his recognition by the father-creator (father atonement), his own divinization (apotheosis), or again — if the powers have remained unfriendly to him — his theft of the boon he came to gain (bride-theft, fire-theft); intrinsically it is an expansion of consciousness and therewith of being (illumination, transfiguration, freedom). The final work is that of the return. If the powers have blessed the hero, he now sets forth under their protection (emissary); if not, he flees and is pursued (transformation flight, obstacle flight). At the re- turn threshold the transcendental powers must remain behind; the hero re-emerges from the kingdom of dread (return, resurrection). The boon that he brings restores the world (elixir)."*

Kaidan Meguri

In Buddhism the ritual of *Kaidan Meguri* is similar to those initiations in the Great Pyramid of Egypt. Translated as *Traversing the Path of Buddha* (Kaidan Meguri), this is a ritual involving passage through a pitch black tunnel, filled with sacred images. When emerging in the light at the other end, one is considered purified and reborn. The journey is thus completed.

Desire Brings Death: Rebis, Anima & Animus

Desire Brings Death is a fifteenth-century painting by the German artist Sebald Beham. It depicts a serpent coiled upon a tree - in this case a skeleton - which is symbolic of the formation of the human spinal cord in the *mysteries*, and further represents the Kundalini energy, literally meaning *snake* in Sanskrit, rising through the blossoming flower-like chakras of the plant body.

It is through *desire*, symbolized as the *realization* of flesh, i.e., incarnation, after man eats of the poisoned apple, that he *falls* from divine grace into *daily life* and *suffering*. These hardships of life must be overcome, the demons conquered, and the dragon slain, before man is able to reunite with the *Cosmic Mind*. Until then, man is soul-spirit crucified to the *World Tree* like Odin, nailed to the cross like Christ, and hanging on the spine like the serpent hangs on a tree. And this is where western spirituality meets eastern philosophy, since giving up *desire* is a key tenant of Buddhism. The *desire* to *be like God*, like the same held by Lucifer, is what *breeds* death of *soul-spirit*. As James 1:15 warns:

Desire Brings Death, by Sebald Beham.

As Hall wrote: *"Desire breeds death."*

"Then, after desire has conceived, it gives birth to sin; and sin, when it is full-grown, gives birth to death."

Encapsulated here is a symbol commonly referred to as the *caduceus*. As it was in the ancient world, the serpent coiled around a staff is still the symbol of contemporary physicians. Known as the *Staff of Hermes* (Greek) or *Staff of Mercury* (Roman), it depicts two serpents twisted around a staff. This image is that of human DNA. Along with DNA we also have RNA and mRNA (messenger RNA). DNA is a building block of life and is found in every cell in our body. The ancients preserved this knowledge in certain images. The Greeks personified DNA and *creation* as the god Phanes, who can be seen with serpents around his body inside the *Cosmic Egg* or *Mandorla*, while surrounded by the zodiac. As mRNA carries messages in the body, Hermes-Mercury, with his *caduceus* staff, carries messages between heaven and earth. These two serpents, like the thieves crucified on either side of Christ, represent opposing forces and their *equilibrium*. They also conceal the symbol of *infinity*, which represents *perfection* and *wholeness*. The wand, pole, or rod represents *power* and *authority*, and like the staff of Moses it is an *umbilical cord* between man and God. It represents the *Tree of life*, human spine, and *World Axis*. It is a tool of all medicine men, magi, and shamans.

Phanes

A *caduceus* is usually accompanied by the wings of Hermes-Mercury, signifying the physical and symbolic flight of the soul-spirit. Often confused with a *caduceus* is the *Wand of Aesclepius,* which usually has only one serpent. Aesclepius is the Greek god of healing, and his staff looks strangely like one of our modern symbols for money. Mercury rules Gemini, the serpents, and the mythical pair of children: Romulus and Remus, Castor and Pollux. The *primal couple* is Adam and Eve, and the *Universal Androgyne* or *Universal Hermaphrodite* can be found in the symbol of the *Rebis*.

Known as *Twofold Matter*, the **Rebis** comprises the male and female, and sun and moon, in perfect harmony. The same concept is mirrored in the Chinese *Yin Yang* Indian *Yab Yum*, and Japanese *In Yo*. To the right of the man's head, and left of the female, are the sun and moon, like the moons *Chesed* and *Geburah*, the fourth and fifth spheres in Kabbalah. The androgynous figure stands upon the back of a fire-breathing dragon like Isis upon snakes, the dragon itself perched atop of the world. The dragon is the great beast that must be defeated. The globe is provided wings to signify its relationship between heaven and earth just as the solar disc is often gifted wings like those of Hermes-Mercury. Inside of this figure is a cross, its four arms denoting the four directions and elements, the fifth of which is found within the central dot. This point, or crossroads, is what leads into the *underworld*. In the right hand of the figure is held the compass, used for tracing and designing, and in the left hand is the square, a symbol of exactitude. Both are essential elements in Freemasonry. Above the couple is a hexagram that shares relations with Saturn, its astrological house of Capricorn represented by the cross sigil depicted just below the left breast of the female. On its opposite side is the sign of female and directly above is that of male. The above star also is a symbol of the hermetic axiom: *As Above, So Below*. The oval shape is representative of the *Cosmic Egg*, a symbol of *regeneration*. These two figures further represent the *animus*, or unconscious masculine within a woman, and the *anima*, the unconscious feminine within a man.

The *animus* and *anima* from a 17th-century alchemical manuscript.

Famed psychologist Carl Jung described these two elements as such: *"The shadow can be realized only through a relation to a partner, and anima and animus only through a relation to a partner of the opposite sex, because only in such a relation do their projections become operative."*

Poisoned Fruit & Man's Fall

The apple and pomegranate are fruits that have come to represent *desire, degeneration,* and *mortality.* The apple is poisoned with *realization* of *individuality* (nakedness), a temporary and perceived separation from *source,* a droplet of water in a vessel floating in the sea, and an amnesia of our *divinity* like Prince Adam in *Beauty and the Beast.* Apples are also symbols of pure *wisdom;* their consumption, or that of the pomegranate, metaphorically grants *mortality.*

In the *Garden of Eden* these apples grew from "the tree of the knowledge of good and evil." In Genies chapter 2, verses 17-18, the "Lord God" warned man that if he ate from this tree he would "certainly die." In the Biblical account Eve is *tempted* by the *serpent* to eat of the *poisoned fruit.* The serpent tells her, as is written in Genesis chapter 3, verse 5: "*For God knows that when you eat from it your eyes will be opened, and you will be like God, knowing good and evil.*"

Being like God would be to become wise like Odin, realizing good and evil. Trying to become more like God is likewise what caused Lucifer, as a great angel, to fall into the lowest depths of the *pit.* We can read this story in Isaiah 14:12-15 (note: the referenced material in context refers to, in verse 3-4, a *"king of Babylon"*):

> *"How you are fallen from heaven, O Lucifer, son of the morning! How you are cut down to the ground, You who weakened the nations! For you have said in your heart: 'I will ascend into heaven, I will exalt my throne above the stars of God; I will also sit on the mount of the congregation on the farthest sides of the north; I will ascend above the heights of the clouds, I will be like the Most High.' Yet you shall be brought down to Sheol, To the lowest depths of the Pit."*

Wisdom is an attribute given nearly everywhere in the world to *serpents.* In the story of the *Quest for the Golden Fleece* a serpent described as "terrible" guarded the "Golden" fleece, which was hung on a tree in a sacred grove. In this story the serpent was described as "subtle" or "shrewd".

Serpents are true symbols or wisdom, for they tempt man with knowledge of self, which results in man's disobedience of God. Without disobeying, however and acquiring *original sin,* man cannot be redeemed by the *blood of Christ.* All *evil* is, in a sense, necessary so far as it encourages upward and inward growth.

The Greek legend of *Hepera* (Hespera), a paradise-like *Garden of Eden* at the western end of the world, also housed serpents guarding golden apples of wisdom on a Tree of Knowledge. The Greek myth of the *Hesperides,* or nymphs of the sunset, describes their job in caring for this garden, which belonged to Hera, the wife and sister of Zeus. If consumed, the apples that grew there would grant *immortality.* Anyone eating this fruit would surely "be like god."

Hera did not trust the nymphs, though, and instead sent a one-hundred-headed dragon named *Ladon* to protect the "Garden."

Some ascribe to the serpent, fruit, and the embarrassment Adam and Eve felt in the Garden, to the *awakening* of *sexual desire.* In this case the serpent is the phallus, the fruit is sexual pleasure and the shameful nakedness of the two is guilt. We can also note that our offspring are sometimes referred to as the *fruit of your loins.*

Disobedience and *pride* greatly contributed to the fall of Lucifer from heaven and man in the Garden. Philosopher Alan Watts describes in <u>Beyond Theology: The Art of Godmanship</u> that Adam's spiritual *pride* was a result of his *desire* "*to become as a god 'knowing both good and evil,*" and in disobedience "*he was warned not to eat from the Tree.*"

Lucifer's fall from heaven has been also attributed to his spiritual pride and his objection to contamination of soul-spirit with *flesh*. Watts continues: *"Lucifer would then be the force against creation, the agent of death to all that is not pure spirit."*

Of the symbolism of *paradise*, simply defined as without knowledge of "good and evil" – without any *desires* - there are many examples. In other words, Lucifer is the thing that exemplifies glamour and vanity by way of the burning fire of *desire*. Whereas the Devil, opposed to the warmth of life, is cold death. Satan, on the other hand, is an adversarial force, or necessary evil.

Author M. Don Schorn in his book <u>Garden of the Elder Gods</u>, writes of an Egyptian belief in *"an island paradise, a Garden of the Gods, which was called Ta-Neteru, a land later destroyed by a natural cataclysm."* Earlier Egyptian beliefs were held in a region called *Sekhet-Aaru*, where *"the dead went to 'live' in a manner quite similar to which they had existed on Earth."*

The Egyptians spoke of this as the *amdwat*, the land of shadow in the west also known as the land of the dying sun. In contrast, Japan is known as the "land of the rising sun." In Welsh mythology this land was called *annwn*.

We are, of course, talking about SET and HORUS, the eternal battle between good-light and dark-evil. It is a battle taking place both internally and externally. The goal of magicians, alchemists, and many religions is to reconcile these conflicts.

After all, even the highest demonic authority is subject to the lowest angel. We have all tasted the fruit, but its *flavor* should not *bind* us in *guilt* nor justify *nihilism*.

The *fall of man*, from the *poisoned apple*, further signifies a change in man's relationship with the world. Where once the *animal nature* of man dictated his every action by *impulse*, now he would become more reflective and take on the tremendous responsibility of becoming more like God, but not GOD; the responsibility of attempting to overcome *bestial desires* through conscious *realization* and *reflection*; becoming aware of *death* and learning to maneuver with a more aware conscience; following God's *divine plan* by working with *natural law*. Alan Watts describes the consumption of the *fruits of desire*:

> *"Those who ate the fruit would become 'as gods', for they would know how to control events and how to make things happen. This is why Adam's fall and expulsion from the garden involves the curse of work, of once you start controlling things according to your deliberations, you can no longer rely upon impulse. You must stop playing, and be serious. You must think of the future, and plan for it, and thus become aware of death in an altogether new way…*

> *"We began to play God - that is, to control our lives instead of letting them happen… But we were like the Sorcerer's Apprentice, and didn't really know what to do. Thereupon pain ceased to be ecstasy and became punishment. At the same time, we began to feel responsible for dying. Death was no longer the transformation and renewal of life, the shuffling of the pack for a new deal. Death became the mark of failure, the wages of sin, and the result of our incompetence in playing God."*

The *serpent* on the *tree* offering this fruit is both representative of the penis itself, while its open mouth is vaginal.

According to Joseph Campbell, the *word of creation* is spoken through the sexual metaphor of the *teeth* and *tongue* acting as *vagina* and *penis*. He says, *"out of their forming words together all the gods, the heavens, and the world are brought forth."*

On that same note, Hall adds that the WORD is made of the seven vowels of the Elohim which are the decree that *"issues as a host of living powers from the 'lips of the Creator'."*

Man Crucified to Matter

One of the most famous crosses in the world is the Egyptian *Ankh*, or *Crux Ansata*, a symbol which denotes and bestows life. Isis famously holds this cross with her hand slipped through the top loop. The word *ankh* translates to *life bestowing,* which is precisely what this Queen of Heaven embodies, the power of birth, nurturing life, and setting it free to flourish. It is Isis, the Universal Mother, who bestows life to all her children.

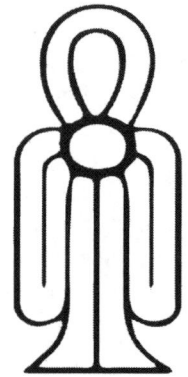

Crux Ansata　　　**Tjet**

Ankhs are sometimes accompanied by the *Tjet*, another symbol of fertility, motherhood, medicine, and life. Also called the *knot of Isis* or *blood of Isis*, a *tjet* looks like an *ankh* but with arms at its side rather than spread outward like wings. When Isis holds the ankh, it is like she is merging with Osiris, whose head protrudes from its mummified wrappings like the circle adorns the top of the Tau cross of *life bestowing*. In other words, *ankhs* are symbols of Osiris and *tjets* are symbols of Isis. Combined they are amulets of protection.

In Egypt these were also symbols of *salvation*, just like the *Christian Cross, Celtic Cross, Latin Cross*, Swastika, and even the *Wheel of the Year* denoting the changing seasons.

Although an inverted cross has come to represent a rejection of Christianity, traditionally it was a symbol of Saint Peter, who felt unworthy be crucified in the same manner as Christ. Choosing to be nailed upside down, Peter's cross became known as the *Petrine Cross*. For Catholics, it signifies deep humility.

The cross is historically derived from the *Zodiac Wheel*, comprised of houses that the *Grand Architect* and archetypical *Carpenter* build. The cross therefore divides the *world* into parts with individual *winds*, while each division of *time* has its own season.

THE CROSS is talismanic and certainly an amulet of protection for Christians today. It is that thing one holds, kisses, places around the neck, hangs on the wall, puts on their car, etc., hoping to acquire the protection of Christ in all things. This *traditional and basic cross* is essentially an umbilical cord connecting the children of God *below* with their Father *above*. This can be said of the *scepter* and *Staff of Moses*, or of the *Hermit's Staff* in general. These are symbols of man's earthly authority which has only been ordained by powers above.

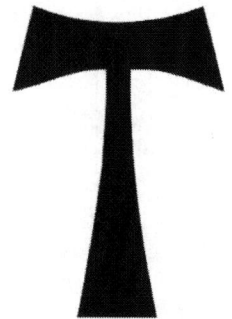

Celtic Cross　　　**Tau Cross**

As with the four corners of the world and their winds, and the four changing seasons, the four elements are ripe for mentioning. When breaking down a hexagram, or six-pointed star, there are two triangles – one upright and one facing downward. The upright triangle symbolizes the phallus and fire. The downward facing triangle symbolizes the womb and water. This symbol further relates to the Hanged Man in tarot, a character upside with his feet touching heaven. Placing a line at the top of the upright triangle gives you the symbol for air and placing a line at the bottom of the downward facing triangle gives you earth. Combined into the hexagram you have the four elements.

If the triangle is ascending upward, it represents man's attempt to connect with the heavens, and when descending, it signifies God reaching down to his creation. More abstractly these triangles represent the superior and inferior worlds touching at a single point like God and Adam in Michelangelo's painting, "The Creation of Adam."

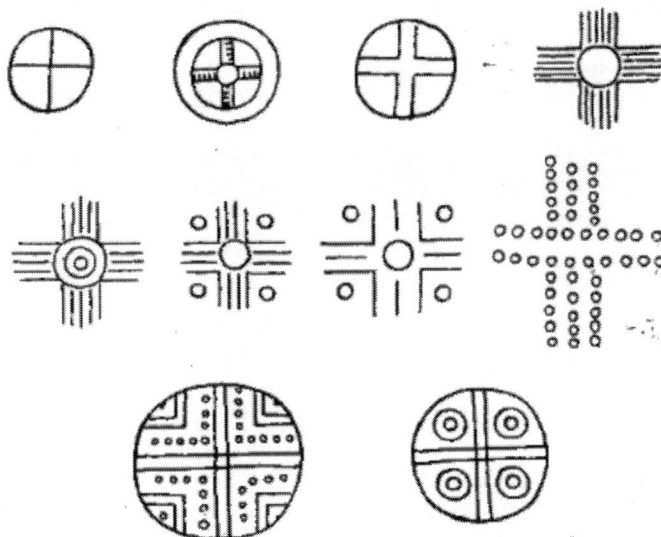

As published in <u>The Complete Book of Amulets & Talismans</u>, by Migene González-Wippler, 1991, we find some of the first crosses.

When the elements of fire and water are about to merge in certain occult imagery there is often a serpent slithering between the two. This is the serpent of the *Staff of Moses*; it is *Astral Light*, reconciling the superior and inferior worlds.

ALEPH א is the first letter of the Hebrew alphabet. It expresses unity but represents hieroglyphically the dogma of Hermes: *that which is above is also like that which is below.*

The Hebrew letter has two arms, one pointing to earth, as with the pyramid based in heaven pointing to downward, or God reaching to man, and one arm pointing to heaven, as with the pyramid based on earth ascending upward, or man reaching to God.

The *Great Work* of alchemy is accomplished by fixating the *Astral Light* through a sovereign act of *will*. It is represented by the piercing of a serpent with an arrow, otherwise depicted as ALEPH א. It is the Kabbalistic *Yesod* manifested downward into *Malkuth*. Eliphas Levi explains here the use of a triangle within the circle of evocation:

> "…a triangle was usually traced, and the side towards which the upper point should it be erected was a matter for careful observation. If the spirit were supposed it to be from heaven, the operator placed himself at the top, and set the altar of fumigations at the bottom; but if the spirit came from the abyss this method was reversed."

The *pentagram* or *pentangle* is comprised of the four elements in its lower points, and upon the fifth, like that of the *ankh*, is signified *intelligence* rising upward from the lower four corners of the infernal world. An ascending pentagram is thus the rising of consciousness to obtain dominion over the four elements. A descending pentagram is just the opposite; the allowance of carnal pleasures to sink the soul-spirit further into the abyss of *matter*. Could the image of Christ *crucified* to a *cross* not represent the *suffering* of all *souls-spirits* crucified to the *body*, or *placed* into the tomb of *matter*, like that of Plato's Cave? Jesus on a Cross suffering in pain symbolizes the cruelty we inflict upon ourselves, as we are often *our own worst enemy*. Watts writes of the latter:

> "*The God-Man on the Cross sums up in one image all the cruelty we inflict by being alive, all the ravages of human selfishness and thoughtlessness.*"

The crucifixion of Christ is a representation of the suffering man inflicts upon himself and his environment, just as mythological characters represent far more than the values attributed to them for entertainment. Crucifixion is acute consciousness; an intense form of awareness, overwhelming to those who easily succumb to *temptation*. From this view, we are all hanging upon the cross of materiality like Jesus and Odin, nailed to the four corners of the world.

Jesus represents an archetype of the great mythological hero who fights the enemies of a nation and slays its greatest beasts like Osiris. He does battle with evil and darkness to ensure our salvation through a lighted pathway provided by the Hermit's hexagram lantern light on the tarot card. This path is split and often referred to as the *Pythagorean Y*.

To the left is a path of temptation and carnal pleasure, which leads to further submersion in the crypts of the underworld. Those ultimately upon this path are, in a sense, punished for their misdeeds and cast into a Hell of the mind.

Only those reflecting and learning from hardships will grow to earn the rewards of Heaven through adversity. To the right is a path of redemption and salvation represented by the ankh and cross.

The *miracle* of Christ's birth, crucifixion, and resurrection are preserved in the *Holy Trinity* and *universal cross*. It would serve mankind well to recognize that both the literal interpretation of the latter and the mockery of the same are likely equally as absurd.

That Jesus Christ as a man, who certainly went by other names, was the *Son of God,* and that he was placed on a cross and then into a tomb, is proof of all our divinity as *children of God*. From the genitals to head, and every inch of the spine between, the *Tree of Life* is our body, and our soul-spirit is nailed upon its branches. Watts further observes:

> "*Only if Bethlehem (the 'House of Bread') becomes the human body, does it mean anything to sing: O holy Child of Bethlehem! Descend to us we pray; Cast out our sin and enter in, Be born in us today.*"

> "*The meaning of the miracle is as important for the age which takes miracles for granted, as for the age which takes them with skepticism; in either age, the fact of the miracle is of no great consequence.*"

The Universal Cross

In an article on the cross published in the <u>Encyclopedia Britannica,</u> Thomas Macall Fallow explains the antiquity of this ideograph:

> "*The use of the cross as a religious symbol in pre-Christian times, and among non-Christian peoples, may probably be regarded as almost universal, and in very many cases it was connected with some form of nature worship.*"

Quetzalcoatl was the civilizer and savior deity Central America. His name means either "feathered snake" or "plumed serpent." He is said to have come out of the sea, bringing with him the *cross* in one form, specifically the red cross worn on his garments. Some may relate these crosses with the pre-Columbian travels of the Knights Templar, thought to have explored much of North, Central, and South America long before Columbus arrived. But the image of the cross is far older, especially when you consider the North American usage of one variety or anther of swastika.

Hall mentions the arrival of Cortez to this land in The Secret Teachings of All Ages, and thus the arrival of the Christian cross which was already in use:

> "When Cortez arrived in Mexico, he brought with him the cross. Recognizing this, the natives believed that he was Quetzalcoatl returned, for the latter had promised to come."

On the crucifixion of the feathered serpent, Lord Kingsborough writes further, referencing both the crucified serpent and that this god was also cut into pieces like Osiris:

> "May we not refer to the seventy-third page of the Borgian MS., which represents Quexalcoatl both crucified, and as it were cut in pieces for the cauldron, and with equal reason demand, whether anyone can help thinking that the Jews of the New World [Lord Kingsborough sought to prove that the Mexicans were descendants of the Jews] applied to their Messiah not only all the prophecies contained in the Old Testament relating to Christ, but likewise many of the incidents recorded of him in the Gospels."

The Crucifixion of Quetzalcóatl, from Codex Borgianus, Kingsborough's Antiquities of Mexico, mid-1800s

In Anacalypsis, Godfrey Higgins expands on the symbol of the cross in the Americas, specifically referring to a beautiful cross known to the Inca Empire. Interestingly, some believe that the word INCA is an anagram for CAIN, and this idea shares a parallel with what Lord Kingsborough believed may be true of the Mexican peoples further north – the Inca Empire having encompassed what today is modern Peru, Chile, Ecuador, and Bolivia:

> "The Incas had a cross of very fine marble, or beautiful jasper, highly polished, of one piece, three-fourths of an ell in length, and three fingers in width and thickness. It was kept in a sacred chamber of a palace, and held in great veneration. The Spaniards enriched this cross with gold and jewels, and placed it in the cathedral of Cuzco. Mexican temples are in the form of a cross, and face the four cardinal points. Quexalcoatl is represented in the paintings of the Codex Borgianus nailed to the cross. Sometimes even the two thieves are there crucified with him… In the Codex Borgianus, (pp. 4, 72, 73,

75,) the Mexican God is represented crucified and nailed to the cross, and in another place hanging to it, with a cross in his hands."

A very thorough overview of the *cross* is provided in J. E. Cirlot's <u>A Dictionary of Symbols</u>, a reference of which is provided in part here:

"The complex symbolism of the cross neither denies nor supplants the historical meaning in Christianity. But in addition to the realities of Christianity there are two other essential factors: that of the symbolism of the cross as such and that of the crucifixion or of 'suffering upon the cross'. In the first place, the cross is dramatic in derivation, an inversion, as it were, of the Tree of Paradise. Hence, the cross is often represented in mediaeval allegory as a Y-shaped tree, depicted with knots and even with branches, and sometimes with thorns. Like the Tree of Life, the cross stands for the 'world-axis'. Placed in the mystic Centre of the cosmos, it becomes the bridge or ladder by means of which the soul may reach God. There are some versions which depict the cross with seven steps, comparable with the cosmic trees which symbolize the seven heavens. The cross, consequently, affirms the primary relationship between the two worlds of the celestial and the earthly. But, in addition, because of the cross-piece which cuts cleanly across the upright (in turn implying the symbols of level and of the axis of the world), it stands for the conjunction of opposites, wedding the spiritual (or vertical) principle with the principle of the world of phenomena. Hence its significance as a symbol for agony, struggle and martyrdom. Sometimes the cross is T-shaped, further emphasizing the near-equilibrium of the opposing principles."

Simple, primordial figure denoting orientation on a plane surface.

St. Andrew's cross: union of the Upper and Lower Worlds.

Arrow-headed cross denoting centrifugal forces.

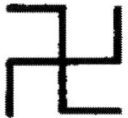

Gammadion (fylfot or cross cramponnee) denoting the path of peripheral forces.

Doubled cross, expressive of parallel forces.

Maltese cross (or cross of eight points), expressive of centripetal forces.

The Cross, from J. E. Cirlot's <u>A Dictionary of Symbols</u>, 1958

The Crucifixion by Bartolomé Estebán Murillo (1675).
&
Odin hanging on the World Tree

The **Orpheus Amulet** – Joseph Campbell writes: *"It is clear that, in Orpheus and Christ, we have exactly the same archetype, with the motif of leaving the physical world, still symbolized with a cross in astronomy, for the spiritual. They leave the Earth, symbol of Mother, to go to the realm of the Father."*

Templar Cross

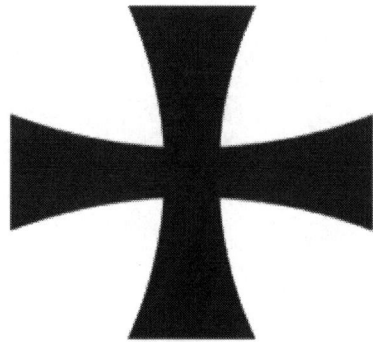

Maltese Cross

The **Templar Cross** has distinctive ends that are "fishtailed" with eight specific points. Eight is also the infinity sign of the Leviathan Cross, and represents the cycle of life, death, and rebirth. It is a symbol of the Knights of St. John, a chivalrous Order originating during the Crusades. Also known as the Knights Hospitaller, these men set up hospitals in Jerusalem in 1080 to provide care for pilgrims traveling to and from the Holy Land. The Templar Cross is also known as the Cross of St. John, Campaign Cross, Regeneration Cross, or Fishtail Cross. The **Maltese Cross** was also used by the Knights Templar and was later known as the Iron Cross.

The **Leviathan Cross** is often referred to as *Crux Satana* for its association with the Church of Satan, although there is little detail to confirm this. It was, however, used by the Cathars and Knights Templar. Alchemically it is a symbol of sulfur. The two bars signify balance, the third identifies the bars with the *Holy Trinity*, and the horizontal eight, or infinity, is a symbol of completion or unity, as depicted by the single circle of an ouroboros.

The **Labarum Cross** is an early emblem of an ancient Chaldean sky-god. Later it was used on Roman Christian tombstones. It is said to have appeared to Constantine in a dream and is typically interpreted as the first two letters of Christ's name in Greek. It holds the *chi* and *rho* of the Greek word ΧΡΙΣΤΟΣ – *Christos*.

Leviathan Cross

Labarum

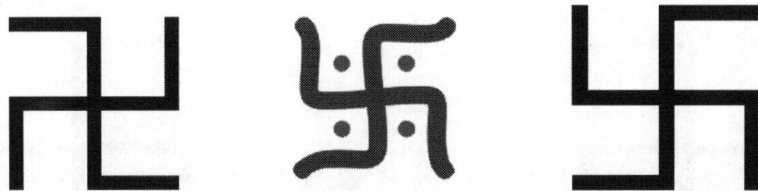

The *swastika* is one of the oldest known symbols in the world, especially as it relates to the *Cross* or *Zodiac*. It is found in the sand paintings of Navajo Indians. Native American medicine men use the *Whirling Log* symbol in their ceremonies (far right). Used in a variety of forms it has played a role in the workings of medicine men, which use the symbol for healing purposes. This makes sense considering the Sanskrit word *swasti* actually means "well being" or "so be it." To the (left) of the *Whirling Log* is the *Hopi Rattle* with swastika.

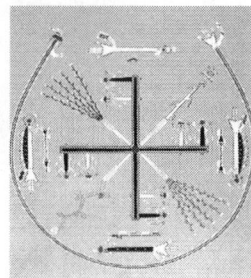

Like any symbol, the orientation of the swastika changes its meaning. When rotated clockwise (*deosil*) it represents the sun. To the Hopi Indians this meant the earth.

When depicted counterclockwise (*widdershins*) it represents the moon. In this latter format the swastika is sometimes referred to as a *sauvastika*. The Hopi used the reverse of this image to represent the sun.

Either way this symbol is turned it has positive meaning. If clockwise, it signifies love and mercy. If counterclockwise, it stands for intelligence and strength. Unfolding the arms will reveal a standard cross with four quadrants. The arms are bent as the wheel turns.

Seen throughout the Hindu world, the *bindhu* dot is often used between each arm of the swastika (Top Middle). An offshoot of Hinduism called *Jain* also uses this symbol. The Chinese-Japanese *Manji* looks like a painted swastika with simple brush strokes. It represents the ancient solar principle, and the word literally means "Chinese symbol for eternity." Variations of this image abound in the form of the sun cross/wheel, Odin's Cross, or Thor's Hammer. Even the dance of Shiva is stylized as a swastika. Shiva dances like Pan, and like the sun across the heavens. This dance is performed likewise by RA and Amaterasu.

Another common cross is for the Irish goddess of spring named Brigid. She presided over the festivals of Imbolc in early springtime and aids women in labor. During the spring celebrations an item was fashioned called a *Brigid Cross* (Middle Right), which shared similarities with the swastika.

The Greeks, Romans, and Ancient Egyptians consumed small circular wheat cakes in celebration of spring, which, representing the sun and moon, were divided into four quadrants like a cross. The cross is also found in the astrological sign of the planet Saturn, with a hook; it relates heavily to the symbolism of the cube and the material world (Middle Right). The Zig-zag cross of the Zia Pueblo is yet another symbol of the sun (Bottom Right). When the sun moves the arms bend.

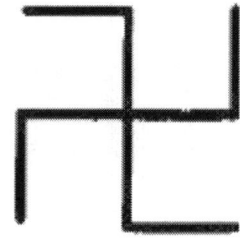

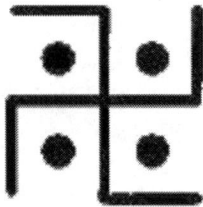

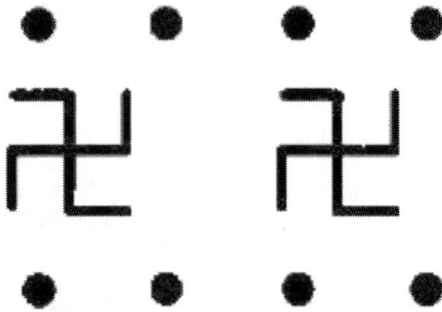

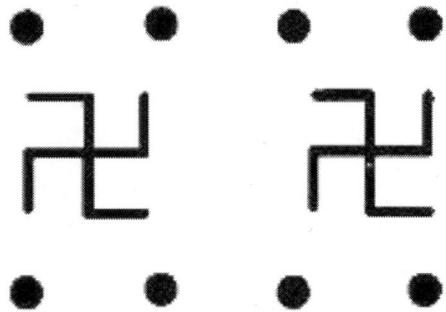

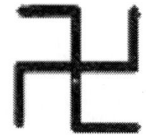

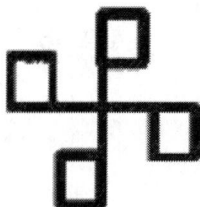

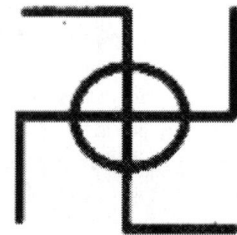

Various versions of the cross or swastika from the 1991 book, <u>The Complete Book of Amulets & Talismans</u>, by Migene González-Wippler.

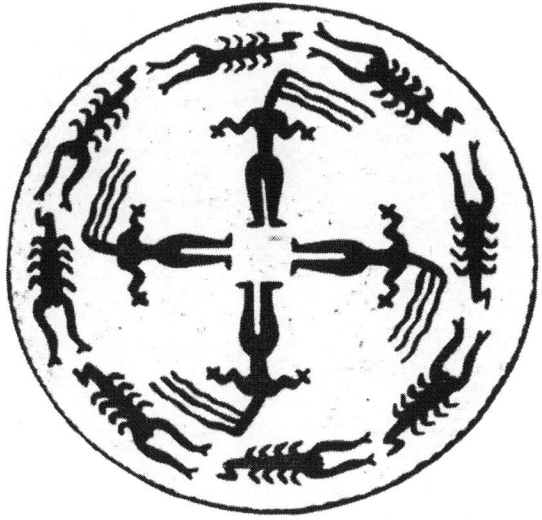

Swastikas on pottery printed in J. C. Cooper's, <u>Illustrated Encyclopaedia of Traditional Symbols</u>

Four goats stylized as a swastika and painted on Sumerian pottery.

Four women and their hair create the swastika on a piece of Sumerian pottery from the 5th millennium B.C.

Engraving of a Norse deity on a coin called a *braceate*. In the upper left of the gold-foil coin is a swastika.

A symbol of the philosophy and spiritual practice of *Falun Gong,* representing balance and harmony of mind, body, and spirit.

gentes præfertim in Urbe *Nepal*, Luna XII. *Badr* 元章, feu *Bhadòn* त्त्देखं *Augufti* menfis, dies feftos aufpicaturæ Dei *Indra* ξ 章. erigunt ad illius memoriam ubique locorum *Cruces* amictas *Abrotono*. Earum figuram defcriptam habes ad lit. 8 Tabula pone fequenti. Nam A effigies eft ipfius *Indræ crucifixi* figna *Telech* in fronte manibus pedibufque gerentis.

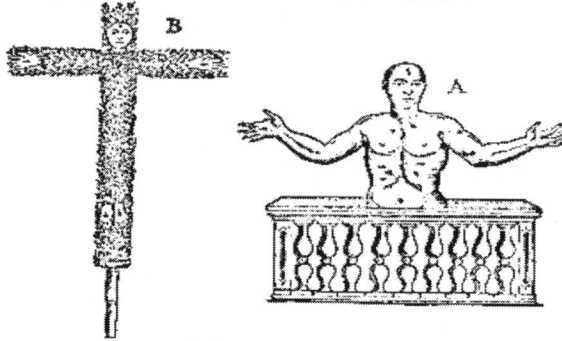

LXXXII. Statuam *Indræ* ex editis locis, pulpitifque confpicuam Indigenæ Nepallenfes adorant, peregrini vero tanquam infigne quoddam fuperftitionis portentum mirantur & obftupefcunt. *Telech* Jovem forte *miniatum* exhibent: notæ facræ funt *effluvia purgationum naturæ* fignificant, iifque Regum pariter frontem, manus pedefque, in folemni eorum inauguratione confignant. Sed *Indra* Deus eft Cæli inferioris, nubium Rector, pluviarum,

Cc 2   inun-

A page from <u>Alphabetum Tibetanum</u> (1762), by the monk Augustinus Georgius

Included are two images of *Indra* as he was depicted in Nepal. One shows the god crucified to a cross while the other shows him resurrecting from a chest like Osiris..

The Hanged Man

When Odin hangs from the *Yggdrasil* (World Tree) "for nights full nine" with "the spear" wounding his side, he is not only crucified, but providing us with what we know in Tarot as the *Hanged Man* symbol. A similar account is held by the Yakuts of Siberia of their supreme being Yrynai-tojon tethered to a gigantic tree. Just as the cross is *physical matter* and the *crucifixion* is our *soul-spirit* placed on the *matter-cross* with *nails of illusion*, Odin's suspension from the tree signifies, as Hall relates, *"the human spirit which is suspended from heaven by a single thread."*

The reward of this sacrifice is wisdom:

> *"Wisdom, not death, is the reward for this voluntary sacrifice during which the human soul, suspended above the world of illusion, and meditating upon its unreality, is rewarded by the achievement of self-realization."*

> *"The myth of the dying god is the key to both universal and individual redemption and regeneration, and those who do not comprehend the true nature of this supreme allegory are not privileged to consider themselves either wise or truly religious."*

The Body & Blood of Immortality

The Greek myth of Dionysus, also known as Bacchus in Rome, tells the story of the god of wine. Thebes was his birthplace, born to Zeus and a Theban princess named Semele. Dionysus was said to bring either kindness or cruelty upon man, certainly a reference to what alcohol does to some. Thus, his worship was focused on two ideas: freedom and savage brutality. Dionysus is a blessing to man, but he can also cause ruin to the same. For as men may be made cheerful or drunk by the consumption of alcohol, some men find it an occasional delight while others are consumed by the drink itself. Since alcohol was once referred to as *spirit*, since the process of fermentation was not widely understood, one was truly being *possessed* - in Greece the possessor was Dionysus. William J. Fielding writes in <u>Strange Superstations and Magical Practices</u> of this scientific process:

> *"We still commonly speak of distillations of various kinds as 'spirits.' Thus, distilled liquors, such as whisky, brandy, gin, etc., are known under the generic term of 'spirits,' or 'spirits of wine.' There are also 'spirits of nitre,' 'spirits of camphor,' and many other similar essences and quintessences. When these terms were first used they had a literal meaning. Distillations were first the monopolist work of the magicians and alchemists, and it was popularly believed that the 'spirits' which pervaded the universe had entered into these mysterious transformations, which of course they did not recognize as chemical processes."*

It was not just an external change in the behaviors of those who partook of his wine; their insides were also changing, too, making the whole story perhaps a primitive explanation for how alcohol was processed by the body. Overall, men were said to literally transform into Dionysus, a story of how men are turned into gods, or *water into wine*.

Bland men (water) could be transmuted into a different person (wine) by the drinking of alcohol, though not always for the better. The true self would be suppressed during the possession of Dionysus only to be resurrected when the *spirits* wore off. Edith Hamilton, in <u>Mythology,</u> writes of this of wine and the gods:

> *"The momentary sense of exultant power wine-drinking can give was only a sign to show men that they had within them more than they knew; 'they could themselves become divine'."*

The celebratory festival for Dionysus took place in spring, sharing a parallel with the Lesser Degrees of the *mysteries* at Eleusis, Greece, when the vine puts forth its branches. It lasted for five days, all of which were to be joyful and peaceful days overflowing with wine. Much like the Roman *Saturnalia* celebration when no war could be declared, slaves and masters reversed roles, or became equals, and presents were given, the festival of Dionysus also prompted the ceasing of all business activities. Prisoners were released to participate in the celebration and no other person could be placed in prison during that day. This was a time of rejoicing for all men.

The honoring festival of Dionysus was unique in that it did not take place in the wilderness or any sacred temple, necessarily, nor by a feast or other similar festivity. It usually occurred in a theater with the ceremony being a dramatic performance or play. Everything about the performance was sacred; the spectators, performers, and writers were all engaged in a form of *worship*. *Comedies* were produced, but most common were *tragedies* since these more closely resembled the life and death of Dionysus. He was both *divine* and *the-vine*. Mirroring the story of Persephone's descent into the underworld, and Demeter's subsequent neglecting of the crops during the winter months, the life of Dionysus was ended by the arrival of colder temperatures, resulting in the death (retreating) of vines. Unlike Persephone's journey to the underworld, though, the death of Dionysus was far more brutal. He was torn into pieces by the Titans, in some stories upon orders from Hera, the wife of Zeus, much in the way Orpheus was dismembered by a band of Maenads. The same horrible fate befalls Osiris and, as we read earlier in this section, Quetzalcoatl as well. But as Edith Hamilton rightfully declares: *"He was always brought back to life; he died and rose again."* She adds:

"In his resurrection he was the embodiment of the life that is stronger than death. He and not Persephone became the center of the belief in immortality."

In the death and resurrection of Dionysus-Bacchus we thus find the dying-god motif. There are common themes here of dismemberment, trees and crucifixion, blood, suffering, death, redemption, resurrection, etc. We can see these Dionysian themes in the stories of Osiris, Jesus, Iapetus (Prometheus), Odin, Adam, and others like Attis, Mithra(s), Orpheus, Pyramus & Thisbe, Adonis, etc. Just as the story of Persephone beautifully explains the changing of seasons and that time of year when earth is left barren before its inevitable regeneration or resurrection, the story of Dionysus-Bacchus explains what happens to vines when grapes are harvested and when frost halts the growth of crops in the fields. To dismiss these stories as mere *myth*, now defined as simple imagination, is both oddly and ironically accurate, yet this provides no context or justice to the ancients and their ability to weave science and myth together in an elegant way for all to appreciate, but for few to fully understand. Yes, they are *myths*, but they are so much more than that. These were stories that, if improperly unveiled, could have gotten you killed in ancient Greece. Hall explains the significance of grapes and their unique juices for which Dionysus and Bacchus were representatives:

"The juice of the grape was thought by the Egyptians to resemble human blood more closely than did any other substance. In fact, they believed that the grape secured its life from the blood of the dead who had been buried in the Earth."

In various traditions all over the world *wine* was consumed as the *blood* of a fallen god, whose *flesh* was also consumed in the form of *bread* or *cake* made from the last harvested wheat. The origin of the Christian *Last Supper*, and also tithing, are based on this harvest, symbolic gestures of thanks to nature – they are agricultural artifacts. The concept of *eating flesh* and *drinking blood* is a practice from antiquity and is accepted today as the orthodox Christian ritual of *Eucharist*. Simply referred to as *communion*, the *juice* and *crackers* act as magical tools to impress the essence of *flesh* and *blood* on participants. It is a magic ritual plain and simple, yet the *Eucharist* is often separated from the Catholic Transubstantiation, which uses the same emblems but holds that they are literal. In the Biblical book of John, chapter 6:53 we read:

"Very truly I tell you, unless you eat the flesh of the Son of Man and drink his blood, you have no life in you."

And just before in the book of John, 6:46-48, Jesus says, *"No one has seen the Father except the one who is from God; only he has seen the Father. Very truly I tell you, the one who believes has eternal life. I am the bread of life."* We are reminded of these verses when reading of the Jicarilla Apache hero Killer-of-Enemies, who says in myth: *"Whoever believes me, whoever listens to what I say, will have long life. One who doesn't listen, who thinks in some evil way, will have a short life."*

The grapes and wheat are nourished by the sun and rain. Grapes are turned into wine and wheat into flower and bread. Grapes and wine, and wheat and bread, are then translated metaphorically into blood and flesh as symbols of the transformations of nature, and the resurrection of the dying-god – *Green Man.*

Edith Hamilton explains the connection made between

The Last Supper, by Peter Paul Rubens, 1632

crops and blood, and therefore, the subsequent justification, for some cultures, of sacrificing a villager in hopes of fertilizing the ground with their blood. The same ritual was symbolically conducted with animal blood during the Roman fertility festival of Lupercalia, what we know call Valentine's Day, when dog or goat hide was dipped in blood and used to transfer the essence of those animals, i.e., fertility, to other animals, women, and the land:

> *"Mankind had only a dim feeling that as their own life depended utterly on seedtime and harvest, there must be a deep connection between themselves and the earth and that their blood, which was nourished by the corn, could in turn nourish it at need."*

Hall adds that many ancient cultures believed grapes *"first sprung out of the earth after it was fattened with the carcasses of those who fell in the wars against the God."*

In the story of Adonis, drops of his blood help sprout plants; the drops cause a crimson flower to grow where they strike the ground. A parallel is found when Mithra(s) slays the bull or when the Greek Cronus is attacked and his blood falls to form Giants. The blood of Raktabija is prevented from sprouting demons by the tongue of Kali in Hindu mythology. It is said how the blood of Dionysus sprouts the pomegranate, which is the fruit Persephone eats in Hades.

Some may consume literal blood with the intention to pervert and alter such sacred practices, or because they believe they are acquiring the true essence of the creature from whence the blood was taken. Warriors throughout history, and certainly within certain tribal societies, would drink the blood of fallen warriors to absorb their strengths. They may also eat certain organs for the same purpose. History preserves how the Scythian peoples, a nomadic tribe originally from the area of modern Iran, would first kill the men, butcher the women, and then drink the blood of those killed in battle. In this case, the reason may have been barbarism. It is thought the Mongols would drink horse blood while fighters in Ethiopia would consume the blood of cattle to obtain vitamins.

The Hittite cult of modern Turkey would *drink the god* at any of their sacrificial celebrations, which clearly was a form of sympathetic magi and communion.

Issues of cannibalism are certainly relevant here, though not all cannibals were completely irrational. Some tribes believed that eating certain parts of a dead family member would prevent the body-soul-spirit from rotting in the cold ground. Some also knew the dangers of this so friendly tribes, with far less blood relations, would eat the organs, flesh, or drink the blood instead. Other tribes were outright cannibalistic, eating other tribes and especially any foreigner, even well-meaning missionaries. The disease known as *kuru,* a neurological sickness, was made famous by the Fore peoples of Papua New Guinea, who practiced their share of cannibalism.

Blood has always been considered a container for the *life force* of a living creature and was thus forbidden for any kind of use in the Bible. As the book of Leviticus 17:11 confirms:

> *"For the life of a creature is in the blood, and I have given it to you to make atonement for yourselves on the altar; it is the blood that makes atonement for one's life."*

And in Hebrews 9:22 we read about the cleansing power of blood, as a literal substance but also as a metaphoric tool, such as wine, for redemption:

> *"In fact, the law requires that nearly everything be cleansed with blood, and without the shedding of blood there is no forgiveness."*

Philosopher Alan Watts writes of blood: *"Blood was to be the life-essence of men and animals, and thus the property of God alone, so that every animal killed for food had to have its throat slit and the blood poured to the ground."* He adds that under the Covenants between man and God:

> *"The sacrifice is a communion meal, between God and his people in which they take the flesh and he takes the blood. But under the New Covenant, instituted by Jesus, the people are to have both the flesh and the blood of the sacrificial lamb."*

All the talk of animal and human sacrifices, so far as they relate to blood and burnt offerings, can be redirected to the sacrifice of the animal nature and the pouring out of one's life in the service of Christ. In many ways, this is precisely what the Church did, redirect barbaric practices into the *Eucharist* and reappropriate the old *holy days* as *holidays.*

Janet Wolter and Alan Butler write of the harvest-communion in their book <u>America Nation of the Goddess</u>:

> *"To partake of this bounty humanity had to effectively 'kill' the god and consume his body in the form of cereal grain and his blood as wine."*

Here is referenced the ritual killing of the god, or the *killing of the king,* an ancient custom, the meaning of which has been mostly lost today. As James Frazer points out in <u>The Golden Bough</u>:

> *"Every purpose, therefore, was answered, and all dangers averted by thus killing the man-god and transferring his soul, while yet at its prime, to a vigorous successor."*

Watts proceeds to explain that the *"…bread and wine offered at the altar for Mass (brought, in ancient times, by the people themselves) represent ourselves, our flesh and blood, and the work, the sacrifice, and the guilt, which they involve."* J. E. Cirlot explains in <u>A Dictionary of Symbols</u>: *"Juice or sap represents life-giving liquid. It is a sacrificial symbol connected with blood and also with light as the distillation of igniferous bodies, suns and stars."*

We find throughout the world not only the earthly communion, but the heavenly one too. In India the gods consume *amrta* on the Mountain of Sumeru. Joseph Campbell explains other parallels in his book The Hero With A Thousand Faces:

> *"Mt. Olympus rises to the heavens; gods and heroes banquet there on ambrosia, In Wotan's mountain hall, four hundred and thirty-two thousand heroes consume the undimininished flesh of Sachrimnir, the Cosmic Boar, washing it down with a milk that runs from the udders of the she-goat Heidrun: she feeds on the leaves of Yggdrasil, the World Ash. Within the fairy hills of Erin, the deathless Tuatha De Danaan consume the self-renewing pigs of Manannan, drinking copiously of Guibne's ale. In Persia, the gods in the mountain garden on Mt. Hara Berezaiti drink immortal haoma, distilled from the Gaokerena Tree, the tree of life. The Japanese gods drink sake, the Polynesian ave, the Aztec gods drink the blood of men and maids."*

Searching for eternal life by means of physical concoctions, infernal intervention, or specific locations is to misunderstand what is meant by achieving *immortality*. The *Watercress of Immortality* sought by Gilgamesh, and the *Everlasting Island*, the Greco-Roman *Islands of the Blessed*, the Chinese *Pill of Immortality*, Ponce de Leon's *Fountain of Youth*, or the one written about by Herodotus, are to be found, like the *Philosopher's Stone*, safely stored within the self. Campbell says that the basic problem is thus: *"To enlarge the pupil of the eye, so that the body with its attendant personality will no longer obstruct the view. Immortality is then experienced as a precent fact: 'It is here! It is here!'"*

Ritual Intoxication

Blood, especially communion wine, is obviously symbolic of the sacrifice made by the dying-savior-god, so that we may all be *born again* in him, and he in us. Intoxication by *drink*, through the transformation of *water into wine*, is reminiscent of the various substances used in many of the *Mystery Schools* to invoke spiritual experiences or to predict the future. This was the nature of the Oracle of Delphi, those priestesses who went into a trance after inhaling the noxious vapors that were rising from a crack in earth, over which her tripod seat was situated. Intoxications, "that of being drunk or under the influence of drugs," were either sublime experiences of the spiritual sort or delusional states brought about by convulsions and heavy inebriation. Narcotics were used probably more widely than the specially prepared psychedelic drugs or hallucinogens.

The legendary **Mandrake Root** must be uprooted by its intended user, but caution should be exercised due to the supposed death-inducing scream emitted when it is removed from the ground. It is used for support in everything from finances to sexual issues. It was also used in the *Mystery Schools*.

In the *mysteries*, these substances were meant to *expand* and *open* the mind. For the commoner, and perhaps in the corrupted *mysteries*, these substances were used, as they are today, in a reckless and dangerous fashion to induce pseudo-spiritual experiences.

The psychedelic variety of drug was usually administered in the *Mystery Schools* only after careful and deliberate perpetration.

This was no joke, laughing matter, or game. As with the true *secret teachings* of the Dionysus-Bacchus myth, if improperly unveiled, the origin and nature of these drugs could have likewise gotten you killed.

MANDRAKE

What we know: Libations in the Persian cult of Zoroastrianism were made from the herb *Peganum harmala,* the seeds and root containing psychoactive alkaloids that induced psychedelic visions. In Mithraism, another Persian cult, the herb was called *haoma.*

The Maya of Central America partook of a mildly intoxicating beverage called *balché,* made with the bark of a leguminous tree. If fermented with honey for several days, the drink becomes a narcotic. *Ayahuasca* of South America and *peyote* of Central and North America have the same types of effects on the body and mind.

One of the most famous of these substances is the Egyptian blue water lily known as *Nymphaea Caerulea.* So popular was this substance that it was placed on the tombs of some pharaohs. It may be used as a tranquilizer in small doses, but in larger amounts psychosis could be induced. As referenced already, William Emboden, Professor of Biology at California State University, believes that the *blue water lily* (*blue lotus*) of the Nile River may have been used to induce hallucinatory states in Egypt, alongside poppy and mandrake root as well. *Poppy* and *Mandrake Root* were also used to induce trances and altered states of awareness by countless other cultures.

In the final rite of initiation in the Greek Mysteries a cup with some type of narcotic substance was given to the initiate. The ceremonial cup is called *kykeon* and the narcotic was made from a distillation of *ergot*, a fungus growing on cereal crops with mild psychoactive effects if consumed. Consumption can also cause *ergotism*, resulting in a very severe sickness. This is why the preparations had to be precise.

Just as blood, or its symbolic counterpart, can induce feelings of spiritual awareness or delirium, the female menstrual cycle and its blood has a similar nature. The word *menstrual* is derived from the Latin word *mensis,* meaning *month*. This lunar connection to the months, or *moonths*, means that the body, blood, and emotions of a woman can be altered by the moon, which further controls the oceans (em-oceans). It can, and does, influence men too, hence the word *lunatic* or *lunacy*, i.e., *insanity*.

An Astrological Misunderstanding

The story of Jesus is an allegory of "astronomical" proportions. Jesus is said to have been betrayed by Judas with a "kiss" before dying on a cross and being placed into a tomb for three days, whereupon he was resurrected in a celebration later referred to as Easter.

Each year the physical sun is reborn in like manner from the cave of the earth. Due to the tilt and wobble of the earth, this solar orb seems to pass through the twelve houses of the zodiac. It does this as part of a yearly cycle and a much larger cycle lasting roughly 26,000 years, or more specifically 25,920 years, wherein the sun rises in each zodiac house for a division of said time. Upon completion a new cycle begins: *the wheel continues turning.*

Throughout the solar year the sun grows in age, strength, and light, to overcome the cold and darkness of winter. From birth and youth to maturity and death the sun is anthropomorphized as a man. In some cases, the sun is considered a penis, going from flaccid to erect until ejaculation results in it becoming flaccid once more. After reaching its strongest point during summer, when the sun is *Most High*, it begins to lose strength as it sinks lower in the sky in the proceeding months.

The full demise of the sun is realized in autumn, and it is said that the *light of the world* eventually will be extinguished, in part, during winter. Rather than being extinguished totaly, the sun, or universal truth, is only being locked away in the Osirian chest.

In mid-December the sun lowers into the lowest portion of the northern hemisphere and symbolically dies; it ceases visual movement for *three days*. At this point it rests near the *Southern Crux* constellation, from one point of view on earth. After three days, the sun begins moving northward again, but only by a few degrees, until it is reborn on December 25th. From this astrological fact it can be said that the sun-son dies on the Southern Cross, and certainly on zodiac wheel, remains dead for three days in the tomb of earth, and is then resurrected or reborn upon the conclusion of the winter solstice.

The story of Jesus details his birth to a virgin in a manger surrounded by animals. He is born in Bethlehem and his birth as flesh is signaled to the *magi* by a star. This is the same *Burning Star*, or *Eastern Star*, met through initiation into the *mysteries* upon exiting the temple to greet the rising sun. For magicians it is the *Great Arcanum* and for Kabbalists the *sacred pentagram*; it is that symbol marked ascending on the idol Baphomet for which the Templars were said to kneel in worship - accused by a man named Esquian de Horian of worshiping this graven image, spitting or trampling upon the cross, and eating roasted babies.

The star signifying the birth of a divine child may also be interpreted as Sirius, while the three Wise Men or Magi are likely the three stars of Orion's Belt, which, on December 25th, partly aligned so that it is possible to follow them to the birth of the sun when it rises northward.

When the sun is born-reborn-resurrected on December 25th, it resides in the constellation *Virgo* - the Virgin. This interpretation is debatable depending upon where you view the sun during that time of the year. It would be made more universal to express the virgin birth as an infant coming *out of the world* and *into what we call life*. We say *virgin birth* always thinking of the mother but rarely of the virginal baby or the nature of virgin motif as it relates to the "face of the deep" in Genesis.

The birth of Jesus is symbolic of, among many things, a renewed earth. Like *Baby New Year* it is a *virgin world*. The anthropomorphized image of the constellation is a virgin holding a sheath of wheat, thus relating to bread. The reason bread is important is because *Bethlehem* translates to become the zodiacal *House of Bread*. The *house* is one of the twelve divisions of the zodiac constructed by the *Grand Architect* and *Carpenter*. The animals in the nativity are the other *houses* of the zodiac.

The twelve disciples are also the *houses* or *signs* of the zodiac. Judas, the *betrayer*, is he who kisses Jesus on the cheek to alert the Roman guards of his identify. This is a strange story considering the relatively small size of such a town at the time, and considering the presence of Jesus whose whereabouts would likely have been known already.

Either way, the *betrayer* played by Judas signals the upcoming death of Jesus. In the heavens it is the constellation *Scorpio* that takes the place of Judas astrologically while Jesus is obviously the sun. Scorpions have a tail stinger and are known to leave a second puncture mark from another part of their tail. This dual sting is a symbol of *two lips*. The approach of the summer solstice is preceded by *Scorpio,* and the *kiss* bestowed upon Jesus was thus the *kiss of death*. Since the scorpion stings from behind it is known as the *backbiter*, from where we derive the word *backstabber*. Judas backstabbed Jesus and *kissed* him with death, much like *Scorpio* marks the sun with imminent death in the closing months of the year – around Samhain or Halloween. This astrological occurrence is described in Mark 14:43-46, detailing Judas, and his betrayal:

> *"While He was still speaking, Judas, one of the Twelve, suddenly arrived. With him was a mob, with swords and clubs, from the chief priests, the scribes, and the elders. His betrayer had given them a signal. 'The One I kiss', he said, "He's the One; arrest Him and take Him away under guard'. Then they took hold of Him and arrested Him."*

Of important note: Matthew 26:47-49, Luke 22:47-48, and Mark 14:43-45 all relate that Judas kissed Jesus, but John 18:3-5 relates that Jesus identified himself while Judas merely stood nearby:

> *"So Judas came to the garden, guiding a detachment of soldiers and some officials from the chief priests and the Pharisees. They were carrying torches, lanterns and weapons. Jesus, knowing all that was going to happen to him, went out and asked them, 'Who is it you want?' 'Jesus of Nazareth', they replied. 'I am he', Jesus said. (And Judas the traitor was standing there with them.)"*

What can be inferred here is that although Judas (Scorpio) issues the *kiss of death*, Jesus (sun) is involved, with Judas, in a cyclical heavenly dance wherein the powerful sun (son) must wane to wax once more, i.e., *rise again*. This story does not mean Jesus and Judas were not real, but merely that their stories were aligned with pagan knowledge of astronomy to assimilate that latter cult into Church doctrine. Therefore, the sun-son was born on December 25th of the Virgin-Virgo in Bethlehem, the House of Bread, or Constellation Virgo holding wheat. The three Wise Men/Orion's Belt then followed a bright star, Sirius, Venus, or the pentagram, to the birth of the sun-son on that significant Solstice-Yule date. Astrologically it is also relevant that the sun enters each sign of the zodiac at 30 degrees and as such the ministry of Jesus begins around age 30. In her book The Christ Conspiracy, D. M. Murdoch explains the metaphor of Jesus as a carpenter:

> *"The Sun is the 'Carpenter' who builds his daily 'houses' or 12 two-hour divisions."* She adds, *"As the mythos developed, it took the form of a play, with a cast of characters, including the 12 divisions of the sky called the signs or constellations of the zodiac. The symbols that typified these 12 celestial sections of 30 each were not based on what the constellations actually look like but represent aspects of earthly life. Thus the ancient peoples were able to incorporate these earthly aspects into the mythos and project them onto the all-important celestial screen."*

Earlier on we learned about the Agee of Pisces, or two fish, being the Age of Jesus Christ, and that the proceeding age is that of Aquarius. In Matthew 28:18-20 we learn the meaning of this astrological misunderstanding in full detail, as the presence of Jesus Christ represents the full length of the sun's stay or movement in a single house of the Zodiac during precession – approximately 2,160 years:

> *"Then Jesus came to them and said, 'All authority in heaven and on earth has been given to me. Therefore go and make disciples of all nations, baptizing them in the name of the Father and of the*

Son and of the Holy Spirit, and teaching them to obey everything I have commanded you. And surely I am with you always, to the very end of the age'."

This is not to say, however, that Jesus Christ was not living or that he was not a prophet. The detail to be extracted here is that the *sacred science* was personified in Jesus and he in astrology. We find additional references to the Zodiac in John 14:1-3 with its notes on *houses* and *rooms* that are, of course, constructed by a *Great Architect* in heaven, or a *carpenter*:

Aries	♈	Libra	♎
Taurus	♉	Scorpio	♏
Gemini	♊	Sagittarius	♐
Cancer	♋	Capricorn	♑
Leo	♌	Aquarius	♒
Virgo	♍	Pisces	♓

The Signs of the Zodiac.

Sun	☉	Jupiter	♃
Moon	☽	Saturn	♄
Venus	♀	Uranus	♅
Mars	♂	Neptune	♆
Mercury	☿	Pluto	♇

"Do not let your hearts be troubled. You believe in God; believe also in me. My Father's house has many rooms; if that were not so, would I have told you that I am going there to prepare a place for you? And if I go and prepare a place for you, I will come back and take you to be with me that you also may be where I am.

These *houses* and *rooms* are those of the sun, but the moon also has many mansions in the heavens. Otherwise called *Moon Stations,* these *Lunar Mansions* are considered ancient astrological concepts. The Chinese called them *hsiu* and the Indians called them *nakshatra,* the 28 divisions of the sky. Encyclopedia Britannica documents this of the mansions:

"At least four quadrantal HSIU that divided the sky into quarters or quadrants were known in China in the 14th century BCE, and 23 are mentioned in the YÜEH LING, which may go back to 850 BCE. In India a complete list of NAKSHATRA are found in the Atharvaveda , providing evidence that the system was organized before 800 BCE. The system of lunar mansions, however, may have a common origin even earlier in Mesopotamia."

The Second Coming

For centuries Christendom has been watching the skies and waiting for the return of Christ. They await the *Parousia* not in a manger, but in the morning or night skies where the sound of Gabriel's trumpet shall herald the *Second Coming,* while other religions tremble to the one true God. Interestingly, the Norse mythology records that Ragnarök, the final battle, will also begin when a "shrieking horn" is blown to gather the warrior sons of Odin. After a great deal of time many have perhaps given up hope while others cling, perhaps bitterly, to an eventual return of the one they call *King of Kings* with his *host of angels.* It seems, though, that those holding the Parousia to be literal may be more than slightly mislead. They are searching in the wrong place, looking in the external world and not the internal *Kingdom of God.*

The flashes of lightning, opening of the heavens, and all else that follows, is metaphoric of the sprouting of a divine seed within. It is a revitalization of spirit awoken to its true nature and purpose. The *Second Coming* in this context thus refers to the flashes of light that appear with new openings of consciousness and the renewed activity of soul-spirit incarnated. We read in the biblical book of Matthew 24:23-27 that the true Messiah will not appear to demonstrate his powers:

"At that time if anyone says to you, 'Look, here is the Messiah!' or, 'There he is!' do not believe it. For false messiahs and false prophets will appear and perform great signs and wonders to deceive, if possible, even the elect. See, I have told you ahead of time. 'So if anyone tells you, 'There he is, out in the wilderness,' do not go out; or, 'Here he is, in the inner rooms,' do not believe it. For as lightning that comes from the east is visible even in the west, so will be the coming of the Son of Man."

The *Son of Man* is elevated from a *Son of Woman* to become a *Son of God* under the guidance of the *Widow Isis*. For no man may come to the perfection of alchemical transformation without knowing the principles of it; without *knowing thyself*, the *I AM*, the Sanskrit *tat tvam asi*, and without obtaining the glories of redemption. Of this fact, Agrippa says that once it is obtained man will *"ascend to so great a perfection, that he is made the son of God, and is transformed into that image which is God, and is united with him."*

The *second coming* is thus the awakening of the inner-higher-divine, or godly, SELF: some may refer to this as *being born again* or *living resurrection*. It is the goal of the transformative hero's journey. Krishna says in the Bhagavad Gita: *"I am the Self, seated in the hearts of all creatures. I am the beginning, the middle, and the end of all beings."* The Egyptian Book of the Dead instructs the soul similarly: *"I am Horus the son of Osiris, and I have come to see my father Osiris."* And the Egyptian Coffin Texts instruct the dead to say: *"I am Atum, I who was alone; I am Re at his first appearance. I am the Great God, self-generator, who fashioned his names, lord of gods, whom none approaches among the gods. I was Yesterday, I know tomorrow."*

The Fountain of Life

The Wheel of the Zodiac is comprised of twelve houses separated by a cross into four quadrants of three. The outer portion contains the symbol of each sign, the next circle expressing the name of that zodiac section. Below is another concentric circle with the astrological sign of each house. In the center is a sun crucified on the cross, the points expressed as the four corners of the world and the four directions. Each division signifies one of the four seasons: winter, spring, summer and autumn. The term *Zodiac* comes from the Greek *zōidiakos,* and from *zōidion,* meaning a sculptured animal figure. The wheel itself is known as the *animal wheel.* These "animals" were those attending the birth of Jesus, the sun/son of God, when he was born after the Winter Solstice in the House of Virgo, the Virgin - *Bethlehem.*

Sign	**Dates**	**Element**	**Ruling Planet**	**Meaning**
Aries	March 21 - April 20	Fire	Mars	Impulsion
Taurus	April 21 - May 20	Earth	Venus	Perseverance
Gemini	May 21- Jun 20	Air	Mercury	Polarity
Cancer	June 21 – July 22	Water	Moon	Passivity
Leo	July 23 – Aug 22	Fire	Sun	Creation
Virgo	Aug 23 – Sept 22	Earth	Mercury	Differentiation
Libra	Sept 23 – Oct 22	Air	Venus	Balance
Scorpio	Oct 23 – Nov 22	Waters	Mars/Pluto	Passion
Sagittarius	Nov 23 – Dec 21	Fire	Jupiter	Cultivation
Capricorn	Dec 22 – Jan 20	Earth	Saturn	Conservation
Aquarius	Jan 21 – Feb 19	Air	Saturn/Uranus	Adaptability
Pisces	Feb 20 – March 20	Water	Jupiter/Neptune	Intuition

The Seed of Life & *Quinta Essentia*

The four corners of a cross can be associated with the *four rivers* described by Greek hierophants. These include the river of silence, *Cocytus*; the river of forgetfulness, *Lethe*; the river of irresistible swiftness with black icy waters called *Acheron*; and a river flowing in the opposite course made of fire called *Phlegethon*. The latter shares characteristics with the *lake of fire* described in Revelation 20:14, *"And death and hell were cast into the lake of fire."*

The horizontal bar of a cross represents the dividing point between the *infinite* and *finite*, the *above* and *below*. Where this bar meets at the vertical axis, symbolic of the universal spine and umbilical cord, there is a *nexus point*. The vertical bar is the creative and active principle described in sexual terms as a *phallus*. In the same terms, the horizontal bar is the creative and passive principle known as *yoni*. The horizontal and vertical bars, in still further terms, relate to that *active spirit* that animates passive *matter*. These two bars are like the *Yin Yang*, *Yab Yum* and *In Yo* – one is time (female) and the other is eternity (male).

When a circle encloses this *sacred cross*, philosophers and psychologists term the symbol the same: *quinta essentia*. Within the circle, sphere, or disc - the *symbol of totality* - we find various forms of treasure, and even the greatest gold of all in that of the *human spirit* or *world soul*. To the alchemists this would be called the *Philosopher's Stone*. Famed psychologist Carl Jung also explains the *Powder of Projection* as being divided into four quadrants like the *world* itself:

> *"It is the circle divided into four with the centre, or the divinity extended in four directions, or the four functions of consciousness with their unitary substrate, the self. Here the quaternity has a 3 + 1 structure: three animal-daemonic faces and one human one."*

> *"The square, being a quaternity, is a totality symbol in alchemy. Having four corners it signifies the earth, whereas a circular form is attributed to the spirit. Earth is feminine, spirit masculine."*

In her book <u>The Secret Doctrine</u>, Helena Petrovna Blavatsky explains how by removing the circle we are left only with the phallic symbol and a sign of man's *fall* into *matter*.

> *"The Cross within a circle symbolizes pure Pantheism; when the Cross was left uninscribed, it became phallic."*

A similar archaic symbol may be derived by placing a single dot within the center of a circle. Here we are essentially erasing the horizontal and vertical bars of *quinta essentia*. This is the *First Manifestation* of the *Cosmic Mind* which draws out the circumference of *creation*. Some refer to this image as the *Eye of God*. Philosophers say it is *infinity*, i.e., all of creation expanding outward from *source*. Blavatsky goes on to say that when a circle encompasses a Tau cross, which has the horizontal

bar at its top, it becomes known as Thor's Hammer, the *Jainer*, or *"Svastica [swastika] within a circle."* She says the Tau was the oldest form of the letter "T" and represented the *"fall of man"* when there was a separation of sexes, symbolized by a circle with a vertical line directly down the center. This *fall* was a tumultuous time, characterized by disorder, chaos, and storms. Gods like Thor, Susanoo, Baal, Yahweh, and even Shangdi, personify these qualities.

The *hammer* of Thor, Mjölnir, which assists in directing thunder and lighting, is thus a perfect symbol, and tool, of the previous chaotic times and those of future tempest, both internally and externally. The *trident* serves the same purpose, as a control mechanism over water, oceans, and emotions (em-oceans). Far away from Norse mythology is the story of Susanoo in Japan, who, alongside Tsukuyomi (moon) and Amaterasu (sun), comprises a sort of trinity. As a god of storms and rain, it makes sense that his shrine today offers a good luck charm in the form of a hammer or mallet. Such a symbol is also found in freemasonry. Not to be confused with a *Common Gavel*, the *Mallet* of the *master* symbolizes the correcting of imbalances in one's emotions and *temperament*, the latter word sharing root with *tempest*. Baal carries a thunderbolt spear as a storm god like Yahweh, otherwise known as *He Who Rides in the Clouds* or *Lord of the Heavens*. Shangdi is an ancient Chinese deity with similarity to both Yahweh and Jesus Christ. He is the deity of victory, harvest, and weather, and also the architecture of the universe, tracing out creation with his masonic tools. In Buddhism we find the *vajra*, a thunderbolt equivalent to Mjölnir or the thunderbolts of Zeus. Guardians of the threshold in the east often carry thunderbolt spears. In the South Rhodesia creation story there is the *ngona horn* which has the power of fire and lighting, to create and destroy.

When the circle splits into two circles (cells after conception) the image created is *vesica piscis.* By extending the arms of this cross within a circle one acquires the solar disc resting on the divided year and zodiac. The circle with horizontal bar *"symbolizes a divine immaculate Mother-Nature within the all-embracing absolute Infinitude."* From here we return in our analysis to the "mundane cross" of Blavatsky, or the *quinta essentia.*

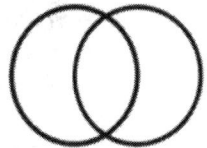

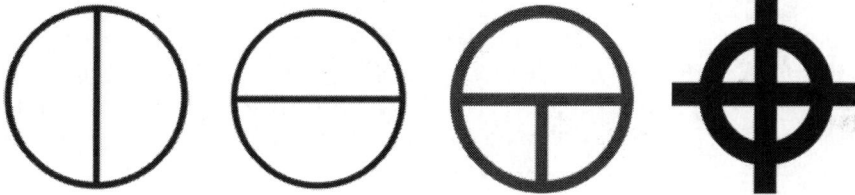

The cross, or *Tree of Life*, was a symbol by which the entire world was made manifest. A third century Bishop of Rome named Hippolytus once remarked that the tree was as *"wide as the heavens itself,"* and *"has grown up into heaven from earth."* He said that the symbolic characteristic of the tree, *"is the foundation of the round world, the center of the cosmos. In it all the diversities in our human diversities in our human nature are formed into a unity. It is held together by the invisible nails of the Spirit so that it may not break loose form the divine."* From nature we can see how trees and the stems of flowers, for example, grow vertically toward the sun, while their branches and leaves essentially grow horizontally. Man grows the same with two legs vertical and two arms horizontal. When Osiris is wrapped as a mummy his head still protrudes like the apex of the pentagram, and as god of agriculture like Demeter-Ceres and Saturn-Cronus, he symbolizes the internal *Osirian Seed*. Gnostic teachers spoke of a *divine spark* or *spiritual seed* inside every human, which was waiting to be watered with *cosmic dew*. David Fideler writes of this immortal seed of potentiality: *"By properly cultivating the inner seed it is possible to realize our true identity."*

Egyptologist E. A. Wallis Budge notes in his book <u>Osiris and the Egyptian Resurrection</u>, the same theme found in Egypt:

"The germination of the grain typified the germination of the spirit-body of the deceased."

The internal *seed* is both metaphor and allegory and was spoken of in Matthew 13:31-34 in a parable expressed by Jesus:

"He told them another parable: 'The kingdom of heaven is like a mustard seed, which a man took and planted in his field. Though it is the smallest of all seeds, yet when it grows, it is the largest of garden plants and becomes a tree, so that the birds come and perch in its branches'. He told them still another parable: 'The kingdom of heaven is like yeast that a woman took and mixed into about sixty pounds of flour until it worked all through the dough'. Jesus spoke all these things to the crowd in parables; he did not say anything to them without using a parable."

And Luke 8:11 says: *"Now the parable is this: The seed is the word of God.'"* The *Parable of the Sower* in chapter 4 of Mark preserves this same motif in the seeds which fell in different places or were distributed otherwise. The *seed* is *truth* and *potentiality*, and as Hall explains:

"Some receive the truth and others reject it; some distort it, and others permit it to be plucked out by impulse and words; by weeds are to be understood the appetites and passions of the lower emotional nature; by the birds of the air, thoughts; by the sun, pride; and by the stony ground, such as are not yet ready to receive the law."

Fideler writes further of this symbolism in <u>Jesus Christ Son of God</u>, discussing how it is part of a geometric higher pattern:

"The literal-minded, like the proponents of materialism, see the world as through the lower diagram and see no further: literalism reads the letter of the law but does not grasp its spirit; materialism holds matter to be the only reality, but does not see that it is merely the effect of a higher cause. Those with the spark of gnosis, however, catch an occasional glimpse of the higher pattern – the Universal Logos, the intelligent pattern of order and harmony which informs all existence."

If we turn the *quinta essential* sideways we then see an x within a circle, and thus a symbol denoting treasure: *x marks the spot*. Initiates of the *mysteries* were symbolically crucified sideways on the four quadrant cross in the form of an **X**. Contrary to popular opinion, the Romans typically used the **T** cross as opposed to the standard Latin **✝**. Literal crucifixions were rarely ordered for anything other than serious theft and murder. Religious offenses were typically punished by sword or stoning.

Symbolic Crucifixions are probably older than ancient Egypt and became a common symbol in the *Mystery Schools*. This image shows the hierophant holding a staff and an ankh. He is flanked on both sides by participants wearing the heads of lions, bulls, and birds. Behind these higher degree initiates stand other participants with headdresses signifying illumination and with the *uraeus* serpent rising from the center of their forehead.

The candidate is tied to an **X** - a common practice in Japan too - above a coffin and two illuminated pillars. The symbolism of the entire scene should be obvious to the reader as one of *Living*

Resurrection. Upon removal from the cross, the candidate is then placed inside the coffin for three days before being pulled out of *death* by the strong grip of the *Lion's Paw*, and then exiting the temple on the middle path between the twin pillars, and through the eastern gate to greet the morning star and rising sun. And thus, as is uttered in *Ali Baba and the Forty Thieves* to open the den of robbers, "open sesame" – *seed.*

The symbolic crucifixion of the *mysteries*.

Hieros Gamos: The Sacred Marriage of Man & Woman

"Some say the lord died first and then ascended. They are wrong.
He rose first and then he died.
Unless you are first resurrected, you will not die.
As god lives, you would already be dead."

~ The Gospel of Philip ~

The Talpiot Tomb & Secret Doctrines of Antiquity

Objective investigation without pre-conceived notions will uncover evidence that there really was a man named Jesus (Joshua, Yeshua) who existed within the confines of the Biblical narrative, and who performed certain miracles that very well may have been in violation of the *mystery tradition* oath. This does not mean he was able to physically heal the blind by touch or turn water into wine literally, nor does it mean he was physically crucified and resurrected three days later. He was, however, a serious and powerful man the likes of which even Muslims and their prophet Mohammed have held in the highest regard.

When preparing to build an apartment complex in the 1980s, a construction crew discovered a tomb in the south suburb of Talpiot, located in the Old City of Jerusalem. Known as the *Talpiot Tomb*, this find essentially proved to be as significant as the finding of the city of Troy though it was met with far less fanfare.

One archeologist conducting research on the site, Dr. Arye Shimron, revealed the following details: he found that Jesus, "son of God," was buried with 9 other people, including "Judah, son of Jesus." The ossuaries in the tomb also contained inscriptions: Maria, Mariamne Mara, Yose (Jos'e or Joseph), and Matia (Matthew), along with the description, "Jesus, son of Joseph," and on the James Ossuary, "James, son of Joseph, brother of Jesus".

This evidence suggests that the physical Jesus fathered a child, and that no literal resurrection from death took place. There may have even been more than one person with the title *Messiah*, *Christ*, and *Jesus*, i.e., Zeus. Although these facts would seem to demolish the entire Christian doctrine, careful consideration will provide relief from this fear and establish a new fact: Jesus Christ was *real*, walked the earth, and although he was not physically resurrected from a literal tomb, there is ample evidence he was a great prophet who was undoubtedly initiated into the *secret teachings* through a process of *living resurrection*. Atheists and detractors of Christianity can be rebuffed by this *truth* and a real discussion of the *Ministry of Jesus* can thus be held.

Many will argue against what is written here, providing John 8:58 as proof of our blasphemy, wherein Jesus claims:

"'Very truly I tell you,' Jesus answered, 'before Abraham was born, I am!'"

In this verse, Jesus is referring to himself as the *Almighty God* – I AM. But these sorts of claims are precisely why Jewish leaders began persecuting him in the first place, i.e., he claimed to be the ALL incarnated in flesh, or that is how they perceived his *teachings*. Such a notion is blasphemous to nearly every religion with a concept of GOD ALMIGHTY at its core. The term "I AM" was exceedingly offensive since it is how God named Himself to Moses through the burning bush in Exodus 3:14, which says:

> *"God said to Moses, 'I am who I am.' This is what you are to say to the Israelites: 'I am has sent me to you.'"*

In John 14:6, Jesus says, *"no man cometh unto the Father, but by me."* Far be it from an intended declaration of his position in relation to God, such a verse directly implies that the *Son of God* is merely walking in the footsteps of his *Father*. This verse is nearly identical to the inscription of Isis and her *veil* in Egypt.

Mythologist Joseph Campbell explains that when Jesus refers to himself as "I AM" he is simply saying: *"I have identified myself with the all."* Such an idea is more understood in the east than it is in the west, but even today *"anyone who says, as Jesus is reported to have said (John 10:30), 'I and the Father are One,' is declared in our tradition to have blasphemed."*

Matthew 26:39 seems to offer further confirmation of these facts, as Jesus speaks to the Father as a separate part of himself:

> *"Going a little farther, he fell with his face to the ground and prayed, 'My Father, if it is possible, may this cup be taken from me. Yet not as I will, but as you will'."*

The Quran is also filled with references to Jesus, and books (chapters) on Abraham (14), Mary (19), and Noah (71). There is therefore great irony in the fact that while Jews and pagans made horrible accusations against Jesus, it is well understood in Islam that Jesus truly was a miraculous prophet. In the Holy Quran chapter of *The Family of Imran* 4:45-51, we read of angels speaking to Mary, the teachings of Jesus, and the middle pathway called the *straight-way*:

> *"And when the angels said: 'O Mary! Allah gives you the glad tidings of a command from Him: his name shall be Messiah, Jesus, the son of Mary. He shall be highly honoured in this world and in the Next, and shall be one of those near stationed to Allah. And he shall speak to men in the cradle and also later when he grows to maturity and shall indeed be among the righteous.' She said: 'O my Lord! How shall I have a son when no man has ever touched me?' The angel answered: Thus shall it be. Allah creates whatever He wills. When He decides something, He merely says: 'Be' and it is.*

> *"And He will teach him the Book, the Wisdom, the Torah, the Gospel, and he will be a Messenger to the Children of Israel.' (And when he came to them he said): 'I have come to you with a sign from your Lord. I will make for you from clay the likeness of a bird and then I will breathe into it and by the leave of Allah it will become a bird. I will also heal the blind and the leper, and by the leave of Allah bring the dead to life. I will also inform you of what things you eat and what you treasure up in your houses. Surely this is a sign for you if you are true believ-ers.*

> *"And I have come to confirm the truth of whatever there still remains of the Torah, and to make lawful to you some of the things which had been forbidden to you. I have come to you with a sign from your*

Lord; so have fear of Allah and obey me. Surely, Allah is my Lord and your Lord; so serve Him alone. This is the straight way.'"

According to the Holy Quran, which most Christians refuse to open, just as most Muslims refuse to open a Bible, it was actually Judas Iscariot who was arrested in the dark when Roman soldiers came for Jesus. The Quran 4:157-158 relates:

"And they did not kill him and they did not crucify him, but it appeared so to them. And surely those who disagree about it are certainly in doubt about it - they have no knowledge about it except that they follow speculation. And they did not kill him for certain - but God took him up to Himself. And God was every Mighty, Wise."

Muhammad 'Ata' ur-Rahim and Ahmad Thomson also write in their book Jesus Prophet of Islam, how the Romans may have simply tried to make an example of anyone that the rebellious nature of the Christian prophet would not be tolerated:

"If the Romans did become aware of the true identity of their prisoner when he was brought before Pilate, the Roman Magistrate, then it is possible that the dramatic turn of events may still have satisfied everyone. The Romans would have made an example of someone - whoever that someone was - which was sure to act as a deterrent. The majority of the Jews would have been happy for, due to a miracle, the traitor was standing in the dock instead of Jesus. Even the pro-Roman Jews would be happy, for, with the death of Judas, the proof of their guilt would be destroyed. And furthermore, with Jesus officially dead, he would be far less likely to come out into the open to give them trouble."

The *Gospel of Barnabas,* named after Bare Nabe, a Jew from Cyprus who became a leading disciple after Jesus disappeared, is a very intriguing text that is known in the Muslim world but not so much in Christendom. In chapter 218 we learn that the body of Judas, after the crucifixion, was stolen to spread word that Jesus had risen. In chapter 219 we learn about Mary returning to Jerusalem to find her son; eventually she discovers that Jesus is indeed still alive. In the very next line from chapter 220 we learn that Jesus had *"not been dead at all."*

In the following chapters 221-22 we learn that Jesus informs Barnabas to tell the truth about Judas so that *"everyone may believe the truth."*

Jesus then proceeds to connect Barnabas with John and Peter *"who saw everything,"* so that they could provide the author with all the details of the death of Judas.

He then *"reproved many who believed that he had died and risen again"* before being taken up to heaven by four angels.

As the disciples departed for different regions, this gospel informs us that "evil men" perpetuated a falsehood that is the cornerstone doctrine of Christianity, i.e., that Jesus died and rose again and that he was the "Son of God."

Yet, Jesus Christ was dead spirituality, he was resurrected while alive, or *born again*, and he was walking in the footsteps of his *Father*. He did all these things in the name of the *secret doctrines of antiquity*. Others simply preached falsehoods that Jesus had died and never rose again. These things, Barnabas writes, were preached by men *"pretending to be disciples."* The opposite of this became basis for the *teachings* that Jesus literally rose from the grave and ascended to heaven. It is thus difficult to see the modern Church, particularly the Vatican, or any demonization thereof, as anything expect *pretend*, filled with *false prophets* making false profits. This is despite the wonderful work such an institution is no doubt responsible for in general: we are not talking about *Inquisition*, but the preservation of a *secret doctrine* for all to read today. The *Gospel of Philip* from the *Gnostic Bible* also confirms what Islam and the *Gospel of Barnabas* say about the controversy surrounding Jesus:

> *"Some say the lord died first and then ascended. They are wrong. He rose first and then he died. Unless you are first resurrected, you will not die. As god lives, you would already be dead."*

It seems as if *truth* is found crucified between two thieves, i.e., by following the *straight way* or *middle path*. This is the *WAY* of Buddha, Jesus, and *Allah*, the latter of which many forget is simply the Arabic word-name for God. Likewise, the word *Islam* means "submission," but only to the will of Allah (God). The notion of decapitating infidels is greatly misunderstood too; as Rumi wrote, *"What is 'beheading'? Slaying the carnal soul in the holy war."* The same can be said about animal-human sacrifice in the Bible. The word religion itself, from the Latin *religare*, means "to bind," just as the Japanese unifying source – *musubi* – means to "to bind." We are bound to God; when we follow the middle way and slay the beast, we overcome death.

The Talpiot Tomb indicates that Jesus was married and had children, key details documented in the <u>Gospel of Philip</u> from the <u>Gnostic Bible</u>:

> *"And the companion of the Savior is Mary Magdalene. But Christ loved her more than all the disciples and used to kiss her often on her mouth. The rest of the disciples were offended by it and expressed disapproval."*

Although there may be several meanings derived from this text, the most obvious to a superficial thinker is to either deny it as heresy or accept it as literal kissing and marriage. To the philosopher it may be extrapolated that this *companionship* was a metaphor referring to the *wedding* of *initiates* to the *maternal principle* within subterranean *Bridal Chambers*. The child resulting from this *divine copulation* was a *new man* born from and within his father, i.e., a *rebirth*, being *born again*, the next incarnation of oneself. This *initiate* was *reborn* like a phoenix out of their own ashes. They were Horus, born of Osiris through the magic of Isis. A chief sacrament of Valentinus (died AD 161), the foremost Gnostic scholar, was a ritual held in the *Bridal Chamber*. It was here that the *devout* witnessed the celestial marriage of *Sophia* and the *Redeemer*. One magical formula used during this ceremony reads as follows:

> *"I will confer my favor upon thee, for the father of all sees thine angel even before his face… we must now become as one; receive now this grace from me and through me; deck thyself as a bride who awaits her bridegroom, that thou, mayest become as I am, and as thou art; let the seed of light descend into thy bridal chamber, receive the bridegroom and give place to him, and open thine arms to embrace him. Behold, grace has descended upon thee."*

When asked why he kissed Mary and loved her so dearly, even over all the disciples, Jesus replied:

> *"Why do I not love you like her? If a blind man and one who sees are together in darkness, they are the same. When light comes, the one who sees will see the light. The blind man stays in darkness'."*

In the <u>Gospel of Mary</u>, Simon Peter says to Mary Magdalene, speaking in a manner that could be interpreted as literal or metaphoric:

"Sister, we know that the savior loved you more than other women."

Later in the same Gospel, Peter is disagreeing over a vision Mary had of the savior, wherein he spoke to her in private without the knowledge of the rest of his students. Peter asks:

"Did he really speak to a woman secretly, without our knowledge, and not openly? Are we to turn and all listen to her? Did he prefer her to us?"

"Levin answered, saying to Peter, 'Peter, you are always angry. Now I see you contending against this woman as if against an adversary. If the savior made her worthy, who are you to reject her? Surely the savior knows her very well. That is why he loved her more than us."

Mary, Melissa & CHiram Abiff

The name 'Mariamne Mara' on the ossuary tomb at Talpiot is Mary Magdalene of the Gnostic scripture. The word *Mara* is Greek and means *teacher* or *master*, the same titles we apply to Christ.

Mara signifies Mary's relationship to the *essence* of Christ in that she herself was a *teacher* held in such high regard to the historical Jesus that the other disciples became irritated. It is critical to remember here that we are talking about a time where the influence of women in public was primitive in comparison with modern political movements. Despite this, women played perhaps the most important roles in the *Mystery Schools*, because, if we are being frank, they hold the *key* to *life*.

The *mysteries* were those of *birth* and *fertility*. The value of *saving oneself for marriage* and only having children within such an arrangement is sacred; as is the question: *Will You Mary (marry) Me?*

~ *Mary Magdalene* is the *Mystical Mother* of the *Mysteries* ~

As with titles like *Messiah* or *Christ*, many holy women held the title of *Mary*, which refers to one brought up in a monastic environment. It is a surname of *magdal-elder*, for which we derive *Magdalene*, meaning *Watchtower of the Flock*. The latter is what Jesus preside over as the shepherd.

The Irish goddess *Brigid* (also *Brighid*) presided over the festival of Imbolc, an early spring holy day celebrating the end of winter. Known as the *Exalted One*, she was a goddess of healing, fertility, and birth. From <u>The Ultimate Encyclopedia of Mythology</u>, authors Arthur Cotterell and Rachel Storm confirm this:

"Brigid, sometimes known as Brigit, was a goddess of healing and fertility who was believed to assist women in labour."

As an assistant to "women in labour" she therefore was the divine representative of earthly female priestesses assisting initiates in the *Bridal Chamber* with being *reborn*. She later transformed into Saint Brigid but also appears in Celtic lore as *Brighde*, the root of our word *bride*.

Put simply, Brigid presided over the rebirth of nature in the spring and the rebirth of initiates in the *Mystery Schools*, as well as the *sacred wedding*.

Of marriage, The Gospel of Philip relates the following.

Marriage:

Great is the mystery of marriage!
Without it the world would not be.
The existence of the world depends on marriage.

The marriage of Jesus to Mary - Christ and his Bride - was a ritual of symbolic sexual union - possibly literal - which became perverted and profaned as an orgy. Modern witch covens still practice this sexual union, though usually between a married couple in private. Some, no doubt, choose to violate all the sacred elements of these traditions. It was for good reason, to some, that the act of sex and the entire issue of fertility was degraded to acts of filth and guilt by institutional dogmas: there are immense creative powers operating here. However, this is not taken as justification for the orgy. The Gospel of Philip continues:

"Think of sex. It possesses deep powers, though its image is filthy."

Great is the mystery of marriage and fertility! The Greek name for this union is *hieros gamos*, or the *sacred marriage*. In agricultural societies, at least once a year, humans acting in the image of the gods would engage in sexual intercourse to guarantee fertility for the land and people, and to bless the community.

The Greek historian and Neoplatonist philosopher, Porphyry, described how the temples of Demeter (Roman Ceres), Artemis (Roman Diana), and Aphrodite (Roman Venus), etc., were overseen by human priestesses referred to as *bees*. One symbol of the Greek Aphrodite was a golden *honeycomb* and the souls of her priestesses were said to inhabit the bodies of bees. These women were called *Melissae*, a word rooted in the same source as *honey* and *bees*.

Melissa was one of a group of *bee nymphs* whose duty it was to teach civilization and elevate men from their state of spiritual death and ignorance. These were *civilizing nymphs*, just like the role played by Osiris or Quetzalcoatl. In Minoan mythology - a Bronze Age civilization centered on Crete (c. 3000–1050 BC) – the goddess Melissa, patron of bees, appears as half-woman and half-bee. The name *melissa* means *bee*, which itself comes from *meli*, meaning *honey*.

A *nymph* is the personification of the female *creative force*. The Greek root for *nymph* is *nymphe*, which also means *doll* or *veiled*, as in the veil worn by Isis: *No Mortal Man Hath Ever Me Unveiled*.

Nymphe, like the root of *Brighde*, also means *bride*. From this word we acquire the contemporary *nympho*, or a *woman with strong sexual urges*. The latter is often misconstrued as derogatory, but it may be that by "sexual urges" is to be understood a less than excessive urge to procreate. As for *nymphomania* there is certainly a relationship to orgiastic ceremonies performed at the time of the full moon in certain sects.

The nymphs, also much like Brigid, presided over all things relating to death, fertility, and birth, i.e., those things relating to the resurrection of candidates in the *Mystery Schools*. From The Illustrated Signs & Symbols Sourcebook by Adele Nozedar there is further explanation of a *nymphe*; she was an unmarried girl acting as priestess in sacred temples: *"In Ancient Greece, temples at sacred springs were presided over by priestesses, all unmarried girls, also called 'nymphs', and the temples themselves,"* what are called *Nymphaeae*, *"were used specifically for performing wedding ceremonies."*

Porphyr wrote that when a *Melissa* refused to reveal the secrets of initiation she was torn to pieces like Osiris, who was cut into fourteen fragments; Dionysus, torn into pieces by the Titans; Orpheus, dismembered by a band of Maenads; Quetzalcoatl, *"both crucified, and as it were cut in pieces for the cauldron;"* Shamans, known as *wounded men*, are often dismembered in altered states of consciousness. In the Eddic account, a giant hermaphrodite named Ymir was torn apart by the trinity of Othin, Vili, and Ve. In Babylon the same story was told of Marduk killing Tiamat and separating her body. So too was Chiram Abiff, murdered by three ruffians in the masonic tradition.

During the building of Solomon's Temple, the three murderers known as Jubela, Jubelo, and Jubelum, awaited the exit of their Grand Master from the unfinished *sanctum sanctorum*, where Chiram Abiff had gone to pray at high noon. Each stood at the gates of the temple ready to strike fatal blows upon their master who had refused to divulge the word of the Master Mason.

As Chiram concluded a prayer, he went to the south gate and was met by Jubela. Upon refusing to reveal the secrets of the Master, he was struck with a twenty-four-inch gauge across the throat. Chiram then attempted to leave through the west gate where Jubelo, holding a square, asked the same question. Refusing to answer once again, Jubelo struck him in the chest with the square. This was repeated once more at the east gate where Jubelum struck him between the eyes with a mallet. In that moment, CHiram Abiff fell to the floor dead, the secrets he possessed lost. This story tells of how the soul-spirit ascends from the underworld in the south to the land of shadow in the west, before being resurrected in the east. Soul-spirit is struck dead by birth in the south, only to be awakened and raised like the morning star and rising sun in the east. It should be clear that the soul-spirit is synonymous with the birth, death, and resurrection of the physical sun.

Each gate of the temple represents a position of the sun in relation to the temple of *Solomon*, a name that can be broken down into three parts that all relate to the solar principle: sol-om-on. The term *Sol* relates to *Solus* or *Solar* and means *sun*. In Sanskrit the term *om*, the Hindu sound of creation, or *Aum*, refers to heat, and a similar sound, *on*, is an Ethiopic term referring to the solar principle manifested. The term *Aum* is like the Egyptian god *Amon-RA* or *Amen-RA*, Chief of the Gods and the source of the term *amen* said at the end of prayers. Jerusalem, the location of Solomon's Temple, also means *City of Peace*, and is referred to as the *Holy City*. The word *Holy* is like the word *hely*, which is rooted in the Greek word *Helios*, meaning *sun*. This also reminds us of the Egyptian *Heliopolis*, or the *city of the sun*. The three solar parts are personified by the triune characters of the Egyptian sun: *Khepri*, the morning sun; *Ra*, the mid-day sun; and *Temu* (Atem or Amen), the setting sun.

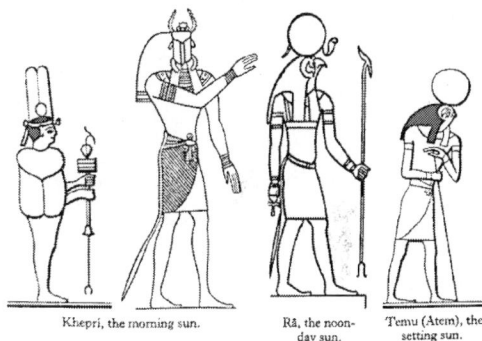

Khepri, the morning sun.　　Râ, the noonday sun.　　Temu (Atem), the setting sun.

E. A. Wallis Budge, From Fetish to God in Ancient Egypt.

The three ruffians (criminals) in our Abiff story likewise represent life divided into three distinct parts: growth, maturity, and decay - birth, life, and death. The striking of the head with a mallet is part of an ancient ceremony called the *opening of the mouth*, which was believed to help the spirit-soul circumvent the trials of the underworld. It was performed in Africa, Mesoamerica, and Japan among other ancient cultures. Shaving of the head in certain schools fulfilled the same purpose.

When *Melissa* refused to reveal the *secrets of initiation*, and was torn to pieces, her remains birthed a *swarm of bees*. Here is yet another common, and very universal, story. Teardrops from the Egyptian sun god RA were also said to turn into bees upon striking the earth.

The Beehive & Honeycomb

The *bee* itself represents a form of *regeneration* acquired through rites of initiation. The teardrops of RA represent the emanating rays of God sometimes referred to as *morning dew*. In like manner, we have the redeeming blood of the Mithraic bull, Attis, Dionysius-Bacchus and Jesus Christ, among many others. The pollen bees collect for food while gathering nectar is called *ambrosia* or *bee bread*, and the excess pollen on their bodies falls off in flight like drops of blood that pollinate surrounding plants. For the Indians of the American Southwest, pollen is collected and used to drive away evil. It is a symbol of spiritual energy. A similar motif can be found in the story of Kali who licks up blood drops to prevent them striking the ground and birthing demons.

Even non-masons have noticed the curious use of bees and beehives by the *Order* of these *sons of the widow*. Anyone traveling through the Mormon state of Utah in the United States have noticed such symbols adorning road signs too. Mormonism was heavily influenced by masonry and both organizations see the *beehive* as a symbol of brotherhood, community, and fraternity.

Bees are a Greek symbol of work and obedience, and in some traditions, *bees* are said to have erected the second temple at Delphi. In Orphic teachings, and Indro-Aryan and Moslem tradition, the migration of bees from the hive was representative of the swarm of souls from *Source*.

The honeycomb is a symbol of personal insight, divinity, and the harmony of nature. Each individual segment of the honeycomb is a hexagon (with six sides). These shapes are the geometric equivalent of the six-pointed hexagram known as the *Star of David* or *Seal of Solomon*. This symbol is also concealed partly within the Masonic square and compass. J. E. Cirlot's A Dictionary of Symbols relates the following about bees:

> *"In Egyptian hieroglyphic language, the sign of the bee was a determinative in royal nomenclature, partly by analogy with the monarchic organization of these insects, but more especially because of the ideas of industry, creative activity and wealth which are associated with the production of honey."*

The *Hierodule, Goyim* & Boiling Excrement

The Sumerian goddess of love and fertility was named Inana (Inanna), often depicted with sunbeams radiating from her body like Amaterasu in Japan. Known as Ishtar in Babylon, Inanna was considered a *sacred woman* under the title **hierodule**.

This was also a title awarded to the Sumerian high priestess presiding over the most sacred ceremonies within the *Bridal Chamber*. From their positions as *sacred women*, they administered the final sacraments leading candidates to their *living resurrection*.

Because of associations with bees and honey, those elevated to such a state may be said to enter the *land flowing with milk and honey*. The source of this statement can be found in the Biblical book of Number 14:8, which relates:

> *"If the LORD delights in us, then He will bring us into this land and give it to us, 'a land which flows with milk and honey'."*

The land of "milk and honey" may also be called the *Promised Land*, and as Joseph Campbell points out, this is *"not a place to be conquered by armies and solidified by displacing other people."* The *Holy Land* of legend, myth, and theology is instead *"a corner of the heart, or it is any environment that has been mythologically spiritualized."* Likewise, exile *"was not a location away from the homeland, but a condition that is not salvation."* Through these initiatory rites, *"salvation would include the resurrection of the dead."*

The robes worn by a **hierodule** priestess were scarlet red and meant to represent *ritu*, a Sumerian word meaning *erect* or *truth*. It could also mean to be *upright and honest*. The word *ritu* clearly is very close to our word *ritual*, or *"a religious or solemn ceremony consisting of a series of actions performed according to a prescribed order."*

We even read about such fine robes in the Samuel II, chapter 1, verse 24, which records David speaking to the "daughters of Israel," telling them to weep for the now dead Saul, *"who clothed you in scarlet and finery, who adorned your garments with ornaments of gold."*

Before the Bible was translated into English the word **hierodulai**, from where **hierodule** is derived, was mistranslated into **harlot**. Any women wearing red thus became identified as **promiscuous** or a **prostitute**. Interestingly, the word *prostitute* is derived from the Middle English word **pautenere**, which means **promiscuous woman**. Pautenere is our word for *partner*, as in a man or woman we enter a relationship with. It is therefore advised that if you wish your relationship to last, beyond the obvious implication of **partners** parting ways, that you should choose marriage instead of a **partnership**.

Goddesses like Inanna and Ishtar thus took on the label *Whore of Babylon*. From Revelation 17:1 we get the image:

> *"That great whore is described, with whom the Kings of the earth committed fornication. She is drunken with the blood of the Saints. The mystery of the woman, and the beast that carried her is expounded. Their destruction. The Lamb's victory."*

The image of the *sacred woman* is also described in Revelation 12:1-3, wherein we read a description of what amounts to Isis, or the Greek goddess Europa who is crowned with twelve stars:

> *"A great sign appeared in heaven: a woman clothed with the sun, with the moon under her feet and a crown of twelve stars on her head. She was pregnant and cried out in pain as she was about to give birth."*

~ GREAT IS THE MYSTERY OF BIRTH! ~

So true is this *mystery* that perhaps we can better understand the restrictions commanded in the Biblical book of Leviticus, chapter 18, verses 22-24:

"Do not have sexual relations with a man as one does with a woman; that is detestable. Do not have sexual relations with an animal and defile yourself with it. A woman must not present herself to an animal to have sexual relations with it; that is a perversion. Do not defile yourselves in any of these ways, because this is how the nations that I am going to drive out before you became defiled."

Those like Mary, the mother of Christ, are called *whores* and *prostitutes* in the *Talmud*, a collection of ancient and modern guidance for Jews. **Sanhedrin 106b** of The William Davidson Talmud states as fact:

"*This woman* [Mary] *was descended from princes and rulers, and was licentious with carpenters.*"

Of Jesus Christ himself, **Shabbat 104b** says he learned magic from Egypt and that he was not to be trusted:

"*We learned in the mishna: If one unwittingly scratches letters on his flesh on Shabbat, Rabbi Eliezer deems him liable to bring a sin-offering and the Sages deem him exempt. It was taught in a baraita that Rabbi Eliezer said to the Rabbis: Didn't the infamous ben Stada take magic spells out of Egypt in a scratch on his flesh? They said to him: He was a fool, and you cannot cite proof from a fool.*"

The name "Ben Stada" is almost always agreed, like many other similar names in the Talmud, to refer to Jesus.

In **Gittin 57a** we read of a conversation between Onkelos, a man seeking guidance on the Jews, a man named Balaam, another name for Jesus, and the actual spirit of Jesus raised from the dead by *necromancy*. We learn that anyone who "distresses Israel" will suffer the following:

"*Every day his ashes are gathered, and they judge him, and they burn him, and they scatter him over the seven seas.*"

The same tract goes on to say that "*Onkelos then went and raised Jesus the Nazarene from the grave through necromancy,*" a practice not uncommon for the Jews. What Onkelos learns is that Jesus now finds the Jews to be a very "important" people and that his punishment for doubting their authority is to burn forever in boiling feces. Anyone following in the footsteps of Jesus Christ is likewise to be punished with boiling excrement:

"*Who is most important in that world where you are now? Jesus said to him: The Jewish people. Onkelos asked him: Should I then attach myself to them in this world? Jesus said to him: Their welfare you shall seek, their misfortune you shall not seek, for anyone who touches them is regarded as if he were touching the apple of his eye (see Zechariah 2:12).*"

"*Onkelos said to him: What is the punishment of that man, a euphemism for Jesus himself, in the next world? Jesus said to him: He is punished with boiling excrement. As the Master said: Anyone who mocks the words of the Sages will be sentenced to boiling excrement. And this was his sin, as he mocked the words of the Sages.*"

Prior to raising Jesus from the grave, Onkelos raises Balaam. Asking the same questions, Onkelos is given essentially the same answers we read above, except that the "boiling excrement" is exchanged for boiling semen:

"*Onkelos asked him: Should I then attach myself to them here in this world? Balaam said to him: You shall not seek their peace or their welfare all the days (see Deuteronomy 23:7). Onkelos said to him: What is the punishment of that man, a euphemism for Balaam himself, in the next world? Balaam said* to him: He is cooked in boiling semen, as he caused Israel to engage in licentious behavior with the daughters of Moab."

The *sacred female* thus became identified as a *harlot* or *whore*, just as Jesus Christ was condemned to "boiling excrement" or "semen." Men later replaced the women as emissaries of God and *living resurrection* was replaced with institutional dogma and *vicarious atonement*. We should also remember that in those days, and even within the *mystery sects*, it was obviously still considered odd to place such emphasis on women, as Simon Peter asks: *"Did he"* the savior *"really speak to a woman secretly, without our knowledge, and not openly? Are we to turn and all listen to her? Did he prefer her to us?"* It is no wonder that revealing the *mysteries* in public was punishable by death. Considering Jesus and his *Bride*, it is therefore no surprise he was condemned to death by various groups - Jewish and non-Jewish alike.

Furthermore, all the followers of Jesus Christ are also condemned to having their ashes scattered while their nonmaterial self is to be burned in feces and semen. In **Tractate Soferim 15** we learn that non-gentiles in general - heathens - are condemned to death because of their supposed wickedness:

"Kill the best of the heathens in time of war; crush the brain of the best of serpents. The most worthy of women indulges in witchcraft. Happy is he who does the will of the Omnipresent."

The impurity of gentiles, according to the Talmud, is universal and especially relates to woman. In **Avodah Zarah 22b** we read the following:

"One may not keep an animal in the inns [befundekaot] of gentiles because they are suspected of <u>bestiality</u>. Since even gentiles are prohibited from engaging in bestiality, a Jew who places his animal there is guilty of violating the prohibition: "You shall not put a stumbling block before the blind" (Leviticus 19:14). And a woman may not seclude herself with gentiles because they are suspected of engaging in forbidden sexual relations. And any person may not seclude himself with gentiles because they are suspected of bloodshed. A Jewish woman may not deliver the child of a gentile woman, because in doing so she is delivering a child who will engage in idol worship. But one may allow a gentile woman to deliver the child of a Jewish woman. Similarly, a Jewish woman may not nurse the child of a gentile woman, but one may allow a gentile woman to nurse the child of a Jewish woman while the gentile woman is on the Jewish woman's property."

Jews are instructed to have no sexual relations with gentiles either, something that historically could be understood due to the small numbers of Jews then as now. But **Avodah Zarah 36b** goes further, suggesting that gentile women are unclean and impure, and that they are to be kept separate from Jews:

"The court of the Hasmoneans decreed that a Jew who engaged in intercourse with a gentile woman bears liability for transgressing four prohibitions, represented by the mnemonic: Nun, shin, gimmel, alef. These letters stands for: Menstruating woman [nidda], maidservant [shifḥa], gentile [goya], and married woman [eshet ish]. By rabbinic law, a man who engages in intercourse with a gentile woman is considered to have violated the prohibitions involved in having intercourse with all four of these women."

Even sexual relations with children is discussed in the Talmud. **Sanhedrin 54b** indicates that it may be acceptable to have intercourse with children, a common perverse accusation against Muslims and Christians:

> *"The Sages taught: With regard to intercourse with a male, the Torah does not deem a younger boy to be like an older boy; but with regard to intercourse with an animal, the Torah does deem a young animal to be like an old animal. The Gemara asks: What does it mean that the Torah does not deem a younger boy to be like an older boy? Rav says: It means that the Torah does not deem the intercourse of one who is less than nine years old to be like the intercourse of one who is at least nine years old, as for a male's act of intercourse to have the legal status of full-fledged intercourse the minimum age is nine years. And Shmuel says: The Torah does not deem the intercourse of a child who is less than three years old to be like that of one who is three years old."*

Later Jews and Rabbis were likely very aware of the perceived filth and perversity of their *Talmud* and thus adopted the Egyptian and Babylonian *mysteries* as an antidote. Michael D. Swartz writes in an essay titled 'Magical Piety in Ancient and Medieval Judaism', how the mystical *"Kabbalah was"* really *"meant to be a stabilizing influence in relation to Jewish tradition."* Perhaps it was meant to make up for the perversity of the *Talmud* and Jewish beliefs of superiority.

Today the global capital of homosexuality is Tel Aviv, Israel, something used as a weapon against the gentile (goyim).

Sacred Locations: Grottos & Cathedrals

Of the *Bridal Chamber* and *Universal Androgyny*, the <u>Gospel of Philip</u> relates the following:

> *Among the forms of unclean spirits are male and female ones.*
> *Males have sex with souls who inhabit a female shape, and females mingle*
> *promiscuously with souls in a male form. No one escapes those spirits:*
> *they seize you, unless you take on the power of male or female,*
> *of groom and bride. This power resides in the mirrored bridal chamber.*

The locations of these *Bridal Chambers* were not always in subterranean crypts, but instead within both natural and artificial temples. The *chamber* itself was meant to mimic the *primordial womb* that nurtured mankind in the *beginning*. One could also call this the *earth* or *cosmic egg*. In addition, the *chamber* represents the *womb* of the *Universal Mother*.

Commonly used natural environments include grottos (caves), which were sacred to Mithra(s); dense forests, sacred to Diana (Greek Artemis); and, of course, any place with a sacred spring, river, etc., as water represented the *birthing fluids*. The Nile River, for example, was the urine, sweat, spit, sexual fluids, and birthing fluids of Isis. These waters are the origin of *baptismal rites*, or the purifying and cleansing of literal dirt, as well as spiritual dirt called *sin*. John the Baptist, who is considered a forerunner to the Christian movement and Jesus Christ, used water sacraments to purify initiates. Hence, they were 'John the' *baptized*.

Many natural *sacred sites* were used in conjunction with the *energies*, i.e., the gods and goddesses, finding homes there. To speak with God, one visits the high mountain tops and to enter Hades one passes through underground crypts.

Many artificial *sacred sites* were later constructed on top of previous *holy* areas in nature, and thus many churches are built upon *sacred grottos* while countless monuments from antiquity are built over even older *sacred locations*. The *Great Pyramid of Giza*, otherwise known as the *Womb of Isis*, is itself built on an even more ancient spring. Water from the Nile would even be channeled into the massive complex.

To commune with the gods of these sacred locations it was customary to align oneself with their energies through various forms *ritual sympathy*. In other words, wearing associated colors and presenting certain related symbols. Singing and dancing were also integral parts of these rituals, therefore preserving and expressing that which is not verbally explainable. To dance was to put the body in motion with the planets and nature.

In Anacalypis, Godfrey Higgins expresses the theory that music, poetry, and dance were the three great elements of primitive ritualism. He suggests that these elements were used before the discovery of writing and were utilized for religious practices. Before the invention of writing, the knowledge of ancient peoples was told in story form, often through poems. Bards committed to memory these narratives, even those of incredible length, and recited them verbatim at feasts and other celebrations. This is famously true of Indian holy men going back over ten thousand years. Manly Hall explains in Lectures on Ancient Philosophy what happened to the art of memory after the art of writing became common practice:

> *"After the invention of writing, the most important records were either carved into the surface of stone or engraved upon golden plates. Thus deprived of their primal dignity the interpretive arts became elements of amusement rather than instruction."*

If you have ever spent time in nature *forest bathing*, visited a beautiful *cathedral*, or walked through a *Buddhist temple*, then you will be aware of the *energy* of these places. The sensitive among us may even feel the vibrations. It is believed that much of this energy is rooted in the *intention* of the *ritual practices* that include prayer, singing, dancing, and honoring the divine. This *energy* is also said to be a result of what some mystics call *ley lines*, which are the crossing of lines at a *sacred site* resulting in a nexus and the birth of a singular point of great energy.

The Sioux Native Americans call them *skan* and in India and Egypt they were described as *snakes*. Material science may call them *conductivity discontinuities*. Where these lines intersect, we acquire the infamous *crossroads* for which the Greek goddess Hecate was associated. Here you will find ghosts, phantoms, and often black magicians and sorcerers attempting to contact infernal forces, all things known to Hecate. She is often associated with Selene (Roman Luna) and all things that come from the shadows of the *Great Reflector* in the sky – our moon.

From the *crossroads* to *Bridal Chambers,* we are dealing with the same ideas: communing with the spirit world.

One of the most famous of all artificial *wombs*, besides pyramids that are found all over the planet, is the *Gothic Cathedral*. These fabulous pieces of architecture are constructed with oval doorways, large pillars, and incorporating vast wisdom on sacred geometry. The oval doorways are called *visica pisces*, also known as a *yoni* or *yonic*, which is a symbol of the female reproductive system.

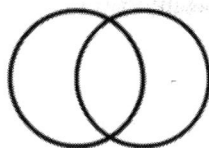

This is the *portal* or *doorway* for life to be birthed. The two towers, famous at Notre Dame in France, and the oval opening can also represent the raised legs of a female and the vaginal opening during the process of giving birth. Use of this symbol dates to the Egyptian hieroglyph *RU*, i.e., birth-portal, or *mouth*.

Remember Joseph Campbell assessed that the *word of creation* was spoken from the mouth through a sexual metaphor of the teeth and tongue. Out of this unification, "all *the gods, the heavens, and the world are brought forth.*"

Despite efforts to conceal these sexual metaphors, women with exaggerated sexual organs can be found in architecture all throughout Europe, from cathedrals to castles. This image is called *Sheela na gigs*.

It is common to see Jesus Christ standing within the *visica pisces*, a symbol which may also relate to the pineal gland. It is also called *Mandorla*, which is Italian for *almond*.

Rose windows are also symbolic of the female and stand as symbolic vaginas for penetration of the male phallus, symbolized by a ray of sunlight. As light penetrates the rose, those in the

Jesus in the vesica piscis with his body surrounded by the *Mandorla*, from Chartres Cathedral, also known as the Cathedral of Our Lady of Chartres. Behind his head is the *Nimbus* and zodiac cross. Surrounding his body is the bull, the lion, the eagle, and angelic man, collectively known as the Tetramorph, otherwise associated with the Four Evangelists or Four Beasts.

cathedral's womb, symbolic of the womb, are nurtured and brought to new life. They are *reborn* as they exit through the oval doorway.

The towers are further symbolic of the pillars of Solomon's Temple, Boaz and Jachin: beauty and strength; the sun and moon; Chesed the white moon, and Geburah the black moon; the duplicated symbols of God in the <u>Zohar</u>; active and passive principles; and fire and water. They represent the philosophical doctrines of Sir Francis Bacon in the study of science and philosophy and are depicted on the symbolic title page of that author's <u>Instauratio Magna</u>. Author and magician Eliphas Levi helps extend our understanding of their meaning:

> *"These two pillar represented man and woman, reason and faith, power and liberty, Cain and Abel, right and duty. They were pillars of the intellectual and moral world, the monumental hieroglyphic of the antinomy inevitable to the grand law of creation."*

These opposing forces generate natural support for each other and the Temple, which is physically supported as a result. One implies the other, and both are required for stability. In other words, life implies death, pleasure implies pain, and *one-thing* implies *no-thing*. This is why Jesus was crucified between two thieves, who mislead us into extremes.

The High Priestess card in tarot depicts a goddess holding a scroll and sitting between these two pillars. That scroll is the *sacred science* and the *teachings of Christ*. As author Mark Booth relates, *"knowledge of the secret doctrine of the Mystery schools was denoted by the holding of a rolled scroll."* Such imagery is found all throughout antiquity right up until modern times.

Along with the *sacred symbolism* of the *divine feminine* concealed in countless cathedrals, with yonic openings, two pillars, rose windows, and large open-womb spaces, there are, of course, images of the *Holy Mother* (vagina and womb) and *Cross* (phallus) of *redemption*, i.e., *resurrection* from *death* and *sin*. The cross itself is a merger of the *vertical* and *horizontal* sexual organs. Hall confirms this in <u>The Secret Teachings of All Ages</u>, writing how the cross *"itself is the oldest of phallic emblems, and the lozenge-shaped windows of cathedrals are proof that yonic symbols have survived the destruction of the pagan mysteries."*

These oval entrances share something in common with *beehives*, too, and possible proof of this can be found all over the world. On the southwest cliffs of the island of Malta in the Mediterranean Sea, the temples known as Ħaġar Qim and Mnajdra, which have beehive like features, were almost certainly used for resurrection ceremonies. Although it may be the rock itself, the Temple of Mnajdra seems to have a beehive look.

Malta is also home to the Ħal Saflieni Hypogeum, an underground crypt almost certainly used by *Mystery Schools*. The same can be said of the megalithic Ġgantija, technically on the island of Gozo to the north. If the beehive features of Mnajdra are not convincing, it should be remembered that the temple itself is, like all grottos and cathedrals, essentially a *beehive* wherein the workers of the mysteries congregate. The beehive structure can be seen also at Newgrange in Ireland and at the temple complex of Deoghar in India.

The Temple of Mnajdra

Newgrange in Ireland has a passageway leading to a beehive-like chamber.

Ishibutai Kofun

In Nara prefecture of modern day Japan there are a series of ancient sites that archeologists inform us must have been tombs for royalty or powerful clan leaders. One such example is Ishibutai Kofun; built, it is estimated, in the 6th-century as the resting place for Soga no Umako from the clan by that name (Soga). There is little doubt that several other sites in the area around Asuka were used for the archeologically approved narrative, and although countless ancient sites have been repurposed for reasons such as burials of prominent leaders, it is hard to ignore Ishibutai's characteristics as they relate to Newgrange in Ireland, the Giza Pyramids in Egypt, or the Hypogeum and Ġgantija of Malta and Gozo respectively. The layout of Ishibutai is centered on a mound that reminds us of the ones constructed in the Americas. In the center of what looks like the first layer of what could be a stepped-pyramid, are thirty megalithic blocks stacked on and against one another to create a slightly submerged chamber. Visitors may recognize that the information signs merely allude to what is assumed about the structure despite the lack of evidence to support those claims. A stone sarcophagus near the mound would appear to be a relic, but in reality it is merely a reproduction based on an assumption. The sign reads, *"no sarcophagus was found during the excavation."* Ishibutai Kofun is considered the largest megalithic site in Japan.

Jesus sitting inside the *Mandorla*, surrounded by the *Four Evangelists*: St. Matthew (man), St. Mark (lion), St. Luke (bull), and St. John (eagle). This image is from a medieval illuminated manuscript.

Mormon Masonry, Beehives & Remphan

All three of the major world religions - Christianity, Islam, and Hinduism, not to mention Judaism - employ these sorts of symbols. In Hindu mythology the bee is a divine assistant to humans, acting to keep all life in order.

The Mormon Church of *Jesus Christ of Latter-day Saints*, founded in 1830 by Joseph Smith, incorporates these same powerful symbols, from bees to those timeless images of the sun and moon.

The headquarters of the Mormon Church is Temple Square, Salt Lake City, Utah. Even a simple glance at the magnificent structure will reveal images of the sun, phases of the moon, hexagrams, honeycombs, beehives, and bees. The sun adorns the top of the main temple from one side to the other in a beautiful trim. Below it is the moon in its various phases, and where the moon is shadowed there is honeycomb relief. The main entrances and exits are located to the east and west, and above each are five-pointed stars - pentagrams. These stars are also found below each sun and above each moon around the entire structure.

Upon the door handles are beehives and above them in metal relief is a larger beehive with six bees. The number of bees is an interesting choice considering that the there is a hexagon (six) water fountain with obelisk in the middle located within Temple Square. There is smaller temple constructed with the remaining material from the main building that also has a glass hexagram (six-pointed star).

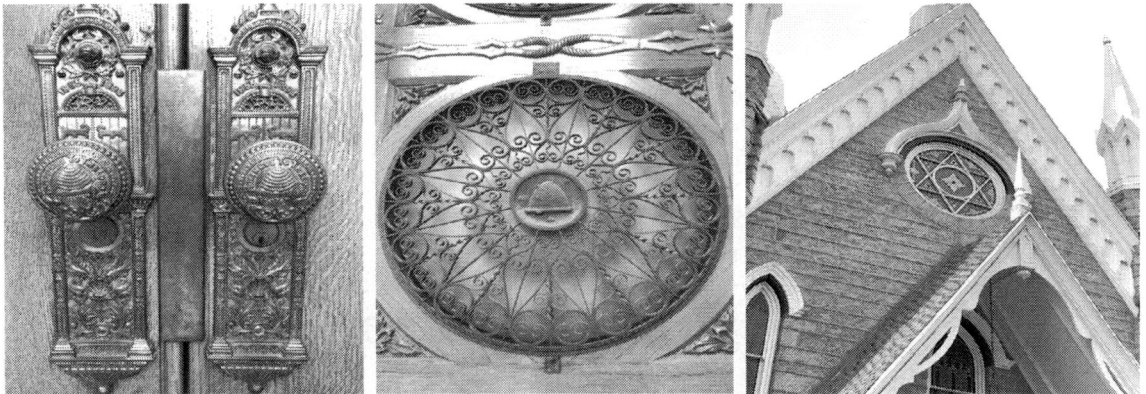

There is yet another water fountain located across from the hexagon fountain. This water fountain is in the shape of a shell, or more specifically, a scallop shell. The significance of the scallop shell is found visually in a Sandro Botticelli painting, *The Birth of Venus*, where the goddess is standing upon the shell on the shore of a great ocean. The name *Aphrodite* (Greek Venus) literally means *foam born*, i.e., *born from the sea*. Some may recall that the *papal court* at the Vatican is called the *Holy See* (Sea), and that the Pope wears a *fish hat* and *fish ring*. Here we are reminded of the Age of Pisces once again.

These symbols relate both to the concept of man's evolution from the oceans, in one interpretation, and the baptismal waters of John and Isis in another. Venus especially is directly associated in astronomy with that above-mentioned pentagram.

Birth of Venus by Sandro Botticelli (c. 1484-86)

As with the hexagon fountain and hexagram window, Temple Square is to be associated with the worship of Saturn, god of time and death. He is known as the Grim Reaper of the harvest and his *Platonic Solid* is the cube. As the *black god* like Osiris, signifying fertile soil, Saturn's relationship with time has much to do with the cycles of planting and harvesting crops.

The *Saturn Star* is often called the *Star of David*, which incorporates the four elements, or building blocks of the cubed three-dimensional world. Few recognize its perverted form, however, as detailed in the Biblical book of Acts 7:41-44, wherein the Jews were accused of worshiping a wicked god named Remphan:

> *"And they made a calf in those days, and offered sacrifice unto the idol, and rejoiced in the works of their own hands. Then God turned, and gave them up to worship the host of heaven; as it is written in the book of the prophets, O ye house of Israel, have ye offered to me slain beasts and sacrifices by the space of forty years in the wilderness? Yea, ye took up the tabernacle of Moloch, and the star of your god Remphan, figures which ye made to worship them: and I will carry you away beyond Babylon. Our fathers had the tabernacle of witness in the wilderness, as he had appointed, speaking unto Moses, that he should make it according to the fashion that he had seen."*

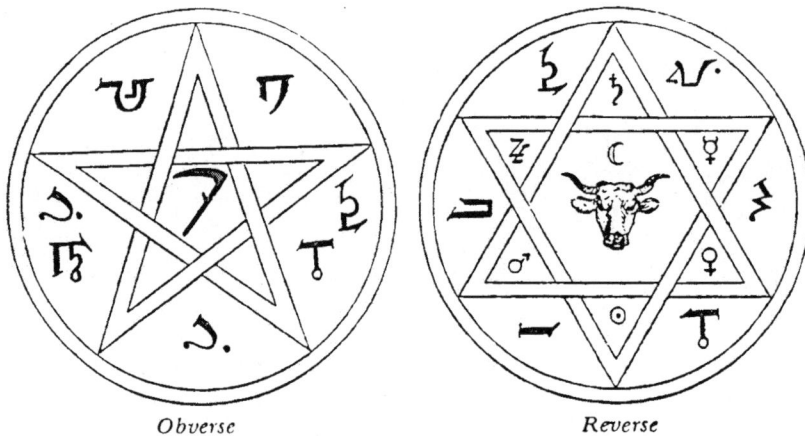

Obverse   *Reverse*

**Talisman of the planet Saturn,
otherwise known as the *Star of Remphan* (Moloch)**

Remphan is simply another name for Chiun, which translates to Saturn. The Babylonians worshipped him as Kiyun, a word referring to a *statue* or *idol*, as did the Arabs, Assyrians, and others honor him under different names. The Jews did not have a star, besides the one they adopted in the wilderness as a *false idol* – some refer to this idol as Chiun (Saturn), Apis (an Egyptian bull deity), and others as the brass bull-headed deity Molech. The "tabernacle of Moloch" is a direct reference to Leviticus 18:21, and the warning:

> *"'Do not give any of your children to be sacrificed to Molek, for you must not profane the name of your God. I am the LORD."*

It is more than coincidence that he main entrances and exits of the Mormon Temple are located facing west and east.

In the *Mystery Schools*, initiates entered the temple from the *western island, or land of shadow,* from which the sun sets and the evening star rests. They were then taken through a series of tasks, as Booth pointed out earlier, and required to do things such as: *"fall down a well, undergo trial by water, squeeze through a very small door and hold logic-chopping discussions with anthropomorphic animals."* They may have been required to swim underwater in the dark or even commune with poisonous or dangerous creatures like snakes and crocodiles. Upon exiting the temple to face the eastern rising sun, a *Son of Man* became a *Son* [sun] *of God*.

In the occult sciences of India, candidates for initiation, the *Brahmatchary*, were led through a ritual that ended with the rising sun in the east. Afterwards, a young neophyte would be referred to as a *Douidja*, which means *twice born*.

Admissions into the *Mystery Schools*, be them at Memphis, Egypt, or Eleusis, Greece, were paid by the surrender of body and soul-spirit to the priesthood. Descending through dark subterranean regions, an initiate would be led by flaming pyres over bridges and through narrow passageways. Initiation into most *schools* began with self-purification (baptism), the building up of intellectual powers (meditation and reading), and a sacrifice of *desires* and *passions* to the *divine* (giving up meat, alcohol, sex, social interactions).

Levi further alludes to the practice of carrying a lamp that must not be extinguished during initiation:

> *"He who trembled, he whom fear overcame never returned to the light."*

If one cannot be trusted with the *light*, and mistreats it, they are pulled again back into darkness. In the story of Orpheus, we read how he looks back to find his love Eurydice, just as daylight breaks, being pulled back into the darkness of the underworld. The likeness of this story is also told in the myth of Cupid and Psyche; that love cannot dwell where there is suspicion. Others may recall Matthew 14:29-31 when Peter doubted Jesus, or Genesis 19:26, the story of Lot and his wife, which shares a similar motif with a Persian city "enstoned in stone" because its people refused the commands of Allah (*The Thousand Nights and One Night*):

> *"But Lot's wife looked back, and she became a pilar of salt [smoke]."*

When Inanna was about to ascend from the Netherworld, she was seized by the gods who said, *"Who has ever risen from the Netherworld? Who has ever risen from the Netherworld alive? If Inanna wants to ascend from the Netherworld, let her give a substitute as substitute for herself."*

The same story is told of Izanagi's wife Izanami in Japan.

This is a 5th century B.C. coin from the ancient Greek city of Ephesus, now modern-day Turkey. The city was located on the western coast of Asia Minor and was the site of the temple of Diana.

On the coin are the Greek letters *Epsilon* ε and *Phi* Φ. In the center is a giant bee, the emblem of Ephesus, and symbol of the great mother. Her priestesses were called *melissae* - the *bees*.

Persian Mysteries & the Full Armor of God

By the teachings of Persian mystics, first degree candidates were given a crown upon the point of a sword and instructed in the power of the *Unconquered Sun,* Mithra(s), who was also born in a grotto (cave) and met by shepherds like Jesus. His rites were thus administered within a sacred cave called *Mithraeas.*

In the second degree the neophyte would be given the *armor of intelligence and purity* before being sent into the darkness of a subterranean pit. The weapons and armor of *light, intelligence,* and *purity* were meant to fight the beasts of *degeneracy, passion,* and *uncontrolled desire.* Some may recall the Biblical armor, or "full armor of God," worn to *"stand against the wiles of the devil"* (Ephesians 6:11).

These pieces include the "breastplate of faith and love," the "shield of faith," the "helmet of salvation," and "sword of the Spirit."

In the third degree of the Persian mysteries initiates were given a cape covered in signs of the zodiac with other astronomical symbols that related to the cloak of Mithra(s) himself. As associated with the seven classical planets, here are the seven grades of the Mithraic cult in Persia: *corax* (Raven), *nymphus* (Bridegroom), *miles* (Soldier), *Leo* (Lion), *Perses* (Persian), *heliodromus* (Courier of and to the Sun), and *pater* (Father).

Upon completing these trials with the *full armor of God* an initiate would be hailed as having risen from the dead. Hall adds additional insight, writing:

> *"Candidates who successfully passed the Mithraic initiations were called Lions and were marked upon their foreheads with the Egyptian cross."*

These "lions" relate back to the *Lion's Paw* of Egypt, used to raise initiates from literal and metaphoric tombs. Lions are also the terrestrial animal of the sun. The "Egyptian cross" placed on the foreheads of Mithraic initiates was known to Moses as the *Yahweh Mark,* a common thing placed on the foreheads of Christians on *Ash Wednesday.* This day of the week is named after Woden, or Odin, the god who first created man and woman from the *ash tree* in German and Norse mythology.

In Hinduism we find *vibhuti* (sacred ash) smeared all over the body of Lord Siva as a sign of his divinity and his choice to mingle with the mundane world like Jesus. The sacred ash in Hinduism is usually worn on the forehead but sometimes smeared over the entire body.

Jesus *Christ* the *Messiah*

The name JESUS is very similar to the Greek *Zeus* and is closer to being both a title and moniker for a god rather than a real name. Although we believe that "Jesus Christ" certainly *existed,* his true name in Hebrew was *Yeshua.* From Hebrew to Greek the translation becomes *Iesus,* which is nearly identical to the *Sky Father* Zeus. When the New Testament, written in Greek, was translated into English his name became *Jesus.* As was customary in those days to place an origin of birth at the end of your name, we also get the title *Jesus of Nazareth.* As for the letters IHS, these stand for the first three symbols of *Jesus* in the Greek alphabet (ΙΗΣΟΥΣ). There are some

sources linking this monogram to Dionysius-Bacchus, too, which would be an interesting correlation considering their ability to also *turn water into wine*. We could further summarize that IHS is yet another version of the *Holy Trinity*. The <u>Gospel of Philip</u> helps confirm what is written here, documenting how *Jesus* is a hidden name altogether:

> *"Jesus is a hidden name, Christ is an open one. So Jesus is not a word in any tongue but a name they call him. In Syriac the Christ is messias, in Greek he is Christos. All languages have their own way of calling him. Nazarene is the revealed name for what is secret."*

The name *Yeshua* was furthermore a common title held by many people during the time of *Jesus the Christ*.

The name CHRIST, like JESUS, is itself a title denoting the one who is *Messiah*, or he who is anointed by God. In Greek the term is *chrīstós* and from this word we derive the meaning of *the Anointed One*.

Christ or *Christos* was a titled also applied to priests of Judah and various other savior gods such as *Krishna* of the Hindu tradition. An incarnation of *Vishnu the Preserver*, he was associated with the sun, as is Jesus and Mithra, the son of the Persian god Ahura Mazda (Ormazd) - the creator spirit in Zoroastrianism. *Mithra* was later to be especially venerated by Roman soldiers as *Mithras* and the *Unconquered Sun*. Vishnu was a protector of *dharma* - moral and religious law - and had ten Avatars, reminiscent of the five pairs of Poseidon's children, who ruled Atlantis. These ten Avatars of Vishnu correspond numerically to the *Sephiroth* of the Kabbalah, those emanations revealing *Ein Sof* that are depicted by ten spheres. Vishnu was born of a virgin in his incarnation as Krishna and his annual festival was held in August under the sign of *Virgo the Virgin*. He was also known as the *Christos* (*Kris-h-tos*), since *kris* is the Hindu word for *Christ*, and yet another title for the sun.

The name *MESSIAH* is denoted from *Christ*, translates to something like *"liberator of people,"* and in the Hebrew Bible it is a title given to a king or High Priest anointed with holy oil. Egyptian Pharaohs were anointed with oil extracted from the fat of a crocodile. This substance was called *messeh*, another origin for the famous word. D. M. Murdoch writes in <u>The Christ Conspiracy</u> of these titles and the *anointed one*:

> *"…anyone anointed would be called 'Christ' by the Greek-speaking inhabitants of the Roman empire, who were many since Greek was the lingua franca for centuries…in Greek, Krishna is also Christos, and the word for 'Christ' also comes from the Hindu word 'Kris,' which is a name for the sun, as is evidently 'Krishna' in ancient Irish."*

According to Joseph Campbell, the entire idea of a Jewish Messiah *"had nothing to do with the end of the world"* but instead with a *"king who would reestablish Israel among the nations."*

The accepted name or title JESUS CHRIST was the result of translations from Hebrew and Greek, and official declarations stemming back to the Council of Nicaea in 325 AD.

Although many consider this event the defining moment in what would be considered the foundation of Christendom, there were other councils throughout the years leading up to 325 AD that played as important a role.

The Council of Arles (314 AD) was the first time Emperor Constantine introduced the omnipotent God of the Christians as his personal sponsor. He then wove together a growing spiritual and political movement with infamous pagan traditions more commonly practiced in Rome. The day of the sun – SUN DAY - became a Christian *holy day* and the *cross* became an exclusively Christian symbol. This morphing of several different religious or spiritual doctrines was Constantine's goal in founding a unified and universal world religion called *Catholicism*, meaning "universal." He then opened the Lateran Palace to the bishop of Rome, creating the early Vatican, and around 324 AD, he ordered the construction of the first Church. What Constantine accomplished was to unify multiple religions and then attach them to the government for religious-socio-political control, while still maintaining his membership as a high priest of the *Unconquered Sun*.

At the Council of Nicaea (325 AD) it was decided what would become *Cannon Law*, including most of the books allowed or disallowed in the finalized Bible. Discussion included the nature of Jesus himself and his relationship to the Father (Trinity), as well as the official date of the *resurrection*. The council decided upon a day for Easter, certainly basing their decision on already popular traditions: what we know as Easter today was already at the time dedicated to the Greek god of vegetation named Attis, who was tied to a tree and later resurrected three days after his death. His blood ran down to redeem the earth in similar fashion to the story of Mithra(s), who ushered in the new age by the slaying of Taurus.

This cycle of *birth, life, and death* was already highly regarded as a *sacred mystery* before it was merged into the *Holy Trinity* by Church Fathers.

The *Fleur-de-Lys*, which is found in ancient art all over the world, is a sacred symbol representing this divine compilation. The trinity is found in many forms: mother, father and child; mother, maiden and crone; morning, noon and night; black, white and gray; below, above and in-between; hot, cold and mild; past, present and future; mind, body and spirit/soul; happy, depressed and tranquil; beginning, middle, end; and in the cycles of the moon there are full, waxing and waning.

The **Fleur-de-lys** is a French symbol of royalty and the trinity. Some feel that it originated from the *bee*, as seen here, rather than a flower.

Babylonian priests knew the *source* of all things as *Ilu*. From Him came all other gods. Ilu formed the sacred and holy trinity of active principles: *Anu* (time), *Nuah* (intelligence), and *Bel* (coordinator). Each of these former gods corresponds also to a passive feminine divinity: *Nana*, *Belit* and *Davkina*. From these emanations came a second trinity, involving the progeny of the all the former: Bin (atmosphere) is the son of Anu; Samas (Sun) is the son of Nuah; and Sin (Moon) is the son of Bel. There is considerable disagreement about whether Rome itself, in its many incarnations, was as harsh in resisting the Christian cult early on as we have been led to believe. For example, during the time of Jesus something like crucifixion was only reserved for large thefts and murders, whereas civil offences like religious crimes were punishable by sword or stoning.

By the time of Emperor Julian, thirty years after the Nicaean Council, Rome was still highly tolerant. A student of classical philosophy, Julian was known as a generally tolerant and noble man, but he did grow rapidly intolerant of Christianity. Julian regarded the Church's concept of *sin*, in that of punishment and reward, or sinner made saint, as an encouragement of delinquency and corruption. He strongly disagreed with the concept that all men were sinners, and that Christians possessed the *sole truth*. For a supposedly intolerant state, Rome still welcomed Greek, Egyptian, and Persian rites for centuries, but it was the new Christian movement that had intolerantly condemned all these gods as demons and their teachings as frauds and sacrilege. If the countless battles within and outside of orthodoxy today are any indication of the past, then it surely was the Christian church itself that persecuted its own from the beginning, through both religious frenzy and political provocation. As Hall points out, it is even thought among some scholars, and based on building evidence, that *"it was actually the Christians who burned Rome during the reign of Nero."*

At the Council of Laodicea (364 AD), only about a year after Emperor Julian left the seat of power, it was decided to further provide structure to the Biblical Canon, an organized effort usually associated only with the Council of Nicaea. Here the decision was made to change the Sabbath from Saturday – SATURN'S DAY - to Sunday, the day of the Sun. An approach was also developed at this council on how to handle heretics.

The Council of Carthage (397 AD) was held in Africa, and along with other councils, was where the agreeable books of the Bible were further transformed into the *Official Word of God*. Many books were intentionally left out, such as the *Book of Enoch*, while others were not found until much later. Two examples are the controversial *Gnostic Codices* found near Nag Hammadi in Upper Egypt around 1945 and the *Dead Sea Scrolls* which were first uncovered in Qumran (Israel-Palestine) in 1947.

~

Author Burton Mack in <u>The Lost Gospel of Q</u> writes of the title *Christ* before the foundation of the Roman Church and helps us to understand a bit more of this confusing, convoluted, and controversial history:

"In the course of Christian history, to take one example of a series of social and cultural shifts, the Christ has been refigured many times over. In the period before Constantine, when bishops were taking their place as the leaders of the churches, the Christ was commonly depicted as the good shepherd who could guide the flock to its heavenly home. After Constantine, the Christ was pictured as the victor over death and the ruler of the world. During the medieval period, when the church was the primary vehicle of both social and cultural tradition, the story of Christ's ascent from the cross (or the tomb) to the seat of sovereignty, judgment, and salvation in heaven focused the Christian imagination on a Christ of a truly comprehensive, three-decker world. Somewhat later we see the Gothic Christ appear, and then the Christ of the crucifix, the man of Galilee, the cosmic Christ, the feminine Christ, and so on."

That *"Christ was pictured as the victor over death and ruler of the world"* is a direct result of his merging with the *Unconquered Sun* cult popular across the Roman Empire. Each new sun is renewed, reborn, and virgin, be that each morning or every solstice. Such symbols apply to the physical sun but also the spiritual sun too.

For complex historical reasons, Jesus Christ himself has become the ultimate *false idol* today, an irony considering Biblical proscription against such a thing. Leviticus chapter 26:1 says:

"'Do not make idols or set up an image or a sacred stone for yourselves, and do not place a carved stone in your land to bow down before it. I am the LORD your God."

Yet the literal image of *Jesus Christ*, separated from *God the Father* in the Gospels, and as rightfully observed by famed philosopher Alan Watts, has *"become far more of an idol than anything graven in wood or stone, so that today the most genuinely reverent act of worship is to destroy that image."* Therefore *"to cling to Jesus"* as a historical character is to essentially *"worship a Christ uncrucified, an idol instead of the living God."*

Watts adds in <u>Beyond Theology: The Art of Godmanship</u> that our *"attempts to 'demythologize' the Gospel and get down to the authentic, historical facts about Jesus of Nazareth are actually as irrelevant and superstitious as trying to concoct pseudoscientific proofs that the Virgin Birth and the bodily Resurrection were physical events. Both are quests for a Jesus 'out there in the past, and,"* in referencing the angels observing the empty tomb, *"why do ye seek the living with the dead?"*

Levi also expounds on this in his <u>The History of Magic</u>:

"To say that there is no God or to define what He is, constitutes equal blasphemy."

Watts explains how the *end times* rhetoric of Christendom, and other religions, is truly foreign to the concept of a *source*-God:

"In the terms of Isaiah II's messianism and of post-Maccabean apocalyptic visions of the coming end of the world, a theology strangely alien to the mystical sense of union with God."

The *Virgin Birth*, or the mythological motif of the *search for the unknown father*, occurs within one's own heart as we begin to live a spiritual life called *Christ*. On this journey to discover our *father* we become *reborn*, something traditionally carried out in puberty rites wherein the little boy symbolically dies and is born again as a young man.

The *Virgin Birth* is also another *Parousia*, or *Second Coming*; that unfolding and sprouting of the *seed within*. This is the moment in Matthew 17:2 when Jesus *"transfigured before them. His face shone like the sun, and his clothes became as white as the light."*

A *Virgin Birth* is representative of the byproduct of the "Spirit of God" moving "upon the face of the waters," the formless void that was earth in Genesis 1:2. The void is passive, abysmal, and dark, and it is the active, creative, light that impregnates this womb. Joseph Campbell explains how, *"the procreating power is everywhere. And according to the whim or destiny of the hour, either a hero-savior or a world-annihilating demon may be conceived."* In modern scientific terms many would refer to this as the *big bang*.

A *baptism* functions to purify and water this internal *seed* while awakening the individual to their *destiny*, which, as Campbell points out, *"is the secret cause of your death."* Baptism is thus attempting to *"pull something out of you."* This concept of *death* as a fulfillment of life *"underlies the sacrifices of the great planting societies"* and *"the idea of the Crucifixion of Jesus."* As per the *mysteries*, Campbell adds: *"…when you have identified yourself with the consciousness, the body drops off. Nothing can happen to you."* It is the *realization*, not of *consciousness* itself, but of the *unconscious* that sets you free. As with the Greek maxim of *know thyself*, the Sanskrit maxim *tat tvam asi* says *"though art that,"* referring to an individual's relationship with the *Absolute*. In other words, the *Kingdom of Heaven* is within everyone, and the *Promised Land*, as Campbell points out, is therefore, as we already noted, *"not a place to be conquered by armies and solidified by displacing other people."* The Holy Land of legend, myth, and theology is *"a corner of the heart, or it is any environment that has been mythologically spiritualized."* Heaven is of similar consideration.

The Word of God & its Perversion

"The Word became flesh and made his dwelling among us. We have seen his glory, the glory of the one and only Son, who came from the Father, full of grace and truth."

Bible - John 1:14

"The Creator rules over boundless infinity. Nothing existed before the Creator. No one ruled before the Creator. The Creator is without Form."

The sacred and varied Japanese text, *Kujiki-72*

"Then came the word. Tepeu and Gucumatz came together in the darkness, in the night, and Tepeu and Gucumatz talked together. They talked then, discussing and deliberating; they agreed, they united their words and their thoughts. Then while they meditated, it became clear to them that when dawn would break, man must appear."

The mythology and history of the Mayan peoples, *Popol Vuh*

The *Word* of God

After the *fall from God's Paradise*, man decreasingly relied on *impulse* and increasingly relied on *thoughts*. These things cultivated further *desires* and began to cause what we call *suffering*. As Genesis 3:23 relates:

"So the Lord God banished him from the Garden of Eden to work the ground from which he had been taken."

This is the *sacred philosophical doctrine* of the evolution of man. Prior to the *fall* or *creation*, God, or the *Cosmic Mind*, first had to mold *matter* into a workable substance. Thus, in John 1:1 we read:

"In the beginning was the Word, and the Word was with God, and the Word was God."

The WORD is a translation of the Greek LOGOS, meaning *principle*, *speech*, or *thought*. The *logos* also indicates *order* in all things, and the acquisition of knowledge. In John 1:2-5 we read further:

"He was with God in the beginning. Through him all things were made; without him nothing was made that has been made. In him was life, and that life was the light of all mankind. The light shines in the darkness, and the darkness has not overcome it."

If you are baptized in fire, i.e., the *light shining in the darkness*, you are purged of *Original Sin* (ignorance) against *God* (truth). *Truth* and *balance* stem from *logos*, too, as indicated by *order*. In Latin the word is *Verbum* – so, *in the beginning was also the Verbum*. The WORD can therefore be extrapolated as the *intellect of God* or the *Cosmic Mind* over, and creating, *matter*. Our *soul* is the *image* of this *intellect* and *mind*, and our *word* is the *image* of the *soul*. Since the *world* is made in the *image of God*, then man is himself made in the *image* of the *world*, and by extension, *made in the image of God*. Genesis 1:27 reads as such:

> "So God created mankind in his own image, in the image of God he created them; male and female he created them."

Egyptian hieroglyphics tells us that the WORD *"creates all things: everything that we love and hate, the totality of being. Nothing is before it has been uttered in a clear voice."*

The *image* of man is merely a reflection of the *divine*, as can be seen in the *Great Kabbalistic Symbol of the Zohar* and *The Great Seal or Symbol of Solomon*. Furthermore, *vibration* is the *Word of God*, and so *speaking*, and particularly of *esoteric philosophy*, is an expression of *consciousness*. It is the method by which divine names or words are intoned to attract their associated corresponding energies. Spoken words begin as *concepts* and *thoughts*, then are expressed as *vibrations* out of *body* and *mouth*. For "God said" in Genesis 1:3, *"Let there be light."*

In Sanskrit we find the word *Anāhata-śabda* - an awareness of *pure sound* beneath *audible*

Great Kabbalistic Symbol of the Zohar

sound. The word *anāhata* means *unhurt* or *unstruck* and relates to the *heart chakra*, while śabda means *speech* or *sound*. We therefore obtain the translation of *unstruck speech or sound*. Many interpretations could be provided here but we will focus on the simplest. An *unstruck* sound is one that resonates within or beyond. An *unstruck form of speech* is that which requires no verbalization by man – perhaps it emanates from the *mind of God*. Perhaps the refences here is to *pure thought*. In Japanese we find the word *kotodama* - *spirit of a word* or *soul of a word*. It is the idea of mythical power behind *spoken words* and *sacred sounds*. The Romans called this authority *voces magicae*, or *magic words*.

Languages and *Alphabets* are comprised of symbols we call *letters*, a written or printed communication that resonates to certain frequencies or vibrations. The sounds of animals, insects, the playing of instruments, and the human voice are all an expression of symbols in auditory form. As philosopher Alan Watts writes of the power of language and words:

> "Language in its broadest sense, including words, numbers, signs, and symbols of all kinds, is what peculiarly distinguishes men from animals, and enables us to know that we know. Language is the symbolic echo of direct experience, lending to it resonance that enhances it - as a great cathedral, with its subtle reverberations, lends an other-worldly magnificence to the voice of a choir."

Author Francis Barrett explains in his classic book <u>The Magus</u> how powerful our spoken word truly is:

"…the virtue of man's words are so great, that, when pronounced with a fervent constancy of the mind, they are able to subvert Nature, to cause earthquakes, storms, and tempests."

The most barbarous and unintelligible words are said to have the most powerful nature in *black magic*. Beautiful language, and kind words, has a power unlike that of the darker arts.

Roger Bacon (1214-1294), the English philosopher and scientist, writes on the power of words in relation to the soul:

"We must consider that it has great force; all miracles at the beginning of the world were made by the word. And the peculiar work of the rational soul is the word, in which the soul rejoices. Words have a great virtue when they are pronounced with concentration and deep desire, with the right intention and confidence. For when these four things are joined together, the substance of the rational soul is moved more quickly to act according to its virtue and essence, upon itself and upon exterior things."

David Frankfurter writes further in his essay, 'Narrating Power: The Theory and Practice of the Magical Historiola in Ritual Spells', that the power of narration is *"a 'power' intrinsic to any narrative, any story, uttered in a ritual context, and the idea that the mere recounting of certain stories situates or directs their 'narrative' power into this world."*

This is why *spells*, *curses*, *incantations,* and even *intonation* are considered so powerful. The naming of a *disease* or *demon*, often the purveyor of the former, is critical because it gives the magician, or doctor in this case, a knowledge of the *evil* to be *exorcised*. Since demons have usually been associated with *sickness*, and many of us *exercise* to stay healthy, we thus *exorcise* the demon with *incantation*.

We can satisfactorily conclude this section with a brief story from the Greek philosopher Socrates, which brings us from the *spoken word* to *written word*. Thoth, the Egyptian god of writing, approaches Amon, King of all Egypt, and urges him to introduce the practice of writing for all people to enjoy:

"O King, here is something that, once learned, will make the Egyptians wiser and will improve their memory; I have discovered a potion for memory or wisdom."

Amon responds with a warning about written language, that it is a destructive force against memory and wisdom. He says, *"it will introduce forgetfulness into the soul of those who learn it."* Amon concludes his comments with respect to the great god Thoth:

"Your invention will enable them to hear many things without being properly taught, and they will imagine that they have come to know much while for the most part they will know nothing."

Even the *written word* is powerful, hence when we SPELL a word, we are practicing magic. The same can be said about the elegant writing called *cursive*, or to *set* or *cast a curse*. Even the word *grammar* has similar origins. It comes from the Greek *grammatikē*, defined as the *"art of letters,"* and *gramma*, a thing that is written. In Old French, *grammatica* became *gramaire* before eventually transforming into the word we know today as *grammar*. The word *gramaire* also had the meaning of *magic* or *enchantment*. This is the basis for why *grammar* in its many forms eventually led to the forming of the word *grimoire*, or the sorcerer's *book of spells*. And Philosopher Alan Watts observes of language in a broad sense:

> *"Language in its broadest sense, including words, numbers, signs, and symbols of all kinds, is what peculiarly distinguishes men from animals, and enables us to know that we know... The verbal description of the world is a simplified, albeit oversimplified, model of the world. But it provides us with a platform apart from the world itself, upon which you can stand and take a new look at the world. Words representing things make it possible to have thoughts about experiences, to deal with life in terms of symbols as we deal with wealth in terms of money."*

The *Logos* Made Flesh

Further along in the book of John chapter 1, verse 14, we learn what happens next with the *Word of God*:

> *"The Word became flesh and made his dwelling among us. We have seen his glory, the glory of the one and only Son, who came from the Father, full of grace and truth."*

By this we are to understand that *order* slowly developed in the form of *matter* and *life*, organizing these things by the *Divine Plan*, otherwise known as *Tao*, the source and law of *being*. Also, that *thought* preceded *matter*. The word *matter* comes from the Sanskrit root *matr*, meaning *to measure*. And it is by *measurement* that the *Grand Architect*, *Carpenter*, and *Ancient of Days* traces out *creation*. The *physical world* stems from the Greek *physis*, meaning *nature*. But the world is not made of *matter* or of any specific *form*, per se. These qualities, Watts writes, *"are two clumsy terms for the same process, known vaguely as 'the world' or 'existence'."*

Joseph Campbell explains TAO as such: *"Tao is the way of course of nature, destiny, cosmic order; the Absolute made manifest."* In Hinduism *The Way* is also called *Bhakti Marga*, a practice in which one acts in daily devotion towards personal deity.

The oriental YUM or YIN is *female* and *time*, whereas YAB or YANG is *male* and *eternity*. One is *measurement* and the other is *infinity*. What we are really debating here are the semantics of etymology and *esoteric philosophy*. All can be understood as being of the *Cosmic Mind*, which in the *secret sciences* preceded *matter* and unfolds all things therefrom.

The WORD MADE FLESH is this androgynous character: Adam and Eve, the Greek Hermaphrodite, Eros, Baphomet, and the Half-Woman Lord Ardhanarisha (Shiva united with Shakti).

Perversion of the *Logos* & Decline of the *Mysteries*

A great many are provoked irrationally to *paranoia* and *fear* by certain images such as the goat. Although there is something to be said of its relationship to Saturn by Capricorn, the goat has throughout history commonly been burdened with crimes, fear, sins, and then sacrificed for communal *atonement*. Here we find part of the basis for the *scapegoat*, which was originally a literal goat stressed with all the sins of a community and then driven from the people and killed.

The goat itself is largely representative of the *animal instinct*, i.e., fertility and reproduction. Its horns are like those of the Celtic Cernunnos and Greek Pan, or the astrological Aries and Taurus. They are the basis, as we noted earlier, for "Devil Horns" and the arousal of sexual excitement.

So far as any *animal sacrifice* goes, we may be discussing a literal *burnt offering* or one that is a result of shining light on darkness, whereupon one is purged of *sin*. The *offering* of the animal-self is *burnt* by its exposure to the *Light of God*.

There are those in the *dark arts*, or those of *lesser wisdom*, who believe, however, in barbaric sacrifices, as has been demonstrated all throughout human history. These are not just *black magicians*, followers of Goëtia, or sorcerers, but those holding strong beliefs in the proscriptions of Biblical books like Leviticus 1:9, instructing:

> *"You are to wash the internal organs and the legs with water, and the priest is to burn all of it on the altar. It is a burnt offering, a food offering, an aroma pleasing to the Lord."*

Author Paul Carus writes in The History of the Devil that as these practices progressed with human development, many became merely symbolic actions:

> *"the victim, be it a child, a virgin, or a youth is offered up without slaughtering, and has a chance either to escape by good luck or to be rescued by some daring deed."*

Some may feel ill at the suggestion of even a symbolic sacrifice of a "child, a virgin," or of a "kid," but rest assured these were codewords used in magical texts. It should be known that the term KID is really a baby goat. None of this has prevented the literal sacrifice of either definition of a kid, however, as we know from the Leviticus 18:21 passage pertaining to *the fire of Molech*. Author and magician Eliphas Levi wrote of these and other horrid practices:

> *"The sorcerer devotes himself to fatality, adjures reason, renounces the hope of immortality, and then sacrifices children."*

To achieve that which is desired, *"all must be dared in order to achieve all."* In other words, one essentially sells their soul with the sacrifice of such pure innocence, or with the diabolic horrors of all forms of *black magic*.

Along with monotheism and polytheism arise *monodiabolism* and *polydiabolism*. The *fire stage* of any primitive people *demonolatry*, whereby the fear of evil is met with horrid actions such as human sacrifice. Later, humans were replaced with animals, and it was not until the arrival of the Christ that there would be a sufficient sacrifice for all ages to come. From The Greater Key of Solomon is provided this statement on sacrifice:

> *"For animal sacrifices white animals are for good spirits and black for evil. These sacrifices consist of blood and sometimes of flesh."*

Concerning sacrifices to the spirits and how they should be made, The Greater Key of Solomon says:

> *"They who sacrifice animals, of whatsoever kind they be, should select those which are virgin, as being more agreeable unto the spirits, and rendering them more obedient."*

From The Grand Grimoire is given the reasoning for the sacrifice of a KID (baby goat) - to obtain virgin parchment for making the grand Kabbalistic circle of magic operations. You are to buy *"a young virgin kid"* for an offering, and after a short prayer you are to *"skin the kid and take its skin, putting the rest of it in the fire until it is reduced to ashes,"* which then you are to gather and *"throw to the rising sun pronouncing another short prayer to the great ADONAY."* The skin is then to be used in making the grand Kabbalistic circle for your undertaking. This process is explained in more agreeable terms within Edward Waite's The Book of Black Magic under the title, *The Rite of Lucifuge*:

> *"In common with the Key of Solomon, and all the Grimoires, the work of Honorius prescribes the sacrifice of a virgin kid, with the object of ensuring the possession of a virgin parchment by the operator. Now, Lévi affirms that when the "abominable author" mentions a kid, he means really a human child. In this interpretation he has not even the excuse of the humorous analogy which has been instituted in vulgar English, for his acquaintance, had he any, with our language was exceedingly slight. There is not a particle of foundation for the charge; the sacrifice in the case of the Grimoire of Honorius means, and can mean, no more than in the case of the Key of Solomon. There was a defined purpose in connection with the slaughter of the victim, which was the same in both instances."*

Any proscription for spilling blood, offering children to the fires, and the like, is to be considered *wicked* and *perverse*. Over the years these practices, as they are literally interpreted, contributed to the corruption of the *Mystery Schools,* and resulted in the proliferation of charlatans.

Other practices of *human sacrifice* had less to do with magic and demons, and more to do with raw superstition, i.e., paranoia and barbarism.

The *hitogaki,* or *human hedge,* sacrifice in Japan involved burying alive several people around the burial location of a high-ranking official. They would eventually die of course, but this was considered an honor and not a horror. The same is true about servants who have been entombed with royalty throughout the world. Committing suicide for this honor was called *junshi.* Perhaps the most famous ritual sacrifice is called *hari-kari.* This ritual sacrifice came in many forms, including the infamous *seppuku,* or suicide through disembowelment by sword. Babies have been used since time immoral in *sympathetic black magic* because of their youth, health, and assumed divine protection. Burying an infant in the structure of a building would thus protect the structure. Offering a baby to Molech would provide protecting for those bringing the sacrifice. Manly Hall details the deterioration of the *mysteries* and their associated temples as darkness slowly crept in:

> *"Though the temples of Thebes and Karnak be now but majestic heaps of broken and time-battered stone, the spirit: of Egyptian philosophy still marches triumphant through the centuries. Though the rock-hewn sanctuaries of the ancient Brahmins be now deserted and their carvings crumbled into dust, still the wisdom of the Vedas endures. Though the oracles be silenced and the House of the Mysteries be now but rows of ghostly columns, still shines the spiritual glory of Hellas with luster undiminished. Though Zoroaster, Hermes, Pythagoras, Plato, and Aristotle are now but dim memories in a world once rocked by the transcendency of their intellectual genius, still in the mystic temple of Freemasonry these god-men live again in their words and symbols; and the candidate, passing through the initiations, feels himself face to face with these illumined hierophants of days long past."*

Hall's mention of the *Vedas* is warrant for brief pause. The word *Veda* translates into *knowledge*. These four sacred texts known as *Vedas* are a compilation of four major sets of text known as Samhitas (union or collection). The most recognized book of Rig Veda is a text of sacred hymns and verses meant to impart sacred knowledge - the word *Rig* meaning "hymns and verses."

Sama Veda is a book of sacred song. Yajur Veda is a book providing sacrificial and ritual formulas. The Atharva Veda is a text not unlike the Egyptian Book of the Dead in that it imparts magical formulas, spells, and incantations. Depending on the reference source, it is believed at base minimum these texts are a few thousand years old, dating anywhere between 2,000 BC and 1,200 BC, though recent research suggests they are up to 8,000 years old, or a date of 6,000 BC. However, since India has a long tradition of orally transmitting sacred information, as do many other cultures, rather than putting it in "on paper" as we say, it is likely that although the *Vedas* may have been codified within this timeframe the information that they contain is far, far more ancient. In other words, codifying such sacred information on any physical medium between 3,200 BC and 6,000 BC indicates a cultural necessity arising that required the preserving of such knowledge for future generations, perhaps due to some form of natural cataclysm, or social and cultural deterioration. Traditionally it is believed that the *Vedas* were preserved in memory by the *Seven Sages*. After the passing of each age, or *Yuga*, which involves a *pralaya*, or destruction by fire or water, these sages then transmit this sacred knowledge to the next age of mankind. Author Graham Hancock confirms this in his book Underworld:

> "The function of the Seven Sages is to ensure that the Vedas are not lost during these periodic episodes of destruction."

The *Vedas* were not believed, *"even by those who recited them in antiquity, to be the first Vedas but rather a younger recension separated by countless aeons from the original…"*

As Sanskritist David Frawley confirms based on his research into Yogic tradition, *"By my interpretation civilization was founded by yogis, seers and sages."*

Now we are in the fourth and final age of the *Kali Yuga*, before the inevitable *pralaya*. This is an age of wickedness and perversion of the *sacred*, much of what we have seen happen to nearly every written *mystery* from every conceivable culture. In a letter to Robert Freke Gould, the Freemasonic general Albert Pike writes also of the deterioration of the mysteries, and the preservation of certain symbols and doctrines:

> "It seemed to me like the Pyramids in their loneliness, in whose yet undiscovered chambers may be hidden, for the enlightenment of coming generations, the sacred books of the Egyptians, so long lost to the world; like the Sphynx half buried in the desert. In its symbolism, which and its spirit of brotherhood are its essence, Freemasonry is more ancient than any of the world's living religions. It has the symbols and doctrines which, older than himself, Zarathustra inculcated; and it seemed to me a spectacle sublime, yet pitiful – the ancient Faith of our ancestors holding out to the world its symbols once so eloquent, and mutely and in vain asking for an interpreter. And so I came at last to see that the true greatness and majesty of Freemasonry consist in its proprietorship of these and its other symbols; and that its symbolism is its soul."

In Masonic lore, through the perfecting of *thoughts*, *desires*, and *actions* we go forth a *Master Builder* under the tutelage of Solomon and the *Widow*. Many neglect their personal tools of development and suffer a collapse of the temple in like manner to Samson pushing apart the twin pillars - philosophy and science or truth and beauty - which results in *true reason* being buried.

The methods of purification and study, seclusion and memory, trials, and the conquering of personal demons, all assist the student in mastering his animal self, exposing it to the burning light of truth - *burnt offering*. Often this *animal self* is depicted as a beast or dragon to be slain. This dragon represents *animal desire* made *manifest,* like the WORD was made FLESH. Physically the *Great Dragon* is that of the *reptile brain*, the oldest part of the brain which rests at its base in the dark of the skull temple. The reptile brain is the seat of our *animal* qualities and the spirit, i.e., the emotional body. As it resides in the darkness, we are reminded of the eternal serpentine predator always lurking in the shadows of our bodily Eden. In fact, Jean Doresse points out in <u>The Secret Books of the Egyptian Gnostics</u>, that the body preserves the *mysteries*, since *"the membranes enveloping the brain,"* are *"the heavens; the head of man,"* is *"Paradise, etc."*

      The goal of the *mysteries* was to follow in the footsteps of the *Son of God* and to be *born again* as a *Sun of God*; to return to the *Garden of Paradise* from the *Garden of Hallucinations*, which, in essence, is a *dream world*. Let the *mysteries of life* be preserved, not perverted!

God as Architect, from the <u>Codex Vindobonensis</u> (Bible Moralisee)

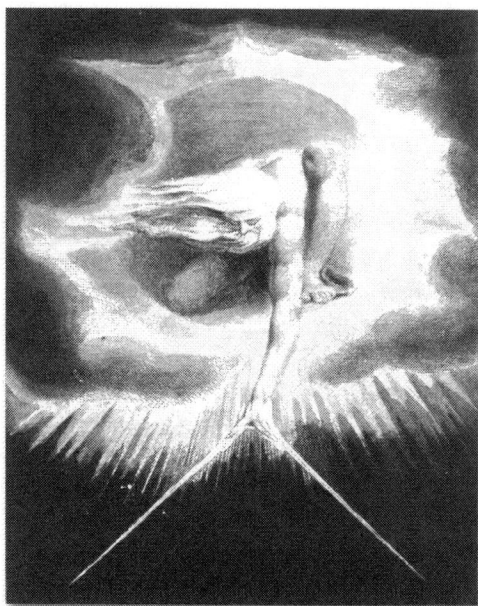

God creating the Universe, by William Blake

In this image we see the *Son of God* using a compass to design our world; using this tool to set the mathematical foundations of *Natural Law*. A compass is one of the key symbols of the Masonic Order and plays various roles both symbolic and literal. It is a tool for material and spiritual masons alike.

The disc behind his head signifies his relationship to the *Sun of God*.

Blake has depicted the *Creator* measuring with compass the borders of his creation, setting forth the fundamental mathematical laws of the world. The long white beard of the *Grand Architect* shows His relationship to *Father Time*, and thus, the *Grim Reaper*. He also shares attributes with the Scandinavian Odin, who lives in the north, and the multi-named *Santa Claus* or *Father Christmas*. In Mesopotamia he was known as *Great Misfortune*.

As Above So Below

The Great Seal or Symbol of Solomon represents the micro-macro-cosm of the earth reflecting the heavens; the inferior reflecting the superior. The bearded *Grand Architect* is depicted through reflections from the higher realm as we may recall from Genesis 1:27: *"God created man in his own image."*

Also, **the Great Kabbalistic Symbol of the Zohar**, the chief text of the Jewish Kabbalah, is an allegorical or mystical interpretation of the Pentateuch.

That God created "male and female" is synonymous with the androgynous nature of *source* separated into *many*.

The description above the shaded area and triangle of the inferior sphere, and below that triangle of the superior sphere, reads from Latin something to the translation of: *As Above, So Below*. Some authors like John Gilbert write about the origin of this axiom from the Emerald Tablet, explaining how the original text was mistranslated for generations and that it should actually read: *"the above is from the below, and the below is from the above."*

This symbol is the fusing of upward and downward triangles, or pyramids, often described as being the phallus and yoni, the passive and active principles united for the purpose of generation. When right side up the triangle represents man's attempt to connect with the heavens. When upside down the triangle expresses the interest of the superiors in the affairs of the lower world. At the very bottom is another triangle reaching above to touch the lower descending triangle. More abstractly these triangles represent the superior and inferior worlds touching at a point between which is often depicted a serpent, or staff, the umbilical cord linking man with heaven. The staff represents this link, which is why it is often carried by the wise, be it Moses or the Hermit.

In the center of the image we find the Star of David or Saturn Star derived from the *Magical Square of Saturn*. Central in this symbol is the Maltese Cross. We find the intelligence of Saturn with human or godly attributes, commonly depicted with a white beard as *Father Time*, or the *Grim Reaper* with a scythe, relating to agriculture. The Demiurge is the Creator and Grand Architect as depicted in this Seal.

What is above is also like that which is below, something we can witness in the micro world of atoms and storms into the macro world, or higher celestial sphere, of solar systems and planets.

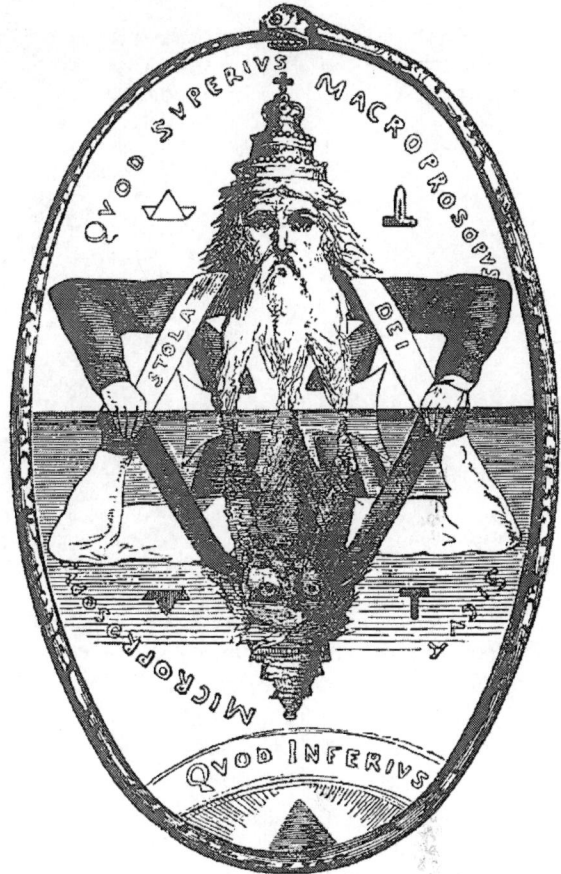

We can see the proof of this *design* in everything from the relationship fruit and vegetables have with human organs to the similarities between veins of a leaf, blood vessels in the body, and rivers when seen from above.

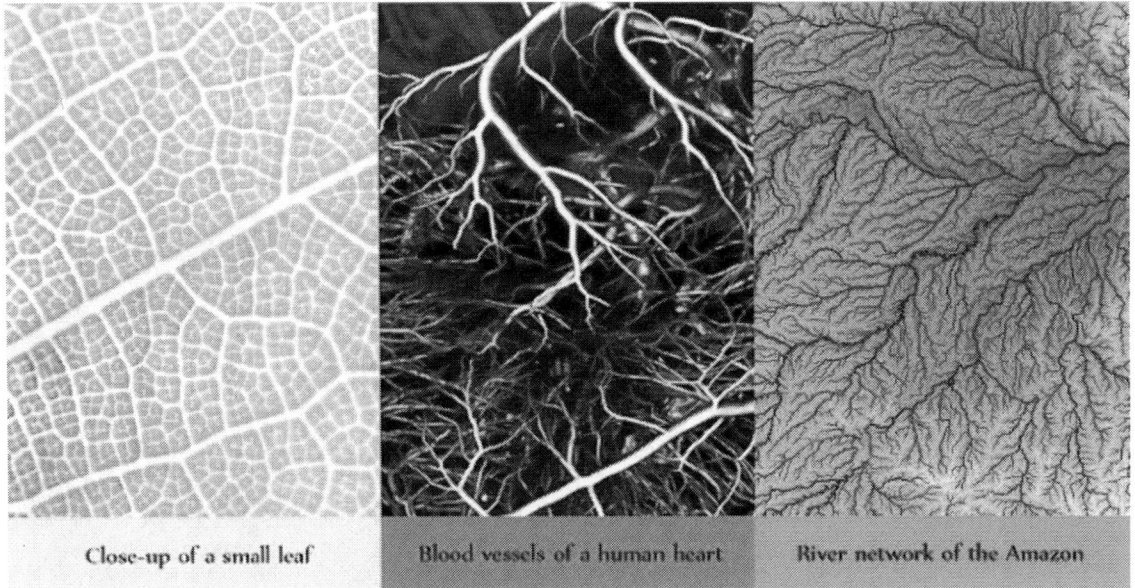

| Close-up of a small leaf | Blood vessels of a human heart | River network of the Amazon |

The *micro-macro-cosm* is nature mirrored and reflected, like God looking into the reflecting pool. Mechanisms found beyond earth are mirrored in those on earth, from solar systems to atoms. Galaxies rotate around a super-massive black hole mimicking a hurricane circulating around a central eye. The rotation of our spiral-armed galaxy around the center of a super-massive black hole is like the planets in our solar system orbiting around our star. On an even smaller scale are the electrons orbiting around the nucleus of an atom. Comets with their tales may be harbingers of death to some, including modern man, but like any space debris they may also bring the elements of life to a barren world – *panspermia*. The notion of *panspermia* offers an interesting correlation between comets and sperm cells, or mechanical science and occult science, what we now call human biology. Comets may penetrate a planet, impregnating or fertilizing it for life, while sperm cells penetrate the female egg. This seemingly complex understanding of biology, microbiology, physics, astronomy, astrology, mathematics, geometry, etc., was to be understood, advanced, and maintained in secret by certain societies to prevent its perversion.

Astronomy has been studied alongside of astrology for thousands of years. The latter was practiced as a *science*, its practitioners some of the most influential persons of their time. Sure, there were frauds, but the general practice is rooted in *magical science*. Astrologers were consulted during national emergencies and other occasions, just as similar men were used for dream interpretation, something described throughout various holy texts, including the Bible, as in the story of Belshazzar and the "writing on the wall" in Daniel 5.

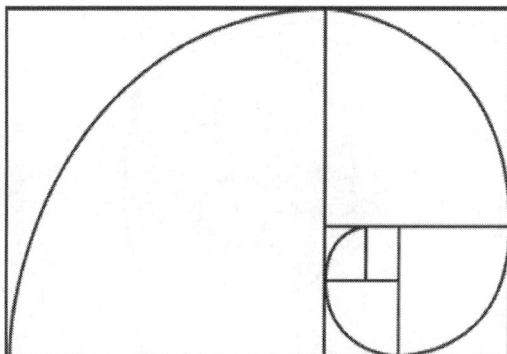

The understanding of the *micro* and *macro* worlds came from observing nature and cataloguing its patterns. So derived was *sacred geometry* from the *mysteries* of nature. The *Golden Mean* may be observed in seashells, flowers, pinecones, beehives, and even the wings and flight patterns of insects. Even our DNA shares a similar relationship to the spiraling and twisting of energy expressed in biological code as numbers and letters. We call it the double helix and it is represented in the Staff of Hermes or Mercury.

In mathematics it is called Golden Ratio or Phi, also known as the Golden Section. The *Golden Mean* is the ratio of two qualities equal to the sum of the whole when added together. It is an irrational number, approximately 1.68 033 988 749 894.

Similar in nature is the *Fibonacci Series* name after the Italian mathematician Leonardo Fibonacci. Beginning with the number one, each new number in the sequence then becomes the sum of the two before it: 1, 1, 2, 3, 5, 8, 13, 21, 34, 55, etc. This is observed in flowers and is also to be found in the unfolding of the spiral arms of a galaxy, or the rotation of a hurricane. Rivers resemble human blood vessels while tree branches and roots mimic bolts of lightning.

Even foods demonstrate this esoteric reality: carrots resemble the eyes; kidney beans for the kidneys; tomatoes for the heart; walnuts for the brain; ginger for the stomach; sweet potatoes for the pancreas; mushrooms for the ears; grapefruit or other forms of citrus for the breasts; and grapes for the lungs. Some foods represent several parts of the body.

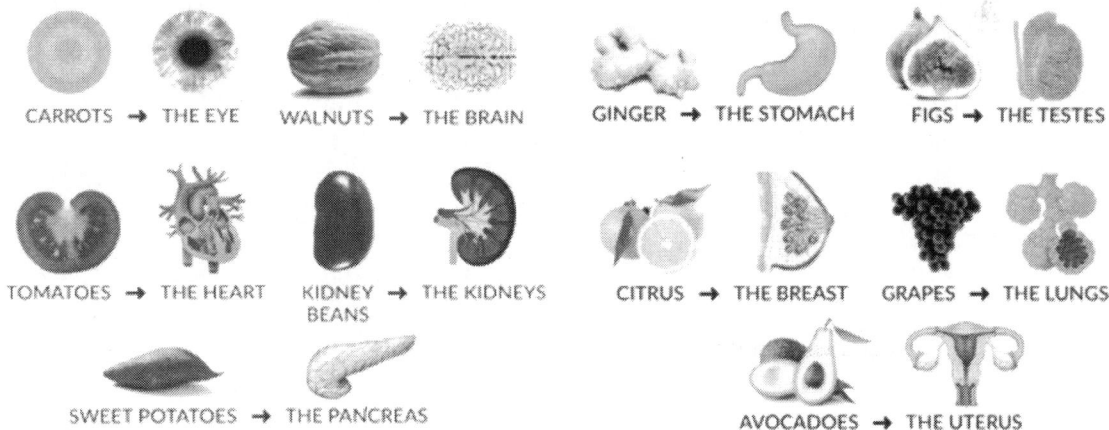

CARROTS → THE EYE   WALNUTS → THE BRAIN   GINGER → THE STOMACH   FIGS → THE TESTES

TOMATOES → THE HEART   KIDNEY BEANS → THE KIDNEYS   CITRUS → THE BREAST   GRAPES → THE LUNGS

SWEET POTATOES → THE PANCREAS   AVOCADOES → THE UTERUS

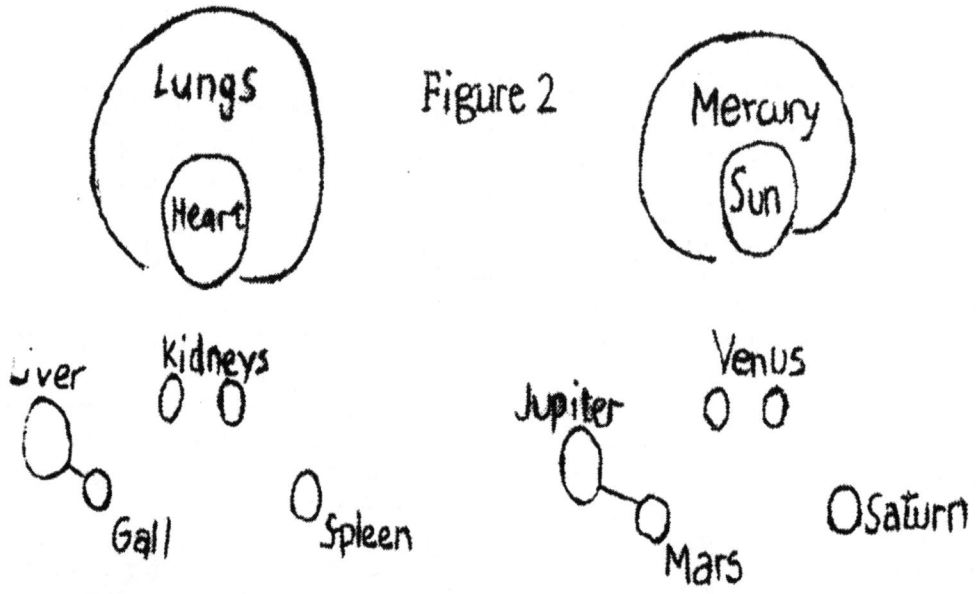

Lungs
Heart

Figure 2

Mercury
Sun

Liver
Kidneys
Gall
Spleen

Jupiter
Venus
Mars
Saturn

A drawing after the likes of Rudolf Steiner depicting human organs in association with the planets.

Slaying the Great Dragon, Opening the Mouth & Lifting the Veil

"The hostile attitude of conquering nature ignores the basic inter-dependence of all things and events – that the world beyond the skin is actually an extension of our own bodies – and will end in destroying the very environment from which we can and upon which our whole life depends."

~ Alan Watts ~

The Image of Isis

Inscription from the Static Isis in Egypt:

"I, Isis Am All That Has Been, That Is Or Shall Be; No Mortal Man Hath Ever Me Unveiled."

By the words "no mortal man" we are to understand those uninitiated novices not yet instructed under the *wings of Isis* to become *Sons of the Widow*. Having never been "unveiled" by these mortal men we are to understand that no man has ever been bestowed the wisdom of the *mysteries* without partaking of the proper course of initiation. The uninitiated are considered "dead" or called "corpses" for not having resurrected their spirit in *rebirth*. Far be it from an insult, such philosophical doctrine was merely meant to preserve *sacred sciences* from those who may abuse them. Nevertheless, of course, the *mysteries* themselves were eventually perverted, and the idea of the "profane" became an insult used by the elite to demean the commoner. In the Biblical book of John chapter 14, verse 6, we find a similar statement to the *inscription of Isis* made by Jesus: *"I am the way and the truth and the life. No one comes to the Father except through me."* The "Father" is *source*, and we are unable to unveil its mysteries, those of life, and be "born again" unless we follow the "way" of Christ or Isis, i.e., the portal of the sun representing *truth*. We read similarly in the <u>Bhagavad Gita</u>, when Krishna speaks, *"He who does My work and reads Me as the Supreme Goal, who is devoted to Me and without hatred for any creature - he comes to me."* Saint Martin's personalized path of spiritual self-cultivation was termed *the way of the heart*, which corresponds to Robert Fludd's depiction of the sun residing in the heart, the Christian conception of *asking Jesus into your heart*, and Plato's contention that man, who enters life in an amnesiac state in need of remembering his divinity, must contemplate the Good - symbolized by the life and order of our sun.

There is a parallel metaphor about the goddess veil concealed in a popular story about Diana. On a hunting trip, the curious Actaeon wandered off alone and found a thicket of cypress and pine trees concealing a forest-grotto. Peering inside he saw a beautiful spring and bubbling water being used by the nude, and stunning, Diana to cleanse herself. Noticing the unwarranted intrusion, Diana's nymphs attempted to cover her body though it remained visible. An angry Diana told Actaeon, *"now you are free to tell, if you can, that you have seen the goddess nude,"* before tuning the man into a stag to be tracked down by his own hunting dogs. Ripping open the veil is punishable by death. **The face of Isis is veiled by scarlet cloth**, which is symbolic of *ignorance* and *emotionalism* that inhibit growth and stand in way of *truth*. Behind her veil is the virgin world, beauty, and spirit.

Red is also a symbol of *menstruation* and *birth*, be that of a human baby or the baby sun surrounded by an orange, yellow, blood red sky. Red is a color of death and the spilling of blood. We can think of the *birth* and death of the sun as a daily and nightly occurrence, or as a yearly cycle. We can correlate this with our own birth and ultimate death, our alpha and omega, symbolized by the red covering of the Universal Mother. As Joseph Campbell points out: *"The mythological figure of the Universal Mother imputes to the cosmos the feminine attributes of the first, nourishing and protecting presence....The goddess is red with the fire of life; the earth, the solar system, the galaxies of far-extending space, all swell within her womb."* As for ignorance and emotions, red is representative of heat and anger, or uncontrolled passions, which also could include sexuality. The fiery red goddess is creator, preserver, and destroyer – see *Brahma, Vishnu, Shiva*.

  This veil is further representative of the scarlet robes worn by the *hierodule*, or *sacred woman*, of the Sumerian and Babylonian *mysteries*. Their robes symbolize *ritu* (being *upright* and *honest*) and were only later associated with *prostitution* when the word *hierodulai* was translated into *harlot*.

  Isis stands between pillars of contradiction, demonstrating how *understanding* is always found at the balanced point of *equilibrium*, and that *truth* is often *crucified* like Jesus Christ between these *two thieves*. The pillars area also are Boaz and Jachin in Masonic tradition. They *stand* for *beauty* and *strength*, and *philosophy* and *science*, for which the universal temple is upheld.

  Behind her head is the ouroboros, the serpent consuming its own tail, a symbol representing *eternity* and *regeneration*.

  Above the veiled inscription is a sun disc with two serpents situated to appear as horns. They represent opposing forces in like manner to the two pillars on each of her sides. In some depictions of Isis, she wears the horns and disc upon her head, representing horns of the bull and Venus, the evening and morning stars. The horns hold up the sun and give it birth, as with the raised legs of a pregnant woman.

  Beneath her feet is inscribed, *"The Fruit Which I have Brought Forth is the Sun."*

  Her feet are covered with serpents, which represent the dragon from Revelatio,n waiting *"so that it might devour her child the moment he was born."* Here is refence to the devouring force of animal nature, ready to consume innocence.

  The solar sun disc with wings, like the wings Isis is often bestowed with, signifies the transitional point between *soul-spirit* and *matter*, or the *superior* and *inferior* worlds.

  Grapes cover her right breast and wheat the left. These two foods are transformed into the wine and bread of *Eucharist*.

  In her left hand is the *sistrum*, a musical instrument with metal frame and rods that rattled when shaken. Priestesses of *Ise Jingu*, the sacred shrine where Amaterasu descended from heaven in Japan, also use nearly identical rattles. **In her right hand is a small boat** denoting her dominion over *water* and *birth*. This boat is thus a symbol the *womb*. **To her left wrist** is attached weight of judgement. **To her right wrist are attached *scales of balance*** relating to the Roman goddesses *Justitia* and *Libertas*, or *Lady Justice* and *Lady Liberty*, for which the *Statue of Liberty* in its many forms is derived – in fact, the one in New York City was inspired by Nubian (essentially Egyptian) iconography. The woman holding a sword, wearing a crown, and holding scales is also used as imagery in Tarot to represent *Justice*. The crown of thorns, or rays, worn by *Lady Justice* represent a solar and nurturing quality that can be found in the Japanese Amaterasu, Persian Mithra(s), Anatolian Attis, Hindu Surya, Aztec Tonatiuh and, of course, the Christian Jesus, not to mention the son of Isis we know as Horus. The crown of Isis usually includes elements of agriculture, like those associated with Demeter-Ceres. Scales further symbolize the astrological sign of *Libra*, a name like *liberty*. The thorns are likewise those of the rose; beauty and danger. *Truth* is found in *balance*, and the Egyptian goddess of truth and justice, *Maat*, balances the heart upon these scales like Anubis weighing the heart against a feather in the *Hall of Judgment*. In this case, the heart represents *conscience* weighed against *justice*, represented by an ostrich feather. This place of judgment was also known as the *Hall of Both Truths* and according to the verdict issued here the dead would receive everlasting life or suffer punishment for their wrongdoings.

In Mexican culture it is Santa Muerte who carries the balancing scales of judgement. In Christendom there is Saint Michael the Archangel holds these scales like the *Black Horse* of judgement.

Such imagery demonstrates that the *mystery traditions* prized *truth* and *justice* above all else, concepts that are considered foreign for such a period of antiquity – though we know this is not entirely true.

Those with a weighted heart were not directly condemned to damnation with *original sin*, however, and instead given an opportunity in the Egyptian Book of the Dead to learn the appropriate magical formulas, incantations, and secret names of demons necessary to pass through the underworld challenges. Even if an individual was an unsavory figure during life, they were still able, by uttering the correct phrase by proper intonation, to find favor in their judgment. There were even included incantations for those who had lost their voice. In some cases, a beetle with charm was placed on the breast of the mummy to pacify the heart: *"O my heart, rise not as a witness against me."*

Within the *heart* thus resides our *desires* which are to be overcome in search of *gnosis* – "knowledge of the spiritual mysteries." These *desires* can furthermore be associated with *beasts* and animals of lesser consciousness, as within us we are comprised of an animal body and mind.

Additionally, Egyptian myth informs us that the Egyptian god Thoth (Greek Hermes), otherwise known as

Weighing the Evil and the Good of the Soul - about 1150 from the Cathedral of Autun, France.

The Christian Last Judgment, reproduced from *The History of the Devil*, by Paul Carus.

Thoth weighing the heart against the feather.

Djehuti, *scribe of the gods*, hid his immense wisdom of *gnosis* in numerous *sacred books*. Hence his names included *The Lord of the Divine Books* and *Scribe of the Company of the Gods*. Perhaps these are physical books or perhaps, as he himself was an expression of *knowledge,* what Thoth inscribed were basic laws of nature that anyone can see when they pay attention. He would then be an expression of God's *Divine Plan*. Thoth (Djehuti) has the head of an ibis and body of a man. *Tehu* is Egyptian for *ibis*. As a god of the moon, astronomy, time, wisdom, writing, science, and like Hermes-Mercury, a messenger to RA, his wife is naturally Ma'at, the goddess of truth, justice, and order, signifying that through *justice* and *truth* comes *wisdom*, or through Ma'at comes Thoth.

In <u>The Egyptian Hermes</u> we read that Hermes (Roman Mercury) also preserved his wisdom and teachings *"by inscribing them in sacred books which he then hid here on earth, intending that they should be searched for by future generations but found only by the fully worthy."* By "fully worthy" perhaps we are once again dealing with immortal men *unveiling Isis.*

The Egyptian ritual *Coming Forth By Day* has been renamed <u>Book of the Dead</u>. It contains images of the Osirian *Hall of Judgment* ritual overseen by Thoth, while Anubis weighs the heart against that of a feather. Behind Thoth is a monster known as the "eater of the dead," a creature part crocodile, hippopotamus, and lion, that would immediately devour the heart if it weighed more than a feather. It is to be understood by the *heart* all *desires* of flesh and animal, and by the *feather* our *soul* ready to transcend the *infernal world*. Here are also found the genii, *Shai* and *Ranen*, of misery and happiness. In the *Hall of Judgment*, the brain was discarded, and the heart was weighed against that of a feather on a scale overseen by Anubis. If the heart was "heavy with sin" the balance of the scale would be tipped, the judgment written by Thoth on his palette, and the candidate for initiation denied access to the root of the ancient *mysteries - eternal life.*

Such a ritual was played out as a drama.

Justice is the Eighth Tarot card of the Major Arcana. It denotes *soul* and the notion of *equilibrium*, by *balancing scales* and a seat *between two pillars*. A crown upon the head with solar emblem signifies *truth* and *light*. The sword is a link between heaven and earth, being used as scepter of power granted by God. In this way the card signifies both divine and earthly justice. The sword and scales interpreted together represent a universal symbol for justice, who is often blindfolded, an obvious reference to what should be impartiality in *judgment*. Swords can mean both protection and war, or defense and offense. Sometimes referred to as *Lady Justice,* this image shares relationship to the Egyptian goddess of truth, Maat (mät), a female personification of *justice* and *cosmic order*. The Static Isis is similarly depicted with balancing scales, signifying her power over universal matters.

Left to Right: Egyptian *Horus* or *Ra*, *Jesus* Crucified, Aztec *Tonatiuh* (16th century Codex Telleriano-Remensis), Hindu solar deity *Surya* (Tanjore School 19th Century), *Attis*, *Mithra(s)*, *Amaterasu* (Utagawa Toyokuni III, Kunisada, 1857), *Statue of Liberty*, and offerings to the Egyptian sun god *Aton*.

Opening the Mouth & Stellar Rebirth

In Central America the followers of Quetzalcoatl believed that upon death their god was reborn as a star. The same was true for Mesoamerican leaders. In Egypt the soul, especially one of a Pharaoh, was to be reborn as a star.

Originally known as the ritual ceremony *Coming Forth by Day*, the Egyptian Book of the Dead acts as a guide for the soul in overcoming the dangers of the afterlife. To *come forth by day* is a reference to the tradition of initiates in the *mysteries* exiting the underworld to greet the rising sun in the east.

In both Central America and Ancient Egypt, it was believed that the *soul* of the dead made its journey by boat, accompanied by guides like the Greek *Charon* who ferried it to and from each stage or level. As with the boat held by Isis, signifying her body as the womb, this afterlife vessel was symbolic of the soul's continued journey.

The *boat* is a *vessel* for the *soul* in the afterlife, just as the *body* is the *vessel* for the *soul* in physical life, or the earth is the universal womb for all mankind.

This boat floats on both a symbolic river and the river of the Milky Way where human souls go after their body dies, and where souls emanate from during *incarnation*. Sometimes this waterway is called *the River of Souls*. The Cherokee call the Milky Way *"Where the Dog Ran,"* referring to a myth about a dog that ran away with a meal dripping from his mouth. This trail became *Sky River*. In Egypt the Nile was said to be connected with the *sky river*.

In the Babylonian version of our story, the lady of Hades was called Nin-ki-gal and her residence was situated near a river like the Greek *Styx* that the spirits were required to cross.

Images found in the tomb of Double Comb, an eighth-century ruler of the Mayan city of Tikal, depict an underworld with similar features also found throughout the Valley of the Kings in Upper Egypt. In both these versions of the underworld there is a *"dog or dog-headed deity, a bird or bird-headed deity, and an ape-headed deity,"* as author Graham Hancock documents.

In Central America one level of the underworld was called *Teocoyolcualloya*, or *"the place where beasts devour hearts."* This is like the stages in the ancient Egyptian *Hall of Judgment*, which includes an almost identical series of symbols. In this version the brain was discarded, and the *heart* was weighed against that of a *feather*. If the heart (*desire*) was "heavy with sin," the balance of the scales would be tipped in negative favor and the *eater of the dead* would consume what remains. If the feather (*soul*) were to be heavier than the heart, then the *dead* would be allowed passage to the next stage.

The bird (avian)-crocodile-reptile motif is also present in Japanese mythology with the sea monster-dragon *Wani*. Generally seen as a monster, the kanji 鰐 is translated as *crocodile*. Being a water-locked country, the ocean is especially akin to *maya*, or illusion, for the Japanese. In fact, *maya* means both illusion and mother, and it is the *land of mother* or the *land of the eternal* which exists beyond the ocean of this nation. This land is where the soul-spirit receives *eternal life* according to Shintō, and so it makes sense there is an association with the crocodile *Wani* in this essential under-or-parallel world.

Both the scared Quiche Maya book Popul Vuh and the Ancient Egyptian Book of the Dead document a belief in "stellar rebirth" – the ability to be reincarnated as a star. Part of this process included special rituals like the *opening of the mouth* ceremony. In Central America this was called *p'achi*, a word meaning "human sacrifice" and *to open the mouth*. In Egyptian rituals, taking place within pyramids or other temples, a cutting tool called *peshenkhef* was used to open the mouth of the physical body. In Mexico, the sacrificial location was also within a pyramid and the ritual was conducted by a high priest and four assistants. A sacrificial knife was used to strike a hard blow to the head of the *dead-victim*, which was thought to free the *soul* to ascend directly into the heavens.

Part of initiation into certain *mysteries* included a similar ritual called *tonsure*, meaning to shave the head. It is based upon the idea of releasing spiritual consciousness from the body and allowing the soul to, as in Egypt, take up journey with Osiris. In the latter underworld, Osiris is accompanied by Anubis, the dog or jackal-headed deity, and in Central America Quetzalcoatl is accompanied by Xolotl, another dog-headed companion, as he attempts to retrieve the skeletons of those killed in a great deluge.

We often find Anubis is associated with the cemetery or death god known as *Upuaut*, a name which translates to *Opener of the Ways*. Osiris and his followers were associated with the constellation Orion just as Isis was associated with the *dog star* Sirius (Sopdet). As with Sirius, Orion has a dog companion known as *Canis Major* – the *Great Dog* following the *Great Hunter*.

To reach the heavens in these stories a "rope ladder" was said to extend down like a hand of God. Such a rope is also used by shamanistic cultures to depict how their shamans reached into other worlds.

In the sacred Hindu text <u>Satpatha Brahmana</u> we are informed of how the Seven Sages (or Rishis) - responsible for guiding Kings in ancient India like the Heliopolitan priests guided kings in ancient Egypt - were known in former times as the *Rikshas*, or bears. They therefore shared a relationship with those stars comprising the *Big Dipper* within the larger constellation of the *Great Bear – Ursa Major*. Also known as the Plough, the *Big Dipper* has another more sacred name, the *Seven Sisters*. A fascinating relationship can be recognized thus with ancient Egyptian *mystery* traditions since these *imperishable stars*, as they are known, are referenced in the Pyramid Texts: *"Make your adobe among the imperishable stars…"*

This is where the Pharaoh calls home after death and a *stellar rebirth* sometimes associated with Orion if not the Plough. The latter also relates to the Pharaoh as an extension and embodiment of Osiris. Whereas it was the goal of a Pharaoh to maintain *ma'at*, expressed as a goddess (Ma'at) of cosmic harmony and balance, the Seven Sages of ancient India likewise attempted to maintain what Hindus still today refer to as *dharma*, or cosmic harmony and balance. Both *ma'at* and *dharma* share another interesting correlation with the *mystery* tradition known as *The Way*, or simply "right way," found everywhere from the ancient Americas and Egypt to the Middle East and Japan.

We likewise find that the *Yellow Emperor* of China, a man credited with founding Chinese culture and traditional Chinese Medicine, took to the heavens as a dragon at the end of his life so that he would be reborn as a star.

The same is said about the people conquered by Jimmu, Japan's first emperor. Those people were called the Mononobe clan, descended from Nigihayahi, who came down from *Takamagahara* in a "flying ship."

Birthed from Ursa Major is not only a home for Pharaohs and Rishis, or for Mesoamerican kings, but the fierce and cunning tiger. The Chinese consider the tiger to be the true *king of the jungle* and believe they live for 1,000 years. The demonic spirit Buer (Bauer), known from a 16th-century grimoire, is known to appear as a lion or tiger. Interestingly, Buer is a great archer like the hunters Orion and Osiris, and is associated with Jupiter Ammon, or just Amon (Amun), later to become Amun-Ra. Interestingly, earlier Mexican cultures used the double-puma, found in Uxmal, which is a mirror of the Egyptian *Akeru*, the lion gods of *yesterday* and *today*. They are like the later Roman god Janus who has two faces. These double-faced-headed deities hold *open* heavenly gates by which the sun passes each day from east to west. Similar images are found throughout the world relating to various flood myths; a breastplate at Tiahuanaco in Central America depicts two felines held at the throat by a Gilgamesh-like hero; a Knife from Egypt shows two lions held by a similar hero figure in the same manner; motifs from Mesopotamia depict the same, and artwork of the Indus-Sarasvati civilization also depicts two tigers being held by the throat.

The practice of *opening the mouth* also stunningly stretches into the ancient Japanese world. Antony Cummins explains in <u>The Dark Side of Japan</u> how *"when a local person dies, the village will put money together to call a shaman and have them perform the ritual of 'opening the mouth of the dead' to help the soul on its way."*

There are, as always, numerous ways in which such a ceremony may be interpreted. Here we have a literal image brought to mind of the barbaric smashing of a human skull, fueled by some primitive belief that it would be released from the body. Contrary to this interpretation is a more symbolic, or metaphoric, one. We find here an appropriate manner by which *Shu*, god of air, was invoked, since it was he who stood between heaven and earth, propping up the sky goddess *Nut*. This ceremony was performed on a statute of the dead that had been erected and placed in their tomb. The mouth of said statue was then *opened* by priests, according to the ascribed ceremony, and as told in the <u>Book of the Dead</u>. Author Kurt Seligmann explains in <u>The Mirror of Magic</u> that the statue was placed on a mound, which symbolized the "funeral mountain." It was there placed against an arch *"beyond which the mummy lay."* Next, it received fluid, or the KA of the deceased, *"that entered the image through the nape, causing the statue to come to life."* The mouth was opened!

The Egyptians described the soul by the separate elements of *KA*, *BA*, and *AKH*. The BA appears in the form of a bird, symbolizing mobility after death as the soul passes into the life thereafter; the KA also survived the death of the body and is said to reside in a picture or statue of the deceased. The KA remains with the mummy and reflects *life* in the grave. All those seemingly silly ornaments placed in tombs were used by this part of the soul. Images, statues, and worldly materials were placed near the dead to attract the KA. More specifically, these replicas become *real* through magical operations. As for the AKH, or *spirit*, it had to travel through the *underworld* and stand up to the *Final Judgement* before being granted access to the *afterlife*.

~

To circumvent the trials of the underworld was to conquer death and be *born again*. It is to be understood that the *heart* was a symbol of all *desires* of *flesh* and *animal instinct*, and only by a *feather* was the soul ready to transcend the *infernal world*. Those still maintaining attachment to spiritual death, i.e., *life*, were not granted access to the *Temple of Wisdom* because their *hearts* were heavier than their *souls*. In other words, their *desires* for flesh outweighed their *desires* for spirit. *The eater of the dead* consumed those *souls* still trapped by the material beast - all those considered spiritual dead, but physically alive.

The belief in *Stellar Rebirth* was a metaphor for the process of *initiation* into the *secrets of nature*. Great irony exists in teaching that these were barbaric rituals and literalisms believed in by some primitive fools, since such symbols were a highly sophisticated theology, theurgy, and psychology. To *open the mouth* by striking a blow to the head was symbolic of allowing the soul to freely ascend through the Crown Chakra, Kether, etc., to *source*. This was portrayed in the drama of the *mysteries* when an initiate after *three days* would be lifted by the *Lion's Paw* to greet the rising sun. And thus, they were *born again* as a *Son of God*; birthed by the *universal mother* a second time, but now under the tutelage of the *Widow*. Beneath the feet of the *Static Isis* is also inscribed: *"The Fruit Which I have Brought Forth is the Sun."* This *fruit* is the sun, the *redeemer* who gives us opportunity to be saved from darkness and ignorance.

On the right is a priest with his wand about to "open the mouth" of an effigy, as reproduced from Kurt Seligmann's, <u>The Mirror of Magic</u>.

The Egyptians separated the soul into three parts: KA, BA and AKH. Here we see part of the soul escaping from the body in form of a bird, while leaving the Mummy behind.

Published in Kurt Seligmann's, <u>The Mirror of Magic</u>.

The Dragon & Stella Maris

The conquering of our *ego* and *instinct*, or rather its subduing, is expressed in the allegory of slaying a great beast or dragon. This lower form of consciousness ravages our soul, dragging us into the underworld of *desire* like Hades does Persephone. And such desire is truly *hell*, an underworld which represents the foundation for the *fall of man*.

When one slays the dragon, it is said they have slain the *beast of material influences* and gained access to its store of treasure. The Biblical book of Revelation, chapter 12:1-4, describes both the *Universal Mother* and the *Great Dragon*. It is appropriate to again provide the first few verses here, and then continue with the next:

> *"A great sign appeared in heaven: a woman clothed with the sun, with the moon under her feet and a crown of twelve stars on her head. She was pregnant and cried out in pain as she was about to give birth. Then another sign appeared in heaven: an enormous red dragon with seven heads and ten horns and seven crowns on its heads. Its tail swept a third of the stars out of the sky and flung them to the earth. The dragon stood in front of the woman who was about to give birth, so that it might devour her child the moment he was born."*

The woman clothed with the sun, with the moon at her feet, and stars crowned upon her head, is the goddess in one of her many forms. Her face is covered with a veil, symbolic of *emotionalism* and *ignorance*, which forever stand as obstacles to the *truth* found in the scattered pieces of her lost husband. The veil, again, signifies that which conceals *wisdom* from the spiritually dead: *"No Mortal Man Hath Ever Me Unveiled."* She is *Stella Maris*, the star of the sea and guardian of the ocean like Aphrodite, who was born of its foam, or as Venus was born of the shell. She is the *World Soul*, or nurturer all of creation. She rules over the moon and thus water, menstruation, fertility, birth, and so on. This explains why she stands on a crescent moon (waxing or waning) for Selene-Luna influences the water upon Earth and plays a vital role in the development of life. Also, the Latin *crescere* comes *crescent*, a word meaning "to grow."

The dragon standing in front of the woman is chaos in its adversarial form known as the Hebrew *śāṭān*, among other similar characters that represent the same. The serpents around the feet of our Static Isis represent the same dragon Typhon-Set, that monstrous beast ready to devour her child upon birth.

Truth is a savior from the chaos of deception and confusion, of ignorance and darkness. Every child is born into the same world of illusion, hunted always by the predator, and swallowed up by tempest. Even as adults many of us are still children drowning in a vast ocean and encircled by leviathan. This is the origin of Jesus saving Peter from the wind and waves in Matthew 14.

The woman's child is the savior of mankind, collectively and individually, representing the sun in the macrocosm and rebirth in microcosm.

As the dragon waits to devour her child, we are reminded of the light extinguishing properties that darkness seems to have, despite the power of even a single candlelight. As it prepares to "devour her child the moment he was born" we are also reminded of the calls for infanticide ordered by King Herod and King Kansa.

Manly Hall writes of the goddess, and particularly of Isis, how she was *Nature personified* in all aspects:

"The statues of Isis were decorated with the sun, moon, and stars, and many emblems pertaining to the earth, over which Isis was believed to rule (as the guardian spirit of Nature personified). Several images of the goddess have been found upon which the marks of her dignity and position were still intact... The deity was generally represented as a partly nude woman, often pregnant, sometimes loosely covered with a garment either of green or black color, or of four different shades intermingled-black, white, yellow, and red."

Pertaining to the "crown of twelve stars on her head" we may figure the associations with signs of the zodiac. The flag of the European Union includes twelve stars and refers to the goddess.

The Labyrinth & Poimandres

Europa was a princess of Tyre, courted by Zeus in the form of a bull. She bore him three sons, one of which was Minos, the legendary king of Crete, whose wife Pasiphaë gave birth to the *Minotaur*. This creature was half-man-half-bull and confined in a labyrinth made by Daedalus. The monster represents our *animal self*, or the dragon, that comprises part of our being. He was slain by Theseus, the son of Poseidon.

A labyrinth represents the difficult path placed before all students of occult philosophy in navigating the many passages and secret chambers that conceal *truth*. It also represents the common difficulties of life. Those able to overcome and learn from such difficulties are said to slay the Minotaur like Theseus, and those unable to do so are themselves killed, or lost in the labyrinth of illusion. By completing the maze, a student is to find that at the center is *self* and that all answers come from the *divine* within. Killing the Minotaur is an *animal sacrifice* of the *ego* and a *human sacrifice* of *passions* to God.

The symbolism of the bull directly relates to the horns of Isis, the Egyptian bull Apis, and that bull killed by Mithra(s) to bring about the age of Pisces.

When Hermes was able to free his consciousness - like the slaying of Minotaur - from the bondage of bodily senses, and the illusions of the material world, his divine nature revealed to him the *mysteries* in the form of a *great dragon*. This dragon spoke to Hermes identifying itself as *Poimandres*, the *Mind of the Universe* and the *Creative Intelligence*. This dragon provoked Hermes to hold its image in his mind, and immediately the creature's form changed. When the dragon spoke, it explained:

"I Thy God am the Light and the Mind which were before substance was divided from spirit and darkness from Light. And the Word which appeared as a pillar of flame out of the darkness is the Son of God, born of the mystery of the Mind. The name of that Word is Reason. Reason is the offspring of Thought and Reason shall divide the Light from the darkness and establish Truth in the midst of the waters."

Hall relates that what the dragon explained to Hermes was how light formed in the spiritual universe:

> *"Where it had stood there was a glorious and pulsating Radiance. This Light was the spiritual nature of the Great Dragon itself. Hermes was 'raised' into the midst of this Divine Effulgence and the universe of material things faded from his consciousness. Presently a great darkness descended and, expanding, swallowed up the Light. Everything was troubled. About Hermes swirled a mysterious watery substance which gave forth a smoke like vapor. The air was filled with inarticulate moanings and sighings which seemed to come from the Light swallowed up in the darkness. His mind told Hermes that the Light was the form of the spiritual universe and that the swirling darkness which had engulfed it, represented a material substance."*

Siegfried slaying the dragon of material *desires*,
as reproduced from Mark Booth's, The Sacred History.

Esoteric Nursery Rhymes & Fairy Tales

It has been made clear so far that the stories of *Sleeping Beauty*, *Cinderella*, *Snow White*, and *Beauty and the Beast*, among others, although considered mere entertainment, contribute a deep message to the *divine seed* ready to be *sprouted* within us all. So too is the fairy tale of *Mother Goose* similarly related. The goose or swan is a symbol of *purity*, especially when white, which holds an association with the *sun*, and sometimes the *moon* since it reflects sunlight.

Two swans are said to represent the goose in books on symbols, while legends say that a goose called *hamsa*, an aquatic bird of passage like the goose, or a swan, laid the egg from which the entire universe formed. *Maternal nature* is thus present in these birds and directly associates them with Isis. The Greek goddess of love, beauty, fertility, and sexual love, Aphrodite, is also depicted riding a swan.

In Hindu belief, the swan lived between the physical and spiritual worlds, perhaps relating to the journey of an initiate into the underworld, and they therefore share relation with Hecate, goddess of crossroads. Her counterparts are the moon goddesses known in Greece as Artemis and Selene, or in Rome as Diana and Luna.

As with the Roman legend of Romulus and Remus, the personification of Gemini, the Greeks told stories of Castor and Pollux. Their moth was Leda, who was seduced by Zeus while she was in the form of a swan. Encyclopedia Britannica explains further:

> "*Variant legends gave divine parentage to both the twins and possibly also to Clytemnestra, with all three of them having hatched from the eggs of Leda, while yet other legends say that Leda bore the twins to her mortal husband, Tyndareus. Still other variants say that Leda may have hatched out Helen from an egg laid by the goddess Nemesis, who was similarly approached by Zeus in the form of a swan.*"

Aphrodite riding a swan, from a Greek vase.

Romulus and Remus (Castor and Pollux), published in The Secret History of the World, by Mark Booth.

Mother Goose is considered a *fairy tale character*, defined as a child's story about magical and imaginary beings, but she is also an *archetype* of the feminine principle. In Boston, Massachusetts, there is a tombstone of one *Mary Goose* at the Old Granary Burying Ground. Some believe that she is the author of countless nursery rhymes attributed to the famous "Mother Goose." Although local legend tells of Elizabeth Foster Goose, who entertained children with songs and rhymes, the date of burial is 1690 and does not relate to the actual "mother" of so many of these popular poems, songs, and stories. The character may have also evolved from the 8th century with Bertrada II of Laon, the mother of Charlemagne, first emperor of the Holy Roman Empire. She was the patroness of children and obtained the title of "Goose-foot Bertha" or "Queen Goosefoot" due to a malformation of her foot. By 17th-century France, the term "Mother Goose", or "mere l'oye", was a phrase referring to a woman who captivated children with colorful stories. It is likely that the legend from Boston is a branch of the evolving

A nineteenth-century illustration of Mother Goose fairy tales published in <u>The Secret History of the World</u>, by Mark Booth. Mother Goose is Isis, a moon goddess like Selene-Luna, and priestess of the *secret philosophy*.

concept of a *mother goose*, as is the usage of the phrase in 17th century France and its later association with "nursery rhymes" in general. The latter terminology was not used until the late 18th and early 19th centuries referring to songs and poems of a traditional nature.

If we trace the title of a "mother goose" into the popular ideas and myths of previous civilizations, then we find its exact, and probably obvious, *archetypical* meaning. A "mother" is obviously nurturing to her children, and the archetype of the mother represents a nurturer in general.

The "goose" is considered a message giver and, like Hermes-Mercury, provides divine communications – a baby is birthed as a soul from the divine realm.

Its feathers are typically used for making writing quills.

Geese are said to lay the golden egg of the sun, which is symbolic of new life, children, and the nurturing qualities of the sun.

In Greece the goose was a guardian of home and children. The feathers of a goose were used for bedding.

All these symbolic relations preserve the archetype of a mother caring for her children, singing them to sleep, placing them in bed, and watching over them like the sun and moon.

These classical nursery rhymes were first published as a *Mother Goose* collection with other folk tales in 1697 by Charles Perrault. Some of the story fragments are more accurately defined as parables though as they illustrate a moral or spiritual lesson. Others are like myth in that they preserve certain historical elements in the form of entertaining poems, songs, and stories.

An English nursery rhyme and children's song "It's Raining, It's Pouring" should be considered more of a parable, in that it tells of an old man who has perhaps had too much to drink, hurt himself, and never woke up again. The rhyme may be reinterpreted from a variety of perspectives, and thus take on a life of its own. This allows for, once again, the use of imagination and visualization in unlocking the *mysteries*:

It's raining. It's pouring.
The old man is snoring
He went to bed and bumped his head
and didn't get up in the morning.

In the case of "Humpty Dumpty" we have more of a historical account. For Humpty was not an egg or person, but a massive siege cannon used by Royalist forces - the king's men - during the English Civil War. It was placed on a church tower but when the structure was destroyed Humpty fell and could not be put back together again:

Humpty Dumpty sat on a wall,
Humpty Dumpty had a great fall;
All the king's horses and all the king's men
Couldn't put Humpty together again.

The "Muffin Man" is another traditional nursery rhyme with historical context, because a muffin man would, like a butcher, take his product to market, ring a bell and attempt to attract customers:

Oh, do you know the muffin man,
The muffin, the muffin man,
Oh, do you know the muffin man,
That lives on Drury Lane?

One nursery rhyme was written as a couplet, first published in 1806 as "The Star." It was later set to the music of a popular French nursery rhyme from an earlier date, which also forms the basis for a work of Mozart:

Twinkle, twinkle, little star,
How I wonder what you are,
Up above the world so high,
Like a diamond in the sky.

"Three blind mice" has a darker origin, as it relates to three protestant bishops who unsuccessfully conspired to overthrow Queen Mary I of England. As punishment they were burned at the stake:

Three blind mice,   *She cut off their tails*
Three blind mice.   *With a carving knife.*
See how they run,   *Did you ever see*
See how they run!   *Such a sight in your life*
They all ran after   *As three blind mice?*
the farmer's wife

Other darker origins include perhaps the most well-known basis for "Ring around the Rosie," which is centered on the suffering felt from what we call the *Black Death* (which was ultimately not caused by rodents, but unsanitary conditions coupled with the earth passing through the tail of a comet). The "ring around the rosy" was a red rash that appeared on those afflicted, while a "pocketful of posies" were bunches of flowers used to conceal the smell of rotting flesh and death. It goes without saying that "ashes" and to "fall down" refers to death:

> *Ring around the rosy,*
> *A pocketful of posies,*
> *Ashes, Ashes,*
> *We all fall down.*

The rhyme "Ring around the Rosie" has a dark and historical origin, but one that is a result of what might be called a natural disaster. In the case of "Mary, Mary, Quite Contrary" we have both a dark and historical origin, too, but one that is a result of the psychotic Queen Mary I of England, otherwise known as "Bloody Mary." Her reign of power from 1553 to 1558 is remembered by the execution of hundreds of protestants. Her garden, which is really a cemetery, grows with "silver bells" and "cockle shells" which are both instruments of torture.

Silver Bells were thumbscrews placed onto both thumbs and turned until the bones were crushed. *Cockle Shells* were vice-like grips attached to the genitals and slowly tightened. Her pretty "maids" were based on "The Maiden," a device used for decapitation before the guillotine:

> *Mary, Mary, quite contrary,*
> *How does your garden grow?*
> *With silver bells, and cockle shells,*
> *And pretty maids all in a row.*

In the story of Snow White, we find reference to the resting *seed* of *purity*, i.e., our soul, in the form of *the fairest of them all*. She is a beautiful woman with *lips red as blood, hair black and ebony* and *skin as white as snow*. The *poisoned apple* is Edenic and preserves the alchemical and transmutative *red* (apple skin) and *white* (internal body of apple). After the witch eats the non-poisoned bit, Snow White eats the other half and falls into a coma like *Sleeping Beauty* and *Persephone*. Snow White's story also includes the *Magic Mirror*, reminding us of Alice and Through the Looking Glass, that portal to another world. We also find the *seven dwarves*: Dopey, Happy, Bashful, Sleepy, Grumpy, Sneezy, and Doc. These characters share a relationship with the seven classical planets, and days of the week. Furthermore, they relate to the seven earth demons in Scandinavian myth: Toki, Skavaerr, Varr, Dun, Orinn, Grerr, and Radsvid. The number may also relate to the *Seven Sins* and *Seven Virtues*. Originally a German fairy tale first published in 1812 by The Brothers Grimm, *Snow White* was known by the title *Sneewittchen* or *Schneewittchen*. As the *fairest of them all*, a symbol of absolute *purity*, Snow White is thus equivalent to the goddess Isis, as, again, is *Cinderella*.

The *glass coffin* motif is *memento mori*, a reminder of *death*. Snow White is the purity of our soul in a deep rest like Sleeping Beauty or Osiris in his chest.

Schneewittchen by Alexander Zick

  The story of <u>Beauty and the Beast</u> was published in 1740, preserving a similar *secret philosophy* to *Mother Goose, Sleeping Beauty, Snow White,* and so on. It is attributed to the original fairy tale written by Gabrielle-Suzanne Barbot de Villeneuve of Paris called *La Belle et la Bête,* although the most common version was written by Jeanne-Marie Leprince de Beaumont. As we have noted in early chapters, the apple from Eden and Snow White is poisoned with *realization* of *individuality* (nakedness), a temporary and perceived separation from *source*, a droplet of water in a vessel floating in the sea, and an amnesia of our *divinity*. Such is Prince Adam in *Beauty and the Beast* a divine turned animal. His *castle* is our physical body as described in 1 Corinthians 6:19-20, which relates:

> *"Do you not know that your bodies are temples of the Holy Spirit, who is in you, whom you have received from God? You are not your own; you were bought at a price. Therefore honor God with your bodies."*

The character *Belle* represents the *bell,* an instrument which rings with harmony to calm all wickedness. This is one reasons churches ring bells, besides to alert the community that service is about to begin. *Brass Bells* in particular have been used for centuries to ward off evil, demons, and general malevolence. Just as kind words with positive attention attract beauty, and mean words with negative intention attract ugliness, harmonious sounds attract he sympathy of similar energies or spirits. The same is true for colors, suffumigations (incenses), candles, metals, herbs, plants, etc.

Belle must therefore *calm the beast* with her beauty, implied harmony (bells), and love, and the Beast himself must learn such things and become deserving of their graces.

Beauty and the Beast by Jeanne-Marie Le Prince de Beaumont (Illustration by Walter Crane)

In the book written by Jeanne-Marie Le Prince de Beaumont, and illustrated by Walter Crane, *Beauty* is depicted in the red robes of *hierodule.* The scarlet robe of beauty, as with the red rose, is the *truth* by which *ignorance* is overcome by the redemption of the blood of Christ; it is birth and death – what is given by woman to man. In *Beauty and the Beast,* we find Christ's rose wilting, which is symbolic of the rotting of *soul* in *matter,* as it awaits redemption from the *true love* of *beauty* and the redeeming red blood of the loving savior. Keen observers and *students of ancient philosophy* may have noticed another peculiar similarity between these esoteric stories. In the cases, for example, of Belle (Beauty and the Beast), Alice (in Wonderland), Dorothy (Wizard of Oz), Snow White, Cinderella, and Jasmine (Aladdin), each woman is wearing blue and white. In the cases of Belle through Snow White, each is wearing an almost identical white top with blue cover. In the case of the latter two, each are wearing similar blue and white clothing. There could be several interpretations of this fact, though it is not coincidence, considering the clear preservation of an *esoteric tradition* within these most iconic and culturally recognizable stories. *Blue* typically symbolizes vigilance, perseverance, and justice, or those things which sit on top of the *white* purity of soul-spirit, represented by the *flawless goddess* we know as Isis or Mother Mary.

Mary as Isis, or *The Immaculate Conception of Los Venerables*, by Bartolomé Esteban Murillo, 1678

I, ISIS AM ALL THAT HAS BEEN, THAT IS OR SHALL BE; NO MORTAL MAN HATH EVER ME UNVEILED.

THE FRUIT WHICH I HAVE BROUGHT FORTH IS THE SUN

The Static Isis

ISIDIS
Magnæ Deorum Matris
APVLEIANA DESCRIPTIO.

Nomina varia Ifidis.

Ifis
Minerua
Venus
Iuno
Proferpina
Ceres
Diana
Rhea feu Tellus
Peffinuncia
Rhramnufia
Bellona
Hecate
Luna
Polymorphus dæmon.

Ἶσις πανδεχὴς πολύμορφ@ δαίμων.
Μυειώνυμ@ φύσις, ὕλη.

Explicationes fymbolorum Ifidis.

A Diuinitarem, mundum, orbes cœleftes
BB Iter Lunæ flexuofum, & vim fœcundatiuam notat.
CC Tutulus, vim Lunæ in herbas, & plantas.
D Cereris fymbolum, Ifis enim fpicas innenit.
E Byffina veftis multicolor, multiformem Lunæ faciem.
F Innentio frumenti.
G Dominium in omnia vegetabilia.
H Radios lunares.
I Genius Nili malorum auerruncus.
K Incrementa & decrementa Lunæ.
L Humectat. vis Lunę.
M Lunæ vis victrix, & vis diuinandi.
N Dominium in humores & mare.
O Terræ fymbolū, & Medicinæ inuentrix.
P Fœcunditas, quæ fequitur terram irrigatam.
Q Aftrorum Domina.
R Omnium nutrix.
S } Terræ marifque
M } Domina.

Ἀκρα Θεῶν Μήτηρ ταύτη πολύτιμ@. ΙΣΙΣ.

A woodcut of the goddess Isis made by Athanasius Kircher
and based on the portrayal of her by the philosopher Apuleius.

Sophia & the Serpent

The Goddess of Wisdom, Venus Cults & *Telos*

The regenerative power of the female, and her great wisdom as carrier of life, is a central theme throughout all human history, often expressed by explicit images of genitalia, or as exaggerated figurines of pregnant women. Her fertility aspect was embodied by Venus in Rome and Aphrodite in Greece. Her wisdom was attributed to Minerva in Greece, Athena in Rome, Lakshmi in India, and Cikap-kamuy of the indigenous Ainu people. Owls are still seen as embodiments of wisdom in Japan today, as evidenced at So-sha Shrine in Himeji. The owl was often associated with both fertility and wisdom as a nocturnal creature having access to the *hidden realm* and its spiritual secrets.

Across Britain, Ireland, Spain, and France can be found explicit images of the *Sheela-na-gigs*, a primarily medieval stone figure showing a naked woman spreading her legs and genitals. The word itself comes from the Irish *Sile na gcíoch*, meaning "Julia of the Breasts." What archeologists call the *Venus Figurine* is probably the oldest proof we have of *Mother Goddess* worship, which dates to 40,000 BCE. Between one and four inches, generally, these small statues have been found in Upper Paleolithic sites across Europe and Asia. The *Venus of Willendorf* figurine is considered one of the oldest pieces of "art" in the world despite the object being far more than a simple piece of creativity. These figurines represented a deep understanding and respect for the generative properties of the world and female, hence the reason earth itself became identified as the *cosmic womb* or mother. Despite their name, Venus Figurines predate the Roman goddess by thousands of years. Obviously, this means the Romans simply gave this *cult* their own name. According to World History Encyclopedia:

> *"The name is derived, in part, from theories that associate these figurines with fertility and sexuality, two traits associated with the Roman goddess."*

In Japan there is a *Venus Jōmon* that has been dated to around 3,000 BCE. In considering the far east, we could translate this Roman goddess to either *Inari Ōkami*, the spirit of foxes, rice, and fertility, or to *Kisshōten* (*Kichijōten*), a Buddhist goddess of beauty, happiness, and fertility. In India she is called *Lakshmi*.

Although the Greek goddess of wisdom is Minerva, their

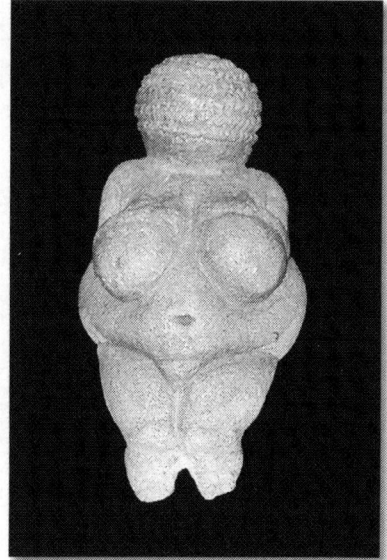

Venus of Willendorf, Austria, 1908. The carving dates back over 22,000 years.

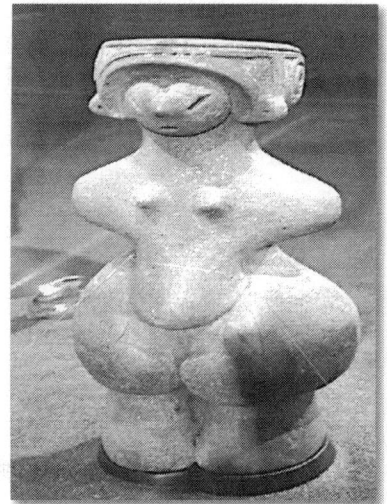

Venus Jōmon, excavated in Nagano, Japan.

Kichijōten painted on hemp.

word for *wisdom* is *Sophia* (Sofia), the essence of which was later personified as being female. Her name is concealed in the sacred practice of *philosophy*, a word taken from the Greek *philos,* meaning "love," and *sophy,* meaning "pure of religion" or "wisdom." From the Greek *philosophia* we obtain the definition, "lover of wisdom." This wisdom was extracted from the *hidden realm* from whence comes the soul-spirit into the womb.

A *sophist* was a paid teacher of philosophy in ancient Greece and the name further comes from *sophos,* meaning "wise." Therefore, the *philosopher* is a "lover of Sophia." This idea was extracted largely from Gnostic writings, including the Pistis Sophia. Wisdom is the central theme in numerous philosophies, including those of Hellenistic origin and the mystic sects of Christianity, Islam, and Judaism: *Gnosticism, Sufism* and *Kabbalah.* Sophia in one carnation is represented by a dove, or the *Holy Spirit* of the Christian Trinity.

Since serpents are traditionally used as symbols of wisdom it is common to find references to Sophia as the "serpent goddess." The color of her manifestation is violet, which has the shortest wavelength and therefore rests at the highest position of the color spectrum. The violet cloth is a common symbol used in Christianity, oftentimes draped over a cross. Violet is traditionally associated with royalty, and it symbolizes the highest realm of visible light, the *Kingdom of Heaven.* Both Sophia and the serpent are expressions of white light, which if broken through a prism or similar atmospheric phenomenon will display the seven colors of a rainbow: red, orange, yellow, green, blue, indigo, and violet. Each chakra, or bodily energy center, also represents a segment of white light. This is what it means to have a "light body" or when someone says that we are all "beings of light."

These colors are further associated with particular parts of the body and its endocrine system; the Base Chakra is red, located at the base of the spine and connected with the adrenal gland; the Sacral Chakra is orange, located at the center of the abdomen and connected with the gonad; the Solar Plexus Chakra is yellow, located near the stomach and connected with the pancreas; the Heart Chakra is green, located in the center of the chest and connected with the thymus; the Throat Chakra is blue, located at the base of the throat and connected with the thyroid; the Brow Chakra is indigo, located at the center of the forehead and associated with the pituitary gland; the Crown Chakra is violet, located at the very top of the head and associated with the pineal gland.

These chakras are the *flowers* and *fruit* of our vegetable body, and the *kundalini,* or *snake energy* of Sophia, is found on our Edenic tree, i.e., our spine.

The chakra colors also relate to the seven classical planets and their metals. The Base Chakra is red, and the base metal is lead. Both are associated with the god of the infernal. The Crown Chakra is violet and pure like gold. Both are associated with the heavenly Sun, the sacred color of which is said to be violet or blue in its association with wisdom.

In the Mayan creation myth of <u>Popul Vuh</u>, the *creator* is surrounded by blue light, which pays reference to those unique Hindu gods with blue skin. The text says, they *"who create, were on the waters as an ever increasing light. They were surrounded by green and blue."* The "increasing light" refers to the seven colors of a rainbow, green preceding blue, indigo, and violet.

Another translation of <u>Popul Vuh</u> says the creators were "hidden under… feathers" of green and blue:

> *"There was only immobility and silence in the darkness, in the night. Only the creator, the Maker, Tepeu, Gucumatz, the Forefathers, were in the water surrounded with light. They were hidden under green and blue feathers, and were therefore called Gucumatz. By nature they were great sages and great thinkers. In this manner the sky existed and also the Heart of Heaven, which is the name of God and thus He is called."*

This is nearly identical to what Hall says the great dragon told Hermes: *"Light was the form of the spiritual universe and that the swirling darkness which had engulfed it, represented a material substance."* In relating these colors to the twelve zodiac signs, Hall says: Aries is assigned pure red; Taurus, red-orange; Gemini, pure orange; Cancer, orange-yellow; Leo, pure yellow; Virgo, yellow-green; Libra, pure green; Scorpio, green-blue; Sagittarius, pure blue; Capricorn, blue-violet; Aquarius, pure violet; and to Pisces, violet-red. He further refers to the theory of solar colors:

> *"The theory so long held of three primary and four secondary colors is purely exoteric, for since the earliest periods it has been known that there are seven, and not three, primary colors, the human eye being capable of estimating only three of them. Thus, although green can be made by combining blue and yellow, there is also a true or primary green which is not a compound. This can he proved by breaking up the spectrum with a prism."*

Of the previous it has traditionally been preserved that *consciousness*, *intelligence*, and *force* are related to specific colors that further correspond to the constitutions of man, and triune nature of eternal states:

Consciousness	Blue	Spirit	Heaven
Intelligence	Yellow	Mind	Earth
Force	Red	Body	Hell

According to Helena Blavatsky the seven sacred colors are related to the septenary constitutions of man and the seven states of matter:

<u>Color</u>	<u>Principles of Man</u>	<u>States of Matter</u>
Violet	Chaya, or Etheric Double	Ether
Indigo	Higher Manas, or Spiritual Intelligence	Critical State called Air
Blue	Auric Envelope	Steam or Vapor
Green	Lower Manas, or Animal Soul	Critical State
Yellow	Buddhi, or Spiritual Soul	Water
Orange	Prana, or Life Principle	Critical State
Red	Kama Rupa, or Seat of Animal Life	Ice

Here are listed the *Auric Colors* and their *indications*, as extracted from <u>The Secret Doctrine of the Rosicrucians</u> by Magus Incognito (a pseudonym):

Black indicates hatred, malice, revenge, and similar depressed feelings.

Gray (bright shade) indicates selfishness; (ghastly shade) indicates fear and terror; (dark shade) indicates melancholy.

Green (bright live shade) indicates diplomacy, worldly wisdom, suavity, tact, politeness, and "polite deceit" in general; (dirty, muddy shade) indicates low deceit, low cunning falsehood, and trickery of a low order; (dark, dull shade) indicates jealousy, envy, and covetousness.

Red is the color of passions in general, but there are a great variety of its manifestations: (dull and appearing as if mixed with smoke) indicates sensuality and the lower animal passions; (appearing as bright flashes, sometimes light lightning in form) indicates anger. Red is usually shown on a black background when anger arises from hatred or malice and on a greenish background when the anger arises from jealousy, envy, etc., but without any background when the anger arises from "righteous indignation" and the defence of what is believed to be righteous cause. Red (crimson shade) represents love and varies in shade according to the character of the type of passion named. For instance, a dull and heavy crimson shade indicates a gross, sensual love, while the brighter, clearer, and more pleasing shades indicate love blended with higher feelings and accompanied by higher ideals. The highest form of human love between the sexes manifests as a beautiful rose red.

Brown (reddish shade) indicates avarice and greed.

Orange (bright shade) represents pride and ambition.

Yellow, in its various shades, represents intellectual power in its various forms. A beautiful, clear, golden yellow indicates high intellectual attainment, logical reasoning, unprejudiced judgment, and discrimination. A dark, dull yellow shade indicates intellectual power concerning itself with thoughts and subjects of a low, selfish order. The shade between the two just indicated denotes the presence of higher or lower thought, respectively, with the dark representing the lower, and light the higher.

Blue (dark shade) represents religious emotion, feeling, and tendencies in general. The dull shades, however, indicate religious emotion of a low order, while the clearer brighter shades indicate religious emotions of a high order. These shades vary and range from a dull indigo to a beautiful bright violet. Light Blue indicates spirituality. This spiritual blue is of clear, transparent, and luminous appearance, which is difficult to describe in words.

The latter is *Sophia*. We know that the body also emits visible color radiations, accompanied by infrared radiations, radiations of ultra-violet, and those radiations beyond ultraviolet. These radiations form the color(s) that surrounds the human body, i.e., the *aura*. This *energy shell* is believed to be formed of radiating thoughts and emotions that span from violet to red. Many people believe this is what can be captured with *Kirlian Photography*.

In the Pistis Sophia it is explained how *true wisdom* extinguishes the seed of the serpent, a situation identical to how Mary crushes the head of that same infernal creature with the birth of her son. In both cases it is the darkness of winter, ignorance, and life in general that begs for salvation in the forms of warmth, light, wisdom, and renewal.

Explained elsewhere is Leviathan, a great sea monster referenced in several texts to have been defeated by God. We find in the Zohar a description of how *"the magical serpent, the son of the Sun, was about to devour the world,"* here represented by the ouroboros, *"when the Sea, daughter of the moon, set her foot upon his head and subdued him."* For this reason, Venus was daughter of the sea and Diana was daughter of the moon. Therefore, even a *Mary* signifies the salt of the sea, while the moon is called *Mother*.

Of Sophia's role with the serpent, some stories explain how she accidentally gave birth to what Gnostics call *Demiurge*, which took credit for all the past accomplishments of Her creative force. The Gnostics referred to these creators, who were really distorters, as the *Archons* and observed that this *Demiurge* called *Ialdabaoth* was the god Yahweh. They saw him as a false and misleading god wishing to keep humanity in bondage. Author and researcher M. Don Schorn explains this of the false god in his book Legacy of the Elder Gods:

> *"The Gnostics identified that later god [Ialdabaoth] as Yahweh, the demiurge or 'living spirit,' the one declared by many to be the god of the Old Testament. It was thought that such as 'false god' made every effort to keep humanity in a state of ignorance, by concentrating only on material desires and goods, thereby keeping the celestial truth hidden from humans."*

The Demiurge (Ialdabaoth or Yahweh) is considered by some the "false prophet" and "trickster," deceiving mankind and separating him further from Sophia. In another way, he is the oppositional hardship that sprouts spiritual growth. In the Gnostic text known as On the Origins of the World, the Demiurge proclaims: *"I am God, and no other one exists except me."* To this his mother Sophia replies: *"You err, [blind god]. An enlightened immortal humanity exists before you!"* In other words, the physical world is merely an extension of *source*. The Greeks called this *Telos*, the *purpose* or *goal* pondered by philosophers. Many refer to *archons* as the seven planetary spheres.

The Pistis Sophia describes how Sophia is held captive after falling from her position on high, which parallels the myths of Persephone and Eurydice. She is rescued, according to general Gnostic writings, by Christ, her divine counterpart called *syzygy*. In other words she is Christ's bride.

In Japan this *source* is *musubi*, that which binds and ties like *religare* and *aslama*. Here we also find the *mother* still present today as the sun goddess Amaterasu, and her likeness in the root of the German sun, *die Sonne*. In Jainism, a nontheistic religion dating to the 6th-century BC

Nure-onna from the Gazu Hyakki Yagyō by Toriyama Sekien.

in India, which preaches salvation through multiple lives and non-injury to living creatures, we find the *Cosmic Woman*. In Finnish tradition the virgin of air, Ilmatar, is the creative spirit.

Within these stories is an underlying truth about birth, life, and death. The woman gives us life, but by extension guarantees us death. Life and death are competing forces and it is also possible to *love something to death*, and in death perhaps love is found. Love gives us life which gives us death, which in turn reminds us to love. Mary crushes the head of the serpent, who she took liberties with, by birthing the savior. The Japanese yokai Nure-Onna, a human devouring serpent usually with female head, like the serpent on the tree in the Garden, draws references to this fact.

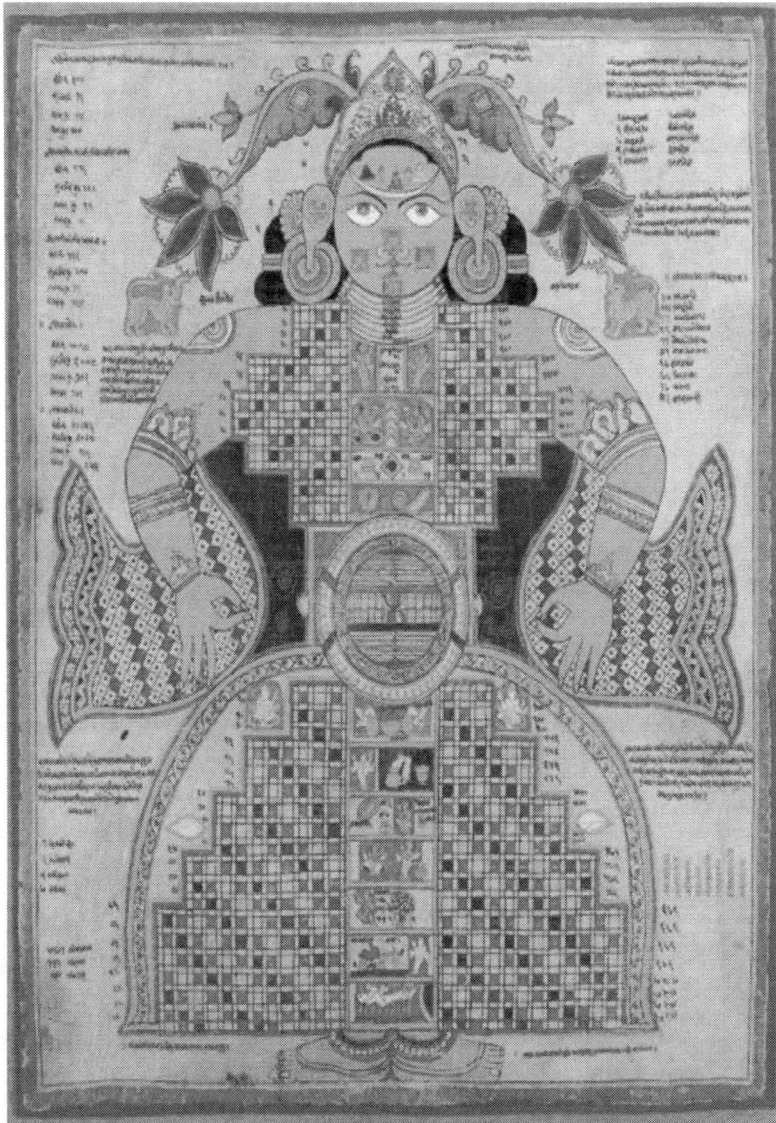

Cosmic Woman of Jainism.

The Lion Man & Little Green Men

"Let us come to the point now. It would be nice to hold on to the common belief that the UFOs are craft from a superior space-civilization, because this is a hypothesis science fiction has made widely acceptable, and because we are not altogether unprepared, scientifically and even, perhaps, militarily, to deal with such visitors. Unfortunately, however, the theory that flying saucers are material objects from outer space manned by a race originating on some other planet is not a complete answer. However strong the current belief in saucers from space, it cannot be stronger than the Celtic faith in the elves and the fairies, or the medieval belief in lutins, or the fear throughout the Christian lands, in the first centuries of our era, of demons and satyrs and fauns. Certainly, it cannot be stronger than the faith that inspired the writers of the Bible — a faith rooted in daily experiences with angelic visitation."

~ Jacques Vallée, <u>Passport to Magonia: From Folklore to Flying Saucers</u> ~

Discovered inside a German cave sometime in 1939, the "lion man" statue stands at 12 inches tall. Carved from mammoth tusk and estimated to be around 40,000 years old, the artifact is one of the earliest proofs of religious belief in the world – predating *Venus of Willendorf* by about 20,000 years, though she was an object of reproductive veneration. Rock art (paintings) in Indonesia, however, preserves evidence of other therianthropic beings dating to over 51,000 years ago. Although not perpetual in nature, it is likely that the evidence of mankind's earliest religious and spiritual beliefs will eventually be proven to be substantially older, and likely the result of his use of a combination of plant sources to make contact with the spirit world. Dr. Rick Strassman opens his classic work, <u>DMT: The Spirit Molecule</u>, with the following assessment:

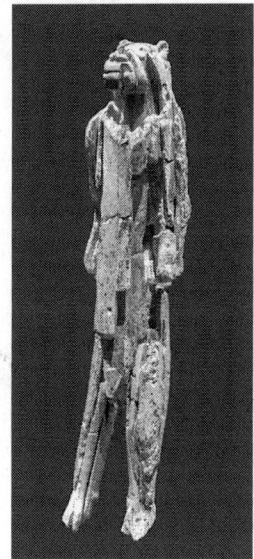

Lion Man was found in a German cave in the year 1939.

"The history of human use of plants, mushrooms, and animals for their psychedelic effects is far older than written history, and probably pre- dates the appearance of the modern human species. Ronald Siegel and Terence McKenna, for example, suggest that our apelike ancestors imitated other animals by eating things that caused unusual behavior. In this way, they discovered the earliest mind-altering substances. There is growing physical evidence that many ancient cultures used psychedelics for their effects on consciousness… Some authors have proposed that language developed out of psychedelically enhanced appreciation of, and associations with, early hominid mouth sounds. Others suggest that psychedelic states formed the basis of humans' earliest awareness of religious experience."

Under the influence of certain substances it is common for humans - we do not know about animals, though we can watch them under the same influences – to see grid patterns, spirals, windows, the double helix, garden-like environments, and half-human half-animal *therianthropes*.

Sometimes these geometric patterns are kaleidoscopic and are relatable to the art or language of Mayan, Aztec, or Islamic cultures. Other times these languages are more pronounced, looking like Arabic or Russian Cyrillic script. Perhaps psychedelic influences are indeed responsible for the development of language, further derived from those "*hominid mouth sounds.*"

Based on Dr. Strassman's study, the influence of DMT also produces interactions with highly sentient spiders, insectoids, reptilians, bees, dwarves, elves, clowns, tall beings, and beings that mimic the saguaro cactus. These beings are usually interested in emotion and will probe the body and mind to learn more. One volunteer even reported that one of the beings had "an elongated head" like those of the people who practice artificial cranial deformation.

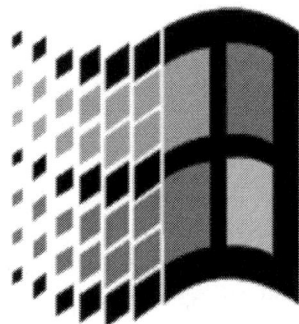

Paintings of window-like devices and dots (pixels) from El Castillo Cave in Spain, compared with Microsoft Windows logo.

The story of the Garden of Eden preserves details of a paradise garden with a half-human half-serpent creature (Lilith) that some may identify as *Mother Ayahuasca*. Considering that "a tree of life and knowledge" is often seen under the influence of DMT makes this consideration all the more powerful. It also lends credibility to the theory that the Revelation of St. John may have been induced by similar substances

These *plant spirits* can be personified as *little green men* or *fairies*, both having much in common with the current usage of the former identifying characteristics as they relate to *flying saucers* or *Unidentified Flying Objects* and their assumed inhabitants. The first object of this variety in myth is most certainly the *flying disc* of the sun, which rises in the east, is seen in the sky, and then crashes in the west. The associated spirits or entities are either anthropomorphic, therianthropic like the *Lion Man*, or fetal-like projections of our unconscious self.

We recover the *flying disc* wreckage by preserving its divine blessings in the form of myths, statues, paintings, carvings, and recognizing the sun's warmth, light, and protective fatherly qualities. The wreckage today, it is said, would be taken to a

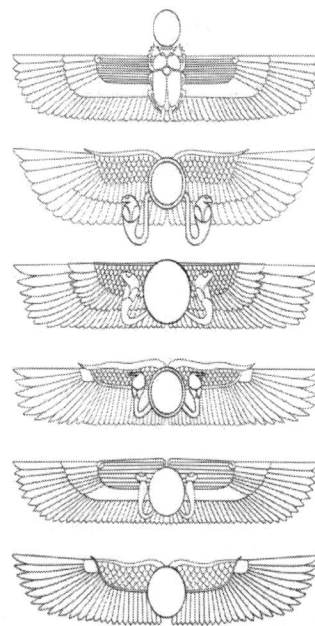

military or corporate base and reverse-engineered for divine gifts from some other more technologically advanced species – or God.

The *little green men* of today's lore are not unlike those of the plant kingdom from whence we obtain much about the nature of fairies, those small creatures that are almost always dressed in green. The classic UFO abduction story is indistinguishable from the same stories of fairy abductions: strange lights are seen in a field, the woods, or in the sky (a ring of lights defining the outline of a UFO, and *fairy circles* or *fairy lights*, which parallel *crop circles*); the victim is kidnapped, usually from a remote area and usually during the night, and taken to a strange place underground or in the air up high; they are subject to experiments, sometimes unknown and other times sexual, the latter often leading to offspring being produced; the victim is given knowledge - usually about healing themselves, their people, or the planet – or warnings about how humans should be careful of their technological developments, something that parallels our own societal fears like the use of atomic weapons. Usually the abductee is then returned home with limited to no memory of the encounter unless it is conjured.

What has just been described is not only a fairy abduction and a UFO abduction, but the oldest religious experience in the world: a *shamanic journey*. What the shaman experiences can also be directly likened to the suffering, torture, and transmogrification of Jesus. Images that preserve this fact, of a body pierced like the side of Jesus, Odin, or Prometheus, are called the *wounded man*. The only major difference between fairies, UFOs, and shamanism, is that shamans intend to embark on these journeys and usually climb the *sky rope* willingly and converse with the entities intentionally.

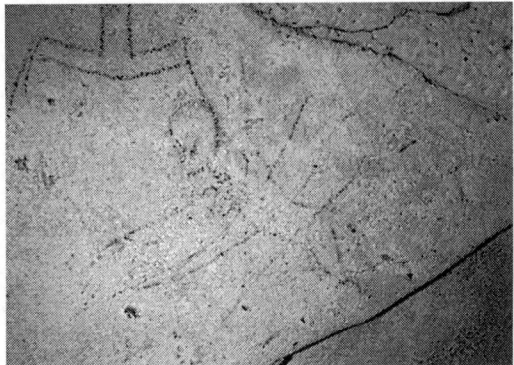

Wounded Man - Pech Merle cave in

Ethnobotanist Terence McKenna described some of these otherworldly beings as *"self-transforming elf machines."* He believed, based on countless experiences, that they are made from "syntax-divine light" and that their language is in essence sound that you can see manifest; *"it is made out of sound, it is sound, but you see it."* We recall: *God said, let there be light.*

In <u>The Mysteries and Secrets of Magic</u>, C. J. S. Thompson describes the *fairy* as being *"clad in green, heath-brown or grey,"* while often riding *"invisible horses and occasionally real ones whom they force to a great speed."* As for the *elf*, they are *"skilled in the mechanical arts"* and their home is within *"the celestial regions."*

These cosmic realms are not dimensions we can interact with under normal states of consciousness. We must either partake of the various *plant medicines,* under appropriate and safe conditions, or fall under the influence of the body's natural production of the same – like DMT. Under the influence of excess amounts of endogenous (occurring within the body) DMT or by the taking of some other psychedelic, our perception is opened to these celestial realms. Dr. Strassman suggests that this naturally occurring DMT in the body can produce *"states of mind associated with birth, death, near-death, entity or alien contact experiences, and mystical/spiritual consciousness."* By the influence of DMT, like any other psychedelic, our mental functions change. This results in our perception of the world, and our emotions, thoughts, bodily awareness, etc., being temporally aligned more directly with the *celestial regions*. Under these conditions a person may experience one of many different extremes in our emotional or physical centers, feelings that are identical to the countless stories of *"entity or alien contact experiences."* These include being either frightened or enlightened, losing time, being carried into the air, feelings as if the body is being transformed or experimented on, paralysis, and a sense that the entities one perceives around them are telepathically communicating. Listed here are a few samples of what Dr. Strassman explains as being the general psychedelic experience:

> *At the extremes lie terror or ecstasy.*

> *Time collapses: in the blink of an eye, two hours pass. Or time expands: a minute contains a never-ending march of sensations and ideas.*

> *Our bodies are hot or cold, heavy or light; our limbs grow or shrink; we move upward or downward through space.*

> *We experience others influencing our minds or bodies - in ways that are beneficial or frightening.*

"DMT" in particular, Dr. Strassman writes, "is physically immobilizing and produces a flood of unexpected and overwhelming visual and emotional imagery." This also could describe the often terrifying twilight zone between waking consciousness and unconscious sleep that we call *sleep paralysis*. Whatever the cause, being consciously aware of your body's paralytic state, and partially aware of the dream state, can produce waking *dreams* whereby a person often feels a heavy or evil presence. This is likely the origin of the *nightmare* (night-mare), once thought to be an evil spirit that oppresses people during sleep. The *mære* is usually a small spirit that lies upon the chest, therefore associating it with the *little people* we know as *fairies* or *green men*.

The most likely time for proper dreaming is about 3 A.M., otherwise known as the *witching hour*. It is around this time – in the middle of the night – that we often experience entities such as *hat man*, *dog man*, *little people*, and *demons* (incubus and succubus). Especially in the case of *dog men*, something equivalent to the Egyptian Anubis, we are reminded of the 40,000 year old *lion man*.

Therianthropes psychologically speak to our animal nature just as the reptile brain speaks to ancient and modern myths alike pertaining to serpent creators and predators. Space is vast, dark, cold, and unknown, which are all the things that humans fear. It is an infinite realm from whence the vicious predator has always lurked, going back to the Garden of Eden. But the eternal predator, usually in the form of a dragon or serpent, is hiding not necessarily in some outer darkness but within the internal darkness of self – and literally at the base of the brain in a division called the *reptile brain*.

The predator hides within the very code of life we call DNA - the double helix - and its image is preserved in both ancient creation stories and the modern symbol of caduceus. It is cold-blooded, venomous and often deadly. It is mechanical in its thinking and programmable in its attack. These are qualities that associate the serpent with modern machines, too, i.e., computers. Carl Jung gets to the root of this issue in his assessment of UFOs called <u>Flying Saucers: A Modern Myth of Things Seen in the Skies</u>:

> *"Undeterred by rationalistic criticism, it thrusts itself to the forefront in the form of a symbolic rumour, accompanied and reinforced by the appropriate visions, and thus activates an archetype that has always expressed order, deliverance, salvation, and wholeness. It is characteristic of our time that the archetype, in contrast to its previous manifestations, should now take the form of an object, a technological construction, in order to avoid the odiousness of mythological personification."*

It therefore makes sense that under the influence of DMT, which we should be reminded is produced by the body, we may see spiraling DNA and interact with technologically advanced reptilian beings who have an interest in human emotions. One of Dr. Strassman's volunteers for the DMT study, Karl, said that what he experienced was like *"some kind of core of reality where all meaning is stored."* This *core* realm is usually described as being filled with vibration, machines of a strange nature, and even as volunteer Aaron said, a "space station" with "androidlike creatures." Another volunteer named Jeremiah interestingly noted:

> *"It may not be so simple as that there's alien planets with their own societies. This is too proximal. It's not like some kind of drug. It's more like an experience of a new technology than a drug."*

As with shamanism and UFO abductions, some of the DMT volunteers were possibly implanted with technology, or experienced intimate sexual contact. Ben said, *"I felt like something was inserted into my left forearm."* Dimitri reported, *"They activated a sexual circuit, and I was flushed with an amazing orgasmic energy."* Volunteers also reported feeling childlike, being in a "nursery," or feeling a sense of rebirth by the unburdening of worry about life and death. This was precisely the idea of the ancient *mystery schools* – to overcome fear, especially that of death.

Of particular interest is the relationship these experiences have not only with the UFO mythos, but with the spiritual, mystical, and theological. Consider both the following quote from a famous German mystic and a popular Bible verse:

Meister Eckhart

"If you fight your death, you'll feel the demons tearing away at your life, but, if you have the right attitude to death, you will be able to see that the devils are really angels setting your spirit free."

Psalm 80:19

"Restore us, O Lord God of hosts! Let your face shine, that we may be saved!"

Now consider what Rex, another of Dr. Strassman's DMT volunteers, said about his experience:

> *"The more I fought, the more demonic they became, probing into my psyche and being... There were rays of psychedelic yellow light coming out of the face of the reassuring deity."*

If we follow the axiom of *that which is above is like that which is below* and *that which is without is like that which is within* we will find that as we blossom out of nature it likewise grows out of us. Therefore our interactions with these entities are probably more often the result of interactions with our internal self, whether the experience results from taking a substance, intense introspection and examination of the psyche, a natural production of DMT in the body, or a byproduct of conditions caused by conflict and stress. On the last point we can understand the explosion of UFO sightings alongside world wars, threats of nuclear annihilation, and natural disasters.

As Jung points out, the ruling ideas of civilization have again changed dramatically in the 20th-century, and thus, *"created a situation that resembles a tabula rasa"* where *"almost anything might appear on it."* Under these conditions *"the phenomenon of the Ufos may well be just such an apparition."* In league with Jung's analysis, Vallee calls it *"folklore in the making."*

Perhaps the psychological view of Jung can be merged with the chemical and psychedelic view of Strassman, i.e., the body deals with severe stress and its likeness by producing excess DMT that overloads normal levels. These higher doses, coupled with stressors, produce the hallucinations and/or real otherworldly phenomena of angels, demons, aliens, monsters, etc. – maybe the exposure of *real* parallel realities.

The identifying nature of these unidentified craft changes over time too. Today we assume they are spaceships since this parallels our own developments, in the same way that the idea of extraterrestrials invading earth became a popular thought as humans readied to invade the moon at the turn of the late 1950s into the 1960s – although this idea was not unheard before. Consider the 1902 classic movie *A Trip to the Moon*.

Prior to spaceships, the UFO was a star, angel, pillar, shield, canon, chariot, basket, cauldron, sea boat, and anything else identifiable to the observer of whatever century. The floating illuminated ball has always been a symbol of the *anima mundi*, or *world soul*. The elongated cigar craft (*ghost rockets*) is penial while the ball of light (*foo fighters*) is yonic.

It seems the shared concerns we have with our space brothers and sisters, who seem particularly and oddly interested in human affairs, are largely based in our subconscious. We project less developed versions of ourselves outward, hence why the *grey aliens* tend to look *fetal* - as partly evidenced by Aleister Crowley's channeled entity named LAM. They are the *homunculus* growing in the human vessel that has been thrust into a world of decay. These are the necessary components of the alchemical process: placing semen and other materials inside a vessel and then putting that container in manure to putrefy and grow the *little person*. The more we study these strange creatures and their modes of transportation, the more we will learn about ourselves and the nature of reality. The more we study therianthropic imagery, the more we will understand the origins of spiritual thought. And that truly is a gift from above.

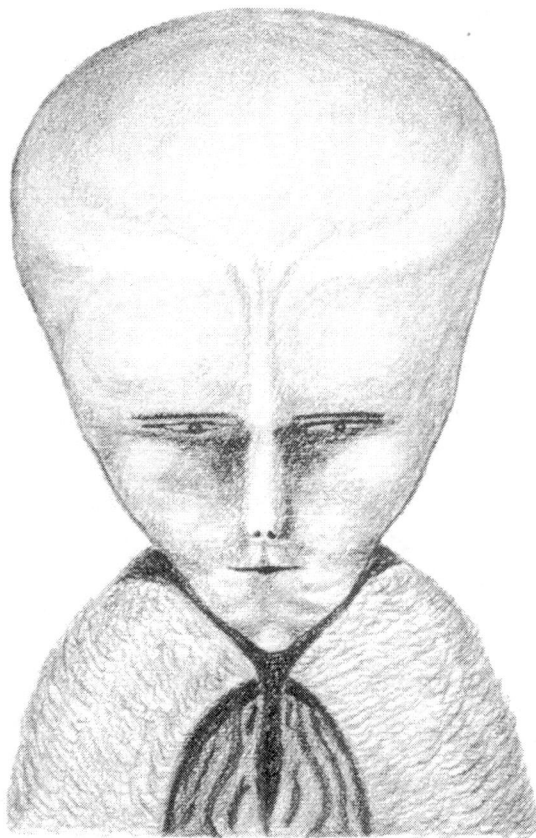

LAM

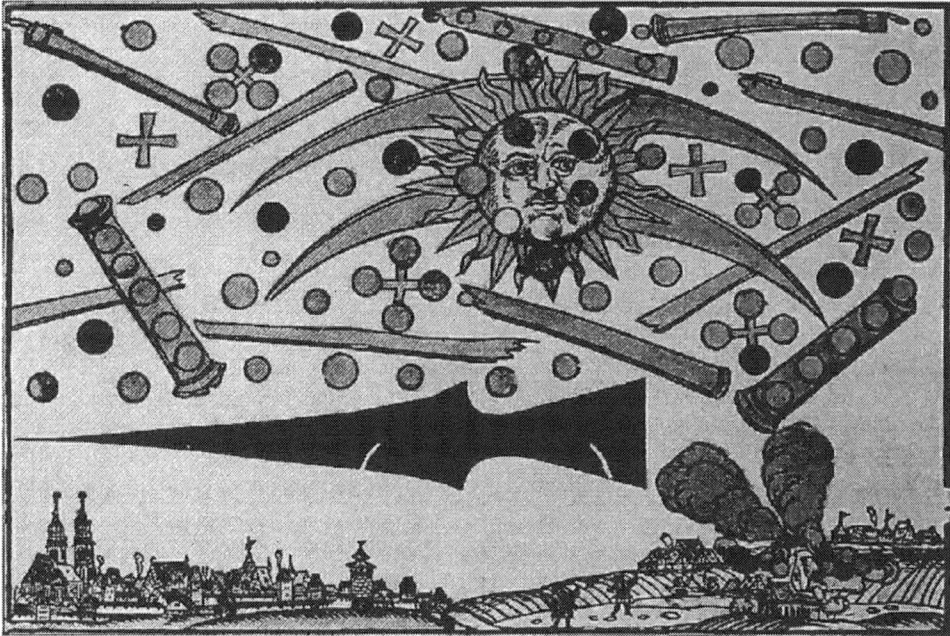

Nuremberg, Germany (1561) – flying spheres, cigar-shaped 'mother-ships', and long cylindrical objects fill the sky in what some interpret as combat. As with the modern spaceship theory of UFOs, witnesses of this heavenly display likened the smaller objects to cannon balls being shot out of the larger cylindrical objects (cannons).

Basel, Switzerland (1566) – white and black spherical discs fill the sky, alongside the sun.

DO NOT GIVE OUT FROM
ASO/W-A

~~SECRET~~
~~Security Information~~

REPORT OF MEETINGS OF SCIENTIFIC ADVISORY PANEL

ON UNIDENTIFIED FLYING OBJECTS

CONVENED BY OFFICE OF SCIENTIFIC INTELLIGENCE, CIA

January 14 - 18, 1953

25X1A

███████████

~~SECRET~~
~~Security Information~~

Declassified by _____008887_____
date _21 JAN 1975_

49

The 1953 <u>Robertson Panel Report</u> was a psychosocial experimental playbook put together by the military and intelligence communities. The report describes how to debunk the UFO mythos while maintaining official investigative interest:

> *"The 'debunking' aim would result in reduction in public interest in 'flying saucers'… This education could be accomplished by mass media such [as] television, motion pictures, and popular articles. Basis of such education would be actual case histories which had been puzzling at first but later explained."*

The report further states that an "advertising expert" would be very helpful in debunking efforts, and: *"The Jam Handy Co. which made World War II training films (motion pictures and slide strips) was also suggested, as well as Walt Disney, Inc. animated cartoons."* The report even suggested using *"amateur astronomers"* as *"a potential source of enthusiastic talent 'to spread the gospel'."* As for civilian UFO groups: *"It was believed that such organization should be watched because of their potentially great influence on mass thinking if widespread sightings should occur. The apparent irresponsibility and the possible use of such groups for subversive purposes should be kept in mind."*

Occult Origins of Lord of the Rings, Harry Potter, & Dune

"Fear is the little-death that brings total obliteration."

~ Frank Herbert ~

More Esoteric Stories & the Lord of the Rings

There is an interesting story involving to the characters Loki, Odin, and Honir (Odin's brother), in Norse mythology. Walking on earth one day disguised as men, they came upon a waterfall and Loki noticed an otter on a flattened rock. He picked up a smooth pebble and throwing it at the otter killed it instantly. Odin and Honir applauded his skill, picked up the otter, and continued their journey. Soon the group arrived at a large hall where a dark-skinned man wearing bejeweled robes greeted them. The man identified himself as Hreidmarr the magician. Pretending to be poor travelers, Loki said they had no gifts to impart but instead could offer the dead otter. Upon the presentation of the body, two other dark-skinned men pinned down the travelers, as the magician hovered over them with an axe. Nervous and confused at this immediate display of hostility, Loki begged to know what they had done wrong. Hreidmarr responded by saying his youngest son would turn himself into an otter when he went fishing, to which Loki pleaded ignorance and penance. After deliberation, the magician offered a plea deal: he would accept in exchange for their transgression enough gold to cover the skin of the otter so that no hair could be seen.

While Odin and Honir were left chained, Loki went to fetch the gold. He retraced the group's earlier steps, arriving at the same waterfall where the otter had been killed. In his contemplation, Loki noticed a glint in the water, which provoked him to take a closer look. Upon doing so he found a pike fish hiding in the entrance to an underwater cave. But this was no common fish. Loki immediately recognized the pike to be a dwarf named Alberich, the famous guardian of a store of treasure. After fetching a net, Loki pulled the fish from its water and threatened by knowledge of Alberich's true identity that he would kill him unless the dwarf handed over his treasure. Alberich obliged. Loki then watched Alberich emerge from the water several times with great armfuls of gold until his store was exhausted.

The treasure was then piled on the same flat rock upon which the otter was killed, and just as the dwarf turned back upon permission of his freedom, another glint caught Loki's eye. It was a golden ring. Loki, feeling drawn to it, demanded the last piece of the dwarf's treasure. This time Alberich protested; for the ring was not ordinary, it was a "magic ring" meant to restore his supply of treasure and gold. And it would only work if worn by a dwarf. But Loki took the ring anyway, and as Alberich swam away, he placed a curse on whomever it was that wore the *magic ring*.

Loki then carried all the gold back to the hall with Alberich's sacred ring on his finger. When he arrived, Odin immediately demanded the ring. Obtaining it, he slipped it on his finger.

The main store of gold was laid on the otter-skin until it eventually covered every hair, except one on the snout, as pointed out by Hreidmarr. Single hair or not, Hreidmarr's intention was to obtain the ring that was now on Odin's finger. Eventually he wrestled it from the group.

Sometime later, and due to the ring's curse, when Hreidmarr refused to share the new gold with his two sons they killed him. After a falling out between the brothers, one turned into a dragon to keep the ring and all the treasure for himself. The other brother, Reginn, was too weak and cowardly to fight his brother so he sought someone else to do his bidding. The young man conscripted for the job was named Siegfried.

Reginn befriended the man first, knowing he possessed a sword forged from the fragments of the one Odin gave to his father. He then filled his head with stories of a dragon guarding a large sum of great treasure and together they went to the dragon's cave and began keeping an eye on the beast. Reginn observed the dragon daily going to a nearby river to drink and so informed Siegfried that he should dig a trench along that route to hide so that when the dragon slithered across, he could stab the creature, plunging his sword into its heart. This is exactly what Siegfried did.

As Reginn ran to hide at a safe distance, though, an old man appeared in a blue cloak to warn Siegfried that the dragon's blood was venomous and acidic and would kill him if he were touched by it. Siegfried took the man's advice and acted to dig a second trench to channel away the creature's blood.

When Reginn emerged from hiding after the dragon fell dead, he told Siegfried to cut out its heart and roast it for his consumption. In doing so, Siegfried was splattered by the blood. In serious pain, he put his finger in his mouth to soothe it and recognized he could suddenly understand the language of the birds.

The woodpeckers warned him of the trick being played by Reginn; if he were to consume the heart of his brother, an unmatchable power and cleverness would be gained. He would then be able to rule the entire world.

Soon after, Reginn moved to killed Siegfried so that he could obtain all the power and wealth. The chatter of birds, however, warned of Reginn creeping up from behind, and so Siegfried turned around quickly to slice off his hand, an action that Reginn had intended to do to Siegfried. Author Mark Booth continues this story in his book <u>The Sacred History</u>:

> "Now the birds began to sing a new song, a song of a beautiful young woman bound by the briars of sleep.
>
> "In the morning, as Siegfried saddled his horse, he saw a great light on the horizon. He rode through trackless regions toward it and saw a great wall of flame at the top of a mountain.
>
> "Spurring his horse forward and up the mountain, he leapt over this wall of flame to discover, lying there as if dead, a knight in golden armor. He dismounted and removed the Knight's helmet, to find a sleeping beauty with long golden hair and dazzling white skin.
>
> "As he leaned down to kiss her, he saw the thorn of a hawthorn stuck in her side. When he pulled it out, she awoke. She said she was Brunhilde, and that Odin had put her to sleep, telling her she could only be woken by the man called Siegfried the dragon-slayer. As they looked deep into each other's eyes, knowing they were destined to be together, Siegfried placed the golden ring that he had taken from the dragon's hoard on Brunhilde's finger."

When the *magic ring* was placed on the finger of the *sleeping beauty* Brunhilde, she instantly changed under its curse and told Siegfried he must prove himself before they could be together: he was to conquer a kingdom for her to rule as queen. Booth further explains the significance of the ring as part of an allegory pertaining to the solidification of matter:

"In this way, the evil influence of the dwarf's ring continued to ripple outward… the evil influence of the ring was spreading not only outward but also downward. Life on Earth would often be hard and full of struggle."

From this story we can derive understanding for the fairy tales of *Sleeping Beauty* and *Rapunzel*, who it is spoken: *"Rapunzel, Rapunzel, let down your hair, so that I may climb thy golden stair."* Here the word "golden" is to be associated with *alchemical gold* and *spiritual enlightenment*, while the stairs are those used to ascend to the heavens like *Jacob's Ladder*. The golden hair represents a similarity between *Rapunzel* and various stories of the sun goddess, such as the Japanese *Amaterasu*, trapped and in need of rescue from her brother *Susanoo*. In this very ancient story, Amaterasu emerges from the cave of darkness to bring light back to the world. Japan thus becomes *Land of the Rising Sun* due to its geographic position in the east. There is a great deal more on this story within the "Occult Japan" sections of this book.

More directly related to *Rapunzel* is the Baltic solar goddess Saulė, who is held captive in a tower. The name of *Sleeping Beauty* is *Aurora*, which in Latin means "goddess of the dawn," thus associating the child with goddesses of light and

The Ring of Gyges from <u>Rings for the Finger</u>, by George Frederick Kunz, 1917

the rising sun like Amaterasu. Her deathlike sleep, as with the coma of *Snow White*, is representative of both the *dormant seed of soul* ready to sprout, and the dying solar deity resurrected on the Winter Solstice and Spring Equinox. We are reminded here once more that Aurora's spiritual coma signifies the *soul* submerged in *matter* awaiting the kiss of a prince, the rosy *kiss of wisdom*.

Readers and viewers of J. R. Tolkien's masterpiece series <u>The Lord of the Rings</u> will know the story of a *magic ring* that causes conflict very well. In fact, the fight that occurs between Reginn and his brother is like that of Smeagol (Gollum) and Deagol, who find the ring on a riverbed like Loki. The name *Gollum* is also derived from the Old Norse word *gull*, which means gold.

Such a fascinating origin for a wildly popular story can be found likewise in J. K. Rowling's <u>Harry Potter</u> series. The *house elf* Dobby, for example, is named after a *dobie* (sometime literally *dobby*), a sort of *brownie* (spirit) known throughout the British Isles.

Both the spiders from these stories, *Shelob* and *Aragog* respectively, are known all throughout the world, and in Japanese folklore as *tsuchigumo*.

Whether called the *Philosopher's Stone* or *Sorcerer's Stone*, Harry Potter discovers that he is in possession of this *Powder of Projection* and can only hold it once he has reached a certain level of awareness so as not to abuse its power.

This is exactly the story of *alchemical gold*: the alchemist is unable to obtain the treasure until they have learned to not abuse its power. Only then can they create unlimited *wealth* – when they no longer have such *desires*.

From the above tales we find the common image of a dragon guarding treasure, which signifies our bestial nature that, upon defeat or overcoming, gives access to spiritual gold. In some stories the dragon guards a princess locked away in a tower. She is to be saved by the same brave knight, who will then be united, in the Bridal Chamber, with his consort. The golden hair and tall tower signify the *reward* granted to a brave individual undertaking such a perilous journey. The cursed ring of Alberich represents a form of perverted alchemy, however, turning gods and men into barbaric heathens with purely materialistic desires, such as the lust for physical gold. This is what Tolkien's details in his epic masterpiece. The meaning here is the fact that Loki did not earn the treasure (enlightenment) but had stolen it by ransacking the *temple of wisdom* (a mystical realm with a shapeshifting fish) by force. By tearing off the veil of the *mysteries* from the face of Isis as a mere mortal, one will never be able to comprehend their true meanings: "*No Mortal Man Hath Ever Me Unveiled.*" The great "wall of flame" jumped over by Siegfried is *Mordor*, the *land of shadow* found in the west within many myths. The "tall tower" is reminiscent of the *Eye of Sauron* held between two horns; an identical image found with the winged solar disc above the veiled warning of the Static Isis.

Magic Rings & Invisibility

The magical ring of Alberich is reminiscent of the talismanic jewels found throughout much of world mythology. Moses the Lawgiver is said by Josephus to have made rings of *oblivion* and *love*. Aristotle said that among the Cireneans, the *ring of Battas* was able to procure *love* and *honor*. The philosopher Eudamus was supposed to have made rings against bites of serpents, evil spirits and bewitching. In Plato's account, this ring is known as the *Ring of Gyges*, and in typical *esoteric philosophy* Eliphas Levi explains:

> "*The true Ring of Gyges is the will; it is also the wand of transformations, and by its precise and strong formulation it creates the magical word. The whole secret of invisible as attributed to this magic ring is the power by which to distract or paralyze attention. A person may become invisible by methods not employed by any form of modern science: invisibility induced by distraction or directing of attention.*"

In the Grimorium Verum is explained a direct yet convoluted and seemingly absurd process by which one may become invisible, as if they had placed the above ring on their finger:

> "*Begin this operation on a Wednesday before the sun rises, being furnished with seven black beans. Take next the head of a dead man; place one of the beans in his mouth, two in his eyes and two in his ears. Then make upon this head the character of the figure which here follows. (Omitted in all the Grimoires.) This done, inter the head with the face towards heaven, and every day before sunrise, for the space of nine days, water it with excellent brandy. On the eighth day you will find the cited spirit, who will say unto you: What doest thou? You shall reply: I am watering my plant. He will then say: Give me that bottle; I will water it myself. You will answer by refusing, and he will again ask you, but you will persist in declining, until he shall stretch forth his hand and shew you the same figure which you have traced upon the head suspended from the tips of his fingers. In this case you may be assured that it is really the spirit of the head, because another might take you unawares, which would bring you evil, and further, your operation would be unfruitful. When you have given him your phial, he will water the head and depart. On the morrow, which is the ninth day, you shall return and will find your beans ripe. Take them, place one in your mouth, and then look at yourself in a glass. If you cannot see yourself, it is good. Do the same with the rest, or they may be tested in the mouth of a child. All*

those which do not answer must be interred with the head."

The secret behind the powers of invisibility attributed to this magical ring is the ability to *distract* or *paralyze* attention. As with the *Ring of Gyges* and *Lord of the Rings*, which we are reminded is Saturn, overseeing earth like the *Eye of Sauron*, Harry Potter also possesses a *Cloak of Invisibility*.

A person may become *invisible* through methods not employed by any form of modern technological science: an invisibility induced by distraction or the misdirecting of attention. According to author Arthur Waite:

> *"There are also other processes which are not in themselves Goëtic, but are objectionable on account of the abuse to which they are liable… experiments of this kind will in one Ritual appear under a harmless guise but will in another bear all the marks of diabolism. The experience of Invisibility, with which we are here concerned, illustrates all these points."*

King Solomon likewise had a ring allowing for control of the infernal powers, or those tempting forces, for which he subdued and captured. In the second book of his <u>Republic</u>, Plato describes a ring that when the collet is turned inward renders its wearer invisible just like in Tolkien's version:

> *"They relate that he was a shepherd in the service of the ruler at that time of Lydia, and that after a great deluge of rain and an earthquake the ground opened and a chasm appeared in the place where he was pasturing; and they say that he saw and wondered and went down into the chasm; and the story goes that he beheld other marvels there and a hollow bronze horse with little doors, and that he peeped in and saw a corpse within, as it seemed, of more than mortal stature, and that there was nothing else but a gold ring on its hand, which he took off and went forth. And when the shepherds held their customary assembly to make their monthly report to the king about the flocks, he also attended wearing the ring.*

> *"So as he sat there it chanced that he turned the collet of the ring towards himself, towards the inner part of his hand, and when this took place they say that he became invisible to those who sat by him and they spoke of him as absent and that he was amazed, and again fumbling with the ring turned the collet outwards and so became visible. On noting this he experimented with the ring to see if it possessed this virtue, and he found the result to be that when he turned the collet inwards he became invisible, and when outwards visible; and becoming aware of this, he immediately managed things so that he became one of the messengers who went up to the king, and on coming there he seduced the king's wife and with her aid set upon the king and slew him and possessed his kingdom."*

Collin De Plancy also writes in his masterpiece <u>Infernal Dictionary</u> about King Solomon as being not only wise, but as possessing a powerful ring:

> *"Philosophers, botanists, soothsayers, and astrologers consider Solomon or Soliman as their patron. According to them, God having given him his wisdom, at the same time gave him all natural and supernatural knowledge; and as part of the last one, to evoke spirits and genies, and to control them. Solomon had, they say, a ring with a talisman, which gave him absolute power over all intermediate beings between God and man."*

According to Plancy, *"the ring still exists; it is enclosed in the tomb of Solomon, and whoever will possess it, will become master of the world."* However, this "ring" is probably more akin to the 36,525 books written by Hermes-Mercury, i.e., the number of days in a solar year (365.2422). A *secret doctrine* preserved in nature.

As messenger of the gods carrying the caduceus staff, we may deduce that this god is truly a personification of our DNA, RNA, and mRNA (messenger RNA): a double helix. His image can be further seen inside the egg or cell, as is depicted in images of the Greek god Phanes, a deity of light, goodness, and creation. Manly Hall writes in <u>The Secret Teachings of All Ages</u> of magic rings throughout history:

> *"Josephus also describes magical rings designed by Moses and King Solomon, and Aristotle mentions one which brought love and honor to its possessor. In his chapter dealing with the subject, Henry Cornelius Agrippa not only mentions the same rings, but states, upon the authority of Philostratus Jarchus, that Apollonius of Tyana extended his life to over 20 years with the aid of seven magical rings presented to him by an East Indian prince. Each of these seven rings was set with a gem partaking of the nature of one of the seven ruling planets of the week, and by daily changing the rings, Apollonius protected himself against sickness and death by the intervention of the planetary influences. The philosopher also instructed his disciples in the virtues of these talismanic jewels, considering such information to be indispensable to the theurgist.*

A Closer Look at Harry Potter & Dune

In <u>Harry Potter and the Philosopher's Stone</u>, our heroes are confronted on their journey by a three-headed dog, which initially prevents their passage through a doorway that would lead to the acquisition of the most *sacred stone*. For passage, music is played that lulls the beast into a delicate sleep. Known as *Fluffy* in the latter account, this dog belongs to Hades or Pluto, the god of the underworld. Guarding the gates into Hades, he is known in mythology by the name of *Kerberos* or *Cerberus*. This name will also sound familiar to *Severus Snape*, who acts as a *necessary evil* to push Harry forward on his journey. He ultimately cares greatly for the boy. When passage is granted by the playing of music like that played by Orpheus or Apollo, the main characters gain access to a small door below, which leads to a trap as they jump through. A plant called the "Devil's Snare" grabs hold of the characters tightly, known only to loosen its bind upon the absence of sufficient effort to escape its grasp. It may also recoil away from *heat* or *fire* and cease to move in the presence of a light. This *fire* is the flaming sword preventing man's return to paradise; it typifies the *astral light* which man lost the ability to direct after the *fall*. It is thus the goal of a magician to make subject this force by a *sovereign act of will*. Here we may understand a *flowing of energy* in *life* that is only controllable by *letting go* and *drifting* with its *current*. It will always lead to where we need to be, and those realizing the quality of this *Universal Agent* in nature will be illuminated beyond any reach of darkness. It does no good to battle against this current. We should, as they say, *go with the flow*. We can recall here a famous quote from Frank Herbert's masterpiece series <u>Dune</u>:

> *"The mystery of life isn't a problem to solve, but a reality to experience."*

It may be understood by the three heads of *Cerberus* the qualities of *self* that must be perfected: *thought*, *action*, and *emotion*. These must be controlled before one can obtain the *elixir of life*.

The music played to lull the beast to sleep is symbolic of the Pythagorean qualities of *harmony* and *balance*; an understanding of the *sacred music* emitted by the *heavenly spheres*, and thus the perfecting of *self* through learning *natural law*.

No man passing by this beast in Greece was ever able to return from the underworld. For anyone descending into this dark land can only return to the *spiritual sphere* after a process of *realization* and *enlightenment* has been undertaken and completed in the *physical sphere*: that is to say, once again, when one has been resurrected from the tomb like Christ.

By conquering "Fluffy" it is to be surmised the conquering of a great beast and the slaying of a great dragon. The binding of the "Devil's Snare" represents elements that *tempt* and *constrict* us throughout our life. The more we struggle in our attempts to control nature, the more we find ourselves bound tighter by her grip. The plant will only release its grip when we relax and *go with the flow*. The heat, fire, and light obviously illuminates the *darkness* of *ignorance*, *superstition*, and *fear*. Only then is passage to the next *sphere of heaven*, *level of hell*, and *gate of the underworld* illuminated. Perhaps the most famous quote from Dune relates to conquering fear:

> *"I must not fear. Fear is the mind-killer. Fear is the little-death that brings total obliteration. I will face my fear. I will permit it to pass over me and through me. And when it has gone past I will turn the inner eye to see its path. Where the fear has gone there will be nothing. Only I will remain."*

In the story, Paul Atreides can only rise as *messiah* after he dies in a test of *death*. His death is not literal, however, but instead a result of him taking the life of a *Fremen* named Jamis. Paul again dies and is resurrected after he drinks the poisonous blue liquid called *Water of* Life, reminiscent of Egyptian *blue water lily*. For when one takes a life, they themselves die. This is the moment Harry realizes he has the power to defeat Lord Voldemort and finds the *Philosopher's Stone* on his person. Hall explains the *stone* as a *powder* able to transform the alchemist:

> *"Wisdom is the alchemist's powder of projection which transforms many thousand times its own weight of gross ignorance into the precious substance of enlightenment."*

The mythology, metaphor, allegory, and symbols found in Harry Potter all stem from a fictional work called *Egypt in the 19th Century*, by M. Ed. Guoin. According to this tale, a pilgrim some identify with Plato comes to the banks of the Nile seeking initiation into the Egyptian *mysteries*. Here he undergoes trials in dark caverns within the earth where three men wearing helmets and representing dogs guard an iron door. These men warned of the dangers on the initiate's path, but the neophyte continued anyway passing through terrifying obstacles until arriving at a room lit by hundreds of torches and where sixty priests sat robed in fine linen.

After a retreat of eighty-one days and an additional six months of study, the initiate took an oath of silence to be finally recognized as a member of the *Sacred College*. Just as what was learned in these *Mystery Schools* was never to be divulged under threat of death, the rules of the magical college Hogwarts likewise forbade the practice of *magic* in front of mere humans – the *dead*. The hall lit by hundreds of torches is identical to the *Great Hall* of Hogwarts where students of nourished with food.

In Harry Potter and The Chamber of Secrets, the heroes are confronted with a large snake called Basilisk, a legendary reptilian creature considered to be the King of the serpents. It is said that one stare from this creature will render you dead, and this relates to the story of *Perseus, Pegasus,* and *Medusa*. It is Perseus and Athene who liberate Andromeda, the bride of death, from her captivity by Medusa – another version of the Persephone, Demeter, and Hades, *drama*.

There is more occult significance in the character *Sirius Black,* who turns into a dog and signifies the three-star system of Sirius so important to certain ancient cultures. This three-star system also directly relates to *Cerberus* and Fluffy. Sirius is the brightest star in the sky found within the constellation *Canis Major*, the dog, for which the star receives its nickname: *the dog star.*

Another character in <u>Harry Potter</u> is Minerva McGonagall, named after the goddess Pallas Athena in Greece and Minerva, guardian of State and home, in Roman mythology.

How to Kill Your Dragon

The writings of Philostratus, a Greek sophist or teacher, examine the life of a philosopher named Apollonius. The entire story is formed of parable and symbol, and a dragon guarding the entrance to a *palace of wisdom*. There are three species of dragons to be derived from alchemy: those that live in swamps, dwell on mountains, or reside in marshes. These three locations correspond to the alchemical agents of Salt, Sulphur and Mercury respectively. In their head, which must be severed, is that great *stone of miracles*. These dragons are caught and killed with the help of a *scarlet cloth* embroidered with letters of gold. They are enchanted to lay their head upon this magical fabric, whereupon it is severed. In searching for real dragons in mythology and folklore it is important to note the distinction between not only the *western serpent* and *eastern beast*, but that the Chinese version has five claws, and the Japanese dragon has only three.

Row Your Boat

One day we shall recognize our being surrounded like Daniel by vicious lions, void of understanding, hungered by *wickedness* and *foolishness*. The story of Samson in the Bible is an allegory of similar standing, as read in the book of Judges 16:30, which reads: *"Then he pushed with all his might, and down came the temple on the rulers and all the people in it. Thus he killed many more when he died than while he lived."* The pushing of the pillars of *reason, justice, philosophy, science*, etc., to their destruction is to bring the entire *temple* down upon itself. Masons know this as collapsing temple, one made unstable by the abandonment of *reason*, which brings about a burying *truth* in the rubble. In Kabbalah the two pillars of *strength* and *beauty* represent the *Universal House*, which may fall if these supporting columns are pushed apart by the likes of Samson.

There are several other historical allegories and metaphors that may also be understood likewise: such is the story of Jesus walking on water. There is a literal explanation and another with deeper roots concealed within the magical nature of conquering the elements. If one has mastered fire, then he can walk upon it without pain or burn. He who has mastered navigation of the ocean may be said to have conquered the seas and waters. In the story of Jesus *walking on water* we are to understand his mastery of illusion. We further find further that the physical sun can be seen shining on the water or "walking" across its surface. Once Peter doubted and lost faith in the story, he began to sink into illusion like Jonah being swallowed by the great whale. Peter lost sight of *The Way*, an ancient path of dedication to truth whereby the student adheres to the principles of certain esoteric philosophies. Embodiment of this philosophy was to secure a *moral responsibility*. Through initiation a newly formed hierophant would have realized that life is *death and death is life*. Life is therefore a *grand illusion* and a complex dream.

Here we are reminded of a classic nursery rhyme preserving this *secret philosophy*. In this verse the boat is a vessel by which to experience the physical world and the *stream is life*. By merrily rowing our boat down the stream it is not meant to suggest we cheerfully ignore our responsibilities, but instead that we embrace them and realize that life is a dream, and one that we should experience to the fullest, so long as we fulfill our *duties* instead every impulsive *desire*. This is when the "Devil's Snare" releases us from its grip:

Row, row, row your boat - Gently down the stream
Merrily, merrily, merrily, merrily - Life is but a dream

The Brambles of Mordor remind us of the **Devil's Snare** and the underlying current of the nursery rhyme **Row Your Boat**.

David Day's wonderful book, <u>An Encyclopedia of Tolkien</u>, provides and exhaustive list of the history and myths that inspired Tolkien's world. The image above is *Morgoth* – the *Dark Enemy*. The following is an extract from Day's book: *"In The Lord of the Rings and the War of the Last Alliance, the name of the high king of the Elves, Gil-galad (meaning 'Star of Radiance'), cannot help but conjure up Galahad and the knights of the Round Table. However, most obviously, in Mordred, the Dark Knight, we have the Arthurian villain who is most akin to Sauron the Dark Lord. Consequently, it is ironic that the name Mordred, which one might assume appropriately had its origin in the homonym 'More-dread,' is actually derived from the Latin meaning 'moderate.' However, in terms of Tolkien's nomenclature, Mordred would be a perfect villain's name. Just as Morgoth in Sindarin means 'Black Enemy,' Moria means 'Black Chasm,' Morgul means 'Black Sorcery,' and Mordor (rhyming with 'murder') means 'Black Land.' So, the Middle-earth name Mordred would suggest something akin to his actual Arthurian epithet of 'Black Knight.'*

The Way of Living Resurrection

"Jesus answered, 'I am the way and the truth and the life.
No one comes to the Father except through me'."

Bible - John 14:6

Awakening from the *dream of life* is the *realization* of one's divine *soul* (the *truth*) temporarily suspended in *matter* like the stories of Moses and Osiris placed in a basket or chest: crucified to *matter* by the *nails of illusion* like the story of Jesus Christ.

The finding of *equilibrium* brings about *harmony* in all things and calms the beast, as opposed to the *chaos* brought about by *disorder* and *unreason*.

In the Biblical book of John 14:16 Jesus says that he is *"the way and the truth and the life."* From *truth* will flow *eternal life* and *light* in all its brilliant forms, including the *Holy Trinity*.

The F*ather* is a prototype of *man*, the Cabalistic Adam Kadmon; and the *Son* is *eternal reason*; and *mother* is *spiritual generation*.

The *Path of Isis* is also known as *The Way* of Christ. We read in Psalm 37:5-6 of the same *path* to be followed:

"Commit your way to the Lord; trust in him and he will do this: He will make your righteous reward shine like he dawn, your vindication like the noonday sun. "

Buddha is said to have walked the *Middle Path*. The Kabbalah has the *Middle Pillar of Mildness*. In the Quran chapter *Muhammed 47:5-6*, we read that Allah will likewise show the *way*:

"He will show them the way, and better their state, And will admit them into gardens with which he has acquainted them."

Even before Jesus Christ, the ritual purifications of John the Baptist prepared initiates for *The Way*, a path leading to *Living Resurrection*. Hermes-Mercury, the Greek-Roman *guide of souls*, or *psychopompos*, is commonly depicted as a *Good Shepherd* carrying a goat. This symbolism will be obvious to Christians as found in John 10:11, when Jesus says, *"I am the good shepherd."* Also sacred to Hermes-Mercury was *The Path* or *The Way*. The Greek musician and poet Orpheus was even known as the *Good Shepherd*.

These "shepherds" or "civilizers" of man, as is the case for Osiris and Quetzalcoatl, came in many, though very similar, forms throughout the world. The *Yellow Emperor* of China is said to have founded Chinese civilization and culture, introducing wooden houses, money, weapons like the bow and arrow, and traditional Chinese medicine. He later ascended into the heavens to become as a star. The first Emperor of Japan, known as Jimmu, is said to have direct lineage to the sun goddess Amaterasu. Through his divinely inspired rule, Jimmu united families and tribes, bringing the people together in civilized harmony with the legendary Japanese islands.

The indigenous Japanese practice called Shintō literally means *True Way*. By extension, the adherents of Amaterasu practice *The Way of Ise* in a ritual space called *Place of the Way*.

The Civilizing Way of Japan

Pilgrims in Japan embarked on journeys of initiation up sacred mountains to find *shugendo* – *The Way*. Therefore, the Japanese have much respect for sacred mountains, including Fuji-no-yama, the "Honorable Mountain." One interpretation of the word *Fuji* is *"everlasting life,"* which would fully align with the goal of following *The Way*. The word *shugendo* itself breaks into three parts:

Shu: nurturing

Gen: realization

Do: attainment of *nehan* or Nirvana

Shintoism is Japan's oldest mystical practice – a folk tradition - and is rooted in the *Shén Dào* of China, mean "philosophical path of the spirit." Otherwise known by the name *Tao* or *Taoism*, this is where we derive the popular image of a *Yin Yang* - the *passive* and *active* principles. Taoism professes a spiritual harmony to be found within an individual and is thus associated with *Hermeticism*, or *The Way* of Hermes. One of the most sacred of all Shintō shrines is known as *Ise Jingu*, and in earlier times, its wisdom keepers were the *jinni,* or teachers who embody knowledge of the spirit. These teachers are similarly related to the Persian *Djinn*, known as beings of *luminous fire* without smoke, and share commonalities with the priestesses of Isis. The *fire* signifies their *illumination* as bodies of *knowledge* and *wisdom*. Matthew 17:2 says of Jesus: *"His face shone like the sun, and his clothes became as white as the light."*

The importance of *Ise Jingu* is described in the oldest prehistoric text of Japan known as the *Kujiki-72*. Mount Omei in China shares similarity with this Japanese, as it houses 72 sacred monasteries. The Buddhist Borobudur Temple, located in Central Java, Indonesia, is pyramidal and from the air looks like a *mandala*. Atop the massive complex are 72 stupas (*heap* in Sanskrit) with Buddha statues underneath. The Dwarkadhish temple in India, dedicated to Krishna, is also built with 72 granite columns. All these references remind us of the 72 sacred *names* of God and the 72 years it takes for a constellation to cycle 1 degree in the Precession of the Equinoxes.

Explained in *Kujiki-72* is the story of a heavenly messenger named *Nigihayahi*, who brings ten treasures in the form of sacred teachings, reminiscent of the Ten Commandments or Code of Hammurabi, by which the spiritually *dead* are *brought back to life*. The text also preserves the story of a divine virgin named *Amaterasu*, the female symbol of the sun. She was also a *kami*, a god whose energy emanates throughout nature like Isis. Amaterasu was a goddess of the sun and married to the god of the moon. Each night the sun descended into the western world of shadow and upon each morning arose *reborn* in the east. This daily cycle is still played out each month by the cycles of the moon, and specifically, each year by the cycles of the sun as it loses strength and symbolically *dies* in the winter. Amaterasu is born from the left eye of *Izanagi-No-Mikoto*, companion of *Izanami-No-Mikoto*, Japan's two mythical founders. Being born of the left eye associates her with the Eye of RA or Horus, which represented the sun. We are reminded here also of Odin plucking out his eye at the *Well of Wisdom,* guarded by *Mimir* the wise. After her entombment like Jesus or Persephone, Amaterasu awakens from her deep sleep and restores light to the world like Demeter or Ceres. She then merges with her male *kami* and becomes *Amateru*, before descending to the shrine of Ise Jingu. Located within this shrine is the secluded and restricted area known as the *Izawa-no-miya*. Within this space are two additional temples where adepts live in careful study of *The Way of Ise*, secluded in a lengthy ritual space called *Place of the Way*.

Sacred mounds, which are the womb of the goddess, are as much a part of ancient pre-Japan as they are the Americas, though scholars tend to identify them with simple burial sites – as with complex pyramids anywhere on earth. Even if such an identity could be derived from scant or even abundant evidence, the materials found within do not prove the age of the structure itself. Later peoples could simply have inhabited the mound and used it for one or many things.

The authors of <u>A History of Japan</u> begin their lecture with a look at the current string of Japanese islands which they believe began to form around "20,000 years ago" - in the heart of the last ice age - when that land was cut off from the continent of Asia by melting ice and rising waters. Early on they tackle the fascinating history of Japanese mounds. These mounds are "distinctively Japanese," despite their Chinese influences, but such structures can also be found further west in Europe and the Americas. Perhaps the most famous is *Serpent Mound* in the state of Ohio.

It is likely that the seemingly universal idea of building mounds had a more archaic ritual purpose, and one possibly linked to the entombment of Amaterasu and *Living Resurrection.*

The name *Ise Jingu* relates to *Isa*, the Arabic name for Jesus. It is also directly related to *Iza*, as in the Giza Pyramids, the largest of which is the *Womb of Isis.*

The Civilizing Way of Egypt

Priestesses of the Ise Jingu Shrine (Ise, Mie Prefecture, Japan) may once have employed a rattle that bears resemblance to the *sistrum* instrument used by priestesses of Isis, and by name to the ISTAR (Ishtar) instrument of the Hittite people. If not the instrument, perhaps the same style of music. These goddesses share other striking attributes: were married to a husband-brother, which signified the sacred alchemical marriage; were repositories of divine wisdom; were patrons of fertility and birth; and all oversaw a yearly inundation that brought fertility to the land. In Egypt this inundation was that of the Nile River and in Japan it was the rain that assured a descent rice harvest.

The name Isis plays an interesting role relating to the Pyramids of the Giza Plateau. Considered a place for *ascension,* the Great Pyramid contains the most dominant of all *Bridal Chambers.* It was from here an initiate was to have communion with THE spirits and after deep introspection be *born again.*

ISE - ISA - IZA

The letter "G" relates to *earth*, which was formed on the potter wheel of Ptah and by the geometrical and mathematical designs of the *Carpenter*. Otherwise known as the *Grand Architect*, he is represented by the "G" inside the Masonic square and compass. From these tools the natural laws of existence were calculated. In a painting by William Blake, the Creator can be seen with compass and the long white beard of Saturn or Cronus. From the letter "G" can also be derived Geb, lord of earth, and Gaia, mother of earth. There is further a god named Gob, the king of earth dwellers that we know as *gnomes*.

The pyramid itself is a *tomb* which symbolizes the *womb* of the *earth*. Therefore, the Gise-Gisa-Giza plateau literally embodies the womb of the goddess - sacred location for *Living Resurrections* to be performed.

According to the Inventory Stele, found by French archaeologist Auguste Marietta, the Great Sphinx of Egypt and Giza's Great Pyramid were in existence long before the kings which aligned themselves with those magnificent structures were even alive. Certainly, the three major pyramids were associated with Khufu (Cheops), Khafre (Chephren), and Menkaure (Mycerinus) but association is not evidence of original design. Greek historian Herodotus was likewise informed in his day that the **Khufu Pyramid** was built by the Pharaoh. Considering the Inventory Stele, however, it seems the Ancient Egyptians were living in the presence of something unfathomably ancient in relation to themselves. The stele refers to the Great (Khufu) Pyramid as being related to Isis. It calls her the *Mistress of the Pyramid.*

These incredible structures are furthermore unrelated to the Egyptians by a simple proof that any tourist can immediately identify; there are no decorations, hieroglyphs, spells, elaborate paintings, etc., which one always finds to some extent in the tombs of *dead royalty.* This is especially noteworthy in Egypt as the afterlife trials were such a cornerstone of their religious system. It would be like finding a 'Catholic Cathedral' that has no Bibles, hymn books, candles, crosses, statues of Mary or Jesus, or colored glass windows. The simple fact that these three main structures at Giza can be seen from incredible distances is glaring proof against the tomb theories of orthodox archeologists. Why would Pharaohs want their resting place to be so visible when they wished to remain undisturbed and protected from grave robbers?

The only other evidence of a relationship between Khufu and construction was conveniently found in a totally random place by Colonel Howard Vyse in 1837 when he was just about out of funding to continue his work.

When the King's Chamber of the Great Pyramid was opened in 1818 by Giovanni Belzoni, all that was available for analysis, other than the structure itself, was an empty, polished granite sarcophagus embedded in the floor. Its lid was broken into two pieces nearby.

The 9th-century governor of Cairo, Caliph Al-Ma'mun, initiated his own expedition into the structure largely based on the not-so-ordinary treasures that supposedly were inside. Tradition maintains that there were iron instruments and weapons that did not rust, powerful spells, and glass that could be bent but not broken. Of course, none of this was found.

Moving to **Khafre's Pyramid** there was much the same disappointment found inside. Only an empty basalt sarcophagus with an anthropoid (resembling human form) wooden lid was found. Researchers have noted how it is far too short and shallow to house a mummified king, or really to fit anything else except for an average human under six feet tall. Egyptian men and women are thought to have been no larger than 5ft 6in and 5ft 2in respectively.

The third much smaller, though still magnificent, **pyramid of Menkaure**, which maintained some of its red granite covering, shares an unbelievable relationship not only with the construction of the other two Giza pyramids but with massive structures in South America. Many of its large blocks are cut and fitted closely together in a jigsaw-puzzle form of building that is found elsewhere in places like Machu Picchu or Sacsayhuamán in Peru.

All the major Egyptian structures, including the three Giza pyramids and even the Sphinx, are constructed in this "advanced" way.

Consider the Great Pyramid only for a moment, which covers 13.1 acres at it base and weighs an estimated six million tons. Its sides are oriented almost perfectly with true North, South, West, and East. The precision in length of its sides is nearly perfect, less than 8 inches. Its corners are almost perfect 90-degree angles, something not usually found in modern buildings. Made of an estimated 2.3 million blocks, each weighing on average 2.5 tons, with some far exceeding double digits, the pyramid also maintains an irregularity in its upward construction. For example, the different courses of blocks decrease in height from course 1-18, as author Graham Hancock points out in <u>Fingerprints of the Gods</u>, but then increase again at course 19. In other words, blocks should theoretically get smaller as the structure increases in height towards its apex. This is not the case necessarily. With an original height to 481.3949 feet, and with almost perfect symmetry and alignment, the Great Pyramid is also constructed to incorporate the ratio *pi*, while internally in the King's Chamber to incorporate *phi* or the *golden ratio*. The Egyptians were not supposed to have this information. But it still may be easier to contemplate how the builders incorporated such timeless and universal information into one of the largest temples on the planet than it would be to figure out how they lifted millions of, on average, 2.5-ton blocks, with some far exceeding this load, nearly 500 hundred feet in the air with near perfect precision inside and outside. Egyptologists gloss over such incredible facts with simple solutions such as they used ramps made of mud and wood and employed 100,000 men over twenty years. It was that simple. But as Hancock points out:

> *"Even the minutest error in the angle of incline of any one of the sides at the base would have led to a substantial misalignment of the edges of the apex. Incredible accuracy, therefore, had to be maintained throughout, at every course, hundreds of feet above the ground, with great stone blocks of killing weight."*

All three of the Giza Pyramids at one point maintained, as can be seen partly left on Menkaure, massive stone coverings. The limestone facing of Khufu consisted of an estimated 115,000 polished limestone casing stones weighing each around ten tons. We can only try to imagine how magnificent the structure appeared when this mirrored coating was present.

In 1940 a British Air Force pilot named P. Groves was flying over the Great Pyramid when he noticed, and photographed, *shadows* that revealed indentations of an eight-sided structure. These shadows were only visible from above on the spring and autumnal equinoxes. In other words, based on a trick of light that precisely occurs only twice a year, the Great Pyramid is shown to have eight sides!

In Central America, the Temple of Kukulkan at Chichén Itzá was also constructed so that on the vernal and autumnal equinoxes an illusion of a giant serpent appears on its sides.

The Pyramid of the Sun in Central America was likewise constructed with similar lighting and shadow manipulation. It furthermore contains, like many pyramids throughout the world, the ratio of *pi* built into its body.

Much further away from Egypt and the Americas is the modern Republic of Maldives, an archipelagic state far south of India. Although some believe these lands were once part of India, and particularly part of a lost land called *Kumari Kandam*, they exist in what is now the middle of the ocean, over 600 miles south-west of Sri Lanka. The history of these lands, and their culture, stems from Hinduism, Buddhism, and more recently from Islam. Pyramids called *hawitta* have been identified on many of the islands, though they are heavily overgrown or collapsed. Many are up to 32 feet high. They, too, are oriented to the cardinal directions.

Mr. Hancock details in <u>Fingerprints of the Gods</u> the incredible accuracy of the Great Pyramid's construction, and how it acts as a scale-model of the earth itself. The *equatorial circumference* of the Earth is 24,902.45 miles and its *polar radius* is 3,949.921 miles. The permitter of the Great Pyramid's base is 3,023.16 feet and its height is 481.3949 feet. The scaling down to a 1:43,200 scale model is not perfectly exact, but it is stunningly close. The Earth's *equatorial circumference* scaled down 43,000 times is 3,043.39 feet compared with the Great Pyramid's perimeter base of 3,023.16 feet, an almost exact match. The Earth's *polar radius* scaled down 43,200 times is 482.59 feet compared with the Great Pyramid's height of 481.3949 feet, another almost exact match. Hancock writes, *"the perimeter of the Great Pyramid's base is indeed 1:43,200 of the equatorial circumference of the earth."* He adds, *"the height of the Great Pyramid above that base is indeed 1:43,200 of the polar radius of the earth."* The number 43,200 is not random either. It represents a fragment of the axial precession of the earth. The movement is "*30 degrees (one complete zodiacal constellation) every 2160 years.*" Precession through two zodiacal constellations is thus 4,320 years. Why two instead of one? Likely because it provides, regarding the earth-pyramid relationship, a patterned eternal key to unlocking the mathematical code(?)

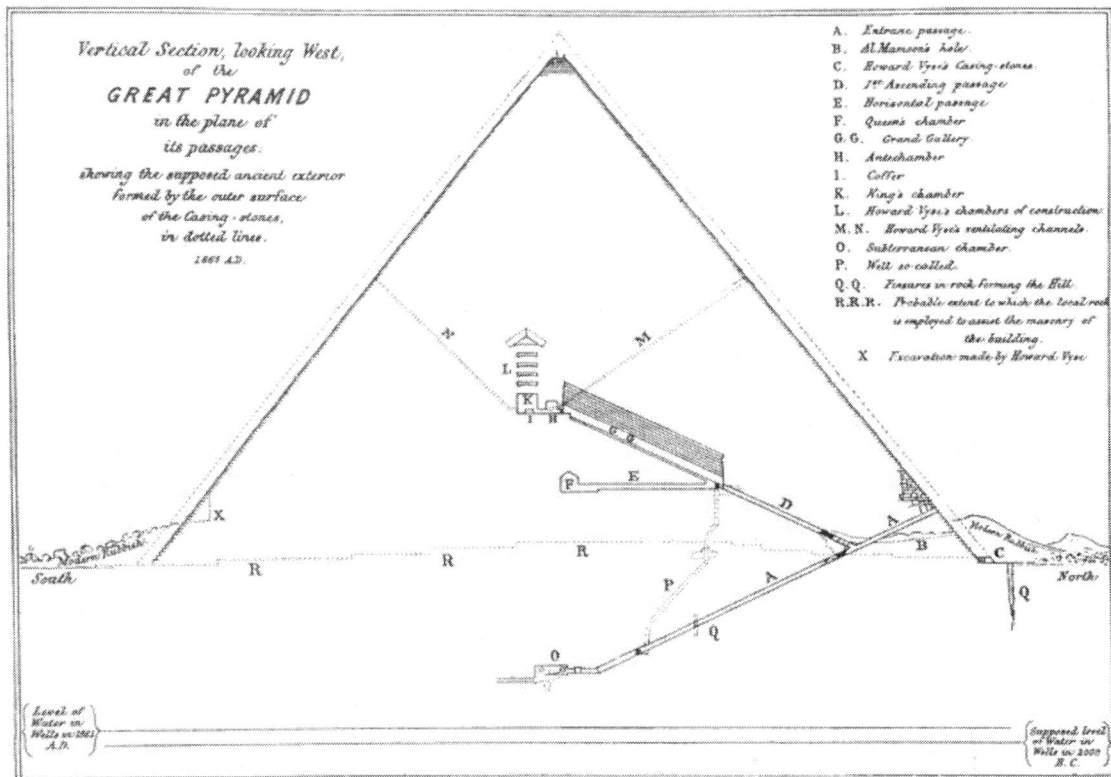

The Great Pyramid with a list of identifying features, from Charles Smyth's <u>Life and Work at the Great Pyramid</u>, and as reproduced in Manly Hall's <u>The Secret Teachings of All Ages</u>.

It was here, among other places, that the *Mysteries* of the *Way* were taught.

The work of Dr Alexander Badawy and Virginia Trimble demonstrated that the southern shaft of the King's Chamber targeted the Belt of Orion at a particular time during the Pyramid Age.

The work of Robert Bauval uncovered how the southern shaft of the Queen's Chamber aligned in the same manner with Sirius during the same age (the same is found of temples on the island of Malta).

Other correlations have been made erroneously, while the above details are oftentimes misquoted and foolishly butchered.

Since King Osiris was associated with Orion, the Great Hunter, and Queen Isis was associated with Sirius, the astronomy and math also align with the theology and myth.

Bauval went further and made highly controversial observations which are either ignored or mocked today. He found that the slight "mis-alignment" of the Giza Pyramidal complex is not a mistake but instead a model of Orion's Belt built on the ground:

> "They're slanted along a diagonal in a south-westerly direction relative to the axis of the Milky Way and the pyramids are slanted along a diagonal in a southwesterly direction relative to the axis of the Nile. If you look carefully on a clear night you'll also see that the smallest of the three stars, the one at the top which the Arabs call Mintaka, is slightly offset to the east of the principal diagonal formed by the other two. This pattern is mimicked on the ground where we see that the Pyramid of Menkaure is offset by exactly the right amount to the east of the principal diagonal formed by the Pyramid of Khafre (which represents the middle star, Al Nilam) and the Great Pyramid, which represents Al Nitak. It's really quite obvious that all these monuments were laid out according to a unified site plan that was modelled with extraordinary precision on those three stars."

The date provided for this alignment is exact, based on computer assessments, and relates to 10,450 BC - around the time the enigmatic Sphinx was likely built in the Age of Leo. Thus, the Milky Way aligned with the Nile River, the Sphinx with Leo on the vernal equinox, and the three main pyramids with Orion's Belt, offset intentionally to align exactly with the heavens. Opposite Leo on the *animal wheel* is the upcoming age of Aquarius, which is perhaps the reason we are just now making these re-discoveries in the transitional end days of the Piscean Age. Bauval writes further:

> "At 10,450 BC - and at that date only - we find that the pattern of the pyramids on the ground provides a perfect reflection of the pattern of the stars in the sky. I mean it's a perfect match - faultless - and it cannot be an accident because the entire arrangement correctly depicts two very unusual celestial events that occurred only at that time. First, and purely by chance, the Milky Way, as visible from Giza in 10,450 BC, exactly duplicated the meridional course of the Nile Valley; secondly, to the west of the Milky Way, the three stars of Orion's Belt were at the lowest altitude in their precessional cycle, with Al Nitak, the star represented by the Great Pyramid, crossing the meridian at 11° 08."

A seeming contradiction does, however, exist in part of Bauval's work, though he believes we are just missing information that would allow us to fully understand this apparent contradiction: the King and Queen chambers of the Great Pyramid align with Orion and Sirius respectively as they were in the sky around 2,450 BC, while the Giza Pyramid alignment with Orion resonates with the sky around 10,450 BC.

Perhaps construction began in the earlier time and was completed more recently? Perhaps, since these dates are based on precession, they relate to an even earlier date going back to 36,000 BC and before?

The important thing to realize, based on what certainly is not sheer coincidence of the similarity between the astronomy, math, theology, and myth, is that after thousands of years we are still asking questions and confirming our own understandings of the universe.

~

The Valley Temple of Khafre, or the Valley Temple, which shares in construction technique with the Osireion at Abydos, is located just behind the Sphinx. As with its apparent architectural counterparts in South America, it was also built with a jigsaw-like pattern of stone. Said to have been built by the gods themselves, an identical account is told of Tiahuanaco in Bolivia, the Valley Temple was known as the *House of Osiris, Lord of Rostau* (an archaic name for Giza).

Much has been written about the Sphinx and we will not make an effort to repeat it here. However, the work of researchers like John Anthony West and Robert Schoch have demonstrated that the ancient monument is really pre-ancient. West argued that signs of water weathering on the Giza monuments were due to long periods of rainfall that occurred closer to the time of the last Ice Age. Shoch confirmed, albeit conservatively so, these findings.

West's initial investigations came after studying the work of French mathematician R. A. Schwaller de Lubicz for his book <u>Serpent in the Sky</u>. Schwaller had proposed in his book <u>Sacred Science</u> that the Sphinx may have already been built when Egypt was experiencing vast amounts of rain and flooding a very long time ago:

> *"A great civilization must have preceded the vast movements of water that passed over Egypt, which leads us to assume that the Sphinx already existed, sculptured in the rock of the west cliff at Giza - that Sphinx whose leonine body, except for the head, shows indisputable signs of water erosion."*

West, who carried out direct investigation of this comment, found it to be accurate. *"If I were asked to place a bet,"* West told author Graham Hancock, *"I'd say that it predates the break-up of the last Ice Age and is probably older than 10,000BC, perhaps even older than 15,000 BC. My Conviction - actually it's more than conviction - is that it's vastly old."* Such a time frame would place construction around when Arthur Posnansky suggested the incredible site of Tiahuanaco in South America was constructed. The Inca, much like the Egyptians in this case, claimed they simply inhabited the site and that it had been built by an early civilization – of which more on later.

Schoch believes the megalith to be dated to around *"7,000 BCE to 5,000 BCE"* – nine thousand to seven thousand years ago conservatively – and defended West's work as did hundreds of others from the Geological Society of America. Robert writes in his book <u>Forgotten Civilization</u> that water erosion present on the Sphinx is *"the result of precipitation and rain runoff, not from flooding or the rising of the Nile."*

But how do we obtain these dates? West and Shoch both have identified severe water erosion on the Sphinx, which only could occur from extended periods of rainfall. The fissures are vertical, too, disputing the claim that they could have resulted from sand and wind. Such sand erosion would indeed make horizontal marks, not vertical ones. The Sphinx itself has also been, even in modern times, routinely covered by blowing sand to the point when preservation efforts had to be launched to keep it above the desert. This is not disputed and has been the condition of the monument for thousands of years. Therefore, erosion could not have come from sand and must have come from water during a time when the climate was more moist than arid.

The Sphinx, which was simply kept and preserved by the Egyptians, shares little similarity with surrounding Old Kingdom structures that have no signs of extensive weathering or erosion. Schwaller's comment about *"vast movements of water"* would explain the weathering. Shoch says that it must *"hark back to a much earlier period when there was more precipitation in the area, and more moisture, more rain on the Giza plateau."*

The timeframe for this "moisture" and "rain" begins around 12,000 - 11,000 BC, the Age of Leo when ice sheets in the northern hemisphere began melting rapidly. The Sphinx after all is very lion-like, is it not?

Egypt's environment may be desert now but it was once a green and fertile land. The Sahara is a very young desert in geological terms, having been green until about 10,000 BC when its wetter and cooler climate shifted. Rains and floods then *"passed over Egypt"* before arid conditions set in until about 7,000 BC. More rains came and as they began to slow after thousands of years, we acquire the desert we know today around the birth of the First Dynasty - 3,000 BC.

We are uncertain of an exact date, though we can be sure it far exceeds the orthodox timeframe of 4,500 years. Construction engineer Robert Bauval likewise proposed that the monuments were built in alignment with certain heavenly constellations – like *Orion's Belt* – at a time coinciding with around 10,450 years ago – around 8,500 BC. Author and curator of the Egyptian Antiquities Museum in Britain, Sir Wallis Budge, also curiously wrote:

> *"The Sphinx was thought to be connected in some way with foreigners or with a foreign religion which dated from predynastic times."*

Perhaps this "foreign religion" was from *Atlantis*(?) Tradition holds, though we can see how distortions take place easily in the modern day, that the Sphinx guarded the *Splendid Place of The Beginning of all Time.* For the Egyptians *time* began in a period known as the *First Time* when the *Neteru* - god and goddesses - brought civilization to Egypt. These gods apparently brought a very high level of civilization with them too.

When we move past the tomb theory and acknowledge the incredible anomalies of just Giza alone there unfolds a different understanding of Ancient Egypt and even *"predynastic times."*

~

Teotihuacan, located in Central America, was the capital of a civilizing god named Quetzalcoatl. Here was considered the birthplace of the fifth sun after the fourth sun was destroyed in a great deluge. From these floodwaters emerged, assuming we are talking about literal *waters* and presuming we are talking about the end of the last *Ice Age*, a global network of unrelated but similar cultures and customs.

The *First Time*, or *Zep Tepi*, occurred after the waters of the abyss receded and the light of civilization emerged again with assistance from the *Urhsu,* or the lesser divine deities called *watchers*, and the powerful gods called *Neteru*. It was later that the Egyptian Osiris went on a civilizing mission around the world bringing knowledge of great things. We can theorize here that Osiris plays a role in the stories of people coming from the waters and teaching civilization, only to return to their homes one day leaving the newly civilized people to worship them in effigy. As a firm but peaceful teacher Osiris is often called *neb tem,* or universal master. His domain, as we see with other gods, "rested on water" with walls made of "living serpents."

Gods appearing on water, as with Jesus Christ walking on the same, could relate to both literal floods of water and of dark periods brought about by war, famine, disease, or massive natural disasters other than floods. Perhaps floods accompanied other disasters such as serpentine rocks called comets or massive volcanic eruptions followed by a blacking out of the sky. Any story relating to boats or caskets on water bringing civilization after cataclysm likewise share a striking parallel to various dramas and initiation rituals from ancient cultures worldwide. These vessels are the physical body, the water is illusion, and the bringer of light and life is the reawakened soul that has been *born again*. Thus, the initiate seeking *reincarnation, stellar rebirth, Living Resurrection*, etc., is not only *made in the image of god* but shares an understandable relationship with the gods themselves.

Such is the case of why a Pharaoh was directly associated with Osiris in seeking rebirth in the Osirian constellation known as Orion. These characters may have been based on real civilizing heroes sharing a common origin, but nevertheless they become the embodiment of a tradition which saves both the *physical man* from *real floods* and the *spiritual man* from *metaphoric floods* of *chaos* and *darkness*.

Teotihuacan was known as the *place where men became gods*, an exact parallel with the Giza structures, where initiates were risen by the *Lion's Paw* and exited to greet the eastern sun with a newly *reborn* title: *Son of God*.

As Hancock points out about the three major Giza pyramids, and in direct opposition with orthodoxy:

> *"Not a single one of these monuments had ever been found to contain the body of a pharaoh, or any signs whatsoever of a royal burial. Some of them were not even equipped with sarcophagi."*

One of the few lesser structures that did contain a sarcophagus, the Pyramid of Saqqara, was untouched by grave robbers and yet was still empty upon excavation.

According to the <u>Pyramid Texts</u> of Egypt, these supposed *tombs* for the Pharaohs were indeed temples of transfiguration wherein a neophyte would be initiated into *The Way*. They turned *dead men* into *immortal beings* by throwing *"open the doors of the firmament"* and making a road so the deceased might *"ascend into the company of the gods."*

The fact that the Great Sphinx is gazing due east towards the equinoctial sunrise is further proof of these facts.

It is said Napoleon Bonaparte spent the night inside the King's Chamber of the Great Pyramid during his conquest of Egypt and afterwards emerged shaken, never officially discussing what happened. Others have spent time there and claim to have witnessed specters or ghosts. The entire room was built to amplify sounds and vibrations, particularly if you are lying within the sarcophagus, as we can imagine Napoleon certainly did.

The massive *red room* is made of granite; 15 massive stone blocks comprise the floor, 100 massive blocks around 70 tons each erect the walls, and the ceiling is constructed of nine blocks weighing about 50 tons each. Back to the incredible accuracy in building, British Egyptologist Flinders Petrie wrote of the King's Chamber how it was incredibly placed *"at the level where the vertical section of the Pyramid was halved, where the area of the horizontal section was half that of the base, where the diagonal from corner to corner was equal to half the diagonal of the base."*

Even the smaller Queens Chamber speaks of the *mysteries* considering the great care in erecting its walls and ceiling but seeming lack of concern with its floor. This indicates perhaps that the roof represented the *divine heavens* and the floor the *mundane earth*.

Although the Giza complex was possessed and marked by many leaders and peoples over thousands of years, it was from some point used as a temple complex to perform rituals of a mysterious and almost supernatural nature. It acted as a doorway to the underworld and a gateway to the heavens, as is the case with similar facilities in the Americas built over caverns or natural springs. One such example is the *Great Pyramid of Cholula*. The sarcophagus acted as the *body* and the individual initiate acted as the *soul*. Upon emersion in the physical and rough tomb - the material body - the initiate would undergo a dark and isolated process of reflection within self (below) and communion with the divine (above). This entire ritual process, which included other steps, is told in the story of Osiris and Set. The rough ground and polished walls and ceilings represented the earth and heavens. Tight and cramped passageways opening into grander areas represented the *ups* and *downs* of life, the good and bad, the *breath of living*. Such maneuvering was required as a physical representation of the soul's journey in the corporeal body, and then its realignment with *source* upon death. Everything culminated in a *resurrection*.

Red walls in the King's Chamber bear a striking resemblance to the megalithic sites of Ġgantija on the island of Gozo, and the Hypogeum on the nearby island of Malta which is subterranean and womb-like. Red within the confines of such rooms likely represents the *pain* and *blood* of *birth*. Other temples contain at their core natural subterranean crypts or artificial chambers that mimic the womb itself. Yet more structures, perhaps including the Osireion, located under the Temple of Seti I, contain water by its construction.

The historian Herodotus documented that the lowest chamber of the Great Pyramid was once connected to the Nile via a channel. He writes of Khufu, *"for the underground he caused to be made as sepulchral chambers for himself in an island, having conducted thither a channel from the Nile."*

A parallel is easily found here with the *Land of the Rising Sun*, Japan, which sees the bloody red sun appear over the horizon of its ocean-locked islands. Japan still uses the red sun on their pure white flag. Blood can furthermore relate to menstruation. Conceptually the red is a symbol of blood, which is taken from the lamb to purify. The blood of Christ washes away our sins. Initiation into the *Mystery Religions* around the world involved red in the various chambers mentioned above as a symbol of the *womb*. After days of gestation a person would be born as a *Son* or *Sun of God*. What is meant by "sun" here is that they would be bright, pure, washed clean, etc. They were a miniature sun, with a fire burning inside - the *soul*. Amaterasu is the *light of heaven*, and each of us is an individual expression of that *light*.

Perhaps the red hats on Rapa Nui (Easter Island) Moai are a sort of solar corona, as is often used to depict Jesus, Mithra(s), Horus, and countless other god-like figures.

We know Pythagoras was also initiated into these *secret teachings* in Egypt within the Great Pyramid of Giza. He was placed in the King's Chamber sarcophagi for three days before being resurrected and offered the hand of an Egyptian hierophant speaking the words "come forth." Recall again John 11:4, which reads: *"And when he thus had spoken, he cried with a loud voice, Laz-a-rus, come forth."* Lazarus was also dead for three days in the tomb of materiality before being symbolically resurrected. The three days are a condensed version of the three stages of living: birth, life, death. Like Pythagoras he was initiated into the *mysteries* through a symbolic process of death and resurrection. Manly Hall writes in <u>The Secret Teachings of All Ages</u> of this ritual drama:

> *"In the King's Chamber was enacted the drama of the 'second death.' Here the candidate, after being crucified upon the cross of the solstices and the equinoxes, was buried in the great coffer. There is a profound mystery to the atmosphere and temperature of the King's Chamber: it is of a peculiar deathlike cold which cuts to the marrow of the bone. This room was a doorway between the material world and the transcendental spheres of Nature. While his body lay in the coffer, the soul of the neophyte soared as a human-headed hawk through the celestial realms, there to discover first hand the eternity of Life, Light, and Truth, as well as the illusion of Death, Darkness, and Sin. Thus in one sense the Great Pyramid may be likened to a gate through which the ancient priests permitted a few to pass toward the attainment of individual completion. It is also to be noted incidentally that if the coffer in the King's Chamber be struck, the sound emitted has no counterpart in any known musical scale. This tonal value may have formed part of that combination of circumstances which rendered the King's Chamber an ideal setting for the conferment of the highest degree of the Mysteries."*

It was through the passageways and chambers of this Great Pyramid that initiates *"entered its portals as men"* and *"came forth as gods."* Here Hall refers to this as the "second birth" out of the "womb of the Mysteries."

We have, too, from Tutankhamun's casket an inscription alongside of an ancient Anubis statue which reads: *"initiated into the secrets."*

The major myths of Egypt are, like they were in many cultures, far more than stories, as author Hancock points out: they *"had been dramatized and performed each year in Ancient Egypt in the form of a mystery play…"*

Such *mystery* traditions that teach *The Way* are as old as the Pyramids and likely predate even the Ice Age dating noted above. The ancient and incredible city of Heliopolis was once considered the center of these *mystery cults*. In Egypt the *City of the Sun* was *Innu* and associated with the nine divine gods, or *Ennead*. In the Egyptian creation story, the sun god RA was formed from *Atum* out of the *nothingness* called *Nun*. He created a divine of the air named *Shu* and a divine of moisture named *Tefnut.* In combing their powers, the god of earth *Geb* and goddess of sky *Nut* were formed. From their unification came Osiris, Isis, Set, and Nephthys.

In some versions of the story this "nothingness" was a period of watery chaos, perhaps associated with the Great Deluge, preceding Zep Tepi. It was here at Innu or Heliopolis that the gods initially began their rule during the *First Time*, and thus this sun city was a storehouse and foundation for a legacy of wisdom handed down from the heavens to earth. Such wisdom was entombed in the greatest temples, pyramids, and *secret teachings* of Africa, India, Asia, South and Central America, and particularly in the guardian of *secrets* that we called the Great Sphinx. Hall informs us of its duty as such: the Sphinx was an *"armed guardian of the Mysteries who, crouching at the gate of the temple, denied entrance to the profane."* In this manner the beautiful Sphinx represented the *"secret doctrine itself"* and protected the mysterious *Hall of Records* which are buried within the enigma of the ancient *Way*.

In the Odinic storyline there were Nine Worlds, and the gods directed our world from *Asgard*. As noted, much like Jesus or Krishna, Quetzalcoatl, Viracocha, Amaterasu, Osiris, etc., Odin's son Balder brought peace and love to the world. One of his twelve disciples was named *Loki*, the manifestation of evil. When Loki had attempted to kill Balder, as Typhon-Set tried to kill Osiris, his light and love vanished from the world. However, the gods attempted to bring him back to life through a process of *reincarnation* or *resurrection*. This *mystery* drama was, as all the others, organized in underground crypts which acted as temples and literal wombs inside of the earth itself. The chambers of these caves were nine, representing the Nine Worlds, as with the Nine Divine in Egypt. Hall writes of this tradition how the Neophyte was taken through a process of initiation identical to that of Egypt, Mesopotamia, and in the Americas:

> *"After wandering for hours through the intricate passageways, the candidate was ushered into the presence of a statue of Balder the Beautiful, the prototype of all initiates into the Mysteries. This figure stood in the center of a great apartment roofed with shields. In the midst of the chamber stood a plant with seven blossoms, emblematic of the planers. In this room, which symbolized the house of the Æsir, or Wisdom, the neophyte took his oath of secrecy and piety upon the naked blade of a sword. He drank the sanctified mead from a bowl made of a human skull and, having passed successfully through all the tortures and trials designed to divert him from the course of wisdom, he was finally permitted to unveil the mystery of Odin--the personification of wisdom. He was presented, in the name of Balder, with the sacred ring of the order; he was hailed as a man reborn; and it was said of him that he had died and had been raised again without passing through the gates of death."*

A disciple of Socrates, Plato consulted the priests of Memphis to be initiated in their *mysteries*, but it is likely his studies were imperfect. By Plato's time (c.428-347 B.C.) many high priests had all but forgotten the meaning of their primeval hieroglyphics, and this lack of proper interpretation continues today in the order of various societies, including Masonry. Having lived close to a century after Pythagoras (c.575-495 B.C) it is not clear whether the latter's initiation was also incomplete in the same manner.

This perhaps most famous land of Egypt is not the only one to contain artifacts, monuments, and *mysteries* from the ancient world that upon unbiased and honest investigation, reveal a level of technical and spiritual advancement exceeding contemporary times. There are also the Americas.

The Civilizing Way of South & Central America

The Olmec people are now thought to be the first civilizers of Central America, pre-dating the Maya by centuries, and ceasing to exist 1,500 years before the Aztec empire. Little is known, or next to nothing, about the Olmec people and culture despite their famous carvings of giant heads with distinctly African features. Some of these heads are between ten to thirty tons each. It is odd enough to find African anything in the Americas prior to a few hundred years ago, let alone thousands of years ago. But there is scant *"paleoanthropological evidence that one of the many migrations into the Americas during the last Ice Age did consist of peoples of negroid stock,"* according to Hancock. Such migration would have occurred around 15,000 BC.

Still, many of these immense heads were quarried from the Tuxtla mountains and moved over sixty miles, indicating the Olmec people were not very primitive. In fact, they are credited with creating the bar-and-dot system of calendrical notation – or they received such knowledge from an even more ancient culture. The infamous Mayan calendar is a creation of the Olmec people, with its starting date of 13th August 3114 BC. and end date of AD 2012.

It was at Coatzacoalcos on the Southern point of the Gulf of Mexico that the civilizing god Quetzalcoatl was said to have originally landed in Central America. At San Lorenzo, just west of Coatzacoalcos, *"the Olmecs had heaped up an artificial mound more than 100 feet high as part of an immense structure some 4000 feet in length and 2000 feet in width."*

Further east at La Venta is found the *Man in Serpent* relief holding a *banduddû bag*. La Venta is also home to a massive fluted-cone pyramid: *"The pyramid was 100 feet tall, almost 200 feet in diameters and had an overall mass in the region of 300,000 cubic feet…"* The site itself is roughly three-square miles and littered with plazas, mounds, platforms, and other smaller pyramids.

Interestingly, the Olmec heads may resemble the head of the Great Sphinx in Egypt, depending on who you ask, and some further suggest to a carving of a humanoid face found underwater off the coast of the extremely Southwestern Japanese island Yonaguni, just east of Taiwan. This latter complex is massive and is yet to be fully investigated.

As for La Venta, Hancock explains from firsthand experiences how it contains sculptures of *"realistic likenesses not only of negroes but of tall, thin-featured, long-nosed, apparently Caucasian men with straight hair and full beards, wearing flowing robes."* These depictions baffle the mind; firstly, due to their African portrayals, but secondly, due to their seemingly European portrayals that fit into the mythological pantheon of both Central and South America.

La Venta is home to hundreds of carved columns made of basalt and quarried from over sixty miles way, each weighing two tons.

Basalt columns, acting more like building blocks, were also quarried, and moved vast distances, then used to build the incredible site of Gunung Padang in Indonesia. The same is true for Nan Madol in Micronesia.

The Maya civilization, believed to have been birthed from the earlier Olmecs, lasted officially from about 300 B.C. until 900 A.D in Central America. Their pyramids were built with similar skill and, like those in Egypt, at one point in history were covered in limestone facing. The Mayan "giza" pyramid of *El Castillo* (The Castle) is located at *Chichén Itzá* on the Yucatan Peninsula in Mexico, where a combination of the Maya and Toltec societies date back more than 1,200 years officially. The structure is also known as the *Pyramid of Kukulkán*, a civilizing deity the Mayan called Quetzalcoatl. As with Khufu, this structure was designed so that on the vernal and autumnal equinoxes a serpent produced by light and shadow would appear on its sides.

Quetzalcoatl is the primary Chief deity in the Mexican pantheon. He goes by many names that include Itzamana, Kukulkan, and Gucumatz (Quiche Maya), and shares similarities with the great civilizers Votan and Osiris. The names Quetzalcoatl, Gucumatz, and Kukulkan translate to "Plumbed" or "Feathered Serpent," while both Votan and Itzamana are symbolized by a *serpent* and a *rattlesnake* respectively.

From *quetzal* comes "paradise bird" and from *coatl* comes "serpent." In Peru he goes by the name Amaru, or our *Amaruca*, which Hall points out literally means *"Land of the Plumèd Serpent."* According to the Ancient Maya texts known as <u>Books of Chilam Balam</u>:

> *"…the first inhabitants of Yucatan were the 'People of the Serpent'. They came from the east in boats across the water with their leader Itzamana, 'Serpent of the East', a healer who could cure by laying on hands, and who revived the dead."*

Quetzalcoatl was a great teacher, imparting knowledge on masonry, engineering, mathematics, metallurgy, astronomy, and general civilization. He was described and depicted as being fair with white skin and a long beard, a broad forehead, and a long robe reaching down to his feet.

Votan, the great civilizer, and Itzamana, the healing god, were both described as having a beard, robe, and pale white skin too. Osiris can also be seen wearing the white robe, as was he depicted with a curved beard, and although African his skin was green to signify an association with the *teachings of agriculture*. Sylvanus Griswold Morely, American archeologist and student of the Maya civilization, describes the history of these gods:

> *"The great god Kukulkan, or Feathered Serpent, was the Mayan counterpart of the Aztec Quetzalcoatl, the Mexican god of light, learning and culture. In the Maya pantheon he was regarded as having been the great organizer, the founder of cities, the former of laws and the teacher of the calendar. Indeed his attributes and life history are so human that it is not improbable that he may have been an actual historical character, some great lawgiver and organizer, the memory of whose benefactions lingered long after death, and whose personality was eventually deified."*

The Toltec people (900 A.D. - 1200 A.D.) developed from the Maya. Their society proceeded with producing incredible monuments and structures, too, as official history concludes.

Their "giza" is the *Pyramid of the Sun* located at Teotihuacan, Mexico, one of the biggest in Mesoamerica. This sun pyramid, as it is called today, is oriented to the eastern sky and rising sun.

At Teotihuacan is also the *Pyramid of the Moon* and the immense astronomically aligned roadway called the *Way of the Dead*. Although these names may set our imagination off with assumptions, but the *Way of the Dead (Calle de los Muertos)* was named as such by the Aztecs without any knowledge of its origin. The Citadel complex at Teotihuacan housing the Pyramid of

Quetzalcoatl was named by the Spanish – *La Ciudadela* – under an architectural assumption. The entire complex was reportedly ancient even to the Aztecs. Hancock says, *"the colossal edifices and avenues were already old beyond imagining"* when they arrived on the scene much later.

Central American tradition maintains that Teotihuacan was the *place where men became gods*, as was Giza. Such a notion rings in harmony with *mystery* cults around the ancient world, with remnants remaining today in various secret societies and myths. Egypt is the most well recognized, as detailed above. Teotihuacan also has another fascinating secret. The city was built with canals and branching waterways, *"artificially dredged into straightened portions of a river, which… ran all the way to Lake Texcoco, now ten miles distant but perhaps closer in antiquity,"* according to Professor Rene Millon.

The *Pyramid of the Moon* contains a drainage system of interlocking "carved rock pipes," writes Hancock. Others have proposed similar things about the Great Pyramid of Giza, that it acted as a water pump or functioned more like a machine.

The *Pyramid of the Sun* was constructed so that during the equinoxes *"rays from south to north resulted at noon in the progressive obliteration of a perfectly straight shadow hat ran along one of the lower stages of the western façade."* This light and shadow work, recall, was built into the Temple of Kukulkan at Chichén Itzá and the Great Pyramid at Giza.

The *Great Pyramid of Cholula* in Puebla, Mexico, is larger by volume than both Giza and El Castillo. Teotihuacan, Giza, and the Cholula pyramid all share the similar feature of either being built over subterranean caverns or water systems beneath. Ground penetrating radar indicates there are similar chambers, likely manmade, within the terraced structure of Gunung Padang in West Java, which dates potentially to over 25,000 years old. Turkey's Göbekli Tepe is the previous official record holder at 11,000 years old.

Teotihuacan was not only the *place where men became gods* but the capital of Quetzalcoatl, being also the birthplace of the fifth sun after a great deluge wiped out the fourth.

Tiahuanaco in the Andes of Bolivia was one of Viracocha's capitals, as was Cuzco, and it, of course, shared a similar purpose, having been built long before the Inca.

From Central America we now travel to South America where there are nearly identical stories about a creator god named Viracocha, who was known to the pre-Inca and the Inca people of Peru. Creator of the sun and moon, Viracocha was responsible for bringing civilization to the region with a tender kindness and love which seemed out of place in such a remote past – based on contemporary assumptions. From North to South, he performed miracles like *Christ*. According to an early Spanish chronicler:

> *"They say that this man travelled along the highland route to the north, working marvels as he went and that they never saw him again. They say that in many places he gave men instructions how they should live, speaking to them with great love and kindness and admonishing them to be good and to do no damage or injury one to another, but to love one another and show charity to all."*

Much like Quetzalcoatl, Viracocha went by other names including Ticci Viracocha, Kon Tiki, Thunupa, Taapac, Tupaca, Illa, and, as his name (*Viracocha*) translates into, *Foam of the Sea*. There seems to be little connection otherwise, but the Greek goddess of love Aphrodite was also known as *foam born*, i.e., *born from the sea* - the Greek *aphros* means *foam*. Much like Christ, he was a teacher and civilizer, moving about to heal the *sick* – in whatever capacity *physically* or *spiritually*. The maternal creator in Finnish folklore is the virgin daughter of the air who descends into the primeval waters where she resides for many years. All of this may be a reference to an early version of the concept of evolution, as also evidenced in the stories of Dagon and Oannes.

Hancock writes, *"Viracocha was also a teacher and a healer and made himself helpful to people in need. It was said that 'wherever he passed, he healed all that were sick and restored sight to the blind'."* Followers of the Biblical *Jesus* will recall Chapter 9 in the Book of John when Jesus healed a man who was born blind. Jesus performs other similar miracles in the books of Matthew, Mark, and Luke.

As a founder of law and writing, Quetzalcoatl in Central America and Viracocha in South America share similarities with the Egyptian deities Thoth and Ma'at, and the famous Hebrew law-giver Moses. Both left in the same manner they had arrived, by the ocean – Quetzalcoatl to the eastern sea after being vanquished by Tezcatilpoca, *the smoking mirror*, at Tollan, and Viracocha to the Pacific Sea after being conspired against like Osiris. As Hancock concludes:

> *"Quetzalcoatl promised his followers he would return one day to overthrow the cult of Tezcatilpoca and to inaugurate an era when the gods would again 'accept sacrifices of flowers' and cease their clamour for human blood."*

In the case of Quetzalcoatl his watery vessel was a *raft made of snakes*. Stunningly, on the other side of the world, we find Osiris, the universal master and teacher, with a domain made of "living serpents" that "rested on water." All three of these gods from South and Central America to Egypt taught agriculture. Osiris, the *Green Man* associated with Orion, shares a very human connection to the land since the name *'ourien'* also means semen. Teaching agriculture is one thing but mixed in with such knowledge were apparently universal themes of human, not plant, procreation.

The battle between Quetzalcoatl and Tezcatilpoca parallels an India myth detailing how Lord Shiva was attacked and driven out of his holy city of Dwarka by King Salwa (Salva). Located in Northwest India, Dwarka is an ancient, submerged city, thought to be the home of Krishna, the Hinudu *Krist* or *Christ*. Krishna's city was also thought to be myth until its discovery just off the coast of India in the Arabian Sea around 1963. Legend says that Salwa used an *illusion* to confuse his enemies, mirroring *the smoking mirror*, or Tezcatilpoca. He flew into the sky and attacked from above, shooting bolts of lightning or energy reminiscent of the *xiuhcoatl* (fire serpents) used by the gods of ancient Mexico. Hancock describes how they *"emitted burning rays capable of piercing and dismembering human bodies."*

Viracocha shares a distinct relationship with the Egyptian Osiris as well, having been likewise championed as a civilizer and struck down in a jealous conspiracy. As Osiris, whose body was placed in a coffin on the Nile, Viracocha was placed in a boat made of totora rush (papyrus reeds in Egypt) and set adrift on Lake Titicaca from whence he originally arrived. This occurred after he was conspired against by jealous and envious enemies in the likeness of Typhon-Set. Hancock goes on to explain the parallel use of these boats for transport in South America and Africa:

> *"Both had also been used for the long-distant transport of exceptionally heavy building materials: obelisks and gargantuan blocks of stone bound for the temples at Giza and Luxor and Abydos on the one hand for the mysterious edifices of Tiahuanaco on the other."*

The story of Noah and the Great Flood, as many have easily overlooked, is another version of the Osiris, Quetzalcoatl, and Viracocha legends. Noah was trapped on waters in an ark made of wood, like Moses in the basket and Osiris in the golden coffin, only to later emerge bringing civilization back to the world with the assistance of God.

~

From the Olmecs to the Maya, Toltecs, Aztecs, and Inca the precision in science, engineering, astronomy, architecture, agriculture, etc., stuns contemporary minds that are all too often inclined to dismiss these ancient advancements by ignoring the obvious or assigning them to some extraterrestrial assistance.

Similar structures are found all over the world, implying that a global society and culture utilized the exact same knowledge and practiced the exact same rituals – likely from a common "civilizing" source.

One of the most incredible sites is in Bolivia where the Inca claim that Viracocha and the gods were responsible for building what they merely occupied generations later.

Tiahuanaco sits on the shores, though much more distant shores, of Lake Titicaca. Within the site are the Akapana Pyramid, Kalasasaya, and the famous Gateway of the Sun, a roughly ten foot tall, thirteen foot wide, intricately carved piece of single stone weighing ten tons. In the center is the god Viracocha.

All indications point to Tiahuanaco being an island at one point. The surrounding area of the lake is littered with fossilized seashells though it is now situated more than two miles above sea level. Conventional history tells us the site is 1,500 years old despite the work of respected scientists like Professor Arthur Posnansky of the University of La Paz finding a construction date closer to 17,000 years ago – 15,000 BC.

Inside **Kalasasaya** there are carvings of fish gods with garments of scales and belts of crustaceans. These are like the Babylonian Oannes or Sumerian Uan, the great civilizer of Mesopotamia on the other side of the world. As a civilizer, he brought wisdom to mankind just like Adapa, the god of wisdom and hero of the Sumerian *fall of man* story.

Legend says Uan lived under the waters, emerging from the Persian Gulf in the morning to civilize mankind. Oannes is said to have *emerged from the sea* with *Seven Sages* to teach the *arts of civilization.* The Mayan word *uaana* interestingly means *"he who has resident in water."* Viracocha, remember, came from Lake Titicaca with knowledge of civilization.

The Sumerian goddess of oceans, Tiamat, was dismembered from a state of chaos into a state of order by the celestial hero Marduk. In Central America, Quetzalcoatl plays the part of Marduk and Cipactli, the Great Earth Monster, plays the part of Tiamat. Tiamat's dismemberment reminds us of the same fate befalling Osiris, Melissa, Orpheus, Dionysius, and Quetzalcoatl, who was *"cut in pieces for the cauldron."*

Kalasasaya is also home to idols holding strange objects in their hands like the Assyrian reliefs and *Apkallu* civilizers, of which there were seven, in Mesopotamia. In South America similar images are thought to depict Viracocha at Tiahuanaco – known as the *Viracocha Pillar.* Nearly identical stonework can be found on Rapa Nui, thousands of miles away westward into the ocean from Chile, Peru, and Bolivia, and nearly nine thousand miles away at the incredible site of Göbekli Tepe in modern Turkey. These sites depict the image of a character with arms and hands stretched around their belly.

The Aboriginal Australians are perhaps the oldest and longest consistent culture in the world today. Their creator-god and civilizer is known as *Rainbow Serpent*, who comes out of the "water hole" to bring civilization and life. His name relates to the life-giving essence of water. As for the snake itself as a *civilizer*, rather than a tempting *evil* force, we can look at its traditional role as a healer, wise voice, and *"prototype of the Universal Savior, who redeems the worlds by giving creation the knowledge of itself and the realization of good and evil,"* as per Manly Hall.

A few hundred meters southwest of Kalasasaya is a site called the *Puma Gate* or **Puma Punku**. Some of the remaining stones here, as many seem to have been blown apart and moved in a sudden and great cataclysmic event, weigh hundreds of tons – one is estimated at 440 tons. I-shaped metal clamps were also used, though found nowhere else officially in South America. However, they have been found in Upper Egypt on the island of Elephantine. Crosses were likewise found at Puma Punku, which were dated to some 1,500 years old, about the official dating of the site. Hancock points out how *they had been carved here, by a people with absolutely no knowledge of Christianity, a full millennium before the arrival of the first Spanish missionaries on the Altiplano.*

Legend holds that Quetzalcoatl, and by extension Viracocha, brought the cross with him to found civilization. Considering how the Christian Europeans were seen by the locals, it is possible that this fact is a result of mingling ancient myth with more contemporary history. Either way, we can be certain that all civilizer gods have an association with the *cross*.

Northwest of Lake Titicaca in Peru is another incredible site never discovered by the conquistadores – *Machu Picchu.* Dated to around 1,500 years roughly, the work of Rolf Muller, professor of Astronomy at the University of Potsdam, found a date closer to around 6,000 years–about 4,000 BC. There clearly were builders with immense storehouses of knowledge, presumably accumulated over thousands of years prior, constructing these complexes anywhere between the end of back to the heart of the last Ice Age.

~

Despite all the terrible things done by Francisco Pizzaro in the South America and Hernan Cortez in Central America, it was purely because of their European features that local Indians did not see them as a threat. Quetzalcoatl had promised to return from the Eastern Sea with his followers and then arrived the Spanish. But the Spanish slaughtered thousands, six thousand alone at Cholula, they merely matched the bloody rituals of the Aztecs in which tens of thousands were murdered to prevent the *end of the world*. The great civilizers of Central and South America taught the exact opposite and ironically both Pizzaro and Cortez played the part of the *trickster* Tezcatilpoca, whose cult demanded bloody human sacrifice.

Although Europeans are generally and historically condemned for what their ancestors did in Central and South America, it is important to recognize that these atrocities were only allowed by the great populations there due to religious and mythological traditions of white men with beards and robes who spread peace, love, and civility.

All these *civilizers* brought astronomy, art, mathematics, architecture, agriculture, metallurgy, law, peace, love, etc., to the Americas long before even the famous Knights Templar were an Order sailing the sea. Interestingly, the Templars did spread their European influence in white robes adorned with red crosses and long beards to much of the same regions roughly a hundred years before Cortez or Pizzaro began their conquests in the early 1500s.

Levitating Stones

Anthropologists, archeologists, historians, and the like, remain baffled that long before the Spanish arrived Central American cultures were using the essential Christian Cross. Having seen the similarities in building styles and designs with Egypt, a culture with the famous *Crux Ansata*, it should be no surprise. As we witnessed earlier, Kingsborough's <u>Antiquities of Mexico</u> depicts the Christ-like *Crucifixion of Quetzalcoatl* (Codex Borgianus). Such symbols were also found in South America. Perhaps the reason "experts" are so unwilling to confirm the obvious, is because of the associated stories about gods that seemed very Caucasian and human, or those of giants and dwarfs.

In Uxmal, Mexico, there stands the site of the *Pyramid of the Magician*. Myth records that the structure was erected by the supernatural powers of a dwarf in a single night. Stories attest to the ability of someone or something a very long time ago being able to manipulate massive stone and earth with relative ease.

Mayan legend says *all they had to do was whistle and heavy rocks would move into place.* In South America, stone blocks used to build Tiahuanaco were *carried through the air to the sound of a trumpet.* Such knowledge has apparently not been entirely lost either.

In the 1920s, Ed Leedskalnin began construction on the famous *Coral Castle* in Florida. A small and thin man, Ed refused to allow anyone to watch him construct the megalithic structure. He used no obvious modern machinery and instead maintained a mysterious box, stating that he had *learned the secrets of the pyramids.*

In Egypt magicians were said to be able to easily lift massive stones into the air. Imhotep, a priest from Heliopolis, was said to have been an architect with magical abilities who built ziggurats like those at Saqqara where was also found the powerful spiritual inscriptions called the Pyramid Texts.

Pacal's sarcophagus lid found within his tomb inside the *Temple of Inscriptions* at Palenque, Mexico.

At the *Temple of Inscriptions* at Palenque, Mexico, one of the most incredible finds has to this day sparked wild speculation about these ancient peoples and their ancestors. The 7th-century ruler of Palenque was named Pacal. When his tomb was found in the pyramid, his sarcophagus shared a striking similarity with an Egyptian mummy casing. The lid was ten inches thin, twelve feet and six inches long, and three feet wide. Hancock relates, having examined it himself, that it *"seemed to have been modeled on the same original as the magnificent engraved blocks the Ancient Egyptians had used for this exact purpose.* As can be seen in images, here is his description of the scene carved on top of the sarcophagus of Pacal, the Maya king:

> *"a clean-shaven man dressed in what looked like a tight-fitting body-suit, the sleeves and leggings of which were gathered into elaborate cuffs at the wrists and ankles. The man lay semireclined in a bucket seat which supported his lower back and thighs, the nape of his neck resting comfortably against some kind of headrest, and he was peering forward intently. His hands seemed to be in motion, as though they were operating levers and controls, and his feet were bare, tucked up loosely in front of him."*

Such imagery is reminiscent of the Olmec relief *Man in Snake* from La Venta. It seems mechanical and inorganic. Near the skeleton of Pacal was also found a small statuette of what appeared to be a Caucasian in long robs and a beard – the civilizer who brought *The Way* to these earlier cultures.

Mysteries of Xibalba & the Grand Medicine Society (*Midewiwin*)

One particularly fascinating story comes from Guatemala in Central America and mirrors the *mysteries* of the Odinic and Egyptian religions, and the Persian *mysteries*.

This is the story of **Xibalba**, or the cavernous underworld. The princess of this subterranean palace – not unlike the Greek story of Persephone and Hades – sends out owl messengers, guardians of wisdom, to two initiates named Hunhun-ahpu and Vukub-hunhun-ahpu, informing them to attend a ceremony in the sacred mountains of Guatemala.

Upon failing the tests, they were killed and buried together, with Hunhun-ahpu's head being placed in a calabash tree. This reminds us of Osiris and the tamarisk tree, which protected his coffin and body. A virgin girl named Xquip later approached the tree seeking its fruit – not unlike Eve in the Garden. Reaching for the food some saliva from her mouth fell onto the head of Hunhun-ahpu and she later found herself pregnant. The saliva here is identical to that which the *Spider Woman* used in the Hopi creation myth. The pregnant virgin needs no further explanation. Her father was angry and did not believe her story, thus demanding that her heart be placed inside an urn. As she was taken by executioners, she convinced them to substitute her heart for a piece of fruit, which was then burned while emitting a beautiful fragrance.

Onlookers believed this was her heart burning, a story sharing similarity, in part, with the Greek and Egyptian underworlds. Her two sons, Hunahpu and Xbalanque, attempted to avenge what amounted to their father's death. The princess of Xibalba was angry and so sent for the two men later in their lives.

From here are formed the seven stages of the *Xibalbian Mysteries*. Initiates, Hall tells us, *"crossed a river of mud and then a stream of blood"* in like manner to the trials of the Pyramids in Egypt.

This first ordeal ended in the *House of the Shadows* wherein the second trial began. The third trial took place in the *House of Spears*, the fourth in the *House of the Cold*, the fifth in a *Great Chamber* filled with tigers (*House of the Tigers*), the sixth in the *House of Fire*, and the seventh in the *House of Bats*. Each house had an important symbolic meaning wherein an alchemical transformation was meant to occur. Here we are reminded of the seven days of creation, the seven classical planets, and the seven grades of the Mithraic cult in Persia: corax (Raven), nymphus (Bridegroom), miles (Soldier), Leo (Lion), Perses (Persian), heliodromus (Courier of and to the Sun), and pater (Father).

A *Midewiwin Record of Initiation* from Alice Palmer Henderson,
as reproduced in Manly P. Halls <u>The Secret Teachings of All Ages.</u>

Initiates of the **Midewiwin**, or Grand Medicine Society of the Ojibwas, underwent near identical ritual initiations, as is also preserved in masonic ritual. These Indians were far away from South America, residing in the Northern U.S. and Southern Canada. Certainly, they were far removed from Egypt.

Hall explains the *Xibalba Mysteries* in greater detail within the pages of his masterpiece, The Secret Teachings of All Ages. He also goes on to explain how the *Midewiwin Mysteries* were transmitted:

> "*According to legend, Manabozho, the great Rabbit, who was a servant of Dzhe Manido, the Good Spirit, gazing down upon the progenitors of the Ojibwas and perceiving them to be without spiritual knowledge, instructed an otter in the mysteries of Midewiwin. Manabozho built a Midewigan and initiated the otter, shooting the sacred Migis (a small shell, the sacred symbol of the Mide) into the body of the otter. He then conferred immortality upon the animal, and entrusted to it the secrets of the Grand Medicine Society. The ceremony of initiation is preceded by sweat baths and consists chiefly of overcoming the influences of evil manidos. The initiate is also instructed in the art of healing and (judging from Plate III of Mr. Hoffman's article) a knowledge of directionalizing the forces moving through the vital centers of the human body. Though the cross is an important symbol in the Midewiwin rites, it is noteworthy that the Mide Priests steadfastly refused to give up their religion and be converted to Christianity.*"

We are clearly dealing here with the same sophisticated system of philosophical and spiritual development whether we investigate Hinduism, Buddhism, Christianity, Judaism, Islam, or any of the world's other *schools of wisdom*; be them found in Japan, Egypt, South America, Central America, India, Greece, or Rome. In all these cultures and myths, we find *mountains*, and caves or constructed temples, held as sacred places to commune with the gods, receive guidance (commandments), and become *enlightened*.

An Olmec relief from La Venta, Mexico
depicts a serpent around a human holding the banduddû.

Magdalin of West & East: *Vastu Shastra & Feng Shui*

Many women have gone by the title of *Mary* - one raised in a monastic environment. It is a surname for *magdal-elder*, meaning "watchtower of the flock." In the *Kujiki-72*, a sacred Japanese text, the universe is regulated by five constitutions comprising *seventeen ways*. Whoever embodies these "ways" comes to embody *The Way of the Protector*, and if they choose to be a teacher of neophytes, *The Way of the Watchtower*. Following this "way" consists of rediscovering the *lost word* of the *Grand Master*, which has remained buried in the rubble of the collapsed temple since the death of Chiram Abiff. Let us not forget that in Luke 10:1-2 Jesus Christ sends out "seventy-two" new disciples.

Equilibrium brings about the realization of the *Universal Agent* by which the alchemists could resurrect the spirit and finish the unfinished temple. This *balance* is found between *two thieves* like Christ and in the temple so long as Samson does not bring down the pillars. As Levi explains:

> "The law of equilibrium in analogy leads to the discovery of an universal agent which was the Grand Secret of the alchemists and magicians in the middle ages."

It is ultimately found with the *Alchemical Marriage* of Christ and his Bride. *The Way* is the center path of Buddhism, also known as the *Middle Way*. It is the realization of the "god within" rather than a god outside. By finding what is within, one is embodying the Greek philosophy: *Know Thyself*. This axiom is attributed to the philosopher Socrates (469-399 BC), and his disciple Plato (429-347 BC), who taught Aristotle. In Kabbalah this path is the *Middle Pillar of Mildness*. In the Quran it is "the way" of Allah (God). In the far east there is Tao, the source and law of being (Divine Plan), or The Way. In Hinduism *The Way* is called *Bhakti Marga*. The *Path of Isis* continues after physical death, too, since the orientation of the human body-temple, like that of manmade temples, was in many cultures critical for the soul. In Hindu tradition, the physically dead were placed with their head pointing north, since this is where the soul supposedly can exit the world. This is like the *Opening of the Mouth* ceremony in Central America, Egypt, and Japan. Other traditions such as those of the *Vastu Shastra*, hold that your head should be oriented during nightly sleep in the west, east, or south, but never to the north unless one wishes to lucid dream or travel in the astral realm. East is considered idea for students as it enhances memory. West benefits those seeking vain success. South is optimal, they believe, because it is the realm of Yama, who will assist in you obtaining restful sleep. Vastu Shastra is used also for architecture and room arraignment, relating the practice to Chinese *Feng Shui*. For example, a Buddha head should only be placed in the north and east corners of the room to bring protections. Placing it in the west, where the sun dies in the *land of shadow*, or in the south, the direction of the *land of death*, will not be optimal.

One of the oldest examples we have of the importance of direction in *ritual* is found in the remotest antiquity of 7,000 BC, or earlier, at a place called Mehrgarh in modern Pakistan. Funerary rites held here confirmed that the posturing of the dead was done in alignment with west-east, the head connecting with the *eastern sun* and the feet with the *western sun*. Put another way, the head rises like the top of an Ankh cross or pentagram, while the feet are rooted in the *land of shadow*. Hancock makes this observation from the collected evidence in his work <u>Underworld</u>, which is a masterpiece of investigative journalism:

> "The bodies were carefully arranged in a 'flexed' or embryonic postures, oriented with the head towards the east and the feet towards the west, surrounded by personal effects and sometimes by

offerings of food and drink for sustenance on what was clearly believed to be some form of afterlife journey of the soul."

The Sanskrit *tat tvam asi*, or "thou art that," is the purest expression in Hinduism of man's relationship with the *Cosmic Mind*. In Greece the philosophy of *Know Thyself* was directly associated with the Oracle of Delphi.

The Oracle of Delphi

The word *Olympic* is derived from the Greek *Olympia* where the original Olympic Games were held in honor of Zeus, who lived on the highest elevation of Cyprus known as *Mount Olympus* (Olympos). It is at the top of sacred mountains like these where man has for millennium gone to have contact with the *divine*: from Mt. Sinai (Jabal Mousa) to Mt. Fuji, and from Gunung Padang to Mt. Kailash and Mt. Meru. Greece is also the location of another highly sacred mountain called Parnassus. This is where the famous *Oracle of Delphi* is located: Alexander the Great once visited her for consultation during his military campaigns.

Its original name was *pytho* or *pythia* since its chambers were initially home to a great Python. The name *Pythoness*, or Pythia, was given to a female hierophant of the oracle. It literally relates to those thrown into a frenzy by inhaling noxious fumes from decomposing matter. The author Alexander Wilder derives the name *Delphi* from *Delphos*, meaning *womb*.

When Apollo climbed Mt. Parnassus and slew the serpent after lengthy combat, he became the *Pythian Apollo* and began giving oracles. He also shared with Dionysus the honor of being a patron god of Delphi. Serpents remained a symbol of the Oracle in their shared association with Apollo, the sun god. For the great king of the sky is an *eagle* and its natural enemy is the *python*.

The *oracle* was seated on a tripod formed by the twisting bodies of three serpents. Although it was widely held that the priestess would inhale vapors emanating from cracks within the earth to deliver her prophecies, other myths relate that she was forced to stare into the eyes of a serpent before speaking with *fascination* and the *voice of God*. Initially she was taking up the tripod once every seventh birthday of Apollo, but as demands grew, she was forced upon the tripod once every month or more. Philosopher Iamblichus describes how the spirit of the *oracle* - considered a demon by some and a God to others - took control of the priestess of Apollo at Delphi and manifested through her to speak:

> *"But the prophetess in Delphi, whether she gives oracles to mankind through an attenuated and fiery spirit, bursting from the mouth of the cavern; or whether being seated in the adytum on a brazen tripod, or on a stool with four feet, she becomes sacred to the God; whichsoever of these is the case, she entirely gives herself up to a divine spirit, and is illuminated with a ray of divine fire. And when, indeed, fire ascending from the mouth of the cavern circularly invests her in collected abundance, she becomes filled from it with a divine splendour. But when she places herself on the seat of the God, she becomes co-adapted to his stable prophetic power: and from both of these preparatory operations she becomes wholly possessed by the God. And then, indeed, he is present with and illuminates her in a separate manner, and is different from the fire, the spirit, the proper seat, and, in short, from all the visible apparatus of the place, whether physical or sacred."*

Oracles were routinely approached before declarations of war or during a war to determine troop movements, and if a city should be attacked; if so, at what time on what day. On more than one occasion it seemed that the *oracles*, particularly at Delphi, acted as unofficial ministers of war and in some capacity as an ancient secretary of foreign affairs.

Although the *Oracle at Delphi* inhaled awful fumes, other *oracles* provided divination in a sober state. This is true for the Oracle at Dodana, where information was received without frenzy, madness, or hallucination. On the other hand, in the ancient Greek city of Argos, the *oracle* would partake of the blood of a lamb to provide insight.

Delphi might be most famous, but there were other *oracles*: Tenarus *in Locania, Dodona in Epirus*, and *Lebadea in Boeotia*.

The Oracle of Delphi Entranced, by Heinrich Leutemann (1824-1905)

Noxious fumes from inside the earth are thought to be responsible for the convulsions and hallucinations experienced by the High Priestess at the Delphi temple of Apollo. But at other sacred locations, such as Eleusis about one hundred miles away, another substance was used.

Those seeking guidance at Eleusis were to first drink a substance called *kykeon* upon entering the temple. The beverage was made of water, mint, and barley; or rather the psychoactive *ergot* fungus growing on the latter. There are also other wild grasses growing in the Mediterranean basin that support such fungal growths, along with the Syrian *rue* and the *acacia* of the Middle East. Ergot fungus is the same fungus that Albert Hoffman used to synthesize LSD in 1938.

Eleusis was sacred to the cult of Demeter, the agricultural goddess often referred to as *Erysibe* – meaning *ergot*. The purple color of the fungus explains robes of the same color worn by this goddess, as does it explain the divine nature of the color itself in its relation to *wisdom and guidance*. The Egyptian *blue lotus* and *Mandrake Root* were of identical consideration, as were poppy seeds, which were also sacred to the Greek Demeter (Ceres).

In Zoroastrianism was the herb *Peganum harmala* and in Mithra(s) cult was *haoma*. The Maya of Central America took *balché*, which was extracted from tree bark like the South American *ayahuasca*. In northern Mexico and North America there is the small cactus called *peyote*, which has psychoactive properties. In the same region we find the Aztecs to have used *morning glory seeds* called *ololiuqui*, along with *teonanactl*, or mushrooms known as the "flesh of the gods."

It is perhaps from the *plant spirits* more than any other source that we acquired *divine assistance* or *oracle* from the world beyond our own. This *plant guidance* is yet another archetype of the great *civilizing* gods who spread their wisdom over much of the earth after a great cataclysm in human pre-history; and one that relates to the *dying-god* myths found within all mythology.

Such is the nature of *shamanism*.

The Civilizing Way of Plant Spirits

Around 35,000 years ago in Europe and about 27,000 years ago in Africa, beautiful and thought-provoking art began to appear seemingly from nowhere in caves and on rocks. It appeared in an established and sophisticated form without any evidence of pre-formation. As archeologist David Lewis-Williams suggests, the catalyst for human spiritual development *"was the cultivation of altered states of consciousness, most probably first experienced by our ancestors through the accidental consumption of plant or fungal hallucinogens."*

The stories of *divine knowledge* being imparted to mankind from spirits, gods, goddesses, *ascended masters*, wise teachers, and today by *ancient aliens*, etc., in myth especially, is well preserved within the study theology and theurgy.

Muhammed was visited by the Angel Gabriel and revealed the text of the *Holy Quran*. Moses famously talked with God by means of a burning bush and later met him face-to-face when receiving the *Ten Commandments*. The *Revelation of St. John* was received in similar manner. In fact, John was writing on the Greek island of Patmos, home to very famous *magic mushrooms*. Joseph Smith, the founder of Mormonism, received golden plates from the angel Moroni that contained the *Book of Mormon*.

The *Bible* itself is the "word of God" and Ezekiel, like the Prophet Enoch, had direct contact with the *divine*. Ezekiel's famous "wheel" itself may be attributed to later *fairy circles, fairy lights, crop circles*, and *flying discs* with rotating lights. These things have been documented in some capacity for tens of thousands of years by shamans around the world, who are given knowledge of how to *heal* or *civilizer* their people better.

Psychoactive plants are not always needed to enter these *other worlds*, or *altered states of conscious*, either, especially considering that we all produce DMT (Dimethyltryptamine) naturally.

One 1979 study published in *Journal of the American Medical Association*, 'Increased Excretion of Dimethyltryptamine and Certain Features of Psychosis', found that with more DMT in the body the more likely a person was to experience episodes of psychosis or schizophrenia:

> *"Dimethyltryptamine excretion was greatest in schizophrenia, mania, and 'other psychosis' and tended to decline as clinical state improved. Psychotic depressives excreted smaller amounts of DMT more akin to those excreted by neurotic and normal subjects... Syndromes suggesting elation, perceptual abnormalities, and difficulty in thinking and communicating were most correlated with raised urinary DMT excretion."*

Dr. Rick Strassman's famous medical trials at the University of New Mexico found that subjects given controlled doses of DMT would report not just *aliens* and *fairies*, but also spaceships and clowns. Strassman explains in his book <u>DMT The Spirit Molecule</u> how the *other worlds* are simply not detectable to scientific instrumentation, but that they are accessible through these types of substances:

> *"These worlds are usually invisible to us and our instruments, and are not accessible using our normal state of consciousness. However, just as likely as the theory that these worlds exist 'only in our minds' is that they are, in reality, 'outside us' and freestanding. If we simply change our brains receiving abilities, we can comprehend and interact with them."*

A small number of shamans are gifted enough to experience these other worlds by slipping into altered states of consciousness naturally and without the need for hallucinogens. DMT is likely playing a significant role here, outside of certain *sacred ceremonies*. Hancock relates these holy men to abductees of the unidentified flying object:

> *"These special gifted shamans, the spontaneous trancers, obviously provide the closest parallel to UFO abductees, whose experiences are also spontaneous and not deliberately induced."*

If we are talking about *plant spirits*, which come in a variety of forms, perhaps these *Green Men* of the forest, like the *little green fairy men* of legend, are the basis for ufological *little green men*.

The shamanic journey is essentially the same: *whether contacted at an early age or not to be a shaman or abductee, the individual will be floated into the sky, or climb there themselves, or be taken to an underworld, where they will interact with therianthropes, serpents, and spirits, experience what we may term 'medical experiments', have crystals or other objects implanted, be dismembered, be given special knowledge and then finally returned home having willfully sacrificed themself like Jesus Christ or Odin for the betterment of their people.*

Necromancy

There are many forms of divination, including the reading of *tealeaves*, *nigromancy* or *necromancy* (also *psychagogues*, *nigrumencia* and *nekromantie*), *cartomancy*, and *haruspicy*, the study of entrails. Some forms are obscure or bizarre, including divination by moles on the body.

Necromancy, from Greek meaning "corpse divination," has two forms; one by evocation of prayer, perfumes, and magical objects; and the other by blood, curse, and sacrilege. Francis Barrett documents in <u>The Magus</u> these two kinds as such: *necromancy* includes *"raising the carcasses, which is not done without blood,"* and *sciomancy*, when *"the calling up of the shadow only suffices."*

Necromancy divination is conducted by using the carcass or its parts, for in these are spiritual qualities friendly to spirits. Souls may love their body even after death, so goes this *magical philosophy*, especially those souls having left their bodies by sudden violence. Barrett explains necromancy further:

> *"Necromancy has its name because it works on the bodies of the dead, and gives answers by the ghosts and apparitions of the dead, and subterraneous spirits, alluring them into the carcasses of the dead by certain hellish charms, and infernal invocations, and by deadly sacrifices and wicked oblations."*

When some read the word *necromancy*, they are ready to put additional crosses around their neck and hold their <u>Bible</u> even tighter, despite that same book preserving accounts of *dream interpretation* and *necromancy*. In 1 Samuel 28 is the famous story of *The Witch of Endor*. The Christian fetish for Judaism also ignores the story of Onkelos, as detailed earlier, who in tract 57a of the <u>Talmud</u> literally conjures Jesus Christ from the grave and from his eternal suffering in *"boiling excrement."*

But *necromancy* is no more a horrible operation than the misunderstood nature of sacrificing a *kid*, i.e., baby goat.

There have been great injustices in reporting the works of *magicians* throughout the ages, as has there been the same committed against the *mysteries* of antiquity. Those accusing the Greeks of consulting the Devil at Delphi are usually the same as those consulting their God to: *show me a sign that I am on the right path* or *making the right decision*. Although this is not to disparage or denigrate Christianity or Judaism. Levi says of this fact:

> *"Horrible histories were circulated concerning the Magi; sorcerers and vampires cast upon them the responsibility of their own crimes; they were represented as feasting on infants and drinking human blood."*

In another statement he speaks of the quintessence of *profane beliefs* relating to the killing virgins or kids:

> *"Prophetic inspirations adorn it, while it is the hatred of innocence and virginity which promoted Goëtic Magic to sacrifice children, whose blood was regarded notwithstanding as having a sacred and expiatory virtue."*

The practice of *necromancy*, however, without doubt produced awful operations carried out by insane practitioners. It has therefore come to represent all acts of *black magic* in general. Yet the practice itself, "communication with the dead, especially in order to predict the future," is something we do every time we leave candy out for Halloween or cookies and milk by the fireplace on Christmas Eve. Every prayer to a dead relative for *guidance* or *protection* is an act of *necromancy*.

General *Divination* & *Superstition*

Divination comes in many forms, including the common game of apple bobbing or throwing a bouquet of flowers at a wedding. These two acts constitute a practice aimed at *predicting the future*, even if undoubtedly some will cry foul and suggest these games are merely fun and symbolic. They will be called *superstitious*, although the word *superstition* comes from a Latin word referring to *"something that survives."* Superstitions persist even in contemporary times with some buildings in the west still constructed without that misunderstood number thirteen – as in a thirteenth floor. In the east, such as Japan, it's the number four, since its pronunciation is *shi* – the word for death.

Those biting the apple in water, or upon a string since they are sometimes suspended, are participating in a practice of predicting the future even if it is *just a game*. The winner usually receives a prize, perhaps candy or a toy, or maybe the apple itself. In the old world, it may have been the apple itself or the reward of *future knowledge*. If I can bite this apple, then (blank) is true or not true. The apple motif clearly takes us back to Eden too. Whoever catches the bouquet of flowers at a wedding is the next to be married.

The breaking of a mirror and the passing of a black cat still grasp our attention today, as does the concern for those about to walk under a ladder.

Superstition is not always about unseen forces, though many "games" we "play" today are literally superstitious traditions we still practice with a nervous laugh for "fun" and "just in case." They are things that also play on the imagination and act as suggestible influences upon the mind much like a *placebo*.

In the story of Parmenides, master of Pythagoras, the former kneels to drink from a spring and afterwards can predict an earthquake. How is one to determine natural causes by merely sipping water from a spring? There cannot be a reaction with first there being an action, going all the way back to the first emanations of the *Cosmic Mind*. Or are we dealing with *miracle*?

This is the misunderstood nature of *occult science* because *action* is *reaction*, and *reaction* is *action*; they are one in the same. For there is nothing "magical" about tasting the presence of bituminous and sulphureous flavors in water, especially if the water tastes different on other occasions, and being alerted to possible subterranean activities. In this way, again, *magic* and *divination* were truly forms of *science*. If nature imparts some unseen quality or scientific wisdom, then the *miracle* becomes classifiable as a *law of nature*.

Birds have long foretold future events, and through understanding their flight patterns and nesting habits, one may predict weather phenomena like rain. Studying their digestive and respiratory systems, as with any animal, may help determine atmospheric influences, and here arises the purpose behind the practice of *haruspicy*.

Levi suggests that without being familiar with the usage of a divination tool it is only by chance that any prophecy may come to pass:

> "It is followed also at this day by adepts of cartomancy who make use of the great magical Tarot alphabets, for the most part, without being acquainted with their values. In such operations accident only chooses the signs on which the interpreter depends for inspiration, and in the absence of exceptional initiation and second sight, the phrases indicated by the combinations of sacred letters or the revelations of the combined figures prophesy according to chance."

Here we would partially disagree with the author because, even by chance, such operations acting on the imagination may bring about the very prophecy through a form of self-fulfillment. Conversely, without knowledge of the *secret science* it would indeed be difficult to see the "sacred letters" as anything more than a fun or superstitious game.

The common greeting "have a nice day," and the common response, "you too," are forms of *magic* and even *divination*; wishing someone to have pleasurable or pleasant experiences by impressing the idea upon their mind with your *will*. The same is true for "happy birthday" and the numerous reasons why one would "congratulate" another.

~

The word *science* is itself is derived from the Latin *scientia*, from *scire*, which means to *know* something. What is usually considered its opposite, i.e., magical intuition, is its own definition. The word *intuition* comes from the Latin *intuitio*, from *intueri*, meaning to *consider*. Science thus means *to know something*, perhaps immediately, and intuition means *to study and consider* something. In other words, when one receives an *oracle*, they are being provided with information of the future without ever having to *consider* its validity, and it is only their *faith* which maintains the belief.

Divination is therefore no more *superstitious* and vulgar than modern practices of *science* that rely heavily on assumptions, faith, and the sacred words of their own *oracles*.

Whether information is obtained by divinatory means, superstitious practices, consulting oracles, or the like, *faith* and *belief* can cultivate what is foretold.

~

In this myth of the *Quest of the Golden Fleece*, the adventurer Jason symbolizes a candidate for initiation into the *mysteries*. Embodying the inconsistencies and weaknesses of mankind he is only considered a hero through his valor.

Upon acquiring the Golden Fleece Jason does not simply obtain wisdom, however, because he only acquires the gold through a form of theft. He owes its mastery to treason and his search for material wealth, making Jason's adventures akin to the Ring of Alberich story. Hence the virtues of the Golden Fleece will not, and are never to be, understood by the likes of Jason and all he exemplifies, but only to the disciples and students of Orpheus may its wisdom be attained.

Hercules, who is a savage force in the story, strays from the path in pursuit of other loves, a clear inclination of all who make the same journey.

Orpheus was able to prevent a shipwreck during the voyage by playing his lyre and drowning out the voices of the lovely Sirens that otherwise would have drawn the initiates to sure destruction - collapsing the temple upon *reason* and *truth*.

Levi explains how during the Quest, *"Medae betrays here father like Ham and assassinates her brother like Cain."*

Thus Medea, like the Greek enchantress Circe, is a representation of *Malefic Magic*. She is the shameless prisoner who makes nature an accomplice in her crimes.

Levi goes on to explain that these creatures are not merely confined to myth: the enchantresses known as Circe and Medea *"inspire nothing but brutal passions; they exhaust and disdain you."* Therefore, they are to be handled in the ways of Ulysses, by obliging them into obedience through releasing *fear* and by being able to leave them without *regret*.

Such defiling creatures are the sirens of antiquity, conquered by the harmonious music of Orpheus for which Pythagoras defined as the true nature of God; *absolute truth* cloaked in light and the *true Way*. Only through *harmony* and *equilibrium* can one conquer the three heads of Cerberus: ignorance, fear, and superstation.

In relation to the Static Isis quote, *"No Mortal Man Hath Ever Me Unveiled,"* Hall famously writes: *"Wisdom is not bestowed, it is achieved."* Whether by civilizer god or oracle, the quest must be undertaken by an individual who is upright and true, never drawn from *The Way* by siren songs or a *desire* to hasten the necessary quest.

~ **Ignorance is overcome by** *civilization*, **Fear by** *realization*, **and Superstition by** *wisdom* ~

Sacred Groves & Wise Trees

As with Delphi, small groves and large forests were the domain of the protector Diana-Artemis, lady of the woods. Any group of trees, even a small orchard, was sacred to her and it was within these natural temples that the goddess would provide *guidance*.

As depicted Tolkien's <u>Lord of the Ring</u>, trees were powerful and wise forces. Another interesting "ring" connection can be made here as trees themselves have layers of rings for each year of their life. These rings can symbolically be attributed in part to Saturn, too, since the Roman festival of *Saturnalia*, December 17-23, was to honor this god with trees and gifts. Trees are upright and firm, making them another relatable symbol to the penis, or *Green Man of the Woods*: Osiris-Orion, i.e., *Ourien* or "sperm."

Trees directly relate to the mystical Kabbalah where we find the *Sephirothic Tree*. We also know of the *Tree of Life*, *World Tree*, and the *Flower of life*, which springs forth from the *Seed of Life* and *Monad* (source). Many ancient people explained how the universe was a tree growing from a singular point in space, which relates to the apex of a pyramid extending into heaven. Hall writes here of trees in their inverted state:

> *"The medieval Qabbalists represented creation as a tree with its roots in the reality of spirit and its branches in the illusion of tangible existence. The Sephirothic tree of the Qabbalah was therefore inverted, with its roots in heaven and its branches upon the earth. Madam Blavatsky notes that the Great Pyramid was considered to be a symbol of this inverted tree, with its root at the apex of the pyramid and its branches diverging in four streams towards the base."*

These four "streams" represent the four corners of the earth, the four winds, four elements, and the four seasons and *Horsemen of the Apocalypse*, which all correspond to the four aspects of the sphinx. As the tree is symbolic of the *Macrocosmic Universe*, we must remember that the universe reaches down to us in the form of an inverted pyramid, just as we reach up to God in the form of an upright pyramid from the *Microcosmic Universe*. Trees were considered sacred by almost every culture, especially to the Celts and their Druidic priests. In African-Haitian Voodoo they are called *reposoir*. Trees extend their branches upward into the heavens and extend their roots downward into the earth like bolts of lightning. Hall explains once more:

> *"According to the esoteric doctrine, man first exists potentially within the body of the world-tree and later blossoms forth into objective manifestation upon its branches. According to an early Greek Mystery myth, the god Zeus fabricated the third race of men from ash trees. The serpent so often shown wound around the trunk of the tree usually, signifies the mind – the power of thought – and is the eternal tempter or urge which leads all rational creatures to the ultimate discovery of reality and thus overthrows the rule of the gods. The serpent hidden in the foliage of the universal tree represents the cosmic mind; and in the human tree, the individualized intellect. The concept that all life originates from seeds caused grain and various plants to be accepted as emblematic of the human spermatozoon, and the tree was, therefore, symbolic of organized life unfolding from its primitive germ. The growth of the universe from its primitive seed may be likened to the growth of the mighty oak from the tiny acorn. While the tree is apparently much greater than its own source, nevertheless that source contains potentially every branch, twig, and leaf which will later be objectively unfolded by the processes of growth."*

Groves are also held sacred by *black magicians* and *sorcerers*, even if this association has more to do with the history of *witches*, i.e., women practicing herbology and visiting the woods for their botanical studies that included medicine and cooking. Since trees produce oxygen, it is believed that spiling the blood of an animal or human in the presence of trees makes that *life force* extra potent and energizing. Practitioners of Chinese medicine say that *chi* is made more potent by fresh oxygen, too, hence the reason breathing is so important in ancient Chinese, and Indian, practices. These groves are home to various practices relating to nature and have commonly been the scene of fictional accounts of witchcraft or sorcery. Otherwise, we find that the *sacred groves* of Diana-Artemis were simply denigrated with rumors and lies to disparage the *mysteries* as pagan heathenism. Hall writes in <u>The Secret Teachings</u> about the usage of sacred groves for ceremonial purposes:

> *"The worship of trees as proxies of Divinity was prevalent throughout the ancient world. Temples were often built in the heart of sacred groves, and nocturnal ceremonials were conducted under the wide-spreading branches of great trees, fantastically decorated and festooned in honor of their patron deities. In many instances, the trees themselves were believed to possess the attributes of divine power and intelligence, and therefore supplications were often addressed to them."*

Today we call these ceremonies *forest bathing* and make them a part of our busy lifestyles without a second thought about their *sacred* or *diabolic* origins.

The Creation of Man, Earth & Natural Law AND Ancient Maps

"The universe, and all that it contains, was produced by Absolute Truth, is maintained by Absolute Truth, and is moved inevitably toward ends determined before the processes of creation had brought forth the world."

~ Manly P. Hall ~

The Dark Father & Triumphant Son

In Greek mythology and *esoteric history*, the first creatures to have the appearance of *life* were the children of *Mother Earth* (Gaea) and *Father Heaven* (Ouranos). Ouranos found little joy in his children, however, since they were deformed with one hundred hands and fifty heads. He hated them so much they were imprisoned within the earth. Only the Cyclopes and Titans were left to roam free. Gaea was so displeased with the treatment of her children that she appealed to them individually for help in stopping their wicked and hateful father. No child was brave or bold enough to take a stand except for the Titan Cronus.

After waiting on his father one day, Cronus wounded him terribly, producing blood drops that sprang forth a fourth race of monsters known as the Giants.

Here we can recall the falling of blood drops of Dionysus, from whence sprout the pomegranate; or the *nama sebesion* (sacred fluid) of Taurus the bull, slain by Mithra(s) to bring in the next *age*. The wife of Shiva from the Hindu trinity, which includes Brahma and Vishnu, is the *black goddess* Kali. Both Shiva and Kali have

Kali defeating Raktabija.

reproductive and destructive qualities. As goddess of time and death, like Cronus and Saturn, Kali, or the Tibetan mKha'sGroma, is commonly depicted with her tongue protruding aggressively from her mouth. In the story of a great battle between the goddess Durga and demon Raktabija, Kali acts to prevent the further birth of demons by licking up each drop of blood as it falls. In the *Quest of the*

Golden Fleece there is an ointment bestowed upon the leader of the group by a female magician, which makes the wearer safe from all harm. Edith Hamilton writes in <u>Mythology</u> about this special ointment and how it would make *"him who rubbed it on his body safe for the day; he could not be harmed by anything."* The plant from whence this magical substance was derived supposedly came from the blood drops of Prometheus. Greek writer Apollonius said the herb grew from the flowing of blood out of the Promethean wound, which dripped to the ground corrupted on the hill Caucasus. In Anatolia mythology, blood from the youthful Attis, whose death and resurrection were celebrated in spring, also fell upon the ground, redeeming the earth like the blood of Jesus Christ. In the Greek story of Adonis, killed by a boar, his blood fell to the earth and gave birth to a crimson flower. When the bee nymph Melissa was dismembered like Orpheus, Dionysus, Osiris, Quetzalcoatl, Chiram Abiff, and the brilliant philosopher Hypatia, her body parts

Mithra(s) slaying the Bull.

birthed a swarm of bees, which produce the honey associated with the crimson rose of Adonis (*Dat Rosa Mel Apibus*). The teardrops of RA likewise were said to turn into bees upon striking the ground; in other words, solar rays penetrate and impregnate the earth so that she can give birth those beautiful spring flowers. These tears are closely associated with *alchemical dew* falling from the head of the *Grand Architect*. The rose flower is, furthermore, thought to have fallen from the hair of Aurora, the Greek goddess of dawn, and later sprouted from the footsteps of Aphrodite. Wild roses are also said to have grown from her tears when they struck the ground.

In Mesopotamia an ointment was used to perform incantations with ghosts and gods. Witches were known to fully hallucinate what became the infamous *Black Mass* by a similar salve, waking up later believing they had communed with the Devil. In the two previous cases we are dealing with substances, i.e., things substituted for *bread and wine*, that relate directly to the *Eucharist* and communion with the Christian God. Their origins are in wheat and grapes, both of which adorn images of the *Flawless Goddess* Isis.

After dethroning his father, the Titan Cronus became lord of the universe with his sister-queen Rhea or Ops. From Rhea, the Greek earth goddess, we can extract Ma-Rhea (Mary).

In similar fashion to the battle waged between him and his father, Zeus, one of the sons of Cronus and Rhea, and known to the Romans as Jupiter, rebelled against his parents. The rebellion of Zeus-Jupiter against his father Cronus-Saturn is preserved in every culture as the archetype of a victorious son over his tyrannical father. In *Star Wars* it is Luke Skywalker who defeats *Darth Vader*, or the *Dark Father*.

Learning that his own child would dethrone him, Cronus began swallowing up his offspring as soon as they were born. Cronus-Saturn is, as an agricultural god, he who *plants in us the seed of our destruction*. He is *Father Time* and the *Grim Reaper* with a ready scythe aiming to cut down crops during the harvest to provide *life* for man through *daily bread* and *wine*. He is a *necessary evil* like all *fathers* who, so long as they are not tyrants, will be eventually and naturally overcome by their offspring. This is why Darth Vader refuses to help the evil Emperor completely kill his son and instead throws him into the pit.

When Zeus (Jupiter) was born to Rhea, she acted quickly to hide him away on the island of Crete, *"giving her husband a large stone wrapped in swaddling clothes which he supposed was the baby,"* writes Edith Hamilton in <u>Mythology</u>. Presented with the large stone wrapped in linen, Cronus swallowed it accordingly. Later, when Zeus was of age, there was a war waged between him, with his brothers and sisters, and Cronus with his Titans. Zeus was able to defeat the Titans in part because he released those terrible beasts imprisoned within the earth by Ouranos. Helping to secure this defeat was also the wise Iapetus (Prometheus) taking the side of Zeus. His brother Atlas bore a different fate, being forever made to hold the crushing weight of the world upon his shoulders. Just as the Greeks and Romans told of how wine was processed in the body by stories of Dionysus-Bacchus, Zeus was the embodiment of atmospheric phenomena and his brother Atlas helped to support all the weight of the sky and world.

Horus is protected in Egyptian myth by his mother Isis from the terrifying beast Typhon-Set. In this story, the monster Typhon imprisons Isis and Horus upon hearing of a prophecy from Thoth that Horus was to take his place as ruler. But Isis finds a way to hide Horus in a papyrus swamp to ensure his safety in like manner to Rhea hiding Zeus and Moses being placed in a basket on the Nile.

In Iran the King was persuaded to kill the infant Zarathustra. In Hebrew tradition the birth of Abraham threatened the rulership of Nimrod, who acted to commit infanticide.

We are reminded here again of the Biblical King Herod and Hindu story of King Kansa, both decreeing infanticides out of fear of losing their power.

In the world of Norse mythology, the lands of *Niflheim* and *Muspelheim* are the realms of the *dead* and *fire* respectively. Edith Hamilton writes that *"from Muspelheim came fiery clouds that turned the ice to mist. Drops of water fell from the mist and out of them there were formed the frost maidens and Ymir, the first Giant. His son was Odin's father, whose mother and wife were frost maidens."* Exactly like these other stories, Odin killed a parental figure to make the earth, ocean, and sky. In this case it was a primaeval giant named Ymir, or Aurgelmir, the *First Being.*

This is how the world was formed. As for time, we return to Greek myth. It is from the greek *khronos*, meaning "time," that we get Cronus and *chronology*, the arrangement of events or dates in the order of their occurrence. Time is critical for determining when to *sow* and *reap* and so are the blessings of the *Green Man*. Although we have reviewed the various relationships this god has with devils and sex, here are a few details as reminder: Capricorn the goat is the astrological house of Saturn and his offspring, humans, can be fierce warriors like *Aries the Ram* and strong like *Taurus the Bull*.

Egyptian Pharaohs herded the ram and bull with their crook and flail, an image most famously known as the *Osirian Pose*, or the arms crossed in an X across the chest. Far away from Africa, the same symbolic gesture was made by Samurai in Japan as part of a ritual for the dead. They would hold a rod in the right hand and the cord of a whip in the left while crossing their breast. We know that Jesus Christ is the *Shepherd of Men* like the *guide of souls* Hermes-Mercury and that both are depicted carrying a lamb, sheep, or goat. Jesus declares in John 10:11, *"I am the good shepherd,"* and Orpheus was sometimes called the *Good Shepherd*.

The *horns* of these characters are also found in the Greek Pan and Celtic Cernunnos. They are the origin of "Devil Horns" and being sexually excited, i.e., *horny*. Cernunnos embodies masculinity, hunting, and nature. Also known as *Cerne* or *Herne*, this horned god is rarely depicted or described historically. Until an inscription was found beneath Notre Dame Cathedral in the ruins of an old

Roman temple in the early 1700s was there even a confirmed description of the god. On what is known as the "Pillar of Boatman", we find a written reference to *Cerne*. A plaque found in Luxembourg refers to the god *Deo Ceruninco*. In depictions he is male, stag-like with antlers, wearing a torc and neck ring, and holding a purse of grains or coins. Accompanying him are often dogs, bulls, and dear.

Pandora's Box & the Wooden Chest

Just as Zeus is the sky and Atlas is its support, Prometheus is *forethought* and his brother, Epimetheus, represents *afterthought*. Epimetheus had created and given superior strengths and qualities to all animals, but he neglected to make mankind any match for these beasts and so sought his brother's help. Prometheus then took over the task of creation, fashioning mankind in a superior image, upright in stature to mimic the gods themselves. This is when he brought the hidden fire of Zeus to man for his protection. That fire was given to man from a torch lit by the sun. Prometheus was punished by being tired to a rock, or crucified in other accounts, and having a bird (eagle) eat his liver, which regenerated, daily. Severe as this torture inflicted was for what Zeus saw as betrayal, he also had other motivations. For Zeus knew fate would bring him a son, who would one day dethrone him just as he cast replaced his father Cronus, who replaced his father Ouranos.

While Prometheus suffered endless torture, the messenger Hermes-Mercury was sent on behalf of Zeus to bid him to disclose what he knew of the mother who would bear that child.

Steadfastly refusing to divulge this secret, like Chiram Abiff, Prometheus continued to suffer the wrath of the gods until it is said Hercules killed the eagle and that a Centaur name Chiron, though immortal, was willing to die in his place.

Although in some accounts it is Prometheus and Epimetheus who are credited with creating mankind, other stories tell a very different story. In one, the gods create men through various metals, starting first with the golden race. Next were to come silver and brass, followed by a race of godlike heroes from the latter. The fifth created was the iron race and the one now said to be inhabiting earth. Edith Hamilton writes of this iron race in <u>Mythology</u>:

> "They live in evil times and their nature too has much of evil, so that they never have rest from toil and sorrow As the generations pass, they grow worse; sons are always inferior to their fathers. A time will come when they have grown so wicked that they will worship power; might will be right to them, and reverence for the good will cease to be. At last when no man is angry any more a wrongdoing or feels shame in the presence of the miserable, Zeus will destroy them too. And yet even then something might be done, if only the common people would arise and put down rulers that oppress them."

In his anger over the love Prometheus had for man, Zeus decided to create woman. She was beautiful, with broidered veil, garlands, blooming flowers, and with a crown of gold. She was then presented to man as Pandora, meaning "the gift of all." Pandora was obviously wondrous to both men and gods when they beheld her beauty. But, in myth, Pandora is the source of all *misfortune*, though only due to her simple *curiosity*. The gods gifted her a box in which each had placed something harmful. They forbid her to ever open it. Curiosity overcame her, however, and once day she lifted the lid resulting in the release of all mankind's sorrows, mischief, and plagues: it was as if Eve had bitten the apple of Eden. The only directly beneficial thing in the box was *hope*: that sole comfort for man in all misfortune and uncertainty. But *hope* itself can be a drug of stagnation and delusion. The euphemistic use of "box" instead of vagina is also a detail that should not be lost when reading this story.

Yet another story of creation included Prometheus, his son Deucalion, and his wife Pyrrha, the daughter of Epimetheus and Pandora. When men grew wicked enough to attract the furry of Zeus, he called on his brother Poseidon, God of the Sea famous for his trident, to help bring about massive a deluge. Together they caused torrents of rains to fall, causing bodies of water to overflow and drown the land. Nearly all was submerged except for the topmost peak of the sacred mountain of Parnassus. Edith Hamilton writes of the deluge:

> "After it had rained through, nine days and nine nights, there came drifting to that spot [Parnassus] what looked to be a great wooden chest, but safe within it were two living beings, a man and a woman."

Those two living creatures were Pyrrah and Deucalion. Their "wooden chest" is not unlike the one of Osiris, or Moses, or even the *Ark of the Covenant*. In the *Kojiki*, or Record of Ancient Matters (Japan - 712 AD), after the first man is created he is also classified as a failure. Izanagi and Izanami then place that child inside a boat-box. Chapter 4:11 of that text records the following:

> "Nevertheless, they commenced procreation and gave to a birth leech-child. They placed this child into a boat made of reeds and floated it away."

Foretelling of the coming deluge, the wise Prometheus acted to protect his family, instructing his son to build a chest, fill it with supplies, and embark upon it safely with his wife. Much later in the story, after exiting the chest, the two used stones to create mankind anew.

Deluges of Water, Ice & Fire

Many will recognize the striking similarity between the aforementioned chest and the ark of Noah in the Bible coming to rest atop Mt. Ararat instead of Parnassus.

Noah was given instruction by God to build an ark for himself and his family, but large enough to accompany two of every animal so that they may survive the coming flood waters. Genesis 6:20 says that Noah is told: *"Two of every kind of bird, of every kind of animal and of every kind of creature that moves along the ground will come to you to be kept alive."*

In Genesis 7:1 the Lord *"said to Noah, 'Go into the ark, you and your whole family, because I have found you righteous in this generation'."*

After several days of heavy rainfall most of mankind had been washed away. Noah then sent out a white dove (a symbol of peace) to find any available land, but there was none to be found at first. Eventually the floodwaters receded, and the ark came to rest on the top of a mountain.

We find the same story preserved in the book 71 of the Quran, or the book of Nūḥ. Verses 1-4 tell of how Noah was sent to warn God's people to repent while verses 25-27 describe the flood:

> "We sent Noah to his people: 'Warn your people before there comes upon them a painful punishment'. He said, 'O my people, I am to you a clear warner. Worship God and reverence Him, and obey me. And He will forgive you of your sins, and reprieve you until a stated term. God's term cannot be deferred once it has arrived, if you only knew'."

"Because of their wrongs, they were drowned, and were hurled into a Fire. They did not find apart from God any helpers. Noah said, 'My Lord, do not leave of the unbelievers a single dweller on earth. If You leave them, they will mislead your servants, and will breed only wicked unbelievers'."

In the *Quest of the Golden Fleece* the Argo and Argonauts escape the sure destruction of Clashing Rocks, the *Symplegades*, also by the assistance of a dove. Edith Hamilton explains that the old man Phineus gave the advice:

"If she [the dove] passed through safely, then the chances were that they too would get through. But if the dove was crushed, they must turn back and give up all hope of the Golden Fleece."

The story of Gilgamesh, a character the Bible associates with Noah, is told in one of the oldest accounts known to man, the Epic of Gilgamesh. The Mesopotamian version of the deluge tells how Utnapishtim was given instructions to build an ark and to save his family and animals from a coming deluge. After the floodwaters receded, he sent out birds in search of land. His boat came to rest on top of a mountain called Nisir. It was there he released a dove, swallow, and raven.

Yet another story originating out of Mesopotamia is the story of **Ziusudra** and the "Great Deluge." The god Enki felt much compassion for mankind, like Prometheus, and so decided to help them. He chose Ziusudra and instructed him in the coming flood and on how to construct an ark to save his family. Ziusudra was also directed to take aboard "beasts and birds." The Encyclopedia Britannica explains the story in the following outline:

"Ziusudra, in Mesopotamian Religion, rough counterpart to the biblical Noah as survivor of a god-sent flood. When the gods had decided to destroy humanity with a flood, the god Enki (Akkadian Ea), who did not agree with the decree, revealed it to Ziusudra, a man well known for his humility and obedience. Ziusudra did as Enki commanded him and built a huge boat, in which he successfully rode out the flood. Afterward, he prostrated himself before the gods An (Anu) and Enlil (Bel), and, as a reward for living a godly life, Ziusudra was given immortality."

Other versions of this same story involve an Akkadian character named **Atrahasis**, one survivor of a great flood. In the *Puranic* (Sanskrit Hindu writings) version of the watery deluge story, the fish god Vishnu warns a human named **Manu** of the coming flood and tells him to prepare Sacred Scriptures in a safe place to pass on important knowledge to future generations. Manu is considered an Indian version of both Moses and Noah. He is a lawgiver and the *civilizing father* of mankind after a great flood. The Mahabaratha says he is a powerful sage or *rishi*.

The sacred Satpatha Brahmana informs us that Manu was instructed by a tiny fish to *"make for thyself a strong ship"* and to *"embark in it with the Seven Sages and stow in it, carefully preserved and assorted, all the seeds"* known and described. The fish sent Manu a ship and told him to load it with two of every living species and the seeds of all plants. His ship eventually came to rest on the Mountain of the North. We learn that the ship is brought to rest atop *"the highest peak of Himavat"* – the Himalayas. The Bhagavata Purana, which specifies that the fish is an incarnation of Lord Vishnu, informs us on how Manu was instructed by the god:

"On the seventh day after this the three worlds shall sink beneath the ocean of the dissolution. When the universe is dissolved in that ocean, a large ship, sent by me, shall come to thee. Taking with thee the plants and various seeds…"

Manu is later granted 64,800,000 years of life by the gods, or about seventy-one complete cycles of four *yugas*. The Mesopotamia Ziusudra is also granted what amounts to eternal life: *"Life like a god they gave him; Breath eternal like a god they brought down for him."*

Manu's relationship with Moses is strengthened by examining the flood story in further detail. The Vedic word for "boat" is NAU, a word also meaning "divine word." Thus, the *place of the binding of the ship - Naubandhana -* in the <u>Mahabaratha</u> also translates to the *place of the protection of the divine word*. It is here, atop the mountain like Moses, that sacred laws are handed down or, in the case of Vedic history, preserved by the Seven Sages for a new generation.

In yet another mythological narrative from Mesopotamia, it is **Utnapishtim** who was told the same thing as Manu by the god Ea, to collect writings and bury them in the city of the Sun at Sippar. In another version of the same story **Xisouthros** is visited by God in a dream and warned of a coming deluge. He is then instructed to build a boat and gather sacred tablets for preservation at Sippar. Interestingly, it was the Egyptian Innu, or the Greek Heliopolis (City of the Sun), which was the storehouse of ancient wisdom.

In Central America it was a deluge which had ended the Fourth Sun or Age. Aztec mythology tells of two humans who survived. **Coxcoxtli** and his wife **Xochiquetzal** were warned of the coming cataclysm and instructed to build a huge boat which eventually came to rest upon a mountain. Another version tells how the *smoking-mirror* god of illusion and human sacrifice, Tezcatilpoca, initiated a great flood to wipe out mankind. **Tezpi** was warned ahead of time to save his wife, children, and a variety of animals, grains, seeds, etc., with which to rebuild civilization after the flood waters had receded. His vessel eventually came to rest on a mountain where he sent out a vulture to search for other land. In the Maya book <u>Popol Vuh</u> is described a massive flood which killed "wooden creatures," or the first people:

"The wooden figures were annihilated, destroyed, broken and killed."

The surviving husband-and-wife pair, with their children and animals, were known to the Maya as the **Great Father** and **Great Mother**.

In South America a deluge was also documented in various accounts. The Chibcas people of Columbia tell the story of an old man of a totally different racial type and a long beard named **Bochica**. His wife Chia played the part of Tezcatilpoca in this story as she used magical powers to cause a flood. Humans fled to the mountains and survived at the highest places.

Canarians in Ecuador talk of two brothers who escaped an ancient flood by finding shelter in the tall mountains.

The Tupinamba Indians of Brazil talk about Monan, an ancient deity who created mankind and then destroyed the world with a flood and fire.

The Araucnaians of pre-Colombian Chile talk of a great flood, with survivors once again finding refuge on a tall mountain called *Thegtheg*.

In Yamana legend the flood was caused by a woman - as with the lady Chia – who was associated with the moon.

Such legends survive in North American Indian mythology within Inuit, Luiseno, Montagnais, Sioux, and Dakota mythologies. In Chickasaw mythology a *single family was saved and two animals of every kind*.

A funerary text from the tomb of Pharaoh Seti I tells of a deluge brought about due to man's wickedness. It was caused by the moon god Thoth: *"This earth shall enter into the watery abyss by means of a raging flood, and will become even as it was in primeval time."*

Similar stories of floods are found in Malaysia, Laos, Thailand, Viet Nam, and Burma. Information discovered by Jesuits in the Imperial Library of China detailed a colossal flood and massive astronomical changes occurring in the past. As reported by Charles Berlitz:

"The planets altered their course. The sky sank lower towards the north. The sun, moon, and stars changed their motions. The earth fell to pieces and the waters in its bosom rushed upwards with violence and overflowed the earth."

A tradition from the Amis tribe of Taiwan tells how four gods of the sea and two gods of the land, Kabitt and Aka, conspired to destroy the world and all mankind. However, two children named Sura and Nakao survived by embarking in a wooden mortar and floating eventually to the Ragasan mountain.

In the *Kojiki* it is also described the failed creation of mankind by the god and goddess pair Izanagi and Izanami. Chapter 5:1 records the following:

"Then the two deities consulted together and said: 'The child which we have just borne is not good. It is best to report [this matter] before the heavenly deities'."

~

Hopi mythology recalls that the first world was destroyed in fire, the second in ice, and the third in a massive flood. They believe that our present fourth world will only be shown mercy if its inhabitants abide by the plans of their Creator. Avestic Aryans also believed in three ages of creation before our own.

Indian, or the Indus-Sarasvati civilization, preserves similar notions within their mythology, theology, and history. Here we find four ages or *Yugas*. The *Krita Yuga* was a golden age of peace and harmony; the *Treta Yuga* saw the decline of virtues; in the *Davapara (Dvapara) Yuga* lying and arrogance spread further throughout mankind; and in the *Kali Yuga* man became his most wicked, only valuing degradation and chaos. Suffice to say it is the age of Kali that we currently reside.

Each *Yuga* or Age ends with *pralaya,* a fire or a great flood, and every cycle of four *Yugas* ends in a larger cataclysm. Thus, at the end of these four ages is the *Kali Yuga,* a time when men are most wicked, and a time when God decides to bring judgement.

The same idea is present in the Biblical book of II Peter 3:5-7, where we read a telling prediction of which much talk of the end of the world today is based:

"But they deliberately forgot that long ago by God's word the heavens came into being and the earth was formed out of water and by water. By these waters also the world of that time was deluged and destroyed. By the same word the present heavens and earth are reserved for fire, being kept for the day of judgment and destruction of the ungodly."

In Joel 2:30 we read of other disturbing prophecy which says, *"The sun will be turned to darkness and the moon to blood before the coming of the great and dreadful day of the LORD."* However, since blood moons occur yearly, and since the sun weakens and dies in the winter, such darkness and lunar change predict only the cyclical nature of the seasons and stars before the *white horse of the apocalypse* rides once again saving mankind from the cold and dark days of winter.

In relation to the Hopi and Avestic Aryan traditions, some may also be reminded of Helena Blavatsky's *Root Races* in theosophical doctrine. In Chinese tradition the five elements (earth, water, fire, wood, metal) are personified as powerful ancient beings: Yellow Ancient, Red Ancient, Dark Ancient, Wood Prince, Metal Mother.

Also, although unconfirmed in authenticity, the enigmatic Takenouchi Documents of Japan, which appeared in 1928, tell of four major dynasties of the world: Genesis, High Ancient, Fukiaezu, Kamu Yamato. In the first dynasty are seven generations like Blavatsky's *Root Races*. In that seventh final generation, the sun god eventually creates a lineage of World-Emperors called *Sumera-Mikoto*. The world was then divided into sections to be ruled by kings, who had dominion over *Five-Colored* Peoples – white, blue, red, yellow, and black. Interestingly, the king of the red people was named Adameve. Forgery or not, there is a deeper meaning present here and it is not simply a merger of Adam, and Eve, who came out of Adam's rib. The name *Adam* in Hebrew does indeed mean *son of the red earth*. Entering the second dynasty of the High Ancient we find the World-Emperor traveling the world like Quetzalcoatl, Viracocha, Osiris, etc., and teaching people civilization. The documents say the World-Emperor made these trips with an *Ame-no-Ukifune*, or "floating ship of heaven."

According to Avery Morrow, a Japanese occult researcher, even the authentic Nihon Shoki records a flying ship called *Ame-no-Iwafune*, something which may remind some of the Hindu *Vimāna*.

Between the second and third dynasties there are great cataclysms on Earth - *tenpenchii* - resulting in a disconnection between the divine and mundane, forcing the World-Emperor to send out additional teachers in his place. We later arrive in the fourth degenerate dynasty or age.

The Takenouchi Documents are reportedly part of a larger tradition connected to the Kojiki and Nihon Shoki, linking with major religions outside of Buddhism like Islam and Christianity. Just as some believe Jesus visited India, there are suggestions that he also traveled to ancient "Japan." In fact, these texts suggest Jesus is buried, believe it or not, in Herai village in Aomori Prefecture. The same goes for Moses, supposedly buried in Hakui in Ishikawa Prefecture.

From Blavatsky to Takenouchi, even an Edgar Cayce reading from 1925 proposed that there were five races of man dating from millions of years ago, despite Cayce, and probably Blavatsky, being unknown in Japan until roughly after World War II. Avery Morrow writes in summary that, according to Takenouchi, *"the laws of Moses and Jesus are founded in the ancient teachings of the Japanese emperors, and therefore the faithful of the world are expressing oneness in spirit with a long-lost true Japan."*

Perhaps this is why the indigenous practice of Shintō in Japan seems to embody the very essence of the *secret teachings of all ages*. An extensive overview of this eastern tradition will be found in later chapters of this book.

There is certainly more than simple coincidence found within all these traditions and myths, and that *truth* may extend beyond the changing seasons or astronomical cycles. As Graham Hancock has suggested throughout his extensive career, these *myths* are clearly preserving *memories* of something fantastic and devastating that shook our ancestors fundamentally to their core.

It is well accepted that a mass extinction of animals occurred because of the last Ice Age. They were, in some cases, violently assaulted alongside of humanoids and trees, then covered with muck and frozen. Such scientific analysis is beyond the scope of this text, but Hancock's books are an excellent refence guide.

All we can say here are that massive ice sheets covering much of the world's landmasses were at their full capacity about 20,000 years ago – *Last Glacial Maximum*. They had begun growing around 60-70,000 years ago.

Suddenly, and for about 7,000 years or so, a period of deglaciation followed causing what we can imagine was a cataclysm of Biblical proportion – a *deluge*. As ice began to melt oceans began to rise quickly. Then, just as suddenly, temperatures plummeted again during the *Younger Dryas*, a cooling period between 12,900 and 11,600 years ago, before eventually reaching deglaciation once more.

For however many *flood* myths persist in sacred texts, oral history, and mythology today, those of which we are analyzing here, destructive events were not confined only to water in the recent past. Perhaps volcanic events darkened the sky with soot, rock, and dirt which cause black rain to fall, as has been reported in various cultures. This would explain how some of the *rain* was like *fire*. A darkening of the sun, or a black sun, would explain how the solar disc disappeared during a dark and terrifying period of pre-history. If such events occurred more than once in a short period of generationally observable time, or over many documenting generations, it would explain the creation and destruction of many suns.

The Mayan <u>Popul Vuh</u> describes such events as including *"much hail, black rain and mist, and indiscernible cold."* Cold and darkness are also characteristics of classical *Hell*–an *ice palace* – which could explain many things: an event that occurred on earth and something now preserved in story form within theology and mythology.

As rainfall continued, and as oceans were upset in huge tidal waves from volcanic eruptions and earthquakes, the world entered a new Ice Age when snow and ice covered much of the inhabitable surface, forcing humans south. Layers of volcanic ash confirm this in the geological record.

Hancock writes in <u>Fingerprints of the Gods</u> how such *"tremendous eruptions"* were *"recurrent throughout much of the last Ice Age, not only in North America but in Central and South America, in the north Atlantic, in continental Asia, and in Japan."*

Flooding from geological upheavals would have caused massive build-ups of water which turned into ice, particularly because areas of rapid freezing have been documented. We also know stories of animals suddenly frozen solid with food still in their mouths or those fossils found standing upright in layered volcanic ash and sand. This deluge of ice eventually melted causing a deluge of water, and it happened rapidly in geological terms. As the ice melted, estimated at "six million cubic miles" in the northern hemisphere, it caused a rapid rising of the sea level.

During peak ice it is estimated the ocean was 400 feet lower than today, but as the ice melted rapidly all that water trigger a sudden rise in sea level.

The Toba Indians of Gran Chaco tell the story of such an *ice deluge*. A figure named **Asin** informs a man to gather wood and cover his hut to protect himself from a coming "great cold."

In the Avestic scriptures from pre-Islamic Iran is the story of ancient Iranian people living in a mythical garden paradise like Edin. The garden of *Airyana Vaejo* was formed by Ahura Mazda, the creator deity in Zoroastrianism. He was happy with his creation, just as *"God was pleased with what he saw"* of his creation in Genesis. *Airyana Vaejo* is said to have experienced seven months of summer and five months of winter before being thrown into chaos by the *black* and *pale* horses, represented by the *Evil One*, known by the name *Angra Mainyu*.

Five months of winter turned into ten months which led to great suffering and death. In this story, too, Ahura Mazda warned a shepherd named **Yima** of a coming "fatal winter."

The usage of wood, which is obviously derived from trees, parallels a Teutonic myth about a wolf-monster chasing the sun and eventually consuming its light and warmth. According to the <u>New Larousse Encyclopedia of Mythology</u>: *"And now all the rivers, all the seas, rose and overflowed. From every side waves lashed against waves... Yet not all men perished in the great catastrophe. Enclosed in the wood itself of the ash tree Yggdrasil... the ancestors of a future race of men had escaped death."*

It is said their only own "nourishment" was "morning dew" – or the *alchemical dew* that nourishes the soul. As flood waters receded, *"slowly the earth emerged from the waves."* Next, *"Mountains rose again and from them streamed cataracts of singing waters."*

A Central American myth tells a similar story about a flood and a tree. In this version of the story two people survived because they were informed by the gods to *bore a hole in the trunk of a very large tree* and take shelter *when the skies fell*.

Falling skies could also relate to raised or falling veils, the *Fall of Man* and our *Fall* season leading us into the cold, dark days of winter. Reference to falling skies or falling stars could likewise indicate space rocks slamming into the planet, or at least getting close enough to cause havoc.

Evidence of underground cities like Derinkuyu in Turkey, reaching deep into the earth because of human carving, could indicate a preparedness for such a cataclysmic event.

Hopi tradition from the American Southwest maintains their ancestors climbed up out of the earth from chambers called *kivas*. Such stories are seasonal but also could overlap with great cataclysmic events that Hancock believes *"may contain accurate records and eyewitness accounts of real events."*

According to the writings of Greek historian Diodorus Siculus, a Great Deluge represented *chaos* incarnate, and he associated this very real event with Deucalion, or the Greek Noah figure.

Civilization began in Egypt when the waters of the abyss receded, and humanity appeared with promethean light to restart civilization. This was the *First Time* known an as *Zep Tepi*. Osiris then went out to share his advanced knowledge with peoples all over the world.

Earth Crust Displacement & Ancient Maps

The theory of *Earth Crust Displacement* was first proposed by Professor and author Charles Hapgood. It suggests that the lithosphere of our planet, a rigid outer layer of the upper mantle and crust, routinely shifts in dramatic and cataclysmic fashion.

Contrary to *plate tectonics*, which involves pieces of the lithosphere shifting over tens of millions of years, Hapgood's theory proposes that sudden and dramatic shifts of the entire lithosphere do occur and have so in recent history. He describes the lithosphere moving over the inner earth *"much as the skin of an orange, if it were loose, might shift over the inner part of the orange all in one piece."* This is no random act either, as Albert Einstein confirmed:

> *"In a polar region there is continual deposition of ice, which is not symmetrically distributed about the pole. The earth's rotation acts on these unsymmetrically deposited masses, and produces centrifugal momentum that is transmitted to the rigid crust of the earth. The constantly increasing centrifugal momentum produced in this way will, when it has reached a certain point, produce a movement of the earth's crust over the rest of the earth's body and this will displace the polar regions towards the equator."*

Other factors contributing to such *"deposition of ice"* include the orbit of earth, the tilt of its axis, etc. Hancock summarizes the obvious implications of such a global cataclysm event to any civilization on the surface of our planet:

> *"In a displacement, those parts of the earth's crust which are situated at the North and South Poles (and which are therefore as completely glaciated as Antarctica is today) shift suddenly into warmer*

latitudes and begin to melt with extraordinary rapidity. Conversely, land that has hitherto been located at warmer latitudes is shifted equally suddenly into the polar zones, suffers a devastating climate change, and begins to vanish under a rapidly expanding ice-cap."

Put simply, this would explain why warmer climates suddenly became frozen and why freezing climates suddenly became warmer and more habitable. Many seemingly overnight. Immense areas of frozen wasteland would have been thrust into warmer temperatures and melted rapidly as a result, causing unimaginable floods.

A shifting of the lithosphere would have caused incomprehensible earthquakes and volcanic eruptions, perhaps blacking out of the sun, just as we read in apocalyptic mythology. Falling stars, or comets and asteroids, or even just their debris, could have contributed to these tumultuous times.

The earth's magnetic polarity has reversed over the past 80 million years more than 170 times and based on the positioning of previous ice sheets there seems to be indication that landmasses have indeed moved relatively quickly in recent history. As Hapgood writes:

"We may conclude that the best theory to account for an ice age is that the area concerned was at the pole. We thus account for the Indian and African ice sheets, though the areas once occupied by them are ow in the tropics. We account for all ice sheets of continental size in the same way."

As a result of *earth crust displacement* many of the world's landmasses are in different places today than they were prior to the movement of the lithosphere. Hence, we obtain the theory that Atlantis, or at least the location of some yet unconfirmed ancient, advanced civilization, may have been a landmass that now is frozen under miles of ice: Antarctica. We do not know what is under the ice with exception of some fossils proving that the landmass was once warmer and more tropical even as early as 100,000 years ago.

An admiral in the navy of the Ottoman Turks, Piri Reis is known famously today as the author of a map drawn in 1513 depicting the northern shores of Queen Maud Land Antarctica without much ice. This is incomprehensible to geographers, cartographers, scientists, and historians because Antarctica was only discovered (rediscovered) in 1820 AD.

Antarctica's coastlines were not free of ice to any large degree until after 4,000 BC and therefore any cartographic attempts at detailing these coastlines would have been thwarted.

According to Charles Hapgood the source maps for Piri Reis came from the Library of Alexandria, which was constructed between 246 and 222 BC. The contents of this library included millions of scrolls, texts, tablets, statues, etc., from all over the world, and from remote antiquity, before it was burned to ash. In other words, Piri Reis got his source maps from ancient sources, which makes his map, among others, even more incredible. Hapgood writes:

"It appears [he concluded] that accurate information has been passed down from people to people. It appears that the charts must have originated with a people unknown and they were passed on, perhaps by the Minoans and the Phoenicians, who were, for a thousand years and more, the greatest sailors of the ancient world. We have evidence that they were collected and studied in the great library of Alexandria [Egypt] and that compilations of them were made by the geographers who worked there."

The 1531 Oronteus Finaeus Map depicts even more incredible details of Antarctica when it had ice-free coasts, at least before 4,000 BC, along with details mountains and rivers which have themselves been confirmed in modern times through seismic surveys.

Gerard Kremer, or Mercator, included these details in his 1569 _Atlas_ along with his own drawings, from his own sources, of Antarctica.

The Philippe Buache Map of 1737 shows no ice at all on the Antarctic continent. It was based on an ancient source, perhaps pre-dating the Reis source, that has been entirely lost as far as we know. Buache's map incredibly shows what we only recently have discovered to be true, i.e., that a waterway divides the continent of antarctica into two landmasses. His depiction of its subglacial topography was only confirmed in 1958. Considering that Antarctica was not officially discovered until 1820, many questions remain unanswered.

We also know that an early 19th-century Russian map shows the world with no antarctica at all, indicating that at that time it had yet to be discovered by those cartographers or known to those drawing the maps the Russian mapmakers used.

It seems that these documents, based on admittedly confirmed much older sources, stem from a culture with knowledge and ability far exceeding what any "primitive" man should have possessed. Since the evidence is simply ignored, or arrogantly mocked, few researchers are willing to acknowledge what these maps and their sources imply. Obviously, we are missing pieces of the puzzle. But just as these proofs of a fantastical history are ignored, we likewise tend to declare that _myth_ has no _memory_, and that it is nothing more than primitive storytelling.

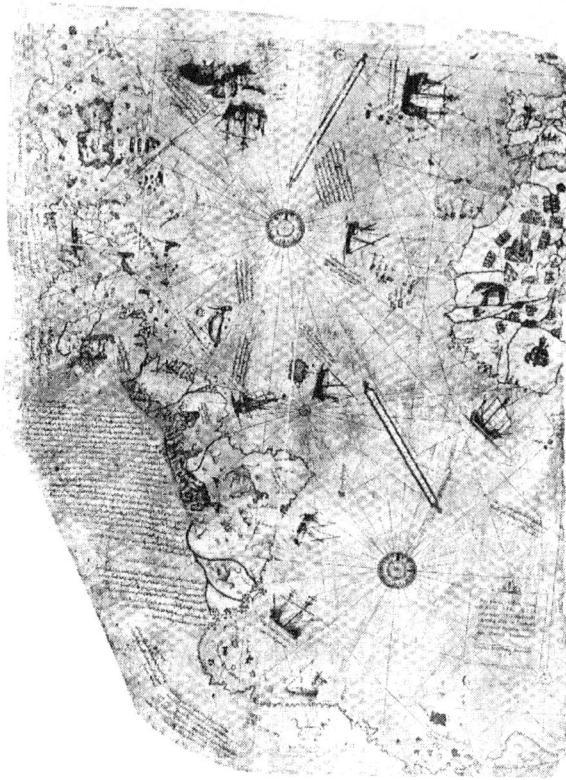

The Piri Reis Map of 1513

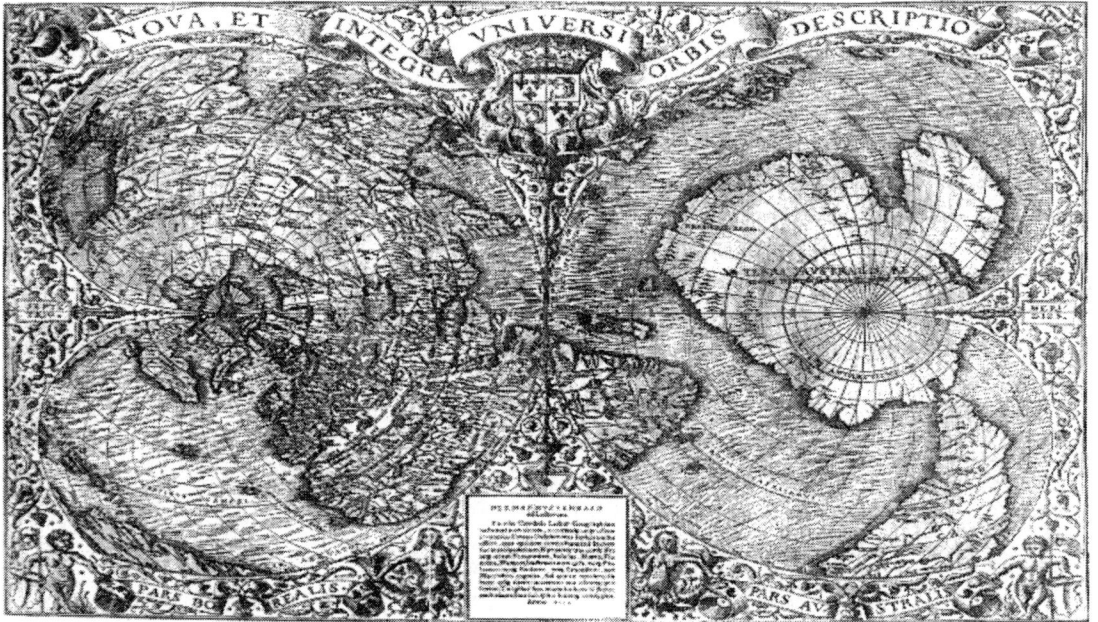

The Oronteus Finaeus Map of 1531 showing Antarctica with mountains & waterways.

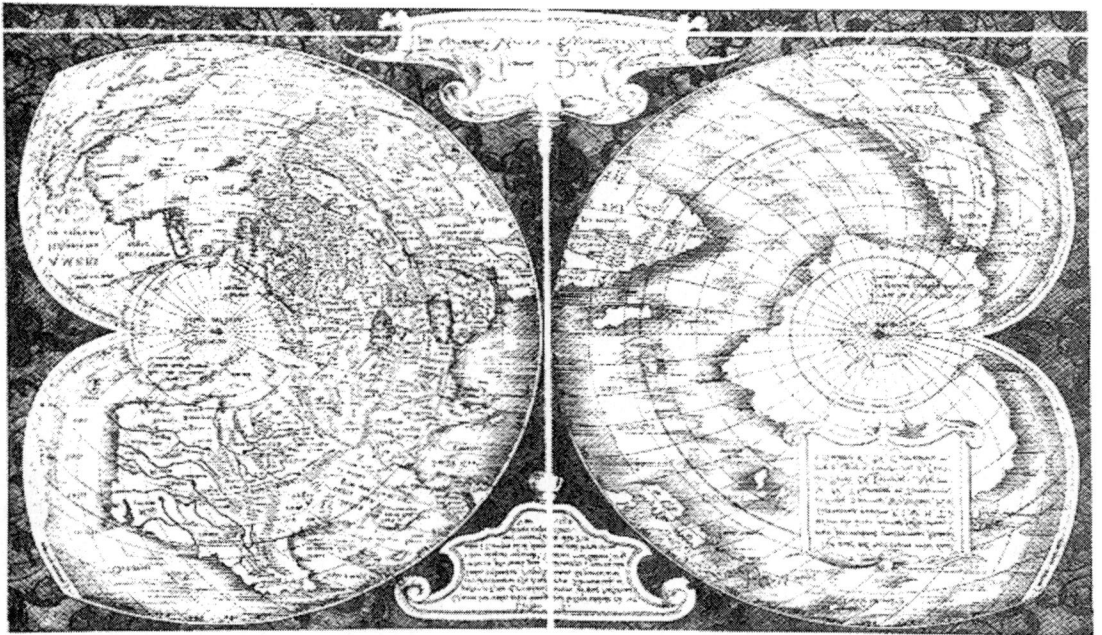

The Mercator Map of 1569 showing the Finaeus version covered in ice.

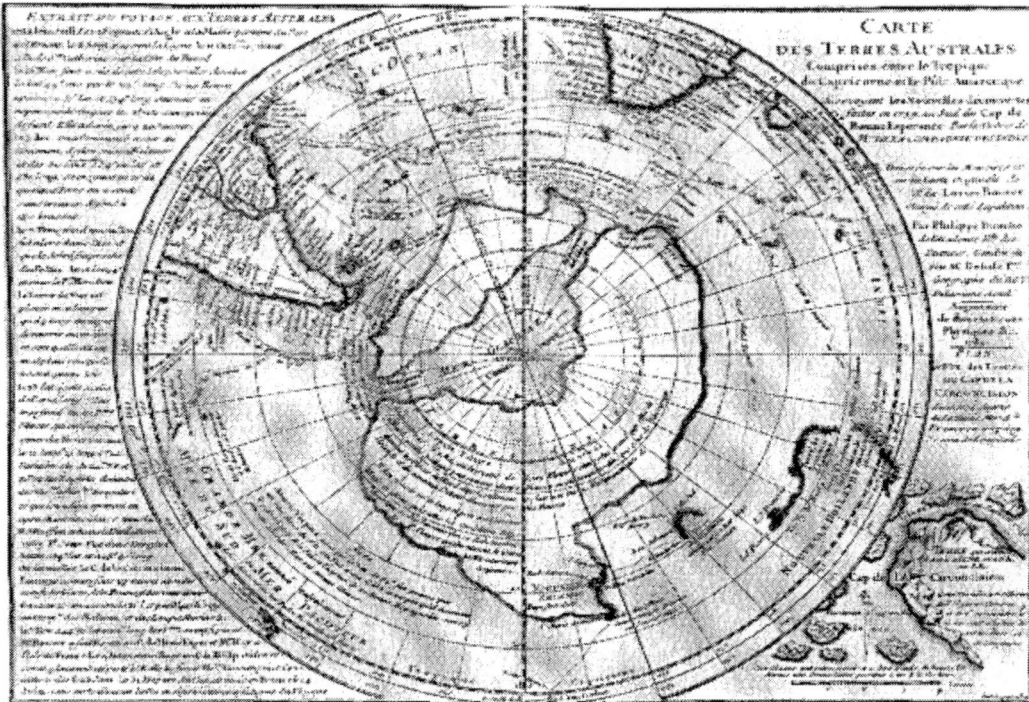

The Bauche Map of 1737 shows Antarctica without ice and with a large waterway separating the two landmasses of the continent just as we now know to be accurate based on recent surveys.

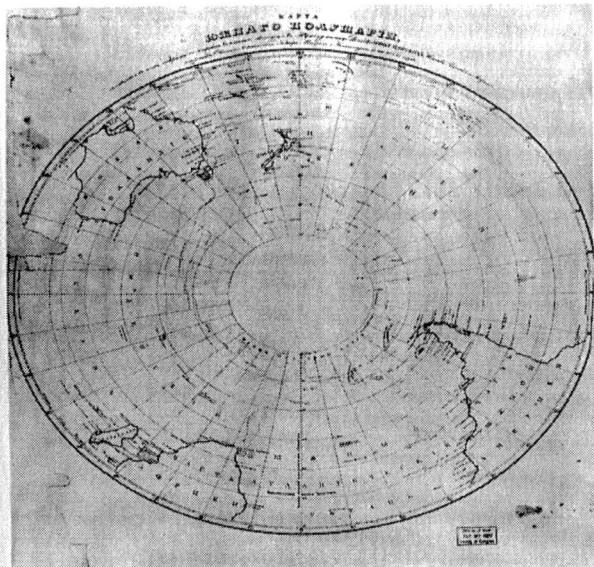

Although Antarctica was discovered in 1820, ancient source maps allowed for Piri Reis in 1513, Oronteus Finaeus in 1531, Mercator in 1569, and Philippe Buache in 1737, to depict various histories of the coastlines and topography of the continent - comprised of two larger landmasses - long before that date Yet, this early 19th-century Russian map still does not show Antarctica.

Biblical Science

The *Great Flood* or *Great Deluge* was followed by darkness on an earth void of sunlight. The Kolbrin Bible - Book of Origins: Chapter Three – The Flood Tale, verse OGS: 3:20-22 preserves the same historical account:

> *"…when darkness did fall, it was not the restful night darkness which soothes work weary men…A vast, black cloud was drawn like a curtain across the skyroof, stretching from horizon to horizon. Rising above it were strange billows of flame and smoke… Then all things ceased movement, all was silent and still; a heavy, ill-boding, brooding silence, the stillness of heart hammering fear.*
>
> *"Then, with awful suddenness came a high wave wall of dark, white-fag-edged waters, sweeping swiftly along in fearsome irresistibility."*

In the myths and ancient texts, we have examined thus far are *memories* of events that can today be explained in very literal scientific terms. In those ages they were an *act of God*. This is not to say that ancient people did not understand natural phenomena, or that God does not show himself today, just that there are no differences between the event(s) being described here, except the way in which they are classified and cataloged.

The Kolbrin Bible is comprised of a series of Egyptian texts compiled after the Hebrew *exodus*, along with Celtic texts compiled after the death of Jesus. In the Kolbrin: Book of Manuscripts is a section titled "The Destroyer," which seems to explain ancient cataclysmic events and the plagues of Egypt as documented in the book of Exodus.

A meteor streaking across the sky and leaving a trail of smoke and debris may be described as a fire-breathing dragon with long tail to some, or perhaps a meteor, but whether the *Destroyer* was a large space rock, or something else, if we are to carefully examine this story, we find the *science* of *myth* explained with the language of our ancestors. A *dragon* to some, others would call it a series of *Plagues sent by God* to punish the Egyptians. The following description describes its approach and all manner of influences that occurred as a result:

> *"Men forget the days of the Destroyer. Only the wise know where it went and that it will return in its appointed hour. It raged across the Heavens in the days of wrath, and this was its likeness: It was as a billowing cloud of smoke enwrapped in a ruddy glow, not distinguishable in join or limb. Its mouth was an abyss from which came flame, smoke and hot cinders. When ages pass, certain laws operate upon the stars in the Heavens. Their ways change; there is movement and restlessness, they are no longer constant and a great light appears redly in the skies."*

The text reveals an understanding of heavenly mechanisms held by priests: *"the wise known where it went and that it will return."* These wise men were the hierophants and magicians that held an understanding of the natural world beyond any knowledge of the profane. The Kolbrin continues with a description of the effects this object caused:

> *"The heavens will burn brightly and redly; there will be a copper hue over the face of the land, 'followed by a day of darkness. A new moon will appear and break up and fall. The people will scatter in madness. They will hear the trumpet and battlecry of the Destroyer and will seek refuge within dens in the*

Earth. Terror will eat away their hearts, and their courage will flow from them like water from a broken pitcher. They will be eaten up in the flames of wrath and consumed by the breath of the Destroyer… The times of its coming and going are known unto the wise. These are the signs and times which shall precede the Destroyer's return: A hundred and ten generations shall pass into the West, and nations will rise and fall. Men will fly in the air as birds and swim in the seas as fishes. Men will talk peace one with another; hypocrisy and deceit shall have their day. Women will be as men and men as women; passion will be a plaything of man."

Referred to as the "Doomshape" in the Kolbrin, "Destroyer" in Egypt, and "Frightener" in Celtic lore, the text specifically states that this object was *"not a great comet or a loosened star, being more like fiery body of flame."* Depending upon the meaning of "comet" or "loosened star" there are still various heavenly interpretations that can be had. Described as a *"fiery body of flame"* by those writers, or as an evil dragon or beast by the profane, an understanding that *"certain laws operate upon the stars in the Heavens"* and that *"their ways change; there is movement and restlessness,"* implies there was something very natural about the *Destroyer*.

Was it a comet? The text says no. But perhaps we need to examine ancient definitions, references, and understandings of comets before we could agree. The object may very well have been a large planetary body, perhaps an ellipse coinciding with other natural phenomena.

"Its movements on high were slow;" perhaps indicating its distances and size. *"Below it swirled in the manner of smoke and it remained close the sun, whose face it hid,"* as might be the case with a large comet. It may have been a massive celestial collision with earth's moon or a reference to some lunar cycle: *"a new moon will appear and break up and fall."* Whatever the source of the destruction and madness that ensued here, we do indeed find a natural explanation for the *Plagues of Egypt* – these were, of course, sent by God. The Kolbrin text reads:

"It caused death and destruction in its rising and setting. It swept the Earth with grey cinder rain and caused many plagues, hunger and other evils."

The plagues of Exodus include those of *water turned blood, frogs, lice, flies, livestock death, boils, hail, locusts, darkness,* and *the killing of the firstborn.* In the Kolbrin version, all of man suffers; even the dead are disturbed in their graves. The *Destroyer* is said to have brought a *"cinder rain"* that *"bit the skin of men and beast until they became mottled with sores."*

As the Earth shook, *"Thick clouds of fiery smoke passed before him [the Destroyer or Dark Lord], and there was an awful hail of hot stones and coals of fire. The Doomshape thundered sharply in the Heavens and shot out bright lightnings."* Here are described boils and sores, and a hail of fire raining down from heaven. Later is described more of this heavenly fire:

"The face of the land was battered and devastated by a hail of stones, which smashed down all that stood in the path of the torrent. They swept down in hot showers, and strange flowing fire ran along the ground in their wake."

Further on is described how *"dust and smoke clouds darkened the sky and coloured the waters upon which they fell with a bloody hue."* Here we find that rivers have turned to blood and that *"the water was vile and men's stomachs shrank from drinking. Those who did drink from the river vomited it up, for it was polluted."* As the water turned to blood, dust *"tore wounds in the skin of man and beast"* and *"all tame beasts whimpered"*; the land *"filled with cries of sheep and moans of cattle."* Here we have the death of livestock. These animals died for the same reasons that men suffered on land; they suffered exposure to acid rain, polluted water, and fire from above.

While fires swept down from heaven and beasts whimpered, *"insects and reptiles sprang up from the Earth in huge numbers. Great gusts of wind brought swarms of locusts which covered the sky… The gloom of a long night spread a dark mantle of blackness, which extinguished every ray of light. None knew when it was day and when it was night, for the sun cast no shadow."* This obviously explains the plagues of locust and darkness: the insects were disturbed and forced to move from burning land, while there was an immense amount of rock and dirt launched into the atmosphere blocking sunlight from reaching the surface of the planet. As blood flowed, fires burned, and the dead lay scattered, one could image the eventual swarm of gnats, flies, and other insects upon the carcasses.

The death of the "first born" may be explained in more precise terms in the Kolbrin by the verse: *"Pregnant women miscarried and the seed of men was stopped."* Since the gravitation of the moon plays upon the waters of earth and menstruation, perhaps the disturbed moon altered the ability of women to carry a child to birth. For something physically was happening to the moon, as described of its *"break up and fall."* If not the moon, perhaps poison in the air caused miscarriages.

Was this object a comet, asteroid, large planetary body, or another mysterious force yet to be identified? The writers of Exodus and the Kolbrin explain these events in different terms, but they are nonetheless detailing the same history. Biblically these plagues were issued forth through Moses from God. In the Kolbrin these plagues are merely the result of what seems to be a natural event rather than some divine judgment. But are these natural events not the result of God's wrath? Moses was initiated into the Egyptian *mysteries*, having grown up in the royal palace, and therefore may have known something about celestial mechanics the Pharaoh did not. Perhaps he *knew of these plagues* before commanding in Exodus 5:1, *"Let My people go."* While some people may have believed Zeus to be responsible for thunder, lightning, wise men knew he was merely their personification.

When we read the story of Genesis 1 how *"God*[s] *created the heavens and the earth,"* what we are really reading is a *scientific philosophy* on how the *"earth was without form"* and *"darkness was upon the face of the deep."* There was nothing, only the *Cosmic Mind.* Modern scientists would call this the Big Bang, yet they struggle the same in proving their belief and so maintain it largely with dogma and faith. The same type of scientific explanation can be extracted from the Quran, in Surat Al-Mu'minum (The Believers), verse 12-14, which talks about sperm:

> *"And certainly did We create man from an extract of clay. Then We placed him as a sperm-drop in a firm lodging. Then We made the sperm-drop into a clinging clot, and We made the clot into a lump [of flesh], and We made [from] the lump, bones, and We covered the bones with flesh; then We developed him into another creation. So blessed is Allah, the best of creators. Then indeed, after that you are to die. Then indeed you, on the Day of Resurrection, will be resurrected."*

Mark Booth discusses in his book The Sacred History about how *evolution* and *creationism,* two classic forms of thought associated with either *science* or *faith,* can be reconciled to be understood as describing the same exact origin story:

> *"It is a sequence in which subatomic particles ("light") are followed by gas ("firmament"), followed by liquids ("the waters"), solids ("dry land"), primitive vegetable life ("grass"), primitive marine life ("the waters bring forth abundantly the moving creature that hath life"), land animals ("the beasts of the earth") and finally anatomically modern humans ("let us make man"). Looked at this way, Genesis is consistent with the modern scientific view."*

Hopi Creationism

The Hopi people of Northeastern Arizona referred to the time-before-time as *Tokpela* (The First World), or the *Endless Space*. Genesis 1:1-2 provides a parallel description of this "beginning" when *"the earth was formless and empty,"* and *"darkness was over the surface of the deep."* Hopi legend describes the Creator *Taiowa* as being the only thing in existence, or what the Bible says is *"the Spirit of God… hovering over the waters."*

The <u>Book of the Hopi</u> describes this *nothingness* as having *"no beginning and no end, no time, no shape, no life."*

It was *"an immeasurable void that had its beginning and end, time, shape, and life in the mind of Taiowa the Creator."*

As the infinite mind of God conceived the finite world, Taiowa created Sotuknang, saying to him *"I have created you, the first power and instrument as a person, to carry out my plan for life in endless space."* Sotuknang's duty was to lay the universes in *"proper order so they may work harmoniously with one another"* according to the Creator's plan. Genesis 1:3 describes this event as God stating: *"Let there be light."* From this creative command, God *"separated the light from the darkness."*

Sotuknang, following the plan of creation, gathered all that which was to be manifest as solid substance, and as the <u>Book of the Hopi</u> describes, *"molded it into forms, and arranged them into nine universal kingdoms."*

The first kingdom belonged to Taiowa, the second to Sotuknang himself, and the reaming *"seven universes for the life to come."* These *seven universes* are the *seven divine rays of creation* and the seven Biblical days of Creation. Taiowa was pleased, saying *"It is very good."* In Genesis 1:10 it is said *"God saw that it [his Creation] was good."*

Hopi tradition says the Creator next separated the waters just as in Genesis 1:6 God says, *"Let there be a vault between the waters to separate water from water."* Taiowa said *"Now I want you to do the same thing with the waters. Place them on the surfaces of these universes so they will be divided equally among all and each."*

Next, Sotuknang was instructed to *"put the forces of air into peaceful movement about all."* This is the Genesis 1:8 parallel in which God *"separated the water under the vault from the water above it,"* calling the upper vault *"sky."*

Taiowa was once more pleased, saying: *"You have created the universe and made them manifest in solids, waters, and winds, and put them in their proper place."* He then instructed the *"first power"* to *"create life and its movement to complete the four parts, Túwaqachi, of my universal plan."*

Sotuknang went into the First World and created a helper deity named *Kokyangwuti*, the *Spider Woman* or *Spider Grandmother*. <u>The Book of the Hopi</u> describes how Kokyangwuti obeyed instruction to create life further. The Spider Woman then took some earth and mixed it with saliva, before molding it into "two beings" named *Poqanghoya* and *Palongawhoya*. It was through the Creation Song, or the *word of God*, that *life* came into existence. The *Spider Woman* then *"gathered earth, this time of four colors, yellow, red, white, and black"* mixed it with saliva, and molded the materials while singing the *Creation Song*.

Human beings emerged from the *"white-substance cape"* known as *"creative wisdom"* which was placed over them in their primal states. It is said that they were created in the image of Sotuknang just as *"God created mankind in his own image,"* as told in Genesis 1:27 when *"male and female he created them."* Spider Woman then created four other beings modeled after her own likeness. These were *"female partners, for the first four male beings."* In Genesis 2:23 this is when Eve was named as a wife to Adam: *"she shall be called 'woman', for she was taken out of man."*

The uncovering of human life is said to be the *"time of dark purple light, Qoyangnuptu, the first phase of the dawn of Creation…"* As humans awakened and began to move around, Hopi tradition tells of the Sikangnuqa, or the second phase of the dawn of Creation, *"when the breath of life entered man."* In Genesis 2:7 we read how *"the Lord God formed a man from the dust of the ground and breathed into his nostrils the breath of life, and the man became a living god."*

The third phase of the dawn of Creation was the time of the red light, when man met his Creator the Sun. Spider Woman tells mankind, *"You are meeting your Father the Creator of the first time."*

Much like in the Garden of Eden, the First People to the Hopi also *"knew no sickness."* It was not *"until evil entered the world"* that *"persons get sick in the body or head."* Perhaps by EVIL we are to understand both an inversion of LIVE and an EVE-IL.

The Book of the Hopi then says *"the First People kept multiplying and spreading over the face of the land and were happy. Although they were of different colors and spoke different languages, they felt as one and understand one another without talking."*

Such a positive Babel-like myth speaks to the meaning of the name Hopi: *the Peaceful People.* In less complex mythology, the Hopi, like countless other Indian Tribes in the Americas, and particularly in the American Southwest, believe that their ancestors came up from under the ground. They were protected by the snake or ant people from falling stars, and what are generally described as massive cataclysmic events.

Maya Creationism

The knowledge possessed by the great Maya civilization was handed down to them from the Olmecs, who may in turn have received the same from an even earlier mysterious culture.

The First Men, as they are called, were civilizers and brought a wealth of wisdom. Balam-Quitze, Balam-Acab, Mahucutah, and Iqui-Balam were their names.

In the Popul Vuh these beings are described as having great vision: *"they saw and instantly they could see far; they succeeded in seeing; they succeeded in know all that there is in the world."* The sacred text explains further how *"they were able to know all, and they examined the four corners, the four points of the arch of the sky, and the round face of the earth."*

In other words, these First Men were wise in geography and astronomy. However, powerful deities were unsettled by their powers and so they said: *"It is not well that our creatures should know all."* Adding, *"Must they perchance be the equals of ourselves, their Makers, who can see afar, who know all and see all?"*

These powerful deities responded by blowing *"mist into their eyes which clouded their sight."* Their vision was stagnated and reduced: *"their eyes were covered and they could only see what was close."* There is no doubt that this Maya text has obviously extracted motifs from the same source as the Old Testament of the Hebrew Bible. In Genesis 3:22 the Lord God says:

"The man has now become like one of us, knowing good and evil. He must not be allowed to reach out his hand and take also from the tree of life and eat, and live forever."

Norse Creationism

According to myth, the world and universe was fashioned from a hoarfrost giant named *Yimir*, whose body was comprised of clouds and mists. This associates him strongly with *Shu* and *Tefnut*. Yimir is said to have been formed further from a great mess of chaos called *Ginnungagap*, a time when, as Manly Hall relates, *"primordial frost giants had hurled snow and fire."* The divine trinity of Odin, Vili, and Ve slew the giant and used his body to create the world and each interconnected part of Nature. Odin then formed the Odinic or Scandinavian Olympus, a place called *Asgard* which was built on top of a mountain. Upon this mountain were also the sacred and famous halls of *Valhalla*, or the *place of the fallen*. Much like Jesus or Krishna, Quetzalcóatl, Viracocha, Osiris, etc., Odin's son Balder brought peace and love to the world. One of his twelve disciples was named *Loki*, in essence the manifestation of evil. When Loki had eliminated Balder, as did Set do the same to Osiris, his light and love vanished form the world. However, the gods attempted to bring him back to life through a process of resurrection. Such *Mystery* traditions were organized in underground crypts which acted as temples and literal wombs inside of the earth. The chambers of these caves were nine, representing the Nine Worlds, as with the Nine Divine in Egypt. The first man and woman in Norse myth were created from trees; man, from an ash and woman from an elm. They were considered the parents of mankind, the divine sexes. Here we have the Garden of Eden with the Biblical parents, or *Universal Androgyny*, known as Adam and Eve.

Egyptian Creationism

In the Egyptian creation story, the sun god RA was formed from *Atum* and sprang out of the *nothingness* called *Nun*. He created a divine of the air named *Shu* and a divine of moisture named *Tefnut*, both of which combined their powers to create *Geb*, the god of earth, and the goddess of sky *Nut*. From their unification came Osiris, Isis, Set, and Nephthys. In some versions of the story this "nothingness" was a period of watery chaos, perhaps associated with a great Deluge. The ruling place of these gods on earth was at Heliopolis, or Innu. From here they went about establishing a legacy of wisdom and passing certain knowledge to mankind.

It is said that Ptah was the creator of physical things, having molded the world on a potter's wheel, and that Thoth was the inventor of language, mathematics, science, magic, and sacred texts. Osiris was the great civilizer and protector, and Isis was the nurturing mother.

As the watery chaos receded, a group of beings called *Urshu* watched over mankind to assist them in rebuilding the world. This process was organized by the divine *Neteru* in the First Time of Zep Tepi. Osiris then went on his civilizing mission around the world, seeking to restart civilization a common sourcebook of knowledge.

From the Osirian cult we obtain information on funerary rites and rituals pertaining resurrection – something that applied civilization and man's spiritual nature. A strange parallel can be found here between Osiris and the Biblical Noah, along with the Central American Quetzalcoatl and South American Viracocha, among others. All four arrived on water bringing civilization back to a planet wrecked by chaos. The Babylonian Oannes is another. With exception of Noah, the other three were later by direct or indirect choice ushered into coffins, caskets, rafts, or boats and forced back onto the waters from whence they came.

Greek historian Diodorus Siculus believed that *"it is probable that the inhabitants of southern Egypt survived rather than any others"* during this previous period of flooding. What seems to be happening here in these accounts of mythology, theology, and fragments of historical record is that there are two "creation" periods. The *Creation* we think of as the universe may itself be different, though closely associated, with the recreation of civilization after a planetary cataclysm. In the first case, or *First Creation*, man became wicked enough to warrant destruction through a chaotic period of earth changes, including floods and harsh cold, now preserved in mythology. In the second place there took place a recreation of the world after such destruction. This *Second Creation* involved the assistance of heroes, demi-gods, and gods, all of which brought remnants of a previously highly developed state of technological and spiritual development.

Such remnants involved law, math, astronomy, agriculture, etc. Since so many of these stories seem to be rooted in a common *source,* it seems as if, as Diodorus wrote, they may come from Egypt. However, the Egyptian versions are themselves taken from some long-lost civilization prior to the Second Creation. Proof of this can be found in the Plato story of his ancestor Solon, a lawmaker from Athens who lived between 630 and 560 BC. Solon claims he learned of Atlantis from an elderly priest in Egypt and that the records of this land were at the time already more than 8,000 years old.

Codes, Commandments & Correlations

Planets were, as are constellations less seriously today, considered to be expressions of, and homes to, certain spirits in antiquity. Each planet has traditionally been considered to have its own energy signature and personality. They are therefore given character traits and have been anthropomorphized. Throughout history we have seen some rulers associated in name and likeness to various gods, and therefore, to certain planets and their spirits. Thus, you may have a king, planet, and mythological deity with the same name and attributes. One is a person, another a planetary body, and the other a symbolic representation of natural forces with human attributes. Such associations hope to draw on the energy of the divine in a form of *sympathetic magic*. When we examine the dictating of *moral codes* by ruling classes, who were controlled by priests in antiquity, as they are today in many ways, there is always the notion that God ordained these laws for man. If a priestly class wrote the laws and enforced them through a King or Emperor, they were to be seen as coming directly from the gods or God, since the throne was the earthly seat of heavenly power. But just as the obeying of God is to work within the confines of *Natural Law*, so too is it to be understood that the commandments dictated to Moses on Mt. Sinai were part of those very laws, albeit a moral variety. It is also important to note, however, that there were dozens more commandments in tradition, and that they likely relate directly to the famous *Egyptian Confessions*.

The *Code of Hammurabi*, King of Babylon from 1795 BC – 1750 BC, was found in 1902 AD carved on diorite. The "code" was extracted from even earlier dictates of a Sumerian King named Ur-Nammu. This find caused much anger in monotheistic religious communities because of its similarities to the *laws* given by Moses, Jesus, and Mohammed: the three major world religions. Other sets of "codes" or "laws" include the *Ten Commandments*; the *Confessions of Ma'at* in Egypt; the *Egyptian Book of Spells,* otherwise known as the *Book of the Dead* or *Coming Forth By Day*; and *The Kolbrin Bible*. Their similarities are striking and imply an effort to strengthen the bonds of society with virtuous teachings. By strengthening said bond one was acting in accordance with *Natural Law* towards constructing a more heavenly world on earth. Symbolically this has been represented in Freemasonic metaphor as the building of a societal temple through the enlightenment of each individual (brick), and the building of individual temples by the refinements of self (bricks). We will also have a look at the seventeen "articles" of Shōtoku issued around 604 AD in ancient Japan.

10 Commandments

thou shalt not take the name of the Lord thy God in vain
honor thy father and mother
thou shalt not kill
thou shall not commit adultery
thou shall not steal
thou shall not bear false witness
thou shall not covet

The Kolbrin Bible

a man will not curse the sacred things
a man will not revile his parents
a man will not slay willfully
a man will not have intercourse with the wife of another man
a man will not rob another with violence or plunder or steal
a man will not utter lies to lead another into error
a man will not pander to the lusts and weaknesses of others

Confessions of Ma'at

I have never cursed God
I have done no murder nor bid anyone to slay on my behalf
I have not lusted nor defiled the wife of any man
I have not robbed with violence and I have not stolen
I have not spoken lies
I have not envied or craved for that which belongs to another

Egyptian Book of the Dead – Coming Forth By Day

I do not offend the god who is at the helm
I do not harm my kinsmen
I do not kill
I am not an adulterer
I do not rob
I do not tell lies instead of truth
I do no wrong or mischief to others

One very often overlooked set of ancient laws were passed to man in 604 AD Japan through Umayado, or Prince Taishi Shōtoku (574-622 CE), who is credited with naming the country *Nihon*, Land of the Rising Sun. His famous *Seventeen-Article Constitution* was not just an advocacy for supporting the authority of the emperor, but they likened such obedience to *Natural Law*. It should be noted, however, that there were reportedly five of these constitutions, one each for Buddhists, Confucianists, shrine workers, politicians, and common people. Although likened to authoritative dictums from the State, such constitutions held the emperor, who was in direct lineage of the Creator, and the state, as subservient to the same virtues.

Taishi Shōtoku, ink drawing, 1878.

US Library of Congress

1. Value harmony and avoid quarreling.
2. Revere the Three Treasures of Buddha, Dharma, and Sangha.
3. Obey the imperial commands, as Earth obeys Heaven.
4. Ministers must behave with decorum, avoiding attention-seeking and flashy behavior.
5. Deal with public matters as a servant of the law, and avoid bribes and corruption.
6. Chastise evil and reward good. Encourage fidelity among your peers.
7. Take responsibility for your own affairs and do not interfere with the duties of others.
8. Come to work early, and work until late, to ensure that all matters are dealt with.
9. Observe good faith toward both superiors and inferiors.
10. Do not regard yourself as a genius and those around you as fools, but quell your anger and approach others with a calm heart.
11. Ensure that good deeds are rewarded and evil punished.
12. There is only one lord in a country. Do not allow local governors or aristocrats to doubly tax the people.
13. Ensure that all officers report for work and carry out their duty with equal diligence.
14. Do not envy those whose wisdom and genius exceeds yours, but honor them.
15. Turn away from that which is private, and be faithful to that which is public, to prevent resentment and corruption.
16. When the people are at leisure in the winter, press them into service for the state; but when they are busy producing their food and clothing, do not employ them.
17. Decisions on important matters should not be made by one person alone, but by consulting with many.

*Note: Ten Commandments plus Seven Deadly Sins equals 17.

These laws, commandments, codes, articles, constitutions, etc., issued by man, but ordained by God, are to be understood as *guidelines* for living a moral life. Their source is rooted in the core of ancient *Mystery Schools*, intended to initiate the few devout intellectuals who possessed both virtue and a willingness to grow in support of civilization.

Commandments of Ancient India, Buddhism & Taoism

While many regard Africa as the origin of civilization, the Torah as the origin of Ten Commandments, and the Jewish Noahide Covenant as sharing much with the latter, it is likely that civilization and its laws, and most of its religious convictions, were instead derived from India. The first lawgiver goes by the name Manu, or Manu-smriti, a figure responsible for imparting to Hindus their *dharma* - obligations for each member of the *varnas* (social classes). These *obligations* are considered *cosmic law*, and they underpin the necessity of social order and moral behavior. So writes Manu, in striking similarity with the Jewish covenant, which came centuries later, that man must abide by the ten virtues:

> *"Resignation, the action of rendering good for evil, temperance, probity, purity, repression of the senses, the knowledge of the Sastras (the holy books), that of the supreme soul, truthfulness and abstinence from anger, such are the ten virtues in which consists duty…Those who study these ten precepts of duty, and after having studied them conform their lives thereto, will reach to the supreme condition."*

Whatever the source of these *virtues* they are most certainly not derived from the Jews, who probably derived many of their *laws* from the Babylonians and Egyptians, who, in turn, derived them from more ancient sources. Writing in her classic work Isis Unveiled, Helena Blavatsky comments:

> *"If Manu did not trace these words many thousands of years before the era of Christianity, at least no voice in the whole world will dare deny them a less antiquity than sever centuries B.C."*

As with the Abrahamic religions, Buddhism finds its source material in India as well. Reading the *commandments* of the Pratimokska Sutra, and other religious texts of the Buddhists, we find vows against killing, stealing, lying, sexual deviancy, and the use of intoxicants. As Blavatsky lays out in her book, the Buddhist tradition, once more, provides us with the same list of commandments:

Thou shalt not kill any living creature.
Thou shalt not steal.
Thou shalt not break thy vow of chastity.
Thou shalt not lie.
Thou shalt not betray the secrets of others.
Thou shalt not wish for the death of thy enemies.
Thou shalt not desire the wealth of others.
Thou shalt not pronounce injurious and foul words.
Thou shalt not indulge in luxury (sleep on soft beds or be lazy).
Thou shalt not accept gold or silver.

"What shall I do to obtain possession of Bhodi? (knowledge of eternal truth)" asks a disciple of his Buddhist master, who replies "Keep the commandments." The disciple then asks, "What are they?" and the Master responds, "Thou shalt abstain all thy life from murder, theft, adultery, and lying." This line of questioning is identical to Matthew 19:16-19 when Jesus is asked how a man may obtain eternal life:

> *"Just then a man came up to Jesus and asked, 'Teacher, what good thing must I do to get eternal life?' 'Why do you ask me about what is good?' Jesus replied. 'There is only One who is good. If you want to enter life, keep the commandments.' 'Which ones?' he inquired. Jesus replied, 'You shall not murder, you shall not commit adultery, you shall not steal, you shall not give false testimony, honor your father and mother,' and 'love your neighbor as yourself.'"*

Unlike some Christians, who abide by the notion of an "eye for an eye, and tooth for tooth, (Leviticus)" both Hindus and Buddhists follow the teachings of *return good for evil*. Then again, in Matthew 5:38 we read that Jesus teaches something similar:

> *'You have heard that it was said, 'Eye for eye, and tooth for tooth.' But I tell you, do not resist an evil person. If anyone slaps you on the right cheek, turn to them the other cheek also. And if anyone wants to sue you and take your shirt, hand over your coat as well.'"*

~

Lao Tzu (Laozi) is famous for writing the foundational text of Taoism called <u>Tao Te Ching</u>. As with Buddhism, which teaches concepts of cosmology and the afterlife, Taoism is also an evolution of Hindu thought. Taoism teaches the path of Tao (*The Way*), the all-powerful but formless force that facilities the eternal cycles of all things.

Many Biblical teachings are clearly extracted from these more ancient principles and philosophies - Taoism dating to around 500 BC and Buddhism to around the same period, roughly. Laozi's work is easily paralleled with Jesus and some of the most famous Biblical verses:

Mathew 22:39 - Love your neighbor as yourself.

Tao Te Ching 13 - Love the world as your own self.

-

Matthew 8:25 - You of little faith, why are you so afraid?

Tao Te Ching 23 - He who has not enough faith will not be able to command faith from others.

-

Luke 6:27 - Love your enemies, do good to those who hate you, bless this who curse you, pray for those who mistreat you.

Tao Te Ching 27 - The sage is good at helping everyone. For that reason there is no rejected person. Therefore, the good man is the teacher of the bad and the bad man is the lesson of the good.

-

John 7:18 - Whoever speaks on their own does so to gain personal glory, but he who seeks the glory of the one who sent him is a man of truth; there is nothing false about him.

Ta Te Ching 56 - Those who know do not talk. Those who talk do not know.

-

Matthew 6:21 - For where your treasure is, there your heart will be also.

Tao Te Ching 70 - The sage wears rough clothing and holds the jewel in his heart.

~

In the occult sciences of India, the Brahmanic Code relates similar things to its adherents: *"thou shall not covet"* and *"a man will not pander to the lusts and weaknesses of others."*

According to Louis Jacolliot's book, Occult Science in India and Among the Ancients, an initiate would need to be able to bear the burden of possessing secrets that may, *"endanger his religious conditions and material observances of the law."* He relates of initiation and the preservation of sacred sciences in India:

> *"Thus, there is no doubt that the initiation in ancient times did not consist of a knowledge of the great religious works of the age, such as the Vedas, the Zend-Avesta, the Bible, etc., which everybody studied, but rather of the admission of a small number of priests and savants to an occult science, which had its genesis, its theology, its philosophy, and its peculiar practices, which it was forbidden to reveal to the vulgar herd."*

The priestly class known as *Brahmins*, the highest of four social groups called *varnas* in Hindu India, were initiated into *mysteries* by three degrees over several decades of study. The first degree included officiating the *pagoda* (temple); the second degree worked as an exorcist, prophet, evocator of spirits and a soothsayer; and the third degree included removal from public relations in exchange for dedicated study of all physical and supernatural forces in the universe. These priests and the *Brahmatchary*, or initiates, were presided over by a *High Council*.

The *Supreme Chief* overseeing this *Supreme Council* of occult study in India was called a *Brahmatma*. This position was only to be selected from members of the council known as *Yoguys*, who had taken vows of chastity. In order for his election to be held valid, *"he had to furnish evidence of his virile power in connection with one of the virgins of the Pagoda, who was given him as a bride,"* writes Louis, who goes on to explain the results of this union with strong parallels to the story of Moses, where, as part of a sacred ritual, if a child was born, they were: *"placed in a wicker basket, and turned adrift upon the river to float with the current. If perchance he was washed ashore he was carried to the temple, where he was at once, and by virtue of that very fact, regarded as having been initiated into the third degree. From his earliest childhood, all the secret mentrams, or formulas of evocation, were made known to him. If, however, the child floated down the stream with the current, he was rejected as a Pariah, and handed over to the people of that caste to be reared by them."* He writes further of similar customs in *"Egypt, which are so similar in many respects to those of the Indian temple,"* proposing an important question: *"Might not Moses, the leader of the Hebraic revolution, have been a son of the Egyptian high priest, who stood at the head of the order of the initiated, and might he not have been brought to the temple, because he had been cast ashore by the Nile?"*

What is told of Moses certainly mirrors that of the occult sciences, or *secret teachings*, of India, and is explained in the Biblical book of Exodus verse two:

> *"There was a man from the family of Levi who decided to marry a woman from the tribe of Levi. 2) She became pregnant and gave birth to a baby boy. The mother saw how beautiful the baby was and hid him for three months. 3) She hid him for as long as she could. After three months she made a basket and covered it with tar so that it would float. Then she put the baby in the basket and put the basket in the river in the tall grass. 4) The baby's sister stayed and watched to see what would happen to the baby. 5) Just then, Pharaoh's daughter went to the river to bathe. She saw the basket in the tall grass. Her servants were walking beside the river, so she told one of them to go get the basket. 6) The king's daughter opened the basket and saw a baby boy. The baby was crying and she felt sorry for him. Then she noticed that it was one of the Hebrew babies."*

The stories of a *Brahmatma* and of Moses are nearly identical to all the other stories we have already documented, from Osiris to the Hindu god Indra. Moses was a lawgiver like Minos of Crete, Manou of India, and Mises from either Syria or Egypt, depending on what author you read. There is also Ieo of China, who was a lawgiver and a "savior" with 70 disciples, which is the alternate to "seventy-two" new disciples of Jesus Christ in Luke 10:1-2.

This "law" was set down to man by God as a guideline for moral development, though there is zero doubt of its corruption and exploitation for worldly power.

But Eliphas Levi does not speak with much veneration for the Indian *mysteries*, calling them *"the Kabbalah in profanation."* He says they do not lead the soul to *"supreme wisdom,"* but that, *"Brahminism, with its learned theories, plunges it into gulfs of madness."* Some say that India was populated by the descendants of Cain, and at a later period, the descendants of Abraham and Keturah. Levi thus refers to India, with a largely magical claim, as *"the country of Goëtia and illusionary wonders."* This could be because by Levi's time India had descended so far form its former greatness that it looked nothing more than a land of *blackness*.

The *Brahmatma*, or supreme chief of the *Supreme Council*, was taken from chastised *Yoguys*. These councils consisted also of 70 members like the disciples of Ieo. *Yoguys*, in should be noted, had a peculiar practice by which they smeared their bodies and foreheads with ashes, like the 40-day lead up to Lent when Christians smear crosses on their heads in remembrance of the death of Jesus and his resurrection on *Ash Wednesday*. The *Seven Sages* of ancient India were also known to smear their entire bodies with ashes.

When Moses is supposed to have left Egypt, he came across a tribe in the desert known as the Midianites or Kenites, worshipers of the god of storms and war. Known as Mars or Aries, the god of war is the deity for which the month of March is named. The Anglo Saxons called him Hlyd-Monat, or stormy month, and the Midianites called him *Yahweh*. His symbol was a crucifix-like motif worn on the forehead, later to become known as the *Yahweh Mark*. Wednesday, referring to Ash Wednesday, is named after Woden, or Odin, the god who first created man and woman from an *Ash Tree*. Like Moses he also established the laws of the Universe. Here we find reference at Dictionary.com:

> *"Woden also created the first man and woman from an ash tree and an alder. As if fashioning the human race wasn't enough, Woden also established the laws of the universe."*

The Seven Esoteric Stages of Creation

The Darwinian model of *evolution*, which includes fish, amphibians, land animals, and humans, is preserved in the *occult sciences* and *stories*, albeit with different interpretations. A wonderful example of this fact can be found in Frank Baum's (a theosophist) classic story <u>The Wonderful Wizard of Oz</u>. Here the different aspects of human nature take form in animal, mineral, and vegetable bodies, i.e., the lion, tin man, and scarecrow, or the primate, mammalian, and reptilian complexes of the brain. From Genesis we are informed that God created the world in six days while on the seventh day He rested. It is common throughout the much of mythology and theology to find the Creator accompanied by seven helpers, often called *divine rays of light*. These seven assistants are the planetary intelligences and ascribed to each is a role to be played in the development of life and consciousness. The rays are the spheres by which the *Cosmic Mind* influences his creation from above.

The first stage of creation is the formation of material substance. It is ruled over by *Rex Mundj*, King of the World, invariably known as Saturn or Cronus, the spirit of which was hovering over a formless and empty world. He is otherwise known as the *Grand Architect*. In the esoteric tradition, darkness had previously suppressed the light and imprisoned the Earth Mother. Mark Booth writes in his book <u>The Sacred History</u> of the significant symbolism of darkness and light, along with the spirit of the former:

> *"The Darkness was the spirit of Saturn…The young Sun-God fought Saturn and vanquished him. Saturn is one of the names of Satan, the spirit of opposition, and creation myths all over the world would preserve a memory of these events in the stories of Saturn oppressing Mother Earth and the Sun god then vanquishing the monster. Saturn was banished to the outer limits, where he lay coiled around the cosmos like a great serpent with his tail in his mouth. He was evil, but a necessary evil."*

This "necessary evil" is obvious to those familiar with *occult sciences* as *ouroboros*, a snake biting its own tail. This symbol represents the pushing back of void so that the common and misidentified impression is created of being *surrounded by darkness and sin*. Without the *ouroboros*, often depicted wrapped around the *Cosmic Egg,* there would be no distinction of *light*. Here is Genesis 1:2 for sake of easy reference:

> *"Now the earth was formless and empty, darkness was over the surface of the deep, and the Spirit of God was hovering over the waters."*

It is written in the <u>Popul Vuh</u>: *"All was immobility and silence in the darkness, and only the creator, the maker, the serpent covered with feathers, they who create, were on the waters as an ever increasing light. They were surrounded by green and blue."*

The "serpent covered with feathers" is the god Quetzalcoatl, also known as the Plumbed Serpent or Feathered Serpent. In the beginning there was only a sea of "un-manifested spirit." From this sea arose the First Spirit, a Serpent or Dragon. Some call this beast the *Serpent Goddess, Serpent of the Tree, Plumed Serpent, Ammon Kematef, Shesha, Kneph,* or various other associated names, per different cultures. Perhaps the most intriguing name is *Mother Ayahuasca,* that serpent lady one sees in the *Garden of Hallucinations* (see my book of the same name). In Japan she has a likeness in the yokai called Nure-onna, a half-serpent, half-female creature.

In Egypt the primal Serpent was *Ammon Kematef*, a reptile creature sharing the likeness of *Typhon* that swam in the cosmic ocean and helped form the Universe. The Serpent appears as *Ammon* or *Agathodeamon* in Greece. The Hermetics also used the Egyptian creation story but changed the name of the god to *Pymander*. The Native Americans recall the birth of this Serpent or Spirit, which they represented as an alligator rising from the *cosmic ocean*. In parts of Central America, the Maya called this dragon *Itzamna*, while others worshiped the god as *Quetzalcoatl*, *Kukulkan* (Amazing Serpent), and *Huracan*, the *Slithering Spiraling Serpent*.

In Peru the serpent was a *Great Dragon* that lived in a large seashell, a symbol of Venus and Aphrodite, the *foam born* of the sea. People in Venezuela worshiped the creator serpent *Puana*, who is credited with creating the world and the *Kuna*, or ancestors of mankind. The aborigines of Australia also recount the *Rainbow Serpent* that lived in a water hole. These beings are directly relatable to the Arabic *Djinn* or the *Djedhi* of Egypt, all of which are interchangeable with *genies*. They are known as *Archons* in the Gnostic Gospels, *Flyers* in Africa, and *Snake Brothers* to the Hopi Indians. They were known also as *Levites* or *Lung Dragons* in China. In India they took the form of the *Nagas*; the root "Nag" means snake or cobra in most Indian languages. *Shesha* was their king.

The Garden of Earthly Delights by Hieronymus Bosch, depicting the various stages of esoteric evolution that include a solidifying of a matter even finer than light, which gradually hardened into the state of nature we know today. Human bodies passed through the same stages with bones becoming solidified from a pink waxy substance, as written about by the Rosicrucian philosopher Jacob Boehme.

Sol rules the second stage of creation; its rays causing the world to cool and solidify. Darkness and night were separated from light and day; there was separation of *The One* into two. A primitive and primordial form of life began to form. Light provided nourishment for these first forms, existing in a state alien to our world today. Elements became minerals and then developed into an early form of plant and animal life, which reproduced through separation and *speciation*. In this stage of creation, the Sun god comes to rescue Mother Earth from darkness, a cycle repeating each morning when the sun rises to save man from the dark, and every spring when days lengthen over nights. Here is Genesis 1:3-5 for sake of easy reference:

> "And God said, 'Let there be light, and there was light. God saw that the light was good, and he separated the light from the darkness. God called the light 'day,' and the darkness he called 'night.' And there was evening, and there was morning – the first day."

In the Zend Avesta, a sacred collection of religious texts known to Zoroastrianism, it is explained the creation of *light*:

> "Ahura Mazda, Spake unto Spitama Zarathustra saying: First I have made the Kingdom of Light, Dear to all life."

Ahura Mazda goes on to create the Preserver, Spoiler, Eternal Life, Death, Wisdom, Ignorance, Work, Idleness, Love, Hatred, Peace, Violence, Power, Weakness, Food, Impure Food, Health, Disease, Man, Inferior Man, Joy, Sadness, Sun, Darkness, Water, Impure Water, Air, Impure Air, Earth, Barrenness. This archetypical battle between darkness and light was told in the conflict spoken of by Persian *magi* through the principles of good and evil, which were manifest under the names *Ormuzd*, or *Ahura Mazda* (creator god), and *Ahriman* (evil spirit). Another name of the conflict is *Armageddon*.

The third stage of creation is the time of the Garden of Eden when *man* lived without *desire*, even for some time after the formation of woman. Before *desire* all needs were met in symbiotic harmony with nature. There was no fear, shame, guilt, dissatisfaction, sorrow or wanting. *Paradise* is the absence of *desire* since for temporal pleasures to be enjoyed there must be an understanding of suffering, which was only brought about by the consumption of the apple and the realization of good and evil. This took place later and it is the apple that many say is a symbol of physical sexual union.

Although not an entirely ancient work, the Popul Vuh is a text written in the 16th-century by an unknown Mayan author. Translated into Spanish by Father Francisco Ximenez, it was first published in Vienna in 1857. The text shares similarities with the Bible and the Quran. It relates the following about man's creation:

> "Let us make him who shall nourish and sustain us! What shall we do to be invoked, in order to be remembered on Earth? We have already tried with our first creations, our first creatures; but we could not make them praise and venerate us. So, then, let us try to make obedient, respectful beings who will nourish and sustain us."

Genesis 1:26 relates the same: "*Then God said, 'Let us make mankind in our image, in our likeness, so that they may rule over the fish in the sea and the birds in the sky, over the livestock and all the wild animals, and over all the creatures that move along the ground'*."

*The "us" here is translated in Hebrew as *Elohim*, which is indeed a plural term. It includes the masculine *ELOAH* and feminine *IM*.

The Quran says in Surat Al-Mu'minum (The Believers), verse 12-14, as shown earlier:

> "And certainly did We create man from an extract of clay. Then We placed him as a sperm-drop in a firm lodging. Then We made the sperm-drop into a clinging clot, and We made the clot into a lump [of flesh], and We made [from] the lump, bones, and We covered the bones with flesh; then We developed him into another creation."

Just as Genesis 2:1-3 says that "By the seventh day God had finished the work he had been doing; so on the seventh day he rested from all his work," we find in the Quran book of Hūd, verse 7, the power of Allah (God) and his creation:

> "It is He who created the heavens and the earth in six spans, and has control over the waters (of life) so that he may bring out the best that [everyone] of you could do."

The Mayan story reports that that the gods were dissatisfied with the ability of their creation to see both the earth and into the heavens. The Biblical story explains this ability as having arisen after the consumption of the *forbidden fruit* and there may even be a relationship to the *Tower of Babel*. The Popul Vuh continues:

> "They were endowed with intelligence; they saw and instantly they could see far, they succeeded in seeing, they succeeded in knowing all that there is in the world. When they looked, instantly they saw all around them, and they contemplated in turn the arch of heaven and the round face of the earth."

In Genesis 3:4-6 it is told the details of how the Old Serpent deceived Eve into consuming the fruit:

> "'You will not certainly die,' the serpent said to the woman. 'For God knows that when you eat from it your eyes will be opened, and you will be like God, knowing good and evil'. When the woman saw that the fruit of the tree was good for food and pleasing to the eye, and also desirable for gaining wisdom, she took some and ate it. She also gave some to her husband, who was with her, and he ate it."

As a direct result of disobeying God, Adam and Eve were punished and removed from the sacred Garden, as detailed in Genesis 3:24:

> "After he drove the man out, he placed on the east side of the Garden of Eden cherubim and a flaming sword flashing back and forth to guard the way to the tree of life."

Similarly, the Popul Vuh describes how the Mayan gods also dealt with a man who had the ability to see beyond their liking:

> "What shall we do with them now? Let their sight reach only to that which is near; let them see only a little of the face of the earth! It is not well what they say. Perchance, are they not by nature simple creatures of our making? Must they also be gods?"

> "Then the Heart of Heaven blew mist into their eyes, which clouded their sight as when a mirror is

breathed upon. Their eyes were covered and they could see only what was close, only that was clear to them."

The Edenic serpent symbolizes not on the *realization of good and evil*, but the further evolution or development of the human body. Its slithering upon the tree signifies the formation of a more upright stature for man, such as the development of backbone. Mankind also developed, or inherited from this metaphoric creature, a reptilian brain so that he would now experience fear, anger, hatred, aggression, compulsion, ritual, and thus, *suffering*: this all results from the opening of Pandora's box by the same *curiosity* that tempted Eve to see the fruit as *"desirable"* and to consume it like Persephone in Hades eating pomegranate seeds. This action brought *shame* and the realization of being naked, i.e., ***the first flicker and glimmer of consciousness***.

Adam's defilement of Eve, the virgin, brought about sins of impurity. Francis Barrett writes in The Magus, *"that man being sowed in the pleasure of concupiscence of the flesh, shall therefore always reap a necessary death in the flesh of sin."* The *impurity* of this action was to be rectified through marriage so that Adam was later able to *"know his wife,"* or that he would be able to reunite with his divine self. The marriage was alchemical and involves a uniting of *consciousness* with the *higher self*. It is the sacred marriage of Jesus and his Bride. The result of Eve's transgression was that she would bring forth life in pain - as it is to philosophers - as would all future generations, yet her privilege was she would crush the head of that same infernal serpent by shining light on the dark through birthing the *sun*. This is Isis standing on the serpents holding her child Horus. Genesis 3:15-15 confirms:

> *"And I will put enmity between you and the woman, and between your offspring and hers; he will crush your head, and you will strike his heel."*

> *"To the woman he said, 'I will make your pains in childbearing very severe; with painful labor you will give birth to children. Your desire will be for your husband, and he will rule over you."*

Adam and Eve are the primordial couple or *androgyny*, symbolized as a hermaphrodite with male and female attributes. Man was to be immortal like the monad, but through the creation of Eve by his rib, he was separated from *source*. The action of *copulation* produces unity in duality, though, for *Original Sin* is sexual unification, yet with defilement of the sacred union by animal tendencies and lust. The monad is the *father* and the duad is the *mother*. The sacred *Trinity* preserves their union with its offspring. Barrett writes further that *Original Sin* was *"bred from the concupiscence of the flesh, but occasioned only by the apple being eaten,"* and that it [the apple] contained a *"lustful property radically inserted and implanted in it."*

But lust is a sin beyond the literalism of sexual union, and this is lost amongst those with superficial consideration, as is the reality of the entire Garden story. Marriage was meant to ratify lust by bringing man and woman together as intended by their Creator. Barrett adds further how "man" is truly a "soul" like the Beast (Prince Adam) calmed by Beauty in the classic story:

> *"Therefore Adam was created in the possession of immortality. God intended not that man should be an animal or sensitive creature, nor be born, conceived, or live as an animal; for the truth he was created unto a living soul, and that after the true image of God; therefore he as far differed from the nature of an anima, as an immortal being from a mortal, and as a God-like creature from a brute."*

From *darkness* and *sin* comes *light* and *absolution*. And from *light* is produced *shadow*.

The fourth stage of creation is ruled over by the moon, which gave rise to the further formation of human awareness by the method of self-reflection. But *reflection* can beget *desire,* too, if one is not careful. It is by *thought* and *self-reflection* of our *decisions*, which come from the great reflector in the sky, that humans can avoid their animal instincts and strive for something more. Through *reflection* we are able to grow as God intended, lit by an internal and eternal flame burning deep within. For some this flame is nearly extinguished and for others it is burning as bright as the sun. The light of Sol, savior of man and earth, was reflected from Luna and cast to the earth; thus, Lucifer was cast out of heaven by Jehovah, the moon god. The Moon is the receptacle of all heavenly influences as they emanate from all the planets and stars. Through them the Moon is made fruitful.

In Zoroastrianism it was *Zrvan Akaran*, or *Boundless Time*, that created all things. Akaran initially produced light by emanations, out of which the first to be born was *Ormazd*, who created a pure world. Second to be born was *Ahriman*, a jealous and angry deity obsessed for power. Because of his envy he was banished, like Lucifer, to the darkness where he was to remain while the battle between light and dark continued. Ormazd created light patterned after the celestial light. He created a source of life called *Bull* and then Ahriman destroyed this being. Its scattered seed led to the creation of the first man and woman. Ahriman also seduced the woman, thus subjecting man to *sin,* by using milk and a kind of fruit. Ahriman then created reptiles and serpents. *Redemption* is said to come on *Judgment Day*. Good and evil will finally be separate and Ormazd, having vanquished Ahriman, will establish his Kingdom on earth. The *dead* will rise, hell will be purified, and everlasting life is to be granted to the pure of heart.

The fifth and sixth stages of this esoteric development were the beginnings of a new age under the rule of Jupiter (Zeus), who overtook his father Saturn (Cronus). This is when animals and primitive life began to form more complexity to resemble something closer to, but not exactly, what we might see today. The immaculate conception of Jesus was by a ray of light, which also penetrates the ground and sprouts vegetation. His birth was indicative of the end of a previous age and the beginning of a new one under the tutelage of Pisces; for we are told in the Bible that Jesus will be with us until the end of time, the aeon, or the age.

After the age of two fish will be Aquarius, the bearer of water, and this is also spoken of in the Bible with the metaphor of a man pouring out water from a pitcher. Words change over time, and their meanings more so, but the consistency of this story remains almost purely astrological. The age of the bull, Taurus, was ended when Mithra(s) plunged his knife into its back. The age of the ram, Aries, also depicted as a sheep for which Jesus was the shepherd, was ended by the birth of the latter bringing in the age of Pisces. There is much overlapping between symbols of one age to the next with Jews to this day still blowing the ram's horn and Christians adorning the *Agnus Dei*.

When the sun began to rise in the constellation Pisces, it was said the first embryonic fish formed. Throughout this age also formed amphibians and creatures with webbed feet.

The next stage saw the wetlands of earth harden into dry land. Primitive humans developed limbs of some sort and began to crawl on that land. This led to the influence of Mars and the evolution of warm-blooded animals.

It is to be understood that although humans developed more identifiable characteristics at this time, their previous existence in the garden was more plant-like than we are aware. Today we still receive assistance from the sun and our nervous system itself mimics developments of a plant.

We maintain our planet nature in the same way we maintain our elemental, mineral and animal nature through water, bone, and instinct.

The *occult sciences* profess how snakes, spiders, and parasitic creatures formed from the dark side of the moon, and this was a time when modern mythological creatures possibly existed. These creatures included humans with the thighs of goats, horns on their head, man-headed bulls, four-headed dogs, and dragon-like beings. Barrett asserts in explanation that Satan instituted a connection *"of the seed of man with the seeds and in the womb of a witch, or sorceress, that he might exclude the dispositions unto an immortal mind from such a new, polished conception."* From this resulted the monstrous generations of Faunii, Satyrs, Gnomes, Nymphs, Sylphs, Driades, Hamodriades, Neriads, Mermaids, Syrens, and Sphynxes, by the constellations *"and disposing the seed of man for such like monstrous prodigious generations."* It was the climax of this age that led to the development of giants called *Danavas* in India and *Miaotse* in China. They were the Nephilim giants of the Bible as told in the book of Numbers 13:33, which states:

> *"We saw the Nephilim there. We seemed like grasshoppers in our own eyes, and we looked the same to them."*

The seventh and final stage of this *esoteric evolution* includes the further condensing of matter, the separation of gods from the physical world, and the forming of a subconscious and *free will*. The final stages also produced the rebirth of higher consciousness that led to the formation of music, math, and language. Each of the previous ages, including our current, are personified not only by astrological characters, but also by various symbols of conscious evolution such as prophets or teachers, themselves represented by the various levels of intelligence expressed through each planetary god. Further described below is a pithy observation containing a general truth, a series of aphorisms that go on to describe the previous processes as preserved by the Rosicrucian Order and expressed in their *Secret Doctrine* republished, in part, by Magus Incognito, a clear pseudonym.

The Seven Rosicrucian Aphorisms of Creation

The existence of Christian Rosencreutz (C.R.C.), the most Illuminated brother and founder of the Order, is arguably unknown. At sixteen years old he traveled to the Holy Land, then to Turkey and Arabia where he was to learn *secret wisdom*. This he preserved in a book written in Latin called *"M."* He then visited Fez in Morocco and acquired knowledge, similar to King Solomon, of all the secrets of nature.

Much of the world at the time rejected his teachings and therefore he returned to Germany, built a modest house, and lived in peace with his studies.

C.R. was supposedly in possession of the famed *stone of the philosophers* but had no desire for riches. Eventually he accepted three disciples to impart his wisdom and plans for his own Order, which expanded to eight members including himself, possibly an amalgamation of various characters. Upon an agreement they would not profess anything except to cure the sick without reward, wear no special garb, meet every year in the House of the Sainted Spirit, choose their own successors, use R.C. as their seal, and remain in secret for increments of one hundred years. It is certain that the mystery of the Rosicrucian Order, their history, symbols, etc., is veiled in a similar manner to Freemasonry, which itself is a pillar of the Order. Their intent was not to obtain wealth or prestige. They instead offered wisdom and help for humanity under the cloak of secrecy.

The original pamphlets published by the group were *Fame of the Fraternity* (1614), *Confession of the Fraternity* (1615), *The Chemical Wedding of Christian Rosencreutz* (1616):

I. The Eternal Parent was wrapped in the Sleep of the Cosmic Night. Light there was not; for the Flame of Spirit was not yet rekindled. Time there was not: for Change had not re-begun. Things there were not; for Form had not re-presented itself. Action there was not; for there were no Things to act. The Pairs of Opposites there were not; for there were no Things to manifest Polarity. The Eternal Parent, causeless, indivisible, changeless, infinite, rested in unconscious, dreamless sleep. Other than the Eternal Parent there was Naught, either Real or Apparent.

II. The Germ within the Cosmic Egg takes unto itself Form. The Flame is re-kindled. Time begins. A Thing exists. Action Begins. The Pairs of Opposites spring into being. The World Soul is born and awakens into manifestation. The first rays of the new Cosmic Day break over the horizon.

III. The One became Two. The Neuter became Bi-Sexual. Male and Female – the Two in One – evolved from the Neuter. And the work of Generation began.

IV. The One becomes Many. The Unity becomes Diversity. The Identical becomes Variety. Yet the Many remains One; the Diversity remains Unity; and the Variety remains Identical.

V. The One is the Flame of Life. The Many are the Sparks in the Flame. The Flame once lighted kindles everything within its sphere. The Fire is in everything and everywhere; there is nothing dark or cold within its sphere.

VI. As Life is the Essence of Spirit, so is Consciousness the Essence of Life. Spirit is One, yet it manifests in many forms of life. Life is One, yet it manifests in many forms of Consciousness. While the forms of manifested Consciousness are innumerable, yet the wise know Consciousness to manifest on Seven Planes: and these Planes of Consciousness are known to the wise as (1) The Plane of the Elements; (2) The Plane of the Minerals; (3) The Plane of the Plants; (4) The Plane of the Animals; (5) The Plane of the human; (6) The Plane of the Demi-Gods; (7) The Plane of the Gods.

VII. The Soul of Man is Sevenfold, yet but One in essence; Man's Spiritual Unfoldment has as its end the Discovery of Himself beneath the Sevenfold Veil.

The Sevenfold soul of man is likewise comprised of the same elements making the seven planes of consciousness. Magus Incognito summarizes the following in <u>The Secret Doctrine of the Rosicrucians</u>:

> *"The student must not fall into the error of supposing that man really has seven separate and distinct souls, either tied together like a bundle of twigs, or else worn as one would wear seven overcoats, one over the other. The symbol is only figurative, and must not be construed literally. There are not seven selves in man – but only One Self concealed by seven veils, each of which while serving to conceal the real nature of the Self yet serves to disclose the presence and power thereof to some degree. It is as if seven planes of variously colored glass, ranging from the darkest to the almost-transparent and colorless, were to be placed before a brilliant light. The darker glass would almost entirely obscure the Light, though yet revealing its presence in some of its rays; the next lighter would reveal more, and obscure less; and so on to the last in which the obscuration was but slight, and the revelation almost perfect. All illustrations of this ineffable fact of the Eternal are, by the very nature of things, imperfect, faulty, and misleading if taken too literally.*

> *"The lesson to the student is that in every man there lie concealed the potentiality of Godhood, and stages less than Godhood though above that of ordinary Manhood; and that in every man also abide the lower phases of manifested existence, even the very lowest of all. The wise man uses the lower, but*

does not allow the lower to use him; he maintains a positive, masterful mental attitude toward the lower planes of being, while opening himself receptively to the influences of the higher planes of his Self.

"In conclusion, you are asked to once more consider the Seventh Aphorism: "The Soul of Man is Sevenfold, yet but One in essence: Man's spiritual Unfoldment has as its end the Discovery of Himself beneath the Seven-fold Veil."

The Seven Hermetic Principles as expressed in *The Kybalion*

The <u>Kybalion</u> suggests and warns to serve life rather than death; to work *with* rather than *against* the laws of nature and to impose *higher laws* over *lower laws*. Be it a pseudo-occult text or not, there is always something to learn:

1. Mentalism

The Universe is a mental creation (as by mediation). It is the Creation of God or the unknown, expressed as the ALL. We are each of the All, but not the All itself. Manifestation of thought, desire, will, etc. is an expression of the feminine principle.

The usage of mental will is an expression of the masculine principle, of impressing one's will over their mind, and those of others, rather than living by the impressions of others. Through mentalism comes all the phenomenon of magnetism, fascination, hypnotism, suggestion, and other mental capabilities.

2. Correspondence

The law of correspondence is expressed by the hermetic axiom of "As Above So Below" or alternately, "As Below So Above." This is a primary law of magic wherein relationships are found between, animals, plants, stones, herbs, planets, organs, etc.

3. Vibration

All things are moving; nothing is at rest; nothing is constant but change.

Differences exist only in rates of vibration.

4. Polarity (the divine paradox of "absolute & reason")

Everything has poles. Opposites are identical in nature but not in degree.

Through the principles of polarity we discover that a lie, even the truth, is merely only half false, or accurate.

5. Rhythm

Similar to the constant and unchanging vibration of things, all things move in patterns of rhythm like the swinging of a pendulum.

6. Cause & Effect

Causes = Effects = Causes, etc., etc.

7. Gender

As witnessed in the principles of mentalism and polarity we find that all things have masculine and feminine principles, and these principles manifest on all planes of existence.

Returning to the Garden

In the Arsenal Library, Paris, there is a manuscript titled <u>The Book of the Penitence of Adam</u>, which deals with Kabbalistic tradition that is presented as an allegorical legend about the Garden of Eden:

"Adam had two sons — Cain, who signifies brute force, and Abel, the type of intelligence and mildness. Agreement was impossible between them; they perished at each other's hands; and their inheritance passed to a third son, named Seth."

"Now Seth, who was just, was permitted to approach as far as the entrance of the Earthly Paradise, without being threatened by the Kerub and his flaming sword."

"It came to pass in this manner that Seth beheld the Tree of Knowledge and the Tree of Life, incorporated together after such a manner that they formed but a single tree."

"When Adam died, Seth, in obedience to the directions of the angel, placed the three seeds in the mouth of his father, as a token of eternal life. The saplings which sprang up from these, became the Burning Bush, in the midst of which God communicated to Moses his Eternal Name signifying He Who is and is to come. Moses plucked a triple branch of the sacred bush and used it as his miraculous wand. Although separated from its root, the branch continued to live and blossom, and it was subsequently preserved in the Ark/ King David planted the branch on Mount Zion, and Solomon took wood from each section of the triple trunk to make the two pillars, Jachin and Boazy which were placed at the entrance of the Temple. They were covered with bronze, and the third section was inserted at the threshold of the chief gate. It was a talisman' which hindered things unclean from entering within. But certain nefarious Levites removed during the night this obstacle to their unholy freedom and cast it, loaded with stones at the bottom of the Temple reservoir. From this time forward an angel of God troubled the waters of the pool, imparting to them a miraculous value, so that men might be distracted from seeking the tree of Solomon in its depths. In the days of Jesus Christ the pool was cleansed and the Jews, finding the beam of wood, which in their eyes seemed useless, carried the latter outside the town and threw it across the brook Cedron. It was over this bridge that our Saviour passed after his arrest at night in the Garden of Olives. His executioners cast him from it into the water; and then in

their haste to prepare the instrument-in-chief of His passion, they took the beam with them, which was made of three kinds of wood, and formed the cross therewith."

The "two sons" are the opposing forces of caduceus. Seth is represented here in a primeval initiation. The incorporation of the trees of *Knowledge* and *Life* signify the harmony of science, religion, and philosophy.

This allegory embodies the great traditions of Kabbalah and the secret Christian doctrine of St. John. It may be derived metaphorically that Moses, Seth, Solomon, David, and Christ each obtained from the same Kabbalistic Tree their scepters, staffs, and pontifical crooks.

The *Tree of Knowledge* does inflict death when its apple is eaten; the golden apples, like those in Greek legend, are the *"glamour that would dazzle people and blind them to higher truths,"* as explained by Booth. This *glamour* is the essence of Lucifer as a serpent of wisdom in the Garden, but an evil necessary for the *realization* of the *soul*.

In Germanic mythology, the *apples of immortality* are given by Freia (Freya), the goddess of love. Her Icelandic counterpart is Idun (the renewer), who gives golden apples to the gods to prevent their aging. The Greek Aphrodite was also associated with golden apples through the pomegranate, which many believe to better represent the *forbidden fruit* offered by the infamous serpent. She is sometimes depicted riding a goose, just as the Hindu god Karttikeya rides a peacock. Although birds are not reptiles, they are symbols of the soul-spirit. Take for example the Egyptian BA. Since Karttikeya fights demons and is associated with fertility, we can infer that there is a further connection between serpent deceivers, birds, forbidden fruit, and life. This is especially true when considering that Apollo, the winged sun, slayed the python serpent. In the east the apples are substituted for *peaches of immortality.*

Serpent worship or veneration has been found all over the world. Serpents were sacred to the Druids, the priests of the Celts, and found in the *Midgard* of Scandinavia, and the *Nagas* of Burma and Cambodia; they were *uraeus* to the Egyptians; *plumbed serpents* of South and Central America; and the *bronze serpent* of Jews.

The serpent in the primordial Garden Paradise symbolizes primal attraction and the eternal predator. This creature tempts the weaker of the two Universal Parents (Eve) causing the other (Adam) to succumb to the same fault. Yet Eve only submits so that she may overcome, for one day she will crush the head of this deceiver by giving birth to the savior or mankind. In this regard, Levi describes how *"man abdicates the realm of intelligence by yielding to the solicitations of the sensitive part."*

Adam profanes the *fruit of knowledge*, the nourishment of the soul, applying it to the uses of carnal pleasures. He thus loses touch with *harmony* and *truth,* and so is clothed like Eve in the skin of the *Beast.* The *Universal Androgyny* is separated into male and female. Both eternal parents then realize their *nakedness*, and in shame, hide from God, demonstrating the forgetting of the divine *source* of their creation.

When cast from the garden they are separated by duality and a cherub armed with burning sword prevents their return to *unity* or *paradise*. The cherub is the bull, and the flaming sword typifies the *astral light* which man no longer has an ability to direct; he became subject to it rather than maintaining sovereignty over this force. Therefore, as per Levi, the *"great magical work, understood in an absolute sense, is the conquest and direction of the burning sword, and the cherub is the angel or soul of the earth, represented invariably under the figure of a bull in the Ancient Mysteries."*

Only upon conquering the *telluric fields* of earth, represented by serpents, and bending the Celestial Fire to one's *will,* can allowance into the Garden be granted once more.

The Five Weights

The Taoist triad of Heaven, Earth, and Man could be seen as yet another sacred *Trinity*. In Confucianism there are the *Three Bonds* of ruler and subject, parent and child, and husband and wife. Buddhism has Buddha, Dharma, and Sangha. Shintoism has the path of *Sōgen*, *Saigen*, and *Reisō*, or the worship of *Seven Divine Deities*, *Five Earthly Deities*, and *Imperial Ancestors*. In Japan the latter three traditions are unified by past, present, and future. Shintō teaches us about the past and beginning of time, Confucianism about maintaining happiness in the present, and Buddhism about the future and afterlife. God is the LOGOS or WORD MADE FLESH; a concept expressed by the Japanese *kotodama* – the *spirit of a word*. The Kujiki-72 informs us:

> *"The Creator rules over boundless infinity. Nothing existed before the Creator. No one ruled before the Creator. The Creator is without Form."*

Unlike the specifics of the Bible or Quran, the Kujiki-72 describes the creation of ALL as appearing in five forms called *WEIGHTS*. These *Five Weights* are *Kami*, *Kokoro* (Mind-Heart), *Principle* (Nature/Behavior), *Qi* (Vital Energy), and *Boundary* (State). Avery Morrow, in <u>The Sacred Science of Ancient Japan</u>, describes these *Five Weights* as: *"kami lives, the mind rules, principles preserve, qi determines our fates, and borders create form."* In books 53-56 of the same Kujiki-72 we learn about how sickness is caused by disharmony in all things and how words, or vibrations, can heal. Avery explains the text from his translation:

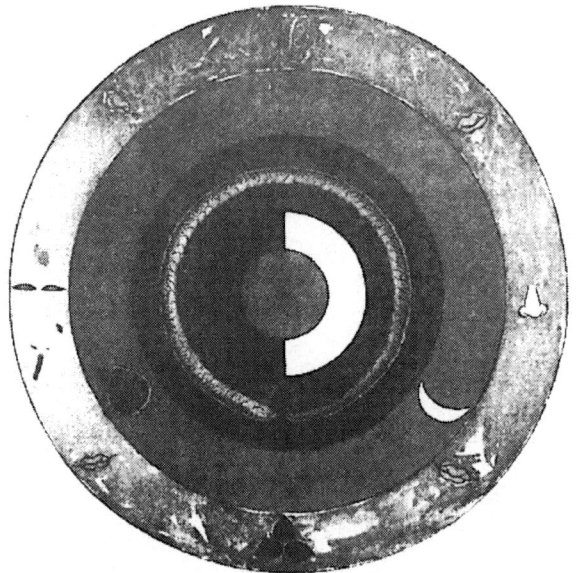

The **Universal** *kokoro*,
according to Sadashizu Yoda.

> *"We learn the sickness is caused by a climate of dishonesty and untruth, that the people in the Age of the Kami avoided illness entirely through honest and frank attitudes, and that if anyone ever got sick their hearts were purified through healing kotodama and other methods, and they would quickly recover."*

From the most eastern of traditions, or from the Land of the Rising Sun (Nihon), we acquire a slightly different view of the manifestation of *matter* and of *Creation*. This version, as could be argued for some parts of the Bible or Quran, too, is both spiritual and scientific. In other words, it is a harmonious balancing of Creation, Life, and what will ultimately be Death. That is to say: past, present, and future. The WORD (*logos*) is CREATION out of VOID. The *Five Weights* therefore represent far more than the Creation of "heaven and earth" (Genesis 1:1), providing us with a deeper look at the *Grand Architect*.

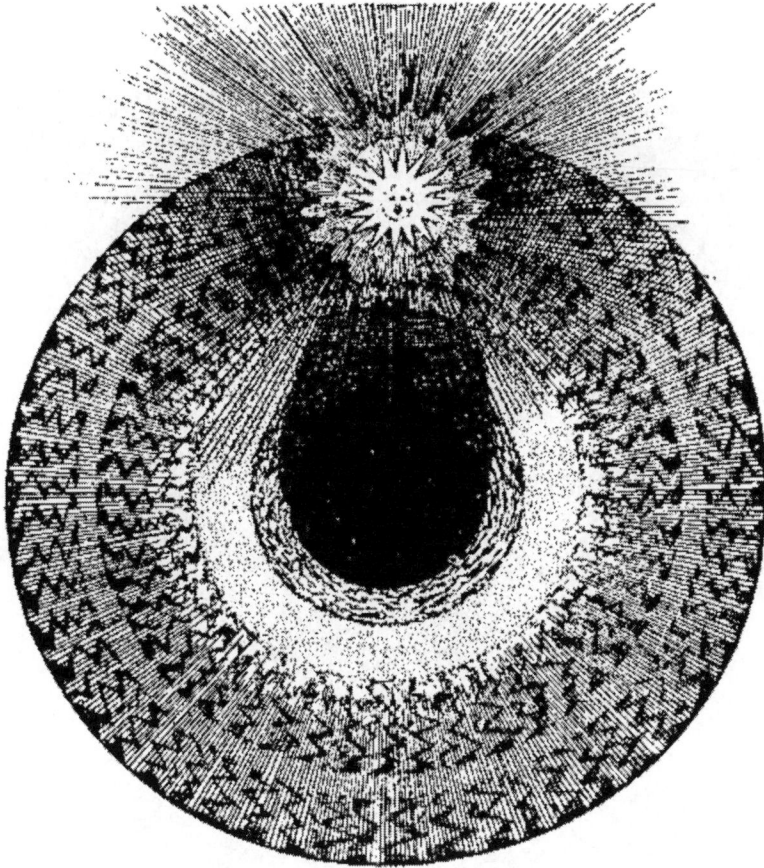

The separation of earth and sun by Robert Fludd, from a seventeenth-century English print.

Depicted here are the *Monad* and *Sun* coming to the rescue of Mother Earth.

The Germ within the *Cosmic Egg* took form and out of *The One* came *The Many*.

Joseph Campbell explains the process of esoteric creation in <u>The Hero With A Thousand Faces</u>, with a slightly similar feel to Mark Booth's above descriptions:

"The emanations have condensed, the field of consciousness constricted. Where formerly causal bodies were visible, now only their secondary effects come to focus in the little hard-fact pupil of the human eye. The cosmogonic cycle is now to be carried forward, therefore, not by the gods, who have become invisible, but by the heroes, more or less human in character, through whom the world destiny is realized. This is the line where creation myths begin to give place to legend—as in the Book of Genesis, following the expulsion from the garden. Metaphysics yields to prehistory, which is dim and vague at first, but becomes gradually precise in detail. The he- roes become less and less fabulous, until at last, in the final stages of the various local traditions, legend opens into the common day- light of recorded time."

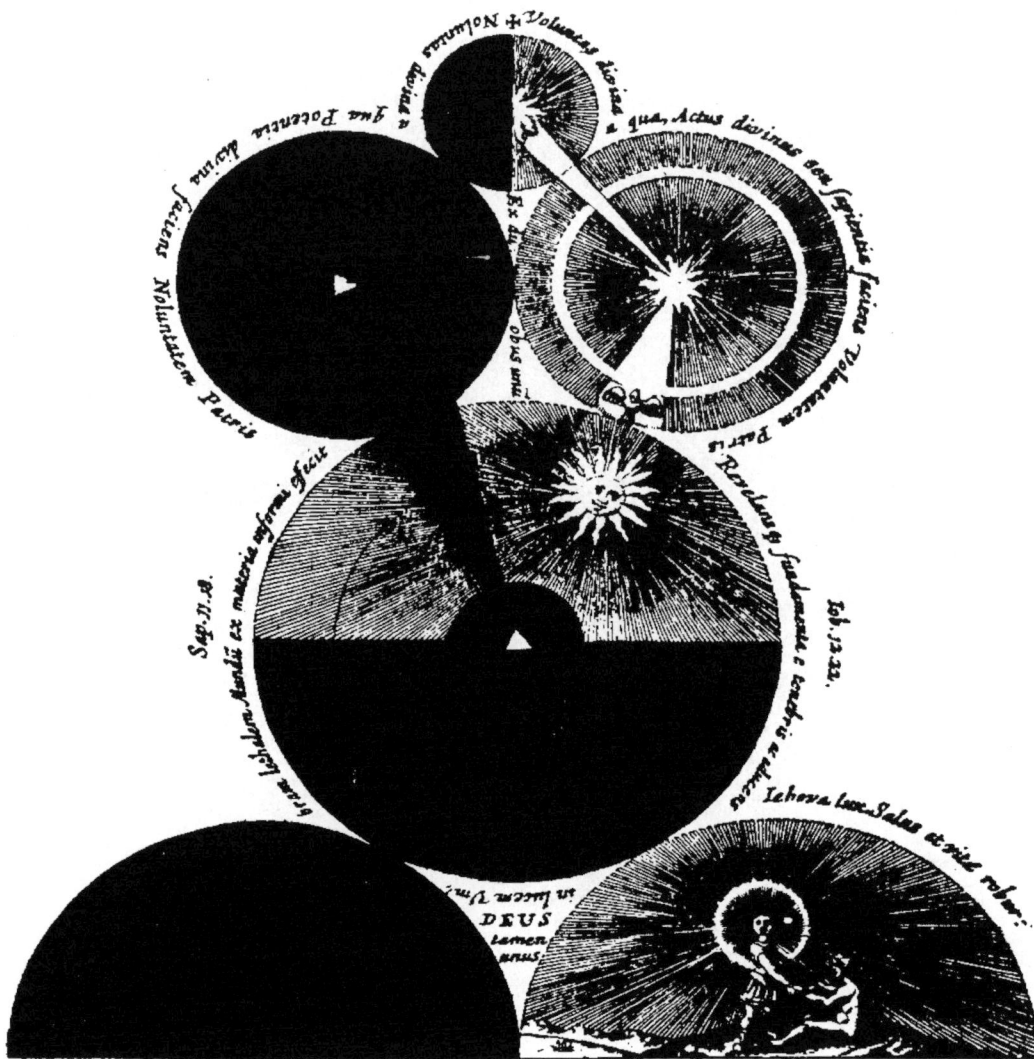

The duality of *light* & *dark* creates the Universe, from Robert Fludd's <u>Philosophia Mosaica.</u>

The smallest globe atop the others represents *Supreme Deity*. It is divided in half with one segment representing *divine darkness* that hides the *Deity* and the other a symbol of the *divine light* of God and His *Creative Powers*.

The larger dark globe on the left is a symbol of the darkness that was upon the face of those primordial waters as Creation began. To its right is a globe of light wherefrom emerges the *First Cause* of the *Supreme Deity* in creating light and forming the mundane world by dissipating darkness.

In the central sphere is divided the *Superior* and *Inferior* worlds in similar fashion to the *Grand Rosicrucian Alchemical Formula*. Below the central sphere are two half spheres. The left bottom globe entirely dark and represents the diurnal hemisphere of the world. The right bottom globe is the nocturnal hemisphere.

The first image is of the Mother Goddess Cybele and the other is of the Buddha. They are credited to Athanasius Kircher, the Jesuit scholar of occult studies. Both illustrate a deep understanding for the vegetable nature of the human body.

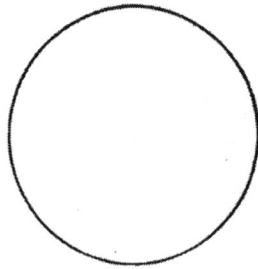

Infinite Unmanifest

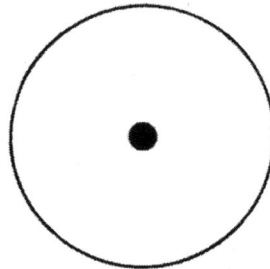

Germ within the Egg

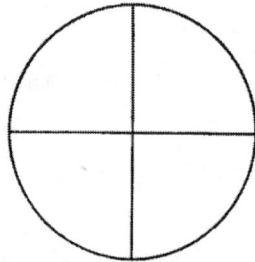

Universal Androgyne

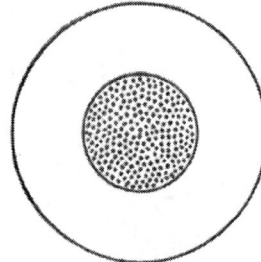

Many in the One

Universal Flame of Life

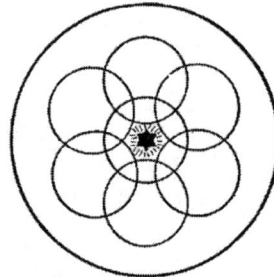

Seven Planes of Consciousness

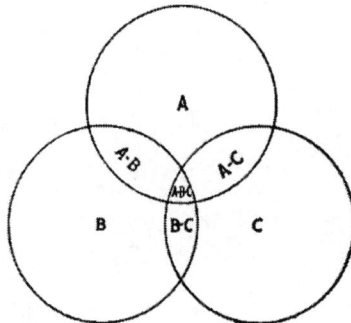

Three Higher Planes of Consciousness

Sevenfold Soul

Conquering the Celestial Fire

"The beautiful kosmos represents a dynamic, harmonic union of the two ideal extremes of Unity and Diversity, Form and Matter, the Limited and the Unlimited Elements."

~ David Fideler ~

The *Middle Path* of *uraeus* and *bindi*

As the Greek philosopher Pythagoras expressed: *"Virtue is harmony."* This implies that those demonstrating *virtue*, a behavior indicative of high moral standards, have more of an ability than others. to overcome their carnal nature, i.e., *to slay the great beast-dragon.*

In the book of Daniel, chapter 6, we learn of how King Darius of Babylon favored Daniel over other presidents and princes. But this caused the wise men to grow jealous. Knowing Daniel prayed to God, the conspirators encouraged Darius to pass a law forbidding such prayer. Punishment for its violation was being thrown into a den of lions. Daniel chose to speak with God anyway and so the king had little choice but to follow his own law, thus casting him to the beasts. King Darius was so worried about Daniel, however, that he fasted all night, hoping to grant him protection in the den. Earlier the next morning we find that Daniel had been protected by an angle sent from God. Daniel 6:22 says:

> *"'My God sent his angel, and he shut the mouths of the lions. They have not hurt me, because I was found innocent in his sight. Nor have I ever done any wrong before you, Your Majesty'."*

These lions in the den did not harm Daniel because neither they nor he were afraid. Daniel's ability to survive came from *an act of God* and his angels, those non-corporeal celestial powers. Some animals are said, in *occult philosophy*, to become docile in the presence of certain *magicians*, those men and women with a lack of *fear*, able to exercise their sovereign *willpower*. This is why the *magi* in stories were said to keep leopards, lions, and tigers in an obedient state within the Kingdom of Assyria.

Lions are traditionally associated with the sun, their mane the solar corona. Therefore, they symbolically hold the qualities of *Celestial Fire*, the solar sphere by which God acts on his creatin. Serpents likewise are emblematic of the electrical and magnetic currents of earth. Anyone mastering such *celestial* and *telluric* forces would be associated with serpents and have power over the same, just as Eve was to *crush the serpent's head* with her offspring in Genesis 3. A serpent in this case symbolizes an ability to direct the *will*.

In Egypt the symbol was called *uraeus* and it was worn upon the forehead, most famously depicted on Pharaoh headdresses called *nemes*. Sometimes the snake is accompanied by a vulture, representing flesh. Uraeus is said to represent an initiate's ability to, like a cobra, strike the fleshy world and make necessary changes. Cobras in general were associated with the goddess *Wadjet*, who protected various parts of Egypt, but particularly royalty. Her significance in myth is greatly overlooked since she nursed Horus and helped Isis protect the child, who would late defeat Typhon-Set, the crocodile-beast-dragon-serpent. Wadjet's sister *Nekhbet* was the goddess of vultures, and the two together were worn on the head. <u>Encyclopedia Britannica</u> shares the following:

> *"Wadjet, cobra goddess of ancient Egypt. Depicted as a cobra twined around a papyrus stem, she was the tutelary goddess of Lower Egypt. Wadjet and Nekhbet, the vulture-goddess of Upper Egypt, were the protective goddesses of the king and were sometimes represented together on the king's diadem, symbolizing his reign over all of Egypt. The form of the rearing cobra on a crown is termed the uraeus."*

Both the *uraeus* and *vulture* are believed to share a relationship with *pineal* and *pituitary* glands, too, both of which are further associated with Adam and Eve respectively. The *third eye* is our *Pineal Gland*, or Adam, and it oversees the *positive* (giving) forces of man, whereas the *Pituitary Gland* is Eve and controls the *negative* (receiving) forces of female.

The Hindus use a *bindi* dot placed in the center of the forehead to represent these same principles. Known as the *Yahweh Mark*, a cross made of ashes is placed on the foreheads of Christians on Ash Wednesday. The exact same practice can be found in the *occult sciences* of India. Mithraic initiates had a cross placed upon their foreheads to signify *spiritual resurrection*. They were referred to as *lions*, since Mithra(s) was the *Unconquered Sun*. There is therefore some reference here to Daniel and the strong grip of the *Lion's Paw* that raised a neophyte from their symbolic death just as Daniel was raised from the den (Daniel 6:23):

> *"The king was overjoyed and gave orders to lift Daniel out of the den. And when Daniel was lifted from the den, no wound was found on him, because he had trusted in his God."*

We are all surrounded like Daniel in the den by lions that are void of *understanding* and famished by *wickedness* and *foolishness*. Only by walking the *Middle Path* of *uraeus* and *bindi* are we able to find *absolution* and *redemption*.

Daniel in the Lion's Den, by the Flemish painter Peter Paul Rubens.

The *Samothracian Mysteries* & Electric Head

Some schools of thought maintain that *Celestial Fire* and *telluric* energies are literal *currents* that can be far more than symbolically controlled. There is even a name for this ability: *transcendental pyrotechny*, the mastering of *Celestial Fire*.

The Greeks are thought to have been familiar with *electricity* - likely knowledge they acquired from Egypt -˙ as are those who built the *Baghdad Battery* in Mesopotamia. These jars of asphalt, iron, and copper still produce an electric charge today, even after 2,000 years! Manly Hall writes in <u>Lectures on Ancient Philosophy</u> on the same theme:

> *"This accounts for the peculiar venerations accorded amber by the early priestcrafts, for this substance had been found to possess the quality of capturing and storing electricity."*

This electricity is certainly literal, but there is far more metaphor to be derived from such studies. Hall expresses similar feelings, stating that among the *Samothracian Mysteries* there are to be found images of what has been called the "electric head." Those faces are surrounded by bands of hair that are standing on end, and in one symbolic group the hierophant is seated in the center like the sun amid the zodiac. Hall says of this depiction that we are observing *"the concentration of the will upon the dissemination of the Great Work."* Such a description may produce memories of *Medusa*, the most famous of three Greek *gorgons*, along with Stheno and Euryale. Her head of serpents is indicative of the "concentration of will" as expressed by *telluric currents*, and those of the body, which slither about the earth, i.e., as *electrical serpents*. Herein lies the essence of *ley lines* and sacred sites, and also of Eliphas Levi's description of the alchemical substance *Azoth*, also

Medusa, by Caravaggio, 1597

commonly symbolized by two serpents - caduceus: *"The secret agent of the magnum opus, the Azoth of the sages, the living and vivifying gold of the philosophers, the universal and productive metallic agent, is MAGNETIZED ELECTRICITY, the first matter of the magnum opus."*

Over four hundred miles away from Greece we find in the middle of the Aegean Sea an island called Samothrace. Here is home to the *Cabiric* or *Samothracian Mysteries*. Among the ancients, these schools were just as important as those in Greece, particularly Eleusis, or Egypt. The word *cabiric* comes from Greek myth and has something to do with a group of obscure deities. Even Hall is uninformed on the subject, writing:

> *"Little is known concerning the Cabiric rituals, for they were enshrouded in the profoundest secrecy. Some regard the Cabiri as seven in number and refer to them as 'the Seven Spirits of fire before the throne of Saturn.' Others believe the Cabiri to be the seven sacred wanderers, later called the planets."*

The *mystery dramas* of Samothrace focus on three brothers named *Aschieros*, *Achiochersus*, and *Achiochersa*, who attack and kill their fourth brother *Cashmala*. These brothers are identified in classical Greek myth with Demeter, Pluto, Persephone, and Hermes, respectively. As Hall points out what should be very clear at this point, these dramas and myths are but a repetition of the *dying-god* motif discussed in greater detail within the works of mythologist Joseph Campbell:

> *"Here again is a repetition of the story of Osiris, Bacchus, Adonis, Balder, and Hiram Abiff. The worship of Atys [Attis] and Cybele was also involved in the Samothracian Mysteries. In the rituals of the Cabiri is to be traced a form of pine-tree worship, for this tree, sacred to Atys [Attis], was first trimmed into the form of a cross and then cut down in honor of the murdered god whose body was discovered at its foot."*

As with the first three *blue degrees* of Freemasonry, the dramas caried out on this Aegean Sea Island were divided into a triune ritual. These *mysteries* were broken into three degrees. In the first degree was a celebration of Cashmala's death at the hands of his three brothers, like the three ruffians in the CHiram Abiff story. In the second degree was the discovery of his mutilated body parts, which had been scattered about like those of Osiris. In the third degree he is resurrected and brings salvation to all mankind. Hall continues:

> *"The temple of the Cabiri at Samothrace contained a number of curious divinities, many of them misshapen creatures representing the elemental powers of Nature, possibly the Bacchic Titans. Children were initiated into the Cabirian cult with the same dignity as adults, and criminals who reached the sanctuary were safe from pursuit."*

Considering this is an island, we should find no surprise in the fact that these rites were concerned greatly with navigation:

> *"The Samothracian rites were particularly concerned with navigation, the Dioscuri--Castor and Pollux, or the gods of navigation--being among those propitiated by members of that cult. The Argonautic expedition, listening to the advice of Orpheus, stopped at the island of Samothrace for the purpose of having its members initiated into the Cabiric rites."*

In this cult drama we have the *"allegory of Self murdered by the not-self,"* something found in every system of mystical philosophy and religious belief. Indeed, *"The philosophic death and the philosophic resurrection are the Lesser and the Greater Mysteries respectively."*

Controlling the Elements

Pythagoras viewed God as essentially being *supreme music*, math, numbers, natural law, etc., just as he said, *"virtue is harmony."* It was this *harmony* or *vibration* emanating from the Creator that transformed the wildernesses of Greece and *tamed* its wild beasts like the lyre or other instruments of Orpheus or Apollo. Of the *taming of beasts*, it may be understood as a state of mind for which mankind views his sovereignty over these other kingdoms. When God says to mankind in Genesis 1:28 that he has "dominion" of the fish, birds, and ground animals, it is to be understood that through such "rule" is not a *right to kill* but a *right to protect* and *utilize* justly:

> *"'Rule [dominion] over the fish in the sea and the birds in the sky and over every living creature that moves on the ground'."*

Man's rule over the water, air, and earth, is his directing of *will* and *authority*, i.e., fire, to conquer the other elements like Daniel survived the den of fiery solar lions.

Furthermore, in metaphoric terms, it is explained by Eliphas Levi in <u>The History of Magic</u> how, *"every animal form manifests a particular instinct, aptitude or vice"* and if we *"suffer the character of the beast to predominate within us"* we may develop external features to an increasing degree like said creature. This is why men of *darkness* will look sickly and as if their body is decaying. Their eyes are dull or black and their skin seems to melt from the bones. They speak with daggers hidden by silk and often they reek with the stench of sulfur and death. Men of light, however, have a pleasant appearance and energy. Their eyes are bright like the sun and their body is kept illuminated by, in philosophical terms, their directing of *Celestial Fire* – that *subtle light* emanating from the center of the cosmos and crystalizing into dense matter.

This certainly explains classic stories of *werewolves* and other cryptid creatures throughout all human history, persisting beyond mere legend and myth. Men and women can transform into other creatures and beasts or become possessed by demons. Those overcome by *animal instincts* and *desire* are consumed by bestiality and can be said to assume the form of their likeness.

Lycanthropy & Lilith

Lycanthropy is a name for the supernatural transformation of a person into a wolf, often defined as a form of *madness*. The word means "wolf-man," but it can also apply to a person assuming the form of any wild animal, or its characteristics. This is why kings are often associated with lions, themselves a *king of the jungle* in the east, and a symbol of the *Most High*, i.e., the sun.

The term "loup-garou" (a Gallic corruption of *wehrwolf*) was more commonly used in Germany and France. The person so transformed, as explained by William J. Fielding in <u>Strange Superstitions and Magical Practices</u>, *"was believed to possess the intelligence of a man, the ferocity of a wolf, and the irresistible strength of a demon."*

The Romans referred to the *wereworlf* as a "skin-changer" or "turncoat." Norse folklore and legend call them *berserk*, a warrior class capable of assuming animal shape, especially a bear or wolf. Hence, we get the phrase *"he went berserk,* or lost control with anger."

There are many stories of the *werefox* or *wervixen* too: African myths preserve tales of *werelions, werehyenas,* and *wereleopards,* while "animal-persons" were called *pondoro* in the Zambezi region; in the history of India are *tiger-men.*; in Japanese legend one could easily become possessed by a fox (*kitsune-tsuki*) or dog (*inu-tsuki* or *inu-gami-mouchi*), while the fox-witch (*Tamamo no Maye*) took the form not of a black cat but of a nine-tailed fox.

Only after the *excitement* or *anger* had been exorcised would these wolves, lions, tigers, foxes, etc., return to their human form. Satisfaction may be met after a foe was killed, in case of the *berserk,* or once one of these therianthropes was subject to a *depressant* or some sort of *pleasure* like music.

Although these transformations are usually thought to involve men only, ultimately by misconception, women are more typically related to the *child-endangering* archetype. When a woman was unwilling or unable to have children in the past, she was seen as embodying the essence of *death* rather than the essence of *life* itself, as found in the *Venus Cult* and the universal *Mother Goddess* cults. The same would be said of a woman who was unable to nurture her children, or lost one due to disease, etc. Such women would thus be possessed by the likes of Lilith or Lamashtu, the tempter of men, aborter of children, and perverter of sexuality and innocence. Sometimes she is called *Ereshkigal,* the Sumerian goddess of *Kur*, the Land of the Dead. Lilith is famous for the two owls accompanying her as she guards the *dead land*. Around her neck can be found a necklace made of rainbow, the inverted bridge, in her case, taking one into the underworld instead of heaven.

In Hindu mythology a parallel can be found in *nature spirits* called *Yakshas*, which are female and sometimes eat children.

In ancient Greece the same concepts are embodied in the child-killing demons of *Gello*, *Mormo*, and *Lamia*, or the Roman *Strix*, which derives from the Slavic *Strzyga* and perhaps even the Slavic *Baba Yaga*. This may recall for some the Mexican ghost *La Llorona*, who drowned her own children.

Academic Sarah Iles Johnston references a fifth-century comic poet named Crates, who portrayed Lamia with a staff symbolizing a penis, explaining how *"some women are busily disguising themselves as men; one woman shows the others the splendid [staff/penis] that she has stolen from her sleeping husband."*

In addition, *"Like her ugliness and dirtiness, Lamia's bisexuality obviously runs counter to the standard of the desirable woman."*

In Japan she is the *Mountain Witch* called Yamamba, the far eastern version of what many in the west understand as the *Hansel and Gretel* witch. She is the *devouring mother* archetype that can be applied likewise to mothers who smother their children and never allow them to suffer consequences.

Lilith is the black veiled Ishtar and the latter is the white veiled former. Isis wears white veils in her pure form and black veils in mourning over her lost Osiris. In Jewish tradition, Lilith is Adam's first wife in the Garden of Eden, with Eve being the second. According to the Wahungwe Makoni tribe of South Rhodesia, Africa, the ritual mating of initial creation is reversed. The moon god Mwuetsi receives first Massassi as a wife and then Morongo, who eventually sleeps with a serpent – the role many believe Lilith played in tempting Eve. And this is the reality of life, that by fertility, creation, and life, will come infertility, destruction, and death.

The Werewolf from *Die Emeis*, by Johann Geiler von Kayserberg, 1517.

The *werewolf* and *lamia* are also, from an anthropological and sociological point of view, much like a standard *demon*, in that they exist between or beyond the boundaries of a community. The monster fails to register as *man* (mankind) or *beast* since they are *both*, and thus operating outside of human comprehension and the natural world. When man acts like a wolf, he becomes a *wereworlf*, and so we obtain some understanding of *lycanthropy*. When a woman snuffs out life by whatever means, she becomes *lamia*.

Likewise, man may draw on the sympathies of the lion for strength, or the reptile for wisdom. In none of these cases is man literally transforming into a wolf, lion, or serpent. Man may also embody the essence of Jupiter or Isis, but he does not become a god or goddess. Detractors of such things are as ignorant as those believing in their literalities.

Wendigos, the Sandman & Night-Mares

A *Wendigo* comes from the folklore of First Nations people in the Americas. In essence, it is *evil* manifest. Wendigos are supernatural creatures described as being the manifestation of a diabolic wickedness that plagues man. It begins when the human body or mind, or the environment, is defiled or polluted, which leads to madness and disorder. As this amorphous creature takes form in the mind it transforms the human into a terrifying force that hunts for new victims. As it consumes the flesh of these victims its hunger intensifies, though it grows weaker. The meaning is obvious and twofold: (1) as man destroys his environment, he kills himself and his fellow man; (2) *evil deeds and deals with the devil* require one to act increasingly wicked to secure the perceptual benefits of delusion.

The Nightmare, by Henry Fuseli, 1781

As darkness consumes the host, it seeks to spread to other victims. The *madness* is like a social contagion, able to cultivate delusion and hallucinations about reality. Some, as a result, allow themselves to be consumed. Others are unwitting victims. After consuming a single host and spreading to another, madness proliferates exponentially. Put simply, it is *chaos* and *destruction*, a polluting of all things natural.

Other names for the *Wendigo* include: *Wetiko* (Cree), *Wechuge* (Athabaskan), and *Skinwalker* (Navajo).

The creature is often depicted in lore as having antlers, horns, and an overtly protruding skeletal structure.

Evil spirits are not always those things that entered our body, so much as they are a symbol of the corrupting of our own soul-spirit by wicked deeds and uncontrolled emotions like in lycanthropy. Through fear and the allowance of ourselves to slip into paranoia or delusion, we become possessed and consumed by this monstrous force.

For some, the spirit is a protector of a natural world corrupted by man, but for others, it is a real monster. For others, it is both. As the human becomes wicked, he is transformed like a *Skinwalker* into a beast; he is transformed like the spirit of a prince into the body of a beast. As the monster symbolically bursts forth from the body, as a thought-form, it spreads to cultivate more suffering and death. Though known by many names, it is EVIL. Only through *harmony* of thoughts, words, actions, and music, can this monster be tamed. Harmony can be found in balance, within nature and within oneself.

Stories of the *Sandman* are like those of *Wendigo*, seeing that he puts his victims to sleep to devour them: when the soul or spirit is suppressed like *Sleeping Beauty*, animal nature and instincts becomes·dominant. Sometimes when we awaken from sleep, perhaps only partially because of the Sandman's work, there is a moment of terror as the body is frozen. This is a natural process which is supposed to prevent us from injuring ourselves while resting. Today we call it *sleep paralysis*. In past years we called it *Mare*, an evil spirit made popular by Germanic and Slavic folklore. The *mare* comes and *night*, hence *nightmare*, and rests or rides on the chest.

Orpheus & the Muses

Orpheus was said to play music so beautiful that it animated nature; trees swayed in measure, water became calm or turned course, and rocks moved while wild animals became subdued. Edith Hamilton writes in <u>Mythology</u> of his music's magical power:

> *"Everything animate and inanimate followed him. He moved the rocks on the hillside and turned the course of the rivers."*

The lyre of Orpheus is a symbol of the archetypical instruments used by man to create beautiful melodies: the *voice* and *lyrics* (lyre-ics). We find in the story of *Snow White* a famous scene where the beautiful princess animates nature with her voice, influencing the animals to participate in her *harmony*.

Orpheus was son of one of the *Muses*, from where we acquire the word *music*. These goddesses of literature and art had no instruments of their own, but like the pure princess, or *femina candida* (white woman), their voices were fantastically beautiful as expressions of *creativity* and *art*. In tradition, Orpheus wooed a maiden name Eurydice with his melodies. The couple were soon married but shortly thereafter she was bitten by a snake and died. Distraught and longing for his bride, he ventured into the Underworld to rescue her, taming the dog Cerberus with his music, and exclaiming:

> *With my song*
> *I will charm Demeter's daughter,*
> *I will charm the Lord of the Dead,*
> *Moving their hearts with my melody,*
> *I will bear her away from Hades.*

The gods decided to call on Eurydice, giving her to Orpheus upon the condition he would not look back as she followed him out of Hades. He was not permitted to see his bride until they both reached the world above. As the story goes, however, he could not help himself and so Eurydice was pulled once more into the *Land of the Dead*. A similar story is told of Cupid and Psyche when the latter allows her *curiosity* and *suspicion* to sabotage her love.

While wandering one day in mourning for his love, a band of *maenads*, the female followers of Dionysus, no doubt drunk on wine, attacked Orpheus and tore his body to pieces like Osiris. And in like manner to the Egyptian story, his head, like the penis or generative aspect of Osiris, was tossed into the river Hebrus. Edith explains how the Muses found his head and buried it at a sanctuary:

> *"His remaining limbs they gathered and placed in a tomb at the foot of Mount Olympus."*

Wherever the body, blood, tears, or dew of the *Celestial Mind* falls, there can be found earthly incarnations like the *rose* or *sunflower*.

Dat Rosa Mel Apibus: The Rosy Apple

The rose symbolizes many things, from love and beauty to *occult philosophy* and the *sacred feminine*. Each color has a different meaning; *red* signifies male energy, passion, and love; *white* represents female energy, innocence, and purity; yellow means compassion; pink symbolizes friendship and thankfulness; orange preserves optimism; black, which does not exist naturally, is a symbol of death and depression.

In Rome this flower was dedicated to Venus and in Greece to Aphrodite. In classical terms the rose had five petals like the apple blossom, which is just one of many varieties found in the rose family. The five petals relate to the pentagram. It is not so common knowledge that *rosaceae*, the rose family, includes the *apple* among other fruits. The Edenic apple handled by Eve, the original mother, then associates both the *forbidden fruit* and *alchemical red-white fruit* with the *sacred feminine*. It is therefore a symbol of initiation into the *mysteries of life*.

As a symbol of Mary, or *Marianne Mara*, meaning "teacher," the rose is directly associated with *hierodule*, the sacred women of the *mysteries* further correlated to the Greek woman *Mellissa*, which means *bee*. From the *bee* we get a *honeycomb*, sacred to Aphrodite and her rose, both symbols relating to *honey* and *alchemical gold*. The name *melissa* itself originally stems from *meli*, meaning *honey*.

In art by Robert Fludd the rose is shown with a stem made to look like a cross. To the left of this image is a square with a cross divider. Surrounding his flower with seven petals, representing the *days of creation*, are bees, and in the background are beehives, indicative of the *Bridal Chambers* wherein *Maras* symbolized by *bees* assisted in ritual dramas of *Living Resurrection*.

When a rose is placed on a cross it obviously implies the redeeming *blood of Christ* and his resurrection. The *Rosicrucian Order* calls this the *Red Cross* or *Rosy Cross*. The *Order of the Golden Dawn* utilizes the red cross above a white triangle to represent *life* and *light*.

Other images famously show a *cross* on a *heart* which is placed within the petals of a *rose*. The cross is our zodiac and thus it represents the solar portal used by the *Cosmic Mind* to rain down (dew) divine influences. Its correlated organ in the body is the heart, where we feel love and *welcome Jesus into our lives*. This is the seat of the *soul* or *sole* (sun). As Ephesians 3:16-17 says in prayer, *"I pray that out of his glorious riches he may strengthen you with power through his Spirit in your inner being, so that*

Christ may dwell in your hearts through faith." The heart is also a *reflection of the sun* and considered the *seat of the soul.* Since the rose is our *sacred feminine* this image represents the *Alchemical Marriage.* Roses are often depicted within a glass case, a common theme in Rosicrucian practices relating to the placement of a body inside of a glass coffin – *memento mori.* In *Beauty and the Beast,* the rose is famously kept in a glass container where it can be seen wilting. In *Snow White,* originally titled *Sneewittchen,* the *fairest of them all* is placed inside a glass coffin.

On the apron of a Master Mason, there are three roses acting as reminders of the *Mystery Trinity* of *faith, secrecy,* and *science.*

On Fludd's famous image is written a phrase that means *The Rose Gives the Bees Honey.*

~ DAT ROSA MEL APIBUS ~

In *The Key to Dante's Divine Comedy,* the rose can be seen within a triangle centered above all lower spheres of the cosmos.

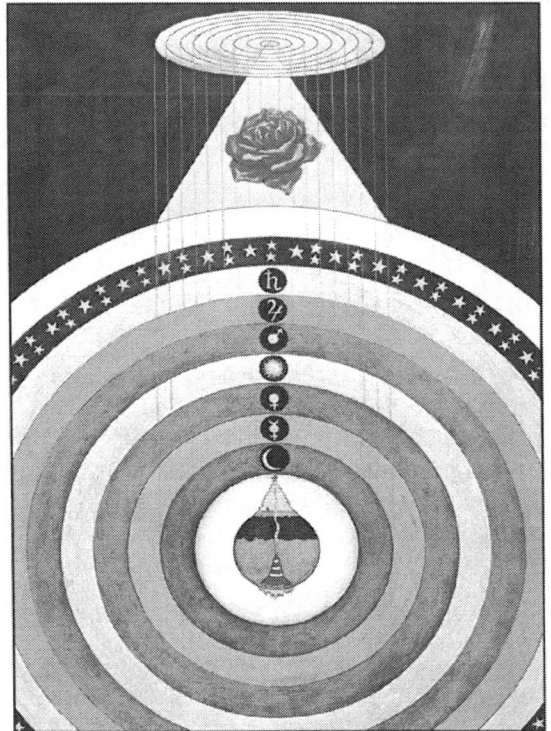

The Spheres of Consciousness, Four Horses & Jacob's ladder

"As Life is the Essence of Spirit, so is Consciousness the Essence of Life. Spirit is One, yet it manifests in many forms of Consciousness. While the forms of manifested Consciousness are innumerable, yet the wise know Consciousness to manifest on Seven Planes."

~ The Sixth Aphorism of the Rosicrucians, Magus Incognito ~

Animal & Human Sacrifice

There are typically two categories of thought pertaining to the *existence* of what we call *the gods*: The first is *superficial*, being either a literal polytheistic belief in multiple gods, a monotheistic belief in a single god, or a denial of all gods. The second is *philosophic*, recognizing that polytheism is a complex form of monotheism; that each individual god is an emanation of the one true God, like the branches of a tree; that to deny the *one true God* is equally as blasphemous as depicting Him with human characteristics.

Likewise, there are two categories of thought pertaining to animal and human sacrifices: The first is *literal*, being either that these sacrifices are a wicked, ordained by God, or that they are confined only to history and no longer occur today. Some may ignorantly wish to kill for the diabolic pleasure and if they have an erroneous fascination with the *dark arts*. The second is *symbolic,* a view that such sacrifices of animals or humans relate merely to our animal consciousness, and thus providing this as a *burn offering* will result in the human dying and being *born again*. This a prerequisite for the *dark night of the soul*.

Manly Hall observes in <u>The Secret Teachings of All Ages</u> this curious misconception about *sacrifice*, which has persisted into contemporary times:

> *"The sacrificing of beasts, and in some cases, human beings, upon the altars of the pagans was the result of their ignorance concerning the fundamental principle underlying sacrifice. They did not realize that their offerings must come from within their own natures in order to be acceptable."*

Some will even justify literal sacrifice based on a story in Genesis 22 when God informs Abraham that he should sacrifice his son Isaac, even though it is considered only a test in the end:

> *"Some time later God tested Abraham. He said to him, 'Abraham!' 'Here I am,' he replied. Then God said, 'Take your son, your only son, whom you love – Isaac – and go to the region of Moriah. Sacrifice him there as a burnt offering on a mountain I will show you'."*

Contrary to popular opinion, the Maya were not entirely warlike barbaric like the Aztecs. In fact, some historians inform us that their powerful civilization lasted for nearly five hundred years without war. It was not until the decline of their empire and its domination by less advanced tribes that literal sacrifices were performed. Even then they were only performed in limited capacity. Hall explains in The Secret Destiny of America that many of these sacrifices were metaphoric in nature and grossly misunderstood:

> *"On the altars of their gods they offered only flowers and fruit."*

On the altars of the *Mystery Schools,* we find *sacrifices* of the human heart as depicted in the Egyptian *Hall of Judgement* and as literally carried out by the Aztecs in honor of their sun god *Huitzilopochtli.* Offering the heart up for judgement is a symbolic action, however, meant to demonstrate that one has no attachments, i.e., *desires,* holding them to their body after death. Only then will the *heart* weigh less than a *feather,* representing the soul-spirit.

Death as we consider it today is truly a *phantom* of *ignorance;* it does not exist. Everything in *nature* is *living* and *dying* simultaneously, and it is only God's grace that places everything in motion from birth to life and death. Eliphas Levi writes on the subject of life and death in nature:

> *"Old age is the beginning of regeneration; it is the labour of renewing life; and the ancients represented the mystery we term death by the Fountain of You, which was entered in decrepitude and left in new childhood."*

The Spherical Guides

Sleep is an experience not unlike *death.* When we sleep the body is paralyzed and deprived of senses that daily allow us to navigate the *mundane sphere.* Like *Sleeping Beauty,* we too are cursed, i.e., granted certain gifts, by the fairies or planetary consciousnesses when we incarnate. In death, these *daemons,* which are divine in nature, tear away at our *impurities,* stripping us of our *sins.* In life we may meet them in *dreams,* and they may help us to follow *The Way.* This is a process of *necessary suffering* that all souls must undergo to gain access into higher spheres of consciousness and eventually *source.* Unless this purge occurs, the soul cannot ascend beyond that which it is attached. Author Mark Booth similarly writes in The Secret History of the World of this process:

> *"Unless the spirit is purged in this way, it cannot ascend through the higher spheres and hear their music."*

The German mystic Meister Eckhart explains how we should never fear these spherical intelligences, since what they consume are *impurities* associated with *death,* and therefore they are nothing more than another version of the crocodile-hippopotamus-lion known as the "eater of the dead" in Egypt:

> *"If you fight your death, you'll feel the demons tearing away at your life, but, if you have the right attitude to death, you will be able to see that the devils are really angels setting your spirit free."*

In author and artist Marlene Seven Bremner's book Hermetic Philosophy and Creative Alchemy, she writes of Hermes and his revelations of *"death and dissolution of the body."*

She explains how *"upon the soul's leaving of the body… it is met by a great daimon (demon) that resides between earth and heaven and has been appointed by God as judge of human souls*

Arthur Edward Waite's <u>The Book of Black Magic</u> also explains something similar, that what we call *demons* or *devils* are no less divine than angels:

> *"In Egypt, in India and in Greece, there was no dealing with devils in the Christian sense of the expression; Typhon, Juggernaut and Hecate were not less divine than the gods of the over-world, and the offices of Canidia were probably in their way as sacred as the peaceful mysteries of Ceres."*

And the physician and alchemist Paracelsus writes something similar, but relating to the duality of God and the Devil, or good and evil:

> *"It is necessary to learn evil things as good, for who can know what is good without learning what is evil?"*

After physical death, the soul ascends through the *seven celestial spheres*, often represented by *gates*, as with the underworld stories in Egypt. This *nether region* of evil forces to Christians was called *duat* in Egypt, both a region of sky that Ra's sun boat traversed each night and day, and the location of those famous and dangerous afterlife trials. The symbol of this realm reminds one of a sea urchin called *Sand Dollar*, or perhaps a pentagram in a circle, i.e., a *pentacle*, which represents the body and earth. The same symbolism can be found in the Americas, specifically on an artifact found at the Moundville site in the U.S. state of Alabama. Known as "The Rattlesnake Disc" it features two serpents, representing earth below and heaven above, with a hand in the middle, itself adorned with an eye centered on the palm. Scholar George Lankford writes of this imagery: *"The hole in the sky is indicated as a slit being pulled apart, and the fact that it is celestial is frequently elaborated by the inclusion of a star circle* [duat] *or dot."*

Throughout our soul's journey, it is said that Mercury, *guide of souls* like Jesus Christ the shepherd, acts as our first chaperon like the ferryman Charon. Mercury helps us gain passage through the daemonic realms wherein we are purified of the seven deadly sins: pride, covetousness, lust, anger, gluttony, envy, and sloth. Lucifer, whose symbol is the pentagram, is then said to take over our ascent to lead us through the spheres of Jupiter, Saturn, and the constellations, soon to be reunited with the great *Cosmic Mind*.

After spiritual death, and upon incarnation, the soul descends back through the constellations and spheres with each planetary consciousness now bestowing at each of the seven gates what was stripped away after physical death. Aristides, a 2nd-century Greek author, comments on the descent of the soul and describes that as it approaches the sphere of the moon it is pulled by its gravity and rhythms to the physical world and incarnation. The soul is then said to lose its *spherical form* and take on a human *shape*: *"The soul, as long as she is seated in a purer place of the universe, in consequence of not being mingled with the nature of bodies, is pure and inviolate, and revolves, together with the ruler of the world; but when, through an inclination to these inferior concerns, she receives certain phantasms from places about the earth, then she gradually imbibes oblivion of the goods she possessed in her former superior station, and at the same time descends. But by how much the more she is removed from superior natures, by so much the more approaching to inferiors, is she filled with insanity, and hurled into corporeal darkness; because through a diminution of her former dignity, she can no longer be intelligibly extended with the universe; but on account of her oblivion of supernal goods, and consequent astonishment, she is borne downward into more solid natures, and such as are involved in the obscurity of matter. Hence, when her desire of body commences, she assumes and draws form each of the superior places some portions of corporeal mixture."*

Inanna's Descent & Ishtar's Garments

In the story of a Sumerian deity named Inanna, we find the goddess of love, fertility, and war, passing each of the seven gates of the underworld and every time being stripped of her clothing until she arrives naked in front of Ereshkigal, Queen of the Dead. The Akkadians and Assyrians later identified Inanna with Ishtar: she was Sauska to the Hittite people, Astarte to the Phoenicians, and Aphrodite to the Greeks. The World History Encyclopedia says this about the goddess:

> "The goddess appears in many ancient Mesopotamian myths, most notably Inanna and the Huluppu-Tree (an early creation myth), Inanna and the God of Wisdom (in which she brings knowledge and culture to the city of Uruk after receiving the meh – gifts of civilization – from the god of wisdom, Enki, while he is drunk), The Courtship of Inanna and Dumuzi (the tale of Inanna's marriage to the vegetation-god), and the best known poem The Descent of Inanna (c. 1900-1600 BCE) in which the Queen of Heaven journeys to the underworld."

In tradition we find that Inanna is not only married to the vegetation god, making her Egyptian equivalent the *flawless goddess* Isis, but that she brought civilization itself, like Osiris, to the ancient city of Uruk. From a poem entitled The Descent of Inanna we read the opening lines:

> *From the Great Above she opened her ear to the Great Below*
> *From the Great Above the goddess opened her ear to the Great Below*
> *From the Great Above Inanna opened her ear to the Great Below.*

Inanna marrying Dumuzi

Neti, gatekeeper of the underworld, opened the entrance but informed Inanna she must remove a piece of clothing at each future gateway. From the first to last gate, seven in all, she removed her crown, rod of lapis lazuli, stones around her neck, stones from her breast, gold ring from her hand, breastplate, and the garments of ladyship. She was then greeted by the Anunnaki, or seven underworld judges, sitting before the throne of her dark sister Ereshkigal. Stripped naked she was turned into a corpse and crucified to a stake for the three days she remained in the underworld.

The garments worn by Ishtar each symbolize those things granted and removed upon the descent and ascent of the soul. Presented here are the gates and their corresponding garment, along with the relationships these share with the chakras and various glands of the body:

First Gate – Cloak of body
(The red *Base Chakra* of the adrenal gland)

Second Gate – Bracelets of hands and feet
(The orange *Sacral Chakra* of the gonad)

Third Gate – Girdle of waist
(The yellow *Solar Plexus Chakra* of the pancreas)

Fourth Gate – Ornaments of breast
(The green *Heart Chakra* of the thymus gland)

Fifth Gate – Necklace of neck
(The sky blue *Throat Chakra* of the thyroid gland)

Sixth Gate – Earrings of ears
(The indigo *Brow Chakra* of the pituitary gland)

Seventh Gate – Crown of head
(The violet *Crown Chakra* of the pineal gland)

These gates also relate to the cleansing of *Izanagi no mikoto* after he visited the land of Yomi to rescue his wife, like the story of Orpheus and Eurydice; he stripped off his clothes and immersed himself in water which soon resulted in the birth of Amaterasu (goddess of the sun), Susanoo (god of earth and weather), and Tsukuyomi (goddess of the moon).

In the first book of the *Corpus Hermeticum*, known as <u>Poimandros</u>, we likewise find a thorough overview of the soul's ascent through the *hebdomad* (seven spheres), *ogdoad (eight sphere)*, and finally to the *Pleroma* (Divine Fullness) after physical death. We find these ideas thoroughly delineated in the works of Pseudo-Dionysius (*On the Celestial Hierarchy*), Proclus (*Elements of Theology*), and Cornelius Agrippa (*Three Books of Occult Philosophy*).

The Seven Spheres of Consciousness

The *seven classical planets* were known to the ancients as the Moon, Mercury, Venus, the Sun, Mars, Jupiter, and Saturn. From these planets and classical myth, we derive the *seven days of the week* which can be clearly correlated with the *seven days of creation*, i.e., the creation and dividing of time into workable segments.

Sunday: day of the Sun, belonging to Mithra(s), Apollo, Helios, Ra, Horus, Shamash, Huitzilopochtli, and Amaterasu.

Monday: day of the Moon, belonging to Diana, Artemis, Selene, Hecate, Khonsu, Coyolxauhqui, and Tsukuyomi.

Tuesday: day of Tyr, the Norse god of war associated with the Greek Ares and Roman Mars.

Wednesday: day of Woden, a southern name for the northern god Odin in Norse mythology. This day is also associated with the Greek Hermes, Roman Mercury, and Egyptian Thoth.

Thursday: day of Thor, the Norse god of weather. He is the son of Odin and Frigga. This is also the day of the Greek Zeus, Roman Jupiter, and Egyptian Amon.

Friday: day of Frigga, Odin's wife, and the mother of Thor. She is also known as Fria or Freya, the goddess of love and beauty, otherwise known as the Greek Aphrodite, Roman Venus, Egyptian Isis, and the Buddhist Kichijoten.

Saturday: day of the Roman Saturn and his Greek equivalent Cronus.

These planets and their associated days of the week, metals, and colors can be found below in a table derived from William J. Fielding's book <u>Strange Superstitions and Magical Practices</u>:

Planet	Day of the Week	Planetary Metal	Planetary Color
Sun	Sunday	Gold	Gold or Yellow
Moon	Monday	Silver	Silver or White
Mars	Tuesday	Iron	Red
Mercury	Wednesday	Mercury	Mixed Colors or Purple
Jupiter	Thursday	Tin	Violet or Blue
Venus	Friday	Copper	Turquoise or Green
Saturn	Saturday	Lead	Black

The number seven can be found all throughout world mythology, theology, and philosophy. It is a sacred number going back to the *beginning of time* and sacred geometry. After enlightenment, Buddha took his next actions in steps of seven. The prophet Mohammed ascended into the seven *heavens* to commune with the divine, and thus the Dome of the Rock Mosque is situated into seven sections. There are seven liberal arts and sciences; seven sacred hills in Rome; seven lions in the den with Daniel; seven orders of angels; seven continents; and seven chakras. There are seven sacred cities; seven pure notes in a diatonic scale; and seven planes of *higher consciousness* (heaven) compared with seven planes of *lower consciousness* (hell).

There are *seven directions*: up, down, west, east, north, south, within; *seven deadly sins*: pride, lust, anger, gluttony, envy, covetousness, and sloth; *seven virtues*: chastity, temperance, charity, diligence, kindness, patience, and humility; seven *gates* or *doorways* into the underworld; seven magical keys; seven sacraments; seven blessings; seven strings of the Greek lyre; seven metals in alchemy; seven vowels in the Greek alphabet; seven African powers; seven colors of the white light spectrum, and seven colors of the rainbow.

There are seven days of the week; six days of creation with the seventh day reserved for rest; seven *rays of light* in theosophy; *seven divine rays* or flames of light emanating from the central cosmos and crystalizing into matter; and the earth is the seventh planet from the outer portion of our solar system. There are seven rows in the periodic table, *Seven Wonders* of the World, and seven stars in the constellations of Pleiades and Orion, which are held sacred to this day. There are seven letters in the sacred creature of wisdom, the s-e-r-p-e-n-t, and *Theon Heptagrammaton*, or *Serapis*, was the god with a name of seven letters like A-b-r-a-x-a-s. Hymns sang to this god were chanted using seven vowels and Serapis was depicted like Mithra(s) with seven horns, or a solar corona of seven rays. Author C. W. Leadbeater informs us in <u>A Textbook of Theosophy</u> about the seven subdivisions of the physical world:

> *"In the matter of the physical world the seven subdivisions are represented by seven degrees of density of matter, to which, beginning from below upwards, we give the names solid, liquid, gaseous, etheric, super-etheric, sub-atomic and atomic."*

The symbol *seven* itself resembles the Hebrew letter *Resh* (meaning *head*) and we do indeed have seven holes in our head: ears, eyes, nose, and mouth. These "holes" relate to the seven classical planets too: the **mouth to Mercury**, the **right ear to Saturn**, the **left ear to Jupiter**, the **right nostril to Mars**, the **left nostril to Venus**, the **right eye to the Sun** and the **left eye to the Moon**. Other correlations may place Saturn over the left ear and Jupiter over the right ear.

In Kanji, used in China and Japan, the number *seven* looks like an upside-down fancy English version with a line. It is pronounced *shichi* or *nana*.

SEVEN   **SCHICHI**   **RESH**

In his first of three books on *Occult Philosophy*, Henry Cornelius Agrippa writes the following on the number seven and its relationship with the conception, birth, growth, life, and old age of a human:

> *"The number seven, therefore, because it consists of three and four, joins the soul to the body; and the virtue of this number relates to the of men, and it causes man to be received, formed, brought forth, nourished, live, and indeed altogether to subsist: for when the genital seed is received in the womb of the woman, if it remains there seven hours after the effusion of it, it is certain that it will abide there for good; then the first seven days it is coagulated, and is fit to receive the shape of a man; then it produces mature infants, which are called infants of the seventh month, i. e. because they are born the seventh month; after the birth, the seventh hour tries whether it will live or no--for that which will bear the breath of the air after that hour, is conceived will live; after seven days, it casts off the relics of the navel; after twice seven days, its sight begins to move after the light; in the third seventh, it turns its eyes and whole face freely; after seven months, it breeds teeth; after the second seventh month, it sits without fear of falling; after the third seventh month, it begins to speak; after the fourth seventh month, it stands strongly and walks; after the fifth seventh month, it begins to refrain sucking its*

nurse; after seven years, its first teeth fall, and new are bred, fitter for harder meat, and its speech is perfected; after the second seventh year, boys wax ripe, and then it is a beginning of generation at the third seventh year, they grow to men in stature, and begin to be hairy, and become able and strong for generation; at the fourth seventh year, they cease to grow taller; in the fifth seventh year, they attain to the perfection of their strength; the sixth seventh year, they keep their strength; the seventh seventh year, they attain to their utmost discretion and wisdom, and the perfect age of men; but when they come to the tenth seventh year, where the number seven is taken for a complete number, then they come to the common term of life--the Prophet saying, our age is seventy years...

"There are, also, seven degrees in the body, which complete the dimension of its altitude from the bottom to the top, viz. marrow, bone, nerve, vein, artery, flesh, and skin. There are seven, which, by the Greeks, are called black members: the tongue, heart, lungs, liver, spleen, and the two kidnies. There are, also, seven principal parts, of the body: the head, breast, hands, feet, and the privy members."

Levi writes of the seven magical animals and their correspondences in his book Transcendental Magic:

"The seven magical animals are: (a) Among birds, corresponding to the divine world, the swan, the owl, the vulture, the dove, the stork, the eagle, and the pewit; (6) among fish, corresponding to the spiritual or scientific world, the seal, the cat-fish, the pike, the mullet, the chub, the dolphin, the sepia or cuttle-fish; (c) among quadrupeds, corresponding to the natural world, the lion, the cat, the wolf, the he-goat, the monkey, the stag, and the mole. The blood, fat, liver, and gall of these animals serve in enchantments; their brain combines with the perfumes of the planets, and it is recognized by ancient practice that they possess magnetic virtues corresponding to the seven planetary influences."

The seven spheres also correspond to the *seven Olympic Spirits*, and various other combinations of birds, fish, animals, metals, and stones. In terms of theological symbolism, each planet corresponds to some aspect of the *mysteries* or *virtue*:

Sun: Word of Truth
Moon: Religion
Mercury: Interpretation & science of mysteries
Mars: Justice
Venus: Mercy and Love
Jupiter: the risen *Savior*
Saturn: God the *Father*

There are seven elements of the human body: marrow, bone, nerve, vein, artery, flesh, and skin; seven black members, according to the Greeks: tongue, heart, lungs, liver, spleen, and kidneys; and seven main parts of the body: head, breasts, hands, feet, and privy members.

The seven classical planets relate as such to the human body, not unlike their correlations to the seven holes in the human head: sun and heart, moon and brain, right hand and Jupiter, left hand and Saturn (*sinister* is Latin for "left"), left foot for Mars, right foot for Venus, and generative organs for Mercury. The *Twelves Signs of the Zodiac* also correspond to members of the body: Aries to the head and face; Taurus to the neck; Gemini to the arms and shoulders; Cancer to the breast, lungs, stomach, and arms; Leo to the heart, liver, and back; Virgo to the bowels; Libra to the kidneys, buttocks, and thighs; Scorpio to the genitals and womb; Sagittarius to the thighs and groin; Capricorn to the knees; Aquarius to the legs and shins; Pisces to the feet.

There are fourteen requisites, seven of the inner life and seven of the outer, necessary for becoming *enlightened*. Anyone achieving a proficiency in these areas of study is granted the esoteric keys to the Temple of Wisdom. The seven requisites of inner life are termed *character* and those of the outer life are called *attainments*. The *character* requisites are as follows: integrity, discrimination, application, patience, moderation, detachment, and relaxation. The *attainment* requisites are as follows: mathematics, astronomy, biology and physics, social-political science, music and art, language and philosophy. According to St. Jerome there are seven levels of initiation in the Mithraic cult, and the Druidic cult, each corresponding to one of the classical planets:

Name of Degree	Meaning	Planet
Pater	Father	Saturn
Heliodromus	Sun-Runner	Sun
Perses	Persian	Moon
Leo	Lion	Jupiter
Miles	Soldier	Mars
Nymphus	Bride	Venus
Corax	Rave	Mercury

According to the *Seven Rosicrucian Aphorisms of Creation*, the soul of man is sevenfold, separated into the souls of elements, minerals, plants, animals, humans, Demi-God and Gods.

Consciousness is found in all the classical kingdoms of life, from the lowest form of "minerals" to the highest form of "God." Each of the seven planes intersect with one another by way of sub-planes. These planes may be visualized as circles, which once connected offer a glimpse through symbolism of the *secret teachings of all ages*. Combining these seven circles or planes creates what those familiar with *sacred geometry* will know as the "seed of life," representing also the *Seven Days of Creation*. Cellular division in the formation of a fetus also unfolds in a similar way. These seven spheres or planes of consciousness are expressed as such, though one may find some animals to be more conscious than humans or some humans to be more conscious than others:

Mineral – Elemental – Plant – Animal – Human - demi-God – God

Writing under the occult name Magus Incognito in <u>The Secret Doctrine of the Rosicrucians</u>, the author explains how man can easily become consumed by the lower spheres of consciousness:

"The more he knows, the more he desires; and the more he desires, the more does he suffer from the pain of not having… He has not only the pain of unsatisfied desires for possession of material things, and physical wants, but also the pain arising from the lack of intelligent answers to the ever-increasing volume of problems presenting themselves for solution to his evolving intellect; and lie also has pain of unsatisfied longings, disappointments, frustrated aims and ambitions, and all the rest of the list.

"And many men are but little above this stage — they are easily satisfied; they are ignorant of the unsatisfied desires which render others unhappy. They have no unanswered questions — they do not even dream of the existence of such questions."

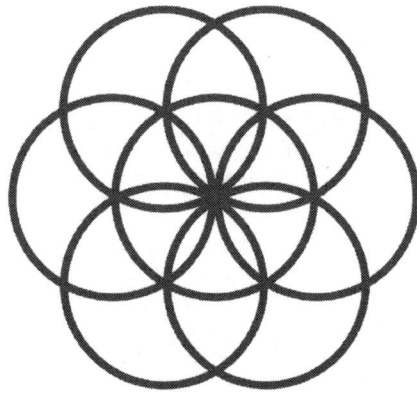

The Seed of Life is comprised of seven circles, six outer and one central, forming the basis for the *Flower of Life*. Each circle represents one of the *spheres of consciousness*, days of creation, and days of the week.

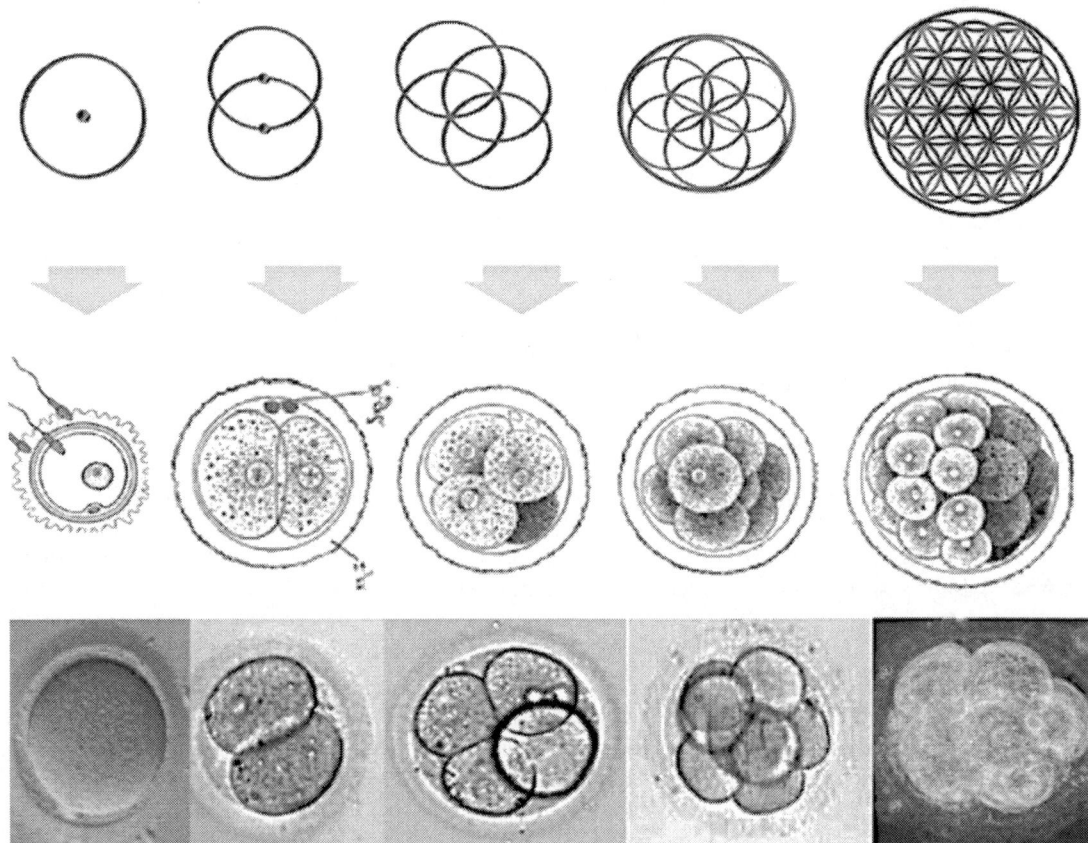

Cellular division in the formation of a fetus unfolds from the *monad*, or unity, symbolized by a dot within a circle, into duality, then into the *Seed of Life* and finally into the *Flower of Life*. The *One* becomes *Many*, while maintaining its connection to *source*.

Magus writes further of this sixth stage, or that of a Demi-God consciousness, that *"the pages of the mystic records are filled with statements of experiences of this kind,"* of course referring to the great poets, musicians, authors, scholars, etc., who displayed almost divine intelligence. These men and women do not have need for the demonstration of worldly facts, per se, because they have manifested a "knowing" intuition of such facts already. Magus writes on the potential genius of man emanating from the *Eternal Parent*:

> *"By a subtle intuition he may, under favorable circumstances, speak, write, paint, act, or produce music representing phase of vital, mental, and emotional activity transcending any actual experience on his own part… This is the secret of the 'genius' of great artists, writers, musicians, poets, and others who express through their own respective mediums or vehicles the messages they receive from the other forms of life with which they are connected by subtle filaments of unity."*

That even higher form of *God Consciousness* is almost entirely inconceivable, though in the *mysteries* one can achieve what we commonly term today, *Christ Consciousness*. Magus adds further, *"the characteristic element of this highest form of all consciousness is the conscious realization of the individual that he IS identical with the Infinite, and is only apparently separated there from by the most tenuous and subtle veil of illusion."*

Those men and women who have been granted even a slight glimpse of this Highest plane of consciousness have been almost *blinded by the light*, an allegorical story expressed biblically in Exodus chapter 33, verses 18-20:

> *"Then Moses said, 'I pray You, show me Your glory!' And He said, 'I Myself will make all My goodness pass before you, and will proclaim the name of the Lord before you; and I will be gracious to whom I will be gracious, and will show compassion on whom I will show compassion.' But He said, 'You cannot see My face, for no man can see Me and live!'"*

Today we may say that some individuals, almost always by choice, are unwilling *to handle the truth*, and instead choose to *live in blissful ignorance* rather than embrace *responsibility* and *growth*. Writing further, Magus discusses how the attachments of the *blissful* are obscuring and corrupting the light within:

> *"Man attaches himself to 'things,' and creates for himself artificial wants which he must labor to meet. His intellect often fails to lead him upward, and too often merely enables him to invent new and subtle means and ways of gratifying his senses in a way impossible to the animals or primitive man. Some men make a religion of the gratification of their sensuality and their appetites, and sink below the level of the beasts in this respect. Others become vain, conceited, and filled with an inflated sense of the importance of their personality. Others become morbidly introspective, and spend their time analyzing and dissecting their moods, motives, and feelings. Others exhaust their capacity for pleasure and happiness, by looking outside of themselves for happiness, instead of within."*

As noted earlier, the Darwinian model of *evolution*, which includes fish, amphibians, land animals, and humans, is preserved in *stories* like Frank Baum's (a theosophist) classic <u>The Wonderful Wizard of Oz</u>. Here the different aspects of human nature take form in animal, mineral, and vegetable bodies, i.e., the lion, tin man, and scarecrow, or the primate, mammalian, and reptilian complexes of the brain. The meanings of Dorothy's dress and her red slippers should, at this point, be clear. The "wizard of oz" is that *madman* or *magician* and his *Emerald City* is that of the hermetic Emerald Tablet, of which more in a later chapter. The city and yellow-brick road represent heaven and the magician is the great architect of the material world, populated by the vegetable, mineral, animal, and human.

From *seven* we acquire a combination of *three* and *four*, which respectively represent the *Holy Trinity* in all things and the four elements of the world. From the latter are associated certain color and animals, according to Fielding:

East	Spring	Blue	Dragon
South	Summer	Red	Bird
West	Autumn	White	Tiger
North	Winter	Black	Tortoise

Four Apocalyptic Horses

Each of the four seasons are associated with these colors: white for spring, red for summer, black for fall, and a pale green for winter. The four season and their colors also correspond to the *Four Horsemen of the Apocalypse*.

The *white horse conquers* the cold and dark of winter with warmth and light as the sun is resurrected on the spring equinox; the *red horse* wages further *war* on darkness in the summer, becoming victorious on the summer solstice; the *black horse* brings about the decline of the sun on the autumnal equinox and *famine* as man harvests for the winter and feasts on the body-bread of God or King; the *pale horse* appears on the winter solstice, is ridden by *death* and followed by hell. The cycle then repeats.

In these images we find *resurrection* of the dead god-savior in spring, his reign in the summer, the *fall of man* and the *apocalypse* (revealing) of autumn, and the *final judgment* in the *end times* (of the year). Many interpret the four horses, and the seven spheres or angels, as demons, elements to be associated with evil; but until we recognize these *"devils are really angels setting your spirit free"* it is impossible to achieve any form of enlightenment.

Although *pale*, the final horse is named *khlōrós*, meaning *green* in Greek. This word eventually was used as a foundation for the French word *chlorophyll*, the green pigment in plants responsible for their absorption of light into energy through the process of photosynthesis. When sunlight becomes scarce and temperatures fall in the latter half of the year, plants and trees are unable to produce as much chlorophyll and therefore their leaves turn yellow, orange, or red depending upon the type of tree.

The *"name that sat on him was Death"* is a reference to what follows the fourth horse and his rider, i.e., the *winter,* and therefore the death of nature and a cold, dark, icy world akin to Hell. The pale green-yellow horse is really the changing of leaves in the fall which heralds the death of nature.

The four horses likewise signify the divisions of human life: childhood (birth), youth, maturity, and age (death). Birth is the rider of the white horse coming forth to conquer; the impetuosity of youth is the red horse that takes peace from the earth; maturity is the black horse weighing all things upon the scales of reason like Lady Justice, Ma'at, Anubis, Saint Michael,

Jesus, and even Santa Muerte; and the final pale horse is death. Writing in <u>The Secret Teachings</u> <u>of All Ages</u> Hall explains the descent of a soul through these stages in like manner with the seven gates or spheres:

> *"In his first and spiritual state he is crowed. As he descend into the realm of experience he carries the sword. Reaching physical expression – which is his least spiritual state – he carries the scales, and by the 'philosophic death' is released again into the highest spheres. In the ancient Roman games the chariot of the sun was drawn by four horses of different colors and the horsemen of the Apocalypse may be interpreted to represent the solar energy riding upon the four elements which serve as media for its expression."*

The horses further share a relationship to the *yugas* in Eastern philosophy and Hinduism. Through our birth, youth, maturity, and death are derived the periods of time granted each horse as a ruler of creation.

In the allegory of the *Four Horsemen* is signified the condition of earth during each stage of the year, and the condition of man during each stage of his life.

Accompanying these stages are the four corners of the world, four elements, and four winds, which relate to the *solar cross* and its divisions of the year and cosmos.

The four seasons and horsemen may also be associated with the red and black colors of playing cards signifying the divisions of a year: spring-summer, fall-winter. Four suits in the deck equate to the yearly seasons, corners of the world, classical elements, stages of life, four horses, etc. The symbols of the Tarot, and the four expressions of the Kabbalistic Tetragram, also relate to the symbolism of four: the Wand represents YOD; the Cup corresponds to HE; the Sword refers to VAU; and the Pentacle is the second HE in *YHVH*.

These horses and their riders are thus used as symbols of the *apocalypse*, which refers to "the complete final destruction of the world" as described in the Biblical book of Revelation. The Greek word *apocalypse* means "uncovering" or "revealing" just like the lifting of the veil of Isis.

The *Seals of Revelation* correspond to the *Four Horses* and four classical planets, with the remaining three seals corresponding to the other three planets and theological principles:

First Seal is the White Horse or Moon
Second Seal is the Red Horse or Sun
Third Seal is the Black Horse or Saturn
Fourth Seal is the Pale Horse or Venus
Fifth Seal is Mars or Blood
Sixth Seal is Jupiter or the Martyrs
Seventh Seal is Mercury or Silence

Revelation chapter 6:1-17 explains the coming of the *Four Horsemen* and the opening of those famous *Seven Seals*:

> *"And I saw when the Lamb opened one of the seals, and I heard, as it were the noise of thunder, one of the four beasts saying, Come and see. And I saw, and behold a white horse: and he that sat on him had a bow; and a crown was given unto him: and he went forth conquering, and to conquer. And when he*

had opened the second seal, I heard the second beast say, Come and see. And there went out another horse that was red: and power was given to him that sat thereon to take peace from the earth, and that they should kill one another: and there was given unto him a great sword. And when he had opened the third seal, I heard the third beast say, Come and see. And I beheld, and lo a black horse; and he that sat on him had a pair of balances in his hand. And I heard a voice in the midst of the four beasts say, A measure of wheat for a penny, and three measures of barley for a penny; and see thou hurt not the oil and the wine. And when he had opened the fourth seal, I heard the voice of the fourth beast say, Come and see. And I looked, and behold a pale horse: and his name that sat on him was Death, and Hell followed with him. And power was given unto them over the fourth part of the earth, to kill with sword, and with hunger, and with death, and with the beasts of the earth. And when he had opened the fifth seal, I saw under the altar the souls of them that were slain for the word of God, and for the testimony which they held: And they cried with a loud voice, saying, How long, O Lord, holy and true, dost thou not judge and avenge our blood on them that dwell on the earth? And white robes were given unto every one of them; and it was said unto them, that they should rest yet for a little season, until their fellowservants also and their brethren, that should be killed as they were, should be fulfilled. And I beheld when he had opened the sixth seal, and, lo, there was a great earthquake; and the sun became black as sackcloth of hair, and the moon became as blood; And the stars of heaven fell unto the earth, even as a fig tree casteth her untimely figs, when she is shaken of a mighty wind. And the heaven departed as a scroll when it is rolled together; and every mountain and island were moved out of their places. And the kings of the earth, and the great men, and the rich men, and the chief captains, and the mighty men, and every bondman, and every free man, hid themselves in the dens and in the rocks of the mountains; And said to the mountains and rocks, Fall on us, and hide us from the face of him that sitteth on the throne, and from the wrath of the Lamb: For the great day of his wrath is come; and who shall be able to stand?"

Next are described the "four angels standing on the four corners of the earth."

In Revelation chapter 8 the seventh seal is addressed: "When he opened the seventh seal, there was silence in heaven for about half an hour. And I saw the seven angels who stand before God, and seven trumpets were given to them."

White Buffalo Woman (Ptesan Wi)

There is an interesting correlation to be made between the *Four Horses*, four seasons, and the lore of certain American Indians like the Sioux, Cherokee, Navaho, Lakota, and Dakota. The birth and symbolism of their *White Buffalo Calf Woman* (Ptesan Wi) is as sacred as the Holy Scriptures.

Upon arrival the woman teaches her people seven sacred ways to pray, which parallel the sacred number seven and the Seven Virtues.

Before leaving, Ptesan Wi promises to return one day to restore harmony to a chaotic world, a parallel to the dying and resurrected god motif.

She then rolls upon the earth four times, changing color each time, before turning into a white buffalo. This is, of course, shares likeness to the changing seasons and Four Horses.

The birth of a real white buffalo is a sign of life's *sacred loop* and therefore a positive omen, especially because, like Jesus, the baby calf is born among the poorest people and in the most unexpected places.

Jacob's Ladder

In the Biblical book of Genesis 28:12-13 is told the story of Jacob's dream and his famous ladder, yet another symbol, like a rainbow, of the stairway or gateway to heaven:

"He had a dream in which he saw a stairway resting on the earth, with its top reaching to heaven, and the angels of God were ascending and descending on it. There above it stood the Lord, and he said: 'I am the Lord, the God of your father Abraham and the God of Isaac. I will give you and your descendants the land on which you are lying.'"

The Ladder of Life as published in Manly P. Hall's <u>Lectures on Ancient Philosophy</u>. *

Summarizing the story, Jacob undertakes a journey to Haran. When night falls, he fashions a pillow out of a large stone and finds rest. While sleeping, Jacob dreams of a large ladder connecting earth and sky. Ascending and descending the ladder are shining beings. Jacob then sees God, who informs him that he shall inherit the land upon which he sleeps. When awakening he discovers that the place where he slept was sacred ground, and a gateway to heaven. Brushing off the morning dew, an alchemical symbol of new life, he raises his stone pillow upright into a pillar called *Bethel* – "the house of God." Similar stones are known in Europe as *betyl* or *betel* and in Celtic lands they are called *menhir*. In India they are called *Sivalingam*. All these megalithic structures are believed to contain the energy of God in some capacity. From this story we can again derive details for the fairy tales of *Sleeping Beauty* and *Rapunzel* with its famous line: *"Rapunzel, Rapunzel, let down your hair, so that I may climb thy golden stair."* Here the word "golden" is to be associated with the *morning dew*, the honey and gold of alchemists, and the *Celestial Fire*.

Traditionally, Jacob's Ladder is depicted as having seven steps corresponding to the seven spheres or planets for which the soul must pass before birth and after death. Jacob's story is allegorical, and perhaps mildly historical. It is an alchemical story of dreaming and awakening to find the blessing of morning dew from the *Cosmic Mind*.

* The ladder of Jacob is commonly depicted with seven steps to indicate the seven spheres or planets. It is a symbol of the ascending and descending forces of heaven, and stages of the soul-spirit. In Masonry it is a symbol of the *Great Work* or *Secret Work*. The *ladder of life* extends from the inferior sphere through the seven planetary spheres, and finally through the wall of the zodiac. It continues upward through the clouds that obscure the *divine*.

Jacob's Ladder, by the German painter Julius Schnorr von Carolsfeld.

Jacob's Ladder by Robert Fludd. The rungs correspond from bottom to top, or earth to heaven, to the senses, imagination, reason, intellect, intelligence, and finally the *Word* itself, or *verbum*.

From the Fool to Death

Dante's vision of the angels in heaven, or *Heavenly Hosts*, was painted by Gustave Doré to resemble the *white rose,* a symbol of *femina candida,* innocence, and purity. On first thought the word *purity* may conjure images of *virginity* and *youth*, but on second thought it could likewise imply the cleansing nature of *necessary evil* and *death*. Again, as Eckhart wrote, *"If you fight your death, you'll feel the demons tearing away at your life, but, if you have the right attitude to death, you will be able to see that the devils are really angels setting your spirit free."*

In Tarot symbolism, the white rose is also held in the left hand of the *Fool* at the beginning of his journey to become *The Magician.* By the thirteenth card there is *Death*, rider of the *pale horse* and carrier of a flag with white rose. By the *death* card should be assumed everything but physical death, alas one worries themself to an early grave through paranoid self-fulfilling prophecy.

Dante's Inferno as illustrated by

Although these symbols and images tend to evoke fear and terror, they merely represent the natural cycles of change occurring throughout what we perceive as time - for humans, the planet, and the cosmos. They symbolize the ascent and descent of the soul through the *seven planetary spheres of consciousness*. As we read in the book of Job 1:21, the following:

"Naked I came from my mother's womb, and naked I will depart. The Lord gave and the Lord has taken away; may the name of the Lord be praised."

Interestingly, the name "Job" means to *weep* or *cry*, and so it is true for most that they view their *work* as a stressful *undertaking* (undertaker) to *earn* (urn) *money* (currency) on *weekdays* (weak days) at a *job* (cry) they don't much care for. We *awake* (a-wake) in the morning (mourning) and if lucky enough, or if we work hard enough, some of us could *earn a killing*.

After the sun completes one full cycle through the twelve zodiac signs, and speaking in numerological terms, the first sign restarts the cycle and may be called thirteen. Just like King Arthur's *12 Knights of the Round Table*, there are *12 Disciples* of Christ, who, like Arthur, was the thirteenth. In the English alphabet our thirteenth letter is "M" and therefore we invoke the name of Mary, the mother *Jesus Christ,* who would be born, live, die, and resurrect in the classic story. Thirteen is therefore symbolized by the number thirteen. Lest we forget that *Mary Magdalene* is the *Mystical Mother* of the *Mysteries*. Her symbol is the red rose, that famous flower of *initiation* which gives the bees honey: *Dat Rosa Mel Apibus.*

Of special note here is the teacher and prophet Moses. The "M" in his name could signify 13, too, while the "OSES" is short for "roses." This could, in very esoteric terms, mean that M-oses means *13-roses*, especially since both the number thirteen and the letter "M" relate to *secret teachings*.

Week-gods, Moon-ths & Holy Days

"Even primitive peoples far back into the mists of prehistoric times must have found the necessity of some division and measurement of time, and doubtless there were many attempts made to fulfill their simple requirements before some really practical system was evolved."

~ William J. Fielding ~

The world is saturated with symbols in the form of colors, insects, animals, alphabets and letters, numbers and geometry, and endless stories of gods and goddesses. Government architecture in the United States capitol calls back to the Roman Empire, with "the Capitol" being a reference to the temple of Jupiter on Capitoline Hill. From classical to more foreign mythologies come names for the days of the week and months of the year. The twelve months are houses to the eight Sabbats as well, which include the two solstices and two equinoxes on the *Wheel of the Year*.

The *cycles* of our moon, which we use to design our twelve months, gives us the word *month* or *month*. The moon is separated into three phases: waxing, full, and waning. From *moon* we also acquire the word *Monday* or *Moon Day*. The *sun* gives us *Sun Day*; Tyre gives us Tuesday; Woden gives us Wednesday; Thor gives us Thursday; Frigga gives us Friday; and Saturn gives us Saturday or *Saturn Day*.

From the pagan *Wheel of the Year*, preserving the eight holy days of the ancient world, we acquire many of our most popular holidays and festivals today, from Valentine's Day to Halloween and Christmas. Although Christianized, the solstices and equinoxes, for example, are anything but evil (as many associate with *pagan*), since they are irrefutable proof of the Grand Architect and his work. The word *HOLIDAY* is itself derived from the Old English *hāligdæg*, meaning *HOLY DAY*.

Holy Days & Months

January is Latin for *Januarius* (*mensis Janus*), named after the deity Janus, who presided over doorways in Rome. He was known as the god of gates (*januae*), amongst other titles, including those relating to time. *Mensis Janus*, of course, means literally *Janus Month*. Janus was worshiped at the beginning of each day, month, and year, his chief festival being held on January 1st, the month that bears his name. Sometimes he was depicted with four heads, one for each direction and season of the year. His twelve altars represent each of the months and houses of the zodiac. In Rome the doors to his main temple were only closed when there was not an ongoing war. This only occurred once between the reign of Numa and Augustus, for which the month of August is named. The most common depiction of Janus is with two faces, back-to-back, one looking forward and another backward. The meaning of this symbolism is derived from his guardianship of time, looking into the past while maintaining a fixed gaze on the present and future.

The God Janus, by Sebastian Münster, 1550.

The two heads of Janus are also meant to represent the sky in its *diurnal* and *nocturnal* states, encouraging the coming of day and night by the directions of east and west for which the sun rises and sets. It was said that Janus opened the gates of heaven at dawn and closed them at dusk. His two heads are further related to the doubled-headed eagle, a symbol of great power, often associated with imperialism. This two-headed bird is important in the myth of Zeus, who let fly two eagles east and west from the ends of the world. They eventually met at Delphi, which proved to be the center of the earth. The eagle, used on various country flags today, and famously in the United States, is itself a modern symbol of the phoenix, which dies and resurrects from its own ashes like the sun. And this is where we acquire the famous image of the winged-solar-disc, soaring above the head of Isis, and carrying RA through the sky like his boat or chariot.

The *flying solar disc* may tell us something about the modern phenomenon of *flying discs*, too, at least in archetypical terms. It is widely popular in Christian iconography, usually with the heart replacing the sun, along with countless other cultures from Egypt to India and North America. The *swastika* is a stylized version of this image, as it represents the solar cross, or wheel, turning. The Germans call it *sonnenrad*, which resembles a bent cross or swastika. This *wheel* motif is recalled also with *Ezekiel's Wheel*, the 12-spoked wheel of creation and destruction in Jainism, the *Chariot Wheel of Krishna*, and the *Ichthys Wheel*, which conceals the name of Christ in Greek: I X O Y E. The latter symbol was used by early Christians as a secret code to identify one another. *Ezekiel's Wheel* allowed for the prophet to interact with the divine directly. Ezekiel 1:15-16 relates:

> *"Now as I beheld the living creatures, behold one wheel upon the earth by the living creatures, with his four faces. This was the appearance and structure of the wheels: They sparkled like topaz, and all four looked alike. Each appeared to be made like a wheel intersecting a wheel."*

The four creatures seen by Ezekiel are *The Four Beasts of Revelation*. The bull, lion, eagle, and man are collectively known as the *Tetramorph*, and otherwise associated with the *Four Evangelists*: St. Matthew (man), St. Mark (lion), St. Luke (bull), and St. John (eagle). They also represent the four elements: water (man), fire (lion), earth (bull) and air (eagle).

One of the most powerful Celtic deities is *Esus*, whose symbol was an all-encompassing circle. According to Encyclopedia Britannica, his victims *"were sacrificed by being ritually stabbed and hung from trees."* Various depictions of the god associate him with the sacred bull, Taurus, of Mithra(s). Since his name means "Lord" he is the *Most High*, i.e., the *solar disc*, and clearly the Celtic Odin.

The *winged solar disc*, and its association with the heart (especially in winged form), is meant to symbolize the worlds of *spirit* and *matter* interacting, just as the two heads of Janus signify the cycles of time. Occultists like Robert Fludd identified the *solar disc* with the *human heart*, where he said the *soul* resides. The heart is therefore the *seat of life* and a microcosmic reflection of the macrocosmic sun. In the first book of his Libri Apologetici, Jakob Böhme writes about the heart and its connection to God:

> *"For we men have one book in common which points to God. Each has it within himself, which is the priceless Name of God. Its letters are the flames of His love, which He out of His heart in the priceless Name of Jesus has revealed in us. Read these letters in your hearts and spirits and you have books enough. All the writings of the children of God direct you unto that one book, for therein lie all the treasures of wisdom. (...) This book is Christ in you."*

The Wheel of the Chariot of Krishna
Temple of Vitala, Vijayanagara, India

Ichthys Wheel

Ezekiel's Vision, by Matthaeus (Matthäus) Merian.

The Egyptians described the *soul* by the principles of *KA, BA, AKH*. The BA appears in the form of a bird, symbolizing the soul's mobility after death; the KA, surviving physical death, was said to reside in a picture or statue of the deceased; the AKH allowed for a soul to visit the earth temporarily for enjoyment. In Egypt the *winged solar disc* was sometimes depicted with two serpents holding up the sun in the middle. One snake faces east and the other west, creating horns like those of Taurus, and unveiling an association with both Esus and Isis.

Ashur (God of Storms & War)

The Assyrians used the same symbol for their sun god Shamash, whose name is like the mythical Tibetan Buddhist city of Sham-bala. Here you have *sham*, as in a sham-an, a medium acting between two worlds, and *bala*, as in Bal or Ba'al, the sun god of the Phoenicians and Canaanites. The Assyrian Ashur was likewise depicted inside of a winged-disc.

It follows that the *seat of the soul* is in the heart, that place where we "welcome Jesus," and the organ associated with the *flying solar disc*. The soul is thus able to ascend and fly away. This was the meaning of BA, or the soul symbolized by a *bird*. Japanese tradition holds that the soul of a person can become a *butterfly* upon death, or just before.

We are often told to "open your heart and let Jesus enter" therein. The Solar Plexus chakra near our heart is known as a "portal for the Sun" and therefore Jesus is to be welcomed into our hearts through the *cakra*, a Sanskrit word meaning "wheel or circle." This is why we feel warmth in our chest with emotions like appreciation and love. When we are betrayed, there may be a sense of cold that descends over the body. Mark Booth confirms this in <u>The Secret History of the World</u>:

> *"The Mystery schools taught that as well as head-consciousness we each have, for example, a heart-consciousness which emanates from the sun then enters our mental space via the heart. Or to put it another way, the heart is the portal through which Sun god enters our lives."*

Manly Hall further explains why the name of God is often found within an inverted human heart, and why this image is sacred:

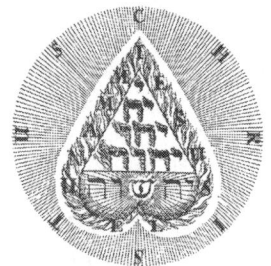

> *"The Tetragrammaton, or four-lettered Name of God, is here arranged as a tetractys within the inverted human heart. Beneath, the name Jehovah is shown transformed into Jehoshua by the interpolation of the radiant Hebrew letter äñ, Shin. The drawing as a whole represents the throne of God and His hierarchies within the heart of man.*

In <u>A Dictionary of Symbols</u>, J. E. Cirlot' writes of the *winged solar disc*, as it relates to the ancient world and today:

> *"The 'winged disc' is one of the most widespread of ancient symbols, which is still in use today in signs and emblems; in the profoundest sense, it represents matter in a state of sublimation and transfiguration. The two small serpents which are often to be seen next to the disk are those of the caduceus, alluding to the equipoise of opposing forces."*

In Buddhist lore, we find *Chavachakra*, the Wheel of Life, or *Wheel of Becoming*. It is held in the hand of *death*, or the Buddhist devil *Mara*, signifying that all life will succumb to demise. This is identical to the agricultural allegory of Saturn *planting in us the seeds of our destruction*. What we call evil is personified in *Mara* as temptation, sin, and death. He is also known as *Papiyan*, the "very wicked," and *Varsavarti*, "he who fulfills desires." It is *desire* that leads to corruption of the soul-spirit, i.e., *suffering*. As in the incarnation *Devadatta* he is associated with Judas Iscariot, or *Scorpio*. The *Devil' Wheel* is sometimes replaced by the *God Wheel*, but either way the imagery can be found from India to Japan.

January is thus, as personified by Janus, the *wheel* of all things in motion.

The Wheel of the Year separates the *holy days* into eight points - the solstices and equinoxes by a *solar cross*, and within the quadrants of the latter are found the midpoints of the year: *Imbolc, Beltane, Luchnassad* and *Samhain*. The summer and winter solstices of *Yule* and *Litha* occupy the northern and southern portions of the cross, while the equinoxes known as *Mabon* and *Ostara* occupy the western and eastern portions. This image also contains *the Twelve Signs of the Zodiac* and an inner circle containing the *Holy Trinity*: birth, life, death. The overlapping lines in the center are called *triquetra*, a very ancient symbol comprised of three interlocking *vesica piscis*, or almond shapes, linked by a circle.

Our lives are in the hands of the *Grand Architect of the Universe*, here seen as either the Devil spinning the Wheel of Life, or as God Supporting the entire world like Atlas.

Indian Wheel of Life *

Tibetan Wheel of Life*

Japanese Wheel of Life*

*Reproduced from Paul Carus

God Supporting the World

by Buonamico Buffamalco

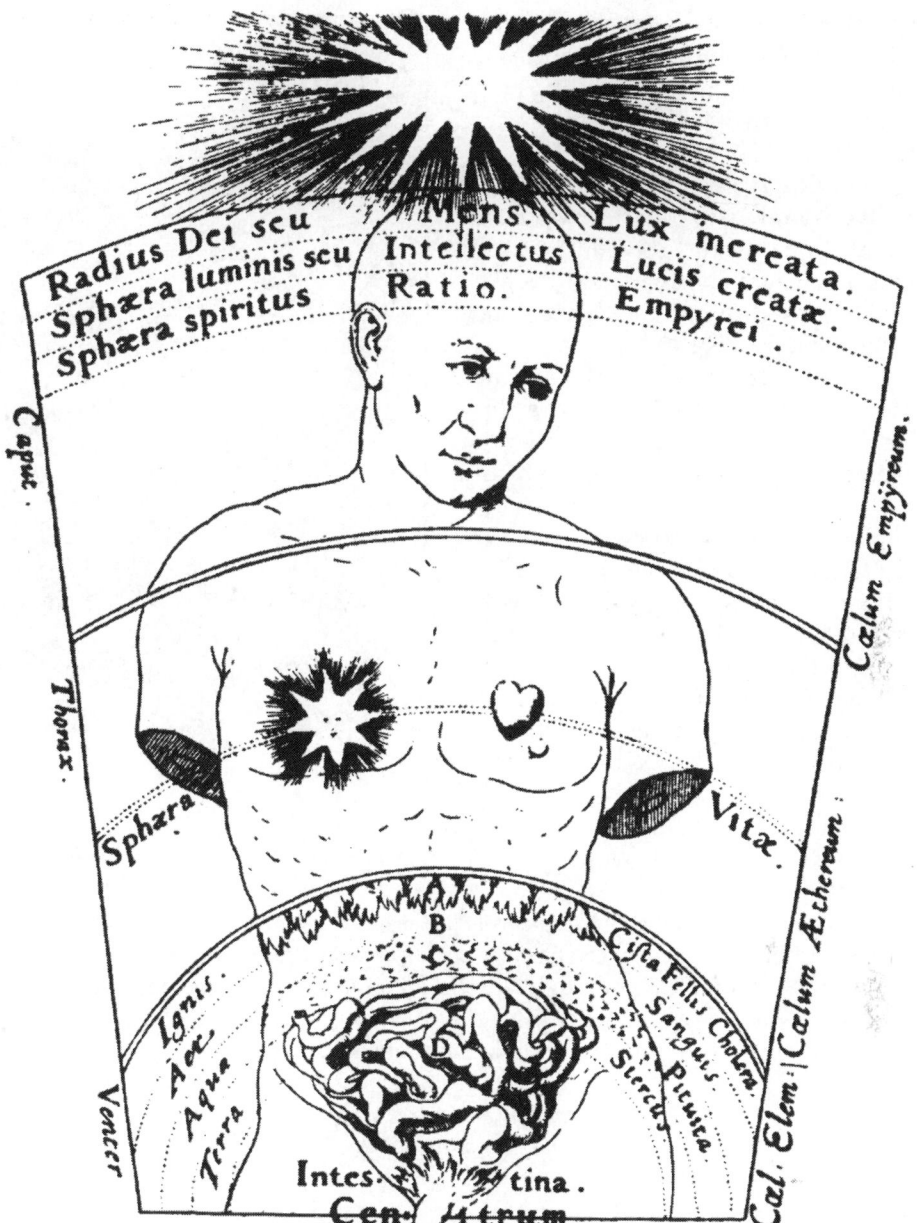

The Solar Heart by Robert Fludd.

The sun is a mediator between spirit and matter.

February comes from the Roman *Februus*, god of *purification*, and *Februa*, a mid-month ritual of *purification* and *fertility*. The name can be further derived from *Faunus*, the god of *purification* and *fertility*.

The word *February* essentially means *purging* and the month is a time set aside for cleaning rituals that were as much about protecting the home, family, and land, as they were about literally cleaning the home. Such rituals were meant to exorcise *wicked spirits*, while simultaneously encouraging fertility and new life. A clean space encourages blessings, and a dirty space conjures devils. From here we derive our "spring-cleaning" ritual that many still practice today.

In Japan, this time was known as the *Bean-throwing Festival* or *Setsubun*. The intent of this eastern tradition was also to expel evil while inviting good fortune into the home by throwing roasted soy beans (*fukumame* – fortune beans) and chanting, *"Demons leave – luck, please enter."*

Februa took place between one and two weeks after the *holy day* of Imbolc, the first sign that winter was ending and spring was beginning. Therefore, *February* is typically considered the last month of winter in the northern hemisphere.

Engraving of Februarius

Wiccans and others celebrate Imbolc as Candlemas (February 2), or simply Brigid, the Celtic goddess of fertility. She also goes by the name *Juno Sospita – The One Savior*.

In northern Scotland, it was thought a good omen if the first three days of winter were dark and cloudy. The weather of a coming season was further said to be determined by clear or foul conditions on Candlemas. Therefore, we read in a famous s couplet:

If Candlemas is fair and clear,
Ther'll be two winters in the year.

According to William J. Fielding in his work <u>Strange Superstitions and Magical Practices</u>, if Candlemas *"passed without a storm, people were sure there would be severe weather before spring and passed, and they expected heavy snow storms before the following Christmas. A showery or tempestuous Candlemas, on the other hand, caused joyousness, for by such omens they were to expect a favorable summer and an abundant harvest."*

A similar divinatory tradition involves using the classic Christmas tree as a symbol of predicting future weather. In certain parts of Ireland, the tree was stripped of decorations and left in place all winter until Candlemas. If the tree kept its green needles through the final waning of winter, then it was said good luck would be found in the coming months.

Although a festival of fire, Imbolc is primarily focused on the reemergence of light as it is the midpoint between Yule (Winter Solstice) and Ostara (Spring Equinox). In Northern England, Candlemas was known as the *Wives' Feast Day*. Food and drink were left out during these celebrations for the goddess Brigid in hopes they would attract her blessings, a similar tradition that relates to Halloween (Samhain) and *trick-or-treating* and leaving food out for Santa on Christmas Eve (Yule). This tradition comes from a variation of the *Last Supper* and all *Great Feasts* had after the final harvest of each year. Around ten percent of such food was traditionally saved in case of failed future harvests, a practice which transformed into *tithing* that same percentage of one's income to the church. On every *holy day*, food is placed out to both appease mischievous spirits and to welcome spirits of family and friends.

If light is the foundational element of this sabbat, Brigid is its foundational goddess. Food was enjoyed in her honor during the *Feast of Brigid* (February 1). She is the bringer of fertility, like Faunus, and known as the Muse-Goddess or *Mary of Gael*. Her attributes where Christianized into a character named St. Brigid, whose day is Imbolc-eve, February 1st, in Ireland. The true historical saint lived between AD 453-523 and all her holy places were merely those of the goddess recommissioned.

Brigid's Cross

It is told in myth that St. Brigid was brought up by a wizard and that she had the power to multiply food and drink, reminding us of when Jesus fed five thousand with two fish and five loaves of bread in Mathew 14:13-21. Just as Jesus turned water into wine, an homage no doubt to the Greek and Roman gods of wine, it is also said that St. Brigid had a miraculous ability to turn her bath water into beer. The Christianized Brigid also shares commonalities with Faunus, both imparting blessings of fertility. When Faunus imparts fertility on cattle his name became *Inuus*. He can be associated with the Greek god Pan. All new life, from womb to earth, is a symbol of renewed time and the New Year.

As with Jesus, one of the most recognized symbols of Imbolc is the *Cross of Brigid*. This powerful symbol of the *turning wheel* was either made of reed or straw and often took the form of handmade doll. A similar cross is used at the Sun God Torii gate Shintō shrine, and others, near the famous Meoto Iwa (Wedded Rocks) on the southwest shore of Ies Bay, Japan. These encircled crosses are rubbed on the body to absorb its impurities and then left at the shrine with a small offering. As with the cross of Jesus, a symbol of salvation, these Japanese crosses are meant to purify one of evil, sin, and general impurity.

Purifying cross found at some Shinto shrines.

February has traditionally been designated as a time for ritual cleansing. Writing in <u>A Witches' Bible</u>, Janet and Stewart Farrar explain the ancient Roman cleaning and fertility tradition:

"In ancient Rome, February was cleansing tie - Februarius mensis, 'the month of the ritual purification'. At its beginning came the Lupercalia, when the Luperci, the priests of Pan, ran through the streets naked except for a goatskin girdle and carrying goatskin thongs. With these they struck everybody who passed, and in particular married women, who were believed to be made fertile thereby."

The Roman festivals of *Februalia* or *Februatio* were held to cleanse the home and community of dirt and crooked spirits. Most homes were ritually cleansed by sweeping them out and sprinkling salt and wheat spelt throughout their interiors. Sometime around February 13th and 15th there was a fertility festival known as *Lupercalia* in Rome, or what we now refer to, in part, as *Valentine's Day*. The Roman festival consisted of a sect of priests called the *Luperci*, who gathered in a sacred cave to perform sacrifices that were meant to expedite the purification of earth, i.e., the return of the sun. This bears resemblance to the still held early mass of the Christian Church and the early "mass" held in ancient Babylon to usher down Ishtar's egg so that new life could be birthed. The person finding her egg was honored with a gift. Brigid would bestow further blessings upon those leaving her a made bed and food.

Lupercalia was also partially celebrated in honor of *Lupa*, the wolf who suckled the mythical founders of Rome. The words *Lupercalia* and *Luperci* stem from the word *lupas*, which means "she-wolf" or "prostitute." Lupercalia is thus known as the "wolf festival." During the festival, *Luperci* gathered to sacrifice a goat and a dog, usually in a cave to represent the womb. The wolf is symbolically a *trickster* and is associated with the Greek gods Apollo and Zeus, representing male energy and sexuality. As a symbol of fertility, the wolf has historically been called upon to help a women conceive children, and this is appropriate seeing that Lupercalia is a fertility festival.

Elsewhere the wolf is *Coyote* in North America or *Reynard* in Europe. In Nigeria the Yoruba know him as Edshu and in Japan he is Inari. The Eskimos of the Bering Strait call him Raven.

In some parts of what we call Russia today, straw wolves were historically made and kept with a young woman to help her conceive. Corn dollies were also similarly made elsewhere by reed or straw, often in the shape of the Cross of Brigid. A wolf also acts as a guide for souls in the afterlife, as does the dog or jackal god known in Egypt as Anubis.

A brief recap of the meaning: The dog is astrologically *Canis Major*, or Orion's dog. Orion is Osiris, the Great Hunter, and Siva (Shiva or Rudra-Siva), and Nimrod, the father of the Sumerian Tammuz. Orion derives from a word meaning *sperm*, something that implies the impregnation of earth with solar rays, and her later giving of birth during the fall harvest. Dogs and wolves both act as guides for the soul and have the ability like the Janus, the keeper of doorways, to see between the physical and spiritual worlds. This ability is commonly referred to as *second sight*. In Teutonic mythology the dog *Garn* guards the gates of Niflheim, the land of the dead. This is like the three-headed *Hound of Hell*, *Cerberus*, who guarded the gates of Hades in Greek myth. The Goddess of the underworld, Hecate, is also depicted with dogs helping her to guard the crossroads. In Welsh myth, souls are led through Annwn by escort dogs and in Egypt the black jackal-headed deity Anubis assists in the *Hall of Judgment*.

The Luperci caves were called *Lupercal* and located on the Palatine Hill where Rome was traditionally said to have been founded. Members of the cult of Mithra(s) also used underground crypts called *Mithraea* to perform their ceremonies.

Lupercalia further connects with the ancient Greek festival of *Arcadian Lykaia*, a ritual held on Mt. Lykaion, or "wolf mountain," in honor of Pan.

Since *Lupas* means *wolf* or *prostitute*, *Lupercalia* may stem from *Luere per Caprum*, meaning "to purify by means of the goat."

The *Luperci* performed sacrifices of a goat and dog as part of the festival, draining their blood and making strips from the hide. The hide was then dipped in blood and used to gently strike women, animals, and the land as a symbolic gesture of *sympathetic magic fertility*. It was believed by some to be literal, and to others metaphoric, that the hide dipped in blood would bring *fertility* by transferring that quality from the animals. Young women in the city would then write their names on something, or make their mark the same, and place it in a container. Some may have used a personal item. Men would then reach inside and choose the name of a woman that he would be temporarily paired with. Sometimes these pairings would end in marriage, but mostly they were for sex. In some cases, it may have been an organized coupling with those already together, as we find in many of the Witch Covens today.

So many holidays today are largely based on Christianized pagan practices since the origins of these holy days would be far too sexually graphic otherwise. Valentine's Day is probably the best example of this fact. We have thus reduced the necessity and sacredness of fertility, sex, and procreation to stories about Saint Valentine, a clergyman, who ministered to persecuted Christians in Rome. After being killed in the 3rd century, his body was buried on February 14, a day known as the *Feast of Saint Valentine*.

As for Cupid, he is often depicted with a bow and arrow, which is symbolic of his connection to Tammuz, Nimrod, Osiris, and many other similar gods. Cupid is Latin for *Amor*, which means love. To the Greeks he was a god of sexual attraction named *Ero(s)*, the son of the Roman Venus or Greek Aphrodite.

Lupercalia, oil painting from 1635.

March is named after a god of war, the Latin Mars, or Greek Ares. From the Latin *Martius* (mensis) is derived the month of Mars. The Anglo-Saxons called this month *Hraed-monat*, meaning "rugged month," or *Hlyd-monat*, meaning, "stormy" month. Storms are to be associated with violence and war. Anglo-Saxons called March "Easter-monat," in honor of the Teutonic goddess Ēostre, a deity of spring and light. As a Germanic goddess of spring, she shares attributes with the Babylonian Ishtar and the Japanese Amaterasu, among many others.

Spring is known as a time of *hieros gamos,* which refers to the sacrificial mating of the god and goddess in ancient times. In the South it is a time of sprouting and in the North a time of sowing.

Most traditions hold that Easter is named for the Teutonic goddess Ēostre, a name in league with Ishtar, Astarte, and Aset or Isis. Contrary to popular belief, what we call Easter was not really imported from the pagan world. If fact, in some places like the British Isles these traditions were imported from Christianity.

Pagans and Wiccans call the spring equinox Ostara, and it is invariably associated with Ishtar and her egg.

Easter is now celebrated on the first Sunday after the first full moon following the spring equinox. Having been born in March, Mars shares much in common with the gods of resurrection, especially because some stories tell of his immaculate conception like Horus and Christ. Encyclopedia Britannica reports that in one myth, *"Hera bore him, without Zeus, at the touch of a magic herb given her by Flora."*

Although the sun resurrects on Yule (December 20-23), or is reborn, and grows to overcome darkness on Ostara (March 20-23), the Christian canon puts the birth of Jesus on the former and resurrection on the latter. Scholars like Ignacio L. Götz propose that Jesus would have likely been born around Ostara. The Eastern Orthodox Church remembers that the crucifixion and resurrection supposedly took place after the Biblical Passover. Some Christians, however, still celebrated the first Easter on the Jewish holiday of Passover and it was not until the year 325 AD when emperor Constantine declared Easter be celebrated on the first Sunday after the first full moon following the spring equinox. Yet another festival of light, the spring equinox equates with the illuminated root vegetables of Samhain, those twinkling lights used at Yule, or perhaps more curiously the bonfires of Litha or Beltane. It marks the midpoint between the winter solstice and summer solstice. Janet and Stewart Farrar explain the same: *"As a solar festival, too, it must share with the Greater Sabbats the eternal theme of fire and light."*

Easter symbols can largely be traced to the moon. As a reflector of light in the sky, our lunar sphere embodies the *triple goddess* qualities of waxing, full, and waning phases, and reflects the triplicity of the sun in its physical, spiritual, and intellectual capacities.

The moon influences water, emotions, menstruation, and is itself egg-like, therefore making it a grand symbol of *fertility*. Since it reflects divine light from the sun, the moon is home to the creation of an *elixir of life*. The Japanese say it is crafted by a rabbit using mortar and pestle on the lunar surface. There may be some connection here to the Hindu elephant-god Ganesha too. The rabbit is a symbol of both fertility and abundance, and sometimes chastity.

The *easter basket* is likewise a symbol of abundance, being the cornucopia of spring. The *Cosmic Egg*, which descends from the heavens with Ishtar, is thought to embody both the creation and renewal of life.

Mesopotamian legend says that each year an egg would fall from heaven and land in the area around the Euphrates River. Ishtar would then burst from the egg, an action symbolizing the birth of spring and renewal of nature. Whoever could find her egg first would be bestowed a special blessing just like those given out by Brigid on Imbolc. We find here the origin of modern Easter egg hunts: these ritual reenactments are symbolic of the hunt for Ishtar and her egg, or perhaps the search by Isis for her husband Osiris. This story then relates, once more, to the various hunter-gods.

The *World Egg* is laid by the *Universal Goddess*, sprouting only when penetrated by solar rays. In other words, women carry eggs and men provide the sperm. Some stories document how this *egg* came from a snake and in various occult depictions the serpent is wrapped around the egg like ouroboros encapsulates the world.

Since the serpent tempted Eve and caused the *Fall of Man*, it can be said that this creature is really the architectural mind behind *matter*.

The idea of sunrise church service is ancient and in those days was meant to symbolically hasten the yearly arrival of Ishtar's egg and its special blessing, i.e., spring and its light.

One Germanic myth says that the goddess Ēostre was one day traveling through a forest when she found a bird dying in the snow, succumbing to hunger and cold. She turned that bird into a hare so it could be warm and find food easier. The hare, once a bird, survived, and when spring came, began laying eggs. The creature in question then decorated every egg and left them for Ēostre as a sign of gratitude, hoping for a blessing from the goddess. From this story comes a tradition of coloring eggs left by a rabbit the night before. Freia, the Norse goddess of love, also held the rabbit sacred.

The phrase "Mad as a March Hare" relates to the beginning of rabbit mating season, as rabbits are specifically known for fertility. A rabbit's foot is considered lucky and a symbol of fertile blessings. White represents the purity of a new day and year, like the innocence of a newborn child. A white rabbit is thus the epitome of Easter iconography because of its fertility and purity. The significance of white can be seen in the myths of a white buffalo or the white apocalyptic horse of spring.

The Achaemenians of the Persian Empire observed the spring equinox with a festival known as *Nowruz*, which means "new day." Prior to Nowruz, the Iranians held a festival called *Chahar-Shanbeh Suri*. This festival encompassed a 13-day period, symbolic of the twelve signs of the zodiac and the beginning of a new cycle with the thirteenth or first.

Rabbit Pounding the Elixir of Life Under the Moon, by Mori Ippo, 1867. The moon is home to the elixir in India and Japan.

The Maya civilization celebrated the spring equinox using their ceremonial pyramid known as El Castillo in the center of the Yucatan Peninsula in Mexico. When sunlight strikes the pyramid on the equinox, as we already know from earlier sections, the god Kukulkan can be seen descending its steps.

The Latin *Aperio*, meaning to open, is a significant part of March because this is considered the first month of spring in the northern hemisphere when things begin blooming and sprouting, i.e., the opening of flowers. Other symbols related to spring include baked cakes decorated with crosses or cakes baked in the shape of a star. These cakes or *hot crossed buns* further relate to wheat and are thus a kind of Eucharist. The latter obviously represents the five-pointed star of the goddess, associating her with Venus and Lucifer, the bearer of the light that is brought back to a dark and cold world after winter subsides. In esoteric tradition, the light of Venus is reflected to earth by way of its moon. Ishtar, Ēostre, and Ostara, all played vital roles in the creation of our modern Easter, as do the numerous dying-gods resurrected in the spring.

In the *Naassene Sermon* from the <u>Gnostic Bible</u>, the *mysteries* of life were explained through a song to Attis, as revealed in the *Mystery Schools*. Attis, like Osiris, was the god of agriculture and vegetation:

> *Whether you are the offspring of Kronos,*
> *Or the blessed child of Zeus or great Rhea,*
> *Hail to you, Attis, at whose name Rhea looks down.*
> *Assyrians call you thrice-lamented Adonis;*
> *all Egypt, Osiris;*
> *Greek wisdom, the heavenly crescent moon;*
> *Samothracians, venerable Adamas;*
> *People of Haimos, corybant;*
> *Sometimes corpse or god or sterile*
> *or goatherd or harvested green sheaf*
> *or flute player whom the fertile almond brought forth.*

Kronos, Saturn, and the Serpent are architects of the physical world, Rhea is the Great Mother (Ma-Rhea), and she looks down at her son; Adonis is lamented three times like Hermes or Thoth, the crescent moon is of the goddess, and sometimes the god is dead, alive, or sterile, or harvested as the *Green Man*. The "fertile almond brought forth" is the female reproductive system and it is encouraged to *aperio*, or open like a flower, to ensure procreation of man and earth. Janet and Stewart Farrar describe the festival of Cybele and her son Attis in their book:

Three Hares

> *"The grim festival of the Phrygian goddess Cybele, at which the self-castration, death and resurrection of her son/lover Attis was marked by worshipers castrating themselves to become her priests, was from 22nd to 25th March. In Rome these rites took place on the spot where St Peter's now stands in Vatican City."*

The motifs of rabbits, eggs, abundance, resurrection, and the moon are found all over the world. The *Three Hares* symbols is an image depicting three hares running in a circle with their ears attached to produce a triangle, or trinity, and it is found everywhere from Europe to China. The earliest example comes in the 6th century AD from a Buddhist holy site. The symbol is thought to originate in the tales of Buddha's lives, or the *Jatakas*. In one story we find the hare to be a previous incarnation of Siddhartha Gautama, who sacrifices himself for a starving priest. As a reward and blessing for his virtue, the hare is cast onto the moon as a sacred symbol. However, there are likely older and more direct associations between the moon and hare, going back to ancient India and likely before. Taoists hold tradition about a rabbit dwelling on the moon, working hard to create the elixir of life - the divine light of the sun cast from the universal mother to her children on earth.

March is also home to the *Ides*. As the saying goes, "beware the Ides of March." The word itself refers to the middle of any calendar month, but mid-March is historically significant because of the assassination of the Roman statesman Julius Caesar.

The Triquetra (Triqueta) is an ancient symbol meaning "three cornered" in Latin. It is comprised of three separate *vesica piscis* symbols interlocked by a circle. In Christianity the symbol is equivalent to the *Holy Trinity*, or Father, Son, and Holy Ghost. In Greek tradition there is monad, intellect, soul. Elsewhere it is symbolic of any three-fold concept such as heaven, earth, and hell, or past, present, and future. It is similarly related to the *Tripod of Life* and *Triple Goddess* of the pagan and wiccan world where it means mother, maiden, and crone. Kabbalists call it the *Supernal Triad*. The Norse called it *Valknut*. The Japanese use it in protective amulets. Psychologists call it mind, body, spirit.

The magical qualities of this symbol are derived from its design since the image can be drawn without utensil leaving the paper.

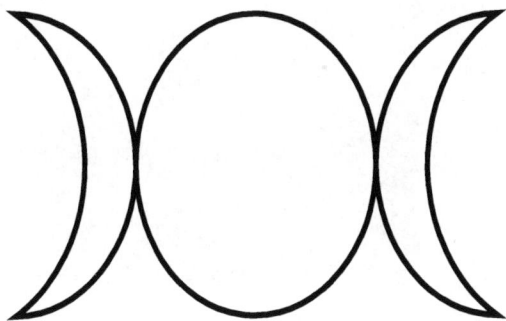

Triple Goddess

Triquetra

The Norse Valknut is comprised of three interlocking triangles

The Japanese Mitsu Domo (Tomoe) amulet offers triple protection against fires, floods, and thieves.

April was associated with Venus by the Romans, who frequently referred to it as "Mensis Veneris," instead of its proper Latin name "Aprilis." This month houses the holy day of *Beltane* (Walpurgis or May Eve) on April 30th, also known as *Walpurgis Night*, a multi-day festival ending on May 1st. Walpurgis night is the English version of the German *Walpurgisnacht*, the eve of a feast to the Goddess and Saint Walpurga. She is a powerful deity across Europe, especially in Germany where she is known by other names such as the "May Queen."

Other Germanic myths refer to her as *Earth Mother*, but she is variously known as the *Universal Goddess*: Aset, Isis, Demeter, Ceres, Ishtar, Mary, Rhea, Cybele, Diana, Aphrodite, Astarte, and Venus, for which the month of April is associated.

The holy day essentially begins around mid-April and lasts until 1st May, but the festival of Walpurgis is April 30th. It is also known as *Roodmas* or *Rood Day*. Although the eve of May is widely known as Beltane, the Wiccan spelling is *Bealtaine*. This word is a combination of an Irish Gaelic word for "May", and of the Scottish Gaelic word *Bealtuinn*. It essentially means "Bel-fire," "Fire of Bel" or "Bel's Fire." Of course, *Bel* is a proto-Celtic god of fire,

Witches Celebrating Walpurgis Night,
by Franz Simm.

derived from *Baal*, a fertility god whose cult was prolific to the Phoenicians and Canaanites. The Jews famously honored this god. He was known as the *Bright One*, a god of light and fire. In his capacity as the "universal god of fertility," Baal went by the name *Lord of Rain and Dew*.

As the summer solstice approaches and the sun matures, Bel-fires or bonfires were lit on hilltops to celebrate and further encourage the full return of light, life, and fertility. Only by light can we see the correct path, and so the sun is *the way and the truth and the life*. As in most traditions, even those outside those of the pagan world, jumping over this fire, or crossing between two fires, was seen as a protection ritual.

A fertility festival would not be such without overt phallic and yonic symbols. Janet and Stewart Farrar explain how things like the *"Maypole, nuts and 'the gown of green' were frank symbols of penis, testicles and the covering of a woman by a man."* Here we can see it is not just Christmas time that is associated with these symbols of nature. The couple go on to explain:

> *"Branches and flowers used to be brought back from the woods on May morning to decorate the village's doors and windows, and young people would carry garlands in procession, singing."*

Opposite *Bealtaine* on the *Wheel of the Year* is Samhain (Sowen or Sowin). One signifies the beginning of summer and the other the beginning of winter. Therefore, May Eve is as much a mischief night as November Eve or All Hallows' Eve. This cyclical turning of the yearly wheel is a process during which the barrier between flesh and spirit becomes thinner. As a result, it is a time of

Perhaps one of the most important elements of Bealtaine is the *Love Chase*, when the High Priest in a witch coven pursues the High Priestess as she playfully flees capture for a short time. The High Priest and High Priestess obviously are physical extensions of the God and Goddess archetypes. Some believe that the legend of such a "chase" was extracted from the stories of Ēostre and Lady Godiva, a famous Anglo-Saxon noblewoman. May 1st was also the day when many Romans paid homage to their household gods known as *Lares*.

May comes from the ancient Italian goddess of spring named *Maia Majesta*. In Rome she was associated with Vulcan. Her days of worship were May 1st and May 15th. She is often confused with the Greek *Maia*, the daughter of Atlas and mother of Hermes. Maia was patron of nursing children. The late Old English, from Old French *Mai*, comes from the Latin *Maius* (mensis) relating to the month of the goddess Maia or May. In the northern hemisphere this is the last month of spring.

Maia obviously is close to Mary, which we know comes from the Greek *Mara*, meaning teacher. We also know that the name Mary was a title granted to certain woman raised in a monastic environment, and a surname of *magdal-elder*, for which is derived *Magdalene*. Her name means *teacher*. These teachers had the duty of assisting in the *Mystery Schools*.

The first of this month is known as *May Day* and is preserved in many parts of the world as a time for traditional spring festivals. A popular image associated with these celebrations is a *Maypole* decorated with flowers that are gathered locally.

Festival participants dance around the pole holding long ribbons attached to the very top. The imagery from above would resemble the monad, alchemical gold (circle with a dot), and sperm penetrating the egg. The ribbons are said to resemble sperm.

A similar Roman festival called *Floralia* was held just before the first of May on April 27th or 28th in honor of the goddess *Flora*. The festival began with theatrical performances and sacrifices to the goddess. Revelers wore garlands of fresh flowers, ceremonially released goats and hares, and scattered seeds to promote agricultural bounty. The young girl or woman crowned during this celebration was known as the *May Queen*. In more modern times the first of May has become a day to internationally recognize workers.

June is named after the Roman goddess *Juno* and the month itself is very favorable to marriage because she was queen of heaven and guardian of the *hieros gamos*. In Roman mythology Juno is considered the most important goddess of the State, particularly considering her relationship as the wife of Jupiter. Traditional myth attributes her to love, marriage, fertility, childbirth, and women's health. Juno was originally an ancient Italian goddess, and her Greek equivalent is Hera, the wife and sister of Zeus. Juno gave birth to Mars, for which the month of March is named.

The Old French *Juin* comes from the Latin *Junius* (mensis) relating to the month of June. It is a variant of *Junonius*, which means something sacred to Juno. The Anglo-Saxons called this month "Sear-monat." June is considered the first month of summer in the northern hemisphere. During June is celebrated Litha, the summer solstice, taking place June 20-23.

June is traditionally considered the first month of rose blossoms. As the sixth month of our current calendar, June plays the part of Wednesday (wed-nesday) in that it is the "wedding" of the first half and last half of the year. In pagan myth this *wedding* is a *battle of brothers* and the *changing of the guard* between the Holly King and Oak King. Midsummer signifies abundance and the height of light and warmth. The ancient Greek sying "Panta rhei, ouden menei" is often associated with this time. It means, *"everything flows, nothing is static."* Janet and Stewart Farrar once again provide an excellent description of this holy day and the *Universal Goddess*:

> *"At the Winter Solstice she shows her Life-in-Death aspect; though her Earth-body seems cold and still, yet she gives birth to the new Sun-God and presides over the replacement of Holly King by Oak King with his promise of resurgent life. At the Summer Solstice she shows her Death-in-Life aspect; her Earth-body is exuberantly fecund and sensuous, greeting her Sun-God consort at the zenith of his powers - yet she knows it is a transient zenith, and at the same time she presides over the death of the Oak King and the enthronement of his dark (but necessary, and thus not evil) twin."*

Midsummer Eve, or the Summer Solstice, is also held by Christians as a feast called Saint John's Day or the *Nativity of John the Baptist.* Celebrations of the mid-point involve, from paganism to Christianity, feasting, dancing, music, fires, and boughs (branches) taken from living trees that are then placed over the doors of houses - like a Christmas wreath or Bealtaine decoration.

The importance of Saint John cannot be overstated. As a forerunner to Jesus Christ, John the Baptist was eventually beheaded like Christ was crucified (meaning the *head* of his movement was removed). Both Jesus and John, as they relate to the physical sun through pagan assimilation into Church doctrine, are thus both given the *kiss of death*. John's feast is on June 24 because this is when the sun begins its southernly decline into the tomb of earth, just after reaching its peak as the *Most High*. Freemasons hold John in high honor and the Knights Templar were accused of being in possession of, and worshiping, *his severed head* – perhaps representative of the *doctrine* he taught. Jesus was also the *head of the Church*, which was his *body* (temple); Ephesians 1:22-23 states:

> *"And God placed all things under his feet and appointed him to be head over everything for the church, which is his body, the fullness of him who fills everything in every way."*

Litha marks the pinnacle of solar radiance and dominance. From this point onward the sun begins its *fall*. In tradition, the *Oak King*, or god of the *Waxing Year*, maintains power from Yule to Litha, when he is killed by his brother the *Holly King*, or god of the *Waning Year*. Janet and Stewart explain in detail this transition of power between the two brothers:

> *"At Midsummer, the Oak King, God of the Waxing Year, falls to the Holly King, his twin, the God of the Waning Year, because the blazing peak of summer is also, by its very nature, the beginning of the Holly King's reign, with its inexorable progression to the dark nadir of midwinter, when he in turn will die at the hands of the reborn Oak King. The Oak King's midsummer death has taken many forms in mythology. He was burned alive, or blinded with a mistletoe stake, or crucified on a T-shaped cross…"*

An old depiction of Juno

July was the fifth Roman month, originally called "Quintilis," named in honor of Julius Caesar. The Latin *Julius* (mensis) literally means month of Julius. Anglo-saxons knew it as "Maed-monat," or the "mead month," because this was the season for obtaining honey and making mead. Historically July 4 has been important for two major reasons: (1) the *Declaration of Independence* established a breaking away from the British Crown by the American colonies in 1776; (2) the 1187 battle of Hattin, when Islamic General Saladin defeated a massive Christian army and beheaded most of the Templars captured by his soldiers.

August was the sixth Roman month, originally called "Sextilis," or "Augustus," named after the Roman emperor Augustus. It is typically considered the last month of summer in the northern hemisphere. *Lammas*, which means "loaf mass" in Old English, is another name for *Luchnassad (Lughnasadh)* or *August Eve*, a festival observed as the beginning of the wheat harvest during which communion bread was made. *Luchnassad* generally takes place on the first day of August and marks the mid-point between the summer solstice and autumnal equinox. The name "Luchnassad" is derived from Old Gaelic, a merging of *Lugh*, the Celtic god of light, and *Násad*, which means "to assemble." The *holy day* is a celebration also of *Tailtiu*, the mythical foster mother who cleared the lands of Ireland to make way for the planting of crops. The light of *Lugh* is also a false light since he is known as a *trickster*. It is believed that *Lugh* can be traced to *Lux*, the Latin word for *light* and where we derive *Lucifer*, the "light bringer." The name *Lughnasadh* literally means "the commemoration of Lugh," easily translated as the "remembrance of the light." The polarity between *Lugh* and *Tailtiu* is like the relationship between the Egyptian goddess of the sky, *Nut*, and the god of the Earth, *Geb*. *Lúnasa* is the Irish Gaelic for the month of August and *Lunasda (Lunasdal)* is Scottish Gaelic for *Lammas*. Janet and Stewart Farrar write that in Lughnasadh, *"we have the autumn parallel to the Bealtaine sacrificial mating with the God of the Waxing Year."* Just as Brigid is the goddess of Imbolc-Candlemas, *Crom Cruach* or *Crom Dubh (The Black Bowed One)* was a sacrificial god associated with Lughnasadh. The last sunday in July is still known to some as *Domhnach Chrom Dubh* (Crom Dubh's Sunday). For a more detailed history on this, one should consult The Witches' Bible. Its authors explain how:

> *"The Sacrifice of Crom himself seems to have been enacted in very ancient times by the sacrifice of human substitutes at a phallic stone surrounded by twelve other stones (the sacrificial hero-king's traditional number of companions)."*

Interestingly, the myth of *Crom Dubh* features the classic motifs of the Christ story: Crom was buried in the ground up to his neck for a total of three days before being released once the fruits of harvest were guaranteed. Like Jesus being placed in a tomb for three days, and the reality of his *Bride*, the Crom Dubh story involves both sacrifice and mating; it is the *hieros gamos* between *Mother Earth* and *Father Sky*. The meaning of these stories can be observed by simply watching rays of sunlight penetrate fertile soil.

September was the seventh Roman month. The Anglo-Saxons knew it as "Gerst-monat," or "barley month," since the barley crop was traditionally gathered at this time. In the northern hemisphere it is considered the first month of autumn. The days of September 20-23 were observed as *Mabon*, a time of giving thanks to the goddess for her sustenance. Mabon is the other mid-point (with Ostara) between the solstices. September is thus historically a time of *thanksgiving*, or of feasts held to honor nature. In essence, Mabon is a salute to the waning powers of solar light and warmth, and a festival to *give thanks* not only for the sun, but for all that the *Universal Goddess* has provided.

October was the eighth month in old Rome, stemming from the Latin *octo* meaning "eight." It was known to the Saxons as "Wyn-monat" or "wine month." Samhain, pronounced *sowin*, is a harvest and fertility festival that takes place towards the end of October on the Gregorian calendar. It is observed on the 31st and therefore is known as *November Eve*. This is the final *holy day* before Yule. Samhain was, and remains, a very important festival. It recognizes the final harvest of the year before the earth falls into darkness and the land became barren; the time when Demeter allowed crops to die in mourning for her daughter Persephone.

As the *Wheel* turns past Mabon and approaches *Samhain*, we witness in the northern hemisphere three things: (1) the *Black Horse* of *Revelation* rides upon the Earth to bring famine, as cold and death are cultivated in place of warmth and life, in both humans and crops - another version of the coal-black horse pulling the chariot Hades as he kidnaps Persephone; (2) autumn brings us *fall*, as in the *Fall of Fan* and the *Fall of the Veil*; (3) the *veil* is lifted in an *apocalypse* to *reveal* what is beyond.

Apocalypse, from the Greek *apokalupsis*, means to "uncover" and "reveal." This *revelation* is the lifting of the veil between the *physical* and *spiritual* worlds. The images of skeletons, death-masks, ghosts, monsters, etc., that we associate with *Halloween,* and similar traditions like the *Day(s) of the Dead*, are all *memento mori*. They are not symbols of death worship. Instead, death is venerated alongside life. The seasonal transitions are part of a larger, natural alchemical process. We are the *microcosm* operating within the *macrocosm* of nature, attempting to align and communicate with the *Cosmic Mind*. Such alignment is a balancing act between opposing forces within and without the *self*. Interestingly, it is the rider of the Black Horse who carries the *scales of balance*, like Anubis and Santa Muerte, which act as a tool of *final judgement* in the *end times* (of the year).

The name *Samhain* comes from the Old Irish *Samain,* which means "summer's end," and it is this Irish celebration that laid the foundation for our modern *holy day* of Halloween. Many of the traditions surrounding this date come from the Catholic Irish when they immigrated to the states in the 1840s due to the potato famine. Although a popular festival, it was not widely celebrated inside of the United States until the early 1900s. The ancient Celts, who referred to this time as the "Witches' New Year," celebrated Samhain as a festival marking the beginning of winter when all things die and are purified. The Druids celebrated their New Year on November 1 instead of during the spring, or on the first day of a new calendar as we know it. They believed October 31 was a time when the boundary between the worlds of the *living* and *dead* became blurred. This resulted in spirits crossing over to roam the earthly plane when the veil lifted. While some of the dead were feared, others were welcomed, such as relatives who had died: two of the various reasons that food was be prepared and left out in appeasement of both types of spirits. It is believed that spirits sought the warmth of Samhain fires and to communicate with their living friends and relatives. Divination therefore became popular and essential. The psychic climate of the shifting seasons is primed for spirit communion and divination, and fear of the coming winter demanded an internal calming of subtle and overt fears and anxieties. Without access to grocery stores, our ancestors could only hope and worship for the renewal of the earth. Janet and Stewart Farrar explain the origin of the name *Samhain* and its proper pronunciation:

> "Samhain (pronounced 'sow-in', the 'ow' rhyming with 'cow') is Irish Gaelic for the month of November; Samhain (pronounced 'sav-en', with the 'n' like the 'ni' in 'onion') is Scottish Gaelic for All Hallows, 1st November."

Samhain is also known as the *"dark counterpart of May Eve which greets the summer."* Celebrations involved divination, feasting, fires, sex, and the like, in defiance of the Black Horse.

Divination provided comfort and a sense of hope for the upcoming cold, dark, winter months. It was accompanied by bonfires and ritual sacrifices meant to appease both benevolent and malevolent spirits. These sacrifices, often chosen by lot, were once ritual killings by fire, as detailed in Celtic and Norse myths about the death of certain heroes and royal figures. Literal killings were later replaced by symbolic sacrifices, a transition no doubt that included a medium of animal killings. Mock sacrifices are still conducted today in performances that mimic dramas.

In the old world, malevolent spirits could cause harm to a community and so protective measures were enacted to protect against such mischief. A fire itself was the best defense, since it illuminates the dark and pushes back cold with its warmth. The second defense involved leaving food on a table or outside the home in hopes a mischievous spirit would eat it and be appeased.

Both fire and food had a secondary purpose, too, since fire could illuminate the path into the physical world for benevolent spirits and the food could provide their nourishment.

One of the popular ceremonial foods eaten on Samhain was called *sowens*, a word like *sowin*. Also spelled *sowans*, this is a Scottish dish of fermented oats. It was a very common practice for young women to use divination in hopes of finding their future husbands during this time. One form involved roasting nuts in a fire, and another involved mirror magic. Other women prepared a lovely meal and left it on a table, hoping that the astral body, or *fetch*, of their future husband would have a bite and thus be stuck with her like Persephone in Hades. Janet and Stewart Farrar further explain an interesting Irish tradition of a bread with embedded tokens that acted as a tool for divination:

> *"In Ireland, 'barm bark', a dark brown loaf or cake made with dried fruit, is as much a feature of Hallowe'en as Christmas pudding is of Christmas and retains the seasonal divinatory function by incorporating tokens which the lucky or unlucky eater finds in his slice."*

A woman might present the best version of herself during these divinatory practices to attract the same likeness in a husband. She may dress in her best clothing for the occasion. Ritual clothing was typically worn on Samhain for the same reasons bonfires were kept burning; beautiful clothing was a sign of respect for benevolent ancestral spirits, while dressing in animal skins and masks would not only disguise you from malevolent spirits but perhaps *scare* away all mischief and bad luck.

Carving traditions stem from bonfire rituals, too, when celebrants would take a burning coal and place it inside of a carved-out turnip to help guide their way home. Many believe pumpkins are prominent in this practice, but the Irish, specifically the Celts, did not have pumpkins - as far as we know. These were primarily a North American food. However, they did have beets, turnips, potatoes, and other root vegetables. The first example of a Jack O' Lantern appearing in American literature was an 1837 story by Nathaniel Hawthorne, who wrote <u>The Scarlet Letter</u>. But the carved lantern did not become officially associated with modern Halloween traditions until around the mid-1800s. One of the most famous stories of this *lantern* is the Irish myth of a man nicknamed "Stingy Jack" (stin-jee). The story goes that Stingy Jack invited the Devil to have a drink, but Jack did not want to pay for his drink so he tricked the Devil into turning himself into a coin that could be used for purchase. Once the Devil did this Jack decided to keep the money instead, putting it into his pocket next a silver cross, which prevented the Devil from returning to his original form. Eventually the Devil was freed, but only after he agreed to not bother Jack for one year nor claim his soul upon death. The next year, however, Jack played another trick on the Devil by convincing him to climb up a tree for a piece of fruit. While he was climbing, Jack carved a cross into the bark, which prevented the Devil from descending. Jack again forced the Devil into a compromise, that he would not bother him for an entire decade. Jack died soon after and due to his cunning nature God would not allow him into heaven. The Devil, who was upset having been tricked twice by Jack, kept his word, and did not claim the soul. Due to his rejection from both heaven and hell, Jack was sent into the darkness of night with only a burning coal to light his way. Legend says that he has been roaming the earth ever since with a carved-out turnip lit by this coal. The image conjures a reminder of the Hermit card in Tarot. Jack clearly falls into the *trickster* archetype.

If roaming spirits like Jack could not be appeased rationally with food or scared by animal clothing, there were other methods used for protection. One of these included the carving out of root vegetables and the placing inside of them lights to illuminate not only a pathway home, but the home itself. Carved pumpkins eventually became deterrents of evil spirits and deceitful characters like Jack. But, again, these lit vegetables could also guide benevolent spirits to their home.

If the Jack O' Lantern was a failure in protecting a home, the food left on a table or outside was the next line of defense outside of scary costumes. The practice of leaving food for roaming spirits is still practiced with the modern tradition of giving candy to children dressed in costumes. Going door-to-door asking for food or candy is today called *trick-or-treat*. It is the drama of dressing in spooky costumes and acting out the roaming of the dead in search of food or warmth.

Stories from England tell of poor citizens begging for food and families giving them pastries called *Soul Cakes* in return for promises to pray for their dead relatives. These cakes remind us of *Hot Crossed Buns.* They further share a relationship with the bread, milk, and blessings of Brigid on Imbolc and the blessings of Ishtar to those finding her egg on Ostara. The Irish people also have *barmbrack,* a bread with raisins and a tiny toy or ring baked within; the person receiving the piece of bread with said prize is to receive an additional blessing. When Samhain transitioned into *All Souls Day*, the Church encouraged the leaving of bread and wine for ancestral spirits. This fact relates to the Saxon name "Wyn-monat," or "wine month," for October.

The tradition known as *trick-or-treat* has further roots in a ritual called *going-a-scowling*, where children would visit the home of their neighbor to be given food, ale, and even money. The literal meaning of *trick-or-treat* is a direct threat to the homeowner. Provide the "treat" or the spirits may harm you, your family, or your home. This is the "trick." Modern participants still take these "tricks" literally on "Mischief Night" when property damage and vandalism have become prevalent. Roaming for treats on Halloween while threatening a "trick" is literally a ritual based on a sort of contractual deal made with the *dead*. It is like Santa's *naughty-or-nice list.*

In some Asian countries there is celebrated the *Ghost Festival* or *Hungry Ghost Festival.* It takes place, according to the Chinese calendar, on the fifteenth night of the seventh month. Some place the date on August 30. It recognizes the opening of the gates of hell which allows for ghosts to roam the earth. They are appeased or welcomed with food and drink. In Mesoamerica we find *Día de los Muertos*, which although now celebrated on November 1st after the Spanish conquest of the Aztecs, was before the 1520s AD held in July-August. Offerings of water, fruit, and sugar skulls to the departed are provided, alongside parades, death masks, and music. In Korea this festival is called *baekjung* and for the Japanese Buddhists it is known as *Obon* or *Bon Festival*, which takes place August 13th-15th. It is likewise believed that the dead walk with the living during this time. The Japanese celebrate such a sacred time with a dance called *bon-odori.* Antony Cummins explains in <u>The Dark Side of Japan</u> how the outside of homes would be lit brightly, and people would *"float small lanterns on rivers to help guide the dead back to the spirit realm."* The *Bommatsuri* - Festival of the Dead - in Japan is celebrated in July between the 13th and 15th. One tradition, as detailed by F. Hadland Davis, involves families preparing their homes *"with a quaint minute meal in readiness for the great company of ghosts."* Davis identifies Bommatsuri with the Indian Śrāddha festival, a ritual for Hindus to pay homage to their ancestors in the afterlife – usually performed on the anniversaries of deaths. In ancient Mesopotamia, ghosts were thought to leave the underworld and visit the living during this time, expecting entertainment upon arrival. This usually occurred in Abu, or the month of our August. J. A. Scurlock writes in <u>Ancient Magic and Ritual Power</u>, how *"the acceptance of a conditional offering by a ghost or demon obligated him to go away and leave the patient alone in the same way that the oath formulae on actual contracts bound the swearing party to fulfill his side of the bargain."*

The Hindus also have *Pitru Paksha* on September 10-25. Although the Japanese *setsubun* takes place in February, as a spring cleaning ritual, it still maintains various elements of what we know as Halloween. The use of *fukumame* (fortune beans) to drive out evil spirits is equivalent to the American lighted pumpkin with scary face, its light illuminating the dark, providing warmth from cold, and driving away general misfortune. The Japanese eat *ehomaki* (lucky direction roll), made from seven ingredients, symbolizing the seven lucky gods, in silence, and face the direction at that time considered luckiest. Adults often wear oni-masks and are driven away from the home by children throwing lucky soy beans. A traditional chant is: "Oni wa soto! Fuka wa uchi!," or "Demons out! Happiness In!"

The red devil costumes of Catalonia, with pitchforks and horns, indicate that it is time for *Correfoc* in Catalonia. These red devils are not unlike the Japanese Oni masks and the dragons and fireworks of this festival may remind one of Chinese New Year.

In Haiti we find *Fèt Gede* (Festival of the Dead), celebrated November 1st, likely due to the same Catholic influences that moved the original date of *Día de los Muertos*. Haitians leave fried plantains, sweet corn, coffee, rum, and other treats for the departed.

Switzerland celebrates *Basler Fasnacht* around February-March, a festival of music, dance, and artificial illumination, usually by a series of lanterns, some very large.

The Nepalese have a tradition called *Gai Jatra*, held in August. The name translates to "cow procession" because those having lost loved ones will lead a cow in procession to symbolize the guidance that animal, as a psychopomp, shows the dead in the afterlife. This festival involves parades, dancing, and even comedy.

In Nigeria, the Igbo people honor the dead as protective spirits by wearing masks and costumes, and providing gifts and meals. Held between September-November this tradition is called *Awuru Odo*.

Two other popular Roman festivals were as follows: *Feralia*, a day in late October when the Romans traditionally commemorated the passing of their dead. The other was related to *Pomona*, goddess of fruit and trees. The symbol of Pomona is an apple, and this is strongly related to the modern tradition of *bobbing for apples*, itself a form of divination like the tossing of a *bouquet of flowers* at a wedding. A similar tradition included trying to bite into an apple while it was suspended from a tree branch by wire.

Many Greek and Roman writers documented Druidic practices of barbaric human sacrifice, especially during Samhain, but these writings are likely somewhat biased depending on the intention and belief of the writer at the time. In an effort to damn the pagan world, writers often fabricated stories with dramatic details. Either way, Irish records inform us that some Catholic monks were obsessed with the Druids. Pope Gregory attempted to reconcile pagan traditions with those of the Church, so he made the proclamation: *"They are no longer to sacrifice beasts to the devil, but they may kill them for food to the praise of god."* In other words, all forms of sacrifice are pagan and barbaric, unless they are given in offering to the Papal God.

Pope Gregory is responsible for designating the *Witches' New Year* (November 1) as *All Saints Day*. Samhain (October 31) became *All-Hallows Eve*. Pope Boniface IV later confirmed these dates. The *All Saints Day* celebration is *All-Hallows* or *All-Hallowmas*. In Middle English "Allhollowmas" literally means "All Saints." The night before became known as *Halloween*. By 1000 AD the Church designated November 2 as *All Souls Day* in honor of all those who had died during the year. This is directly related to the original observations of Samhain. Thus, we can find an absolute thread between pagan beliefs and modern Christian or Catholic practices: Janet and Stewart Farrar also describe how Samhain traditions were Christianized from their deeply seeded pagan origins:

> "The aspect of communion with the dead, and with other spirits, was Christianized as All Hallows, moved from its original date of 13th May to 1st November, and extended to the whole Church by Pope Gregory IV in 834."

During the English Reformation in the 16th-century, All Hallows was banned. It was not formally restored as a *holy day* until 1928 by the Church of England.

Black cats are invariably associated with this *holy day* as spooky and unlucky. As a popular superstition rooted in the Middle Ages, it is still common today to associate black cats with bad luck due to their relationship with witches. There is great irony is this fact. The Dark Ages were a period spanning 500-1000 AD, when much knowledge was snuffed out by force and replaced with institutional and state dogmas. Few are willing to admit that Islamic astronomers preserved that science from destruction, details of which had been received from Greece and Mesopotamia sources. The Celtic peoples, and particularly the Druids, where we acquire the origin for most modern Halloween traditions, were widely educated in these *mysteries of nature*. Where the irony comes in is when the Church attacked these wise men and women as heathens and witches. Due to a lack of understanding, and gross negligence, it was actually the Church itself that formulated much of what we think about pertaining to witches and black magic, while they were the ones that snuffed out not only the *mysteries of nature* but knowledge God's Divine Plan.

Janet and Stewart Farrar further describe the importance of *salt* and *harvested crops* relating to Samhain and magic rituals. Since most herds could not be supported during winter, only the breeding-stock were kept alive while others were slaughtered for meat, which was then salted for preservation. It is likely that this practice forms the basis of salt being a "disinfectant against psychic or spiritual evil." It was just as important to gather all the available crops before Samhain out of fear that hobgoblins would roam the fields searching for food. Any abandoned or unharvested crop was said to be contaminated the nocturnal creature, which tormented both farms and households. This creature was known as *Pooka*.

November was the ninth month in old Rome, stemming from the Latin *novem*, meaning "nine." Known as "Blot-monat" by the Saxons, the "blood" month is when sheep and cattle were killed for food and sacrifice. It is typically considered the last month of autumn in the northern hemisphere. The Latin word *novum*, or "new," can be found famously on the reverse side of the Great Seal of the United States and on the one-dollar bill: *novus ordo seclorum*. The translation: "new order of the ages." On the front side of this Great Seal is the Latin phrase *E pluribus unum*, meaning *"out of many, one."* It refers to the colonies, but in Freemasonry it signifies the *creator* and His *creation*.

December was originally the tenth Roman month, and they consecrated it to Saturn. The name comes from the Latin *decem*, meaning "ten." Our word *decimate* comes from the Latin *decimat*, meaning to "take as a tenth." The Anglo-Saxons called it "Midwinter-monat" and "Yule-monat," the "Midwinter" or "Yule" *month*. They collectively referred to December and January, through which traditional Christmas festivities are celebrated, as *giuli*, like the Icelandic *ylir*. It was the time of the *wild hunt* in Germanic tradition, and of the Scandinavian *Feast of Lights* and *Julbock*. Yule is further derived from the Old Nordic *Jól* or Anglo-Saxon *geol*. The festival honors the birth-rebirth of our sun. In such cold and dark places, *evil influences* were everywhere, and with such harsh winters, superstitions and rituals were literally lifesaving.

On December 17 the Roman festival of *Saturnalia* began. It proceeded for eight days through the winter solstice until December 24, or what we call Christmas Eve. These eight days are identical to the "festival of lights" known as *Hanukkah*. During the former, Jews light candles, say blessings, eat specialty fried foods, play games, give gifts and gelt (money), spend time with family, and sing songs. In far north Scandinavian countries what we call *Christmas Eve* and *Christmas* are known as *Julfest*, and the various days preceding are called *raw nights* or *smudging nights*. These nights are "raw" because of the harshness (rawness) of winter. They are nights of "smudging" because the light of our sun has dimmed, and days have gotten shorter; thus man attempts to invoke protections against the cold and dark, i.e., evil spirits. These *raw nights* are better known as the *Twelve Nights of Christmas* and in contemporary times are celebrated in the lead up to the *holy night* and *holy day*.

Long before the *Twelve Nights,* however, are the final nights and weeks of summer that leave us with increasingly colder temperatures and multi-colored leaves. The *changing of the leaves,* which usually takes place near the mid-to-end of October, is an indicator to most that not only is *Autumn* here, but *Old Man Winter* will be just as quickly to arrive.

Here is critical to combine what we have learned thus far about nature and finalize its meaning: Few realize that despite *end-of-the-physical-world* preaching, Biblical books like Revelation actually preserves scientific information about the cycles of nature, rather than stories of physical war and *Armageddon,* or the last battle between good and evil. *Armageddon* precedes what many call the *Day of Judgment.* Such *judgement* is reserved for a time after the *Autumn*, or *Fall of Man*, i.e., the *fall* of the *veil of nature*, which allows for death and suffering - *winter*. In other words, we are talking about *Hell*. It was common throughout history to see *Hell* as a dark, frozen ice-palace rather than a pit of fire. Cold and darkness are, after all, the opposite of the warmth and light of *Heaven*. Those unprepared for the cold and subsequent *death of nature* may die of exposure or starvation, fighting for the last remaining scraps of food, especially if crops fail. All of this is precisely what we find described in Revelation, chapter 6, verse 8:

> *"And I looked, and behold a pale horse: and his name that sat on him was Death, and Hell followed with him. And power was given unto them over the fourth part of the earth, to kill with sword, and with hunger, and with death, and with the beasts of the earth."*

But the *Pale Horse* referred to in this verse as one of the *Four Horseman of the Apocalypse* does indeed have color. Although pale, the final horse is named *khlōrós*, a Greek word meaning green or yellow. The same word was foundational for the French word *chlorophyll*, that green pigment in plants responsible for their absorption of light into energy through the process of photosynthesis. When sunlight becomes scarce and temperatures quickly fall, many plants and trees are unable to produce as much chlorophyll and so their leaves turn yellow, orange, or red depending on the type of tree. The *Apocalypse* is thus a *lifting of the veil of nature* and *Armageddon* is the *final battle between good and evil*, or light and dark, when the latter conquers light for the time being.

This is *Judgement Day*.

~

It was around 1170 that the term *Weihnachten* (holy night) emerged in German language. Folklorist Adolf Spamer, who wrote <u>Christmas in Old and New Times</u>, believed this "night" was a translation of the Catholic *nox sancta*. According to Spamer, the word *jul* had various meanings ranging from "shout of joy" to the Old Nordic *jek* (to speak), and appropriately to the Middle High German word for "invocation of the sun." Traditional rites during the *Twelve Nights* include smudging (incense) to call upon the favor of the gods in vanquishing evil and in bringing back the sun. Midwinter is dreary but it maintains a promise of *life* and a return to *viriditas*, or the greening power of nature. Fielding writes in <u>Strange Superstition and Magical Practices</u> of the origins of Yule:

> *"The original meaning of the word Yule has been traced to the Islandic Hjol, wheel, indicating that at this period the sun wheels or turns the winter solstice."*

The pagan winter goddess is known as the *Old One*, lover of the *Green Man*. Together they are known as *Frau Holle* (or *Hludna*) and *Wotan*. Their plants are mistletoe, winter palms, and ivy, which symbolizes the *Stairs of Heaven*. Ivy is also dedicated to Osiris. In Greece, flaxseed was also called *Osyris*.

Mother's Night is the darkest time of the year as she prepares to birth the sun from her womb. Authors Christian Rätsch and Claudia Müller-Ebeling write in <u>Pagan Christmas: The Plants, Spirits, and Rituals at the Origins of Yuletide</u> how the Germans began their new year with *Moraneht*. This, of course, made it very *"easy for early Christian missionaries to associate that day with the day mother Mary gave birth to the Christ child."*

It is interesting to note that Christmas and Easter – *birth* and *resurrection* – are comparatively contrary in their dating. Christmas remains static due to its relationship with the sun, while Easter falls on different dates due to its reliance on lunar cycles. Many Church fathers did not agree with the concept of a dated birth for their savior, arguing its relationship to pagan practices and gods. Furthermore, the Romans already held January 6th as a celebration of rebirth, or a new year, consecrated to Janus. This was also the date of Dionysian wine miracles and in Egypt it was believed that water drawn from the Nile on this day would turn into wine.

Janet and Stewart Farrar explain how *"Jerome, the greatest scholar of the Christian Fathers, who lived in Bethlehem from 386 till his death in 420, tells us that there was also a groove of Adonis Tammuz there. Now Tammuz, beloved of the Goddess Ishtar, was the supreme model in that part of the world of the Dying and Resurrected God."*

According to David Fideler in <u>Jesus Christ Sun of God</u>, the winter solstice *"represents the rebirth of the cyclical year and the renewal of time. Before the adoption of December 25 as the birthday of Jesus the Spiritual Sun, the Nativity was celebrated on January 6, the day of 'Epiphany' or 'manifestation' of the Lord."*

Spamer refers to the third king of Norway, Hakon the Good (934-960), as being responsible for situating Christmas within the traditional *Jul* celebrations. Christian Rätsch and Claudia Müller-Ebeling explain that Hakon merged the names *jul* and *fest* into the *julfest* (yule feast). Other sources refer to the Roman Emperor Justinian, a convert to Christianity, *"who changed the date of the feast from*

January 6 to December 25 in 542 CE, to honor the birth of Christ."

For the birth of the physical Jesus, Clement of Alexandria (c.150- c.215) favored May 20, while Hippolytus (c.170-c.236) wanted January 2. November 17, November 20, and March 25 were all considered too. March 21 was also a possible date, as it was believed to be the day God created the sun, but more importantly, it related to the worship of Attis, who was born on December 25th of the virgin Nana, his blood and body consumed in like manner to Jesus. Bishop Polycarp (c.69-c.155) attempted to reason that the birth of Jesus and his baptism likely took place on a Wednesday because God created the sun on the fourth day.

Eventually, the date of December 25 was chosen to merge God's son with the Celestial sun. It was already an important date in Rome, being the birthday celebration of Mithra(s) or *Sol Invictus*, the *Unconquered Sun*. December 25 was thus called "Dies Natali Invicti Solis," or the *Birthday of the Unconquered Sun*. Merging God's son and the Celestial sun allowed for easier assimilation of pagan beliefs into the newly forming Church doctrine. As St. Gregory wrote on this subject:

> *"The Bretons have fixed days for feasts and sacrifices; leave their feasts and do not restrain their sacrifices; leave them the joy of their festival, but from the state of paganism draw them gently and progressively into the estate of Christ."*

Late December was thus commemorated with a celebratory feast known as *Christmas*, also known as *Saturnalia*. It was instituted by the Roman emperor Constantine, who issued the *Edict of Milan*, which welcomed Christianity into the empire. Yet it was not until years later that Pope Julius I declared Christmas to be permanently celebrated on December 25, linking the *new holiday* with the *old holy day*. He declared: *"December 25th, Christ born in Bethlehem, Judea."* The Roman Almanac, the Chronographer of 354 (Philocalian Calendar), indicates that the Church of Rome celebrated the first festival in 336 AD. But the Church of Jerusalem did not officially celebrate Christmas until at least the seventh century. In the 16th-century, Pope Gregory created a new calendar to parallel the Julian one, which meant that Christmas was then celebrated thirteen days earlier than before. This is the calendar most followed today, and December 25 is the date that so many observe as the birth of Jesus based on the Gregorian calendar.

~

Countless contemporary traditions can be traced directly back to the Roman festival of *Saturnalia* and the birthday of the *Unconquered Sun*. From the winter solstice to January 6 feasts, we also acquire our traditions for New Year's. The ringing of bells was a common practice on New Year's Eve, not always for the greeting of the New Year, but on the ending of the old, and it was common practice amongst the English to clear the chimney on New Year's Day so only good luck could descend into the household. Traditionally, chimneys are considered portals to other worlds, especially when fires are burned within. Cleansing them helps to open the *pipes of the house*. A similar practice of yearly resolutions has been maintained to the present day in the form of a custom called "wiping the slate clean."

Christmas comes from "Christ" and "Mass," signifying the anointed one (Christ) and a large gathering of people in worship (Mass). The word "mass" can apply to either a Church service or a family gathering for Christmas dinner. The feast itself is also traceable to a pre-Christian custom of people from the Alpine Austrian state of Carinthian. There they would lay a table for the deceased on the *holy night*, an almost identical practice found in traditional Samhain celebrations.

It is from the winter solstice, Yule, that we acquire *Yule Logs*, which were specifically utilized by Scandinavian people to protect against cold and dark (evil), yet another motif aligning with Samhain and its Jack O' Lanterns. After the *Yule Log* and *Yule Buck*, a braided straw mountain goat (*ibex*) like those which pulled Thor's cart, are burned, their ashes become sacred and are used for medicinal purposes. The *Yule Log* itself is burned in honor of the *Yggdrasil* or *World Tree* where Odin was crucified. To receive blessings from above, people would write letters and place them in the fire. When fire burned the paper to ash it was believed the smoke would carry the message upward, which is the same idea behind burning incense.

From chimney sweeps on New Year's Day to the burning of messages on Yule, here we acquire partial foundations for why Santa Clause enters our home through the chimney so he can deliver the presents we requested by written letters. As a supernatural spirit, Santa is appeased by the leaving of cookies and milk, or vegetables and fruits. Another foundation for this tradition comes from the ancient world of shamans. According to American ethnobotanist Jonathan Ott, the shaman would enter a *"winter dwelling, or yurt,"* through a smoke hole. After descending and performing his duties, he ascended once more up a pole. Ott reports: *"He enters and leaves by the chimney, and he has reindeer. Santa Claus also flies, an accomplishment he shares with the shaman."*

Just as Yule Logs and candles protected from cold and dark, other instruments were employed to obtain protection for the home. One tradition began in 1690 when hollow glass balls, usually with a mirror inside, were placed in windows to frighten witches and other malevolent spirits. It was believed a witch would see her reflection and flee. In the eighteenth century these glass ornaments became known as *Witch Balls*. Hair was sometimes placed inside the balls because it was believed that hair could absorb evil spirits, too, not like traditional Native American *dream catchers*.

Contemporary ornaments come from a variety of places. They represent the savior crucified to the *World Tree*, because a beautiful globe or orb has always been a symbol of the *World Soul*. When we place one on a tree, we are essentially hanging Odin and crucifying Christ. But since the *Christmas Tree* can survive winter, these are symbolic reminders of how the *Green Man* will resurrect on both December 25 and in the spring. To hang an ornament on a tree is to provide the spirits of the woods with a gift in hopes of encouraging nature's renewal. The Japanese place straw rope and zigzag cut paper on trees to demarcate sacred spaces. The rope is called *shimenawa* and the paper is called *shide*.

The practice of ornament placement is obvious to some as a symbol of the apple hanging from a tree in the Garden of Eden. Whatever the case, reasoning, or tradition, man was signaling his veneration for nature. Tinsel is placed on the tree for a similar reason. The sparkling material reminds one of snow, precious metal, and of older traditions where valuable coins were placed under a tree as an offering. Orange slices, one of the most iconic Christmas symbols, are placed on trees as decorations that resemble the heavenly sun wheel and its cyclical movements. Red roses cut from paper have also been traditionally placed on trees for the same reason; they are a symbol of the *sacred feminine*, and thus renewal.

Saturnalia was a festival honoring the sun and celebrating the bounties of nature. The most common traditions then included feasting, drinking, dancing, singing, and giving gifts to one another like the Wise Men placed at the feet of baby Jesus. These "gifts" are symbols of the blessings of Brigid, Ishtar, and the *Celestial Sun*. In Sweden, there is the gift-giving ritual called *Julklapp* and in Siberian shamanism there is a similar ritual known as *Potlatch exchange*. The Three Kings derive their title from the Greek *Magoi*, meaning "astrologer," a title that was taken by prophets of Zoroaster and priests of the Persian god Mithra(s). These kings are Caspar, Melchior, and Balthazar. Caspar brings the gift of myrrh; he represents youth, Africa, and healing power. Melchior brings the gift of frankincense; he represents old age, Asia, and Priestly power. Balthazar brings the gift of gold; he represents midlife,

Europe, and Lordship.

One curious practice of Saturnalia was centered on the altering of societal rules. A game was played called the *Lords of Misrule* where slaves wore the *Pileus* (Pilos), a small hat like a skullcap, which denoted freedom and higher status in society. They were allowed to participate in feasts provided by their masters, who themselves played the part of a slave. By "misrule" it is to be understood the *necessary evil* of Saturn and Cronus, from whence we derive certain aspects for the modern Santa Claus. Others call him *Father Christmas* but in the ancient world he was *Green Man*, and his powers would be preserved with the bringing of plants, branches, and small trees indoors during winter.

The modern *Christmas Tree* is largely derived from Germanic tradition, though it can be found in the far east too, not so famously in Japan. It is symbolic not only of nature, but with its star on top, of the pyramid with *Eye of Providence*. According to the book <u>Pagan Christmas</u>, the original "tree" was called *wintermaien*, while *tannenbaum* is simply German for "fir tree." The authors write:

> *"The world tree grows in the cosmic swamp. The sun and moon hang on its branches, and forest people live in it. Later, the original shamanic world trees became holy trees of pagan religious worship."*

In tradition, the Germans made *Christmas Pyramids* decorated with fruits and gifts. The Christian *Paradise Tree* also became popular as it was decorated with pastries and fruits like apples, which, again, relate to the Edenic apple and *Tree of the Knowledge of Good and Evil* in the Garden of Paradise, along with the mystic Kabbalah and *Tree of Life*. One of the earliest written accounts of the modern Christmas Tree comes from the year 1419, from the baker's guild in Freiburg (Breisgau). Other accounts relate that the fir tree was first used in the Alsatian town of Strasbourg in 1604. Since some smaller plants look like the fir tree they are often called "Christmas Tree." Although the tradition is longstanding and was never a Church-sanctioned practice, it was adopted as such to easily assimilate pagans into Christianity. Augustine of Hippo (354-430 AD) informs us of the newly formed Church doctrine:

> *"Do not kill the heathens – just convert them; do not cut their holy trees – consecrate them to Jesus Christ."*

Interestingly, however, we may also read in Jeremiah 10:3-4 an examination of the tree and its decoration. It is interpreted from these verses that venerating nature is akin to erecting false idols:

> *"For the customs of the people are vain: for one cutteth a tree out of the forest, the work of the hands of the workman, with the axe. They deck it with silver and with gold; they fasten it with nails and with hammers, that it move not."*

Ironically, even in the pagan world, this was often the case! Trees have traditionally been protected as sacred and therefore left untouched in the woods by many cultures. Most pagans decorated their trees outside. In the late fourth century, holy trees were forbidden to be decorated by anyone under the Roman emperor Theodosius the Great. In fact, the practice of bringing an entire tree inside was illegal in most places or considered offensive and sacrilege. Branches were more commonly taken from these trees and placed on the ceiling of a home or over doorways. From Germanic peoples to the Japanese, trees were sacred and traditionally protected from desecration.

Trees, pillars, and stalks have always housed the essence of gods like Osiris, and thus they hold great wisdom. Their rings are another symbol of the *Lord of the Ring*, i.e., Saturn and his Roman festival of Saturnalia. With their upright sternness, all trees are also symbols of an erect penis that mimics the rising of the sun each day and year. They extend their branches upward into the heavens and their roots downward into the earth, touching both the macrocosm and microcosm.

This *vegetation veneration* is largely derived from ancient pagan worship of *evergreen trees* while Christmas itself is probably the richest of all *holy days* in botanicals: spices, incense, flowers, trees, nuts, seeds, etc.

Mistletoe and *Holly* both are natural forms of *living vegetation* that were used in the home during winter. Holly is green (male) with red berries (female), the traditional colors of Christmas, and has little prickly ends that symbolize the phallus and *fertility*. The red berries have come to signify the *blood of Christ*, while in classical myth they represent wine and the blood of Dionysus-Bacchus. Red also has the longest wavelength of the colors in the visible spectrum, and so it relates to the infernal office of Saturn. It also represents fire and heat, like those phallic *Christmas Lights* strung on homes. The Romans used Holly during Saturnalia, alongside the parasitic plant Mistletoe with its white berries (sperm), which in Norse myth was responsible for the death of Balder, son of Odin and god of the summer sun. In <u>World Mythology</u> Donna Rosenberg writes:

Children in red and white carrying **mistletoe** and **holly,** from *Mistletoe* by Mili Weber.

> "Balder is one of a number of fertility gods in various mythologies who are killed, go down to the Underworld, and then come back to life. The pattern of life, death, and resurrection reflects the annual, cyclical pattern in nature of birth (spring), maturity (summer), death (autumn and winter), and rebirth (the following spring)."

A wreath is another common symbol of vegetation veneration, relating directly to the dying-god motif and the sun. Wreaths are typically an arrangement of leaves or flowers used for decoration, commonly placed on graves as a sign of respect for the dead. In the case of winter, it is the sun that has died. But like the flaccid penis, it will resurrect (become erect) once more. In the meantime, we are greeted by the *old man of the woods*, otherwise known as the *Wild Man*.

The image of Santa Claus, whose name shares similarity to Saturn and Satan, was formulated in American culture by Macy's department store and Coca-Cola. In 1931 Santa acquired his widespread contemporary image from a marketing campaign. Through an artist named Harold Sundblom, Santa became very round, jolly, and identified with red and white, the colors of Coca-Cola. Nearly a hundred years prior in 1847, Moritz von Schwind had depicted Santa as "Mr. Winter" carrying a Christmas tree into town. By 1964 Santa was *Coca-Cola Santa*. The English call him *Father Christmas* and in Europe he is known as **Sinter Klass** or **Sint Nicolaas**, the latter based on **Saint**

Father Christmas (as the *wild man*) with tree and pipe, from a nineteenth-century postcard.

Nicholas. In the Netherlands, Belgium, Germany, and Austria, Santa was known as **Sankt Nikolaus**, and in Italy his name was **San Nicola.** The Dutch refer to him also by the name **Saint Nicholas.** Each of these names represents the common collective character now known today as **Santa Claus.** *Father Odin* shares striking similarities not only with the Egyptian Osiris, Christian Jesus, and all those divine beings riding white horses, but also with **Saint Nick**, itself a name traditionally referring to Satan (**Old Nick**). *Nik* was also a name given to Wodan as a *Holly King* figure. Christian Rätsch and Claudia Müller-Ebeling relate that Wotan was the *"ghostly rider who led the ghostly army in the storm during the twelve days around New Year's Day."* He is embodied in the myth of *Rübezahl*, a spirit from the mountains between historic Bohemia and Silesia. Akin to the *wild man of the woods*, this character is a *Great Hunter* and is pictured smoking a pipe like *Father Christmas.*

Santa could also be called *Mr. Winter, Father Time*, or *Father Christmas*. He appears from the woods bringing gifts of a botanical nature: oranges, apples, nuts, seeds, etc. The white horse is also ridden by Father Christmas, according to shamans in Tibet. They even see the elusive *Yeti* to be a forest shaman or *wild man*. Their sacred trees are covered in prayer flags meant to spread prayer of protection through the wind. The Slavic war god St. Veit likewise rides a white horse.

Saint Nicholas was also known as **Nikolaos of Myra** (also **Nicholas**), a fourth-century Christian saint and Greek Bishop, who lived in what is now Turkey around the time when Christmas was first being celebrated. Because of the miracles he supposedly performed, Nikolaos took on the title "Nikolaos the Wonderworker." His portfolio included giving gifts secretly and putting coins in shoes. Wet socks placed over the fireplace to dry became a popular symbol of this gifting process in association with the coins that were placed inside of shoes. Dutch children would put their shoes in front of the fireplace with a small gift for Santa's white horse, hoping to receive their own gifts in return. These became *Christmas Stockings*. Christian Rätsch and Claudia Müller-Ebeling explain further:

> "*In the Netherlands, according to newspaper sources, the eve of December 6 is 'the only national folk feast' in honor of Sinterklass, patron of sailors and merchants. In the second or third week of November, he comes in his boat from Spain to the Netherlands, accompanied by his black servants, the zwarte pieten, who dance on the boat and make jokes.*"

A parallel to Saint Nicholas of Myra can be found in the fourth-century **Nicholas of Sion**, Bishop of Pinora, who founded a monastery in Myra. He was also said to perform miracles and was the patron Saint of children, associated with the traditional Holy Day of *Childermas*, the day of innocent children.

Traditionally *Sinterklass* brings treats such as nuts, oranges, and *spekulator* (spiced biscuits) to the youth. Most of his gifts, as with nearly all Christmas symbols, related to love, fortune, and fertility. The pinecone plays an important role in Christmas due to its abundance of seeds and its ability to be preserved for long periods of time. These qualities give the pinecone, like Poppy seeds, the meaning of *eternal life*. From the bounty of a forest to the *Holy Bread* consumed in Roman times, feasting was one of the most important rituals for every *holy day*, and especially in honor of the *wild man of the woods*. The feast of Saint Nicholas was held in early December, usually on the 6th. One month later, January 6, was held as the day of Dionysian wine miracles; the day of Janus; and the Feast of Epiphany, which means *Little Christmas* or *Three Kings Day*, a celebration of God incarnated as Jesus Christ. Sinter Klass was depicted with a large hat like the Pope's *miter*, which came from Mithraism, fish worship, and the Age of Pisces. Fish symbolism also relates to the worship of the Babylonian Oannes and the Sumerian Uan. An interesting observation, and indirect correlation to Santa and his large bag of gifts, may be made of this god. In Central American Olmec carvings, and those from Mesopotamia, there are depicted humans, gods, and divine emissaries holding a container called *banduddû*, which designates its possessor as having some form of special knowledge. These sacred teachings were given to mankind as gifts from the gods. Likewise, Santa, Ishtar, Brigid, and Jesus all give gifts of some form. Some gives blessings and others provide the gift of *eternal life*.

The robes of Sinter Klass were gold, red, and white, like the red Maltese crosses and white robes worn by the Knights Templar, the Papacy, and the Essene community of which Jesus was affiliated. Other depictions of Santa show him in a sleigh with blue and white robes. The Central American god Quetzalcoatl was also said to have worn white robes with red.

From South and Central America to Mesopotamia there are images of beings holding strange bags called *banduddû*, which means *container*. These bags signify that the possessor holds some form of specialized knowledge or wisdom. Winged figures called the *Apkallu* were a group of emissaries sent by the creator god and entrusted with bringing civilization to man after the great deluge. The *Apkallu* also wear an object on the wrist depicting a wheel with spokes. The same images can also be found at Tiahuanaco in Bolivia. In one depiction an *Apkallu* can be seen holding a container and picking fruit from a tree, like Eden. Another image shows a man wearing fish garb, often associated with Oannes. He too is holding a strange bag. The beings with wings on their backs and the heads of birds are depicted as giving fruit from the *Tree of Knowledge* to certain humans, who then become *enlightened*. The same bag can be found depicted at Göbekli Tepe, Turkey, and on an Olmec relief from La Venta, Mexico.

Many relate Santa, and his clothing, reindeer, and gifts to Shamanism, and specifically to Arctic Shamanism. The tradition goes that these intellectual and spiritual figures of the Arctic, known as *angakkuq*, would distribute special mushrooms on the winter solstice. Since mushrooms, and particularly the red and white Amanita Muscaria (*fly agaric*), are typically found underneath trees, the idea for wrapped presents under a pine tree formed. The clothing of these medicine men, red and white, mimicked the Amanita. The *red* relates to the universal female essence: menstrual blood, love, sex, passion, and magic. It is also the color of thunder and of the Germanic god Donar and Norse god Thor. The white symbolizes snow, light, spirit, purity, and semen, making it *phallic* in parallel to the *yonic* qualities of red. Alchemists sometimes refer to the substance of mercury as that which is red and white. This is appropriate seeing that alchemy is a transformative spiritual process, as is the proper ritualistic taking of certain kinds of mushrooms. Many speculate that the hallucinations induced through these mushrooms allowed for the abundance of reindeer nearby to appear as if they were flying. After taking these mushrooms, as with DMT, it was commonplace to see elves, just like the ones assisting Santa at the North Pole. Furthermore, to dry the mushroom, shamans placed

Fly Agaric mushroom being carried by a chimney sweep from a postcard in 1900.

them on tree branches, thus creating ornaments. The mushroom cap itself also mimics the *Pileus* worn during Saturnalia. It is said that from the lighting and thunder generated from Thor's hammer thunderstones would fall upon the ground and initiate the sprouting of *fly agaric mushrooms*. In legend, this mushroom is called "raven's bread" due to the bird's association with both shamans and the god Odin, who was accompanied by his famous ravens *Huginn* and *Muninn*. The mushroom itself is phallic and said to resemble the helmets worn by Viking warriors. According to the book Pagan Christmas, the Greek Zeus was considered the father of mushrooms.

The *fly agaric* is seen as a lucky symbol while the mushroom itself acts as a gateway to the underworld. Descending into the spirit realm and acquiring gifts of wisdom can be equated with Santa coming down a chimney with presents. Just as Jonathan Ott says a shaman would enter a *"winter dwelling, or yurt,"* through a smoke hole, it is Santa Claus who comes down from the North Pole.

In his relationship with Saturn-Cronus, and thus *time*, Santa Claus is a derivative not only of the *Wild Man*, but of *Father Time* and his white beard. The Norse god Odin is also heavily borrowed from for traditional Christmas symbolism. Perhaps the most significant contribution of these myths is that Odin lives in the North (or the North Pole) and has a white beard. Odin also rides an eight-legged horse named *Sleipnir*, derived from Old Norse to mean "slippy" or "sliding." Here we have a possible origin for *Santa's eight reindeer* and *Santa's Sleigh*, since a sled is used for "sliding." This sleigh and the winter flight of Father Christmas is equated by some to the *fly agaric mushroom* and *shamanistic hallucinations*. It has also been suggested that the origin of Santa's transportation is a white horse, much like the one ridden by Wodan.

~

In Germanic folklore we find the oppositional force of Santa Claus known as *Krampus*. He is increasingly popular today, as he was in various regions of Europe historically. If not by Krampus, you may know him by the name *Ruprecht*. This character is called the "helper" and although he seems to play the part of an elf in that regard, Ruprecht instead carries a sack and hazelwood rod to punish poorly behaved children. The rod itself is a symbol of life affirmation or fertility. It plays a similar role to the broomsticks of both shamans and witches that are used to ritually cleanse houses throughout the year. The ugliness of Krampus provides a warning like the one implied by his rod, i.e., divine punishments exist for the wicked. His ugliness may also be used to scare away other evils, as is the case of those scary masks used for Halloween.

Instead of rewarding children with presents he punishes those who misbehaved during the year with beatings. His name comes from the German *krampen*, which means "claw," and these are one tool he uses to injure children. Santa's *naughty-or-nice list* obviously takes on a role in this story. Other legends say Krampus will deposit coal into your shoe or sock if you are deserving of punishment. There is an occult meaning to be extracted here considering that one version of Santa gives gold

Krampus punishing children.

and the other coal. This, along with the list of the *naughty* and *nice*, urges children to act with virtue and to obey their parents. Those children choosing to act with virtue are rewarded with gold like that found in the streets of heaven while those acting as animals are punished by coal that burns like the supposed fires of hell. The *list* designating reward or punishment is thus representative of the idea of hell or heaven in general, and of the alchemical elements of lead or gold. In fairy legend, the *little people* would often give coal as a gift, and only if one was accepting of these lumps would they turn into gold. In some myths, Krampus is the son of Hel, god or goddess of the underworld. <u>Encyclopedia Britannica</u> provides a concise overview of this monster who, like Satan, plays the role of *necessary evil* or *adversary*:

Krampus on an Austrian postcard, 1910.

"Krampus, in central European popular legend, a half-goat, half-demon monster that punishes misbehaving children at Christmastime. He is the devilish companion of St. Nicholas. Krampus is believed to have originated in Germany, and his name derives from the German word Krampen, which means 'claw.' Krampus was thought to have been part of pagan rituals for the winter solstice According to legend, he is the son of Hel, the Norse god of the underworld. With the spread of Christianity, Krampus became associated with Christmas—despite efforts by the Catholic Church to ban him. The creature and St. Nicholas are said to arrive on the evening of December 5 (Krampusnacht; 'Krampus Night'). While St. Nicholas rewards nice children by leaving presents, Krampus

beats those who are naughty with branches and sticks. In some cases, he is said to eat them or take them to hell. On December 6, St. Nicholas Day, children awaken to find their gifts or nurse their injuries."

Due to the relationship Santa and Krampus share, it is obvious that the *naughty-or-nice list*, like *trick-or-treat*, is really a sort of *threat* and *contractual agreement*. The Santa Claus is really the Santa Clause: an article, stipulation, or proviso in a treaty, bill, or contract. The Greeks referred to Santa as Nicholas. The Germans called him Nikolaus but his general European name is Sinter Klass (or Klaus).

The word *Klaus* is also like the Latin spelling of *claus* and the French *clause*. Determining if someone is *naughty* or *nice* during end year celebrations is paralleled to the idea of *final judgement* or the *weighing of souls* in the *end times* or *end days*.

Drunkenness during the Saturnalia celebration, by John Reinhard Weguelin, 1884.

As with Halloween, when spirits arrive at the home requesting a *treat* and threatening, if they don't receive the offering, a *trick*, the evil Finnish spirts called *nuuttipukki* would go door to door during Yule demanding gifts and leftovers from family feasts. When the nuuttipukki were merged with Santa there developed another Krampus-character called *Joulupukki*, which *means "Yule Goat"* or *"Christmas Goat."* On January 13, St. Knut's Day (*nuutinpäivä*), Joulupukki arrives to deal with naughty children by whipping them with a branch. His red robes, sleigh, and non-flying reindeer are obvious in nature. This is also the date when sweets are finished and in Sweden Knut's day signifies the taking down of Christmas trees - *julgransplundring* which means "Christmas Tree Plundering."

The modern *Elf on the Shelf* toy is an extension of the contractual clause in the form of *The Krampus Box*. This box is filled with

Belsnickel   **Joulupukki**

slips of paper and pictures of family children. Misbehaving children have their names written on the paper or photo and it remains in the box until the next full sunrise, which, considering northern weather in Krampus' region of the world, may be weeks. If a child's name was still within the box on Krampusnacht (December 5), then Krampus would arrive and drag the kids to hell in his sack.

In Southwest Germany there is another character named *Belsnickel*, who appears before children just prior to Christmas and asks them if they have behaved during the year. After throwing candies, cakes, and nuts on the floor Belsnickel, also named *Kriskinkle*, waits to see which children have the self-restraint to control their greed and gluttony. Those unable to do so would be stuck with a whip or stick.

The Italian Christmas witch *Befana* played both roles of gift giver and punisher. On the night before the Christian Epiphany, *Befana* would come down the chimney and deliver gifts into children's boots. Misbehaving children received ashes, coal, or garlic, instead of the customary sweets and candies Janet and Stewart Farrar detail an interesting myth from Italy, where Santa's place is *"taken by a witch, and a lady witch at that. She is called Befana (Epiphany), and she flies around on Twelfth Night on her broomstick, bringing gifts for children down the chimneys."* In old German tradition, the fifth of January was the holy night of *Berchta*, a goddess of winter witchcraft. She is also associated with *Eisenberta*, *Frau Bert*, *Frau Holle*, *Mother Goose*, and *Perchta*, according to Christian Rätsch and Claudia Müller-Ebeling. She belongs to the group of *ghost riders* from the *wild hunt* that takes place during the darkest days of each year. This "hunt" is nothing more than winter storms personified like thunder is said to be the sound of God bowling. In Athens, Yule was celebrated as *Lenaea*, a death and rebirth festival for the Wild Women who killed Dionysus.

In Iceland this witch is *Grýla*, which means "growler," the mother of a family of monsters, who kidnap misbehaving children and turn them into stew. She has 13 large adult sons called the *13 Yule Lads*. Other folklore preserve her troll-like husband and a giant man-eating Yule Cat known to target anybody who doesn't have on new clothes—making a new pair of socks necessary, among other items, though the latter relates to stockings. In essence, remember to wear your winter clothes so you do not freeze. One poem from Iceland describers her as such: *"Down comes Grýla from the outer fields / With forty tails / A bag on her back, a sword/knife in her hand, / Coming to carve out the stomachs of the children / Who cry for meat during Lent."*

The Earth Mother's mourning of her dead sun-son is still reenacted in *Witch Covens* by the High Priest and High Priestess, much like the *Love Chase* of Bealtaine. In the ritual, the High Priestess veils herself in sorrow, mimicking the veil worn by Isis while in search of her lost Osiris. The High Priestess moves around the dead High Priest seven times to mimic the seven circles made by Isis around Osiris. These circles are highly significant to say the least, and in ritual represent the search for the missing pieces of Osiris. The ritual described in <u>A Witches' Bible</u> has the High Priestess state the following:

> *"Now, at the depth of winter, is the waning of the year accomplished, and the reign of the Holly King is ended. The Sun is reborn, and the waxing of the year begins. The Oak King must slay his brother the Holly King and rule over my land until the height of summer, when his brother shall rise again."*

In closing, it is perfectly understandable why institutional religions would shun pagan practices that directly honor nature. To Christians, for example, they may see that idols of nature merely are the substance rather than essence of God. To pagans, on the other hand, they may believe these idols to literally embody the essence of *source*.

Perhaps no better explanation could be given of these various traditions than what Joseph Campbell describes as the celebration of Attis in Phrygia:

> "In Phrygia, for example, in honor of the crucified and resurrected savior Attis, a pine tree was cut on the twenty-second of March, and brought into the sanctuary of the mother-goddess, Cybele. There it was swathed like a corpse with woolen bands and decked with wreaths of violets. The effigy of a young man was tied to the middle of the stem. Next day took place a ceremonial lament and blowing of trumpets. The twenty-fourth of March was known as the Day of Blood: the high priest drew blood from his arms, which he presented as an offering; the lesser clergy whirled in a dervish-dance, to the sound of drums, horns, flutes, and cymbals, until, rapt in ecstasy, they gashed their bodies with knives to bespatter the altar and tree with their blood; and the novices, in imitation of the god whose death and resurrection they were celebrating, castrated themselves and swooned."

Unicorns, Turkeys, Harvest Festivals & Giving Thanks

Here we will examine the traditional *giving of thanks* observed after a harvest, a tradition that extends, likely, to the first people who practiced agriculture. Providing sacrifices of flowers, fruits, animals, etc., however, to "thank" the gods, is a practice that extends far beyond the first agricultural people. In the United States of America there is common belief that *Thanksgiving* is either a strict US holiday, as it is officially, or that its celebration is also the praising of Native genocide. These are typically religious and politically motivated ideologies.

Celebration of mass on September 8, 1565, at St. Augustine, from the State Archives of Florida/Florida Memory.

Debates extend across professions and State line with arguments that this first *holiday* was held in 1621 at Plymouth Rock, while others suggest the first *feast* took place in 1565 at St. Augustine, or forty miles north in 1564 near the current city of Jacksonville. Others further argue that the first *feast* took place in Texas. Each State wants to obtain and maintain historical supremacy with such an important historical event. We will first examine this tradition in the United States of America and then extend our study to the origins of such traditions worldwide.

Spanish admiral Don Pedro Menéndez de Aviles arrived at St. Augustine on September 8, 1565, and was greeted with trumpets and artillery. The captain of his fleet, Father Francisco Lopez, then claimed Florida for his country and God. The local Timucua indigenous tribe likely observed about eight hundred colonists gathering around an altar as Father Lopez presided over a Catholic mass of *giving thanks* for their safe arrival at the new settlement of St. Augustine. The Timucua were even invited by the admiral to join the colonists for their giving of thanks.

Some forty miles north of St. Augustine is the modern city of Jacksonville, where some contend was held the first *giving of thanks*. This *Thanksgiving* is dated June 1564, a year earlier than the St. Augustine meal, and it took place when a feast was held between the French Huguenots and indigenous Timucuans to celebrate the establishment of Fort Caroline along the St. John's River.

The *Texas Society of the Daughters of the American Colonists* has placed their own historical marker near Canyon, Texas. It says that prior to the 1560s, it was here where Father Juan de Padilla held a *Thanksgiving* service in May of 1541 for an estimated 1,500 Spanish conquistadors under the command of Francisco Vasquez de Coronado.

The first harvest at Plymouth Rock was held in 1621 and it was during this time that Governor William Bradford (1590-1657) dedicated the occasion as a special day of prayers and *giving thanks*. That autumn, Plymouth colonists and the local Wampanoag Indian tribe feasted for three days to celebrate a successful harvest. This one instance of giving thanks in 1621 was probably the last official instance of anyone celebrating what most would consider a modern *Thanksgiving* for many years to come. Other states such as Virginia and Maine have also submitted claims of hosting the first *Thanksgiving*. On technical grounds one would find it hard to justify any of these dates as the first official United States *Thanksgiving* considering that the country was not founded for over a century and a half, or more, later.

It wasn't until 1777 that the first nationwide celebration of *giving thanks* was observed. But this day was not to celebrate the harvest or give thanks to a god or goddess. It was to celebrate the defeat of the British during the battles of Saratoga on September 19th and October 17th of that same year. The thanks for these victories were carried on with a celebration, which likely included a *feast of thanks*. One day after the initial battle victory on September 20th begins the Mabon, and October 17th is a week before the harvest festival known as Samhain. So here we find a connection, however unintentional it may have been, to the original harvest festival dates.

So, the first official day of *Thanksgiving* in the United States was celebrated by the 13 colonies to honor the victories at the battles of Saratoga. Congress, in response to the surrender of British General Burgoyne, declared December 18th, 1777, as a national day of *"solemn Thanksgiving and praise,"* in recognition of the military successes. It was the Nation's first official observance of a holiday with the name *Thanksgiving* and is, by this dating, closely related Yule.

The very first *National Day of Thanksgiving* was held in 1789 when President George Washington proclaimed Thursday, November 26th, to be *"a day of public thanksgiving and prayer,"* to especially give thanks for the opportunity to form a new nation, and to establish a revolutionary Constitution. Yet, even after a National Day of Thanksgiving was declared in 1789, it was still not an annual celebration. On October 3rd, 1863, Abraham Lincoln declared a *"General Blessing"* holiday to be on the last Thursday in November. This officially became the first day of *giving thanks* as we know it as a holiday. When President Franklin D. Roosevelt wanted to make this a federal holiday, he moved up the date of celebration so that it would allow for a longer Christmas shopping season and encourage economic growth. Thus, is the birth of our modern *Thanksgiving* celebration in the United States, which ties into the base commercialized themes of most Sabbats such as Samhain (Halloween), Yule (Christmas), and Ostara (Easter). The close associations our modern *holidays* have with ancient *holy days,* coincidence or not, is not dissimilar from the official transitions order by the Church to assimilate pagan traditions with newly formed Christian doctrine, albeit for different reasons.

~

There are several Native American harvest festivals that include dancing, singing, rituals and prayers. One is the *Green Corn Festival* celebrated in the summer by the Cherokee, Seminole, and Iroquois, during the first full moon after the corn crops have matured. This is like the new *Moon Ceremony* celebrated on the first new moon of October with feasts *giving thanks* for the harvest. It is a Cherokee tradition that the world was created in the autumn, which relates directly to the Druidic tradition of November 1 as the true beginning of a year.

Historically any *giving of thanks* was related to the sun and earth. After gathering crops, a feast would be held to *give thanks* to the land (Universal Goddess), spirits, and sun (God). These feasts were also meant to encourage new growth during the next season. After a harvest was collected, ten percent was saved in case of future failures.

As with *vegetation veneration* during the winter months, and since the essence of God existed in crops, dolls called *corn dolly* would be made from the last stalks not harvested. During the next planting season this doll, which preserved the *crop's spirit,* would then be placed back in the ground to encourage new seeds to sprout. In other cases, people would simply exert physical force over the final few stalks by striking them, and the spirit, into the ground.

The corn dolly of the Phrygians, who lived in central Asia Minor, was comprised of thick bundles of grain stalks formed into a large column. Anyone wandering into the area of this corn-column was sacrificed under the belief that the spirit of harvest had lured the person to that spot. The poor soul would then be trapped and beheaded, with their blood thought to purify the field. We have seen many references to this throughout our study, including the rituals of *Lupercalia.*

Sometimes the *dolly* was made into an old woman, or crone, one of the aspects of the *Triple Goddess*, which includes *mother* and *maiden*.

There is an English legend of this sort told of a nature spirit existing in crops. He is known as *John Barleycorn,* or elsewhere as the *Green Man*. John Barleycorn signifies the significance of barely and corn crops. This story is metaphoric of cycles of birth, suffering, death, and rebirth. John suffers and dies so that bread, the body of Christ, can be made. Alcohol is also derived from barley, an association we find with wine and blood of Christ. These motifs are also found in the *Killing of the King* ritual.

Despite the origins of any *giving of thanks*, the associated symbolic elements always include a cornucopia of abundance, be that of food, light, or life. The *cornucopia* is strongly associated with the harvest festival as it symbolizes *abundance* and *prosperity*, all of which are associated with the basis of any *Thanksgiving* festival, but especially of those rooted in harvests. It literally means *Horn of Plenty*. The horn could be that of a goat, which the infant Zeus drank from. Sometimes it is said that a goat named *Amalthea* nursed Zeus and other times a nymph of the same name fed him the milk of goats she fostered. The *cornucopia* is most frequently associated with the goddess of the harvest, Demeter, but is also associated with other gods, including Pluto. It is from the Greek story of Persephone that the ancients explained the changing of the seasons and preserved them. We likewise preserve these traditions and stories in practice, tradition, and myth today.

In Mesopotamian myth we find the story of Tammuz and Ishtar. Tammuz, the young lover or Ishtar, dies and takes leave in the underworld. Ishtar follows him and attempts to assist in his resurrection by removing him from the hands of the infernal powers. Successful, Tammuz returns to life and brings about rejuvenation of land. Ishtar and Tammuz return the strength of day from the darkness of winter, and all vegetation, ceased upon Ishtar descending into death, is renewed.

The Roman goddess of luck and fortune, *Fortuna*, was often depicted carrying a cornucopia and it thus became linked with her nature. Lady Fortuna expressed how life was subject to the whim of chance, good or ill. In ancient Rome, the goddess *Fortuna* was followed by anyone seeking good fortune and by others looking to avoid ill fortune. It was for this reason the goddess *Fortuna* has acquired our modern interpretation as *Lady Luck*. An abundant harvest is fortunate and something to be thankful for.

The *cornucopia* plays another significant role in the stories of Unicorns, once thought to exist while now being considered only fictional characters. There are, in fact, 17th-century newspaper advertisements posted in London giving notice of elixirs being sold that contained "true Unicorn Horn." This is not *snake-oil*, but perhaps *unicorn-oil*. This potion was thought by many to relieve ulcers, fainting episodes, melancholy, scurvy, epilepsy, stomach trouble, lymph node swelling due to tuberculosis, and to protect the body from poison. Nancy Hathaway documents in her book The Unicorn of such a story. She writes of how the English King James I was determined to figure out if a purchased unicorn horn was really from the mystical creature:

Fortuna carrying the cornucopia, by Jean Francois Armand Felix Bernard.

> *"James summoned a favorite servant and instructed him to drink a draught of poison to which powdered unicorn horn had been added. The servant did so, and James could not have been more unpleasantly surprised when the servant promptly expired."*

There are eight references in the Bible to such a creature, found here in the book of Numbers 24:8 and written in one variation as:

> *"God brought him forth out of Egypt; he hath as it were the strength of an unicorn: he shall eat up the nations his enemies, and shall break their bones, and pierce them through with his arrows."*

The verses of Psalm 22:21, Psalm 29:6, and Psalm 92:10, all make reference to the essence of this creature:

> *"Save me from the lion's mouth: for thou hast heard me from the horns of the unicorns."*

> *"He makes Lebanon leap like a calf, Sirion like a young wild ox."*

> *"But my horn shalt Thou exalt like the horn of a unicorn; I shall be anointed with fresh oil."*

If this is of interest, the other verses are Numbers 24:8, Deuteronomy 33:17, Job 39:9-12, and Isaiah 34:7. Translation may vary, not only in English but from the original source.

The Roman naturalist Pliny the Elder writes in his encyclopedic <u>Natural History</u> also of this animal:

> *"The unicorn is the fiercest animal, and it is said that it is impossible to capture one alive. It has the body of a horse, the head of a stag, the feet of an elephant, the tail of a board, and a single black horn three feet long in the middle of its forehead. Its cry is a deep bellow."*

Hunting the Unicorn,
from the <u>Rochester Bestiary</u>,
British Library

Most historians relate this description to the specifics of an Indian rhinoceros, which many believe is the historical foundation for the *unicorn*. This creature, however, does not have a true horn, only hair tissues that have grown together.

In the 7th-century Isidore of Seville wrote of how unicorns were *"very strong"* and how the creature *"pierces anything it attacks. It fights with elephants and kills them by wounding them in the belly."* Far too strong to be captured by hunters, *"except by a trick,"* the only manner one could use in meeting these ends was to use a virgin girl. She is to be seated with exposed breasts in the woods. It is said the unicorn will become less fierce at her appearance and lay its head down on her bosom. Perhaps this was merely a way to trick young maidens into exposing themselves?

There is a marine version of this creature known as a narwhal, which is a medium-sized whale.

The horn here is most significant, however, be it of the unicorn, a symbol of purity, or the cornucopia of fortune and abundance. These things are the cornerstone of harvest festivals, *giving thanks*, *Thanksgiving*, corn dollies and all other related stories, legends, myths, and traditions. Another is the turkey. One of the most common and recognized symbols of *Thanksgiving* in the United States of America is the turkey. Although some of the previously mentioned colonists likely did not eat turkey, the word here refers to *fowl* in general, and it is a staple food and symbol of the *holy festival* made holiday. Turkeys represent fertility and motherhood. The bird is known as the "Earth Eagle" because its life is spent so near the ground. Toltecs

Maiden and the Unicorn, by Domenico Zampieri "Domenichino", 1602.

called it the "jeweled fowl" and reserved it for food only during festivals or certain rituals. When it was eaten the entire bird was used; meat was eaten, feathers were used for ornamentations, and bones were utilized in the making of musical instruments. The Pueblo never ate the bird but kept its feathers. These would be fashioned into prayer sticks and given to families of deceased persons, as the turkey itself was often buried with the dead. As a symbol of the United States of America, the eagle was truly chosen because of its relationship to the phoenix bird. However, it was not the immediate choice of each founding father. Benjamin Franklin instead preferred the turkey to an eagle, which he called a bird of *"bad moral character."*

Saint Patrick's Day

Saint Patrick's Day gets a special note; hence it was not included in the month of March section. Celebrated with parades since before the founding of the United States, Saint Patrick's Day is held every year on March 17. Most people wear green, drink green-dyed beverages, and eat green-dyed foods to honor Irish culture. Famously, it was Patrick who drove all the snakes from the Emerald Isle, though there were no real snakes in Ireland. The "snake" is a metaphor relating to non-Christian communities such as the Druids, who were known for working with the energy currents of the earth. These energy currents are sometimes called *telluric,* and they have traditionally been symbolized by a snake.

The real Saint Patrick was named Maewyn Succat and he wore robes of blue, just like the original Santa Clause, instead of green. He later wore green robes. This is highly ironic considering that the pagan communities were worshiping, in one manner or another, the *green man*. As with Christmas plants, Saint Patrick's Day would not be the same without three-leaf clovers. For the church they represented the Holy

Saint Patrick wore *green man* robes and was accompanied by a solar corona.

Trinity, but for others they signified the renewal of spring. Perhaps a four-leaf clover is "lucky" because each leaf would represent one of the seasons. As for the Leprechaun, or *lobaircin,* which means "small-bodied fellow," we find a relationship with countless other earthen creatures such as fairies, elves, and gnomes. All these characters tend to dwell near or under the earth, often protecting treasures, like the notion of a pot of gold at the end of a rainbow.

The Eight Sabbats, Seven Days of the Week & the Esbat

Of the eight yearly Sabbats, including the two solstices and equinoxes, Fielding writes in Strange Superstations and Magic Practices:

"The Druids observed four feasts of considerable importance each year, those of May-eve, Midsummer eve, the eve of the 1st of November, and the eve of the 10th of March. Dancing around the Maypole is believed to have been carried down from the first mentioned feast, which included the druidical custom of dancing on the green to the song of the cuckoo."

"The legendary lore of old, arising out of supernatural beliefs that live eternal in the primitive subconscious mind, find wide popular expression in carrying on the traditions of St. Valentine's Day, Halloween, and, particularly the old world, May Day and Beltane, not to dwell unduly upon the ancient fold practices associated with Christmas, New Year's and other high days in the ceremonial calendar."

The principal festivals known as the "Sabbat of Witches" were celebrated four times each year: in spring, autumn, winter, and summer. They are not to be confused with the *Witches' Sabbath*, a largely misunderstood and superstitious belief in an assembly of witches, devils, and sorcerers for orgies and certain other diabolic rites.

The *Esbat* is differentiated from the *Sabbat* by being more business related, whereas the latter was centered on religious ritual. For some witches this was a meeting time for business to be conducted that only occasionally required magical assistance. Feasts and dancing called close to both forms of festivities. The word *esbat* is derived from the Old French *esbahir*, meaning to "enjoy oneself." It is similar to *Sabbat*, which is derived from the Hebrew *Shabbath*, meaning "to rest," or according to David Conway has been derived from the Thracian god Sabazius. In Latin it is *sabbatum*.

There are likely many other origins for the *esbat* and the *Sabbat*. Dancing in general, the mimicking of the rotation of planetary spheres by *whirling dervishes*, was an important part of fertility rights, as demonstrated by the *Maypole*. Each Sabbat was meant to promote fertility, and productivity relating to fertilization of crops, humans, and animals.

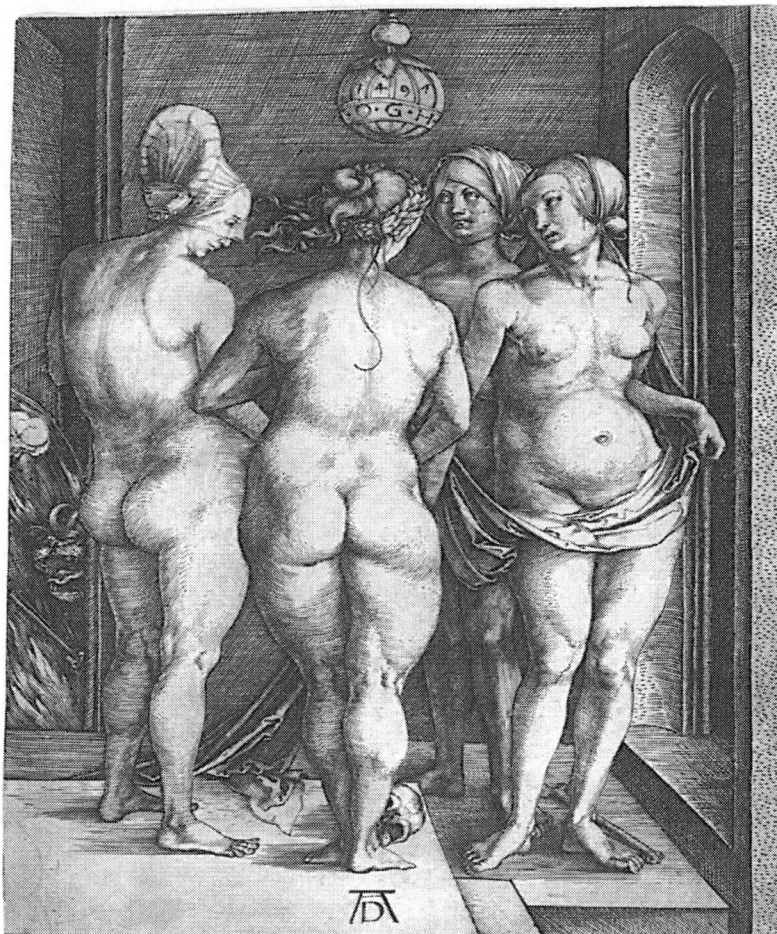

The Four Witches, by Albrecht Dürer, 1497.

Magic Squares, Gematria the Mark of the Beast & the Angel of Death

"There is assigned to each planet an Intelligence, or Good Spirit, and an Evil Spirit or Demon. Each planet has its own seal or signature, as well as the signature of its intelligence and the signature of its demon."

~ William J. Fielding ~

Squaring the Planets & Marking the Beast

The physical sun is triune, consisting of spiritual, intellectual, and material aspects. In Hebrew Kabbalah, the *Intelligence* of the sun is called *Nakiel* (or Nachiel) and given the number 111. The *Spiritual* sun is *Sorath* and given the number 666. Both numbers are derived from the *Magic Square* of the sun. Every planet has an *intelligence* and *spirit*, too, and each of these aspects are given a name: to the Moon are *Hasmodai* and *Malcha betharsithim hed beruah schehakim*; to Mars are *Graphiel* and *Barzabel*; to Mercury are *Tiriel* and *Taphthartharath*; to Jupiter are *Johphiel* and *Hismael*; to Venus are *Hagiel* and *Kedemel*; to Saturn are *Agiel* and *Zazel*.

For more details on this subject consult Francis Barrett and Henry Cornelius Agrippa, whose seals and talismans are at the end of this chapter.

Every classical planet has its own *Magic Square* from whence is derived the number of said planetary *intelligence*. These "squares" are referred to as *Qameoth*, or *Qamea* when singular. Each of these *intelligences* is said to have a *substance*, free of body and flesh, immortal and assisting in all things. Of these *substances* are considered three kinds: *Super-Celestial*: minds separated from body that infuse with the light of God for distributing heavenly duties; *Celestial-Intelligences*: the worldly angels govern every heaven and star; and *Angels*: the ministers for disposing all things below.

The angelic administrators are essentially individual expressions of EL, as in *Elohim*, a plural word denoting several gods: Genesis 1:26 says, *"Le us make man in our image, after our likeness."* This literal plurality can be reconciled with monotheistic belief by understanding the various emanations of a singular *Cosmic Mind*. The word *angel*, which comes from the Greek *angelos* (and Hebrew *melakh*), meaning "messenger," contains the letters *e-l*, found also in Gosp**el** and Chap**el**.

Kabbalists ascribed names to the angels based upon their *activity* or *function*, and then added the suffix "el." For example: the *angel of death* is named Samael (Samil), from *Sam*, a name referring to his destructive tendencies despite the obedience he still pays to God. This means that evil is always subject to good. Samael may or may not have a relationship with Azrael, another Jewish and Islamic *angle of death*, who watches over the dying. But by *death* we are merely meant to understand Azrael's duty in separating the soul from the body and acting as its guide in the afterlife. His name is derived from the Hebrew *Azra*, meaning *pure*, as in the purification of the soul after death.

Angels are thus *emissaries* or *attendants* of God, much like the messengers Hermes-Mercury were in Greece and Rome. Although *Michael* was once considered the only "Archangel" he would later be associated with a host of other angles taking on the same title, each including the name of God. There are *seven archangels* in comparison with the *seven planetary intelligences.*

Since the name EL is plural and indicates several gods, it is appropriate to list the angels as emanations of God's *seven assistants* or *divine rays*: Michael, Raphael, Gabriel, Jophiel, Ariel, Azrael and Chamuel. There are also the archangels as mostly related from ancient Jewish texts: Raguel, Raziel, Zadkiel, Haniel, Jeremiel and Uriel. These angels govern each of the *seven days of the week* and are presented in the table below with their sigils (from the Latin *sigillum,* meaning *signature*), respected planets, and signs. In the Book of Enoch, an ancient Hebrew text, we read of how Enoch had direct communion with the heavnes. He writes of the *Holy Angels* as such:

And these are the names of the holy angels who watch mankind.
Uriel, one of the holy angels, who is over the world and over Tartarus.
Raphael, one of the holy angels, who is over the spirits of men.
Raguel, one of the holy angels who takes vengeance on the world of the luminaries.
Michael, one of the holy angels, to wit, he that is set over the best part of mankind and over chaos.
Saraqael, one of the holy angels, who is set over the spirits, who sin in the spirit.
Gabriel, one of the holy angels, who is over Paradise and the serpents and the Cherubim.
Remiel, one of the holy angels, whom God set over those who rise.

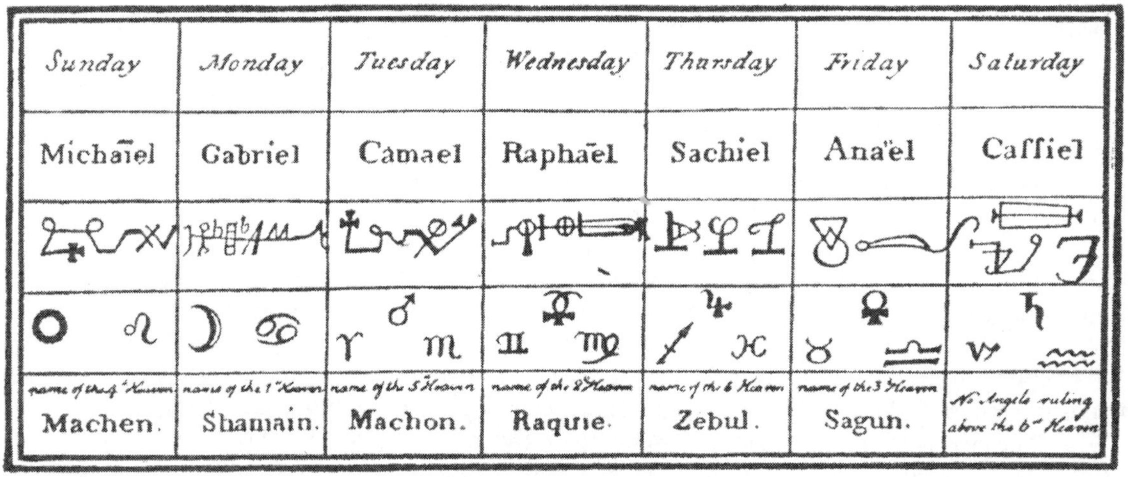

Sunday	Monday	Tuesday	Wednesday	Thursday	Friday	Saturday
Michaël	Gabriel	Camael	Raphaël	Sachiel	Anaël	Caffiel
☉ ♌	☽ ♋	♂ ♈ ♏	☿ ♊ ♍	♃ ♐ ♓	♀ ♉ ♎	♄ ♑ ♒
name of the 4th Heaven Machen.	name of the 1st Heaven Shamain.	name of the 5th Heaven Machon.	name of the 2d Heaven Raquie.	name of the 6 Heaven Zebul.	name of the 3 Heaven Sagun.	No Angels ruling above the 6th Heaven

By drawing upon the *Qamea* of each planet there can be derived a unique sigil that is symbolically indicative of that planet's individual *spirit.* This energy is what magicians call upon through rituals that involve the sympathetic colors, incenses, symbols, and elements of whatever planetary *spirt* they wish to work alongside. Contrary to popular belief, evil spirits, and demons, with their seals and characters, were not typically inscribed upon any talisman unless the intent was to produce a wicked result. Even when the latter is intended, such evil is still subject to the intelligences of good spirits. In preparing evil talismans to bring about *destruction* upon an enemy, a metal is to be chosen in contrast with the signs engraved thereon.

When one calls upon *benevolence* rather than *malevolence* their operation is intended to bring about *harmony* rather than *harm.* As in *law,* we find in *magic* that perhaps the most important element of any operation is *intention.* Without *intention* to create *harmony* the magician either *intends* to cause *harm* or, with no *direction* whatsoever, becomes *victim* to forces that have their own agendas, i.e., *possession*. At the very least, potential for infernal influences. In the latter case (*harm* or *no direction*) we would call this *Black Magic(k)*. In the former case (*harmony*) it would be called *White Magic(k)*. The additional "k" is meant to distinguish ceremonial magic(k) from stage magic, according to Aleister Crowley.

Sigils are inscriptions that may be carved or painted on an item that is then believed to obtain some sort of magical power, as a result of drawing on sympathetic energies. They may be simple or comprise complex designs, but in either case the meaning behind the symbol is the embodiment of an *idea*. Each of the *planetary spirits* has its own *energy*, i.e., *sigil*, derived from the planet's name. The numerical value of that name is how each sigil is extracted from a *Qamea*.

If the Intelligence of the sun, Nakiel, is equivalent to 111, then the separate letters reduce to these specific numbers: N=50, K=20, I=10, A=1, L=30. Added together the value of these letters is 111. If these numbers, minus their zeros, are imposed on the *Magical Square of the Sun*, its sigil can be extracted. There are different systems of *gematria*, or numerical assignments to the letters, along with different names from the start, so be aware of what *system* you are reading.

Magic Square of the Sun							
Day: Sunday		6	32	3	34	35	1
		7	11	27	28	8	30
Color: Gold or Yellow		19	14	16	15	23	24
		18	20	22	21	17	13
Sign: Leo		25	29	10	9	26	12
Metal: Gold		36	5	33	4	2	31

The *Magical Square of Saturn*, which has three columns and three rows, always produces the sum of 15. After counting from one to nine then the *perfect ten* becomes one, and thus proceeding, eleven is two, etc., until fifteen is six. Henry Cornelius Agrippa writes the *perfect ten* in his *Occult Philosophy*, and how all proceeds therefrom:

"*As the number ten flows back into a unity, from whence it proceeded, so every thing that is flowing is returned back to that from which it had the beginning of its flux: so water returns to the sea, from whence it had its beginning; the body returns to the earth, from whence it was taken; time returns into eternity, from whence it flowed; the spirit shall return to God, who gave it; and, lastly, every creature returns to nothing, from whence it was created.*"

In numerology the number 15 equals 6, and therefore Saturn's square, energy, sigil, and signature, are all equal to 666. But the "666" of the *physical Saturn* is not equated necessarily to that same value when derived from the *physical Sun*, which is 111, but would instead relate to the value of the Spiritual Sun, *Sorath*, which is also 666. The latter number is considered the "mark of the beast," which relates to the modern concept of Satan, derived from Saturn. Revelation 13:18 states this as wisdom:

"*Here is wisdom. Let the one who has insight calculate the number of the beast, for it is the number of a man, and that number is six hundred sixty six.*"

If 666 is the number of the *beast,* one could compare this "mark" to the numerical value of the Sun and Saturn. But this "mark" is perhaps better descried philosophically as the identifying feature of physical man living within the *Divine Plan* put into place by the *Cosmic Mind.* All men and women are born with this "mark," and it is the goal of alchemists to transform this "beast mark" into gold, i.e., to move from the *material sphere of Saturn* to the *spiritual sphere of the Sun.* The "*six hundred sixty six*" remains 666, because man's soul-spirit does not change in the process. By "beast" we are to understand "man" and his base element of *carbon,* which has 6 protons, 6 neutrons, and 6 electrons.

Here is wisdom indeed! Interestingly, 666 is considered a lucky number in China.

Magic Square of Saturn

Day: Saturday

Color: Black (the absence of or complete absorption of light)

Sign: Capricorn

Metal: Lead

4	9	2
3	5	7
8	1	6

The individual "6" is further a "number of a man," because he was created in Genesis on the sixth day. This is also the day of our redemption, since Christ suffered on a Friday, the sixth day of the week. Man is also comprised of two legs, two arms, one torso, and one head. Eliphas Levi writes of these magical numbers and squares:

"By casting up each column of these squares, you will obtain invariably the characteristic number of the planet, and, finding the explanation of this number by the hieroglyphs of the Tarot, you proceed to seek the sense of all figures, whether triangular, square or cruciform, which you find to be formed by the numbers. The result of this operation will be a complete and profound acquaintance with all allegories and mysteries concealed by the ancients under the symbol of each planet, or rather of each personification of influences, celestial or human, upon all events of life."

Utilizing these names, numbers, sigils, energies, spirits, days, colors, metals, etc., allows one to invoke that specific planetary intelligence or archangel. If we wanted to call upon Saturn, we would use lead, black, and symbols of time, death, and goats, and perform our rite on a Saturday (Saturn Day). If we wanted to call upon the sun, we would use gold, yellow, and symbols of solar radiance like the lion, and perform our rite on a Sunday (Sun Day). Author Jim Moran observes of the *Qameoth* in his book <u>The Wonders of Magic Squares</u>:

"Magic squares brilliantly reveal the intrinsic harmony and symmetry of numbers; with their curious and mystic charm they appear to betray some hidden intelligence that governs he comic order that dominates all existence. They have been compared to a mirror reflecting the symmetry of the universe, the harmonies of nature, the divine norm. It is not surprising that they have always exercised a great influence on thinking people."

Saturn's Cross, Square & Cube

The *astrological sign of Saturn* (1) is the cross with a hook. The *sigil of Saturn* (2) is essentially the merging of two triangles that in Freemasonry are called the *square* and *compass*, and elsewhere either the *Star of Remphan* or *Star of David* (3). The *star* comprises all four elements in the merging of upright and downward triangles: fire, air, water, earth. From the center of this *Davidic hexagram* can be extracted the six-sided geometric shape known as *hexagon*, which in three dimensions becomes the *cube of the material world*. The physical planet Saturn has even been photographed with a large storm rotating on its North Pole in the form of a hexagon. The two triangles are also representative of Alpha (A), the beginning letter of the alphabet. Saturn's metal is lead, which is also symbolized by two Alphas or triangles. The turning of lead into gold, i.e., the *rising of consciousness*, is the movement of soul-spirit through the seven spheres or gates of the classical planets, from beginning to end, or from the Alpha (A) to Omega Ω. The flipping of the planet Saturn on its side produces a *monad*, a circle (rings) with dot (planet) in the center, or the alchemical symbol of gold and the sun. Some may refer to this as the *Black Sun*, which is sunlight reflected by the mirroring qualities of the moon.

It is relevant to mention that you can take *Saturn's cross*, or the *Latin Cross*, and fold its bars into a box. This cube is the symbol of the *tomb of matter*, that same chest wherein Osiris (agricultural *seed*) was confined.

Christianity, Islam, and Judaism all incorporate this sacred cube into their symbols. Jews sometimes where small black cubes called *Tefillin*, which contain parchment paper with inscriptions from the Torah. One of the holiest sites for Muslims is near the Red Sea in western Saudi Arabia. Located amid two sacred towers is the *Kaaba* (also *Caaba*), a square building in the center of Al-Masjid Al-Haram at Mecca. The cube is black, contains a piece of black space rock, and crosses over into mystic Judaism by sharing a similar name with *Kabbalah* (also Kabbala, Cabala, Cabbala or Qabalah). The fourth book of <u>Popol Vuh</u> concludes with an interesting account of a majestic temple, which also preserves a black divining stone. The temple itself is cubical and called *Caabaha*. Manly Hall documents how the temple was *"all white, where was preserved a secret black divining stone, cubical in shape."* He continues:

> *"Gucumatz (or Quetzalcoatl) partakes of many of the attributes of King Solomon: the account of the temple building in the Popol Vuh is a reminder of the story of Solomon's Temple, and undoubtedly has a similar significance. Brasseur de Bourbourg was first attracted to the study of religious parallelisms in the Popol Vuh by the fact that the temple together with the black stone which it contained, was named the Caabaha, a name astonishingly similar to that of the Temple, or Caaba, which contains the sacred black stone of Islam."*

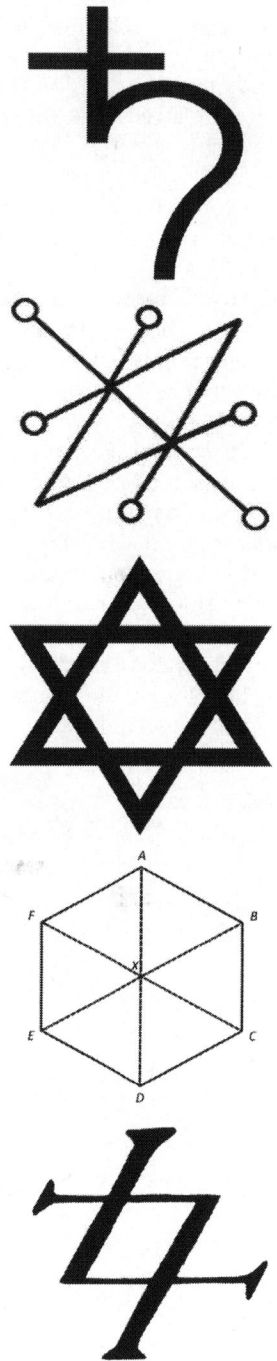

The *Seven Days of Creation* are the seven days of the week, each governed by their respective *planetary intelligence*. A square has four sides, representing the elements, corners, seasons, and so on. The cube has six sides, and they rest on the *seventh*, or center position, as God rested on the seventh day. On a blank sheet of paper if seven lines are drawn south to specific points, there is geometrically depicted the *seven emanations of Source*, or the *seven divine rays* that created all things. Source is a single dot, *monad*, and each day of *creation* is one of the seven lines or *rays* emanating downward from this eighth point. Therefore, from *INFINITY* comes all *FINITE* forms suspended in temporary individuality.

Those with the "spark of gnosis," as David Fideler points out, can glimpse this "higher pattern" of the *harmony* and *order* of the Universe and will therefore be able to see beyond the seven days, or emanating rays, to *the Universal Logos* or *Cosmic Mind*. They will find the eighth point, or *eighth sphere*, to be where the *seven divine rays* emanate from to produce the hexagon in *two dimensions*, itself shown with six rays directed outward and a single point in the center known as the *seventh day* - when God "rested."

The hexagon then is expressed in three dimensions as a cube. The hexagram, or six-pointed star, is expressed in three dimensions as the *Merkabah*, which means *chariot* in Hebrew.

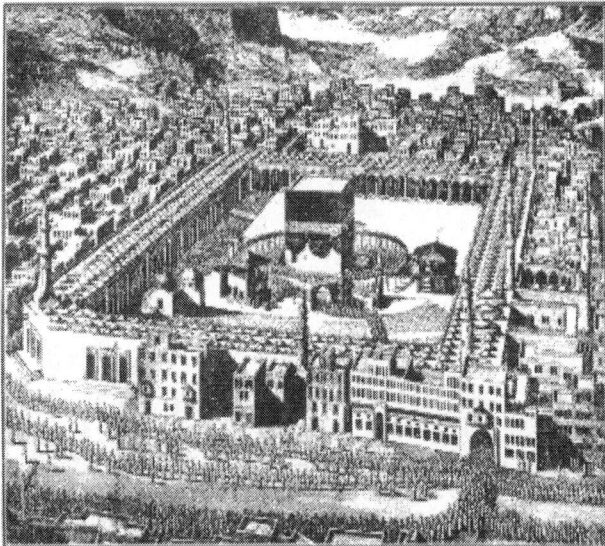

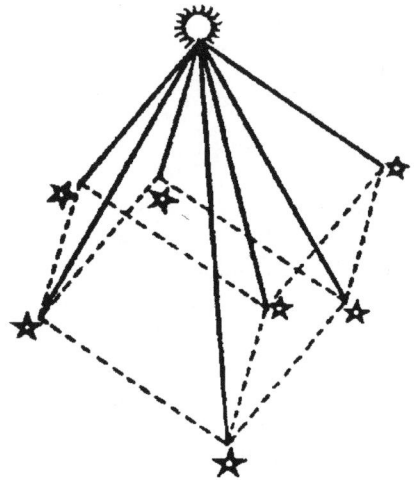

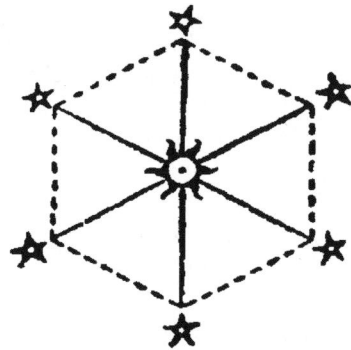

The Seven Days of Creation, as published in David Fideler's book <u>Jesus Christ Son of God</u>.

Kaaba

Tefillin

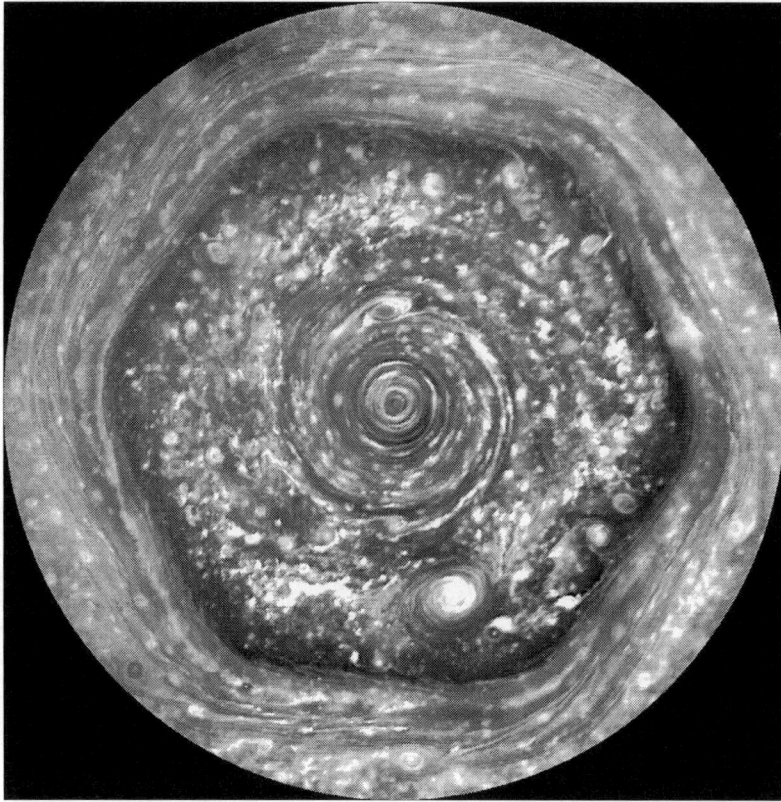

Hexagon storm observed on the north pole of the planet Saturn,
by Cassini in 2012, taken in wavelengths ranging from UV to IR.

(Credit: NASA/JPL-Caltech/SSI/Hampton University)

Here are listed the numerical values of each planet and its associated square when one column is added together either vertically or horizontally. Listed next to the Roman name is the corresponding day of the week and its Greek equivalent.

Roman	**Greek**
Saturn………...15 (Saturday)	Saturn
Jupiter……......34 (Thursday)	Zeus
Mars……….…..65 (Tuesday)	Ares
Sol/Sun……....111 (Sunday)	Helios
Venus……….....175 (Friday)	Aphrodite
Mercury……….260 (Wednesday)	Hermes
Luna/Moon…...369 (Monday)	Selene

8	58	59	5	4	62	63	1
49	15	14	52	53	11	10	56
41	23	22	44	45	19	18	48
32	34	35	29	28	38	39	25
40	26	27	37	36	30	31	33
17	47	46	20	21	43	42	24
9	55	54	12	13	51	50	16
64	2	3	61	60	6	7	57

Magic Square of Mercury

Day: Wednesday

Color: Purple

Sign: Virgo, Gemini

Metal: Mercury

Magic Square of Jupiter

Day: Thursday

Color: Violet or Blue

Sign: Sagittarius

Metal: Tin

4	14	15	1
9	7	6	12
5	11	10	8
16	2	3	13

22	47	16	41	10	35	4
5	23	48	17	42	11	29
30	6	24	49	18	36	12
13	31	7	25	43	19	37
38	14	32	1	26	44	20
21	39	8	33	2	27	45
46	15	40	9	34	3	28

Magic Square of Venus

Day: Friday

Color: Turquoise or Green

Sign: Taurus, Libra

Metal: Copper

Magic Square of the Moon

37	78	29	70	21	62	13	54	5
6	38	79	30	71	22	63	14	46
47	7	39	80	31	72	23	55	15
16	48	8	40	81	32	64	24	56
57	17	49	9	41	73	33	65	25
26	58	18	50	1	42	74	34	66
67	27	59	10	51	2	43	75	35
36	68	19	60	11	52	3	44	76
77	28	69	20	61	12	53	4	45

Day: Monday

Color: Silver or White

Sign: Cancer

Metal: Silver

11	24	7	20	3
4	12	25	8	16
17	5	13	21	9
10	18	1	14	22
23	6	19	2	15

Magic Square of Mars

Day: Tuesday

Color: Red

Sign: Aries, Scorpio

Metal: Iron

Gematria & the Secrets of Harpocrates

In the iconic alphabet of Miletus, adopted in Athens in 403 BCE, numerical values are assigned to different letters (symbols) of the alphabet. This alphabetical numbering system is known as *gematria*, which comes from the Greek word *geometria*, meaning geometry. This is considered a Kabbalistic method of interpreting Hebrew scriptures by the placing of numerical values on letters and words. There are many forms of *gematria* with some being more common than others, like Greek and Hebrew, though some researchers simply mash numbers, words, and names together in an incoherent and foolish manner. The Christian Gnostics, however, made much of the fact that the name Jesus (ΙΗΣΟΥΣ) is equivalent to the number 888 by this numerical alphabet. Just as *carbon* is equated to 666 in the sciences, there are 8 protons, 8 neutrons, and 8 electrons in *oxygen*. So, as Genesis 2:7 relates, the *"Lord God formed man"* from dust and *"breathed into his nostrils the breath of life."*

I = 10
H = 8
E = 200
O = 70
Y = 400
E = 200
_____
888

In Greek gematria we find that A = 1 and Ω = 800. This gives us 801. We read in Revelation 22:13 that the LORD GOD is precisely this: *"I am the Alpha and the Omega, the First and the Last, the Beginning and the End."* Since these letters and numbers comprise the entire alphabet, *"a set of letters or symbols in a fixed order, used to represent the basic sounds of a language,"* then they represent the start of Genesis wherein "God **said**" for there to be many things. As the spoken and written *WORD*, HE begins and ends the alphabet. For as John 1:1-5 says:

"In the beginning was the Word, and the Word was with God, and the Word was God. He was in the beginning with God. All things were made through him, and without him was not any thing made that was made. In him was life, and the life was the light of men. The light shines in the darkness, and the darkness has not overcome it."

The *Word* was also referenced in the Popul Vuh, where the creators came together in thought and meditation to form man:

"Then came the word. Tepeu and Gucumatz came together in the darkness, in the night, and Tepeu and Gucumatz talked together. They talked then, discussing and deliberating; they agreed, they united their words and their thoughts. Then while they meditated, it became clear to them that when dawn would break, man must appear."

Jesus is thus valued at both 888 and 801. In John 1:29 we read that John calls him the *lamb*, who by the implication of his blood has washed away *sin*:

"The next day John saw Jesus coming toward him and said, 'Look, the Lamb of God, who takes away the sin of the world!'"

The lamb is a symbol of *peace* like the white dove or Holy Ghost. The Greek name for *dove* is *peristerá*, and it is also numerically equivalent to 801. Numerically speaking, Jesus is the *dove* (*"The Prince of Peace"* from Isaiah 9:6), *Holy Ghost*, and A & Ω (*Father*). This is the sacred Trinity of so many traditions. Harpocrates, the Greek god of *silence* equated with the Egyptian Horus, is also depicted with symbols of the Alpha and Omega. Perhaps this is the *secret* concealed behind his finger and lip: for *HERE IS WISDOM!* And the spoken *WORD OF GOD.* Amaterasu in Japan is the start and finish of each day, too, and Arjuna speaks the same to Krishna (Visnu), saying *"I behold Thee, infinite in form, on every side, but I see not Thy end nor Thy middle nor Thy beginning, O Lord of the Universe, O Universal Form!"*

The "God above all Gods" to the Gnostics was *Abraxas*, a name with the numerical value of 365 in Greek gematria, or the number of days in a solar year. The name Mithra(s), the *Unconquered Sun*, is also equivalent to 365. Both gods were personifications of the sun, the *flying solar disc*, which makes a cyclical circle each day and year as part of the macrocosmic dimension. Although a circle has a circumference of 360 degrees, readers will recall the story of Nut, RA, and Seb, wherein there were 360 days in a solar year. However, Thoth wins from Selene an additional five days for Nut to bear the children we know as Osiris, Typhon-Set, Isis, Nephthys, and Horus-Harpocrates.

Harpocrates

As a mathematician and keeper of the library of Alexandria, Eratosthenes (276 BCE – 194 BCE) is known for measuring the dimensions of earth. Alexandria was just north of Syene or Sauanu, where, on the summer solstice, the sun was directly overhead at noon. Buildings cast no shadows at this time and the bottoms of wells were illuminated. Considering the distance between the two cities, and the angle of the sun at Alexandria when it was directly overhead at Syene, Eratosthenes calculated the circumference of the earth. The Egyptian hieroglyph *Khekh* ☥ denotes the city of Syene, specifically on June 21. It is a partial triangle with cross in the center and circle suspended below. The triangle is the *Masonic Square & Compass*, and the dangling lower circle is the *plumb bob*, used for measurement and balance. Freemasonry without doubt dates, at minimum, to this period in Egypt and likely far before. In fact, many believe, including Helena Blavatsky, that one of the founders was Enoch:

> "…Enoch, fearing that the real and precious secrets would be lost, concealed before the Deluge in the bowels of the Earth -- were simply the more or less symbolical and allegorical copies from the primitive Records. The 'Book of Enoch' is one of such copies and is a Chaldean, now very incomplete compendium. As already said, Enoichion means in Greek the 'inner eye,' or the Seer; in Hebrew, and with the help of Masoretic points it means the initiator and instructor, חנוך. It is a generic title; besides which his legend is that of several other prophets, Jewish and heathen, with changes of made-up details, the root-form being the same.

A circle with a circumference of 888 houses two other circles: the second has a value of 666, and the third has a value of 769, the *mean* between 888 and 666. The number 769 is the value of the Greek *Pythios*, that god of music and harmony, and the name of Apollo at Delphi.

The ALPHA is also contained in the OMEGA, and as the Gnostic Christ says in the <u>Pistis Sophia</u>:

> "The First Mystery is the 24th mystery from within outwards."

> "He who shall have received the complete mystery of the First Mystery of the Ineffable… shall have the power of exploring all the orders of the Inheritance of Light."

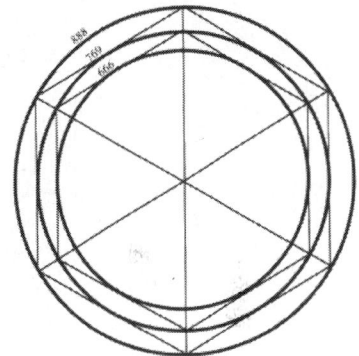

This can be expressed by a cube, as explained by Fideler in <u>Jesus Christ Son of God</u>, his analysis of sacred geometry in relation to the occult teachings of the *mysteries* and *mythology*. We also learn also from C. W. King's <u>The Gnostics and their Remains</u> of the veiled terms of twenty-four *mysteries* contained in twenty-four eons, as further discussed in the <u>Pistis Sophia</u>.

The following summarizes some of Fideler's findings: The volume of a cube with 52900 cubic units has a surface area of 8490 square units and a surface area on each side of 1415 square units. Removing the zero, 532 is the numerical value of ALPHA, 849 of OMEGA, and 1415 is the numerical equivalent of Apollo. Squaring a circle with a circumference of 353 units produces the perimeter of the square inside with a measurement of 318. The circle, 353, is equivalent to Hermes, who is said by Manetho, an Egyptian priest of RA from Heliopolis, to be author of 36,525 books, the exact number of days in a solar year (365.25).

The Adoration of the Lamb (Paschal Lamb) by Jean van Eyck. Revelation 21:9 refers to the lamb as such: *"Then came one of the seven angels who had the seven bowls full of the seven last plagues and spoke to me, saying, 'Come, I will show you the Bride, the wife of the Lamb'."* The *Paschal Lamb* is often depicted with a halo, signifying its relationship to the sun, along with a chalice to collect the blood spewing from a wound in its side like Christ, Odin, and Prometheus.

Magical Seals or Talismans drawn & published by Francis Barrett in in <u>The Magus</u>.

The next three pages include more detailed information pertaining to the symbol, spirit, seal, and intelligence of the planets, as published in the 1991 book, <u>The Complete Book of Amulets & Talismans</u>, by Migene González-Wippler.

MOON

Symbol

Spirit: CHASHMODAI

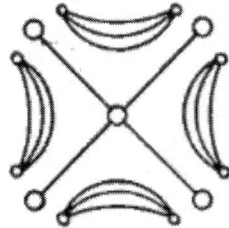

Seal of Planet

Intelligence of the Intelligences of the Moon: MALCAH
BETARSHISIM VE-AD RUACHOTH HA-SCHECHALIM

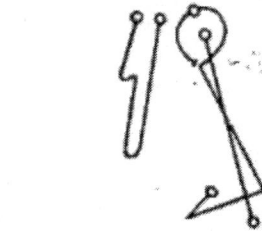

Spirit of the Spirits of the Moon:
SHAD BARSCHEMOTH
HASCHARTATHAN

Symbol and Seals of the Moon

MERCURY

Symbol

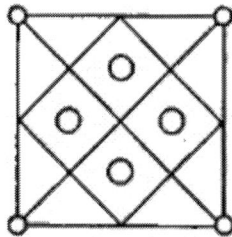

Seal Of the Planet

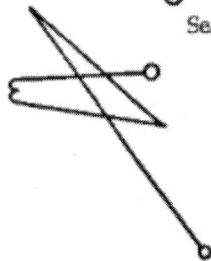

Intelligence: TIRIEL

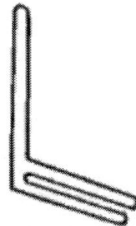

Spirit: TAPHTHARTHARATH

Symbol and Seals of Mercury

VENUS

Symbol

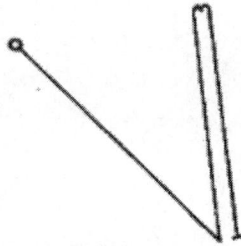

Intelligence: HAGIEL

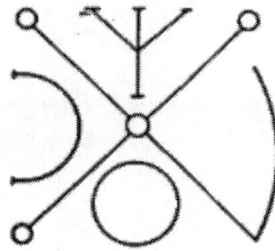

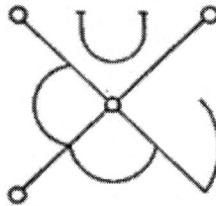

Seal of Planet

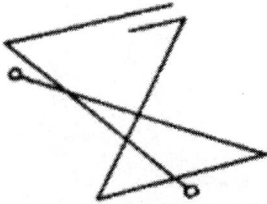

Intelligence: (Choir of Angels)
BENI SERAPHIM

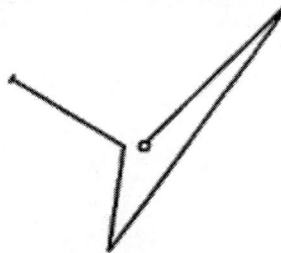

Spirit: KEDEMEL

Symbol and Seals of Venus

MARS

Symbol

Seal of Planet

Intelligence: GRAPHIEL

Spirit: BARTZABEL

Symbol and Seals of Mars

SATURN

Symbol

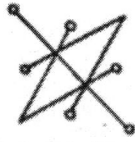

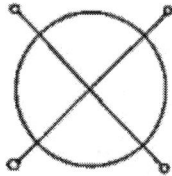

Seal of the Planet

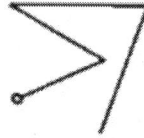

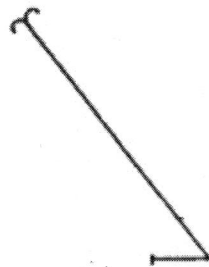

Spirit: ZAZEL

Intelligence: AGIEL

Symbol and Seals of Saturn

JUPITER

Symbol

Seal of the Planet

Spirit: HISMAEL

Intelligence: YOPHIEL

Symbol and Seals of Jupiter

SUN

Symbol

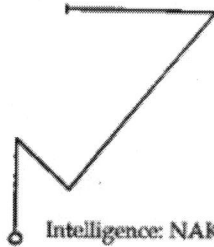

Intelligence: NAKHIEL

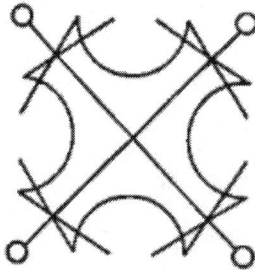

Seal of Planet

Spirit: SORATH

Symbol and Seals of the Sun

Natural Magic:
Stones, Talismans, Charms, Herbs,
Suffumigations, Magnetism,
& the Planetary Pentacles

"From time immemorial magicians have sought to establish the natural affinity that exists between certain planets, metals, jewels, birds, beasts, herbs, colours, flowers and scents. A great deal of patience and ingenuity have been expended on this formidable task, but observation and experiment have also played their part."

~ David Conway ~

Celestial Virtues

Stones, talismans, charms, enchantments, fetishes, etc., are typically associated with magical, and to most, strictly *superstitious*, motivations. Some may attribute their use to delusion, belief in fantasy, or to diabolism. No matter the view, those making such accusations, or scoffing at the mention of such things, are prone to either keep or wear their own version of these items: crosses, jewelry from a deceased mother or grandmother, lucky shirts, four-leaf clover keychains, an item that holds sentimental value, etc. Then there are the brand logos worn on hats, shirts, pants, and shoes. Whether intended to have *magical power* or not, perhaps they are kept or worn "just in case," and without realizing what the item or symbol represents, or from whence it draws its power and influence. Millions of amateur and professional athletes alone wear jerseys, shorts, socks, and shoes with that famous checkmark, and one sincerely wonders how many know that *Nike* was a Greek goddess of victory conjured to assist in winning *competitions*.

Magic is truly a matter of the *power of belief* and *intention*, just as religions rely on *faith* and *intention*. But some beliefs are so firmly fixed that they are seen as neither *supernatural* nor *real*; they just *are*. Although an item is generally thought to only have *magical qualities* if the holder or wearer has *faith* in its power, consciously or subconsciously, some symbols are so powerful they draw on the *faith* of countless people who have used them throughout the ages. In this way, we can see the ancient gods and goddesses as mere *reservoirs of energy* to be tapped into like a *water well*.

When a professional sports team chooses a name and logo, or a grade school chooses the same, they are drawing on the *sympathies* of what they select: horses, bears, lions, tigers, birds, pirates, knights, etc.

Others may dabble in *stones*, for example, believing these items to hold some supernatural power that has nothing to do with their own personal *intentions*. But their power does not reside in *unseen forces*, per se, and instead within *associations* and *correspondences*. For example: to attract solar virtue, one may use those elements associated with the sun. A lion's tooth, *crown of thorns*, yellow fabric, and gold are items to be used on a Sunday, at noon, under the sign of Leo. The *bloodstone* is of use here too. It is known as *heliotrope* (from the Greek *Helios*), obviously deriving its name from the personified sun. The reddish hue this stone gives to water reflects the virtue of the sun's red-orange rays reflecting off the same. As an amulet it is described in the <u>Leyden Papyrus</u>:

> *"The world has no greater thing; if anyone have this with him he will be given whatever he asks for; it also assuages the wrath of kings and despise, and whatever the wearer says will be beloved. However bears this stone, which is a gem, and pronounces the name engraved upon it, will find all doors open, while bonds and stone walls will be rent asunder."*

Some people hold onto physical items with such unyielding obsession that these *possessions* appear to have *possessed* their owner. Even for the person with a lucky shirt there is certainly some part of their mind holding onto what might be the most meager belief in its unseen influence. Whatever the case or reasoning, there is unbridled *danger* in the *absolute belief* and *absolute denial* of such things. One leads to *obsession* and *possession*, the other is akin to *foolishness* and *delusion*.

Although contemporary society is heavily reliant on pharmaceuticals it is far less common to find someone willing to see value in the power of herbs and plants even if their drugs were originally derived from these sources. *Herbology* is seen historically as *witchcraft*, in recent times as the work of *hippies*, and generally today as unnecessary for human health. Perhaps it is the word *herbology* itself, which means to study plants and their history, that is the problem; *botany* is a perfectly acceptable field of study, and it possesses the same definition! The practice of *pharmaka*, or the preparation of biological ingredients into medicines or poisons, was once thought to be an act of sorcery or magic due to the way such things altered the body and mind. The word *pharmaka* comes from the Greek *pharmakeia*, meaning "practice of the druggist," based on *pharmakon*, meaning "drug." From the Greek we derive our words *pharmacy*, *pharmaceutical*, and *pharmacology*. Since men were traditionally hunters, the women would gather roots, herbs, flowers, and plants to cultivate powders, potions, medicines, and poisons. These women were the *witches*.

The purest form of magic is the utilizing of natural tools like plants to induce seemingly supernatural effects. When our ancestors learned how to craft bear, they did so, it would seem, without a complete understanding of fermentation, and therefore it was believed spirits were causing *drunkenness*. This is why we still refer to alcohol as *spirits*. In the case of Dionysus-Bacchus, it was believed the god of wine had an ability to make one joyous or angry, which ultimately is a sophisticated, yet simple, metaphor for explaining intoxication of the body. Without an understanding of plants, herbs, fermentation, and alcohol, such things are, by definition, *magic*: "the power of apparently influencing the course of events by mysterious or supernatural forces."

Magic, mythology, astronomy, and alchemy are to thus be understood as means of scientific observation that gave birth to modern science, astrology, and chemistry respectively.

Sigils are inscriptions that may be carved or painted on an item that is then believed to obtain some sort of magical power by drawing on those corresponding sympathetic energies. They may be simple or comprise complex designs, but in either case the meaning behind the symbol is the embodiment of an *idea*. One can dwell on that *idea* or outright dismiss the same.

We return to certain charms like *crosses* for Christians and *pentagrams* for Pagans so that we may understand the *sigil*. Sigils are inscriptions that may be carved or painted on an item which is then believed to obtain some sort of magical power by drawing on those corresponding *sympathetic energies* related to the art. They may be simple or comprise complex designs, but in either case the meaning behind the symbol is the embodiment of an *idea*. One can dwell on that *idea* or outright dismiss the same. Yet it remains for every person to decide what a solar cross or pentagram means.

If the microcosmic world mirrors the macrocosmic world, then it would make sense to apply the theory of *sympathies* and *antipathies* to our lives. That which is below mirrors that which is above. In his first of three books on *Occult Philosophy*, Agrippa writes of the natural and artificial preparations used to obtain certain *Celestial Virtue*s or gifts:

> *"When the Soul of the World, by its virtue doth make all things that are naturally generated, or artificially made, fruitful, by infusing into them celestial properties for the working of some wonderful effects, then things themselves not only applied by suffumigations, or collyries* [treatment applied to the eyes]*, or ointments, or potions, or any other such like way, but also when they being conveniently wrapped up, are bound to, or hanged about the neck, or any other way applied, although by never so easy a contract, do impress their virtue upon us.*

> *"By these alligations* [physical contact] *therefore, suspensions* [things hung]*, wrappings up, applications, and contacts the accidents* [casual appearances or effects] *of the body, and mind are changed into sickness, health, boldness, fear, sadness, and joy, and the like: they render them that carry them gracious or terrible, acceptable, or rejected, honored and beloved, or hateful and abominable."*

The instrument of *enchanters* is a *breathing spirit* by which they attract or bind those things delighted in or desired. To *enchant* someone is to fill them with *great delight*, i.e., *charm* them. Such an action can be *white* or *black*. As we learned earlier, the *written word* and *spoken word* are both acts of divinely inspired magic. When we spell a word, we are *casting a spell*; when we write in cursive, a magical language where the utensil rarely leaves the medium (these symbols are considered most powerful), we are *sending a curse*. We also know the Greek *grammatikē*, defined as the *"art of letters,"* and *gramma*, a thing that is written, are the basis for our modern word *grammar*. In Old French, *grammatica* became *gramaire*, which eventually transformed into the word we know today. This *gramaire* also had the meaning of *magic* or *enchantment*, however, and it is thus the basis for why *grammar* in its many forms eventually led to the forming the *grimoire*, or a sorcerer's *book of spells*. All such language is an expression of the soul-spirit and an emanation from the *Cosmic Mind*. As with art, beauty sympathizes with *Heaven* and ugliness sympathizes with *Hell*.

Magicianess & the *Tooth Fairy*

There is a natural sympathy and antipathy of things that we may term *Natural Magic* or *Sympathetic Magic*, and this includes the gathering of items that draw on the *Celestial Virtue*s: animals, plants, metals, stones, sigils, etc. Egyptians called this nature *magicianess*, the attraction or repulsion of things alike or different – though sometimes *opposites attract*. Francis Barrett notes how *"each mortal creature possesses a Sun and system within himself; therefore, according to universal sympathy, we are affected by the general influence or universal spirit of the world, as the vital principle throughout the universe."* These living creatures, whether animals, insects, or even the animistic qualities of stones, possess sympathy and virtue with related elements. They also possess antipathy with unrelated elements. Bodily organs relate to planets, as we have seen, and vice versa: there are also further associations to be found between our organs, and body parts, and animals, herbs, stones, metals, plants, and general foods. Such associations, more specifically termed *Sympathetic Magic*, have meaning because the human body is a microcosm of the entire universe. As Lord Amateru (a male version of the Japanese sun goddess Amaterasu) explains in esoteric tradition:

> *"First, the human body is a hinagata, meaning a miniature version, of the universe. Our left eye is the Sun, our right eye the Moon, and our nose is a star. The middle of our body is the world: the heart is the sovereign, the liver is the ministers, and the spleen is the common people. The lungs are the workmen, and the kidneys are the merchants. The heart is like a mirror: it shows your true intentions to heaven and Earth, and soon enough men will know of it. This is why one of the Three Treasures of the Emperor is a mirror, the Yaga-no-Kagami."*

Author and artist Marlene Seven Bremner explains something similar in her book <u>Hermetic Philosophy and Creative Alchemy</u>:

> *"Through the use of sacrifices, hymns, praises, and heavenly sounds, the powers of heaven are drawn down into the statue or idol."*

Barrett writes in <u>The Magus</u> of the magical sympathies: *"whatever things are taken for magical uses from animals, whether they are stones, members, hair, excrements, nails, or any thing else, they must be taken from those animals while they are yet alive, and, if it is possible, that they may live afterwards."*

Aristotle writes in the sixth book of his *Mystical Philosophy*, "*that when any one, by binding or bewitching, calls upon the Sun or other stars, praying them to assist the work desired, the Sun and other stars do not hear his words; but are moved, after a certain manner, by a certain conjunction and mutual series, whereby the parts of the world are mutually subordinate the one to the other, and have a mutual consent, by reason of their great union: as in a man's body, one member is moved by perceiving the motion of another; and in a harp, one string is moved by the motion of another. So when any one moves any part of the world, other parts are moved by the perceiving of that motion.*" The same consideration should be given to a fallen tooth, as it maintains the virtue of its owner. Practices of exchanging this lost part for something of value, a blessing or coin, span much of the world. For some it was a mouse, but for most it is the *Tooth-fairy* responsible for such a transaction: a macabre concept that implies the swapping of human body parts for blessings or money. **On another note**: Divination by fingernails is called *onychomancy*. In the Zoroastrian book known as <u>Vendidad</u> there is given similar consideration to hair and nails. Responding to Zoroaster, the King of Light informs him that when these two ingredients fall to the earth, they produce *Daevas* or "lice."

Abracadabra

Charms and talismans (from the Arabic *tilsam*, meaning *completion*) were traditionally made with *stones* or *jewels* and meant to protect their wearer against disease - one of the most common uses - or to repel poisons and acts of witchcraft the same. They can also be used to attract that which is thought agreeable, such as the *Celestial Virtues* of the planets and gods. For attracting the energies of art or justice one could wear a pendant calling on Minerva-Athena. To dissolve a relationship of any kind, business or personal, the energies of Saturn can be utilized. For winning a competition there is the goddess Nike. The most famous charm is probably *Abracadabra*, an incantation not unlike *open sesame*, used to heal and dissipate disease. The word was traditionally written on parchment and then slowly reduced downward from *ABRACADABRA* to *BRACADABR* and *RACADAB*, and so on, in doing so producing an inverted triangle pulling down on *Celestial Virtues*. In Genesis 11:1 we read that *"the whole world had one language and a common speech,"* and that the people, in attempting to build *"a city, with a tower that reaches to the heavens,"* thus greatly angered the Lord. *"Come, let us go down and confuse their language so they will not understand each other,"* the Lord says. So, the Lord did go about confusing their languages and then scattering *"them from there over all the earth."* Such a story conveys and implies far more than the confusion of mankind over *languages,* which are not specified in the story to be verbal communications. Perhaps the *confusion* stems from the introduction of vastly different *languages* into the human sphere, i.e., some development of *human speech.* The *"one language and a common speech"* therefore could relate to a universal language of symbols, intuition, and a simple *knowing.* After the introduction of *language,* by our modern definition, mankind became confused in his communications and was scattered about the earth. This story is important because it documents man's attempt to reach heaven from an earthly triangle, i.e., his attempt to usurp the authority of heaven and steal the *keys of wisdom.* Abracadabra, on the other hands, draws God's influence down.

When **ABRACADABRA** is used to create a magical charm, talisman, or amulet, it acts as a protective barrier against fever, sickness, witchcraft, and enchantments. It can be written in two forms, both inverted triangles. The first triangle is smaller, formed by removing the first and last letters of the word continually until there is only left one letter, thus dissipating the disease. The second triangle is larger, formed by the continued reduction of the final letter until there is only one letter remaining: *ABRACADABRA* becomes *ABRACADABR, ABRACADAB, ABRACADA,* and so on.

The Syrian word *Abracadabra* has traditionally been used as a magical charm or amulet. The word itself is said to come from Ab, Ben, Rauch, ACADosch – Hebrew for the trinity of Father, Son, and Holy Ghost. The earliest recorded account of its usage was in a poem called *Precepta de Medicina,* by Q. Serenus Scammonicus, a second century Gnostic physician. Its usage was recommended as a preventative measure against fevers originally. Interestingly, gingerbread has also been used in the same way: if written on and eaten properly it is believed to convey a medicinal benefit. If not inscribed on a medal *Abracadabra* can be written on a piece of parchment or paper. This paper is to then be folded into the form of a cross and worn for nine days, and then *"thrown backward before sunrise into a stream flowing eastward,"* according to William J. Fielding. When Abracadabra is worn in some manner next to the heart it is considered protection against the influence of spells and enchantments. There are several ways in which it may be written, but it should always be in the form of a triangle:

ABRACADABRA
BRACADABR
RACADAB
ACADA
CAD
A

ABRACADABRA
ABRACADABR
ABRACADAB
ABRACADA
ABRACAD
ABRACA
ABRAC
ABRA
ABR
AB
A

Abracadabra also conceals the name of the Hellenistic deity *Abraxas*. He is often associated with the name of Demiurge, IAO, the creator of the physical Universe. Typically, he is depicted with the head of a cock, which announces the return of the sun each morning. The sum of Abraxas (Ἀβραξας) in Greek is: A = 1, β = 2, ρ = 100, α = 1, ξ =60, α = 1, ς = 200, equating to 365, the number of days in the year as we have shown. He is a symbol of the 365 *Æons* or *Spirits of the Days* that bring about life and health with each new cycle.

As a symbol of protection, the triangle itself is used in all sorts of *evocations* and *invocations*. If spirits were drawn from *heaven*, a magician is to place himself at the top of the triangle and place the altar of fumigations at the bottom. If the spirit is drawn up from the *infernal*, or the abyss, the magician should place himself at the bottom of the triangle and place the altar above. This is for ceremonial magic. A triangle is one of the strongest structures on earth and holds at its three points the *Holy Trinity*. But no matter the *operation*, it is critical to understand that no amount of correspondence work, or postering of crucifixes and virgin statues, can replace the true *intention* of an operator, as Barret writes: "*…in forming of a charm, or amulet, it will be of no effect except for the very soul of the operator is strongly and intensely exerted and impressed, as it were, and the image of the idea sealed on the charm, or amulet; for without this, in vain will be all the observations of times, hours, and constellations; therefore, this I have thought fit to mention, once for all, that it may be almost always uppermost in the mind of the operator, for, without this one thing being observed and noticed, many who form seals, &c, do fall short of the wished-for effect.*"

~

Students of *Hermetic Medical Theory* recognized seven primary causes of disease and seven ways to treat, cure, or prevent them. The seven primary causes of disease were as follows: evil spirits, derangement of one's spiritual and material nature, unhealthy or abnormal mental attitudes, karma, the motion of heavenly bodies, misuses of the body, and foreign substances, obstructions, or impurities. The cures included *spells*, *vibrations*, *talismans* or *charms*, *herbs*, *prayer*, *prevention* and *purging*. No matter how fanciful or silly such things seem in retrospect, one should be careful to scoff quietly considering how all these measures are still employed today: we *spell* out *Get Well Soon* cards; speak kindly to the sick (*vibrations*); nearly every ambulance and hospital employs *caduceus* (*charms*); *herbology* is at the root of pharmaceutical drugs; we *pray* for better health; we attempt to *prevent* disease; we induce the *purging* of anything making us sick. Manly Hall explains how all "*the inharmonies of the bodies were neutralized by chanting spells and intoning the sacred names or by playing upon musical instruments and singing.*"

Barrett goes on to treat the work and theories of the physician Paracelsus, along with the ideas of philosopher Jan Baptist Von Helmont, by explaining the *healing sympathies* of our body. The idea that blood, hair, or nails retains a connection with the body after separation is ancient. He says that "*blood keeps a concordant harmony with the spirit of the whole, and draws forth from the same the offensive quality communicated, not only to the lips of the wound, but to the whole man, for from one wound only the whole man is liable to grow feverish.*" And Paracelsus directly says of the dark arts:

"*Witches give their hair to Satan as a deposit on the contract they make with him.*"

Kurt Seligmann provides further historical context on the same subject in his book The Mirror of Magic, describing how hair and nails were traditionally hidden, burned, or buried "*to prevent their falling into the hands of sorcery who would use them for evil spells against their former owners.*"

Something like blood contains not only our *life force* (Deuteronomy 12:23), which belongs to God (Leviticus 17:11), but depending on circumstance other parasitic forces as well. In fact, the mystic Rudolf Steiner explains exactly this:

> *"There are beings in the spiritual realms for whom anxiety and fear emanating from human beings offer welcome food. When humans have no anxiety and fear, then these creatures starve... If fear and anxiety radiates from people and they break out in panic, then these creatures find welcome nutrition, and they become more and more powerful."*

Scientists know this fact too: when we are in danger or afraid, *adrenalin* is pumped into our bloodstream as a survival mechanism. *Adrenochrome* is a chemical compound produced by the oxidation of this hormone. Such facts of body chemistry certainly enlighten us as to why the consumption of blood is so strongly associated with the image and idea of Satanic cults, which are usually hell bent on usurping the power of *life* and perverting its essence. These practitioners have no need for Abracadabra and instead choose to build the *Tower of Babel*

Magical Items

Talisman: the word is derived from the Greek *Teleo*, meaning "to consecrate." These objects are believed to have magical powers in attracting positive fortune and protection. They come in many forms, but typically are fashioned as rings or amulets. The components used in creating a talisman for hanging, wearing, or another format, are to be in *sympathy* with its designated purpose. According to Irish tradition, anyone finding a four-leaf clover is destined to obtain the qualities associated with such a symbol: hope, faith, love, and luck. A clover of this nature, or a seashell, stone, root, etc., can be used as a protective talisman.

Apotropaic: any item that has magical power and is used to deny evil influences, deflect harm, and avert misfortune.

Charm: any item can be charmed, be it a necklace, bracelet, or other piece of clothing or jewelry. Typically, these are small ornaments to be worn as an amulet or talisman. Charms are *enchanted* with the purpose of *delight*, i.e., to "charm" someone or "turn on" one's charm in a particular situation. Such *delight* can obviously be used for malicious intent.

Amulet: an ornament or small piece of jewelry offering protection against evil, disease, and other types of danger. Some of the oldest ever officially found date to around 2500 BCE and are mostly of the animal variety. The word "amulet" is derived from the Latin *Amuletum*, which, according to the writer Pliny, is *"an object that protects a person from trouble."* In Egypt, the word for amulet was *udjau*, the *"thing which keeps safe."* Essentially, a *charm* is an *amulet* inscribed with special characters (symbols or sayings), as with a talisman. Colors, numbers, insects, animals, etc., all act as amulets of protection, strength, luck, and health. Animal amulets include teeth, hair, claws, bones, etc. Vegetable amulets include herbs, leaves, trees, roots, flowers, etc. Mineral amulets include precious and semi-precious metals, ordinary stones, soil, sand, rocks, etc.

Enchant: to fill someone or an object with *delight*; to *enchant* something or someone and put them under *your spell*. A master of verbal communication, no matter their intent, can act to *enchant* and *charm* their way into a business deal, sexual encounter, and the like. There should be noted here a difference between those with strong communication and leadership skills, and a person with sociopathic tendencies.

Philtres: these are curious concoctions prepared to arouse feelings of *love* and *desire* in a consumer. Also referred to as a "love potion," the *philtre* acts like a liquid *charm* that has been *enchanted* with *delight* for a specific person. Personal items are to be incorporated into the mixture so that the target is *drinking your essence*. No matter how *loving* such things may seem, however, Arthur E. Waite says these are essentially "evil experiments.

Herbs: plants with leaves, seeds, or flowers used for flavoring food. In magical terms, herbs are appropriately used for perfumes and medicines, and in the creation of certain potions, i.e., herbal remedies and elixirs. With enough knowledge, such things can obviously be used to create poisons. The medicinal properties of plants and herbs are sometimes determined from their corresponding colors. Blue is soothing, yellow is vitalizing, and red is agitating.

Potion: a liquid with healing, magical, or poisonous properties – essentially an *herbal remedy* or *herbal poison*.

Stones: nonmetallic, hard, and solid mineral material of which rocks are made. Many are considered precious or semiprecious when cut and polished. Some stones are engraved, giving them magical qualities. Of certain stones used to attract *celestial virtues*, or to repel sickness and poison, Barrett explains: *"stones inherit great virtues, which they receive through the spheres and activity of the celestial influences, by the medium of the soul or spirit of the world."*

Ring Symbolism

Stones are most worn on rings either for accessory or to signify marriage. A ring, of any sort, has the meaning of *unification, perfection,* and *eternity*. Some rings, *on the other hand*, strictly signify power, although perhaps it is *eternal power*. Leaders throughout history often wore rings with a *signet*, or small seal, to give authentication (by pressed wax) of official documents. They can be made from gold, silver, ivory, amber, alabaster, crystal, etc. A *wedding ring* was originally intended to imply that the wearer had reached a state of *completion* and *equilibrium*, i.e., found their *other half* and completed the *Great Alchemical Work*. As a single band of gold, the ring stands as witness to the sacred wedding, or *Hieros Gamos,* and the ceremony consummating this *union* is the formalizing of the alchemical or hermetic marriage. Wednesday is known as "hump day" and from this day is derived "wed," meaning "to join." And indeed, this day does unite the other six days of the week from a place of balance in the center. Wednesdays would thus be a proper day to be wedded.

Magnetism & Mesmerism

Animal Magic or *Sympathetic magic* are ideas based on the principles of *magnetism*. This could mean *Like Attracts Like* or *Opposites Attract*. What we call *animal magnetism* was made popular by the Austrian physician Friedrich Anton Mesmer (1734-1815), who studied the works of Paracelsus intimately. He believed that the stars had influence on human health through an invisible fluid, and thus that healing powers could be found in one's own hands – *magnetism*. It is from his name that we derive the word *mesmerism*, meaning to *hypnotize* or *mesmerize*. Also published before the time of Mesmer was a work by William Maxwell, De Medicina Magnetica, wherein it was described the following of *material rays* that flow from all bodies in which souls operate:

> *"By these rays energy and the power of working are diffused. The vital spirit which descends from the sky, pure, unchanged and whole, is the parent of the vital spirit which exists in all things. If you make*

use of the universal spirit by means of instruments impregnated with this spirit you will thereby call to your aid the great secret of the Mages. The universal medicine is nothing but the vital spirit repeated in the proper subject."

Magnetism essentially works as such: by taking a new knife and cutting open a lemon while using words of hatred or disgust against an individual, the absent party is said to feel an inexpressible and striking anguish of the heart, along with cold chills and failures throughout the body. Such an act, of course, is baneful and truly causes harm only to the operator with their *spite* – the sorcerers harm themselves while attempting to harm others.

Here are other examples of such foolishness, or misunderstanding: suspending the image of a man by a single thread may induce fear and death; swallowing the warm heart of a bird, mole, weasel, or lapwing is believed to improve intellect through the retaining of their virtues; fear can be induced by the eye of a wolf, or fat of a bear, and love by the blood of doves; the juice of a nightshade, if distilled, will make any party imagine whatever you choose.

From *Mesmer* are certainly derived *hypnotic gestures* and *parlor tricks*, but the idea of *magnetism* itself is to essentially call on *Celestial* and *Earthy* virtues and correspondences. Nevertheless, Mesmer supposedly utilized his theory of *magnetic fluid* in the body to heal enough people to become the target of the medical establishment. He also believed that the stable mind of a physician was as equally important as the treatment itself: *"if the will of an individual could be concentrated and correctly focused, he would inevitably bring about physiological changes in the biological condition of the patient."*

Animal Magnetism, or *hypnosis*, as made popular by the Austrian physician, Friedrich Anton Mesmer.

The signet ring of Pythagoras, from Vincenzo Cartari's <u>Imagini degli Dei degli Antichi</u>.

The five-pointed star is associated with the art of healing. It represents health because the symbol calls upon the *four elements* and the *spirit* for protection. When a circle is added to encapsulate the pentagram it becomes a pentacle, or *a talisman or magical object, typically disk-shaped and inscribed with a pentagram or other figure, and used as a symbol of the element of earth.* The Pythagorean ring was used as a talisman of health with each interior angle assigned one of the letters of the Greek word ΥΓΕΙΑ, or the Latin SALUS, both of which signify *health.* On the subject of the pentagram Hall writes:

> *"The pentagram is used extensively in black magic, but when so used its form always differs in one of three ways: The star may be broken at one point by not permitting the converging lines to touch; it may be inverted by having one point down and two up, or it may be distorted by having the points of varying lengths. When used in black magic, the pentagram is called the 'sign of the cloven hoof,' or the footprint of the Devil. The star with two points upward is also called the 'Goat of Mendes,' because the inverted star is the same shape as a goat's head. When the upright star turns, and the upper point falls to the bottom, it signifies the fall of the Morning Star."*

Magnetic Love

A *love potion* may be part of "evil experiments," because it intends to bind the soul-sprit of another sovereign being, but there are natural methods of meeting the same ends. As with *adrenalin* and *adrenochrome*, mammals and insects release chemical substances called *pheromones* into the environment to attract mates. These chemicals may also repel mates that are not a proper biological or genetic match.

There are social customs as well which are a sort of *love potion*. In cultured societies, a man traditionally "courts" a woman with *charm* by offering objects and symbols that express his feelings. He may write poetry, letters, or sing songs, which are all actions of *casting spells* and performing *sacred dances*. Whether she will be interested or not is another matter altogether. But as per what is *attractive*, from the Latin *attractivus*, is a certain *magnetism* that may also be *repulsive* in nature.

What is most critical to understand here is that *creation* itself is magical and attempting to distill its essence for selfish gains is wicked.

Diamonds are the Devil's Worst Enemy

St. Hildegard, the writer, mystic, and philosopher, held diamonds in great esteem. She believed that they frustrated the Devil fiercely due to their natural power in attracting women into committed relationships. This is opposed to the naked *Black Mass*.

In Egypt and Arabia, the diamond was thought to bring good fortune and luck much like the Irish four-leaf clover. Unlike some stones, however, diamonds are said to only retain their *virtues* if acquired as gifts in the form of rings or amulets. They are said to hold little power if purchased or stolen; they must be gifted to possess power.

In French lore the saliva of gathering snakes is said to form the diamond, i.e., *wise serpents* produce symbols of *purity*. Folklore around the world also associates the diamond with serpents. The Celts had *snake stones* and their priestly class, the Druids, said many snakes would gather around said stone in fascination. In Celtic countries (Irish, Scottish, etc.) these stones were sometimes referred to as *adder-stones*. Diamonds are also held in high regard by alchemists for their natural properties.

A quartz crystal is a similar stone and symbol of purity. Being colorless in nature and consisting of silicon rather than pure carbon like the diamond, a quartz crystal is revered as having magical qualities. The mineral has been used as a prop for magicians from the Aborigines of Australia and Polynesia to the people of North America and elsewhere. Professor Charles Seligman writes in The Melanesians of British New Guinea how *"certain charm stones - as far as my knowledge goes these are always of quartz - are so highly charged with magical power that it is not considered safe for them to be touched with the hand."* Both clear quartz and rose quartz, alongside of diamonds, would make an acceptable wedding ring.

Magical Stones & their Attributes

Amber, especially red-amber, is worn as protection against poisons and pestilence. The oil of amber, or amber dissolved into pure spirit of wine, is said to comfort the womb and stomach. Barrett writes of the latter: *"if a suffumigation of it be made with the warts of the shank of a horse, it will cure many disorders of that region."*

Amethyst is a variety of quartz useful in inducing self-control over sexual passions. This precious stone is used for protecting the wearer from diseases. It is thought to cure drunkenness and also preserve soldiers from the hazards of battle. It is also thought to have a special use for hunters.

Blue Sapphire is efficient in protecting against poisons and pestilence. It also protects from *envy* while attracting virtues from the heavens. For this reason, sapphire is a symbol chosen often by royalty. Barrett writes of this stone: *"A sapphire, or a stone that is of a deep blue color, if it be rubbed on a tumor, wherein the plague discovers itself (before the party is too far gone) and by and by it be removed from the sick, the absent jewel attracts all the poison or contagion therefrom."* **Star Sapphire** was believed by some to provide protection against witchcraft and evils of every kind.

Cat's-Eye is a variety of chrysoberyl, used by natives of Ceylon (Sri Lanka) as a charm against evil spirits.

Emerald, sometimes called *beryl*, like other stones, comes in different forms. Whether green or aquamarine, emerald is sympathetically linked to vegetation and water, i.e., the Green Man and the patron of water – Venus, Aphrodite, Isis, etc. Emeralds are said to be birthed, grow, and die in relation to the seasons. The terms *beryl* or *emerald* are used in the Bible to describe Jesus in the book of Daniel (10:6) and heaven in the book of Revelation (4). Emerald is also described as being the foundation of the New Jerusalem in Revelation 21. **Beryl** is said to preserve happiness and youth.

Moonstone is venerated in India as a sacred stone that brings good fortune. It is an appropriate gift for lovers since the stone is thought to arouse tender passions.

Opal gained a reputation of ill luck in the west, but in the Orient, it is regarded as a gem of good fortune which acts to prevent its wearer from certain diseases. Early writers on the subject called this stone *Ophthalmias* and believed it had tremendous benefit to eyesight. The name is derived from *ophthalmos*, meaning "eye," or *ophthalmius*, "pertaining to the eye." There is a perhaps an interesting relationship between opal and the Greek myth of Zeus involving the *Omphalos* stone, meaning "center or hub of something." Perhaps the "eye" is the one in the *center* of your forehead, i.e., the *Third Eye*. Opal has also been called *patronus furum*, the stone able to render the wearer invisible.

Although they are not *stones*, per se, *pearl* and *coral* share in their qualities. The Gaelic name for **pearl** is *neamhnuid*, relating to "a heavenly thing," and the ancient Persian name for a pearl, *margan*, is defined as "life giver." Pearls therefore are associated with the sacred groves of the goddess and her life-giving qualities. This association is made stronger by the fertilizing waters that birth a pearl, which cause this spherical mass to be regarded as a symbol of fertility. Venus was birthed from the ocean in a shell and her Greek counterpart, Aphrodite, means "foam born." The Romans and Greeks wore pearls to win her favor and blessings. In Norse mythology the pearl, along with amber and other precious stones, was thought to be solidified tear droplets of the goddess Freya, who is identified with Frigga, for which Friday is named. According to Oriental tradition, pearls have medicinal properties. Wearing them is said to clear the skin and enhance beauty. There is a belief in India that burnt powder of pearls, if taken with water, cures hemorrhages, lunacy, general mental illnesses, and defeats those evil spirits working mischief on the mind. The pearl is described in the sacred Hindu scripture <u>Atharva-Veda</u> as such:

> *"With the shell that was born of the sea, foremost among bright substances, we slay the Rakshas and conjure the Atrins; with the shell we conquer disease and poverty; the shell is our universal remedy. Thou art the daughter of the Moon; the bones of the gods turned into the sea-dwelling pearl. I fasten it upon thee that thy life may be long, lustrous and mighty, that it may last a hundred autumns, protected by the pearl."*

Coral is sometimes referred to as the *sea tree* and was likewise considered a symbol of the mother goddess for its association with water. Used as an amulet it provides protection against poisons, sorcery, and glances of the *evil eye*. Opal or *ophthalmos* may provide the same protections. The Romans used coral as a charm against sterility, as per its relationship to the fertilizing qualities of the ocean, and in Asia and Africa it was once a common accessory for women. Coral is said to be particularly effective in curing childhood disabilities, because, again, the mother protects her children. For adults it is an antipathy to pains of the stomach.

~ Relating to other Stones, Gems, & Jewels ~

Agate promotes health, wealth, and longevity; **Carnelian** bolsters courage, while strengthening articulation and self-confidence; **Chrysolite** offers protection against evil spirits if the stone, according to some writers, is pierced, strung on the hair of an ass, and attached to the left arm. If the stone be set in gold and worn as a talisman or amulet it is said to banish terrors of the night. Chrysolite is also supposed to be good for overall lung health. **Garnet** ensures power, grace, and victory; **Hyacinth** is useful for second sight; **Jacinth** is a gem of modesty; **Jade** is indicative of good fortune; **Jasper** promotes courage and wisdom, and protects against bloody-flux (dysentery); **Onyx** is a variety of agate beneficial to conjugal felicity (happy marriage); **Ruby** is a precious stone of charity, divine power, and dignity; **Topaz** supports friendship and fidelity, and is naturally the antipathy of lust; **Turquoise** has the feature of preserving a wearer from injury in case of falling. Eliphas Levi explains the following correspondences between days of the week, their stones and metals, and the types of accessories to be worn by ceremonial magicians, or those seeking similar *Celestial Virtues*:

Sunday: a golden wand in the right hand, set with a ruby or chrysolite.

Monday: wear a collar of three strands of pearls, selenites, and crystals.

Tuesday: carry a wand of magnetized steel and wear a ring of the same metal fixed with amethyst.

Wednesday: wear a necklace of glass or pearl beads that contain mercury and a ring set with agate.

Thursday: carry a wand of glass and wear a ring set with either emerald or sapphire.

Friday: carry a wand of copper and wear a ring set with turquoise; wear a crown decorated with lapis lazuli.

Saturday: carry a wand containing onyx stone and wear a ring set with the same stone, along with a chain upon the neck made of lead.

Here is a more modern account, still dependent for accuracy upon certain opinions, listing the birth month and its associated stone:

Month	Birth Stone
January	Garnet
February	Amethyst
March	Bloodstone
April	Diamond
May	Emerald
June	Pearl
July	Ruby
August	Sardonyx
September	Sapphire
October	Opal
November	Topaz
December	Turquoise

Below are the stones for each of the months, as described by Agrippa in his *Occult Philosophy*, along with their astrological symbol and zodiac sign:

	Astrological Symbol	Month commencing about the 21st of preceding month	Stone
Aries (The Ram)	♈	April	Sardonyx
Taurus (The Bull)	♉	May	Carnelian
Gemini (The Twins)	♊	June	Topaz
Cancer (The Crab)	♋	July	Chalcedony
Leo (The Lion)	♌	August	Jasper
Virgo (The Virgin)	♍	September	Emerald
Libra (The Balance)	♎	October	Beryl
Scorpius (The Scorpion)	♏	November	Amethyst
Sagittarius (The Archer)	♐	December	Hyacinth* (=Sapphire)
Capricornus (The Goat)	♑	January	Chrysoprase
Aquarius (The Water-bearer)	♒	February	Crystal
Pisces (The Fishes)	♓	March	Sapphire* (=Lapis-lazuli)

Gemstones of the Planets, Zodiac, Months & Elements

SUN: Amber, diamond, topaz
MOON: Moonstone, pearl
EARTH: Amber, jade, ammonite
MERCURY: Agate, opal, citrine
VENUS: Malachite, rose quartz, emerald
MARS: Hematite, ruby, spinel
JUPITER: Sapphire, lapis lazuli, turquoise
SATURN: Jet, onyx, coral
URANUS: Opal, amethyst
NEPTUNE: Aquamarine, coral, pearl
PLUTO: Diamond, jade, zircon

ARIES: Diamond, bloodstone
TAURUS: Emerald, lapis lazuli
GEMINI: Agate, citrine
CANCER: Moonstone, pearl
LEO: Peridot, amber
VIRGO: Aquamarine, carnelian
LIBRA: Jacinth, amethyst
SCORPIO: Opal, sapphire
SAGITTARIUS: Turquoise, topaz
CAPRICORN: Onxy, garnet
AQUARIUS: Garnet, aquamarine
PISCES: Amethyst, bloodstone

JANUARY: Garnet
FEBRUARY: Amethyst
MARCH: Heliotrope, jasper
APRIL: Diamond, sapphire
MAY: Agate, emerald
JUNE: Emerald, pearl, agate
JULY: Onyx
AUGUST: Carnelian
SEPTEMBER: Peridot
OCTOBER: Aquamarine, beryl
NOVEMBER: Topaz
DECEMBER: Ruby

Air: Agate, citrine, lapis lazuli, opal, rose quartz, sapphire, turquoise
Fire: Amber, citrine, fire opal, garnet, heliotrope, ruby, spinel, topaz
Water: Amethyst, aquamarine, coral, lapis lazuli, moonstone, pearl, tourmaline, turquoise
Earth: Amber, ammonite, emerald, jet, magnetite, malachite, jade, onyx
Ether: Amethyst, diamond, opal, pearl, rock crystal, sapphire, tourmaline, zircon

Suffumigations & Incense

The active elements of air and fire, and the passive elements of earth and water, are used with *incense* to invoke certain *Celestial Virtues*. As with correspondences for stones, plants, animals, etc., incense is burned according to its planetary associations, and the smoke is carried from the fire up into the airy heavens. Otherwise called *vapors* and *perfumes*, suffumigations (incense) can be *sweet* or *pungent*. This is why one should purify the home with incense, and the body with water and deodorants like essential oils, to attract *angelic influence*. This is also why animal sacrifices are said to call upon malevolent spirits, because the rotting carcass and its blood are pleasing to these infernal energies, i.e., *death*.

Each sign of the zodiac and each planet is given at least one complementary incense: *myrrh* for Aries; *pepper-wort* for Taurus; *mastich* for Gemini; *camphire* for Cancer; *frankincense* for Leo; *sanders* for Virgo; *galbanum* for Libra; *oppoponax* Scorpio; *lignum aloes* for Sagittarius; *benjamin* for Capricorn; *euphorbium* for Aquarius; and *red storax* for Pisces.

Appropriate for Saturn are odoriferous roots: pepper-wort root & frankincense tree; to Jupiter are odoriferous fruits: nutmegs and cloves; to Mars are odoriferous woods: sanders, cyprus, lignum aloes, and lignum balsam; to Venus are flowers: roses, violets, saffron, etc.; to Mercury are parings of wood or fruit: cinnamon, mace, citron peel, bay-berries; to the Moon are leaves of all vegetables such as myrtle or bay tree; to the Sun are all gums: frankincense, storax, and musk.

According to Francis Barret these are the following compositions of perfumes, as appropriate to attract the *Celestial Virtues* of the seven classical planets:

THE SUN ☉

WE make a suffumigation for the sun in this manner: Take of saffron, ambergris, musk, lignum aloes, lignum balsam, the fruit of the laurel, cloves, myrrh, and frankincense; of each a like quantity; all of which being bruised, and mixed together, so as to make a sweet odour, must be incorporated with the brain of an eagle, or the blood of a white cock, after the manner of pills, or troches.

THE MOON ☽

For the moon, we make a suffume of the head of a frog dried, and the eyes of a bull, the seed of white poppies, frankincense, and camphire, which must be incorporated with menstruous blood, or the blood of a goose.

SATURN ♄

For Saturn take the seed of black poppies, henbane, mandrake root, loadstone, and myrrh, and mix them up with the brain of a cat and the blood of a bat.

JUPITER ♃

Take the seed of ash, lignum aloes, storax, the gum Benjamin, the lapis lazuli, the tops of peacocks' feathers, and incorporate with the blood of a stork, or swallow, or the brain of a hart.

MARS ♂

Take uphorbium, bdellium, gum armoniac, the roots of both hellebores, the loadstone, and a little sulphur, and incorporate them altogether with the brain of a hart, the blood of a man, and the blood of a black cat.

VENUS ♀

Take musk, ambergris, lignum aloes, red roses, and red coral, and make them up with sparrow's brains and pigeon's blood.

MERCURY ☿

Take mastich, frankincense, cloves, and the herb cinquefoil, and the agate stone, and incorporate them all with the brain of a fox, or weasel, and the blood of a magpie.

~

When performing suffumigations, the <u>Grimorium Verum</u> (or *The True Grimoire*), published by "Alibeck the Egyptian" in 1517, provides us with an exorcism, oration, blessing, invocation, and method to properly carry out this process appropriate to magical tradition. We are also reminded to be in the grace of God and to have nothing reproachful on our conscience. As evil spirits are raised through profane arts, so those good spirits are called upon through pure minds, prayers, confessions, and works of light. To act otherwise would be to subject ourself to the *will* of any spirit other than our own.

Exorcism of the Incense

O God of Abraham, God of Isaac, God of Jacob, deign to bless these odoriferous spices so that they may receive strength, virtue, and power to attract the Good Spirits, and to banish and cause to retire all hostile Phantoms. Through Thee, O Most Holy ADONAI, Who livest and reignest unto the Ages of the Ages. Amen.

I exorcise thee, O Spirit impure and unclean, thou who art a hostile Phantom, in the Name of God, that thou quit this Perfume, thou and all thy deceits, that it may be consecrated and sanctified in the name of God Almighty. May the Holy Spirit of God grant protection and virtue unto those who use these Perfumes; and may the hostile and evil Spirit and Phantom never be able to enter therein, through the Ineffable Name of God Almighty. Amen.

O Lord, deign to bless and to sanctify this Creature of Perfume so that it may be a remedy unto mankind for the health of body and of soul, through the Invocation of Thy Holy Name. May all Creatures who receive the odour of this incense and of these spices receive health of body and of soul, through Him Who hath formed the Ages. Amen.

Oration of the aromatic scents

God of Abraham, God of Isaac, God of Jacob, God of our fathers, blessed this paper and increase the power of these odors, so that they receive in them the virtue to attract the spirits that I will invoke, and that all deceits may depart from it, through you, O most holy Adonay, who reigns without end. Amen.

Blessing of the aromatic scents

Deign O Lord, to bless and to sanctify these scents, so that they are a health-bringing remedy for us, bringing salvation to our bodies and spirits, with your holy aid, Lord Adonay, God who reigns through the infinite ages. Amen.

Invocation to be said while fumigating

Angels of God be our help, and may our work be completed. Zazay, Salmay, Dalmay, Angerecton, Ledrion, Amisor, Euchey, Or, great angels, Adonay, be present with us here, and grant N. the virtue to receive such force, that through it our work may be accomplished, in the name of the Father and of the Son and the Holy Spirit Amen.

The way to sprinkle and fumigate
Oration that must be said while sprinkling

In the name of immortal God, may God sprinkle you N., and purify you of all deceit and wickedness, and you will be whiter than snow. Amen.

Purify me, O Lord, with hyssop, and I shall be pure;
wash me and I shall be whiter than snow.

Concerning Holy Water

Preparatory Oration - Holy Water

O Lord God Adonay, you who has created mankind out of nothing after your own image and resemblance; although I am an unworthy sinner, I pray that you deign to bless and sanctify this water, so that it is beneficial to my body and spirit, and that all deceit depart from me, O Lord God omnipotent and ineffable, even as your people departed from the land of Egypt, and you allowed them to pass over the Red Sea on dry fee, grant your grace to me, that being purified by this water of all my sins, I may appear innocent before you. Amen.

Sprinkle the holy water, saying

In the name of the Father and the Son and the Holy Spirit Amen.

Of the aspersion of the water

Lord, God almighty Father, my refuge and my life, help me, O holy father, because I put my trust in you, God of Abraham, God of Isaac, God of Jacob, God of the angels, God of the archangels and prophets, creator of all. I humbly pray through the invocation of your name, though I am not worthy to invoke it, and I humbly call upon you to bless and consecrate this water, so that whomever it is sprinkled on, will be restored to health of body [and soul], through you, O most holy Adonay, whose reign is endless.

The Holy Pentacles

Consultation of <u>The Greater Key of Solomon</u>, among other relatable texts on the subject, will provide one with correspondences and procedures for constructing the pentacles of Saturn, Jupiter, Mars, Venus, Mercury, the Moon, and Sun. Of these bodies each has its own set of pentacles to which Saturn, Jupiter, Mars, and the Sun are given seven; to Venus and Mercury are given five; and to the moon are given six.

Concerning the Holy Pentacles or Medals

They are also of great virtue and efficacy against all perils of Earth, of Air, of Water, and of Fire, against poison which hath been drunk, against all kinds of infirmities and necessities, against binding, sortilege, and sorcery, against all terror and fear, and wheresoever thou shalt find thyself, if armed with them, thou shalt be in safety all the days of thy life.

The corresponding colors are as follows: **Saturn** is *black*; **Jupiter** is *celestial blue*; **Mars** is *red*; the **Sun** is *gold* or *yellow*; V**enus** is *green*; **Mercury** has *mixed colors*; and the **Moon** is *silver*.

In constructing the pentacles and characters, it is necessary, according to <u>The Greater Key of Solomon</u>, to burn temple incense. You must have "*ever in your mind no other intention than the glory of God, the accomplishment of your desires, and loving kindness towards your neighbor.*"

Solomon instructs us to never "*profane the things which are divine, for if you do this, far from rendering you a friend of the spirits, it will but be the means of bringing you unto destruction.*"

The pentacles are listed on the following pages, as extracted from that grimoire, and may be referenced with each description below.

A) The Seven Pentacles consecrated to Saturn are here provided in correspondence with their value.
(Figures 11-17)

1. Striking terror in spirits.
2. Is of great value against adversaries.
3. Good for use at night when the spirits of Saturn are called at night.
4. Useful for carrying out experiments of destruction and death.
5. Defense of those invoking spirits of Saturn at night. Chases away spirits guarding treasures.
6. The person for whom this is pronounced shall be obsessed by demons.
7. Useful for exciting earthquakes.

(B) The Seven Pentacles consecrated to Jupiter are here provided in correspondence with their value.
(Figures 18-24)

1. Useful for invoking spirits of Jupiter.
2. Useful in acquiring glory, dignity, honor, etc., and tranquility of mind. Also, to discover treasure and chase away spirits guarding the latter.
3. Defense against those invoking spirits. It forces the spirits to obey.
4. Use to acquire wealth and honor.
5. Serves for visions.
6. Protection against all earthly dangers, especially by devotion and repeating this versicle: "*Thus shalt thou never perish.*"
7. Power against poverty. Drives away spirits guarding treasures.

(C) The Seven Pentacles consecrated to Mars are here provided in correspondence with their value.
(Figures 25-31)

1. Used to invoke spirits of the nature of Mars.
2. Protects against disease.
3. Valuable for exciting war, discord, hostility, etc., and for resisting enemies.
4. Provides virtue and power in war, and victory.
5. Terrifies demons and upon view they will obey you.
6. Used for protection against attacks so that you will not be injured or wounded.
7. In invoking demons you shall see hail and tempest.

(D) The Seven Pentacles consecrated to the Sun are here provided in correspondence with their value.
(Figures 32-38)

1. All creatures obey, and angelic spirits kneel.
2. Represses the pride and arrogance of the solar spirits.
3. Serves to inflict loss and acquire glory, especially by the name Tetragrammaton.
4. Enables you to see spirits when they appear invisible to those who invoke them.
5. Useful in invoking spirits to transport you from one place unto another.
6. Serves for the operation of invisibility.
7. Frees the imprisoned.

(E.) The Five Pentacles consecrated to Venus are here provided in correspondence with their value.
(Figures 39-43)

1. Controls spirits of Venus.
2. Used for obtaining grace and honor.
3. Serves to attract love.
4. Compels spirits of Venus to obey, forces instantly any person desired to come unto thee.
5. It incites and excites love.

(F) The Five Pentacles consecrated to Mercury are here provided in correspondence with their value.
(Figures 44-48)

1. Invokes spirits who are under the firmament.
2. Bring to effect and to grant things contrary to the order of nature
3. Invokes spirits subject to Mercury.
4. Proper to acquire the understanding and knowledge of all things created.
5. Commands the spirits of Mercury; serves to open doors in whatever way they are closed.

(G) The Six Pentacles consecrated to the Moon are here provided in correspondence with their value.
(Figures 49-53)

1. Serves to call upon spirits of the Moon and to open doors.
2. Protects against all dangers by water.
3. Serves against all attacks by night and against every peril by water.
4. Defends you from all evil and from all injury unto soul or body.
5. Serves to have answers in sleep.
6. Excites and causes heavy rains (image not included).

PLATE II.

Fig. 6.

hels, hels, hels, ⊕ ⊻ ✝ A ⌐∟

Fig. 7.

ABIMEGH o≻))≻o

Fig. 8.

Dv ROSA o≺≼⊢o o o o M 3 Λ 3

Fig. 9.

RAZIEL רזיאל

Fig. 10.

NOPA ⟨⟨⟨⫸≻≺≺≺≺ o PADOUS

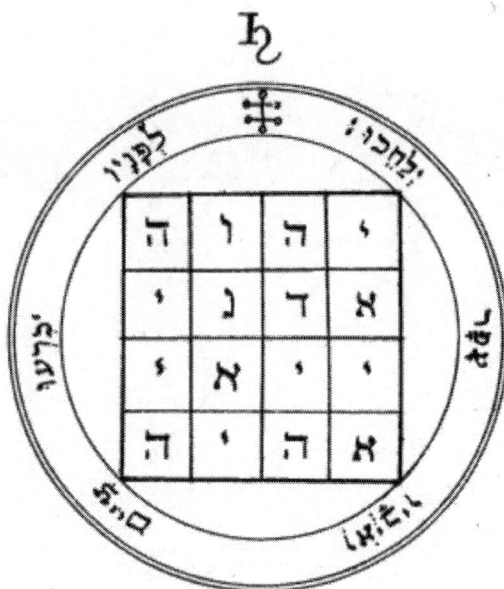

Fig. 11.

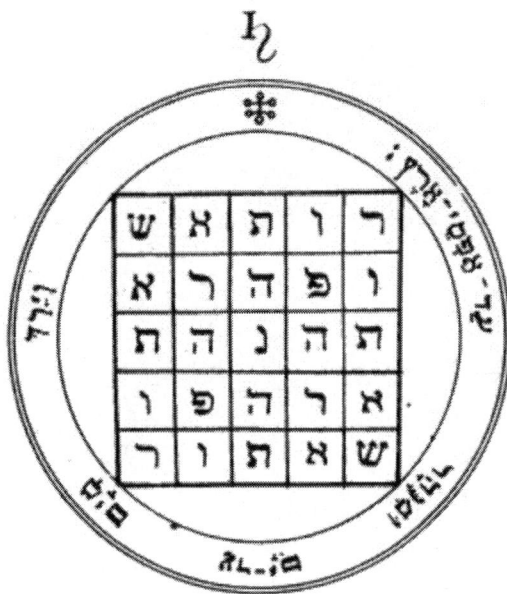

Fig. 12.

Fig. 13.

PLATE III.

Fig. 14.

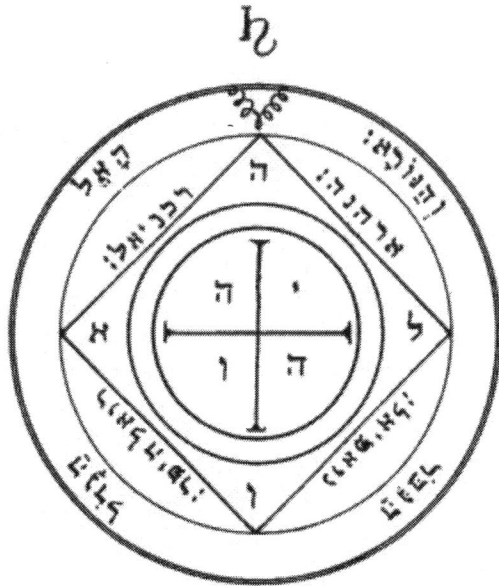

Fig. 15.

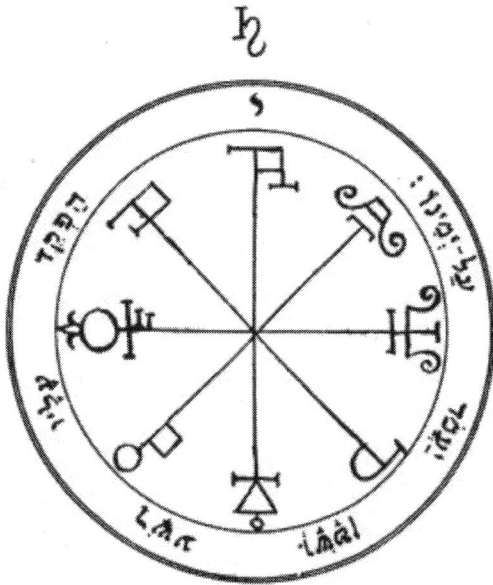

Fig. 16.

Fig. 17.

PLATE IV.

Fig. 18.

Fig. 19.

Fig. 20.

Fig. 21.

PLATE V.

Fig. 22.

Fig. 23.

Fig. 24.

Fig. 25.

PLATE VI.

Fig. 26.

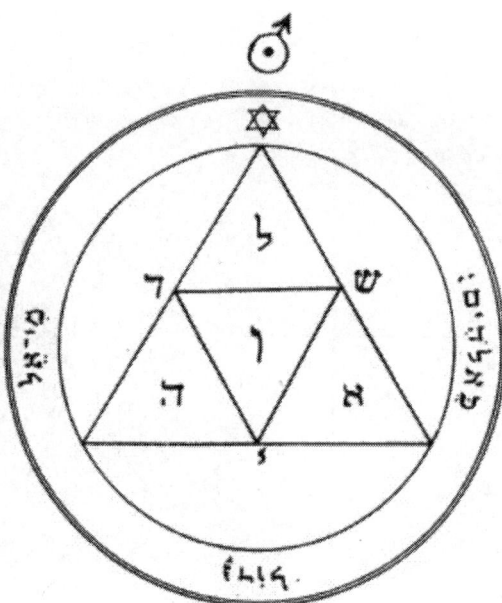

Fig. 27.

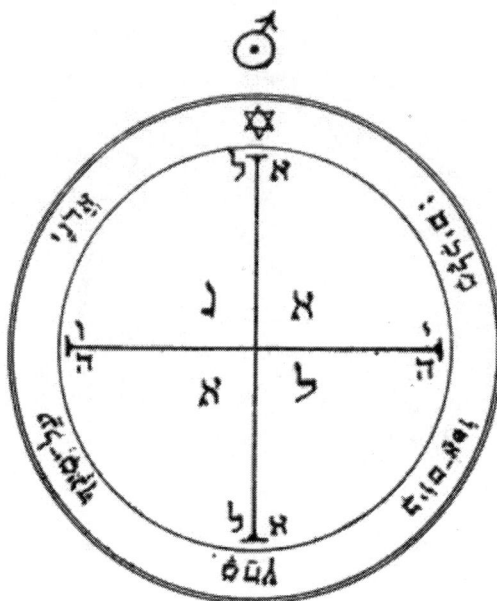

Fig. 28.

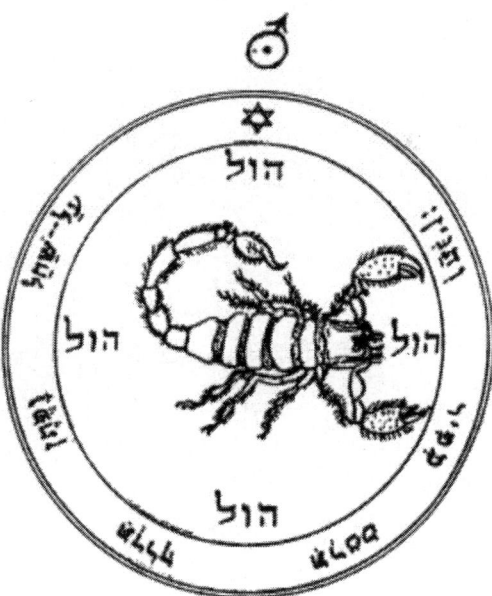

Fig. 29.

PLATE VII.

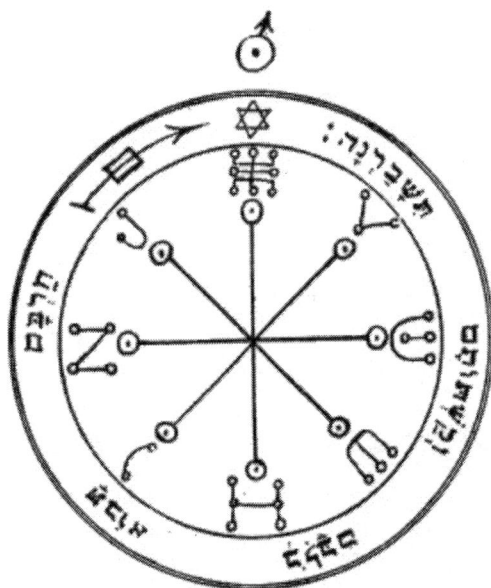

Fig. 30.

Fig. 31.

Fig. 32.

Fig. 33.

PLATE VIII.

Fig. 34.

Fig. 35.

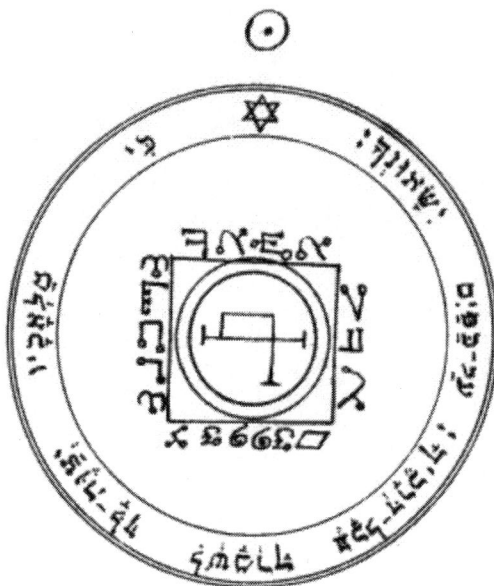

Fig. 36.

Fig. 37.

PLATE IX.

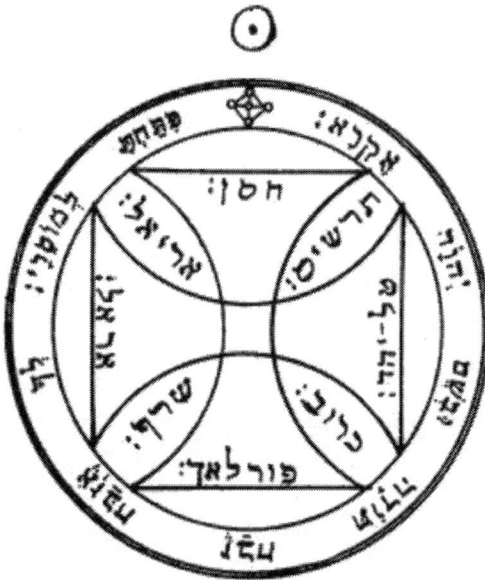

Fig. 38.

Fig. 39.

Fig. 40

Fig. 41.

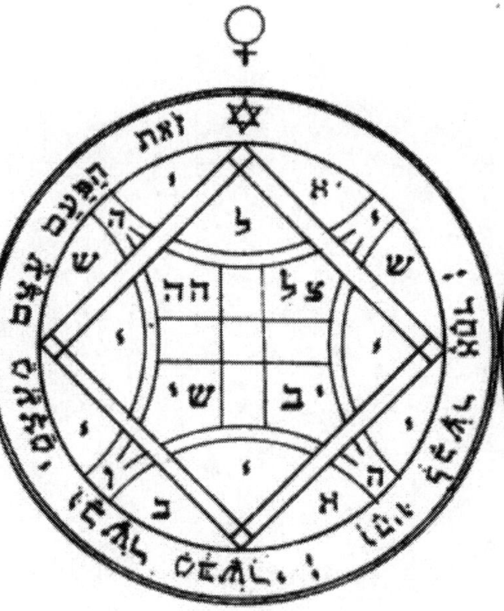

PLATE X.

Fig. 42.

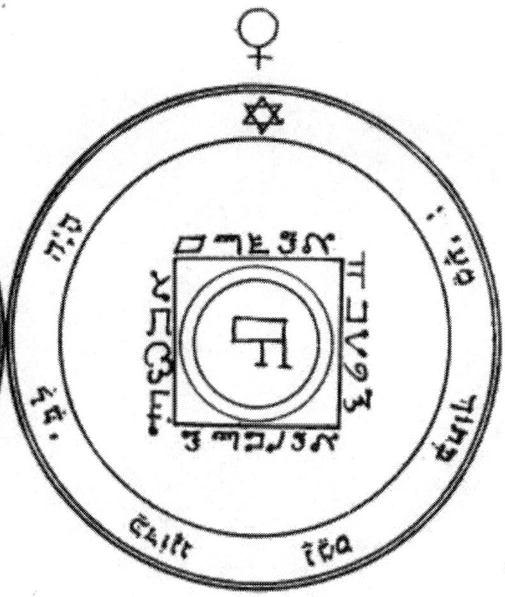

Fig. 43.

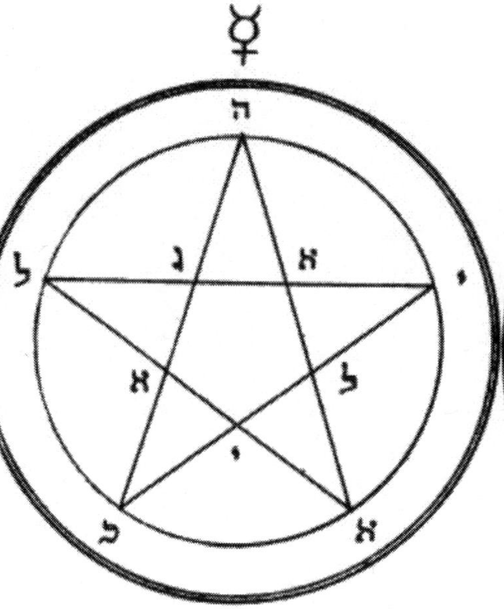

Fig. 44.

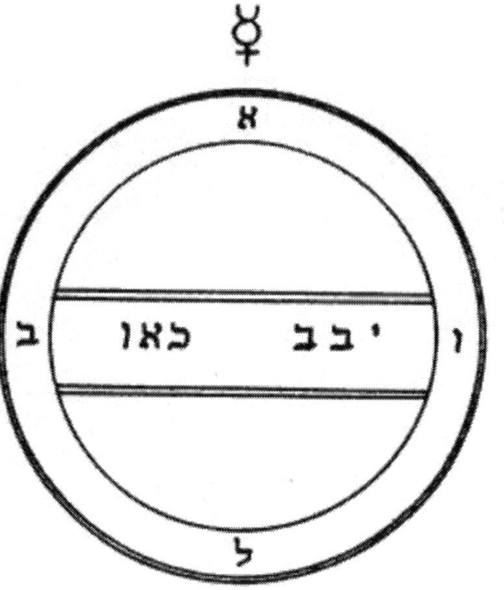

Fig. 45.

PLATE XI.

Fig. 46.

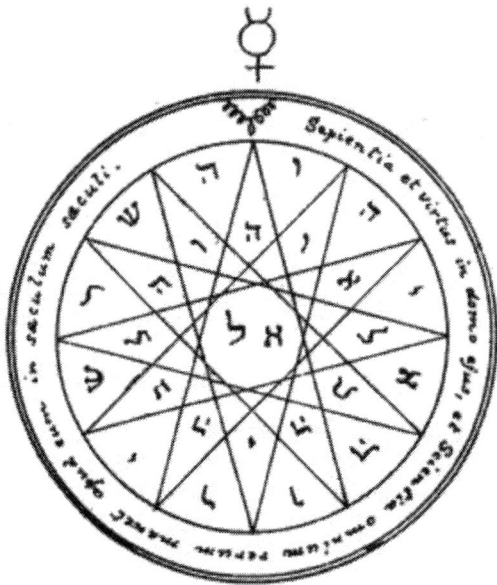

Fig. 47.

Fig. 48.

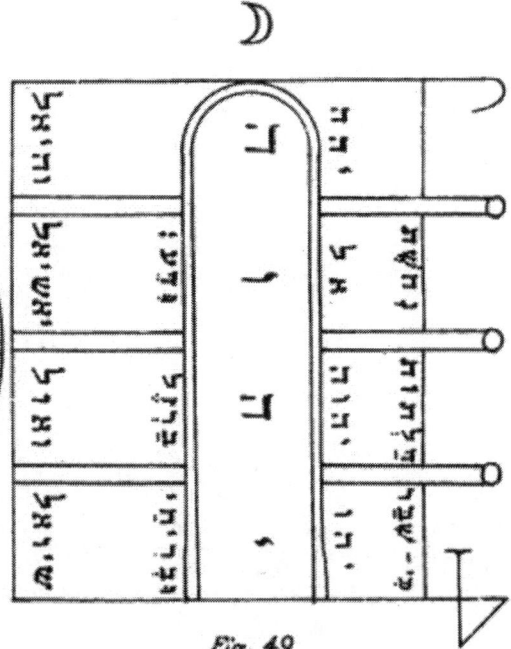

Fig. 49.

PLATE XII.

Fig. 50.

Fig. 51.

Fig. 52.

Fig. 53.

Introduction to the Study of Natural Magic by Kurt Seligmann

To the faithful and discreet Student of Wisdom.

TAKE our instructions; in all things ask counsel of God, and he will give it; offer up the following prayer daily for the illumination of thy understanding: depend for all things on God, the first cause; with whom, by whom, and in whom, are all things: see thy first care be to know thyself; and then in humility direct thy prayer as follows.

Of Natural Magic in General

BEFORE we proceed to particulars, it will not be amiss to speak of generals; therefore, as an elucidation, we shall briefly show what sciences we comprehend under the title of Natural Magic; and to hasten to the point, we shall regularly proceed from theory to practice; therefore, Natural Magic undoubtedly comprehends a knowledge of all Nature, which we by no means can arrive at but by searching deeply into her treasury, which is inexhaustible; we therefore by long study, labour, and practice, have found out many valuable secrets and experiments, which are either unknown, or are buried in the ignorant knowledge of the present age. The wise ancients knew that in Nature the greatest secrets lay hid, and wonderful active powers were dormant, unless excited by the vigorous faculty of the mind of man; but as, in these latter days, men have themselves almost wholly up to vice and luxury, so their understandings have become more and more depraved; 'till, being swallowed up in the gross senses, they become totally unfit for divine contemplations and deep speculations in Nature; their intellectual faculty being drowned in obscurity and dullness, by reason of their sloth, intemperance, or sensual appetites. The followers of Pythagoras enjoined silence, and forbade the eating of the flesh of animals; the first, because they were cautious, and aware of the vanity of vain babbling and fruitless cavillations: they studied the power of numbers to the highest extent; they forbade the eating of flesh not so much on the score of transmigration, as to keep the body in a healthful and temperate state, free from gross humours; by these means they qualified themselves for spiritual matters, and attained unto great and excellent mysteries, and continued in the exercise of charitable arts, and the practice of all moral virtues: yet, seeing they were heathens, they attained not unto the high and inspired lights of wisdom and knowledge that were bestowed on the Apostles, and others, after the coming of Christ; but they mortified their lusts, lived temperately, chaste, honest, and virtuous; which government is so contrary to the practice of modern Christians, that they live as if the blessed word had come upon the earth to grant them privilege to sin.

Purifying the Body & Mind

Expiation of Body, Mind & Instrument

Washing the body is symbolic of cleansing the soul. This is perhaps the most important action to be taken, besides being chaste, if one seeks to practice *pure ritual magic*. The mind must also be washed clean; not troubled, distracted, or filled with guilt. We must have strong willpower, hope, faith, intention, and the like towards that which we seek to accomplish, but be void of carnal desires, distrust, greed, lust, envy, covetous, idleness and excess luxury.

From ink and pen to the wax of a candle, to metal, parchment, incense, our clothes, etc., all instruments must be *cleansed* and *virginal*, i.e., having either been *purified* or never used for any other purpose other than the operation soon to be performed. As was written in Isaiah 1:16 about purification:

"Wash you, make you clean; put away the evil of your doings from before mine eyes; ceases to do evil."

The same is said about animal *meat* and alcoholic *drink*, both historically avoided by initiates of the *mysteries*, and both related to savage instincts bringing one closer to infernal things instead of God. For in Matthew 25:42 it is written:

"For I was an hungered, and ye gave me no <u>meat</u>: I was thirsty and ye gave me no <u>drink</u>."

By cleaning the body, mind, and instruments one is
made worthy of receiving the *Celestial Virtues*.

The *Seven Sages* (or Rishis) of ancient India were strict vegetarians living on fruit and roots. They abstained from meat and spent most of their time in seclusion. It is said that these Hindu sages could obtain Christ-like abilities such as *walking on water*, *healing the sick*, and *restoring the dead to life*, by performing meditation, yoga, and austerities (*tapas*). These abilities, however, required a renouncing of *material desires* and a mastery over body and mind. Through this process a *Rishi* was thought to even be able to escape death itself, as John E. Mitchiner details in his book <u>Traditions of the Seven Rishis</u>:

"One of the aims of the Rsis in performing tapas was to attain to the realm of the immortals and to obtain immortality - even as it is said that the gods and demons themselves performed tapas in order to escape death."

By "escape death itself" we are no doubt referring to the ability of these holy men in *transcending matter* and obtaining *eternal life*, and thus their ability to "heal the sick" refers to a remedy provided to heal diseases of the mind, including ignorance, fear, and superstition. In the Indian *Mystery Schools* as a whole, restrictions upon diet were imposed and in the third degree an initiate was removed from all social relations in exchange for dedicated study of all the physical and supernatural forces of the universe. If the man we call Jesus Christ did venture to India, he certainly learned much from the local sages.

We learn of the land meats, water creatures, birds, and insects allowed or disallowed by God when he speaks to Moses and Aaron in Leviticus 11:

> *"The Lord said to Moses and Aaron, 'Say to the Israelites: 'Of all the animals that live on land, these are the ones you may eat: You may eat any animal that has a divided hoof and that chews the cud'…Of all the creatures living in the water of the seas and the streams you may eat any that have fins and scales…'These are the birds you are to regard as unclean and not eat because they are unclean: the eagle, the vulture, the black vulture, the red kite, any kind of black kite, any kind of raven, the horned owl, the screech owl, the gull, any kind of hawk, the little owl, the cormorant, the great owl, the white owl, the desert owl, the osprey, the stork, any kind of heron, the hoopoe and the bat.' All flying insects that walk on all fours are to be regarded as unclean by you. There are, however, some flying insects that walk on all fours that you may eat: those that have jointed legs for hopping on the ground. Of these you may eat any kind of locust, katydid, cricket or grasshopper. But all other flying insects that have four legs you are to regard as unclean'. 'You will make yourselves unclean by these; whoever touches their carcasses will be unclean till evening. Whoever picks up one of their carcasses must wash their clothes, and they will be unclean till evening'."*

The flesh of *carnivora* is considered unwholesome because of the animal's carnal instincts, and because of the fear and death it likely absorbed during certain types of slaughter. The Bhagavad Gita explains in chapter 14, verse 16:

> *"Slaughtering poor animals is also due to the mode of ignorance. The animal killers do not know that in the future the animal will have a body suitable to kill them."*

The Quran reads similarly, documenting how Allah has only forbidden certain types of foods and substances to his people. In Al-Baqarah (the Cow), verse 168, Allah commands men to *"eat only the things of the earth that are lawful and good."* In verse 173 we read the following:

> *"He has only forbidden you to eat carrion, blood, swine, and what is slaughtered in the name of any other than Allah. But if someone is compelled by necessity – neither driven by desire nor exceeding immediate need – they will not be sinful. Surely Allah is All-Forgiving, Most Merciful."*

In the Quran 4:43 we also read of how one should never approach the sacred while intoxicated: *"Believers! Do not draw near to the Prayer while you are intoxicated until you know what you are saying nor while you are defiled – save when you are travelling – until you have washed yourselves."*

The Bible gives the same proscription in Ephesians 5:18, commanding: *"And be not drunk with wine, wherein is excess; but be filled with the Spirit…"* And in Proverbs 23:20-21 we read further on alcohol and animal flesh: *"Do not join those who drink too much wine or gorge themselves on meat, for drunkards and gluttons become poor, and drowsiness clothes them in rags."*

It should be no surprise to find the same themes in the Bhagavad Gita 5:22, which speaks more directly to all material pleasures: *"An intelligent person does not take part in the sources of misery, which are due to contact with the material senses. O son of Kunti, such pleasures have a beginning and an end, and so the wise man does not delight in them."*

According to the Crata Repoa: Initiations of the ancient mysteries of the priests of Egypt, as reproduced in Hall's The Lost Keys of Freemasonry, an initiate into the *mysteries* would be placed *"on a particular diet, interdicting him the use of certain foods, such as vegetables and fish."* Wine was rarely allowed, *"but after his initiation this restriction was relaxed."* The candidate was then compelled *"to pass several months imprisoned in a subterranean vault, abandoned to his reflections he was allowed to write his thoughts."* Next, he was *"strictly examined to ascertain the limit of his intelligence"* and understanding.

The *magi*, in all their incarnations, traditionally abstained from consuming or using the flesh and blood of certain animals, believing both were vessels of the *life essence*. "Blood is the life," as per Deuteronomy 12:23. Historian Jonathan Z. Smith confirms the Greek stance on these matters:

> *"...there is a high concern for purity in both the rituals of preparation and reception. The practitioner is to abstain from sex, from animal food (including fish), and from 'all uncleanness'."*

According to Euripides, the Greek writer, initiates of the secret *cultus* of Jupiter in Crete touched no flesh or meat, and in a chorus addressed to King Minos, the priests spoke: *"I eat nothing which has been animated by the breath of life."*

The initiates of Eleusis refrained from domestic birds, fish, and certain plant foods like beans, peaches, and apples. Levi says, *"they abstained also from intercourse with a woman in child-bed, as well as during her normal periods."* This is a common theme throughout history, some believing that menstruation was impure. But this is not to suggest that "women" are unclean, only that their cleansing blood was sacred and should remain untouched. Leviticus 15:24 informs us of the same:

> *"If a man has sexual relations with her and her monthly flow touches him, he will be unclean for seven days; any bed he lies on will be unclean."*

And in Hindu tradition husbands avoid sex with their wives outside of their *ritu* (season), a period roughly of sixteen days within the menstrual cycle. Those students of the Greek *mysteries* held very *"high standards of morality which they demonstrated in their daily lives,"* according to Hall. He adds: *"The Egyptians worshiped Nature in the form of the goddess Isis..."* and that *"to the Greeks, she was Kore or Ceres, the mother of the Eleusinian Mysteries. She was the mysterious Diana of the Ephesians. To Christendom, she is Mary, the Virgin Mother of the Messianic Incarnation. Always she is the source of that moral nutriment by which the well-being of the human soul is assured."*

Perhaps these parallels will lend credit to the para-histories, or *koshi-koden,* of Japan. According to Lord Amateru, the *amakami* (Heavenly Lord), who in this story is male rather than female (the sun goddess Amaterasu), one should only consume the right kinds of foods to cleanse the organs and return the body to balanced perfection - *homeostasis*. The *amakami* educates his people on why they should never consume beasts or birds, since doing so would pollute the body with dead spirits. One of the only creatures acceptable to eat was a fish, but only if it had scales. For an ocean-based society this makes logical sense, but the same was commanded by God to Moses! The best thing to consume, says *amakami*, are vegetables, because their energy came directly from the sun.

We are informed of expiations likewise in The Grimoire of Pope Honorius (published 1760), and the same is written in The Greater Key of Solomon (edition published in 1914 by Samuel Mathers):

> *"WHEN the Master of the Art shall wish to perform his operations, having previously arranged all things which it is necessary to observe and practise; from the first day of the Experiment, it is absolutely necessary to ordain and to prescribe care and observation, to abstain from all things unlawful, and from every kind of impiety, impurity, wickedness, or immodesty, as well of body as of soul; as, for example, eating and drinking superabundantly, and all sorts of vain words, buffooneries, slanders, calumnies, and other useless discourse; but instead to do good deeds, speak honestly, keep a*

strict decency in all things, never lose sight of modesty in walking, in conversation, in eating and drinking, and in all things; the which should be principally done and observed for nine days, before the commencement of the Operation."

Levi blends together India, Egypt, and Japan in sharing the practices of the students of Kabbalah. When Levi refers to "unhealthy evocations" he is speaking of drugs, poisons, alcohols, and foolish activates that intoxicate both our ability to reason and our nervous system:

"The Kabalists in their wisdom were on their guard against the dreams of imagination and hallucinations of the waking state. Therefore, they avoided in particular all unhealthy evocations which disturb the nervous system and intoxicate reason. Makers of curious experiments in phenomena of extranatural vision are no better than the eaters of opium and hasheesh. They are children who injure themselves recklessly. It may happen that one is overtaken by intoxication; we may even so far forget ourselves voluntarily as to seek the experience of drunkenness, but for the man who respects himself, a single instance suffices."

He goes on to explain in his book <u>Transcendental Magic</u>: *"So long as the soul's struggle, it is reasonable; when it yields to this species of invading intoxication it becomes mad. To disentangle the direct ray, and separate it from the reflection – such is the work of the initiate."* Adding, *"In all things, the vulgar mind habitually takes shadow for reality, turns its back upon light and is reflected in the obscurity which it projects itself."* We are reminded of the allegory of Plato's cave, suggesting that those focusing on corporeal matters are merely watching shadows cast on the wall of the cave by the spirit world. The *inferior* world is merely a mirrored reflection of the *superior*.

It should lastly be noted that the pineal gland inhibits sexual function through the production of melatonin. A 1984 animal study titled 'Neuroendocrine Basis of Seasonal Reproduction' demonstrated that exposure to constant darkness shrank the sexual organs and inhibited reproductive function, while simultaneously enlarging the pineal gland and increasing production of melatonin. Opposite of this, constant light reduced the size of the pineal gland and melatonin levels, while activating sexual function. As Dr. Rick Strassman assesses in his book <u>DMT: The Spirit Molecule</u>, *"it is as if within the pineal gland there is a powerful dynamic or tension between the two roles it may plan – one spiritual and the other sexual. It is fascinating to note that many religious disciplines believe celibacy is necessary to attain the highest spiritual states."* Others, of course, use sex to reach the same states, or sex mixed with meditative practices – *Tantra*.

Taqwa

Orthodox Christians are supposed to fast on Wednesdays and Fridays, particularly during Lent and on Good Friday: the Catholic *Black Fast*. Hindus fast on certain days of the month such as the full moon and the eleventh day after both the full moon and the new moon. Muslims famously fast for Ramadan between sunrise and sunset. As with Islam, Jews are always forbidden from eating pig flesh. Seventh-day Adventists likewise abstain permanently from pork, along with alcohol, tobacco, and any type of mind-altering substance. They eat a vegetarian diet and drink clean water. Latter-day Saints eat almost exactly the same. The political movement of Rastafarians also adopted, like Voodoo, certain aspects of Christianity and mysticism, including their dietary guidelines. Rastafarians may be the strictest in their diets since they avoid all additives and chemicals, too, all in an effort to reach their version of what Muslims call *taqwa*, i.e., being conscious and cognizant of God.

Temple of the Spirit
& Keys to the Heavenly Kingdom

"The real rewards of magical study are not temporal benefits but a spiritual maturity which affords a more profound understanding of the universe in which we live."

~ David Conway ~

The *Three Fates & Platonopolis*

The *Three Fates* in Greek religion, known also as *Norns, Sisters*, and *Moirai*, were said to weave a living garment that cloaks our spiritual bodies. Their names were Clotho, Lachesis, and Atropos in Greece, and Urd, Verdandi and Skuld in Norse mythology. Each symbolized one of the triune *portions* of existence: birth, life, and death. We further clothe our bodies with literal white garments to signify outer purity. As with the *armor of intelligence and purity* granted in the *Persian Mysteries*, the weapons and armor of *light, intelligence*, and *purity* were meant to fight the beasts of *degeneracy, passion*, and *uncontrolled desire*. Some may again recall the Biblical armor, or "full armor of God," worn to *"stand against the wiles of the devil"* (Ephesians 6:11).

Fully prepared and sure of death, i.e., having confronted the *Moirai*, the initiate approaches the *Temple of Wisdom* hoodwinked by *ignorance* and *bound* by the cable tow of limitation. On arrival, he states his *intention* and *will* to better himself and his society. These symbols are concealed in Freemasonic metaphor and allegory, and the sacred texts of almost all religions, especially the Bible.

The external *temple*, like the external robes, symbolizes the body and its living garment we call the soul-spirit.

1 Corinthians 6:19

"Do you not know that your bodies are temples of the Holy Spirit, who is in you, whom you have received from God?"

John 2:21

"But the temple he had spoken of was his body."

Through the Blue Levels of Masonic initiation, the *Entered Apprentice* may advance as a *Fellow Craft* to finally become a *Master Mason*. This is symbolized in Tarot by the *Fool* inevitably becoming a *Hermit*. In alchemy, *lead* is turned into *gold*. In the Bible, *water* is turned into *wine*. In nature, the sun and rainfall support the growth of *grapes* and *wheat* that are then turned into *wine* and *flower* that becomes bread. In myth, the soul ascends through the *seven spheres of consciousness* prior to incarnation and after death.

The *Great Evils* of *ignorance, superstition*, and *fear* must be conquered like the *Great Dragon* feeding our *ego*. If we are to *perfect* ourselves, becoming square, upright, and true, and thus turning rough ashlar into smooth stone, we must also conquer the elements that otherwise would bring our *temple* crumbling down upon us like Samson. Once the individual achieves a state of *enlightenment*, they act as a brick in the building of *Platonopolis,* or Francis Bacon's *New Atlantis.* Just as a society must operate from a solid foundation of ethics, virtue, respect, and responsibility, so must each individual within that society. Whereas every person must complete their own *temple* with *bricks of action* they must also become a brick in the larger *unfinished societal temple.* The *body* is thus the ultimate force of natural magic. And to this end, Paracelsus once said:

> *"The physical body itself is the greatest of mysteries because in it are contained in a condensed, solidified, and corporeal state the very essences which go to make up the substance of the spiritual man, and this is the secret of the Philosopher's Stone."*

The Revelation of St. John

The two crossed keys of Roman Popes and St. Peter are representative of the *exoteric* and *esoteric* religions. The silver key unlocks the *mysteries* of the mundane world (earth) and the gold key unlocks the *mysteries* of the superior world (heaven). These keys unlock the *mysteries* of the Old Testament and New Testament, and it is the keeper of keys, Janus, who preserves and unlocks the *esoteric tradition* across time.

The *esoteric teachings* are represented by a *head*, usually of St. John the Baptist. The *exoteric teachings* are represented by a body, always of Jesus Christ.

Here is wisdom: The *keys of heaven* are not exclusive to any one religion or philosophy. They are preserved within all mankind like a *seed* or *egg*, despite his corruption and sin, because the *mystery* is mankind.

St. Peter is the rock (*petra*) upon which the Church was built, and thus is the orthodoxy of Christianity and a mostly literal system of belief, Saul of Tarsus (Paul) helped to preserve the mystical nature of Christ's teachings. As Manly Hall says, *"To Peter, the Christian 'mystery' was that of God made flesh. To Paul, it was flesh made God."*

~

James M. Pryse writes in <u>The Apocalypse Unsealed</u> how the *apocalypse* was once subjected to historical interpretation, but without any evidence of such past records, *"it was next interpreted as a history of the future, that is prophecy."* In some ways it can be both history and future, internal and external. Ultimately, the Greek *apokalupsis* means to "uncover, reveal," and so it is the *unveiling* of Isis and her *mysteries,* i.e., the cycles of birth, life, and death.

Pryse says that it is *"unintelligible to the conventional scholar,"* and as such, countless *faithful* today see it in an even less intelligent manner. This is not to say they are dumb, but instead merely ignorant of the context. For it is indeed *"veiled in symbolic language"* and thus *"relates to the Mysteries of the early Christian Society, the esoteric teachings which it was not lawful to reveal."*

The *Revelation of St. John* is truly a masterful work in esotericism which acts as a preservation of early Christian and Gnostic doctrine against institutional dogma and purging. This *secret doctrine* was carefully concealed *"under the most extraordinary symbols, checked off by a numerical key and by similar 'puzzles,' so that the meanings could be conclusively demonstrated from the text itself, and concluding it with a dread imprecation against any one who should add to or take away anything from the book."*

St. John therefore gives the *key* to *gnosis* in every age while transcending *faith* and certain *philosophies* or dogmas. His work is a *"secret science which is in reality secret only because it is hidden and locked in the inner nature of every man, however ignorant and humble, and none but himself can turn the key."* As we have seen, classic fairy tales preserve these same *keys* and *secrets*.

St. John's Revelation is what theologians might call *literal prophecy*, what occultist may call the *mysteries*, and what explorers of thought may call *an altered state of consciousness*. Perhaps the latter two possibilities are one and the same. It is rarely debated anymore that John even wrote the book, with some suggesting that a Gnostic named Cerinthus, who some say took Christ's place on the cross, was the author, a possible fact which would certainly explain its deep occult themes. Either way, when John ascended by way of a symbolic ladder comprised of *seven churches,* he took the shamanic *sky rope* of *Jacob's Ladder* into the heavens. These churches are clearly relatable to Inanna's descent into the underworld and Ishtar's ascent through the *seven gates.* Revelation 4 tells the story of what John sees in Heaven:

St John's Vision of Christ, woodcut by Albrecht Dürer (1497-98).

After the vision of these things I looked, and there before me was an open door in heaven. And the same voice that spoke to me before, that sounded like a trumpet, said, 'Come up here, and I will show you what must happen after this.' Immediately I was in the Spirit, and before me was a throne in heaven, and someone was sitting on it. The One who sat on the throne looked like precious stones, like jasper and carnelian. All around the throne was a rainbow the color of an emerald. Around the throne there were twenty-four other thrones with twenty-four elders sitting on them. They were dressed in white and had golden crowns on their heads. Lightning flashes and noises and thunder came from the throne. Before the throne seven lamps were burning, which are the seven spirits of God. Also before the throne there was something that looked like a sea of glass, clear like crystal.

In the center and around the throne were four living creatures with eyes all over them, in front and in back. The first living creature was like a lion. The second was like a calf. The third had a face like a man. The fourth was like a flying eagle. Each of these four living creatures had six wings and was covered all over with eyes, inside and out. Day and night they never stop saying:

'Holy, holy, holy is the Lord God Almighty.
He was, he is, and he is coming.'

These living creatures give glory, honor, and thanks to the One who sits on the throne, who lives forever and ever. Then the twenty-four elders bow down before the One who sits on the throne, and they worship him who lives forever and ever. They put their crowns down before the throne and say:

> *'You are worthy, our Lord and God,*
> *to receive glory and honor and power,*
> *because you made all things.*
> *Everything existed and was made,*
> *because you wanted it.'*

St. John says he was "in the Spirit," having an experience beyond the physical. He saw the "throne in heaven" and the person seated there was like "precious stones." The surrounding twenty-four thrones and elders are the hours in a day.

The *lightning flashes and noises and thunder* emanating from the throne relate to the power of the internal and the eternal. They are evidence of the *second coming*, i.e., the awakening of consciousness: *being reborn*.

The *seven lamps* and the *sea of glass like crystal* witnessed on John's journey are symbolic of classical septet symbology signifying *completion*, but particularly of the planets, along with the water above the firmament. In other words, the manifest heavens.

The *seven lamps* are the seven illuminated spheres of the classical planets, and the *sea* is the heavens which glistens like *crystal*.

From the *"four living creatures,"* or the four directions, seasons, horses, etc., being "covered all over with eyes" is to be understood the shining stars in heaven; they are *creation* which *"day and night"* repeat *"holy is the Lord God Almighty."*

Therefore, it is to be understood that *"the One who sits on the throne"* is *spirit*, which is what John says he is "in," and the description of this Holy One as "precious stones" is clearly indicative of the *Philosopher's Stone*.

When all bow to the *One* and say *"you are worthy"* we are to understand that the spirt of man, that seed planted in each of us, is the *mystery,* and subsequently, if properly prepared, it will be ready to receive the *revelation* of the *mysteries* by lifting the veil of Isis and peering into the Holy of Holies.

The *revelation of St John* is thus a ritual of *living resurrection*, i.e., being *born again*, as is evidenced from Revelation 20:6 which states:

> *"Those who are raised from the dead during this first time are happy and holy. The second death has no power over them."*

The "second death" refers to *physical death*, our *first death* being the suspension of our *soul* in *matter* at birth. In Revelation 20:13 it is said that the dead will be judged, a fact taken directly from the *mysteries* of Egypt, wherein the *heart* of the *dead* is judged, or weighed, against that of a *feather*. The *sea* is *illusion*, and the *dead* are those *uninitiated*:

> *"And the sea gave up the dead which were in it; and death and hell delivered up the dead which were in them: and they were judged every man according to their works."*

The Kingdom of Heaven

The *REVELATION* is of the *Kingdom of Heaven*, existing in the *Garden of Paradise*, a state of *being* from whence man *fell* into the *Garden of Hallucinations*. The *garden* and its *fruits* are the *body*, and the *trees* are the *spine*. The *base* of the spine is the *fruit* of *sexuality* and *procreation*, or the *Tree of Knowledge of Good and Evil*, while the *crown* of the spine is the skull or temple, the *Tree of Life*, where Christ was crucified at *Golgotha*, i.e., the Hebrew *gulgoleth*, which means *skull*. From the *fruit of desire* to the revelation of *eternal life*, the human spinal column, or tree, with its mystical *thirty-three* stacked vertebrae, is the *cross* that man is crucified on by the *nails* of the senses, i.e., physical illusion. For the "kingdom of heaven is like a mustard seed," as per Matthew 13:31, and as the *Great Mystery* is concealed in Luke 17:20-22, we read:

> "And when he was demanded of the Pharisees, when the kingdom of God should come, he answered them and said, The kingdom of God cometh not with observation: Neither shall they say, Lo here! or, lo there! for, behold, **_the kingdom of God is within you_**. And he said unto the disciples, The days will come, when ye shall desire to see one of the days of the Son of man, and ye shall not see it."

The human body is thus the *Ark of the Covenant*, *Noah's Ark*, *Tabernacle*, *Basket of Moses*, *Chest of Osiris*, *Womb of Isis*, *Temple of Solomon*, and the "boat made of reeds" where the first child in pre-Japan was placed after birth.

Our bodies are *"temples of the Holy Spirit,"* even below the head, and they remain forever unfinished like the pyramid with all-seeing eye. The *Third Eye* oversees this construction from realms beyond the physical kingdom of *malkuth*. This "eye" is the *Pineal Gland*, or Adam, and it oversees the positive (giving) forces of man, whereas the *Pituitary Gland* is Eve and controls the negative (receiving) forces of female.

THE WORLD TREE IN THE HUMAN BODY

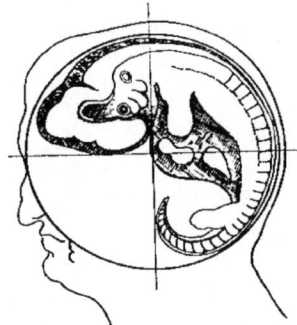

THE BRAIN IN THE FORM OF AN EMBRYO

As a vessel for the Holy Spirit our body should be kept clean and pure, but not worshiped in place of soul-spirit, for this is one of the greatest *false idols*! Manly Hall, in his book, <u>Man: Grand Symbol of the Mysteries</u>, writes of how the brain and spinal cord offer keys to the mysteries of nature:

> "The pia mater (that delicate membrane which invests the brain and spinal cord, forming as it were an inner garment) offers a definite clue to the anatomical arcana of the philosophers. Many scientific terms now in general use have been appropriated from older orders of learning, often with little

understanding and less appreciation of the original meanings. Pia, for example, is the feminine of pius (pious), meaning 'godly' or 'devoted to Deity,' while mater is the 'mother'. Thus, pia mater is the Holy Mother, the Sophia-Achamoth of the Gnostics, containing within herself the foetus of the Heavenly Man. Mater, also interpreted as the origin or the source of, when read cabalistically indicates the brain to be the place where the gods are generated, or where piety or godliness has its seat. When the Cabalists declared the Heavenly Man to be androgynous, they stated only that which is testified to by the inner structure of man himself and by the early development of the embryo. Thus, the foetal creature within the womb of the Holy Mother (pia mater) is the celestial hermaphrodite, whose parts and members may be faintly traced in even the modern terms used to identify the parts of this amazing organ which we call the brain."

Regarding Hall's assessment, we find Augusta Foss Heindel making a similar statement as per the head, brain, and already mentioned glands:

"There is but one fountain of youth, one elixir of life, and that is our food and our thoughts. If we live a pure and simple life of unselfishness, eating lightly of vegetables and fruit, keeping close watch over our desires, then we need not sacrifice the life of the animal to replenish our wasted energy. Ponce de Leon sought the fountain of perpetual youth in far-off lands, while he had two tiny cups within his own brain which, if he had only paid the price of making an exchange of the worldly life of the senses for the spiritual life of purity, would have given him the elixir of life."

We may thus conclude that the *Fiery Red Dragon* of Revelation is far more than an actual monster, or merely a symbol of man's carnal nature. The *DRAGON* is the hopeful devourer of a newborn about to be birthed by the *"woman clothed with the sun, with the moon under her feet, and on her head a garland of twelve stars."* In Revelation 13:2 we learn that *"the dragon gave the beast his power and his throne and great authority,"* and by his fact alone it becomes clear what the dragon and beast, and that newborn, really represent.

The baby is our *POTENTIALILTY* and *RESURRECTED SOUL*. The *RED DRAGON* is the *EGO*, and the *BEAST* is the *ANIMAL SELF*. The WOMAN is also *anima* and the DRAGON *animus*.

The Eternal Predator

At the root of our brain is the *reptilian brain*, which is the seat of *spirit*, i.e., emotion, alongside of aggression and territorialism. In Revelation 13:4 we read that *"people worshiped the dragon because he had given authority to the beast,"* a reference to the same psychological features.

This serpent, from *Eden* to *Revelation*, represents the *eternal predator* lurking in the shadows. He is *ouroboros*, the snake eating its own tail, *i.e., eternity* and the *cycles of time*. He is the *snake* on the *Edenic tree*, tempting with *forbidden fruit*. The *serpent* is thus relatable to *kundalini*, a spiritual energy, while the *tree* is our body and spine, and the fruit is *desire* in all *forms*. This slithering creature is a symbol of *wisdom* because he drives man from the shadows towards the betterment of self. The concept of *ouroboros* comes from antiquity, first appearing in Egypt around 1600 BCE, and although named by the Greeks, it appears in various other mythologies. The Norse serpent *Jormungandr* was big enough to engulf the entire planet while still being able to grasp the end

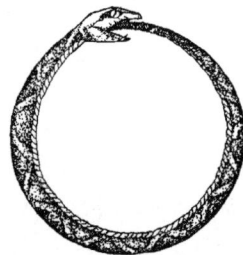

of its tail. In Hindu myth there is the serpent Goddess *Nahusha,* who is responsible for creating, or *measuring*, the world.

As *sexual desire*, the fruit is a symbol of procreation, or the *fruit of our loins*. Otherwise, it is the *fruit of our* labors and the *apple of knowledge*. The *serpent* is therefore penial and must be allowed inside the female; the *serpent* is likewise yonic as the opened vagina resembles the creature's mouth tempting withs whispers. From the latter is also birthed the offspring of man and woman.

That Adam and Eve were made aware of their *nakedness* (Genesis 3:7) we are to understand they were, in essence, *born* and opened their eyes for the first time to a world wherein they could experience both *pleasure* and *pain*:

> *"Then the eyes of both of them were opened, and they realized they were naked; so they sewed fig leaves together and made coverings for themselves."*

The *eternal predator*, usually in the form of a *dragon* or *serpent*, is hiding not necessarily in some *outer darkness* but within the *internal darkness* of *self* – and literally at the base of the brain shrouded in darkness. The predator further hides within the very code of life we call DNA, and its image is preserved in both ancient creation stories and the modern symbol of caduceus. Psychologist Carl Jung writes of this predator:

> *"The serpent is the earthly essence of man of which he is not conscious. Its character changes according to peoples and lands, since it is the mystery that flows to him from the nourishing earth-mother. The earthly (numen loci) separates forethinking and pleasure in man, but not in itself. The serpent has the weight of the earth in itself but also its changeability and germination from which everything that becomes emerges."*

The ABYSS (formless and empty) of our *genesis* is both an oceanic depth and a dry desert, filled with all manner of predators symbolizing *danger*. In Job 41 there is described a terrible beast, a "king of the ocean, king of the deep" that we also know as *Leviathan*, a creature easily associated with *ouroboros*. Both creatures signify the *boundary of creation* and *limitless potential*, even if the POTENTIAL is limitless within the bounds of CREATION. These monsters are *necessary evils* which hold back the DARK from fully consuming LIGHT, a *rhythm* and *breath* like night and day. Hall informs us that the potentiality of life itself stems from darkness, *"true darkness is the womb of Light,"* in the same way that clinical psychologist Jordan Peterson writes, *"everything that emerges from the realm of possibility in the act of creation (arguably, either divine or human) is good insofar as the motive for its creation is good."* Both good and evil, like man and woman, come from *darkness*, as does *light*.

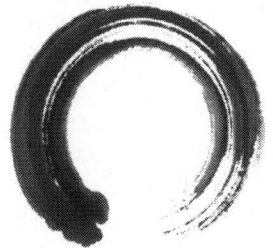

The Enso is a symbol in Zen Buddhism made with a single brush stroke. As simple as the symbol may seem, it takes years of practice in the art of calligraphy to create. It represents eternity, enlightenment, and a perfected meditative state.

Original Sin

These are complex metaphoric and allegorical subjects that relate as much to the physical world as they do to the various layers of the human body and mind. For demons and monsters are not merely an expression of internal conflicts, they are spiritual and psychological forces operating in the same predatory manner as the great serpent of Eden, which is always tempting us with the *sin* of transgression against God. Recalling Meister Eckhart once more:

> *"If you fight your death, you'll feel the demons tearing away at your life, but, if you have the right attitude to death, you will be able to see that the devils are really angels setting your spirit free."*

All *sin* is unmanifest potential and a LIE, which is the opposite of the TRUE WORD of God. Jordan Peterson writes further:

> *"The Word - the tool God uses to transform the depths of potential - is truthful speech. It appears necessarily allied, however, with the courage to confront unrealized possibly in all its awful potential, so that reality itself may be brought forth."*

From this point of view, psychologically speaking, *Original Sin* is our proclivity to reject creation, i.e., the manifesting of our potential, in favor of sinking into the expansive *oceanic* or *desert* abyss, like being swallowed by the whale like Jonah. For the essence of reality, as Peterson concludes, is *"an eternal treasure house guarded by an eternal predator,"* which represents the *"way you are wired to react to the world at the most fundamental depths of your Being."*

We must come to understand the Holy Trinity of body, mind, and spirit (psyche). We must come to understand the demons and monsters within, and then overcome them. We must come to understand the nature of the *Red Dragon* and *Beast* from Revelation, as they relate to our *ego* and *animal nature*. Jordan Peterson explains in further detail the meaning here:

> *"If the Dragon of Chaos and the paired Benevolent and Evil Queen are representatives of potential and of the unknown, the Wise King and the Authoritarian Tyrant are representatives of the structures, social and psychological, that enable us to overlay structure on that potential."*

We must recognize the archetypes of *hero* and *adversary*. We must come to grasp that nature of both a *Kind Mother* and *Evil Queen* or Witch: that nature should be preserved but that it is also there for our use so that we can build protections against its more wicked side. We must come to likewise grasp that society, its institutions, etc., are comprised of a *Wise Ruler* and *Evil Tyrant*, parallel to the mother and witch: that institutions are necessary for civility and order to exist but that too much *order* creates *chaos*, while too much *chaos* eventually inspires *order* – or too much sin eventually inspires absolution.

Made Alive in Christ

In 1 Corinthians 15:50 we read how *"flesh and blood cannot inherit the kingdom of God."* This verse is nearly identical to the inscription above Isis: *"No Mortal Man Hath Ever Me Unveiled."* In 2 Corinthians 4:3-4 we read that even the Gospel is veiled, and especially to those who are dying:

> *"And even if our gospel is veiled, it is veiled to those who are perishing. The god of this age has blinded the minds of unbelievers, so that they cannot see the light of the gospel that displays the glory of Christ, who is the image of God."*

From these philosophical motifs come the notion that the *light of God* is too strong for those not ready to receive its glory, i.e., the *dead*. And in Exodus 33:20 we read likewise, *"you cannot see my face, for no one may see me and live."* Through *sacred teachings*, magicians, philosophers, and alchemists have attempted to extinguish the *Great Evils* of the world and unveil the faces of *Father* and *Mother*:

Ignorance: insufficient knowledge.

Superstition: lacking knowledge superior to a particular situation.

Fear: anxiety of responsibly and the unknown.

Ignorance and superstition, and purely carnal pleasures, destroy our *bodily temple* and pollute the *spirit* inside, as told in 1 Corinthians 6:19, *"Do you not know that your bodies are temples of the Holy Spirit, who is in you, whom you have received from God? You are not your own; you were bought at a price. Therefore honor God with your bodies."* And so, as Hall writes in <u>The Lost Keys of Freemasonry</u>, we must serve a higher purpose to find the greater reason for being:

> *"In spite of the fact that many of us live apparently to gratify the desires of the body and as servants of the lower nature, still there is within each of us a power which may remain latent for a great length of time. This power lives for eternities perhaps, and yet at some time during our growth there comes a great yearning for freedom, when, having to discover that the slurs of sense gratification are eternally elusive and unsatisfying, we make an examination of ourselves and bend to realize that there are greater reasons for our being."*

He writes further in <u>Lectures on Ancient Philosophy</u> how by overcoming fear man can find true liberation:

> *"It is strange but true that all the things man fears become the instruments of his liberation. Man fears the loss of individuality, yet perfection is not it attainable without it. Man fears death, yet death is simply the necessary polarizing life that he may endure until he has learned to exchange the living death of for the deathless life of the spirit. If it were not for the opportunity that death gives us to go behind the scenes occasionally, we might become so obsessed with the dream playing mortal life that we would never wake up to its unreality."*

We shall conclude this section with scripture from Ephesians 2:23, which should be sufficient in providing further the *keys to heavenly kingdom*:

> *"As for you, you were dead in your transgressions and sins, in which you used to live when you followed the ways of this world and of the ruler of the kingdom of the air, the spirit who is now at work in those who are disobedient. All of us also lived among them at one time, gratifying the cravings of our flesh and following its desires and thoughts. Like the rest, we were by nature deserving of wrath. But because of his great love for us, God, who is rich in mercy, made us alive with Christ even when we were dead in transgressions – it is by grace you have been saved. And God raised us up with Christ and seated us with him in the heavenly realms in Christ Jesus, in order that in the coming ages he might show the incomparable riches of his grace, expressed in his kindness to us in Christ Jesus. For it is by grace you have been saved, through faith – and this is not from yourselves, it is the gift of God – not by works, so that no one can boast. For we are God's handiwork, created in Christ Jesus to do good works, which God prepared in advance for us to do."*

The Great Red Dragon and the Woman Clothed with Sun, by William Blake, 1805.

Eschatology, Tribulation & the Triune Sun

The *eschatological* belief in *rapture* consists of the doctrine that the *living* and *dead* will eventually *ascend* upward into heaven and meet Jesus Christ in the clouds. This heavenly *ascension*, meaning "to rise to an important position," relates to all the *sick* and *lepers* Jesus healed, and to the *demons* he sent out of the *dead*. The *second coming*, called *parousia*, is akin to an awakening of our soul's *potential*, while *rapture* is the calling up of the *dead* from the tomb just as Jesus calls upon Lazarus by saying, "*Laz-a-rus, come forth.*" For we all hope to call upon the *Osirian, Mustard*, or *Sesame* SEED.

To *ascend* is to do the opposite of *descend*, i.e., moving upward on the rungs of *Jacob's Ladder* and the steps of the *Stairway to Heaven*. We often call work promotions in business, "climbing the corporate ladder" or "ascending the corporate ladder."

The Apostle Paul wrote in his first letter to the Thessalonians that *parousia* would involve a shout from heaven and the call of a trumpet. We read something similar in the book of Mark.

1 Thessalonians 4:15-17

"For this we say unto you by the word of the Lord, that we which are alive and remain unto the coming of the Lord shall not prevent them which are asleep. For the Lord himself shall descend from heaven with a shout, with the voice of the archangel, and with the trumpet call of God: and the dead in Christ shall rise first: Then we which are alive and remain shall be caught up together with them in the clouds, to meet the Lord in the air: and so shall we ever be with the Lord."

Mark 13:26

"And then shall they see the Son of man coming in the clouds with great power and glory."

The word "rapture" itself is defined similarly to the word "religion." *Rapture* comes from the Latin *raptura*, meaning to "seize." *Religion* comes from the Latin *religio* and *religare*, meaning "obligation or bond" and "to bind," respectively. Islam comes from *aslama*, meaning "submit to God," just as the Japanese unifying source called *musubi* means "to bind."

Eschaton, or the *end days*, is slightly more than a parable; it is a complex and sophisticated mystical allegory. But that is not to say there are no true *final events* in the world. We all die, and in that way face *eschaton*. Scientists believe in the *end times* when our sun will engulf the earth. Religions maintain the *end times* of a literal *rapture*. New Age cults believe in a literal ascension of the soul, but as occurring at some unspecified date that usually has nothing to do with evil, which is what makes these beliefs more dangerous: they deny the fundamental struggle between darkness and light, focusing instead on light without discussing if it is *real* or *false*. In either case, we are judged on the scales of Anubis by the weights of *desire* and *feathered soul-spirit*. When we undergo *death* and *resurrection* while still alive, be it the *Dark Night of the Soul* or call it a *spiritual awakening*, we are *born again*. The process of *ascension* is merely the *transfiguration* of our outlook and appearance, like Christ in the books of Matthew, Mark, and Luke. Realization of *soul-spirit*, over the *false idol* of body, allows us to transcend *matter* so that, as Revelation 20:6 informs, we are risen from the dead: *"The second death has no power over them."* By "trumpet call of God" we may understand a *call to war* or the *sound of victory*. The Latin *triumphus* and Greek *thriambos* are defined as a "hymn to Bacchus-Dionysus," the Roman-Greek god of *turning water into wine*. The *triumph* of such an achievement, equal to turning lead into gold, is matched every morning and year with "a trumpet call of God," a *sound of victory* for the sun's conquering of darkness and cold: *the son's triumph over death.* Jesus is often called the *Lion of Judah* because this animal corresponds to the sun, which is "in the clouds" and walks, or reflects, on water. It is the sun that provides the triune *qualities* of life, light, and heat, according to Robert Fludd. Its *nature* is also triune, comprising the physical, spiritual, and intellectual *suns.* Hall explains this in detail within <u>The Secret Teachings of All Ages</u>:

> *"The origin of the Trinity is obvious to anyone who will observe the daily manifestations of the sun. This orb, being the symbol of all Light, has three distinct phases: rising, midday, and setting. The philosophers therefore divided the life of all things into three distinct parts: growth, maturity, and decay. Between the twilight of dawn and the twilight of evening is the high noon of resplendent glory. God the Father, the Creator of the world, is symbolized by the dawn. His color is blue, because the sun rising in the morning is veiled in blue mist. God the Son he Illuminating One sent to bear witness of His Father before all the worlds, is the celestial globe at noonday, radiant and magnificent, the maned Lion of Judah, the Golden-haired Savior of the World. Yellow is His color and His power is without end. God the Holy Ghost is the sunset phase, when the orb of day, robed in flaming red, rests for a moment upon the horizon line and then vanishes into the darkness of the night to wandering the lower worlds and later rise again triumphant from the embrace of darkness."*

The *rising sun* is correlated with the *resurrection* or *rebirth* of soul-spirit and so its color is blue: the *spiritual sun.* The *midday sun* is correlated with strength and enlightenment, or wisdom, and so its color is yellow: the *physical sun.* The *setting sun* is colored red as it lowers into blackness, preparing for resurrection through introspection: the *intellectual sun.* Just as the *"golden color in the wheat (corn) indicates that in the sunlight or spiritual gold is concealed the first sperm of all life,"* these same solar influences help grow watery grapes into wine. Hall goes on to describe the blue and gold robes worn by *The Initiator* of the Great Pyramid, assistant to a candidate's *second birth*: *"Through the mystic passageways and chambers of the Great Pyramid passed the illumined of antiquity. They entered its portals as men; they came forth as gods. It was the place of the 'second birth,' the 'womb of the Mysteries,' and wisdom dwelt in it as God dwells in the hearts of men. Somewhere in the depths of its recesses there resided an unknown being who was called 'The Initiator,' or 'The Illustrious One,' robed in blue and gold and bearing in his hand the sevenfold key of Eternity. This was the lion- faced hierophant, the Holy One, the Master of Masters, who never left the House of Wisdom and whom no man ever saw save he who had passed through the gates of preparation and purification. It was in these chambers that Plato--he of the broad brow---came face to face with the wisdom of the ages personified in the Master of the Hidden House."*

In Buddhism the ritual of *Kaidan Meguri* is similar to those initiations in the Great Pyramid. Translated as *Traversing the Path of Buddha* (Kaidan Meguri), this is a ritual involving passage through a pitch black tunnel, filled with sacred images. When emerging in the light at the other end, one is considered purified and reborn.

In John we read about *trials and tribulation*, which are those things we all must experience if we are to have the context and authority to achieve a better moral outlook. Matthew tells us of tribulation as a *great distress.*

John 16:33

"I have told you these things, so that in me you may have peace.
In this world you will have trouble. But take heart! I have overcome the world."

Matthew 24:21

"For then there will be great distress, unequaled from the beginning of the world until now — and never to be equaled again."

As Jung once wrote on the same, *"The only thing that really matters now is whether man can climb up to a higher moral level, to a higher plane of consciousness, in order to be equal to the superhuman powers which the fallen angels have played into his hands. But he can make no progress until he becomes very much better acquainted with his own nature."* One must *know thyself*, discover the *I AM*, and realize they are part of the *Absolute*, or *tat tvam asi*, "though art that." Krishna also says in the Bhagavad Gita: *"I am the Self, seated in the hearts of all creatures. I am the beginning, the middle, and the end of all beings."*

Tribulation is the journey of life and represented by the Egyptian trials that compelled an initiate to crawl through narrow spaces, swim in dark water, and be secluded for three days in a dark tomb. Once resurrected as a *son of God*, like Christ, we *ascend* from *matter* by the realization of *soul-spirit*, and thus have our names written in the *book of life*. This occurs internally but also externally when a young man reaches adulthood in a tribe. We find the *tribulation* and *trials* performed by many mythological heroes, most famously as the *Labors of Hercules*. They are also played out in various *underworld* mythologies around the world. In Egypt the trials are detailed in the Book of the Dead. In Greenland the Eskimos describe them as involving boiling kettles and rocks that strike each other and then separate. The Aztecs said a prayer at the deathbed to warn of the journey back to the god of death. All of this speaks of, as Joseph Campbell put it, the *"dangerous journey of the soul"* and the obstacles that it must pass.

Daniel 12:1 - *"'At that time Michael, the great prince who protects your people, will arise. There will be a time of distress such as has not happened from the beginning of nations until then. But at that time your people — everyone whose name is found written in the book — will be delivered."*

Judgement Day

The last battle between good and evil is fought each morning and evening, solstice and equinox, and within even larger cosmic cycles. The battle described in these terms relates to light and dark, of course, or *Ahura Mazda* (creator god) and *Ahriman* (evil spirit), but the same theme can be found within the human experience in terms of happiness and sadness, health and sickness, youth and old age. Cataclysmic events in earth's past, from the Ice Age to its end with rapidly rising oceans, are another example of *Armageddon*, which refers to both a location (hill of Megiddo in Revelation 16:16) and an *event*. A popular them in Christianity, it is called *Malhama Al-Kubra* in Islam, *Ragnarök* in Scandinavian countries, *Kurukshetra* in the Hindu Mahabharata, which laid groundwork for Bhagavad Gita, and in general Germanic mythology it is *Götterdämmerung*. After this great battle will be the *Apocalypse* and *Day of Judgement*. Even in China there is the *Divine Incantations Scripture*, known to be the oldest classic text of that region dealing with the apocalypse. What follows are various sacred scriptures discussing *Judgement Day*.

The Biblical book of Revelation 20:12 says: *"And I saw the dead, small and great, stand before God; and the books were opened: and another book was opened, which is the book of life: and the dead were judged out of those things which were written in the books, according to their works."*

The **Quran** book of **An-Nisā, verse 87 states:** *"Allah, there is no god worthy of worship except Him. He will certainly gather all of you together on the Day of Judgment – about which there is no doubt. And whose word is more truthful than Allah's?"*

And in Ar-Rūm we also read in verse 19 how: *"He brings the living from the dead, the dead from the living, and quickens the earth after it had died. So you will be brought forth (from the dead)."*

The **Bhagavad Gita** **8:18 says something similar:** *"At the advent of Brahma's day, all living beings emanate from the unmanifest source. And at the fall of his night, all embodied beings again merge into their unmanifest source."*

The **Zend Avesta** **agrees:** *"If by reason of these things the better path is not in sight for choosing, then will I come to you all as judge of the parties twain whom Ahura Mazda knoweth, that we may live according to the Right… I recognize Thee, O Mazda, in my thought, that Thou the First art (also) the Last – that Thou art Father of Vohu Manah; -- when I apprehend Thee with mine eye, that Thou art the true Creator of Right [Asha], and art the Lord to judge the actions of life. According as it is with the laws that belong to the present life, so shall the Judge act with most just deed towards the man of the Lie and the man of the Right, and him whose false things and good things balance (in equal measure)."*

And the **Popul Vuh:** *"These, therefore, were the great judges, all of them lords."*

Perhaps the most famous "judgement" outside of the Christian version is the *Hall of Judgement* in Egyptian mythology. It is here that Osiris, Anubis, Thoth, and others recorded the deeds of the living and passed final judgment with scales of balance. Another iconic Egyptian image is the birth of Geb and Nut, earth god and sky goddess respectively, the husband and wife separating the *below* and *above*. Nut is stretched out to create the sky and Geb forms the earth. The pair are pushed apart by Shu, god of air. Paiore, a Chieftain of the Polynesian island of Anaa, documented in the 19th-century his people's (Tuamotuan) creation story, which mirrors the Egyptian depiction of the sky being upheld by Geb and Nut. After the Christian *Tribulation* we learn in Matthew 24:29 of what will happen to the sky upheld by Nut:

> *"Immediately after the tribulation of those days shall the sun be darkened, and the moon shall not give her light, and the stars shall fall from heaven, and the powers of the heavens shall be shaken."*

The best known **Edda** in Norse mythology is called **Völuspá**. Within its poetic lines is described both the creation and destruction of the world, something sounding identical to the Bible:

> *The sun turns black, earth sinks in the sea,*
> *The hot stars down from the heaven are whirled;*
> *Fierce grows the steam and the life-feeding flame,*
> *Till fire leaps high about heaven itself.*
> *No Garm howls loud before Gnipahellir,*
> *The fetters will burst, and the wolf run free;*
> *Much do I know, and more can see*
> *Of the fate of the gods, the mighty in fight.*

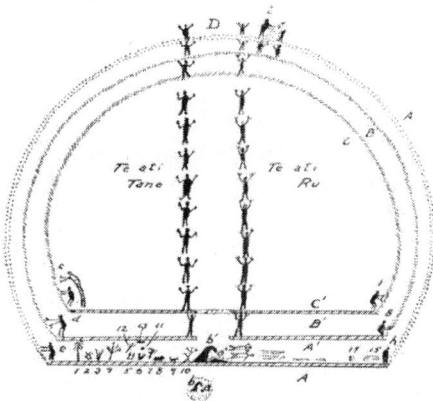

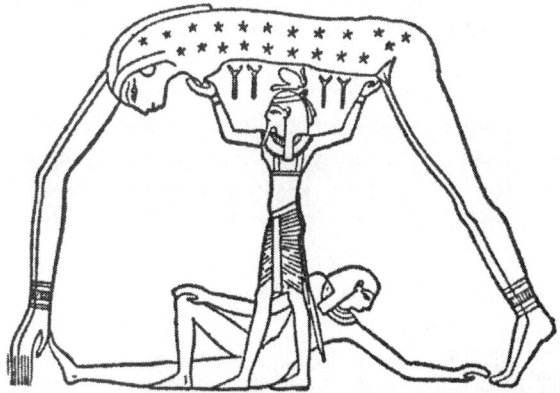

The above images from the Tuamotuan and Egyptian mythologies can also be found in the Greek (Ouranos, Father Heaven, and Gaia, Mother Earth, are separated by Kronos), Sumerian (An, Heavenly Father, and Ki, Earth Mother, are separated by Enlil, god of air), and Māori (Rangi-potiki, Heavenly Sky, and Papa, Mother Earth, are separated by Tane-mahuta, god of forests and air, who stretches out just as Shu does to separate his parents). In Babylon the same story was told of Marduk killing Tiamat and separating by ceiling and floor the waters above and below, a story we read in Genesis 1:6 as well: *"And God said, 'let there be a firmament in the waters, and let it divide the waters from the waters."* The same image can also be seen on "The Rattlesnake Disc" of Moundville, Alabama, which includes a *hamsa*-like figure symbolizing the underworld, not entirely unlike the Egyptian hieroglyphic - a star circle - for the *duat*.

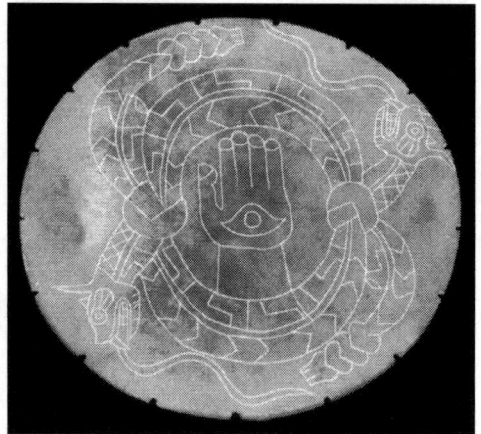

Of the four Mayan manuscripts that still officially exist, the oldest and best preserved is called "Dresden" after the Dresden court library in Vienna purchased it as the "Mexican Book" in 1739. Not until 1853 was it identified as a Mayan Manuscript which now holds the name Dresden Codex. The US Library of Congress has high resolution scans of the document and describes it as such:

> *"The codex depicts hieroglyphs and numerals and figures, and contains ritual and divination calendars, calculations of the phases of Venus, eclipses of the sun and moon, instructions relating to new-year ceremonies, and descriptions of the locations of the Rain God, which culminate in a full-page miniature showing a great deluge."*

The "great deluge" cataclysm is global, as we have seen, and on the very last page of the codex is depicted the *Final Destruction of the World.* Mythologist Joseph Campbell describes the image in his classic work, A Hero With a Thousand Faces:

> *"The serpent numbers which appear toward the close of the text (so-called because of the appearance*

in them of a serpent symbol) represent world periods of some thirty-four thousand years – twelve and a half million days – and these are recorded again and again."

In Hindu mythology, the universe was created by Brahma, who made its substance of Himself. Vishnu is the protector and preserver of that world and all life. As the cycles of nature and time proceed, it is inevitably Shiva who will destroy the universe before its rebirth. In Brahminic opposition, Jainism teaches of the twelve-spoked wheel, an endless recycling round involving heaven and earth.

False Idols & the *Tower of Babel*

The *El-Temen-An-Ki* (Etemenanki), from Sumerian meaning "temple of the foundation of heaven and earth," was a gargantuan ziggurat complex in ancient Babylon. Dedicated to Marduk, chief god of the city, this pyramidal temple is often associated with the famed *Tower of Babel*. Each stage of *El-Temen-An-Ki* supposedly represented one of the seven planets: it's angles, the four worldly corners. Kurt Seligmann confirms in <u>The Mirror of Magic</u> how the *"seven steps of the tower were painted in different colors which corresponded to the planets."* The colors and their correspondences were as follows: black for Saturn; white for Jupiter; brick-red for Mercury; blue for Venus; yellow for Mars; silver for the Moon, and gold for the sun. Each stage thus represented one of the seven classical planetary spheres, the seven garments of Ishtar, and the seven churches of St. John. From the black-lead of Saturn to the yellow-gold of the Sun, the ziggurat preserved in its construction the *stairway to heaven*. Contrary to *Etemenanki* is *Babel*, which Genesis 11:1-9 informs us was built so its summit would reach the heavens:

Etemenanki

> *"Now the whole world had one language and a common speech. As people moved eastward, they found a plain in Shinar and settled there. They said to each other, 'Come, let's make bricks and bake them thoroughly.' They used brick instead of stone, and tar for mortar. Then they said, 'Come, let us build ourselves a city, with a tower that reaches to the heavens, so that we may make a name for ourselves; otherwise we will be scattered over the face of the whole earth. But the Lord came down to see the city and the tower the people were building. The Lord said, 'If as one people speaking the same language they have begun to do this, then nothing they plan to do will be impossible for them. Come, let us go down and confuse their language so they will not understand each other.' So the Lord scattered them from there over all the earth, and they stopped building the city. That is why it was called Babel – because there the Lord confused the language of the whole world. From there the Lord scattered them over the face of the whole earth."*

The underlying lesson from the *Tower of Babel* can be summarized by Hall in the following statement: *"As man attempts to elevate himself spiritually, he gradually separates himself from his material environment."* Conversely, as man lowers himself into materiality, he quickly separates himself from spirit. But it's not so much the nature of *materiality* that is the problem. Issues arise only when man makes himself and his own creations the center of all existence. What results is the worship of the *self* as a *false idol*, i.e., the *Tower of Babel*.

There may have been a true *Babel*, but perhaps it is lost to time and so *Etemenanki* has taken on its likeness in history. Such stories are also archetypical and conceal hidden meaning. The symbolic *towers* they talk about, like Solomon's Temple and its relationship with the human body, can be easily associated with real ziggurats and pyramids.

Mexican history on the other side of the world preserves an identical story to *Babel*, and like *Etemenanki*, the temple in this case is also real. The Great Pyramid of Cholula, or *tlachihualtepetl*, is known as the *man-made mountain*. It resides in Cholula, Puebla, Mexico, and is the largest pyramid by volume known to exist in the world. Its base is 45 acres, and its height is 210 feet. It is, as author Graham Hancock confirms in his monumental work <u>Fingerprints of the Gods</u>, *"three times more massive than the Great Pyramid of Egypt."* Hancock documents the work of a Franciscan named Diego de Duran, who visited Cholula in 1585 AD to document local historical knowledge. Upon interviewing a woman said to be over one hundred years old, Duran explains what sounds stunningly like the Biblical *tower*, but in Mexico, not Babylon:

> *"In the beginning, before the light of the sun had been created, this place, Cholula, was in obscurity and darkness; all was a plain, without hill or elevation, encircled in every part by water, without tree or created thing. Immediately after the light and the sun arose in the east there appeared gigantic men of deformed stature who possessed the land. Enamoured of the light and beauty of the sun they determined to build a tower so high that its summit should reach the sky.* **Having collected materials for the purpose they found a very adhesive clay and bitumen with which they speedily commenced to build the tower** *... And having reared it to the greatest possible altitude, so that it reached the sky, the Lord of the Heavens, enraged, said to the inhabitants of the sky,* **Have you observed how they of the earth have built a high and haughty tower to mount hither,** *being enamoured of the light of the sun and his beauty?* **Come and confound them, because it is not right that they of the earth, living in the flesh, should mingle with us.** *Immediately the inhabitants of the sky sallied forth like flashes of lightning;* **they destroyed the edifice and divided and scattered its builders to all parts of the earth."**

The Great Pyramid of Cholula, Mexico

TURRIS BABEL

The Tower of Babel from Athanasius Kircher's <u>Turris Babel</u>.

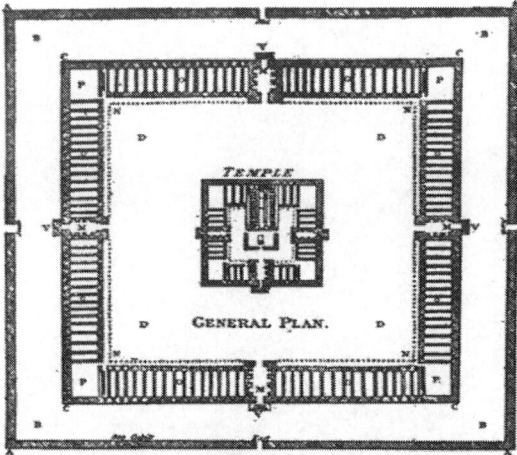

Solomon's Temple, from Hall's book <u>How to Understand Your Bible</u>.

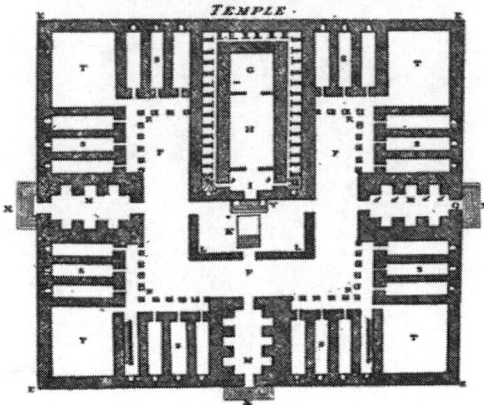

Noah's Wonderful Ark, from Hall's book <u>How to Understand Your Bible</u>.

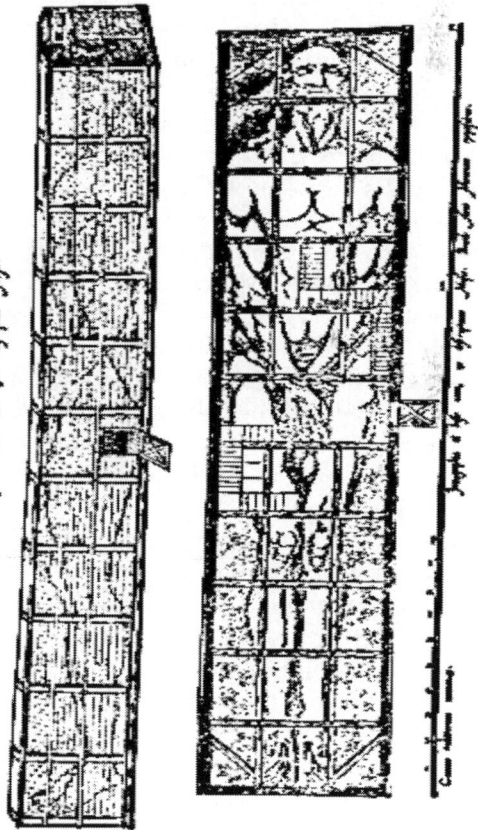

The Manitou

The largest serpent effigy in the world resides in Adams county, in Peebles, Ohio. Built on an ancient impact crater some 8.6 miles in diameter (14 kilometers) the snake itself is 1,348 feet long, and between its tail tip and upper body, aligned to true north, are seven meanders (winding courses) between twenty and twenty four feet wide, which culminate in a stylized head holding an oval object. This *eternal predator* has been noted by many researchers, including Ross Hamilton, author of <u>The Mystery of the Serpent Mound</u>, to be what the Algonquian people call *Manitou*. These are supernatural beings in control of nature, or sometimes defined as a deity or object possessing those same otherworldly powers. It is our intention here to provide merely a brief introduction to the mound itself while focusing on what this serpent symbolizes in regard to our study.

The stylized head and oval are clearly symbolic of the serpent either swallowing the cosmic egg or regurgitating the same. This is another example of ouroboros and the *Orphic Egg*, which features a serpent wrapped around the egg of potentiality. Just as Saturn *eats* his own children, planting in them the seeds of death, so does the

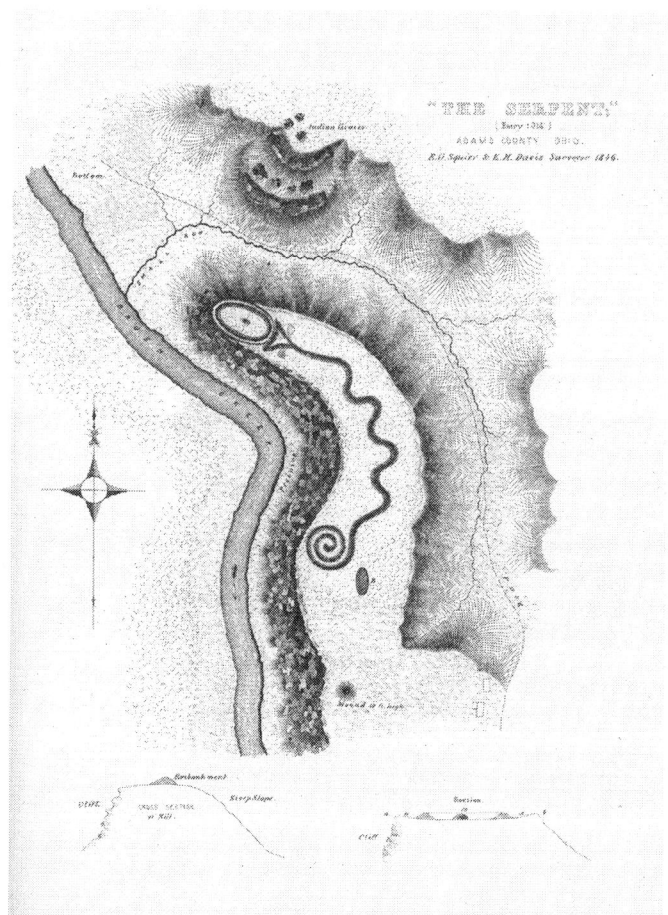

An 1846 survey made by Ephraim Squier and Edwin H. Davis, the first two surveyors of Serpent Mound.

snake look to engulf light and life by swallowing the egg. In the Greek myth it is Cronus who attempts to prevent downfall by eating his own children. The goddess Rhea, however, tricks him into swallowing a stone so that Zeus could survive the infanticide and overthrow his wicked father. Serpent Mound becomes more fascinating when one learns that the effigy's head, which holds the egg, was constructed to face the summer solstice sunset.

Serpent Mound served, and still serves, as a *manitou* over the land. Although the setting solstice sun signifies the downfall of warmth and light, or the swallowing of the egg by the serpent, this solar savior will return once more from the underworld and be reborn. This imagery of a serpent and sun is preserved not only in Adams county, Ohio, but in the story of Apollo killing Python, St. Michael vanquishing Satan, and in the lesser narratives about Theseus killing the Minotaur or Mithra(s) stabbing the bull, the latter two signifying the hero or *Great Hunter* conquering the beast.

Goëtia, White Magic & Sex Magic

"This atrocious history is that of every magician, or rather of every sorcerer who practices bewitchments. He poisons himself in order that he may poison others…"

~ Elphias Levi ~

The Dark Arts

The ancient Greek word *goēteía* means "to charm" or to practice "witchcraft." It involves the poisoning of self and nature, and the summoning of infernal forces to carry out these deeds. From *goēteía* and the Latin *goetia* we derive all manner of awful things, misunderstandings, and madness. Few realize that although the *dark arts* are classified as the *evocation of demons or evil spirits*, some can find themselves just as lost in evocations or invocations of angelic spirits. However, evocation or invocation of angels would not be considered *dark* while every *prayer* is indeed an invocation of the *Higher Self*. We cannot say for sure how our ancestors practiced either *White Magic* or *Black Magic*, only that the former works internally and the latter seeks external power.

It is commonplace today to find truly *black texts* and *pseudo-black texts*, along with politically motivated diatribes, works of banality, and grossly misunderstood *white texts*, on display at used and new bookstores. The works of Aleister Crowley are a wonderful example since they are found easily accessible virtually everywhere, and although some of his writings may impart *magical secrets*, the man was fueled primarily by drugs, sex, and covert government employment. On the other hand, the enlightening works of Manly Palmer Hall, although lauded by those who have read them, are usually tucked into a bottom shelf between other random texts.

As we learned in the last chapter, *creation* itself is magical and any attempt to distill its essence for personal gain, especially at the expense of others, is baneful. As Hall explains: *"magic is the art of manipulating the unseen forces of Nature."* This can be done in subtle ways or forceful ways. The *White Magician* learns to align themselves with *God's Divine Plan*, essentially *going with the flow*. The *Black Magician* attempts to forcibly subject nature to their own will and thus subvert the natural order; this type of sorcerer poisons their own being so that they may have an opportunity to poison others. This is the reason *goēteía* is so fatal, according to the best authorities on the matter.

Baneful magic is the submitting of *self* to excess passions, overwhelming desires, and the feeding of soul-spirit energy to Rudolf Steiner's *"beings in the spiritual realms for whom anxiety and fear emanating from human beings offer welcome food."* Writers like Marquis de Mirville and Eliphas Levi describe how this *excess*, or sickness of the individual, causes atmospheric disorders such as the automatic movement of objects or the levitation of the same. Adolescence is more prone to produce such psychic disturbances, as made famous by the 1974 novel *Carrie* by Stephen King. Philosopher Alan Watts goes on to describe how the actions of a *sorcerer* are intended not merely to hurt others, but to upend the natural order itself:

> *"The grimoire and arcane books of demonology suggest that the true preoccupation of diabolism is not just destroying, but insulting and humiliating the created order of things by upsetting the laws of nature."*

Inversion, perversity, and the love of destruction are instincts of the diabolically possessed that, according to Eliphas Levi, assume *"frequently the form of the hatred of children; an un-known power impels certain subjects to kill them, and imperious voices seem to demand their death."* Of the dark arts in general we obtain a great explanation from Hall's <u>The Secret Teachings of All Ages</u>, wherein he describes how baneful magicians invert the *Divine Plan*, subjecting nature to their own destructive will, and how even acts such as mesmerism and hypnotism, if not used solely for medicinal reasons, are likely baneful:

> *"The most dangerous form of black magic is the scientific perversion of occult power for the gratification of personal desire. It's less complex and more universal form is human selfishness, for selfishness is the fundamental cause of all worldly evil. A man will barter his eternal soul for temporal power, and down through the ages, a mysterious process has been evolved which actually enables him to make this exchange. In its various branches, the black art includes nearly all forms of ceremonial magic, necromancy, witchcraft, sorcery, and vampirism. Under the same general heading are also included mesmerism and hypnotism, except when used solely for medical purposes, and even then there is an element of risk for all concerned."*

Expanding on Hall's interpretation of the *dark arts*, Levi precisely explains the methods by which the diabolic poison is infused into the body and mind, thus creating *madness* of many varieties:

> *"This atrocious history is that of every magician, or rather of every sorcerer who practices bewitchments. He poisons himself in order that he may poison others; he damns himself that he may torture others; he draws in hell with his breath in order that he may expel it by his breath; he wounds himself to death that he may inflict death on others; but possessed of this unhappy courage, it is positive and certain that he will poison and slay by the mere projection of his perverse will.*

> *"The more difficult or horrible the operation, the greater is its power, because it acts more strongly on the imagination and confirms effort in the direct ratio of resistance. This explains the bizarre nature and even atrocious character of the operations in black magic, as practiced by the ancients and in the middle ages, the diabolical masses, administration of sacraments to reptiles, effusions of blood, human sacrifices, and other monstrosities, which are the very essence and reality of Goëtia or nigromancy."*

The Greek philosopher Plato, in <u>The Laws</u>, speaks similarly and swiftly of *goēteía*, calling for the death of its practitioners:

> *"He who seems to be such a man who injures others by magic knots or enchantments, be he a prophet or a diviner, let him die."*

Origins of Goëtia & the *Magus*

In his essay 'Excluding the Charming: The Development of the Greek Concept of Magic', Professor Fritz Graf writes how the *"goēs is a complicated figure."* By *goēs* he is referring to one of the original words denoting a *magician*. Fritz says the goēs combine *"ecstasy and ritual lament, healing rites and divination."* He adds also how *"the goēs has been connected with the world of the shamans."* These were essentially figures connected with the passage of the dead, much like the Greek Morpheus assisted the living in traversing dreams and nightmares, or Chiron ferried souls across the river Styx. Graf confirms that *"goēs is a marginal figure connected with the passage of the dead between worlds."* Furthermore, he writes that *"the combination, finally, of goēteia and mageia occurs for the first time in Gorgias, in his Encomium of Helena."* In combing the Greek term for enchantment, fascination, and wizardry - *mageia* - with the word for invoking angels and demons - *goēteia* - the idea of *magic* took on a new form.

The *goēteía* was thus a combination of practices, angelic and demonic, performed by *goēs*, and it seems that over time it has now come to signify only the darkest subversions of nature.

The Greek philosopher, and disciple of Socrates, Plato, referred to what we call *magicians* as *agurtēs* and *mantis*, or "begging priests" and "seers." Plato says that these men would visit the homes of wealthy citizens and attempt to convince them of a power they possessed that was, of course, for sale: *"a faculty which they obtained from the gods through sacrifices and incarnations."* They would then offer *"to heal them through joy and feasts in case their*

Charon, by Gustav Doré, 1861

ancestors or they themselves had committed some injustice; and in case they would like to harm an enemy, they would be able, at low cost, to injure righteous people as well as unrighteous ones through some incantation and decision because they were able, as they brag about, to persuade the gods to help them." Psychic troubles, or *mania*, could be healed, say the priests and seers of Plato, at *"a low cost"* with purification rituals and mysterious rites. In other words, something akin to *placebo*, meaning "to please," or *stage magic*.

The word *magos* first appears in a Greek text at the end of the 6th-century BCE, though the word is from Persia where the *magos* or *magi* was a priest and practitioner of certain mystical rites. The 'Father of History', Herodotus, was one of the first to speak of these *magoi* or *magi* as a type of secret society. He discusses how the Persian priests engaged in sacrifices and divination, while also conducting funerary rites and dream interpretation. The Greek words *mageia* and *magos* are probably more famous in Latin as *magia* and *magus*.

Plato points out that the teachers of this art of *magoi (mageia)* derived it from *"Zoroaster, son of Oromasdes,"* who was a prophet from the Middle East. Zoroaster is known also as Zarathustra, the founder of Zoroastrianism and author of a sacred scripture called <u>Zend Avesta</u>. This commentary text is older than the <u>Vedas</u> of India, the <u>I Ching</u> of China, and many of the sacred texts from ancient Egypt. The age of the *Vedas*, however, are called into question considering the date of their writing is set from the time they were first written down. In other words, the *Vedas*, like other sacred texts, were kept by holy men in memory long before being inscribed. Many of these sacred texts, or at least the concepts embodied within them, are pre-ancient, and certainly date to Graf's ancient *"world of the shamans."*

Other forms of Magic: Black, White, Grey, Yellow, Placebo

In another essay, 'The Religious, Social, and Legal Parameters of Traditional Egyptian Magic', Robert K. Ritner explains how in a post-Socratic world, "*mageia was held to make use of good daimones (spirits lower than the gods of religion), while goēteia utilized evil daimones, thus producing the categories of good and evil ('white' and 'black') magic.*" Of these two schools we are familiar, but there is also an area of *grey magic* whereby the magician operates between the *selfless* and *selfish*. *Grey Magic* is indeed a more neutral and obscure form of the art, expressed by the descent of *White Magic* to *Black Magic*. If the former is involved in the upholding of the laws of nature, then the latter is concerned with the abuse of these laws to create chaos. But what may be considered selfish is not necessarily a dark art, unless it becomes totally perverse, centered on self at the expense of others, and abusive. Therefore, this *Grey Magic* is only partly selfish and far more obscure in meaning. Hall says it is "*the unconscious or subconscious perversion of power.*" He likewise explains that materiality and some of those things which we do *desire* are not necessarily in opposition to God's plan so long as man understands that it is his responsibility to cultivate them justly. We will learn the same of Shintō in a later chapter:

> "*Man was not intended by God to be rich, wise, beautiful, healthy, witty, of charming personality, or happily married. This does not mean that the Lord has any objection to his being any of these things or all of them. It merely means that if he desires these things he must go forth as Adam was directed to do, earning his bread by the sweat of his brow and not by the sweat of somebody else's.*"

Since "black" is void of color, and due to it being the essence of *Absolute Intelligence*, there is nothing *evil* or *wrong* about it in relation to *magic*. For there is *false darkness* and *true darkness*, just as there is *false light* and *true light*. Hall says, "*true darkness is the womb of Light; the false darkness, the perversion of light that pours out of the true darkness.*" For all *life as we know* it, i.e., all *form*, dies in the light and truly lives in darkness, and thus "*in dying really comes to life, for life as we know it is pure death.*" The archetype of the Devil is but a representative gesture of this *false darkness*, and a symbol of inversion, perversion, and misuse. He is "*not a son of Saturn*" per se, "*but is a son of man and the false darkness on earth.*" Furthermore, "*Man is the incarnation of the germ of mental intelligence,*" and therefore "*black magic is possible only to intelligent beings.*" The nature of crystallized reality is *false darkness* illuminated by external light.

Yellow Magic is the failure, for whatever reason, to prevent perversions of nature. It is falling victim to temptation, even temporarily, while on a path of pure intention – *the road to hell is paved with good intentions*. *White Magic* and *Black Magic* can be summed up as such, according to Hall:

> "*A White Magician is one who is laboring to gain the confidence of the Powers That Be and to prove through the purity of his life and the sincerity of his motive his worthiness to be interested with the great Arcana (the Wand of the Magus).* "

> "*A Black Magician is one who seeks to gain authority over spiritual powers by means of force rather than by merit. In other words, he is one who is trying to storm the gates of heaven; he is one who is sweeping spiritual power and occult dominion with an ulterior motive.*"

~

All magic can scientifically be explained by the *placebo effect* since these practices having more of a psychological benefit to the operator rather than some supernatural outcome. Having *faith* and *belief* in what one does is perhaps the greatest act of magic, especially if a certain degree of *willpower* is needed to move forward. The true and honest purpose of all magical operations, as detailed by Israel Regardie in <u>The Tree of Life</u>, is to surpass the physical senses by occupation, and to guide the soul-spirit to a better outcome. All the robes, wands, symbols, sigils, circles, perfumes, oils, etc., are simply mental assistants to help envision a desired outcome:

> "The magical apparatus is likewise the means-just as incomprehensible to the layman-by which the Magician is able to understand himself, and commune with the invisible but no less real parts of nature. We have already defined Magic as the science having for its objective the training and strengthening of Will and Imagination. More than aught else, it is thought and will which really count in Magic, and the magical hypothesis is that by the use of the instruments of art and the sigillze with which the Theurgist surrounds himself in his ceremonial work that this enhancement of the creative faculties is obtained…"

> "In short, magical ritual is a mnemonic process so arranged as to result in the deliberate exhilaration of the Will and the exaltation of the Imagination, the end being the purification of the personality and the attainment of a spiritual state of consciousness, in which the ego enters into a union with either its own Higher Self or a God. By each act, word and thought, this one object of any particular ceremony is constantly being indicated. Even the sigillz are different for each ceremony so as to indicate its unique purpose, and one kind of symbol is applicable only to the invocation of one species of universal essence…"

> "The elaborate system of God forms, vibration of divine names, gestures and signs, signatures of spirits, the prominence of geometric symbols and penetrative perfumes, besides their ostensible purpose to invoke the desired idea to manifestation, have this auxiliary motive. It is to fully occupy the attention of each of the lower principles, or to exhilarate them, that is one of the functions of ritual, leaving the soul free to be exalted and wing its way to the celestial fire, where eventually it is wholly consumed, to be reborn in bliss and spirituality. In one sense, the effect of the ritual and the ceremony is to keep the senses and vehicles engaged each with its own specific task, without distracting the higher concentration of the Magician. And, moreover, it separates them by assigning a definite task to each. Thus, when the moment of exaltation arrives, when the mystical marriage is consummated, the ego is naked, stripped utterly of all its enclosing sheaths, left free to turn in whatsoever direction it will. At the same time, the most important function of the ceremony is fulfilled ; there being aroused in the heart of the Operator so intense an intoxication as to serve as the preliminary to the ecstasy of union with the God or Angel."

Magical Blessings

Coming from the Latin *superstitio*, the word "superstition" signifies *something that survives*, and to *under* or *over stand* something. Superstitions, as common now as in the ancient world, are remnants of old ideas and ancient knowledge. One of the most famous superstitions is the common blessing delivered almost by reflex when someone sneezes: "God, bless you." Others may use the popular German word "Gesundheit," meaning "good health." Such a practice extends, at least, to medieval Europe between the Plague years of 1347 and 1352.

Sickness has always been seen as the result of malicious spirits or God's punishing hand, and so to wish well upon someone else it was common to ask for God's graces and blessings, especially after a sneeze. The Romans and Greeks saw the sneeze as an ominous sign and thus were careful in saying, *"Jupiter preserve you."*

It is interesting to note that the plant *Hellebore* was dedicated to the planet Saturn and that its root, if prepared properly, is known to induce sneezing. Since the act of sneezing has long been seen as the avoidance of evil influence or as a sign of potential illness, which was usually caused by spirits, it makes sense that *hellebore* makes one sneeze. If the plant of Saturn induces this *evil reaction*, then providing blessings from Jupiter is an appropriate way to combat them. Witches are also thought to utilize this plant for their fabled Sabbath flights.

Exorcising Demons & Driving out the Scapegoat

As we have said, illness and disease were always thought a result of malicious spirits attacking or possessing the body or mind.

Adjuration of demons formally evict them from an object, place, or human vessel. There have likely been exorcisms performed on animals, though in Mark 5:12-13 it is the animal which acts as a vessel for expulsion:

> *"The demons begged Jesus, 'Send us among the pigs; allow us to go into them.' He gave them permission, and the impure spirits came out and went into the pigs. The herd, about two thousand in number, rushed down the steep bank into the lake and were drowned."*

There is likewise a *scapegoat* described in Leviticus 16:8-10, which in Jewish tradition was sent into the wilderness bearing the burden of collective sin. During the ancient Jewish rite of Yom Kippur (Day of Atonement), two male goats were selected for these ritual transfer of the people's sins, one animal for God and the other for the fallen angel Azazel. The goat for Azazel was then driven into the wilderness to its death while the one for God was killed in His honor:

> *"He is to cast lots for the two goats — one lot for the Lord and the other for the scapegoat. Aaron shall bring the goat whose lot falls to the Lord and sacrifice it for a sin offering. But the goat chosen by lot as the scapegoat shall be presented alive before the Lord to be used for making atonement by sending it into the wilderness as a scapegoat."*

The use of scapegoats is not confined to the Bible, nor even to goats. One ancient Greek custom was to drive disease from cities by using a *pharmakoi*,

Azazel, writes Collin De Plancy, is *"one of the angels who revolted against God. Rabbis say that he is chained on. Pointed stones, in dark place of the desert, waiting or the Last Judgment."*

or human scapegoat, which we can assume was killed. If not literally, perhaps the ritual was symbolic. During Apollo's holy day of *Thargelia*, a vegetation ritual in Athens celebrating the first fruits and breads, a young couple would feast before being walked through the town, beaten with sticks, and finally driven from the city. This tradition seems closely related to the Roman Lupercalia, where hide from sacrificed goat and dogs was employed in transferring fertility to animals, land, and women. As Encyclopedia Britannica points out:

> *"Christianity reflects this notion in its doctrine of justification and in its belief that Jesus Christ was the God-man who died to atone for the sins of all mankind."*

As with the *baptism* of the Church, the purifying rites of the Templars, Muslims, Jews, and of the Shintō practice of purification (*harai*) called *misogi*, the waters of Isis, associated with the Nile River, were also used to save the life of baby Horus, who was burned in the *Egyptian Hieratic Papyri* spells:

> *"Your son Horus is burnt in a place where there is no water."*

These "waters" are the birthing fluids of Isis, but also associated with her saliva, sweat, urine, and vaginal fluid, which all flow as the Nile River itself. In a similar spell from Babylon, it is water drawn from the Tigris and Euphrates which carries the weight of *purification*. As Christopher A. Faraone writes in his essay titled, 'The Mystodokos and the Dark-Eyed Maidens':

> *"This use of Nile water to 'save' living patients from disease and discomfort has also been connected with the use of Nile water in the mysteries of Isis, where water apparently played an important role in protecting an individual from the fires of the underworld."*

From the Encyclopedia Britannica we learn more about the history of exorcism, a tradition existing today in the Church that ultimately stems from the expelling of demons by Jesus Christ and then his followers, who drove them out *in his name*:

> *"In the first two centuries of the Christian era, the power of exorcism was considered a special gift that might be bestowed on anyone, lay or cleric. About AD250, however, there appeared a special class of the lower clergy, called exorcists, to whom was entrusted this special function. About the same time, exorcism became one of the ceremonies preparatory to baptism, and it has remained a part of the Roman Catholic baptismal service."*

> *"The exorcism of persons possessed by demons is carefully regulated by canon law the Roman Catholic church, and the elaborate rite is contained in the Roman ritual."*

For a detailed account of Christ's exorcisms, consult Matthew 28, Mark 5, and Luke 8 respectively. From Mark we learn their "name is Legion."

There is much to be said about the words *exorcise* and *exercise*, far beyond their near identical pronunciation. The familiar term *exorcise* obviously is defined as the *driving out* of an *evil spirit* from a person or place. Originally from the Greek *exorkizein*, the word is reduced to "ex" and "horkos" -

out and *oath*. To *exorcise* someone or some place is to adjure a spirit to fulfill its oath to higher authorities and leave, hence why the Lord or some other powerful angelic force is called upon.

The term *exercise* is defined as a *physical effort, carried out to sustain or improve health and fitness.* While we use this word far more often than *exorcise*, the two have much in common. *Exercise* comes from Middle English for *application of a right,* which stems from the Latin *exercitium*, and further from *exercere*, which means to *keep busy. Exercere* is reduced to "ex" and "arcere" in Latin - *thoroughly* and *to keep away.*

Both words thus request a spirit of manifest evil or illness to fulfill its oath, leave, and stay away. The fact we exercise to stay healthy is a direct descendent of the reasons behind why ancient *exorcisms* were performed, i.e., *disease*s were what was usually being *driven out*. We also *exercise* to stay in *shape*, so we do not become *distorted* versions of ourselves.

Just as knowing the name of a demon is supposed to give an exorcist, or even commoner, power over the unclean and corrupt, knowing the name of disease provides for the same power. As Roy Kotansky writes in a detailed essay called 'Greek Exorcistic Amulets', exorcists typically were *"adjuring demons directly by the name of the affliction they cause."*

Call them illnesses, ailments, diseases, demons, chaos, or the unclean, these forces are distortions of creation and thus *"do not belong in the realm of the living but of the dead."*

The "possessor" was sometimes seen as *just an illness*, but like the *spirits* of alcohol such an *ailment* was more often thought to be caused by something *unclean* and *unfit*. By "unclean" we could also easily identify conditions of poor hygiene, unsanitary living conditions, polluted water, spoiled food, etc. The fact we blame *disease* on a virus or bacteria today, and further give them scary or sometime mythological names, is an extension of this ancient practice which largely continues to ignore environmental and lifestyle conditions. From the *crucifix* to a *syringe*, even the consecrated objects are the same today for compelling demons and viruses to vacate the body.

Great proof of the existence of *demons* further comes in the form of those internal conflicts we all face, some more significant than others. We all have the capacity for *good,* but we also have the same capacity for *evil*. As clinical psychologist Jordan Peterson points out, having also worked in the study of alcohol-related social issues:

> *"Continued use of an addictive drug therefore feeds the growth of what can be accurately conceptualized as a living monster in the user's psyche…"*

That internal *living monster* is the *demon*, which must be exorcised; it can be fed with drugs, alcohol, pride, greed, wrath, envy, lust, gluttony, sloth, and even sex.

Sex Magic

Fertility, sex, and birth are the greatest *mysteries* of life itself. Because of its incredible power, particularly the *orgasm* and resulting *pregnancy*, sex has always been an act of *magic*. We still refer to newborn babies as *miracles* from God, an idea that without doubt dates to the most ancient of days. What may be a *miracle* today, however, was an act of *magic* yesterday.

To hasten the fertility of fields or regrowth of vegetation, it was common for priest and priestesses, or King and Queen, to engage in sacred sexual unions to impart their powers onto the fields and nature in general. If royalty is acting through heavenly authority, then their sexual union must extend to the marriage of heaven and earth. Sacred acts of copulation were performed thousands of years ago by the Sumerians, specifically between a king and priestess who were drawing on the powers of Inanna to fertilize. In fact, it was common throughout the ancient world, for different reasons than today, to find prostitutes acting on behalf of the goddess. In temples dedicated to Venus-Aphrodite, these women were priestess-prostitutes, using their bodies to share blessings from above. The Greek poet Hesiod wrote of these women:

> *"She is the bringer of sexual joy and the vessel by which the raw animal instincts are transformed into love and love-making."*

Herodotus writes in his *Histories* of a Babylonian custom compelling all women, at least once in their life, to sit as an attendant on the priestess throne and server strangers in the sacred act of sex:

> *"The foulest Babylonian custom is that which compels every woman of the land to sit in the temple of Aphrodite and have intercourse with some stranger at least once in her life. Many women who are rich and proud and disdain to mingle with the rest, drive to the temple in covered carriages drawn by teams, and stand there with a great retinue of attendants. But most sit down in the sacred plot of Aphrodite, with crowns of cord on their heads; there is a great multitude of women coming and going; passages marked by line run every way through the crowd, by which the men pass and make their choice. Once a woman has taken her place there, she does not go away to her home before some stranger has cast money into her lap, and had intercourse with her outside the temple; but while he casts the money, he must say, "I invite you in the name of Mylitta". It does not matter what sum the money is; the woman will never refuse, for that would be a sin, the money being by this act made sacred. So she follows the first man who casts it and rejects no one. After their intercourse, having discharged her sacred duty to the goddess, she goes away to her home; and thereafter there is no bribe however great that will get her. So then the women that are fair and tall are soon free to depart, but the uncomely have long to wait because they cannot fulfil the law; for some of them remain for three years, or four. There is a custom like this in some parts of Cyprus."*

Some view sex as not merely a union of *male* and *female*, but the direct unification of the gods and goddesses themselves. The offspring produced is the incarnation of a soul-spirit descending through the seven gates of consciousness, being gifted the garments of Ishtar: body, hands and feet, waist, breasts, neck, ears, head.

So true is the *mystery of birth* that it should be obvious to any serious occultist that the Biblical restrictions of Leviticus 18:22 are divinely inspired. For two men and two women cannot, even if performing sex with each other for reasons of love, under no circumstances conceive a child, i.e., *draw down a soul into human form*. By this understanding homosexual sex is without doubt an abomination to the *Laws of Nature*. We say this with zero zealotry.

> *"Do not have sexual relations with a man as one does with a woman; that is detestable."*

Although there were wonderful benefits of the *sexual revolution*, the purpose of sex seems to have been lost with the advent of *birth control*, and thus the act has lost much of its sacred value. It seems we no longer have sex as a culture to conceive new life, or honor the goddess, but instead to fulfill personal pleasures of a carnal nature. Increasingly the number of people even interested in the latter has dropped significantly in the west. On average today it would seem pregnancy is either an anxiety or a mistake, and in either case it is increasingly acceptable to toss those fetuses and infants into the raging fires of Molech under the erroneous notion of *women's health* and *personal freedom.*

These arguments are nothing more than the reemergence of Remphan's cult, one that demands, as Levi writes, "*the hatred of children,*" which involves an "*un-known power*" compelling "*certain subjects to kill them.*" Recall in the book of Acts how the Jews are accused of taking up the "*tabernacle of Moloch,*" that ancient deity associated with child sacrifice. "'*Do not give any of your children to be sacrificed to Molek,*" says Leviticus 18:21, referring to the same Canaanite demon named Baal. Originally associated with fertility and rain, Baal was in constant conflict with Mot, the god of death and sterility. Over time he became a demon of abortion like certain incarnations of Lilith. Collin De Plancy writes of Moloch in his Infernal Dictionary the following:

> "In Milton, Moloch is a horrible and terrible demon covered with the tears of mothers and the blood of children. The rabbis claimed that in the interior of the famous statue of Moloch, the god of the Ammonites, people created seven kinds of cabinets. They opened one for flour, another for doves, a third for sheep, a fourth for a ram, the fifth for a calf, the sixth for a cow, and the seventh for a child. This is what gave rise to Moloch being confused with Mithra, and his seven mysterious doors with seven rooms. When they wanted to sacrifice children to Moloch, they lit a big fire in the interior of the same. But to prevent hearing their plaintive cries, the priests made a great noise with drums and other instruments around the idol."

The idol Moloch with seven chambers or chapels, by Johann Lund, 18th-century.

Moloch, from the Infernal Dictionary

Offering to Moloch, by Charles Foster, 1897

Not only today, but even in ancient Rome, fertility rites are largely reduced to grotesque orgies that strip the true purposes, symbolic or otherwise, away from the act of sex, which itself has become little more than animal debauchery. *"Sensual indulgence for its own sake will not serve the magician's purpose,"* writes author Richard Cavendish. This is not to say highly restrictive sexual practices are any less destructive. But it is sacrilege and infernal to suggest that uninhibited sexual exploits are the true path to oneness or enlightenment, and it is utterly delusional to suggest they are the means by which to fight patriarchy and corruption. In fact, used for these purposes sex becomes a tool of intoxication and perversion. This is why the *mystery* rites in antiquity required abstinence from sex, and why infernal rites required the orgy. Writing on occult traditions of sex and its power, David Conway explains in his Ritual Magic: An Occult Primer:

> *"Occult (or 'esoteric') traditions goes further and insists that sex also releases is own form of power which can then be used in magic to reinforce or propel the elemental power evoked by ritual. Certainly, if all thinking processes generate a form of electro-magnetic energy, then the intensity of feeling that accompanies the sexual act must release its own very special force. In occultism, therefore, ritual sex is thought to possess an intrinsic value in addition to its symbolic and psychological purposes."*

Kama Sutra

Beyond *orgasms* and the *mysteries of fertility, marriage,* and *birth,* are the *mysteries of love.* The Kama Sutra, a classical ancient Indian book on courtship, marriage, and sex, is probably best known for its many depictions of sexual intercourse. But the book also focuses on the power and necessity of *love,* too, and in one translation from Alain Daniélou, we read about the necessity not only of love, but of ethics and spiritual seeking:

> *"Love is necessary to satisfy the mind, ethics to satisfy the conscience, and spiritual seeking for peace of soul. Without food and clothes, the body becomes thin and weak. Without eroticism, the mind becomes restless and unsatisfied. Without virtue (ethics), the conscience goes astray. Without spirituality, the soul is degraded."*

Although *Kama Sutra* is most famous, there are similar texts on the *sacred coupling* consisting of poems, guidelines, and stories, from all over the world. The Italian poet Ovid wrote the Ars Amatoria, or *Art of Love,* poem published 1 BCE, wherein he describes more scandalous forms of seduction. In Arabian poetry are the *ghazals,* short writings on romantic and spiritual love. William Shakespeare's Venus and Adonis is a poem of obvious love and seduction:

> *"Had I no eyes but ears, my ears would love. That inward beauty and invisible; Or were I deaf, thy outward parts would move each part in me that were but sensible: Though neither eyes nor ears, to hear nor see, yet should I be in love by touching thee."*

In another line, *"Ten kisses short as one, one long as twenty."* These writings are highly similar to the following line from *Kama Sutra*:

> *"So long as lips shall kiss, and eyes shall see, so long lives this ,and this gives life to thee."*

Sex is the uniting of man and woman in the bliss of wholeness, something we find depicted in the already discussed symbol of *caduceus*. From China and India to Mesopotamia, the Celtic lands, and the Americas we find this symbol not only concealing the sacred embrace of love making, but the double helix we call DNA, which is precisely what the act of sex is all about: *procreation*. In this symbol is the famous *Yin Yang*.

Yab-Yum: man and woman embrace in this painting from a Tibetan temple banner, 19th-century.

Nü Wa and Fu Xi as twin serpents, from
Han Dynasty (c. 206 BCE – 220 CE).

Basil Valentine's **Azoth**, 1613.

Caduceus on a coin from Turkey (140-144 CE).

Libation Cup of King Gudea
of Lagash, Sumer (2,000 BC).

The Right Hand of God (*Dextra Dei*)
designed from a stone cross in Ireland.

Aztec **Altar of the Caduceus,** from Codex Fejérváry-Maye.

Elementals & Spirit Conjuration

"The stories [of myth] are early literature as well as early science."

~ Edith Hamilton ~

The Golden Dawn System

The *Golden Dawn* was formed in 1888 by a freemason named Dr. William Wynn Westcott. With assistance from Dr. William Robert Woodman and Samuel Liddell 'MacGregor' Mathers, both Rosicrucian masons, the Order was founded at the Isis-Urania Temple in London. Although short-lived - the OGD dissolved in 1903 – many offshoots quickly appeared, including *Alpha et Omega* and the *Order of Stella Matutina*. Its most famous members are Aleister Crowley, Dion fortune, and Israel Regardie. In the *Golden Dawn* system of magic, there are the laws of *willpower, astral light, correspondence,* and *imagination.*

Willpower is the directing of *intention.*

Astral Light is the subtle force being *directed.*

Correspondences are your *tools* and *symbols.*

Imagination is that which one desires to *accomplish.*

If a magician's work is aligned with *Divine Will,* or the *Divine Plan,* then balance can be maintained and ends accomplished. Any deviation from DW results in chaos and a boomerang of destructive energy back on the magician. As Chic Cicero and Sandra Tabatha Cicero write in their book Golden Dawn Magic:

"Golden Dawn magic incorporates a process of memorization, creation, ritual work, and internal work that results in the direct stimulation of the magician's will and imagination."

"An effective ritual is an astrally empowered piece of performance art: a working symbiotic relationship between the magician and the Divine."

One could easily classify *magic* as nothing more than the psychological practice of *visualization,* i.e., meditating on specific ideas.

The Science & Psychology of Magic & Mythology

The willingness to dismiss what is considered *myth,* believed to be mere fantasy or that of wild imagination, has stagnated archaeologists, anthropologists, historians, and scientists. These fields then pass along their dogmas to the next generation of students, who continue in repeating "credentialed" *opinions* as fact, while true *facts* are often dismissed as opinion: biased research leading to faulty conclusions. When *facts* are spoken of by the "un-credentialed," the "credentialed" experts dismiss them as *opinions*. When *opinions* are spoken by "credentialed" experts, they are accepted as *facts*. The latter tend to be *deniers* of any possibility beyond their own rigid faith and preconceived conclusions, which are viscously defended by the status quo. Anything to the contrary is laughed away as impossible. When information is made available through new discoveries, it is protested as a hoax and immediately classified as pseudo-science. In this way, guidelines are established for researchers with clear delineation of what is acceptable and what is off-limits. Yet, it is arguable that those refusing to walk the narrow line of accepted dogma have pioneered the greatest advances in the *liberal arts*. Meanwhile, real pseudo-science dominates the academic landscape through special interests and personal bias.

The power of influencing events through some unseen force is only *magical* if one is ignorant of *cause and effect*. For it is a blasphemy to attribute God's *creation* to infernal powers, though these certainly exist. Magic is an early form of psychology, and along with *mythology*, an early form of *natural science*.

Magic is inseparable from science and psychology, as is astronomy from astrology. It may produce hallucinations, illusions, and the like, just as mechanical science dazzles with machines, computers, engineering marvels, and weapons. Magic may drive one mad or help them to achieve peace of mind, while science may kill or save lives. For as Arthur C. Clarke is famous for saying: *"Any sufficiently advanced technology is indistinguishable from magic."* Eliphas Levi explains further how magic is the *absolute science* of *natural law*:

> *"Magic has been confounded too long with the jugglery of mountebanks, the hallucinations of disordered minds and the crimes of certain unusual malefactors. There are otherwise many who would promptly explain Magic as the art of producing effects in the absence of causes and on the strength of such a definition it will be said by ordinary people — with the good sense which charac-terises the ordinary, in the midst of much injustice that Magic is an absurdity. But it can have no analogy in fact with the descriptions of those who known nothing of the subject; furthermore, it is not to be represented as this or that by any person whomsoever: it is that which it is, drawing from itself only, even as mathematics do, for it is the exact and absolute science of Nature and her laws."*

Nikola Tesla was one of these men of both science and magic. An inventor and researcher, Tesla famously and infamously worked out methods for deriving electricity from *nothingness*, effectively making it free to everyone. He was thus able to harness the telluric energies of earth, making him a master of these electrical serpents. His ideas were so revolutionary at the end of the 19th century into the 20th century, that even in the 21st-century many of them are still not understood nor common knowledge to the public, largely because they have been locked away.

Nikola Tesla is responsible for alternating current, superior turbines and engines, radio transmission, neon lighting, hydroelectric generators, a forerunner to the atom smasher, brighter and more efficient lighting devices, and wireless technology, including remote control devices, robotics, and automata developed in the 1890s. Perhaps his most famous experiments, typically misrepresented or misunderstood, were the *death* ray, a sort of *directed energy weapon* to disable electronics, and his research into the wireless transmission of electricity.

Being knowledgeable about natural and celestial phenomena would make one appear as a god if their audience were ignorant of *cause and effect*. Here Cornelius Agrippa comments on the nature of the magician and his ability to influence by magical fascination:

"Hence a magician, expert in natural philosophy, and mathematics, and knowing the middle sciences consisting of both these, arithmetic, music, geometry, optics, astronomy, and such sciences that are of weights, measures, proportions, articles, and joints, knowing also mechanical arts resulting from these, may without any wonder, if he excel other men in art, and wit, do many wonderful things, which the most prudent, and wise men may much admire."

Joseph Campbell comments on the same, saying that gods are simply agents of a masked mystery, essentially representing the mathematical nature of reality:

"The gods themselves are simply agents of the great high mystery, the secret of which is found in mathematics. This can still be observed in our sciences, in which the mathematics of time and space are regarded as the veil through which the great mystery, the tremendum, shows itself."

The Four Elements & Threefold World

The *four elements* have undergone name changes over the centuries, from personifications to technical terms. Earth has become Carbon; Water has become Hydrogen; Air has become Oxygen; and Fire has become Nitrogen. The personified living man we call God has also undergone transformation into a particle called *Higgs Boson*, i.e., the *God Particle*. The elementals are ruled over by their respective elemental spirits, and by the four archangels: Uriel (Earth), Raphael (Air), Michael (Fire) and Gabriel (Water).

In studying the elements, much of which we can learn from the writings of Agrippa, we find the following qualities: fire is hot and dry; earth is dry and cold; water is cold and moist; and air is moist and hot. Fire is contrary to water and earth to air. Yet fire and air are agreeable since the former requires the latter to burn. Water and earth are agreeable because the former separates the latter. Fire and air are light and active. Earth and water are heavy and passive. They also relate to the four bodily humors: Choler (bile) is hot and dry as fire; Melancholy is dry and cold as earth; Phlegm (mucous) is cold and moist as water; and Blood is moist and hot as air.

There are twelve *secondary elemental powers* given in pairs besides the first four powers of hot, cold, moist, and dry: heavy and light, rare and dense, smooth and rough, hard and soft, thin and thick, acute and obtuse. The elements are given three attributes or properties, too, which by multiplication gives us the number twelve by four and three. The twelve signs of the zodiac fall under each of the elements also in groups of three. *To Fire*: Aires, Leo, Sagittarius; *to Earth*: Capricorn, Taurus, Virgo; *to Water*: Cancer, Scorpio, Pisces; *to Air*: Libra, Aquarius, Gemini.

By mixing each element together they are transformed into different states of matter. When earth mixes with water it becomes a semi-solid liquid viz. mud. This liquid is then evaporated by fire into the air where through that same heat and moisture we acquire rainfall. The air may then be kindled into fire, as with smoke viz. gas, and the fuel and ashes then cooled once more into a solid, or earth. Since nothing is visible without fire, God said, "let there be light," and since nothing is solid without earth it too was created as a base for the other elements. God then placed water and air between fire and earth, *"and made them to have the same proportion so far as was possible,"* writes Plato. In his Timaeus Plato provides us with a description of this process:

"In the first place, we see that what we just now called water, by condensation, I suppose, becomes stone and earth, and this same element, when melted and dispersed, passes into vapor and air. Air,

again, when inflamed, becomes fire, and, again, fire, when condensed and extinguished, passes once more into the form of air, and once more, air, when collected and condensed, produces cloud and mist--and from these, when still more compressed, comes flowing water, and from water comes earth and stones once more--and thus generation appears to be transmitted from one to the other in a circle."

Fire provides superior heat and light, but also parched heat and darkness. The former heat allows for fruitful reproduction and life, whereas the latter heat consumes all and leaves the land barren. In all its various expressions, by heat and light, or candle and bulb, etc., or by Yule log, Christmas lights, Imbolc candles, Beltane fires, or Samhain lanterns, it drives away darkness, cold, and evil or malevolent spirits.

Water is that element by which all things generate, subsist, and are nourished. It is powerful enough to overtake the other elements by extinguishing fire, ascending high above in clouds as rain, and in swallowing the earth by flood. If not with the assistance of heat and air, then condensation, the collecting of water droplets on earthy material, would not be possible.

Air is that vital spirit passing through all things, and from it we acquire the four winds: the southern *Notus*, the northern *Boreas*, the western *Zephyrus*, and the eastern *Eurus*.

From the earth all other elements are founded and made fruitful. It is a receptacle for all influences and contains the seeds or seminal virtue of things. Agrippa thoroughly provides a course on the subject of *the elements* in his monumental text, Three Books of Occult Philosophy:

"The elements are found in expressions of stones, metals plants, animals, personalities, species, and planets, as they come from the same intelligences, and of those still higher. These elemental virtues would include the earthy heaviness of a stone, while there are those stones which have watery properties, or those fiery or airy; the liquid state of metal, or its solid as earth, or if it be light as air, or heated like fire before becoming liquid; the earthy nature of roots grounding a plant or tree, their need for sunlight and water, and air. The same is true for animals and humans. Of animals we find a bird is primarily airy, but can also land upon earth, while it needs the heat of the sun and water to survive. Certain creatures such as a duck are master of the elements; they swim or dive in water,

Air
Masculine
(active)
Moist   Warm
Water   Fire
Cold   Dry
Feminine
(passive)
Earth

fly in air and walk on land. Humans need water, fire, earth and air to survive and these elements are also represented in the personality of man, animal, stone, plant, metal, etc., as described above. Our senses suffice to explain this: sigh is fiery, for which we would not see without light; hearing is airy, for we could not hear without vibration of air; feeling is solely earthly, as this is solid; and smell and taste are watery, since without moisture we would not experience either. Moving from the infernal elements strictly to those of the stars we find planets having the same vibrates: Mars and the Sun are fiery, Jupiter and Venus are airy, Saturn and Mercury are watery, and the Moon and Earth are earthy. These planetary intelligence express emotion, too, by their virtues; Saturn is to sadness, Jupiter to honor, Mars to boldness or anger, the Sun to glory or victory, Venus to love or lust, Mercury to eloquence, and the moon to common life."

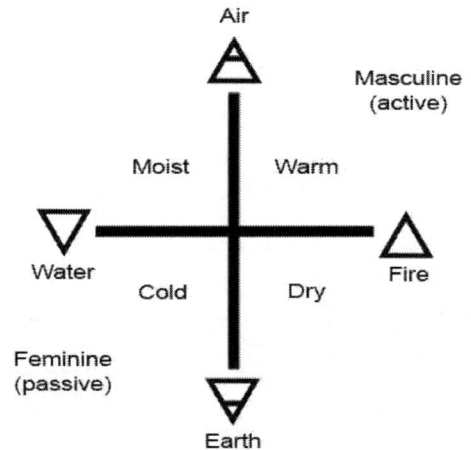

The elements are in all things and in all things are expressed these elemental qualities. In all things inferior are those superior and in those superiors are the inferiors. From the ideas of things to be produced, to intelligences distributing their powers, to heavenly virtues, and to those inferior bodies and gross forms, Agrippa explains this hidden meaning:

> "For God in the first place is the end, and beginning of all virtues, he gives the seal of the Ideas to his servants the intelligences; who as faithful officers sign all things entrusted to them with an ideal virtue, the heavens, and stars, as instruments, disposing the matter in the meanwhile for the receiving of those forms within reside in Divine Majesty and to be conveyed by stars; and the Giver of Forms distributes them by the ministry of his intelligences, which he hath set as rulers, and controllers over his works, to whom such a power is entrusted in things committed to them, that so all virtue of stones, herbs, metals, and all other things may come from the intelligences the governors. The form therefore, and virtue of things comes first from the Ideas, then from the ruling, and governing intelligences, then rom the aspects of the heavens disposing, and lastly from the tempers the elements disposed, answering the influences of the heavens, by which the elements themselves are ordered, or disposed."

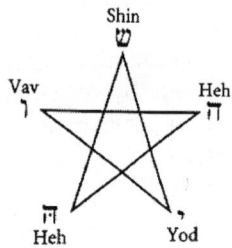

The elements are expressed through their appropriate symbol. Fire is an ascending triangle rooted in earth with its apex in heaven; it is the active male principle and phallus. Water is a descending triangle with its base in heaven and an inverted apex; it is the passive female principle and womb. Air is an ascending triangle with a bar passing through just below its apex. This bar is the base of a descending triangle, rooted in heaven, and so the airy element is nearer heaven. Earth is a descending triangle with a bar passing through the lower portion just above the inverted apex. This bar is the base of an ascending triangle and so the earthy element is the base for the rest. The *four elements* further correspond to four of the five points of a pentagram, with the fifth point representing *spirit*. Another version of this can be seen in the mummified Osiris or Levi's Baphomet. In Buddhism we find the four directions guarded by the Five Wisdom Kings, with the fifth king Acalanatha representing the internal fire of spirit (his image is usually surrounded by flames).

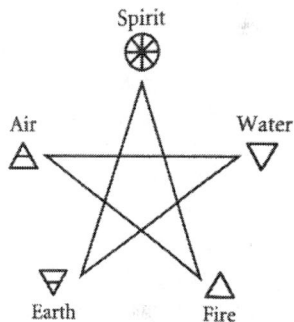

Elementals & Vampires

The *spirits of nature* are thought to exist just beyond human sight in an undefined region called the *Twilight Zone*. However, they make themselves visible by choice or be made visible through certain magical operations. Since *life* is a condition that includes capacity for growth, reproduction, functional activity, and change, even after death, the *elements* and their *spirts* are very much alive! Fire grows and dies, water evaporates, air thickens or thins, and earth condenses or expands. Personified in an understandable form they become the *fairies* and *hobgoblins* dwelling in grasslands; *potamides* in rivers, *nymphs* in marshes, *oreades* in mountains, *humedes* in meadows, *dryades* and *hamadryades* in woods, and *paleae* and *feniliae* in the countryside. The term *fairy* traditionally comprises all these spirits in the west while in the far east the Japanese call them *yōkai*.

From the *spirits of nature* can be derived *plant spirits*, those peculiar creatures, not unlike fairies, appearing in green clothing like the *Green Man*. Their small stature and green clothing, accompanied by their *fairy circle* dances of lights, and abductions of humans, align them directly with modern UFO abductions. Jacques Vallee confirms this in his book <u>Passport to Magonia</u>, writing how the UFO phenomenon is "*identical to the earlier belief in the fairy faith.*" He adds, "*the entities described as the pilots of the craft are indistinguishable from the elves, sylphs and lutins of the Middle Ages.*" Writing editorial notes to <u>The Occult Sciences</u> by Salverte, Anthony Todd Johnson explains fairies as such:

> "*The Fayes and Fairies are evidently of Scandinavian origin, although the name of Fairy is supposed to be derived from, or rather [is] a modification of the Persian Peri, an imaginary benevolent being, whose province it was to guard men from the maledictions of evil spirits; but with more probability it may be referred to the Gothic Fagur, as the term Elves is from Alfa, the general appellation for the whole tribe. If this derivation of the name of Fairy be admitted, we may date the commencement of the popular belief in British Fairies to the period of the Danish conquest. They were supposed to be diminutive aerial beings, beautiful, lively, and beneficent in their intercourse with mortals, inhabiting a region called Fairy Land, Alf-heinner; commonly appearing on earth at intervals – when they left traces of their visits, in beautiful green-rings, where the dewy sward had been trodden in their moonlight dances.*"

Gnomes are of the earth and get their name from the Greek *gnomus*, which means "earth dweller." They preside over rocks, dirt, trees, and all other associated elements. They are ruled over by a king named *Gob*, who they revere and love. His subjects are known as *goblins*. These "earth dwellers" were given the northern part of creation. The most recognized *gnome* is a *brownie* or *elf*, a mischievous character no larger than two feet in height. Their dwellings are usually within caves, ground holes, or the stumps of trees, and sometimes they are seen merging or disappearing within the trunks. They often appear very aged with long white beards and canes for support. Since earthen material is considered masculine, gnomes are mostly male spirits. Their rugged appearance signifies a personification of earth. Gnomes work through us by way of our physical body and environment.

Gnomes, from Gjellerup's
<u>Den Ældre Eddas Gudesange</u>

Duendes are supernatural beings in Latin American folklore, akin to *pixies* or *imps*. A *Pukwudgie* is a human-like creature found in Wampanoag tradition. Similar beings are found in the mythos of Hawaiian culture: said to live in forests and valleys, the *Menehune* are excellent builders like the Germanic gnomes we call *dwarves*. Their wisdom and craftsmanship may be further associated with another gnome we call *elf*, which contrary to popular belief is often a tormentor of the home. Some people place gnome statues in their garden or yard as a decorative totem, unknowingly drawing on its protective masculine properties. Future generations may look back at these customs and think us to be far more superstition than we would ever admit, just as we may call the Romans superstitious for using statues of *Lares* or *Penates* to protect the home.

Undines or **Naiads** are water spirits like *mermaids* or *Melusine*, the spirit of fresh waters. They went by various names including *sea maids*, *potamides*, *nereides*, *limoniadoes*, and *oreades*. Their element is water and state of matter liquid or humid ether. While gnomes were rugged and old, the Undines were always beautiful and youthful in appearance. Water has traditionally been seen as feminine in nature due to its nurturing essence, fluidity, and the influences of the feminine moon on its tides, and so these beings were almost always female. They are found in all forms of water: waterfalls, rivers, lakes, ponds, fountains, and the ocean where each wave was accompanied by its *oceanid*. The Undines were ruled over by *Necksa*, whom they honored as the gnomes did Gob, and were given as a kingdom the western corner of creation. Undines work through us by way of our emotions.

Melusine

Sylphs are elementals representing the air or ether. Their state of matter is gas. Female sylphs were called *sylphids*. Not to be confused with the atmosphere of earth, this elemental exists as an intangible and invisible spiritual medium. Their home is in the clouds, surrounding atmosphere, and among mountains. Their leader is *Paralda*. Sylphs are the highest of the elementals since their element has the highest vibratory rate. Unlike the advanced age of *gnomes* or the youth of *undines*, these beings never seem to grow old. Their appearances vary with exception to wings. The Sylphs were given the eastern corner of creation, for which we recall the "eastern wind." Sylphs work through us by way of our mind. Plato preserves in his <u>Phædo</u> a discourse from Socrates on these elementals:

> "And upon the earth are animals and men, some in a middle region, others (elementals) dwelling about the air as we dwell about the sea; others in islands which the air flows round, near the continent; and in a word, the air is used by them as the water and the sea are by us, and the ether is to them what the air is to us. More over, the temperament of their seasons is such that they have no disease [Paracelsus disputes this], and live much longer than we do, and have sight and bearing and smell, and all the other senses, in far greater perfection, in the same degree that air is purer than water or the ether than air. Also they have temples and sacred places in which the gods really dwell, and they hear their voices and receive their answers, and are conscious of them and hold converse with them, and they see the sun, moon, and stars as they really are, and their other blessedness is of a piece with this."

Even St. Augustine wrote about this subject, something that was common knowledge to the learned men of past ages:

> "It is a widespread opinion, confirmed by direct or indirect testi-mony of trustworthy persons, that

the Sylvans and Fauns, com-monly called Incubi, have often tormented women, solicited and obtained intercourse with them. There are even Demons, which are called Duses [i.e., lutins] by the Gauls, who are quite frequently using such impure practices: this is vouched for by so numerous and so high authorities that it would be impudent to deny it."

The alchemist Paracelsus wrote numerous things about these creatures, too, and warned of their dangers:

"I do not want to say here, because of the ills which might befall those who would try it, through which compact one associates with these beings, thanks to which compact they appear to us and speak to us."

Salamanders are the elementals of fire often seen as luminous globes and sometimes witnessed hovering above water. They dwell in the south, commonly associated with heat and hell. Considered the strongest and most powerful of all elementals, their ruler is *Djin*, described as being smokeless, but made of luminous fire. Commonly referred to as genies, they provided a framework for the formation of demons in Christianity, Islam, and Judaism. Salamanders could be felt and seen with fire and incense, which was burned by man in conjuration. Material fire was made of their essence and could not exist otherwise. Hall says they work through our emotional nature by means of *"body heat, the liver, and the blood stream."* Paracelsus writes of the fire spirit, saying *"Salamanders have been seen in the shapes of fiery balls, or tongues of fire, running over the fields or peering in houses."* Today we may call them *ball lightning*.

Salamanders, from Parcelsus' <u>Auslegung Von 30 Magischen Figuren</u>

~ PUT SIMPLY ~

It is from the *Gnomes*, those elementals of earth, rock, dirt, wood, etc., for which we get stories of goblins and their leader Gob in the north.

Undines occupy water and invoke imagines reminiscent of western sirens and mermaids, especially of the freshwater nymph called Melusine.

Sylphs are considered entirely intangible and invisible, but they provide us with the idea of the *great eastern wind*, as this was their creative domain.

Salamanders are northern elementals of fire similarly related to the beings of smokeless fire known to the Arabs as *Djinn*, and wherefrom we derive the idea of *genies*.

Our *emotions* are driven by Undines, *thoughts* by Sylphs, *physical* body by Gnomes, and our *passions* by Salamanders.

Hall explains further in <u>The Secret Teachings of All Ages</u> how these *spirits of nature* were eventually gathered up and collectively titled "demon" by the Church:

"The Christian Church gathered all the elemental entities together under the title of demon. This is a misnomer with far-reaching consequences, for to the average mind the word demon means an evil

thing, and the Nature spirits are essentially no more malevolent than are the minerals, plants, and animals."

Although Hall suggests the harmlessness of these spirits, Paracelsus would disagree it seems. And Levi concurs with Paracelsus, writing how Kabbalists view these spirits in their *"most secret books"* to be *"the children of the solitude of Adam."* He says they were born before the creation of woman when man was dreaming of companionship. As also theorized by Paracelsus, menstrual blood and nocturnal emissions create *phantoms* or *larvae* that are known as *elementary spirits*. Levi writes of these phantoms: *"such larvae have an aerial body formed from vapor of blood, for which they are attracted towards spilt blood and in older days drew nourishment from the smoke of sacrifices."*

These *elementary* spirits are distinct from the *elemental* spirits of this section, thus reconciling Hall's description with those of Paracelsus and Levi. The *elementals* are benevolent while the *elementary* spirits are usually malevolent and vampiric. In fact, they are said to be the *incubi* and *succubi* of legend, those vampires draining the vital heat or energy of healthy persons. If the *life force* of a creature resides in the blood, as is commonly believed, then the *sucking* or *draining* of energy through an act of vampirism may be associated with the *drinking of blood*. Certain parasites can be treated with garlic and so we may derive from here the origin of using the bulb to protect against parasitic vampires.

Dictionary of the Infernal & The Magus

At the core a *demon* or *demonic classification* is a cultural determinate of societal limitations and values. People falling outside these boundaries are usually seen as *cursed, possessed, crooked, wicked, demonic,* and further as *wizards, sorcerers, magicians,* and witches. We may also say that a *miracle* within a religious community is proof of God at work whereas outside that same religious group it is an act of wicked *magic* and condemned as *demonic*. Sarah Iles Johnston put it simply in her essay 'Defining the Dreadful', how in this paradigm *"'normal' demonic behavior = abnormal human behavior."* One of the best examples of this comes in the form of demonic female spirits or ghosts seeking to harm children, an archetype of women incapable of pregnancy or unwilling to give birth, and even to those whose children die in accidents. Sarah goes on to write:

> *"Demons are clay with which people mold images of their fears and anxieties; in order to express the fears and anxieties of the moment effectively, that clay must remain malleable. It is not until those who stand outside of a community begin to make lists of its demons (i.e. demonologies) for their own purposes that any real consistency of traits and imagery is obtained, and it is artificial consistency, born form a scholar's desire to organize, a magician's desire to control or a missionary's desire to devalue and eventually overcome."*

From the ancient Greek words *daimonion* and *daimōn*, we acquire our word *demon*. A *daemon* is a "divinity or supernatural being of a nature between gods and humans," and thus akin to *elemental spirits* that Hall says are *"no more malevolent than are the minerals, plants, and animals."* The more common *demon* is akin to the *elementary spirits* that Levi calls *"children of the solitude of Adam."*

If we are doing any kind of internal work of a magical, religious, spiritual, or psychological nature, intended to elevate our moral standing, then we are drawing on *Celestial Virtues* and the *Cosmic Mind*. If we are doing the same work to fulfill selfish desires only, or to bring harm to others, then we are calling on the spirits of the infernal. On this point, Agrippa explains something similar:

> "Whosoever therefore doth the more exactly imitate the celestial bodies, either in nature, study, action, motion, gesture, countenance, passions of the mind, and opportunity of the season, is so much the more like to the heavenly bodies, and can receive larger gifts from them."

Jacques Collin de Plancy was an occult author and demonologist, who published Dictionnaire Infernal in 1818. In his writings he explains how the Devil received most of his deformities from man just as we said the Church is primarily responsible for fabricating most the horrors of the *Black Mass*.

Years earlier, in 1801, it was the professor Francis Barrett, author of The Magus, who began to remove these exaggerated details. He drew numerous demons and spirits in a manner more human: Apollyon, Belial, Asmodeus, Astaroth, Abaddon, and Mammon, among others, and his work should be consulted for further review. Barrett's treatment of these spirits is reminiscent of the *werewolf* and *wendigo*. He writes in his classic book:

> "An intelligence is an intelligible substance, free from all gross and putrifying mass of a body, immortal, insensible, assisting all, having influence over all; and the nature of all intelligences, spirits, and angels is the same. But I call angels here, not those whom we usually call devils, but spirits so called from the propriety of the word, as it were, knowing, understanding, and wise."

Every man is given a *good spirit* and an *evil spirit*, and each seeks union with our soul-spirit. Each of these spirits attempts to attract our spirit to it through *angelic* or *diabolic* methods like the *shoulder angel* and *shoulder demon* representing *conscience* and *temptation* respectively. In the Graeco-Egyptian religion we find the *kakodaemon* (evil) and *agathodaemon* (good).

There are *nine degrees* of evil spirits in contrast with the *nine orders* of angels.

In first order are the *False Gods* usurping the true name of God and requiring sacrifices amongst other dark practices; of these is known *Beelzebub*.

Next come the *Spirits of Lies* and *Vessels of Iniquity*, the latter being inventors of evil things and wicked arts.

The *Revengers of Evil* are ruled by their prince *Asmodeus*, the cause of judgments.

The *Deluders* imitate miracles, serve sorcerers, and are ruled by their prince *Satan*.

The *Aerial* powers cause pollution of the air and the spread of pestilence; their prince is *Meririm*.

Shoulder Angel, attributed Guido Reni, 17th-century.

The *Furies* are powers of evil, war, and devastation, and are ruled by the Greek *Apollyon*, or Hebrew *Abaddon*, names that mean to "destroy" or lay waste.

The eighth and ninth degrees are known as *Accusers* or *Inquisitors* and *Tempters and Ensnarers*. *Astaroth* is prince of the Accusers and *Mammon*, meaning covetousness, rules the Tempters.

Each of these demonic spirits, easily associated with angels, are given authority over certain parts of the mind (psyche) and world, and many acquire their names first from real cities that were historically wicked, as is the case with Astaroth.

In Islam there are three created intelligences under Allah: Angels of light, Jinn of subtle fire, and Man of the earthly dust. Of the Jinn there are three orders: flyers, walkers, divers.

According to the Arbatel grimoire and the writings of Arthur E. Waite, it is best to focus on the office of each spirit rather than their diverse, and often confusing, names or configurations. This is the case with mythology, too, due to countless methods of storytelling and preservation, language variations, cultural differences, and the like, creating confusion in the relationships of gods and goddesses. In The True Grimoire we are further informed of the various appearances of these spirits:

> "The spirits do not always appear in the same form. This is because they meld themselves out of the secret matter, from all the matter and for this reason they need something to lend them a body in order to appear to us, and can take the shape and form that appeal to them."

There are described three spirit types in The Magus: *Super-Celestial* spirits are separated from a body; *Celestial* spirits are worldly angels; and *Angels* are the ministers of worldly things. Of the fallen angels are Apollyon, the deceiver, and Belial, the immoral. Next are described the *Vessels of Wrath*: Theutus, incubus or succubus, and Asmodeus.

Some spirits are *superior* and others *inferior*. The superiors and their titles, according to the grimoires, are Lucifer, the Emperor; Beelzebuth, the Prince; and Astaroth, the Grand Duke. They may be invoked by their sigils, which, it is said, must be written, at least, in the blood of the operator at a certain hour, then worn.

~ the seal and character of each of the three superiors are as follows ~

| Lucifer | Beelzebuth | Astaroth |

Asmodeus is a "destructive demon," writes de Plancy, sowing "dissipation and error." *Aeshma Daeva* is known as *Asmodeus* to the Christians, and in Hebrew as *Ashmadai* or *Asmoday*, here described by Doctor John Wier (1515-1588) in the following horrific manner:

> *"He is a great and powerful king. He appears with three heads, a bull's head, a human head and a ram's head. He has goose feet and a snake's tail. He exhales fire and rides upon a dragon of hell. He carries a spear and a banner."*

Yet, Asmodeus grants knowledge of geometry, astronomy, arithmetic, and mechanics, but only if called upon as such: *In truth thou art Asmodeus.* These are things that may be revealed through dangerous operations that are plagued with dissipation. According to some, de Plancy says *"this Asmodeus is the old snake who seduced Eve."*

From the doctrines of Zoroastrianism, we find a clear delineation of the spirits of light and dark. Lord Ormazd (Ahura-Mazda) is the King of Light and Ahriman (Anra-Mainyu) is the Prince of Darkness. There are six archangels and archdemons under Ormazd and Ahriman respectively. Of the kingdom of light: Divine Wisdom, Righteousness, Dominion, Devotion, Totality, and Salvation. Of the kingdom of darkness: Anarchy, Apostasy, Presumption, Destruction, Decay, and fury.

Other Zoroastrian demons leading away from Ormazd, or reason and light, include: Vereno (lust), Paromaiti (arrogance), Zaurvan (Decrepitude), Mitox (fallen spoken word), and Akatasa (meddlesomeness).

Lower in this hierarchy are the Drujs, Yatus, Nasus, enchantresses, malevolent begins, deceivers, and monsters. Of the Nasus we find a female demon in form of a fly, embodying impurity and decay, like *Beelzebub*, who was worshipped by the Canaanites. Hebrews called him *Prince of Demons*.

The Zoroastrianism accounts of these things allows us to do what Waite suggested, that we focus on the offices of these spirits instead of their appearances. Any man or woman is therefore said to be "possessed" by a demon when displaying characteristics associated with their offices. *Mammon* possesses a covetous man. *Asmodeus* possesses the lustful. *Apollyon* creates conflicts in relationships. *Meririm* is a sickness or poison in the air. When we understand the hierarchal offices of demons it becomes completely clear how to place their correspondences, influences, and locations. Unclean spirits like *Belphegor* require offerings of feces and urine from the slothful. Since blood belongs to God, as we have seen, using it to attract spirits is diabolic. Impure spirits are attracted to blood, semen, feces, urine, and the smoke of animal or human sacrifices. Here we can understand Crowley's *Cake of Light*, comprised of blood, honey, and oil, and Marina Abramović's *Spirit Cooking* performance, comprised of blood, semen, and breast milk. Richard Cavendish explains the same thing in The Black Arts:

> *"The best-known type of imitative magic relies on creating a link with its victim by making an image of him in wax, clay, rags or whatever material is to hand, usually including his hair or nail clippings, blood or sweat, which retain their connection with him."*

The blood contains *life force*, semen contains *life seed*, and breast milk contains *life's nourishment* like honey and oil. From here we can read Rudolf Steiner's assessment of spiritual vampires that feed off human anxiety and fear:

> *"There are beings in the spiritual realms for whom anxiety and fear emanating from human beings offer welcome food. When humans have no anxiety and fear, then these creatures starve. People not yet sufficiently convinced of this statement could understand it to be meant comparatively only. But for those who are familiar with this phenomenon, it is a reality. If fear and anxiety radiates from people and they break out in panic, then these creatures find welcome nutrition, and they become more and more powerful. These beings are hostile towards humanity. Everything that feeds on negative feelings, on anxiety, fear, and superstition, despair or doubt, are in reality hostile forces in supersensible worlds, launching cruel attacks on human beings, while they are being fed. Therefore, it is above all necessary, to begin with, that the person who enters the spiritual world overcomes fear, feelings of helplessness, despair, and anxiety. But these are exactly the feelings that belong to contemporary culture and materialism; because it estranges people from the spiritual world, it is especially suited to evoke hopelessness and fear of the unknown in people, thereby calling up the above mentioned hostile forces against them."*

We should instead offer beautiful things, sweet incense, perfumes, prayers, clean clothes, and the like, while we *"imitate the celestial bodies."* In this sense, one could define the *dark arts* as a usurpation of God's authority because they allow mankind to cheat in his search for alchemical gold.

If we wish to call upon any spirit, let us first understand the methods: *imprecation*, prayer for invoking a deity or spirit; *deprecations*, prayers for averting evil; *orations*, prayers of supplication to God; *evocation*, calling upon a spirit; *invocations*, callings upon spirits by incantation; *conjurations*, constraining and compelling a spirit by oath; *obtestations*, charging or beseeching by sacred names; *adjurations*, retractions and renouncing of pacts or oaths.

To better understand these energies, we shall also evoke a statement from Migene González-Wippler's, The Complete Book of Amulets & Talismans:

> *"Spirits, angels, archangels, elementals and demons are likewise electrical impulses that populate the cosmos. They are in a sense thought concentrations, mind entities that exist without the benefit, or should we say, without the hinderance, of a human body. These are the cosmic forces that control the workings of the universe, and to whom we have recourse in times of need. Because they lack a body, and are essentially mental in nature, they must be contacted through the symbolic language of the mind, a language which is universal and all its aspects."*

Magical Images

Contrary to popular assumption, the wearing of a cross, pentagram, or the sigil of Lucifer, for example, does indeed draw on certain powerful reservoirs of energy. The same can be said of statues, books, and even doodles. There is considerable danger to the psyche when one plays with such things, especially if they are in any way mildly serious. In Egypt an image was considered to hold magical powers. This is why some people refuse to be photographed, believing their essence could be trapped in the camera, picture, or video. Kurt Seligmann confirms in <u>The Mirror of Magic</u> how images are endowed with certain magical powers:

> *"Whenever the sculptor's chisel molds the amorphous mass into an image, whenever he portrays an organism, magical power flows into the statue – a power which may be imprisoned within it by incantation and magical gesture, and which gives life to the image as long as it remains whole."*

In paranormal research it is believed that common objects can become possessed by spirits, too, which is an idea similar, but not identical, to the Japanese concept of *tsukumogami*. If not by malevolent spirits, items like statues may be possessed by the benevolent spirit of their likeness.

It is just as common today to keep pictures of our dead relatives or parents in the home, and often even their urns and ashes. When we look at the picture or urn and recall memories, we are essentially performing a type of necromancy, something especially true when we call on our ancestors or dead parents to assist us in life. When objects possessing benevolent or malevolent spirits are broken it is believed the inhabitant vacates the vessel.

Be Mindful of Your Thoughts

Words are by the simplest definition expressions of *consciousness* that result in *creation*. The Hebrew *gōlem,* or shapeless mass, is an illustrative physical example of this process. In one 16th-century story, a man called Elijah of Chelm, with assistance from the mystic Jewish text known as <u>Yetzirah</u>, created one of these creatures. The artificial and shapeless monster came to life having had written the secret name of God on its forehead. In most stories the *golem* comes to life through intention, will, and the Hebrew word emét, which means "truth." To stop this monstrous manifestation, a letter is removed from the word emét so that the inscription reads mét, the Hebrew word for "death."

The word *tulpa* is a creation of Tibetan Buddhist philosophy. These *thought-forms* are manifest either through a deliberate act of will or by unintentional thoughts. Although like a *golem,* the *tulpa* can form because of individual or collective thoughts with no need for additional physical assistance. Hence, you should *be mindful of your thoughts.*

Non-physical entities that manifest by individual or collective thoughts are called *egregore,* from the French égrégore and Greek egrēgoros, which means "wakeful."

Energy flows where attention goes, even if that attention is unintentionally creating monstrous embryonic phantoms unconsciously. We are told to "pay attention" and that transaction is conducted through the medium of our energy, i.e., *currency.* It is with this same "currency" that we "pay" for an item or service. Our money is stored in a bank, which can be found on either side of a river and its *currents.* When we direct our attention towards symbols, images, sounds, ideas, etc., we are feeding them our energy. According to C. W. Leadbeater in <u>A Textbook of Theosophy</u>, thoughts alone are powerful enough to create *embryonic forms*, and although the thoughts of others may drift into our minds, it is our responsibility not to invigorate them:

> "*Every thought builds a form; if the thought be directed to another person it travels to him; if it be distinctly selfish it remains in the immediate neighborhood of the thinker; if it belongs to neither of these categories it floats for a while in space and then slowly disintegrates. Every man therefore is leaving behind him wherever he goes a trail of thought-forms; as we go along the street we are walking all the time amidst a sea of other men's thoughts. If a man leaves his mind blank for a time, these residual thoughts of others drifts through it, making in most cases but little impression upon him. Sometimes one arrives which attracts his attention, so that his mind seizes upon it and makes it its own, strengthens it by the addition of its force, and then casts it out again to affect somebody else. A man, therefore, is not responsible for a thought which floats into his mind, but he is responsible if he takes it up, dwells upon it and then sends it out strengthened.*"

Agrippa writes on the same: "*and his imagination is made most strong, when that etherial and celestial power is poured out upon it, by whose brightness it is comforted, until it apprehend the species, notions and knowledge of true things, so that that which he thought in his mind, cometh to pass even as he thought, and it obtaineth so great power, that it can plunge, join and insinuate it self into the minds of men, and make them certain of his thoughts, and of his will and desire, even through large and remote spaces, as if they perceived a present object by their senses; and it can in little time do many things, as if they were done without time.*"

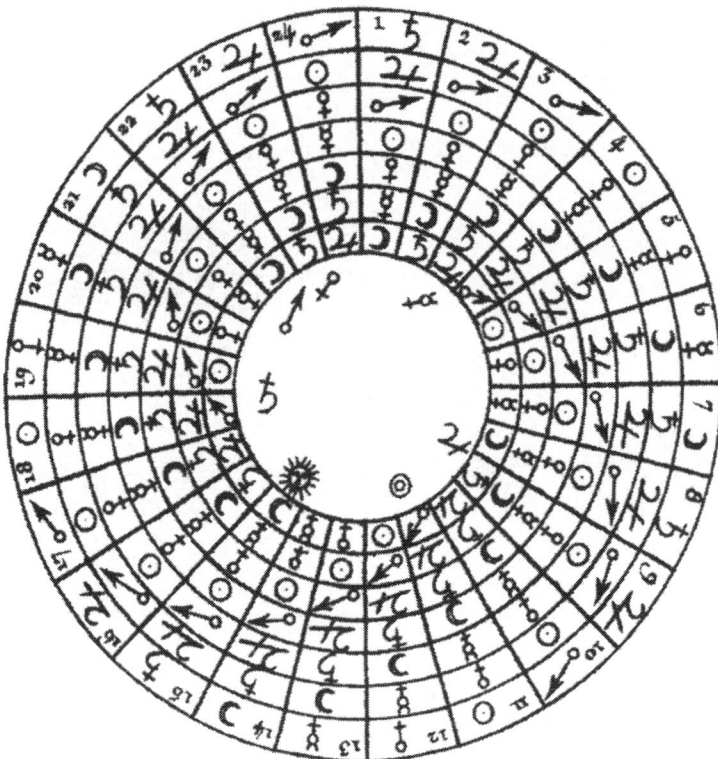

The Great Wheel or Sphere of the Planets, from Grimorium Verum or The True Grimoire.

It depicts the planets assigned to each hour of the week. At the very top outer circle we see the astrological sign of Saturn and a number one, indicating that the first hour after sunset on a Saturday belongs to Saturn; the second hour belongs to Jupiter and so forth. The first hour of Sunday belongs to the Sun.

Of Superior Spirits, their Offices & Subordinates

The *superior spirits* beneath Lucifer, Beelzebuth, and Astaroth, are as follows, along with their offices and subordinates, according to selected grimoires:

Lucifuge, Prime Minster: Bael, Agares, Marbas

Satanachia, Great General: Pruslas, Aamon, Barbatos

Agliarept, General: Buer, Cusgyn, Betis

Fleurety, Lieutenant General: Bathim, Hursan, Eligor

Sargatanas, Brigadier: Loray, Valefar, Farai

Nebiros, Camp Marshal: Ayperos, Naberus, Glosialabolas

These *superior spirits* are here listen as instructed in the <u>Grimorium Verum</u> with assistance acquired from Arthur Waite and <u>The Book of Black Magic</u>:

Lucifer (Emperor): Pu Satanachia & Agaliarept.

Beelzebuth (Prince): Tarchimache & Fluerety.

Astaroth (Grand Duke): Sargatanas & Nebiros.

From <u>The Grand Grimoire</u> we extract the names and officers of the *superior spirits*: to the right are their characters from <u>Le Dragon Rouge</u>:

Lucifuge Rofocale (Prime Minister): grants wealth and treasures.

Satanachia (Commander in Chief): has power over women.

Agallarept (Commander): helps uncover the arcane.

Fleurety (Lieutenant General): assists in labors by night.

Sargatanas (Brigadier Major): opens locks and helps to transport.

Nebiros (Field Marshal / Inspector General): informs on mineral and plant virtues.

LUCIFER, Empereur.

BELZÉBUT, Prince.

ASTAROT, Grand-duc.

LUCIFUGÉ, prem. Ministr.

SATANACHIA, grand général.

AGALIAREPT., aussi général.

FLEURETY, lieutenantgén.

SARGATANAS, brigadier.

NEBIROS, mar. de camp.

The <u>Grimorium Vernim</u> provides us here with the 17 subordinate spirits:

Clauneck: bestows wealth and hidden treasures.

Musisin: has power over lords.

Bechard: has power over winds, rain, lightning and hail.

Frimost: has power over maidens.

Khil: causes earthquakes.

Mersilde: will transport thee wherever.

Listheret: has power to alter night and day.

Sirchade: has power to produce animals.

Segal: causes unnatural things to become visible.

Hiepacht: may bring a distant person to location.

Humots: transports books.

Frucissiere: brings the dead to life.

Guland: causes all manner of disease.

Surgat: opens locks.

Morail: makes all worldly things visible.

Frutimiere: prepares festivals.

Huictiigarra: has power over sleep, wakefulness and insomnia.

~

Other serviceable spirits of use are mentioned by Arthur E. Waite:

Serguthy: has power over wives and virgins.

Heramael: teaches medicine; gives knowledge of plants, and of diseases and their cures.

Trimasel: teaches chemistry and sleight of hand; imparts secrets of the powder of projection.

Sustugriel: teaches the magical art.

Elelogap: has power over water.

Hael: instructs in the art of writing and speaking in many tongues.

Table of Planetary Hours

Chic Cicero and Sandra Tabatha Cicero break down the hours of the day in their book <u>Golden Dawn Magic</u> the following:

"Divide the total time between sunrise and sunset by 12. This will give you the length of the Magical Hours of the day. Dividing the time between sunset and sunrise by 12 will give you the length of the Planetary Hours of the night."

The four seasons are governed by angels, as are the days of the week and the hours of those days. The angels of *spring* are Caracasa, Core, Amatiel and Commissoros; of *summer*, Gargatel, Tariel and Gaviel; of *autumn*, Tarquam and Guabarel; and of *winter*, Amabael and Cetarari.

The angels of the seven days of the week are here listed, along with their perfumes, and below is a table, as reproduced from <u>The Magus</u>, of the names angels and planets, and their days and times.

Sunday: Michael, Dardiel, Huratapel (Perfume: Red Sanders); **Monday**: Gabriel, Michael, Samael (Perfume: Aloes); **Tuesday**: Samael, Satael, Amabiel (Perfume: Pepper); **Wednesday**: Raphael, Meil, Seraphiel (Perfume: Mastic); **Thursday**: Sachiel, Cassiel, Asasiel (Perfume: Saffron); **Friday**: Anael, Rachiel, Sachiel (Perfume: Pepperwort); **Saturday**: Cassiel, Machatan, Uriel (Perfume: Sulphur).

Hours Day.	Angels and Planets ruling SUNDAY.	Angels and Planets ruling MONDAY.	Angels and Planets ruling TUESDAY.	Angels and Planets ruling WEDNESDAY.	Angels and Planets ruling THURSDAY.	Angels and Planets ruling FRIDAY.	Angels and Planets ruling SATURDAY.
	Day.	*Day.*	*Day.*	*Day.*	*Day.*	*Day.*	*Day.*
1	☉ Michael	☽ Gabriel	♂ Samael	☿ Raphael	♃ Sachiel	♀ Anael	♄ Cassiel
2	♀ Anael	♄ Cassiel	☉ Michael	☽ Gabriel	♂ Samael	☿ Raphael	♃ Sachiel
3	☿ Raphael	♃ Sachiel	♀ Anael	♄ Cassiel	☉ Michael	☽ Gabriel	♂ Samael
4	☽ Gabriel	♂ Samael	☿ Raphael	♃ Sachiel	♀ Anael	♄ Cassiel	☉ Michael
5	♄ Cassiel	☉ Michael	☽ Gabriel	♂ Samael	☿ Raphael	♃ Sachiel	♀ Anael
6	♃ Sachiel	♀ Anael	♄ Cassiel	☉ Michael	☽ Gabriel	♂ Samael	☿ Raphael
7	♂ Samael	☿ Raphael	♃ Sachiel	♀ Anael	♄ Cassiel	☉ Michael	☽ Gabriel
8	☉ Michael	☽ Gabriel	♂ Samael	☿ Raphael	♃ Sachiel	♀ Anael	♄ Cassiel
9	♀ Anael	♄ Cassiel	☉ Michael	☽ Gabriel	♂ Samael	☿ Raphael	♃ Sachiel
10	☿ Raphael	♃ Sachiel	♀ Anael	♄ Cassiel	☉ Michael	☽ Gabriel	♂ Samael
11	☽ Gabriel	♂ Samael	☿ Raphael	♃ Sachael	♀ Anael	♄ Cassiel	☉ Michael
12	♄ Cassiel	☉ Michael	☽ Gabriel	♂ Samael	☿ Raphael	♃ Sachiel	♀ Anael

Hours Night							
	Night.	*Night.*	*Night.*	*Night.*	*Night.*	*Night.*	*Night.*
1	♃ Sachael	♀ Anael	♄ Cassiel	☉ Michael	☽ Gabriel	♂ Samael	☿ Raphael
2	♂ Samiel	☿ Raphael	♃ Sachiel	♀ Anael	♄ Cassiel	☉ Michael	☽ Gabriel
3	☉ Michael	☽ Gabriel	♂ Samael	☿ Raphael	♃ Sachiel	♀ Anael	♄ Cassiel
4	♀ Anael	♄ Cassiel	☉ Michael	☽ Gabriel	♂ Samael	☿ Raphael	♃ Sachiel
5	☿ Raphael	♃ Sachiel	♀ Anael	♄ Cassiel	☉ Michael	☽ Gabriel	♂ Samael
6	☽ Gabriel	♂ Samael	☿ Raphael	♃ Sachiel	♀ Anael	♄ Cassiel	☉ Michael
7	♄ Cassiel	☉ Michael	☽ Gabriel	♂ Samael	☿ Raphael	♃ Sachiel	♀ Anael
8	♃ Sachiel	♀ Anael	♄ Cassiel	☉ Michael	☽ Gabriel	♂ Samael	☿ Raphael
9	♂ Samael	☿ Raphael	♃ Sachiel	♀ Anael	♄ Cassiel	☉ Michael	☽ Gabriel
10	☉ Michael	☽ Gabriel	♂ Samael	☿ Raphael	♃ Sachiel	♀ Anael	♄ Cassiel
11	♀ Anael	♄ Cassiel	☉ Michael	☽ Gabriel	♂ Samael	☿ Raphael	♃ Sachiel
12	☿ Raphael	♃ Sachiel	♀ Anael	♄ Cassiel	☉ Michael	☽ Gabriel	♂ Samael

From the 1914 edition of <u>The Greater Key of Solomon</u>, by Samuel Mathers, here is reproduced, in part, *Chapter II - Of the Days, and Hours, and of the Virtues of the Planets.* It provides us with the correspondences of which hour and day, and which planet, best is suited for certain operations:

WHEN thou wishest to make any experiment or operation, thou must first prepare, beforehand, all the requisites which thou wilt find described in the following Chapters: observing the days, the hours, and the other effects of the Constellations which may be found in this Chapter.

It is, therefore, advisable to know that the hours of the day and of the night together, are twenty-four in number, and that each hour is governed by one of the Seven Planets in regular order, commencing at the highest and descending to the lowest. The order of the Planets is as follows:

ShBThAI, Shabbathai, Saturn; beneath Saturn is TzDQ, Tzedeq, Jupiter; beneath Jupiter is MADIM, Madim, Mars; beneath Mars is ShMSh, Shemesh, the Sun; beneath the Sun is NVGH, Nogah, Venus; beneath Venus is KVKB, Kokav, Mercury; and beneath Mercury is LBNH, Levanah, the Moon, which is the lowest of all the Planets.

It must, therefore, be understood that the Planets have their dominion over the day which approacheth nearest unto the name which is given and attributed unto them-viz., over Saturday, Saturn; Thursday, Jupiter; Tuesday, Mars; Sunday, the Sun; Friday, Venus; Wednesday, Mercury; and Monday, the Moon.

The rule of the Planets over each hour begins from the dawn at the rising of the Sun on the day which takes its name from such Planet, and the Planet which follows it in order, succeeds to the rule over the next hour. Thus (on Saturday) Saturn rules the first hour, Jupiter the second, Mars the third, the Sun the fourth, Venus the fifth, Mercury the sixth, the Moon the seventh, and Saturn returns in the rule over the eighth, and the others in their turn, the Planets always keeping the same relative order.

Note that each experiment or magical operation should be performed under the Planet, and usually in the hour, which refers to the same. For example: --

In the Days and Hours of Saturn thou canst perform experiments to summon the Souls from Hades, but only of those who have died a natural death. Similarly on these days and hours thou canst operate to bring either good or bad fortune to buildings; to have familiar Spirits attend thee in sleep; to cause good or ill success to business, possessions, goods, seeds, fruits, and similar things, in order to acquire learning; to bring destruction and to give death, and to sow hatred and discord.

The Days and Hours of Jupiter are proper for obtaining honours, acquiring riches; contracting friendships, preserving health; and arriving at all that thou canst desire.

In the Days and Hours of Mars thou canst make experiments regarding War; to arrive at military honour; to acquire courage; to overthrow enemies; and further to cause ruin, slaughter, cruelty, discord; to wound and to give death. The Days and Hours of the Sun are very good for perfecting experiments regarding temporal wealth, hope, gain, fortune, divination, the favour of princes, to dissolve hostile feeling, and to make friends.

The Days and Hours of Venus are good for forming friendships; for kindness and love; for joyous and pleasant undertakings, and for travelling. The Days and Hours of Mercury are good to operate for eloquence and intelligence; promptitude in business; science and divination; wonders; apparitions; and answers regarding the future. Thou canst also operate under this Planet for thefts; writings; deceit; and merchandise.

The Days and Hours of the Moon are good for embassies; voyages envoys; messages; navigation; reconciliation; love; and the acquisition of merchandise by water. Thou shouldest take care punctually to observe all the instructions contained in this chapter, if thou desirest to succeed, seeing that the truth of Magical Science dependeth thereon.

The Hours of Saturn, of Mars, and of the Moon are alike good for communicating and speaking with Spirits; as those of Mercury are for recovering thefts by the means of Spirits.

The Hours of Mars serve for summoning Souls from Hades, especially of those slain in battle.

The Hours of the Sun, of Jupiter, and of enus, are adapted for preparing any operations whatsoever of love, of kindness, and of invisibility, as is hereafter more fully shown, to which must be added other things of a similar nature which are contained in our work.

The Hours of Saturn and Mars and also the days on which the Moon is conjunct with them, or when she receives their opposition or quartile aspect, are excellent for making experiments of hatred, enmity, quarrel, and discord; and other operations of the same kind which are given later on in this work.

The Hours of Mercury are good for undertaking experiments relating to games, raillery, jests, sports, and the like.

The Hours of the Sun, of Jupiter, and of Venus, particularly on the days which they rule, are good for all extraordinary, uncommon, and unknown operations. The Hours of the Moon are proper for making trial of experiments relating to recovery of stolen property, for obtaining nocturnal visions, for summoning Spirits in sleep, and for preparing anything relating to Water.

The Hours of Venus are furthermore useful for lots, poisons, all things of the nature of Venus, for preparing powders provocative of madness and the like things.

But in order to thoroughly effect the operations of this Art, thou shouldest perform them not only on the Hours but on the Days of the Planets as well, because then the experiment will always succeed better, provided thou observest the rules laid down later on, for if thou omittest one single condition thou wilt never arrive at the accomplishment of the Art.

For those matters then which appertain unto the Moon, such as the Invocation of Spirits, the Works of Necromancy, and the recovery of stolen property, it is necessary that the Moon should be in a Terrestrial Sign, viz.:--Taurus, Virgo, or Capricorn.

For love, grace, and invisibility, the Moon should be in a Fiery Sign, viz.:--Aries, Leo, or Sagittarius. For hatred, discord, and destruction, the Moon should be in a Watery Sign, viz.:--Cancer, Scorpio, or Pisces. For experiments of a peculiar nature, which cannot be classed under any certain head, the Moon should be in an Airy Sign, viz.: -- Gemini, Libra, or Aquarius.

The 72 Solomonic Spirits & Seals:

Baal: imparts wisdom and invisibility.
(appears with a human, toad or cat head)

Agares: teaches all languages; causes earthquakes; makes runners stand still.
(appears as an old man upon a crocodile)

Vassago: declares things past, present and future; finds what is lost or hidden.

Gamygyn: teaches liberal sciences.
(appears as a horse, donkey or human)

Marbas: causes and cures diseases; reveals things kept hidden or secret.
(appears as a lion and human)

Valefor: leads those to theft.
(appears as a many headed lion)

Amon: discerns past and future; procures love; reconciles friends and foes.
(appears as a wolf with serpent head vomiting flames)

Barbatos: instructs is sciences; reveals treasures, and things past and future.

Paimon: teaches art, science and secrets; makes men subject to magicians.
(appears as a crowned man)

Buer: teaches philosophy, logic, and virtues of herbs; heals disease.

Gusion: gives honors; discerns past, present and future things.

Sytry: procures love between sexes.
(appears with a leopard head)

Beleth: procures love between men and women.
(appears upon a pale horse)

Lerajie: visits battles.
(appears as an archer)

Eligor: causes war; kindles lust and love; uncovers what has been hidden.
(appears as a knight with lance and scepter)

Separ: inflames women with love for men and has the ability to make them barren.

Botis: reconciles friends and foes; discerns things past, present and future.
(appears as a viper and also as a human with horns)

Bathin: teaches the virtues of herbs and precious stones; transports men.
(appears as strong man with serpent tail upon a pale horse)

Saleos: promotes love between sexes.
(appears as a soldier riding a crocodile)

Purson: provides answers concerning things of a human and diving nature.
(appears with a lion head holding a viper)

Morax: teaches astronomy and liberal sciences; gives knowledge of herbs and stones.

Ipos: imparts wit and courage.
(appears as an angel with lion head or with rabbit tail and feet of a goose)

Aini: imparts cunning and gives answers to matters of a private nature.
(appears with many heads)

Naberius: teaches arts and sciences; restores lost honors.
(appears as a crowing cock)

Glasyalabolas: teaches all art and science; incites homicide.
(appears as a winged dog)

Bune: gives riches, wisdom and eloquence, and brings forth other demons.
(appears as a dog or dragon and has the head of a man)

Ronobe: teaches rhetoric and knowledge of many tongues.

Berith: turns metals into gold and provides true answers to questions.
(appears as a soldier riding a red horse)

Astaroth: gives skill in liberal sciences; uncovers secrets.
(appears as an angel carrying a viper)

Forneus: causes men to be loved by their enemies.
(appears as a sea monster)

Foras: teaches virtues of herbs and stones; teaches logic, ethics and imparts wisdom.

Asmoday: grants invisibility; indicates where treasures are hidden; teaches geomancy.
(appears with the head of a bull, ram or man, with goose feet and the tail of a serpent)

Gaap: teaches philosophy; excites love and hate.

Furfur: incites love between a man and wife; raises lightning and wind.

Marchosias: gives true answers to all questions.
(appears as a wolf with serpent tale)

Solas: teaches astronomy and the virtue of herbs.
(appears as a raven)

Phoenix: teaches poetry, all sciences and is obedient to orders.
(appears as the bird of legend)

Halpas: kills the wicked and burns towns.

Malpas: destroys desire and thoughts; deceives those making sacrifices.
(appears as a crow)

Raum: steals treasures, destroys cities; grants love of friends and foes.

Focalor: drowns men and has power over winds and seas.

Sabanack: builds and fortifies towers, camps and cities.

Vepar: governs water and ships.
(appears as a water spirit)

Shax: steals money; destroys sight and hearing.

Vine: makes known the past, present and future; reveals witches.

Bifrons: conveys knowledge in astrology, geometry and mathematics.

Vual: procures love of women.

Hagenti: grants wisdom; transmutes metal into gold and water into wine.

Procel: teaches geometry and the liberal sciences.
(appears as an angel)

Furcas: teaches philosophy, rhetoric, astronomy, logic and pyromancy.
(appears as an old man)

Balam: imparts wit and invisibility.
(appears with the head of a bull, man or ram)

Allocen: teaches astronomy and liberal sciences.

Caim: imparts understanding of the songs of birds and of barking dogs.

Murmur: teaches philosophy and forces souls to appear from the dead.

Orobas: informs on divinity and creation.

Gomory: discovers treasures.

Ose: gives answers to questions pertaining to secrets; teaches liberal sciences.

Amy: teaches astrology and deals with hidden treasures.
(appears as a flame and then in human form)

Orias: informs on the virtues of the planets.

Vapula: teaches skills in manual professions.

Zagan: turns water into wine like Hagenti; turns blood to oil, and oil to water, makes fools wise.

Valac: gives answers to hidden treasures; finds and provides serpents.
(appears as a little boy, sometimes with wings of an angel)

Andras: kills the unwary and sows discord.
(appears as an angel with the head of a raven)

Flauros: burns and destroys enemies.

Andrealphus: teaches geometry, astronomy and turns men into birds.
(appears in the form of a peacock)

Cimeries: discovers things lost; teaches grammar, logic and rhetoric.
(appears as a soldier on a black horse)

Amduscias: makes trees fall.
(appears as a unicorn)

Belial: second only to Lucifer; causes favors of friends and foes.

Decarabia: informs on the virtues of herbs and stones; control birds.

Seere: discovers those that have committed theft and transports instantly.

Dantalian: teaches all art and science; kindles love.

Andromalius: returns stolen goods and finds the thief.

Here follows the replication of seals for the seventy-two spirits that King Solomon shut up in a brass vessel and concealed in a lake:

Baal

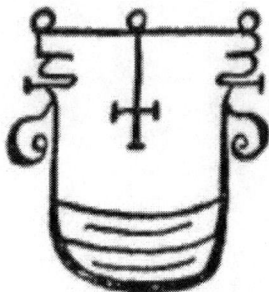

Agares

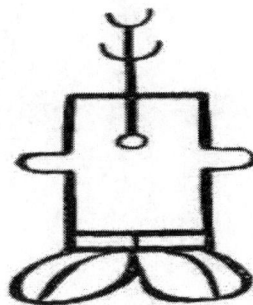

Vassago

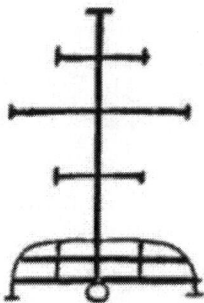

Gamygyn

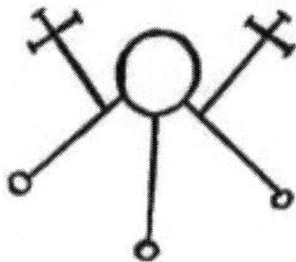

Marbas

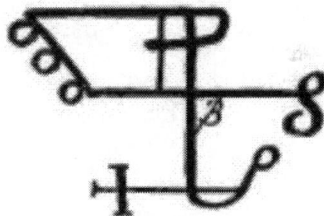

Valefor

Amon

Barbatos

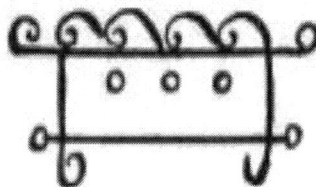

Paimon

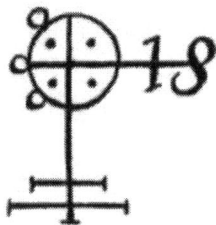

Buer

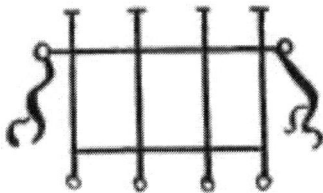

Gusion

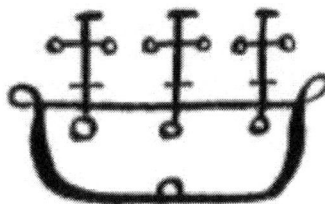

Sytry

Beleth

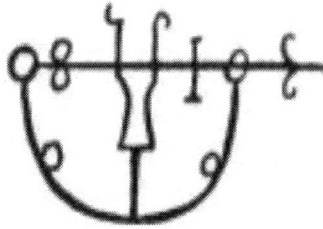

Lerajie

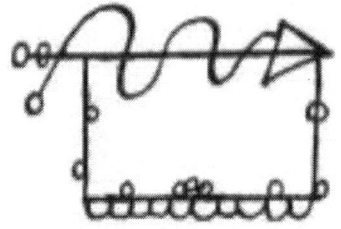

Eligor

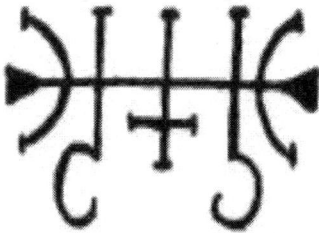

Zepar

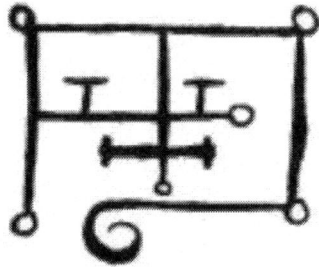

Botis

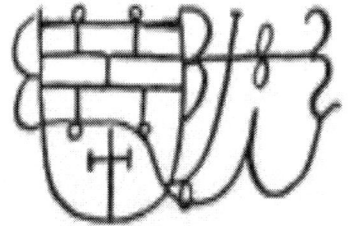

Bathin

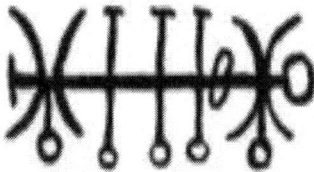

Saleos

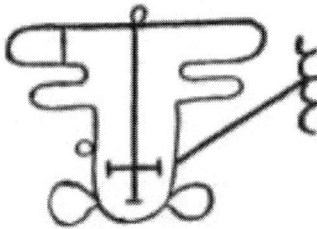

Purson

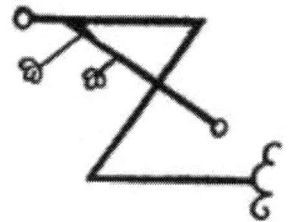

Morax

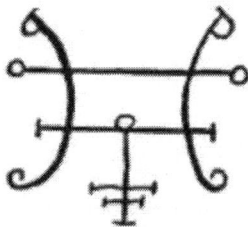

Ipos

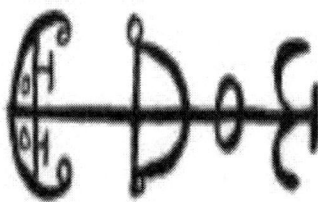

Aini

Naberius

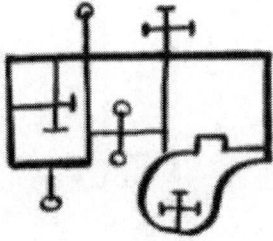

Glasyalabolas

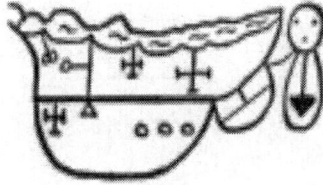

Bune

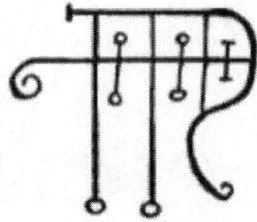

Ronobe

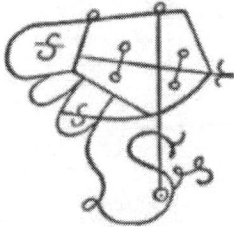

Berith

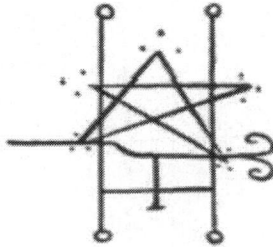

Astaroth

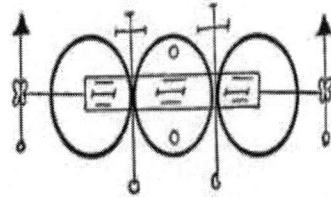

Forneus

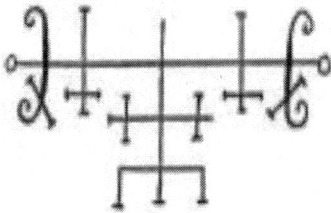

Foras

Asmoday

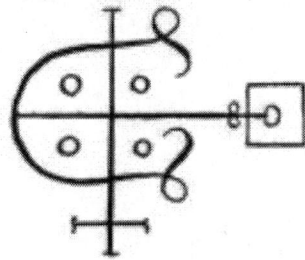

Gaar

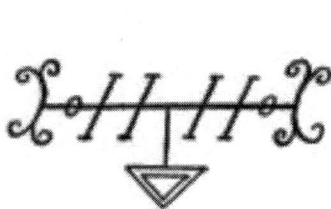

Furfur

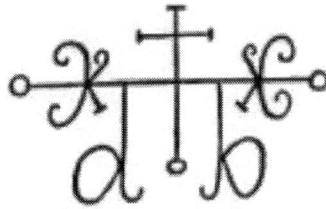

Marchosias

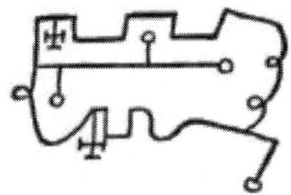

Solas

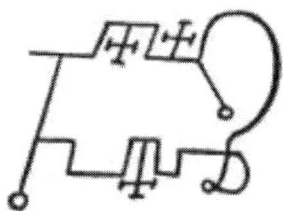

Phoenix

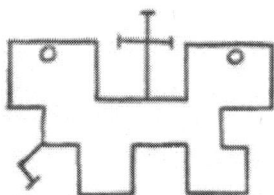

Halpas

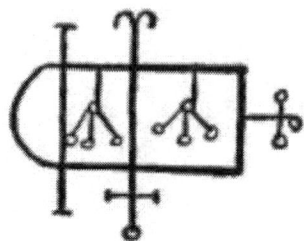

Malpas

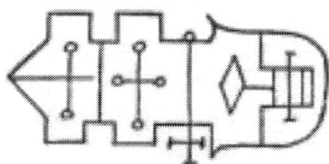

Raum

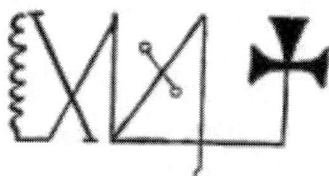

Focalor

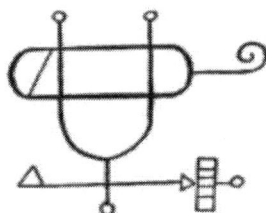

Sabnack

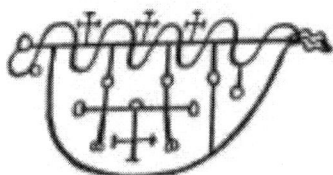

Vepar

Shax

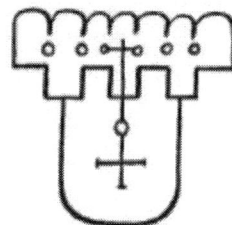

Vine

Bifrons

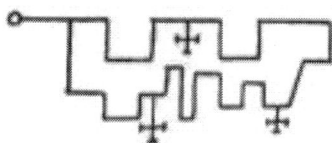

Vual

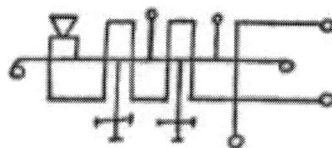

Hagenti

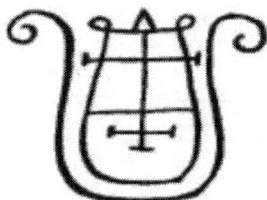

Procel

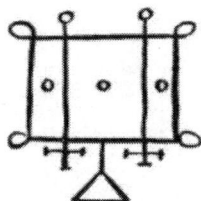

Furcas

Balam

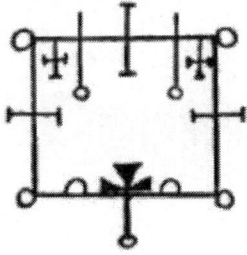

Allocen

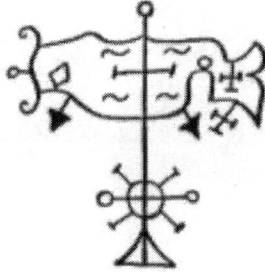

Caim

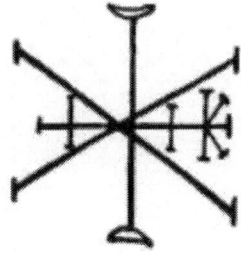

Murmur

Orobas

Gomory

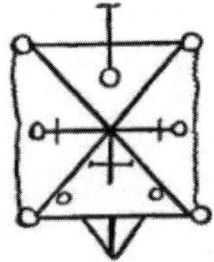

Ose

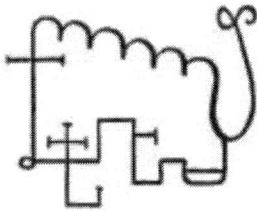

Amy

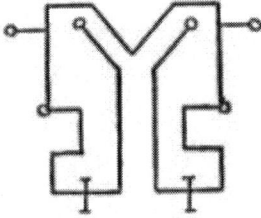

Orias

Vapula

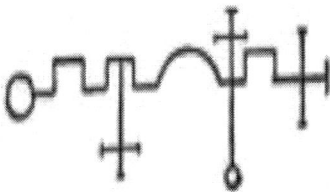

Zagan

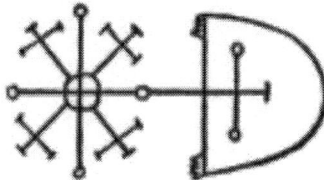

Valac

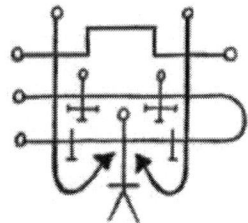

Andras

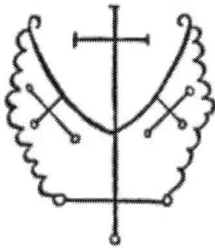

Flauros

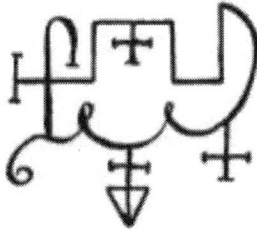

Andrealphus

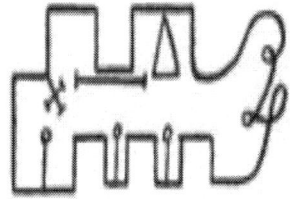

Cimeries

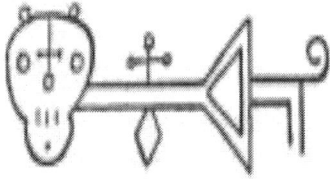

Amduscias

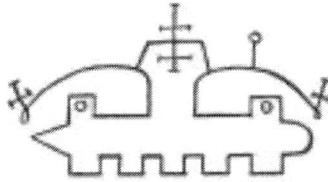

Belial

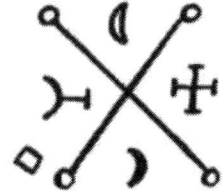

Decarabia

Seere

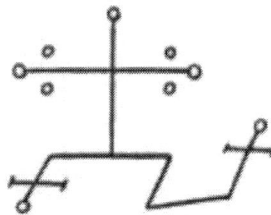

Dantalian

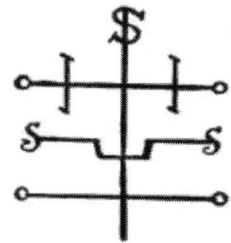

Andromalius

There are, according to the Arbatel, and as outlined by Arthur Waite, **Seven Olympic Spirits**: Aratron, Bethor, Phaleg, Och, Hagith, Ophiel and Phul. Their characters are here reproduced from The Book of Black Magic along with their offices:

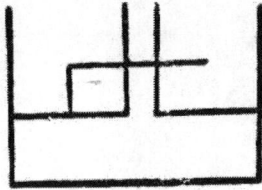

Aratron (Saturn)

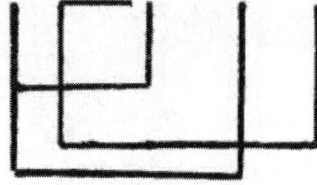

Bethor (Jupiter)

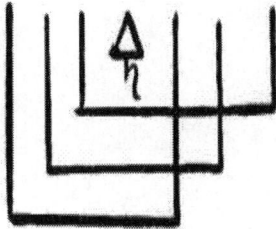

Phaleg (Mars)

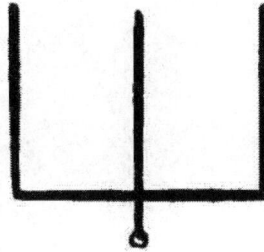

Och (Solar)

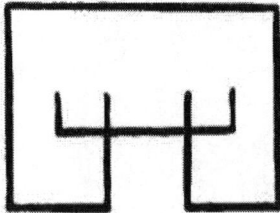

Hagith (Venus)

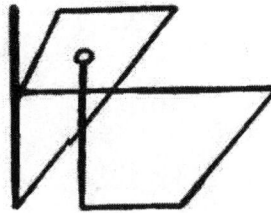

Ophiel (Mercury)

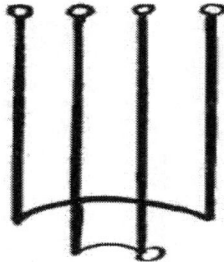

Phul (Lunar)

The Demons from Collin de Plancy's, *Dictionnaire Infernal*, 1863.

ABIGOR
GRAND DUKE OF HELL

ABRAXAS

ABRAMELECH
HIGH CHANCELLOR OF HELL

AGUARES
GRAND DUKE OF HELL

ALASTOR

ALOCER
DUKE OF HELL

AMDUSCIAS
GREAT DUKE OF HELL

AMON
MARQUIS OF HELL

ANDRAS
GREAT MARQUIS OF HELL

ASMODEE
GREAT KING OF HELL

ASTAROTH
DUKE OF HELL

AZAZEL

BAEL
FIRST KING OF HELL

BALAN
GREAT KING OF HELL

BARBATOS
GREAT DUKE OF HELL

BEHEMOTH
DEMON OF GLUTTONY

BELPHEGOR
Demon of Discoveries

BELZEBUTH
Prince of Demons, Lord of the Flies

BERITH
Great Duke of Hell

BUER
Great President of Hell

CAACRINOLAAS
High President of Hell

CAYM
High President of Hell

CERBERE
Marquis of Hell

DEUMUS

EURYNOME
Prince of Death

FLAGA

FLAUROS
Grand General of Hell

FORCAS
High President of Hell

FURFUR
Count of Hell

GAAP
High President and High Prince of Hell

GOMORY
Duke of Hell

HARBORYM
Duke of Hell

IPES
Prince and Count of Hell

LAMIA

LECHIES
Demons of the Woods

LEONARD
Grand Master of the Sabbaths

LUCIFER
King of Hell

MALPHAS
Grand President of Hell

MAMMON
Demon of Avarice

MARCHOCIAS
Great Marquis of Hell

MELCHOM
Demon Who Carries the Purse

MOLOCH
Prince of the Land of Tears

NICKAR

OROBAS
High Prince of Hell

PAYMON
King of Hell

PRUFLAS
High Prince and Grand Duke of Hell

RONWE
Marquis and Count of Hell

SALLOS
Great Duke of Hell

SCOX
Duke and High Marquis of Hell

STOLAS
High Prince of Hell

UVALL
Great Duke of Hell

VOLAC
High President of Hell

XAPHAN
Demon of the Second Order

Angels over the Planets

Saturn - *Zaphiel*
Jupiter - *Zadkiel*
Mars - *Camael*
Sun - *Raphael*
Venus - *Haniel*
Mercury - *Michael*
Moon – *Gabriel*

Angels over the Winds

Gabriel – Northern Wind
Nariel – Southern Wind
Raphael – Western Wind
Michael – Eastern Wind

Angels over the Elements

Fire – *Seraph*
Water – *Tharsis*
Air – *Cherub*
Earth – *Ariel*

Angels over the Signs

Aries - *Malahidael*
Taurus - *Asmodel*
Gemini - *Ambriel*
Cancer - *Muriel*
Leo - *Verchiel*
Virgo - *Hamaliel*
Libra - *Zuriel*
Scorpio - *Barchiel*
Sagittarius - *Advachiel*
Capricorn - *Hanael*
Aquarius - *Cambiel*
Pisces - *Barchiel*

Angels over the twenty-eight mansions of the Moon

Geniel, Enediel, Anixiel, Azariel, Gabriel, Dirachiel, Scheliel, Amnediel, Barbiel, Ardefiel, Neciel, Abdizuel, Jazeriel, Ergediel, Atliel, Azeruel, Adriel, Egibiel, Amutiel, Kyriel, Bethnael, Geliel, Requiel, Abrinael, Agiel, Tagriel, Atheniel, Amnixiel.

Evil Spirits over the Four Parts of the World

Egin (Mahazuel) – King of the North
Amaymon (Azazel) - King of the South
Paymon (Azael)– King of the West
Urieus (Samuel) – King of the East

Witchcraft, the Art of Conjuration & the Afterlife Trinity

The Pagan & Christian Witch

Of this practice there is much to say, but little to be understood by the casual observer. Its modern definition wrongly associates all actions of magic, i.e., the use of meditation, visualization, non-religious prayers, invocations, incantations, talismans, herbs, etc., with *diabolism*. The definition is usually: *"the practice of magic, especially for evil purposes."* This form of *witchcraft* is also wrongly considered an attribute of *wicca*, a pagan practice whereby the changing seasons are observed with special focus on the major (mid-points) and minor sabbats (equinoxes and solstices). Although the word "wicca" literally means "witch" in Old English, these witches are largely unrelated to those of the *black mass*. A *wiccan* or *pagan* is simply someone with an affinity for nature, usually a person without adherence to major religions. Traditionally a *pagan* was a person living remotely. The idea of the *witch in the woods* is a mythological archetype that probably developed from the oddity of a woman choosing solitude over a husband, or remarriage if she had been married previously. Existing on this fringe of society she became a *witch*, and so it was

Witch Summoning a Demon,
from Sebastian Münster's
Cosmographia Universalis, 1544.

imagined all manner of horrible *dark arts* she performed in the forest with Satan. These women, and sometimes men, were usually experts in botany and herbology, and thus were knowledgeable on poison and medicine. When one uses the word *hex,* they are referring to the German *hexen*, which means "to use witchcraft." But these darker actions are not motivated by external demons, they are driven by internal ones. Such dreadful individuals do indeed "sell their soul," but to their poisonous passions and frenzied actions. Their *energy* is thus transferred to the image of the diabolic in whatever form it takes.

For the sake of simplicity, we shall refer in this section to botanical witches as "white" and selfish witches as "black."

The *black witch*, like any practitioner of the *dark arts*, is involved in poisonous activities that pollute the soul. While some may embrace these perversities others are engaged in a deceptive form of witchcraft whereby it is publicly called *female empowerment* but privately known as an *attempt to fulfill selfish desires*. Other times it is the proud use of *baneful* binding spells to curse politicians. Today when a woman engages in witchcraft it is almost certain that her practice is only in name for show. If otherwise, it is highly likely she is practicing the *dark arts* with the politically correct motivation of *empowerment*, i.e., selfishness.

The *white witch*, like any practitioner of the *light arts,* is involved in elevating their soul and finding empowerment in developing the self with moral pursuits. It is almost ironic today that a woman who embraces her *femininity*, and especially if she chooses a non-political conservative path of monogamous partnership and childbirth, is far more a witch than those rejecting their biology. A mother by choice with a committed man is sincerely *drawing down the moon* in ways the *black witch* cannot.

What has just been described is precisely the historical line between what made a witch *white* or *black,* i.e., embracing femininity and childbirth or rejecting it outright.

Additional irony can be found in the fact that witchcraft is almost exclusively embraced by those rejecting the *Universal Mother* for the *Father of Lies,* usually based on the rhetoric that men are unnecessary or toxic, and that a women should never give them birth. This is an idea that is rooted in antiquity too. What is truly ironic about this fact is that those embracing the *Universal Mother* would typically consider themselves religious today, and therefore in no way pagan, a word derived from the Latin *paganus,* meaning "villager." This is especially true for Catholics venerating the Virgin Mary! The pagan miracle of birth in pre-Christian times is now considered blasphemous and magical, despite a Christian also referring to birth as a *miracle* from God. Furthermore, both a pagan and Christian would certainly agree that the *miracle of life* is a form of now understood magic, i.e., science. They would both agree that artificially extinguishing life is *wrong* unless we were discussing the natural cleansing of a forest by fire. Paul Carus explains in his book <u>The History of the Devil and the Idea of Evil</u> how the line between magic and miracle is drawn by the identity of the cult:

> *"…a religion of magic is based on a belief in the contra-natural, and as soon as a religion of magic becomes an established institution, it will develop the notion of witchcraft by a discrimination between its own miracles and those of other people who are unbelievers."*

At one point or another, though, both paganism and Christianity were *religio paganorum,* or the "religion of country people."

Witchcraft Lore: Familiars, Wandering Dames & the *Black Mass*

Of the witch there is much from popular lore we can learn, such as their apparent ability to transform into an animal. Their master Satan often appears as a goat or black cat himself, the latter a popular familiar of witches. Here we return once more to the *werewolf* or w*endigo* motif, whereby a person with uncontrolled passions and desires becomes like an animal. Since the *black witch* flaunts her sexuality and gives herself to countless men, and Satan, she becomes the epitome of animal sexuality, i.e., the goat.

Their ability to fly arose sometime in the 13th-century when tradition tells us it was common for a witch to mount a besom (broom made of twigs) and take to the air as a "wandering dame." These *night flights* made arrival at the *Black Mass* more convenient. The symbol of a broom here is obvious because it was the woman who cleaned the home. But brooms are also phallic in nature and thus associated with sex and the *witch orgy.*

Although we have said that the Church is highly responsible for the imagery of the *Black Sabbath* it was also the witch herself who had similar hallucinations, which resulted from a toxic pomade smeared over her body. We may say, then, that like the Oracle of Delphi these witches became so frenzied that they fell to the ground in convulsion only later awakening with memories of their travels. Ulrich Molitor (1442-1507), a legal scholar and German witch hunter, agreed that these gatherings were merely hallucinatory. Despite these facts, regarding the stories and imagery, Kurt Seligmann assures us that these gatherings *"did without doubt occur."*

The Sorcerers' Feast from Fr. M. Guaccius, Compendium Maleficarum, Milan, 1608.

As per the *Black Mass* itself we refer to Francesco Maria Guazzo, an Italian monk, who described the feast as having normal decor but with nude devils carrying food to the witches. They ate meat, bread, and drank wine, symbols also of the Eucharist, though this was an unholy communion. Although these gatherings took place "without doubt," we can assume no witch arrived by flying besom. We can also assume that these dark feasts and orgies were later organized because of the legends. In Strange Superstitions and Magic Practices William J. Fielding writes of the *Black Mass* and what was accomplished at these gatherings:

"A routine procedure of the services at the Witches' Sabbath consisted of the Black Mass, a parody and inversion of the ceremony of the Christian mass. Devotions were paid to the demon who presided, or a representative in the form of a dog, goat or other animal."

It is important to note here that there is indeed an ancient Christian custom called *Black Fast*, but it obviously has nothing to do with the *black feast*. When practicing this *fast* you would consume no food or drink during the day, while at night it was acceptable to drink water and eat a vegetarian meal without meat, eggs, dairy, or alcohol.

Every seven years there would be held a *Great Sabbath* attended by local covens, but otherwise meetings revolved around the major and minor sabbats, as Fielding explains:

"While the local meetings of the coven were held once a week, usually on a Thursday, the 'Sabbath of Witches' was celebrated four times a year. These principal festivals were, in the spring, May Eve (April 30th), called Roodmas, or Rood Day, in Britain, and Walpurgis-Nacht in Germany; in the

autumn, November Eve (October 31st), called in Britain, All-hallow Eve. Between these came, in the winter, Candlemas (February 2nd), and in the summer, the Gule of August (August 1st), called Lammas in Britain. The festivals of the solstice were also celebrated - Beltane at midsummer, and Yule at midwinter."

Upon arrival at these *dark feasts,* it was common for witches, as per legend, to offer a human child for sacrifice. The ceremonies then supposedly involved a chanting of the Lord's Prayer and the reading of commandments both in reverse. There was also produced a book called *The Wicked Bible.* Since this form of witchcraft was directly opposed to creation, life itself, and Christianity, or so the Church said, St. Hippolytus informs us of what the *black witch* must say as her prayer:

"I deny the creator of heaven and earth. I deny my baptism. I deny the worship I formerly paid to God. I cleave to thee, and in thee I believe."

Insults and impieties were to be committed against God and Church, and the witch was to abstain from any further usage of the cross, holy water, or consecrated bread and salt, unless its use was sacrilege. Witches were even required to step on the cross in mockery of Christ. One should be reminded of the power of such items, as was the case with St. Anthony who, tormented by demons, was able to secure his personal protection from a cross.

Satan is then said to mark his witches with a claw and reverse their baptisms, which as a purifying ritual causes the *black witch* to become impure and filthy. A *blasphemous baptism* is then organized whereby a witch is made further impure by dirty water under the darkness of night. After denying the sacraments and bathing in filth, the *black witch* receives her new name. To complete the transaction and deal it is said Satan requires a piece of clothing or other personal item, because these, like hair or nails, maintain the qualities of its host. If one can offer their own child, especially in the womb as an abortion, their powers are said to grow strongest.

The Temptation of St. Anthony,
Salvator Rosa, 1645.

The Old Norse word *mál,* meaning "speech" and "agreement," is the origin of *blackmail,* the action of demanding payment in exchange for the concealing of personal information. Since the word *black* implies "nothing, we could translate *blackmail,* regarding the *witch pact,* as being a "silent agreement" or "black speech," i.e., a contract with Satan.

Witches would swear allegiance to Satan (*I cleave to thee, and in thee I believe*) within a circle drawn upon the ground. Their names were then inscribed in the *Book of Death.* To retain her powers, granted in exchange for her soul in the form of a personal litem, the *black witch* was said to have a monthly requirement to harm the innocent.

The Witches' Sabbath engraving by Michael Herr, German, 17th century.

Sorcerers offering a child for sacrifice and trampling on the cross.

Persecuting Witches with a Hammer

Much of the lore pertaining to witchcraft is nonsensical, superstitious, and paranoid, which is largely what we acquire from Heinrich Kramer's 1486 classic, Malleus Maleficarum (the *Witch-Hammer*). This text codified the legends of our witches and was dedicated to Exodus 22:18, wherein we read:

"You shall not permit a sorceress [witch] to live."

Part one of the *Witch Hammer* documents the perversity of witches, while condemning non-witches to the same heresy for questioning or denying demonology. Part two discussed the activities of witches, including their sex lives and diabolic pacts. Part three provided legal procedures to follow at any *witch trial*, including methods that were anything but legal or moral. Of course, from here we obtain the idea of a *witch hunt*.

Denying guilt during a witch trial was itself considered a crime, but confessions were usually extracted by their own crimes. Few accusations against witches could be more abhorrent or barbaric than the methods of torture used to find guilty parties. Torture was not only common but sanctioned by texts like Malleus Maleficarum. Francis Hutchinson concluded in his 1718 Historical Essay on Witchcraft how torture itself was one of the primary driving forces of sorcery:

"I have shown plainly that accusing and prosecuting and hanging in that case does not cure but increases the evil; and that when a nation of people in are such a state, they are under a great calamity."

Men like Johannes Weier, Meyfart, and Cornelius Loos, all rejected the trials. The Jesuit Friedrich Spee (1591-1635) was an ardent opponent of the *witch trials*, too, and here is his opinion summarized.

"Often I have thought that the only reason why we are not all wizards is due to the fact that we have not all been tortured. And there is truth in what an inquisitor dared to boast lately, that if he could reach the Pope, he would make him confess that he was a wizard."

As Grillot de Givry writes on a similar subject in Witchcraft, Magic & Alchemy, it is no wonder diabolic resistance to the Church grew rapidly:

"It is no matter for wonder or indignation to see, during the whole time that Catholicism had the spiritual direction of Europe, a veritable Church of Evil opposed to the Church of Good, a Church of the Devil defying the Church of God, and possessing, like the latter, its rites, its cult, its books, its congregations, and its supernatural visitants."

~

Pierre de Lancre, a French judge, was able to describe intimate details of the *black sabbath* based on information he derived from the accused witches. In one account is told the story of a young teenage girl who was forgiven her deeds after a full admission of her participation in the *dark arts*. In confession she also declared to have an ability to detect other witches and wizards by their body *marks*. Appointed to examine suspects of the craft, she sent many innocent people to the stake, as if, ironically, under the influence of the Devil.

The lawyer Matthew Hopkins applied similar "skills" in finding these *marks*, operating in several countries during the seventeenth century under the title of "Witch-finder General." He even received a license of empowerment to examine those suspected of witchcraft, which resulted in countless people being tortured and forced under torment to confess to crimes either not committed or impossible. Each confession brought more authority to the inquisitors and likely more women to real covens that acted as a community for the abused. Hopkins also claimed that upon tricking the Devil he received a pocketbook with the names of all the witches in England, and of those consulting the same for assistance. There could be no greater irony than accusing innocent people of *dark arts* and murder, or of making deals with the Devil, and then sentencing them to death based on a magical book received from their supposed master!

The *mark of the witch*, as it is known, was used to identify witches during inquisition and trial. It was, of course, subjectively detected, often coming in the form of a birthmark or mole. Another method of extracting guilt involved a pin stuck in the body. If the accused did not express pain nor bleed, then their invisible diabolic mark was confirmed. Said pin could be so small as to not cause pain or bleeding, or it could have been applied literally behind the suspect's back, so they were unaware of whether the device had been used or not! Hopkins applied a more sophisticated method: a device placed on the skin whereupon the point retracted as if it had entered the body. Feeling no pain, and without bleeding, the witch or wizard, and their *mark*, were considered discovered. When blood did run from a would it was indeed evidence, but not of the suspect's guilt. That blood was extracted by a different type of sorcerer in their own form of frenzy. Fielding explains the process of determining a witches' guilt:

> "The accused person, whether young or old, modest or wanton, was stripped of all clothing and made to sit cross-legged on a stool or table placed in the center of some old barn. If resistance was shown by the person on trial, force and binding with cords was resorted too."

Hopkins also popularized an infamous method for determining the identity of witches called "swimming the witch." It was based on the belief that pure water would not receive a person who renounced their baptism. If the accused sank, having been accepted by the water, they were absolved of guilt even though they still likely drowned. Those who floated were of course considered guilty and put to death soon after. Even the few sinking witches were then brought up and murdered anyway *just in case*. In a twist of ironic fate in 1677, Hopkins himself was seized and put to his own test. But he floated and was therefore judged guilty of being a wizard before being hanged.

The story of Matthew Hopkins is interesting for another reason: the *witch hunting license*. All elements of this hysteria were made economic with persecution of witches and wizards becoming an industry that would only be made obsolete by application of *reason*. The industry employed judges, jailers, lawyers, spies, hunters, torturers, executioners, etc. For the *witch hunter* it was beneficial to demand the accused name their accomplices, which often provided dozens of others to be tried likewise. Witch trials throughout history, not just the infamous ones at Salem, were turned into a circus. They were operated like sporting or gladiator events with food stalls, shops, and souvenirs. This absurdity even resulted in a horse being put to death because its owner had taught him a few uncommon tricks. Thousands were burned at the stake, hanged, or drowned. Others were boiled alive in what amounts to a cauldron! In other words, it was *frenzy* and *paranoia* that created our modern conception of the witches' gathering.

During the Salem trials in Massachusetts between 1692 and 1693 more than two hundred people were accused of witchcraft and twenty were executed. The most famous witness at these trials was a woman named Mary Walcott, who bore witness to the afflicted.

Nearly every element of a *Black Mass* can be found in the *witch trials* themselves. Hopkin's magic book was acquired through communion with the Devil; the licenses for hunting witches identified these zealots like the *mark of the witch*, often a mole, supposedly identified the sorcerers; the methods of torture and death, including fires and boiling cauldrons, are precisely how the witch was seen sacrificing a victim or preparing a poisonous concoction; and it is said that many women in particular were grabbed in the middle of the night for arrest and trial, something akin to the "wandering dames" themselves!

The central figure is supposedly Mary Walcott, from an 1876 illustration of the Salem *witch trials*.

All these images and ideas were largely a result of ecclesiastical insanity, which itself provided the descriptions for the master of all witches, as per de Givry:

"The Church propounded the existence of the Devil not in derision or as a jest, but as an article of faith, and as the illiterate mass of the populace could not go to the theological books, which were restricted to the learned, for the details necessary to an exact idea of the Prince of Darkness, his effigy was profusely reproduced, for the benefit of the crowd, in the tympana of cathedral doorways, the stained-glass windows of churches, the bas-reliefs of the periphery of choirs, and among the tiers of gargoyles and waterspouts. These last, beside, swarmed with a whole fantastic fauna repenting the presumed forms of the inhabitants and rulers of Hell."

Suppositions of Witchcraft

Francis Barrett provides us in <u>The Magus</u> with what are still suppositions today pertaining to witchcraft and the infamous *Black Mass*.

The First Supposition

First of all, thou shalt take notice, that Satan is the sworn and irreconcilable enemy of man, and to be so accounted by all, unless any one had rather have him to be his friend; and therefore he most readily procures whatsoever mischief he is able to cause or wish unto us, and that without doubt and neglect.

The Second Supposition

And then although he be an enemy to witches themselves, forasmuch as he is also a most malicious enemy to all mankind in general; yet, in regard they are his bond-slaves, and those of his kingdom, he never, unless against his will betrays them, or discovers them to judges, &c.

Let it be noted: The absolute power of a witch, as with any sorcerer, does not belong to Satan. For if the latter where indeed the executioner of these *midnight crimes*, he would not need an assistant to carry them out. His involvement is a matter of enjoyment in watching man destroy himself. Whether directly involved in what would be classified as an act of witchcraft, or involved in self-destructive behavior, the sorcerer condemns God by abusing His laws, and thus subjects himself to a living Hell.

DESCRIPTION DE L'ASSEMBLÉE DES SORCIERS QU'ON APPELLE SABBAT

The Black Mass, by Nicholas Gosselin, 1710.

Witches Sabbath, by Francisco de Goya, 1797 1798.

Satan Presiding at the Sabbath, from Paul Christian, *Histoire de la magie,* 1870.

The Afterlife Trinity: Heaven, Purgatory & Hell

The "hell" of Satan or the Devil, which we know are distinct characters, is that fire encompassing earth and consuming all it produces like Saturn or Cronus. This infernal serpent is ouroboros and his progeny inhabit the earth in telluric energies. By the domain of Saturn, we are surrounded by darkness and sin, i.e., temptation and emotional turmoil. In <u>A Dictionary of Symbols</u>, J.E. Cirlot says of this image:

> "In some versions of the Ouroboros, the body is half light and half dark, alluding in this way to the successive counterbalancing of opposing principles as illustrated in the Chinese Yang-Yin symbol for instance."

The half-black serpent signifies earth and night, while the half-white serpent symbolizes heaven and light. Here we find a relationship to the white moon *Chesed* and black moon *Geburah*.

In Mesopotamia we have the Sumerian goddess of the moon, *Nanna*, who is affiliated with the Akkadian moon god *Sin*. In Norse mythology we find the exact same name used to identify the consort of Odin's son Balder. Her name is *Nanna*. We also find in Norse myth the personification of the underworld in the goddess *Hel*. It is here, like in Hades, that *Heimdall* goes to rescue *Idun*, like the story of Orpheus and Eurydice. In other accounts the underworld itself is called *Niflheim* and it is ruled by *Hel*, like Persephone rules Hades or Izanami rules Yomi. Hel's home was bitter cold and not warmed by the sun, a heat only to be found in the "Land of Fire," *Muspelheim*, located in the south. We are clearly talking about the hemispheres of the earth.

The Old English *hel* or *hell* has a root meaning "to cover or hide," or "to conceal." And so does the terror of Hell conceal a great truth, but one of the mind rather than the body. Just as we feel warmth with love, we feel cold with betrayal. Like the *shoulder angel* and *shoulder demon* these are the two forces pulling us apart while holding us together. The angel offers us peace while the demon offers temptation and sin.

Heimdall Desires the Return of Idun from the Underworld (*Hel*), by Emil Doepler, 1881.

The word "sin" is also likely derived from the Old English *synn* and relates to the Latin *sons* or *sont*, meaning "guilty." It may relate to the Akkadian god *Sin* too. The final destruction of the Jerusalem Kingdoms came around 586 B.C. under the Chaldean controlled Babylonians, when many Jews became captives and were taken to Babylon. Here they would have learned of the Chief deity *Bel* or *Bal*, a fertility god worshiped in the Phoenician and Canaanite lands. The name in Hebrew is *ba'al*, which means "Lord." The Jewish religion borrowed heavily from the Babylonians, and much of the Kabbalah itself came from the mystery teachings of the Chaldean temples. Their captivity in

Egypt, likely caused by the *Hyksos* enslavement of Northern Egypt, produced not only Apis worship, or the golden calf, but must have also contributed greatly to the mystical Jewish tradition in general. Followers of Yahweh, who was originally considered a lunar god (Jehovah), would have seen competition in the newly introduced gods like *Sin* and therefore would consider their adherents to be *sinners*.

It must be noted that Hell has not always been depicted as a burning pit, but instead a dark and cold ice-palace like *Niflheim*, or a feeling like loneliness. Dante Alighieri described Hell as a palace of ice in Canto XXXIV (34) of his *Divine Comedy*, where he relates:

"How frozen and how faint I then became,
Ask me not, reader! for I write it not,
Since words would fail to tell thee of my state.
I was not dead nor living. Think thyself
If quick conception work in thee at all,
How I did feel. That emperor, who sways
The realm of sorrow, at mid breast from th' ice
Stood forth; and I in stature am more like
A giant, than the giants are in his arms."

The King of Hell Frozen in Ice, by Gustave Dore, 1885.

In opposition to this Land of Darkness is the Land of Light, i.e., Heaven, an adobe for the gods like *Asgard* or Olympus. Heaven is a feeling of love and appreciation. Those living in a personal mindset of Heaven, one that is not delusional, will more easily commune with angelic spirits. Hell is a feeling of betrayal and loneliness. Those living in a personal mindset of Hell, one that is always delusional, will without much work commune with demonic spirits. David Fideler, writing of magic, says something similar:

> *"People who have a low-minded view of things will discover this reflected in the events of their lives, thus confirming their perspective, while others who are high-minded and invoke the spirit of excellence find themselves capable of attracting it."*

As for what we call *Purgatory* much can be said. From the Latin *purgatorius*, meaning "purifying," this place or state of mind is more akin to the *seven spheres of consciousness* which purify the soul-spirit. We can say with certainty that this intermediary between Heaven and Hell has been used as encouragement to *guilt* one into subscribing to the Church of Good or the Church of Evil. Otherwise, it is a state of failure likened to Hall's description of *Yellow Magi*, i.e., the failure to prevent perversions of nature. C. W. Leadbeater writes something similar of man's own responsibility in creating this *Afterlife Trinity*:

> *"Man makes for himself his own purgatory and heaven, and these are not places, but state of consciousness. Hell does not exist; it is only a figment of the theological imagination; but a man who lives foolishly may make for himself a very unpleasant and long-enduring purgatory."*

Making Pacts

Here we will address the subject of making a *pact*: "a formal agreement between two parties." These parties could be a magician and a spirit, or a sorcerer and the Devil. Whereas witches and wizards were slaves to the infernal, the ceremonial magician with pure intention to obtain wisdom exercises authority over the same. Of pacts with any spirit there are considered two types, according to the <u>Grimorium Verum</u>: the *tactic* and *manifest*. By other names they are known as *implicit* and *explicit*. And in these operations, spirits come in two forms: the first are "employed" and the others are "not employed." Spirits that are "employed" require you provide them a personal item when making a pact. The "unemployed" do not require an item. But the <u>Grimorium Verum</u> issues warning on the former:

> *"Whoever makes a friend his superior, makes himself an enemy."*

Although our goal in this section is to discuss the ceremonial nature of conjuration in general, which is more often an operation of *black witches*, it must be stated that a magician operating with pure intention may also draw upon the assistance of *superior intelligences* for less nefarious means. All commerce with evil spirits, however, is founded on the law of exchange whereupon personal items are traded for power, wealth, or the accomplishment of those things seemingly beyond the power of nature or man. In seeking power over nature, the magician is *black*, but in seeking alignment with nature the magician is *white*. J. G Frazer explains the two principles of thought upon which magic is founded as the individual laws of "similarity" and "contagion." The *law of similarity* is founded on the idea of producing an effect by imitating an effect, as in *sympathetic magic*. The *law of contagion* renders one able to manipulate persons by far simply by acting upon some object that they have touched, or more specifically, one of close value to them; this may also involve teeth, blood, sweat, nails, and hair. These items are desired by the infernal as a form of *blackmail*. They are the gateway by which *possession* occurs, i.e., through a person's *possession* that maintains their life essence. Kurt Seligmann says of this phenomenon:

> *"Whatever a man calls his own is magically a part of him…objects with which he has shared contact are imbued with his personality; and his name is just as much a part of him as a limb is of his body."*

Once a *pact* is made there is typically a set period for which the operator will be granted something in the temporal for the exchange of their soul after death. This will often lead practitioners of the *dark arts* to engage in all manner of experiments to extend their life and prevent the inevitability of their damnation. There are, however, methods given in certain magical texts for averting such exchanges and acquiring without damnation, what one *desires*. But it is this *desire* that makes these operations perverse in the first place. For those wishing to obtain the wisdom of Solomon only, to never use nor abuse the *Philosopher's Stone*, are more easily granted heavenly blessings. Agrippa says, *"let us desire nothing of God, which we think uncomely to wish for."* And as Luke 11:9-13 famously says:

> *"And I say unto you, Ask, and it shall be given you; seek, and ye shall find; knock, and it shall be opened unto you."*

If a *deal* has been struck with the infernal, the damnation which follows is usually a result of paranoid delusions, or conditions described more easily by psychology than magic(k). If a deal be struck with God and his angels, however, the results are usually uplifting and spiritually reassuring. In case of the former, there are many ways said to dissolve said contract: prayers, adjurations, deprecations, exorcisms, and by an even simpler method described in the <u>Vocabulaire Infernal</u>:

> *"If you are disposed to renounce the devil after having entered into a compact with him, spit three times on the ground, and he will have no further power over you."*

The Roman scholar Pliny also wrote of the usefulness of *spitting* as medicine, which is obviously a form of *purging*:

> *"We ask pardon of the gods, by spitting in the lap, for entertaining some too presumptuous hope or expectation. On the same principle, it is the practice in all cases where medicine is employed, to spit three times on the ground, and to conjure the malady as often; the object being, to aid the operation of the remedy employed. It is usual, too, to mark a boil, when it first makes its appearance, three times with fasting spittle."*

Since cats were considered sacred in Japan, killing one was thought to bring very bad luck and even a familial curse lasting seven generations. In Akita Prefecture it was a common practice to spit three times on a cat that you accidentally killed. You were to then walk around the carcass the same number of times to dispel evil. In Okinawa Prefecture it was common to hang the dead body from a tree, or bury it, at the crossroads. Whether spitting or walking the number *three* certainly refers to one version or another of the *Holy Trinity*. This is also where we derive the custom of *knocking on wood*, i.e., the wood of Christ's cross.

Making a *pact* with a spirit is often described as *"selling your soul to the Devil."* But whether these stories are literal or figurative, they are indeed common throughout history. The nature of the contract is likewise to be delineated along lines similar to those between *magic* and *miracle*. In the simplest terms, most of us have engaged in these agreements at one point or another in our lives without realizing the fact. Santa's *naughty-or-nice list* and the tradition of *trick-or-treating* are both contractual agreements we make with supernatural characters on Christmas and children imitating roaming spirits on Halloween.

One of the first documented cases of a diabolic pact is believed to have been a deal between St. Theophilus of Adana and Satan in the 6th-century AD.

St. Theophilus was archdeacon of Adana, Cilicia, located now in present day turkey. Upon being elected Bishop he chose to reject the position out of humility. This was a decision he later regretted when the new Bishop deprived him of his then position as archdeacon. By anything other than humility St. Theophilus sought to contact Satan so that he could regain his powerful position in the Church. The deal St. Theophilus made with Satan provided him with that which he sought, but only for a price. In exchange for becoming Bishop, he was to renounce Christ and the Virgin Mary. The contract was to be signed in his blood, a common practice, because we know it maintains the *life force* and is thus a symbol of the *soul*.

St. Theophius later regretted the deal he made with Satan and resorted to intense prayer in seeking forgiveness from the Virgin Mary. After several days of fasting and prayer

The Devil Presenting St. Augustine with the Book of Vices, by the German painter and sculptor Michael Pacher (1435-1498). It reportedly shows, depending upon the source, the Devil interacting with Saint Augustine or Saint Wolfgang; others say this is a depiction of Saint Theophilus making his pact with Satan.

Mary appeared to him and granted absolution. Satan was supposedly reluctant to void the contract, however, but after three days St. Theophilus awoke to find the bloody documented upon his chest. He proceeded to take the contract and have it burned by the legitimate Bishop. In other versions of the story, it is merely "silver and gold" the archdeacon desired. Upon receiving it he was miserable.

Johann Georg Faust (1480-1540), an alchemist, astrologer, and magician of the German renaissance, supposedly sold his soul for twenty-four years of service from Satan. After sixteen years had elapsed Johann attempted to void the deal, but was instead murdered, as the story is told, brutally by Satan.

Father Urbain Grandier (1590-1634), a Catholic Priest from France, was convicted of witchcraft, tortured and then burned at the stake. As priest he ignored vows of celibacy and gained a reputation as a philanderer. Nuns had accused him of sending the "Prince of Lechery," Asmodeus, to commit sexually perverse acts upon them. At the center of this controversy was Joan of Angels who had been smitten by Grandier and longed for him in her dreams. Exorcists were sent to the nunnery and ceremonies were performed to identify and drive away the devils. Joan convulsed and the other nuns were sure she was possessed. She spoke gibberish, eventually uttering the name Grandier, which confirmed him as the diabolic operator in their minds. After being accused, Grandier made an appeal to the archbishop of Bordeaux who sent a doctor to declare that the nuns were not possessed. Soon after a trial was called and by the hand of Joan, in automatic writing, a promise was composed and signed by the demon Asmodeus warning against any exorcism:

"I promise that when leaving this creature, I will make a slit below her heart as long as a pin, that this slit will pierce her shirt, bodice and cloth which will be bloody. And tomorrow, on the twentieth of May at five in the afternoon of Saturday, I promise that the demons Gresil and Amand will make their opening in the same way, but a little smaller - and I approve the promises made by Leviatam, Behemot, Beherie with their companions to sign, when leaving, the register of the church of St. Croix! Given the nineteenth of May, 1629."

At the trial of Father Grandier it is said that the very contract with Satan and his demons was presented as evidence. It was found at his house, written in backwards Latin and supposedly included the signature not only of Grandier, but of various demons and Satan HIM-SELF. From the acronym HIM we acquire *His Infernal Majesty.*

Johann Georg Faust (1480-1540) making a deal with Satan (*Mephistopheles*) for his temporary service. This image is from the title page of the 1631 chapbook of Christopher Marlowe's play *The Tragical Historie of Doctor Faustus.*

EFFIGIE DE LA CONDEMNATION DE MORT
& execution d'Vrbain Grandier, Curé de l'Eglise S. Pierre du Marché de Loudun, atteint
& conuaincu de Magie, sortileges & malefic le uel a cité bruflé vif en ladite ville.

The Execution of Urbain Grandier, or *L'Execution d'Urbain Grandier,* 1634.

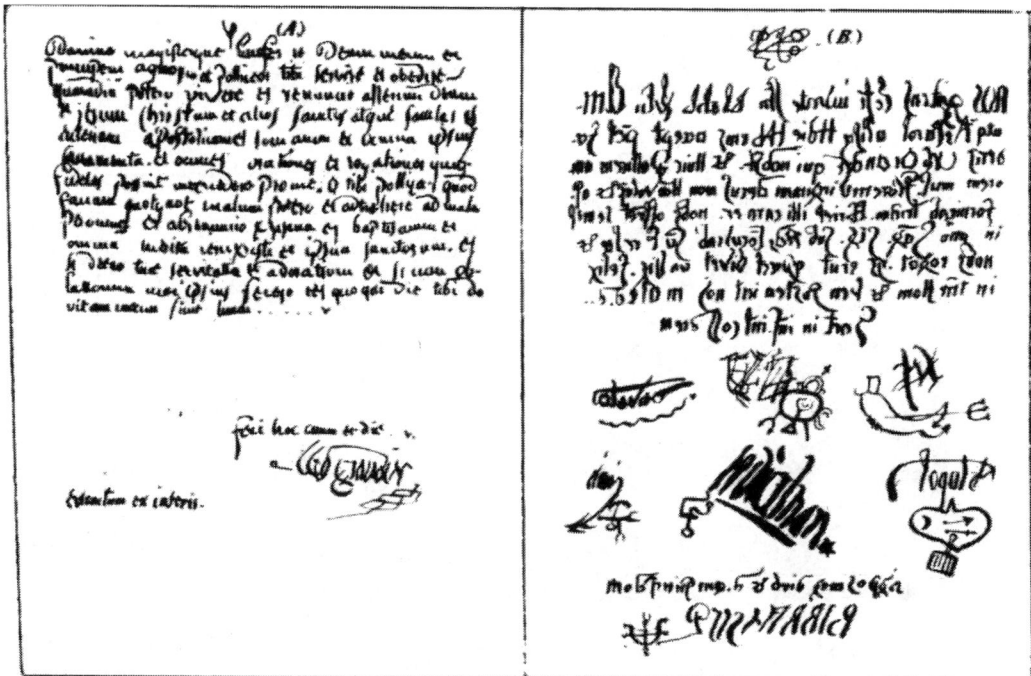

Father Grandier's diabolic contract with the signatures of demons.

The Legend of Theophilus, from Monk Conrad's illuminated MS

Secret of the Black Hen from Le Poule noire (1820), as published in Grimorium Verum or The True Grimoire; Le Véritable Dragon Rouge, 1521.

According to the author of the Black Pullet, to call upon demons a magician must carry a black hen, having never laid an egg, to a crossroads. At midnight he is to cut the bird in half and pronounce these words:

"Elohim, Essaim, frugativi et appellavi."

Next, he must turn to face the east while kneeling, and pronounce the great appellation while holding a cypress staff. If done properly it is believed that the Devil will immediately arise. This is not to be advised for numerous and obvious reasons.

Lucifuge Rofocale leading to the Treasure, from The Grand Grimoire & Le Véritable Dragon Rouge, 1521.

Although the Devil may give physical treasures, it is known that this wealth does not come with any lasting value. It turns into ashes or excrement in time or ignites into flames when poured upon the ground.

Psychic Abilities & the Evil Eye

Extrasensory Perception

The *thoughts* and *feelings* of others may be discerned from a distance by accessing, in some form, their *electromagnetic field*; feeling by *intuition*; understanding *human psychology*; and observing *body language*. Becoming proficient at any of these methods is what some call *telepathy* or *mind reading*, the ability to obtain information without any physical interaction and without the use of traditional sensory channels; *precognition*, the ability to foresee future events; and *clairvoyance*, the ability to access information about a person, place, or thing, through extrasensory perceptions: what is more commonly referred to as ESP.

Perceiving *thoughts* and *feelings* from a distance is a *realization* that can be made when one has a close relationship with a family member, based on behaviour patterns, or a romantic partner, based on the latter and the physical-spiritual bond one makes during sex. Carl Jung's concept of a *collective unconscious* may come into play here when discussing the "electromagnetic field," because it is something we are all part of without conscious realization.

All forms of ESP, and any ability to *perceive* without the traditional *senses*, are classified as *PSI* abilities. The twenty-third letter of the Greek alphabet is *psi* Ψ and it is used here like the algebraic X to signify what is unknown. The letter or symbol itself is interestingly a trident Ψ making it a very appropriate symbol in relation to the nature of *magic*.

According to Louisa Rhine who, along with her husband, coined the term *extrasensory perception*, there are four types of ESP: *realistic*, *unrealistic*, *hallucinatory*, and *intuitive*.

Realistic experiences are typically perceived in a pictorial form, as in the case of a photographic event seen with realistic detail.

Unrealistic experiences are more fictionalized accounts that may be symbolic in nature with archetypical characters present during the experience, such as during a dream.

Hallucinatory ESP experiences typically occur during a waking state, but some manifest while the subject is entirely awake, i.e., a hallucinatory vision separate from a dream-like state. The former type of vision is often referred to as a *daydream*. Hallucinations are defined separately from *extrasensory perception,* though, when something or someone is perceived to exist momentarily although nothing is physically there to be sensed otherwise. Louisa Rhine writes of how PSI hallucinations are *"different from other hallucinations in that they usually are experienced by perfectly normal people who are not in abnormal mental states caused by drugs or illness."* Because of this we can determine that unexplained hallucinatory experiences are not always the result of a state of delusion or inebriation. Furthermore, we may feel physiological effects, such as another person's bodily discomfort, even at great distances. Strong relationships between friends, couples, or family members may result in shared physical discomfort through a type of *telepathic communication* or *telepathic empathy*. Others may call it *sympathy pains* if it involves menstruation or pregnancy. *"Such experiences,"* writes Louisa *"are often of the telepathic type. It seems as if the person projects in his own organism either a replica of the sensations being felt by the distant person or his own interpretation of what those sensations are."* This form of *extrasensory communication* could account for cases of telepathy, clairvoyance, precognition, and even biolocation if there is a strong enough subconscious projection at work. Famous examples of hallucinatory ESP may also include *Mariana Apparitions*, the most famous of which is the *Our Lady of Fatima* case that occurred in 1917 Portugal.

Intuitive ESP experiences involve no traditional dream or hallucination in the waking state. Intuition comprises a simple and sudden "knowing" of information or details that otherwise could not have been known. It could come in the form of random bits of information or a compulsory action, which may just as well be the body reacting by reflex to something one is unaware of consciously. In fact, the same can be said of the these "random bits" since our brain processes only so much information at any given time. We may have been considering an idea and although we moved on consciously to something else, the brain is still processing those thoughts, which may later re-emerge suddenly as a form of intuition. None of this is meant to deny that there is a seemingly supernatural intuition that does occur, though it is likely related to the abovementioned electromagnetic field and light.

Writing in <u>Hidden Channels of the Mind</u>, Louisa Rhine describes the difference between *thoughts* and *things* in relation to *perception*:

> *"A world of difference separates thoughts form things. Thoughts are not material. Those of another person can never be known by one's sense perception unless the other person converts them into speech, writing or overt gesture of some kind. Things, on the other hand, are material, and we can easily sense them, provide barriers are removed and the distance is not too great."*

Whether or not *thoughts* can be accessed through *light transference* is debatable, but the nature of ESP is not. Although *telepathy* is more widely observed and often attributed to all *PSI* phenomena, the word *clairvoyance* is much older. Interest in telepathy has traditionally been accompanied with skepticism for clairvoyance, as the latter was concerned with discerning future events only. This, however, would be more accurately defined as *precognition*. Nevertheless, interest in telepathy has been maintained throughout history. There are likely two reasons for this: one, it does not as directly imply a breaking of any universal laws, per se; and two, it seems to provide more *grounded* applications for reading the minds of others.

Psychometry allows for an operator to obtain information about an object or person through simple touch, something that further explains how a husband or wife may say to one another, *you read my mind.*

Poltergeists & Telekinesis

Psychic abilities have been exaggerated by those exerting tremendous energies for their demonstration, while true *psychics* exhaust little energy in obtaining their abilities though they may be drained after using them. In other words, true magicians have no need to demonstrate their abilities and real alchemists tend to live impoverished. Emotions have a dramatic effect on the body, too, resulting in stress and sickness or peace and health. Happiness, peace of mind, and love may play upon the electromagnetic field in a manner to produce a bodily glow or halo. Anger, anxiety, and hatred may play upon electromagnetic fields so powerfully that the energy of the body is able to overload external mechanisms. This phenomenon is especially prevalent in adolescence and can be documented as the disruptions of electronics. We call the former *poltergeist activity* and attribute it to spectres and ghosts. We call the latter *bad luck.* The most powerful form of *electromagnetic charge* outside anger involves sexual excitement.

Telekinesis is the ability to influence objects without direct physical interaction.

The *Evil Eye* & Protective Symbols

Symbolic actions have the power to act upon the *imagination* through *intention*, as is demonstrated by most human rituals like a wedding or graduation ceremony. Another great example of this is the "evil eye." As Eliphas Levi writes of *"the basilisk who slays by a look,"* it is indeed a magical allegory and not a mere fable. In Latin the name is *Nvidia*, a sense of the strong gaze of envy associated with the "evil eye." Romans used this name for the Greek deity *Nemesis*, i.e., ruin.

Those we have not met may still alter the direction of our life through a mere glance, and so protections were used against these influences throughout history: amulets, talismans, charms, sigils, and perhaps the most powerful *Eye of Horus*. Witches are said to possess this ability naturally. They can bewitch others with a mere glance, or what we call *be-witching*. In Italy the evil eye was known as *mal d'occhio* or *iettatura*; in Greece it is *Baskanos*; in the Arab culture is the eye of envy known as *ain al-hasad*; and in Mesopotamia the *IG-HUL* was the evil eye.

The Roman author and naturalist Pliny the Elder wrote that the *evil eye* could be averted with the sharp-sighted essence of an animal like a hyena, and therefore, the skin of this animal would provide needed protections. The same could be said of a hawk. Most employ necklaces and earrings as defensive tools against the *evil eye* because these accessories draw attention to the jewelry itself rather than the wearer.

Some sorcerers are believed to possess an ability to kill or cause severe harm by a mere glance, too, while others have traditionally burned images of enemies, or punctured them with pins, depending on the amount of harm intended. Against the *evil eye* incantations have been used, such as the following one from <u>La Magie chez les</u>, translated by François:

> *He who forges the image, he who enchants -*
> *The spiteful face, the evil eye,*
> *The mischievous mouth, the mischievous tongue,*
> *The mischievous lips, the mischievous words,*
> *Spirit of the Sky, remember!*
> *Spirit of the Earth, remember!*

From the same source we are offered another incantation but this time against the abuses of nature in general:

> *They fall on one land after the other,*
> *They raise the slave above his rank,*
> *They cast the freewoman out of the house where she gave birth,*
> *They cast the young birds out of their nests into emptiness,*
> *They drive the oxen before them, they drive away the lamb,*
> *The evil, the cunning demons.*

Fascination is a type of *binding* caused by the eyes whereby the observer takes possession of the intended body and overpowers the same. We may call this *intimidation* today. Those easily fascinated are also likely to be easily influenced by *impression*, i.e., they are *impressionable*. By appealing to belief, emotion, ego, safety, etc., and by certain states of excitement induced and then reduced, a form of breath, one can be placed in a state of trance and made vulnerable to *suggestibility*.

These suggestible soul-spirits are easily swayed as if by a force of magical influence. Fascination is more popularly known as *mesmerism* or *magnetism*. Daniel likewise survived being torn apart by lions in the den through *magnetism*, as per the esoteric reading, and his conquering of *Celestial Fire*, for which the lion is a symbol. Those able to control this fire are said to possess the ability of **Pyrokinesis.**

To *bind* something or someone in magical terms means to exercise authority over that thing or person. A *binding* is thus similar to the influence of the *evil eye*. This form of magic is usually *dark* in nature with one of its most famous examples being that of an object used to assist in burglary. Known as the *Hand of Glory*, the object is a literal hand taken from a gibbeted man (executed by hanging) who lies dead. When the candle attached by wax or glue is lit, and the hand is placed near a house, the item is meant to prevent the occupants of a home from awakening while the thieves do their work. Its power lasts if the candle burns. Writing about bindings, Cornelius Agrippa says:

The Hand of Glory

"*Fascination is a binding, which comes from the spirit of the witch, through the eyes of him that is bewitched, entering into his heart. Now the instrument of fascination is the spirit, vic. a certain pure, lucid, subtle vapor, generated of the purer blood, by the heat of the heart. This doth always send forth through the eyes, rays like to itself; those rays being sent forth, do carry with them a spiritual vapor, and that vapor a blood, as it appears in blear, and red eyes, whose rays being sent forth to the eyes of him that is opposite, and looks upon them, carries the vapour of the corrupt blood, together with itself, by the contagion of which, it doth infect the eyes of the beholder with the like disease.*"

Unlike the *glory hand* there are other hands used as amulets of protection against *fascination*, *binding*, and the glance of an *evil eye*. From the Americas to Arabia, we find them in gestures, bronze statues, and diagrams.

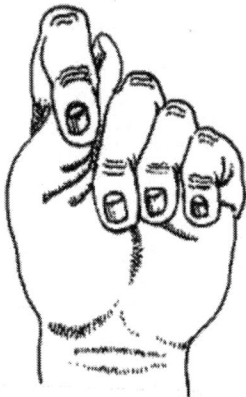

The **Figga** or **Fico** is an amulet used commonly in Latin America against the *evil eye*.

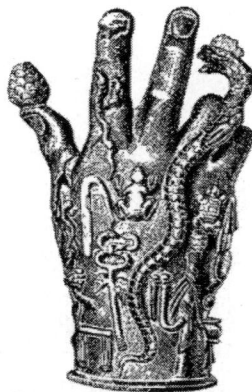

A magical bronze hand from Egypt, meant to protect from the *evil eye*.

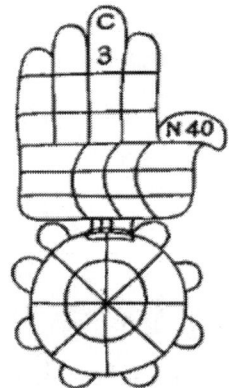

A diagram of the **Hand of Fatima**, named after Mohammed's daughter.

Further east in India and China we find the use of an *evil eye charm* often placed in a home or worn as a necklace. It is common in the west, too, consisting of a black dot inside a blue sphere, surrounded by a white line and thicker blue circle. All these charms have the same role as the *four-leaf clover*, *Eye of Horus*, or *Bagua Mirror* in Feng Shui.

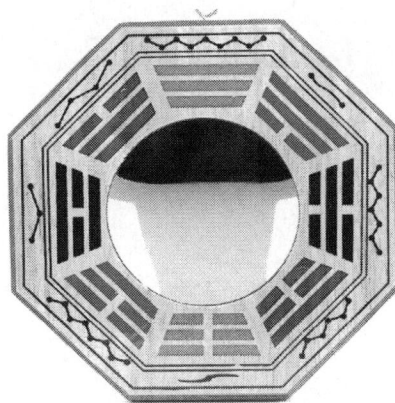

Two versions of the Feng Shui *Bagua Mirror*, meant to transform negative *chi* into positive *chi*.

We know *thought forms* can manifest into monsters: *Tulpa, Golem, Egregore, Aquastor*. These creatures are personifications of *a thought, train of thought, obsessive thought,* and *compulsive thinking*. Each *thought* is expressed through *words* and by these vibrations there are etheric shapes that take form, further organized by one's actions. It is easy to see when someone is happy or seems *to be followed by a dark cloud;* when someone is in love or depressed from loneliness; when someone is actively listening or clearly distracted by their own thoughts.

These *thoughts* are said to take the shape of an etheric body which may become visible in serious situations. This may also explain biolocaiton, the phenomenon where a body seems to appear in multiple locations at once. In popularized terms this can be explained as the projection of the astral body beyond the physical body, something that usually occurs during sleep. David Conway comments on this in <u>Ritual Magic: An Occult Primer</u>:

> *"The fact that the physical self is usually asleep when bilocation occurs suggests that consciousness may sometimes be transferred from the physical body to its astral counterpart."*

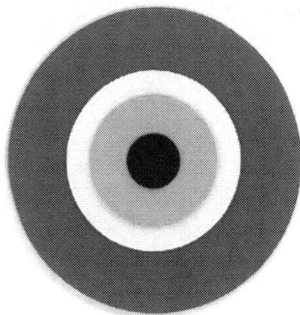

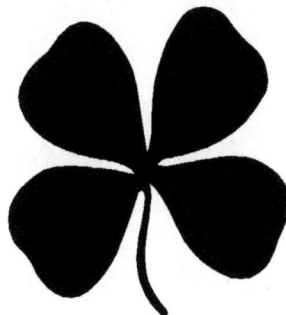

Divination, Fate, Augury & Runes

"Not all events of human life are caused divinely nor are they all inevitable; neither do they all stem from a single relentless fate, as there are also natural events. Man is subject not only to disasters inherent in his own personality, but also to those born of general causes - plagues, floods or fires, which destroy multitudes. Such occurrences must be explained by the absence of any opposing heavenly influences which might prevent them. Whoever exercises prognostication must take care to foretell only those events belonging within the realm of natural causes."

~ Kurt Seligmann ~

General Divining

We know that certain psychic abilities and forms of magic can be explained in scientific terms. Now it is important to project these understandings on *divination*, the practice of *seeking knowledge of the future*. Divination is also known as *manteia* (touched by the divine). Although this is typically done by conjuring spirits or consulting the dead through *necromancy*, divination may also be performed, and usually is, by modern scientists. Weather forecasters use computers to "predict" the weather just as economists use data and simulations to predict market trends. With these two forms of divination, we learn if we should bring an umbrella or perhaps invest in a stock. Earlier we also learned that common games and traditions like *apple bobbing* or *throwing a bouquet of flowers* at a wedding are themselves methods used for divining the future. Some may deny this fact because these traditions are simply fun, but if this be the case then why should those same folks deny the use of a *Ouija* board? Divination comes from the Latin *divinatio* from *divinare*, which means "to predict." From the word "divination" we extract *divinei*, which has meaning of "guesswork" or "intuition," and of "magical insight into the future by supernatural means." The word also relates to God or the gods, and thus the nature of divine works and supernatural guidance. We get the word *science* from the Latin *scientia,* which comes from the word *scire,* meaning "to know." This means that *science* is not mere *observation* but is in fact defined etymologically in the same capacity as we define *intuition*, meaning "to know." The word *intuition* stems from the Latin *intuition* and *intueri*, which means "consider." This means that *intuition* is essentially a process of consideration, something more akin to our modem view of science, while the latter is an ability to simply *know* something, or what we call *intuition*. *Divination* is thus the use of *science* and *intuition* to find patterns and formulas embedded in the fabric of God's creation. These could include microcosmic cycles of the moon or macrocosmic seasonal cycles that expand upward into increasingly larger cycles.

Astrology

Reverend John Butler said about astrology, which was no doubt practiced by the Christians, Jews, and Muslims:

"And while I study thus I find that next unto Theology, nothing leads me more near unto the sight of God, than this sacred astrological study of the great works of nature."

Astrology was without question cultivated and practiced in every ancient culture, including by the ancient Hindus, Chinese, and Jews. Manly Hall writes in The Story of Astrology of this fact and then goes on to quote a Jewish Encyclopedia on the same issue:

"Much of the religious inspiration of Christendom is derived from the ancient Jews and it is not amiss to realize that astrology was greatly cultivated by the wisest among the ancient Israelites… even by Moses himself, who must need have been proficient in it because he was a priest of the Egyptians."

"Abraham, the Chaldean, bore upon his breast a large astrological tablet on which the fate of every man might be read; for which reason - according to the Haggadist - all kings of the East and of the West congregated every morning before his door in order to seek advice."

We can also assume, as was the case in Egypt, Greece, Rome, India, the Americas, and Asia, that astrology was used to diagnose and even cure diseases, i.e., it was used to *cast out demons*. Out of the study of astronomy came an understanding not only of the planets, but also of the signs of the *zodiac*, largely the offspring of Chaldean astrologers. The six original figures still in use today are the Lion, Balance, Twins, Scorpion, Bull, and two Fish. According to Kurt Seligmann writing in The Mirror of Magic there are certain cases of star interpretation where *"a planet or a fixed star might be replaced by a consolation or zodiac figure."* He provides us with an example: *"Saturn might be replaced by the Balance, by Cassiopeia, by Orion or by the Raven."*

By the stars were derived *information* about future events, answers to general questions, data useful to the military, and pretty much anything else desired. Richard Cavendish simplifies the issue:

"The universe is a whole, a great design. Any event which occurs is part of the design and can be used to predict events in the future because they are also parts of the design."

Astrology was not merely an ancient magical practice based on ignorance, but one that incorporated mathematics, geometry, and science into the same category. It is not, except by ignorant and uninformed opinion, a superstition, though many have made it their own. Those seeing it as such must be children of atheism wherein *fear of creation*, i.e., responsibility and logic (God), is replaced by a willful ignorance that sees the body as a distinct and separate unit apart from a nature they believe exerts no influences on the former. However, astrology is certainly inundated with charlatans and wishful thinking. But for it to have any value whatsoever the calculations must be precise and a person's knowledge of the heavens considerable. If these conditions are not met, then astrology is nothing more than a game. As Helena Blavatsky wrote:

"Astrology is a science as infallible as astronomy itself, with the condition, however, that its interpretations must be equally infallible…"

With the separation of astronomy and astrology there was also an absorbing of one by the other. Astronomy has gobbled up the relevancy of astrology and promoted itself as an absolute science by which we can see distant planets through magical lenses. Astrology has gobbled up all the irrelevancy of astronomy and been relegated to small sections in newspapers, phone applications, and mockery. The irony is that, once again, the scientific version is only able to see those distant planets either by magical technologies or through computer generated images that are simply meant to give an impression of what some artist thinks a distant speck of light may really look like! Without doubt our ancestors, though not perfect in these pursuits, were far more inclined to take both arts seriously, as Seligmann notes:

> "They were masters in the arts of prescience, predicting the future form the livers and intestines of slaughtered animals, from fire and smoke, and from the brilliancy of previous stones; they foretold events from the murmuring of springs and from the shape of plants… Monstrous births of animals and of men were believed to be portents, and dreams found skillful interpreter."

> "Atmospheric signs, rain, clouds, wind, and lightening were interpreted as forebodings; the cracking of furniture and wooden panels foretold future events."

The above-mentioned "cracking of furniture" is known as *Assaput*, or *Prophetic Voice*. Signs, symbols, and omens existed, and exist, everywhere, as do the spirits that communicate through them. From insects and animals to weather and chance meetings, these are all signs of esoteric messages. There are no coincidences in journalism nor in the occult sciences.

If we take a trip back to the Garden of Eden we can learn how Adam, the first man, was himself instructed in astrology. By this tradition we might suggest that man was given a certain authority over the stars to understand *God's Plan* and live in harmony with the same. In fact, as Genesis 2:19-20 states, man was given authority to name the animals. Perhaps Adam was given the power to name the animals not only of the earth but of the zodiac (animal wheel) as well:

> "Now the Lord God had formed out of the ground all the wild animals and all the birds in the sky. He brought them to the man to see what he would name them; and whatever the man called each living creature, that was its name. So the man gave names to all the livestock, the birds in the sky and all the wild animals."

Oracles & Predestination

There are many forms of divination, which range from *astrology* and reading *tealeaves* to playing with cards and reading *entrails* or organs like the *liver*. All these, and many more, are generally called "oracles."

The oracle has been made most famous by the one at Delphi, but such a word has more useful meaning if we define it as "sacred words." The word "oracle" comes from the Latin *oraculum* and *orare*, meaning "to speak." These "words" were often derived from a priest or priestess embodying the very essence of celestial authority. In fact, these men and women are themselves the *oracle* or *medium* just as they may *give oracle*.

Spinning thread on a spindle and weaving on a loom are connected allegorically by *fate*: the development of events seemingly outside of one's control. The *weaving* is related to the fabric of matter itself. The *spinning* of thread is related to the motions of the heavens, the whirling dervishes, and the cyclic nature of life. Hindus believe in the doctrines of *Samsara*, the continuous cycle of life, death and reincarnation, and *Karma*, or the universal law of cause and effect. We can find evidence of this cycle in the Tibetan Buddhist <u>Book of the Dead</u> which teaches that it takes 49 days for the soul to reincarnate after death, precisely the amount of time it takes an embryo to form the pineal gland and determine male or female gender. The doctrines of *Samsara* and *Karma* share a relationship with the *Three Fates* of Greece: Clotho, Lachesis, and Atropos. Similar are the *Three Norns* of Norse mythology: Urd, Verdandi, and Skuld. These *sisters* sit at the center of our world spinning our fate and cutting the string like Saturn with his scythe when *our time comes*. They represent "what was," "what is becoming," and what should become," all things that humans attempt to understand by asking for assistance from the divine. We do this by asking God for strength or dabbling with tools promising us a glimpse of what comes next.

Fate is considered *predestination*, a belief that all things are preordained by supernatural or divine forces. Yet one does not need to believe in such a thing specifically, but only generally, to understand the nature of divination. From predestination we may extract *destiny*, something that *will* happen at some future point in time, but not something that must occur specifically. We will die but the cause of our expiration is unknown. By our *will* we may avert certain occurrences, even those fortunes found unfavorable, which are merely a *possibility* and not an *absolute* certainty. How you arrive at the destination is different from the inevitability of reaching the same. Nigel Pennick writes of matter and energy:

> "*The dynamic relationship between matter and energy naturally take certain forms, which can be expressed in mathematical forms or geometric patterns.*"

We find meaning here that *matter* and *energy* share a relationship that expresses the divine through mathematics and geometry, or sacred geometry. These "mathematical forms or geometric patterns" are the basis of astronomy-astrology. If one interprets *fate* in such a way, then predestination is not merely God's unchanging *Divine Plan*, implying that life is purposeless, but instead a *plan* that implies, perhaps, the very opposite, that life is filled with purpose to be discovered through mastery of self; that fate is merely the end of such an experience and one may reach its conclusion in infinite ways mapped out in the fabric of reality by the mind of God.

~

Martin Luther's reformation of the Church essentially abandoned even the beneficial elements of Catholicism in that of confessing sin, rectifying wrongs, and doing good works for the community. Although these forms of penance have become a matter of heavenly credit today, the basic ideas behind such actions were the betterment of self spiritually and the betterment of one's community. Luther instead taught that an individual had no control over his or her salvation, which was dependent entirely upon God's grace. From these teachings came the contemporary view that the only way to obtain absolution was through blind faith in Jesus Christ. Luther helped develop the idea that if one holds this belief in Jesus, then his suffering upon the cross would atone for all their sins, effectively providing an unchecked moral licensing that has resulted in a perverse corruption of the Church. In other words, no matter what one does in life they can find salvation by simply filing for a form of spiritual bankruptcy that moment fate finally catches up. Today we hear Christians say that they are assured of their fate because they hold a belief in Jesus Christ, and so it does not become immediately necessary for them to fight evil since they have already been saved!

Predestination as taught by John Calvin preached that God had already decided before birth who was to be spiritually saved. Those unlucky enough to have been pre-selected for a life of feudal suffering were not an "elect" like John Calvin and the other elite-elect Calvinists.

Puritans believed that conflict was a permanent element in *existence*. There is nothing necessarily inaccurate or wrong with such a belief unless it is used to wage perpetual warfare in the name of good versus evil, and especially if it taught that the horrors of war are perquisites to spiritual salvation. In simpler terms that are less violent, struggle certainly "makes a man" and hardship hopefully breeds character. Hijacking such a notion is yet another exploitation of the sacred nature of existence in that of playing upon the unseen to wage war on the visible. This is also the political doctrine of Marxist philosophy known as *dialectical materialism,* or the idea that class warfare is inevitable and should even be provoked as the first stage in bringing upon a collective classless society. As in all human history, the future was always uncertain, especially during the winter. It was during these times of chaos, natural or manufactured, that man sought assistance from the unseen. Due to temptation and sin, billions continue to seek assistance from crosses, moons, stars, holy books, and prayers to celestial forces. Others seek foreknowledge of future events out of fear for their own mortality.

Listed below are a variety of divinatory practices in summary, some more famous than others, followed by a more complex overview of certain forms, including *Runes*, which serve a phonic as well as a pictorial, or symbolic, purpose.

Many Types of Divination

Alectromancy: divination by means of a rooster is thought to be a precursor to the *Ouija* or *Talking* board. It is conducted by placing a rooster (fowl) in the center of a circle composed from letters of the alphabet over which you place pieces of grain. The rooster then chooses the grain, and thus the letters, which are then interpreted. The Syrian Neoplatonist philosopher, Iamblichus, who was also the biographer of Pythagoras, is credited with developing this method of divination.

Astragali: divination using the knucklebones of animals; a forerunner to dice.

Astromancy: divination by winds.

Bibliomancy: divination by interpreting random passages from a book, especially the Bible. Some believe that the Bible was used for determining the guilt of suspected witches. He or she would be literally weighed against the book and only if lighter would they be considered innocent. This is reminiscent of the weighing of the heart against a feather in the Egyptian *Hall of Judgment.*

Capnomancy: divination by interpretation of smoke from a burnt offering on a sacrificial altar. In using the intestines of those scarified animals, or the liver as in *Hepatoscopy*, the diviner examines how the parts burnt within the flame.

Cartomancy: the telling of future events by interpreting a random selection of cards from a deck. The most famous form of this practice is known as "reading Tarot" or, erroneously, "playing the Tarot."

Cereoscopy (or ceromancy): divination by wax in which the substance is melted into a brass bowl, stirred, and when fully liquefied, poured carefully into another bowl filled with cold water. Once the wax spreads and solidifies in the water its shape is then interpreted.

Crithomancy: divination by dough or baked items such as bread.

Haruspicy: divination by studying entrails of sacrificed animals.

Hepatoscopy: divination specifically by the liver of a sacrificial offering. The Roman scholar Pliny said of this organ: *"The liver is on the right side: in this part is situate what has been called the 'head of the entrails,' and it is subject to considerable variations."* Since the liver filters blood and breaks down toxic substances like alcohol and drugs, it could be, to the trained eye of a doctor, used to determine if one was sick or ill.

Lecanomancy: divination by pouring water into oil or oil into water. The number of drops formed, and their sizes, are then interpreted.

Libanomancy: divination by smoke from burning incense, wood, or other fuel.

Onychomancy: divination by fingernails.

Oomancy: divination by egg is accomplished by reading the albumen and yolk.

Pegomancy: divination by studying springs or fountains. These magical fountains were believed to provide insight into future events. The practice of tossing coins into fountains, wells, or any water, and making a wish or asking a question silently, is derived from *pegomancy*. Here we obtain the common idea of a *Wishing Well* popular in European folklore, a belief partly based upon the existence of water deities – *undines, naiads,* or *nymphs* - inhabiting the water. Stories from medieval literature associated with *King Arthur* refer to this deity as the *Lady of the Lake*. Another famous water nymph is the female spirit known as *Melusine*, depicted as a fish or serpent below the waste. *Pegomancy* is thus a form of *Hydromancy*, or divination by the element of water.

Plumbomancy: divination by lead dripped into water in like manner to *cereoscopy*. It is a very dangerous practice not to be recommended.

Rhabdomancy (or rhabdoscopy): divination with a wand or stick, commonly called the *dowsing rod*.

Scrying: divination by peering into a medium such as a crystal ball, known as *crystallomancy*, or some form of other lens like a *Black Mirror*, which is prepared with the black volcanic glass called obsidian. The magician looks into that mirror hoping to summon a spirit or acquire a vision to answer a question. These are the famous *magic mirrors*. Today we stare at another black mirror, or screen, in the form of televisions, computers, phones, tablets, etc. Metal is often used to construct these mirrors.

Tsuji-ura: divination from Japan whereby women divine the future by piecing together random conversations of people in public. Some believe this is benign while others equate it to a form of malicious crossroads magic.

Turtle Shells: the second oldest book on classical Japanese history, <u>Nihon Shoki</u>, tells of divination by reading cracks in a turtle's shell. Traditional eastern directional markers are painted on the shell with a *machi* first – North (To), West (Emi), South (Ho), East (Kami) – but flipped in comparison with the west. North becomes south and west becomes east. The shell is then cast into the fire. Once it cracks the markings are read in correspondence to the symbol and their locations on the shell. The purpose was to divine future shrine maidens, a practice like the selection of *Vestal Virgins* in Rome. The latter attended a sacred fire that was never allowed to be retired.

Three additional practices include: **Metoposcopy**, the determining of destiny and fate by lines on the forehead; **Physiognomy**, or the judging of fate and destiny by facial expressions and traits; and **Chiromancy**, Greek for "hand divination," like modern *palmistry*. Chiromancy dates to around 3000 BCE, when it was practiced in China. Metoposcopy is attributed to Jerome Cardan, although his treatise on the subject appeared later than other initial publications.

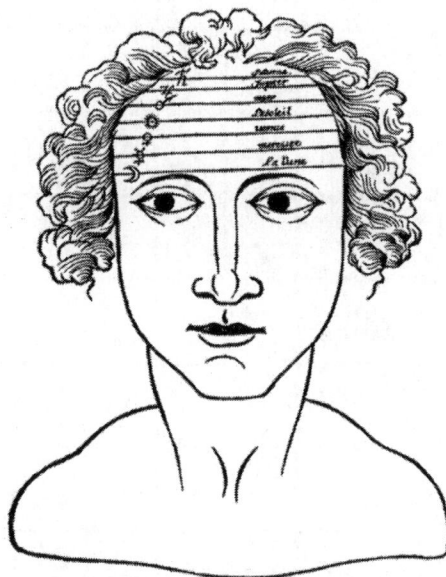

Metoposcopy from Metoposcopia by Jerome Cardan, 1658.

Augury & Geomancy

One of the most famous forms of divination involves interpreting the nearly endless signs of nature, such as the flight patterns of insects and birds or the blowing of wind. These omens were analyzed in a process called *augury* and by priests called *augurs*. Omen interpretation applies not only to the wind but to the other elements as well: air is ***aeromancy***; water is ***hydromancy***; fire is ***pyromancy***; and earth is ***geomancy***.

Augury was historically practiced at the College of Augurs in Rome. There are now considered only two main categories: *ex avibus*, interpreting flight patterns and songs, and *ex tripidus*, interpreting the eating habits of birds. Historically there were five main *augurs*, here mentioned first by name, then meaning, and then specification: *ex coelo* (from the sky): thunder, lightning, meters; *ex avibus* (from birds): broken into *alites*, the flight of birds, and *oscines*, the voice of birds; *ex tripudiis* (from the feeding of birds): birds dropping a kernel while eating was seen as a good omen; *ex quadrupedibus* (from animals): their motions and sounds; *ex diris* (from warnings): any incident foretelling disaster.

Geomancy is a technique practiced in two different forms: *inspection* of the surface of the earth by means of dirt, dust, sand, etc., and the *placement* or arranging of buildings in relation to one another. The latter usage is employed in the Chinese art of placement known as *Feng Shui* or the Indian *Vastuvidya*. It is most often thought of in its most simple form, which involves picking up a handful of Earth, sprinkling it on the ground, and reading the meaning.

The basic process of tapping the earth in a random or intuitive manner and then translating those taps into binary code is commonly seen in geomanic figures of dots or diamonds. There are four lines of these points, from top to bottom, known as head (fire), neck (air), body (water), and feet (earth). They almost resemble *I Ching* hexagrams.

Modern geomancy overtook the Arab *Raml* in name and practice. Otherwise known as *psammomancy*, or 'ilm al-raml, it was the experiment of reading patterns formed randomly in sand, which would indicate messages to an interpreter. One form of technique described is the use of sixteen mathematically related configurations of dots drawn on paper, or using seeds, stones, or whatever else may be proper for such an operation. Agrippa writes of this practice too:

"Geomancy is an art of divination, whereby the judgment may be rendered by lot or destiny, to every question of everything whatsoever…"

Figure	Geomantic figure	Planet	Element	Astrological sign	Quarter	Alternate sigils	Days	Prophet
Populus	(: :) (: :)	☽	▽	♋	N	(four sigils)	Monday / Thursday n.	Moses
Via	(:)(:)(:)(:)	☽	▽	♋	N	(four sigils)	Monday night	Abachim
Tristitia	(two pairs)	♄	△	♒	E	(four sigils)	Saturday	Jacob
Laetitia	(two pairs)	♃	▽	♓	N	(four sigils)	Thursday / Sunday	Adam
Fortuna major	(pattern)	☉	△	♌	S	(four sigils)	Sunday	Noah
Fortuna minor	(pattern)	☉	△	♌	S	(four sigils)	Saturday n. / Noon Thurs.	Mohammed
Acquisitio	(pattern)	♃	△	♐	S	(four sigils)	Thursday	Ousmane
Amissio	(pattern)	♀	▽	♉	W	(four sigils)	Friday	Jesus
Puella	(pattern)	♀	△	♎	E	(four sigils)	Friday / Monday n.	Ladari
Puer	(pattern)	♂	△	♈	E	(four sigils)	Tuesday	Jonah
Carcer	(pattern)	♄	▽	♑	W	(four sigils)	Saturday / Wed. n.	Solomon
Conjunctio	(pattern)	☿	▽	♍	W	(four sigils)	Wednesday / Sat. n.	Ali
Albus	(pattern)	☿	△	♊	E	(four sigils)	Wednesday / Saturday	Idris
Rubeus	(pattern)	♂	▽	♏	N	(four sigils)	Tuesday / Friday n.	Amar
Caput draconis	(pattern)	♃♀	▽	☊	W	(four sigils)	Friday	Madi
Cauda draconis	(pattern)	♄♂	△	☋	S	(four sigils)	Tuesday	Lassima al-Houssein

The Geomantic Correspondences are left to right: figure, geomantic figure, planet, element, astrological sign, quarter of the earth, alternate sigils from geomantic figures, days, Jewish-Islamic prophets.

Throwing Dice

Divination by dice, known as **astragalomancy (astragyromancy)**, is centuries old. Cubic dice have been found dating from before 2000 BCE in Egyptian tombs. Their usage for divinatory purposes stems from their name: singular – *die,* or plural - *dice*. The latter comes from the Latin *dadus,* meaning "given," which references *fates* or *destines* ordained by the gods. Dice have been used for various forms of foretelling future events, even to determine who out of a group of prisoners should be sacrificed or executed. It is common for gamblers to blow on dice before they throw them. This tradition or superstition comes from magic too. When magicians are working to enchant certain things, they often begin by blowing on them, breathing in the virtue of spirit and exhaling *"so that the entire virtue of the soul is directed into the thing enchanted, disposing it for accepting said virtues,"* writes Agrippa. We are also aware of popular phrases such as "the die is cast." Therefore, what is given - or *dadus* - has been ordained by the gods. Fate is indeed predetermined, but only so that we must reach a certain end. It does not dictate how we choose to arrive. The foretelling of future events does not force their exact outcome, but only reflects infinite possibilities. Nigel Pennick explains in <u>Games of the Gods</u>, a great text on this subject and others, of the development and design of dice:

> *"...there are only two possible arrangements, which are mirror images of each other. If a die is looked at so that the faces bearing the numbers one, two and three are visible, the numbers are arranged in ascending order anticlockwise. This is the standard form found all over the world, except in Japan, where a mirror image of this is employed in the game of Mah Jongg."*

From *dice* or *lots* also comes their association with determining ownership of lands; the word *allotment* and *lot* are remnants of a time when land ownership had been selected by *drawing lots*. From this practice may be understood the *drawing of straws*.

Spears and Arrows

Divination by dice in Tibet is known as *Sho-mo.* Another form of divination in Tibet, known as *Dahmo,* and by other names elsewhere, is the method of utilizing arrows. Prayer scepters called *muwieri,* of the Huichol people in Mexico, are also derived from sacred arrows. Stewart Culin was an American ethnographer and author who believed that the game of *chess,* along with card games, was derived from arrow divination. Arrow feathers in traditional archery were taken from selected birds with qualities hopefully transferred to the arrow by the magical law of correspondence. Arrows were used for strategic purposes such as deciding where and when advances in times of war should be made and if a city should be attacked or left in peace. We also find in the book of Ezekiel 21:21 the following:

> *"The king of Babylon stands at the parting of the ways, at the fork of the two roads, practicing divination; he shakes his arrows..."*

Similarly related to *arrow divination* is the same practice of using broomsticks, twigs, bones, spears, other weapons, and so on to determine the best course of action.

Spears: we can find similarity to alectromancy, the art of divining by observing birds and white roosters, in pagan Wendish tradition. Instead of white birds, the Wends used a white horse and in placing spears upon the ground monitored the movements of the animal.

Sacred Games

Those interested in these things should consult <u>Secret Games of the Gods</u> by Nigel Pennick, who gives a most wonderful explanation not necessary for this text.

From the Indian game *Moksha-Patamu* are derived certain religious instructions. The board displays a unification and contrast of opposites: right and wrong. In game play these former "right" actions are called *pap*, denoted by a ladder, and those "wrong" actions are denoted *punya*, represented by a serpent. Of this game, also called the *Game of Heaven and Hell*, is a grid situate to resemble the planets, zodiac, and stars. Although providing more meaning than what is derived from a game of *Snakes and Ladders*, the archetypes of these two symbols still represent virtue and downfall, respectively. Ladders lead to upward movement whereas the serpent denotes a downward fall into animal nature.

A similar game was played in Egypt called the *Egyptian Serpent Game*, details of which have been taken from tomb paintings dating to the third dynasty 2,700 BCE.

Another game goes by the lengthy name of *The Royal and Most Pleasant Game of the Goose*, shortened to simply *Game of Goose*. It was invented in Florence and utilizes dice for play. Its directional game play, as with the former games, relates to advancement or decline in spiritual progression. The game proceeds from the outside towards the middle of the board in an anti-clockwise direction.

In Egypt the center of the board was a serpent's head, but the direction of play is unknown, whether from head to tail or its opposite.

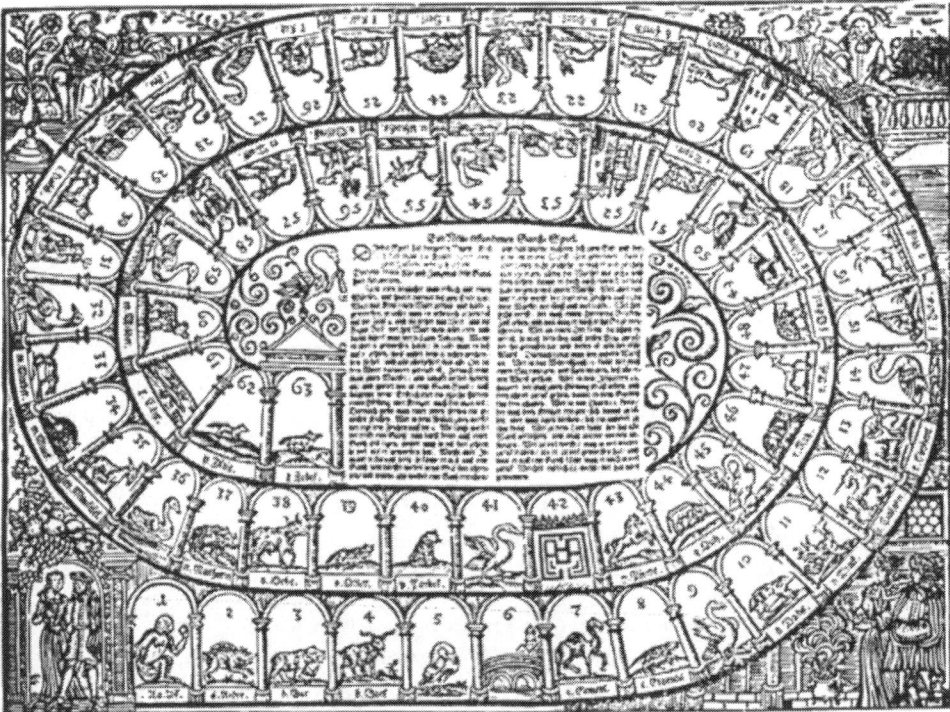

A 17th-century woodcut of *Ganss-Spiel* (**Game of Goose**)

Red String of Fate

Divination can be practiced with tools such as ropes, chains, bracelets, and charms. There is the African chain known as *opele* used for this purpose, and a cord (Witches' Ladder) with forty knots or beads used by wiccans. In traditional wiccan magic a red string or rope with nine knots is used. These methods likely play a role in the popularity of the *Charm Bracelet* and the importance of a *Christian Rosary*, the string of beads also used in other religions. The wiccan red string is of particular interest here, too, because in Japan this item is known as the *Red Cord* or *Akai Ito*. Also called *unmei no akai ito*, meaning "red string of fate," Japanese believe it connects people who are destined to meet. The string essentially symbolizes a cosmic *connection of dots* and can be seen stereotypically on an investigator's wall connecting pictures, news clippings, documents, and photographs.

The Runes

One of the most famous pictorial tools for divination, which also serves a phonic purpose, are the runes. The word "rune" comes from the German *raunen*, meaning something that has a "hidden nature." In Old English the *rūn* was something of a "secret" or "mystery." These now sometimes beautiful works of art were originally derived from pre-alphabetic symbols that were used for divination long before they were used as a script.

In the northern part of Europe, sometime between 1300-800 BCE, symbols in the form of petroglyphs, known as *Hällristningar*, were inscribed on rocks. These characters include variations of the swastika or fylfot, the spiral or labyrinth, wheels, a monad, and commonly recognized geometric shapes and runes. This collection of symbols is often referred to as *Rune-Hoard*, used for divination and other forms of communication. From these inscriptions there developed forms later incorporated into the runic alphabet, *Futhark*, created in about 305 BCE and used between 200 BCE and the late eighth century.

The *Hällristningar* or *Rune-Hoard*

As described in <u>Secret Games of the Gods</u> by Nigel Pennick, there is a significant difference between the "runic alphabet" and other systems of hieroglyphics, like those found in Egypt or Mesopotamia:

"The alphabet, and the Futhark in its use as a script, symbolizes a fully phonetic representation of language in a manner qualitatively different from that of hieroglyphic, ideographic or other non-

phonetic systems of language notation. The transition of the use of runes from their state in the ancient Rune-Hoard, where each character was non-alphabetic and non-phonetic, to their use in an alphabet, marked a changeover in the use of the sides of the brain from right to left, from the intuitive to the analytical/"

The earliest form of *runes* as we know them comes from German-speaking countries and range from 19-23 characters. Later sets or rows of runes were placed at 24, the number being divided for divination into three sets of eight called *aettir,* whereby the first rune in each set rules the others. This is the common row known today as *Elder Futhark.*

When the Frisians and Saxons migrated to England in the 6th-century, they brought with them additions to the common row. Frisians, whose magical system was based on Druidic practices, added four new runes to the 24 for a total of 28. The Saxons further added to the row increasing it to 29 and finally to 33. This process was reversed in Scandinavia where the 24 runes became 16 for a more simplified format. The *Elder Futhark* runes are the most used and recognized form today, but in German-speaking countries a set of 18 runes called the *Armanen Runes* are still popular.

The 16 runic-row used in Scandinavia.

FEOH	UR	THORN	OS	RAD	CEN	GYFU	WYN	HÆGL	NYD	IS
GER	EOH	PEORTH	EOLH	SIGEL	TYR	BEORC	EH	MAN	LAGU	ING
EHTEL	DAG	AC	ÆSC	YR	IOR	EAR	CWEORTH	CALC	STAN	GAR

33 runic characters with their names, by author.

The method of *casting* runes is called *Raed Waen.* Where they are cast is called *Shoat.* Before one can begin it is necessary to take into consideration certain environmental and planetary factors. *Shoat* must be cleansed and a *Stol,* or special cushion, is to be placed behind the caster at what is referred to as the "negative" end of the space. In the direction of *raed waen* is the "positive" end. In the latter place is *Weofodi,* a ceremonially embroidered white cloth, whereupon the *Mearomat,* or personal talisman of the operator, is set. At each of the corners of this space are to be the symbols of the four elements. One of the earliest references to runic divination is preserved by Roman author Tacitus (120 AD) writing in <u>Germania</u>, an account of Germanic nations and their forms of divination:

> "They have the highest possible regard for divination and casting lots. Their procedure in lot-casting is always the same. They break off a brance from a fruit tree and slice it into strips; they distinguish these by certain runes and throw them, as fortune will have it, onto a white cloth. Then the state priest (if the divination is a public one) or the family father (if it is private), after a prayer to the gods and a strong heavenward gaze, picks up three of them, one at a time, and reads their meaning from the runes carved on them."

Another Roman writer, Hyginus, once suggested that writing was developed from monitoring the flight of cranes. Whether there is any truth to this observation it is certainly true that animals were the basis for several forms of martial arts and ancient healing practices like Qigong. Kurt Seligmann wrote similarly, but also of divination:

> "The curve observed in the flight of birds, the barking of a dog, the shape of a cloud are occult manifestations of that omnipotent coordinator, the source of unity and harmony."

Readers will recall Odin's birds *Hugin* and *Munin*, respectively representing *thought* and *memory*. In all endeavors these birds helped the god to explore and learn. It was also Odin who developed, or realized, runes upon his suffering on the *World Tree*. This story is told in the song of *hávamál* from *Utterances of the High One – stanzas 138 and 139*:

I know that I hung on the windswept tree,
Through nine days and nine nights,
I was stuck with a spear, and given to Odin,
Myself given to myself,
On that tree, which no man knows,
From which roots it rises.
They helped me neither by bread,
Nor by drinking horn.
I took the runes,
Screaming, I took them,
Then I fell back from there.

Armanen Runes by Austrian Mystic Guido Von List, from the earlier 20th-century. This image depicts 18 runes arranged around the *Wheel of Time*. This was the standard system used for magic and divination in most German-speaking countries.

Fa   Ursache   Thor   Os   Rit   Ka   Hagal   Not   Is

Ar   Sig   Tyr   Bar   Laf   Man   Yr   Eh   Gibor

Runic Attributes, *Vegvisir* & the *Black Sun*

An alphabet is "a set of letters or symbols in fixed order." Each letter is a symbol with a vibration, proven in auditory form, that when strung together allows for the written or verbal expression of *thought*, i.e., consciousness. The *Word of God*, as we have seen, is the outward emanation of the *Cosmic Mind*. The name of God in Hebrew is articulated as Yahweh, the Tetragrammaton, containing within its spelling the base for *grammar*, or the structure of language. YHVH and Tetragrammaton, or the simpler Yahweh and Adonai, represent the four base elements of fire (ash), water (mem), air (ruach), and earth (aretz). The fifth of these elements is expressed in the sacred pentagram, or *pentagrammaton*, otherwise known as the *pentalpha*. The fifth point is *spirit*, symbolized by a turning eight-spoked wheel.

In Iceland, across the Norwegian Sea from Scandinavia, a special pentacle with eight spokes was used as a protective amulet against harsh weather. The eight points of *Vegvisir* are the *Wheel of the Year*, clearly giving its operator balance and control over the eight *holy days*: Yule, Imbolc, Ostara, Beltane, Litha, Luchnassad, Mabon, Samhain. The word itself is Icelandic for "wayfinder," or sometimes called "Viking Compass," a tool that certainly would have been necessary to assist people in finding their way through that region's harsh winters.

Similar to *Vegvisir* is the *Black Sun*, a symbol of where the physical sun goes each night when it is vanquished to the underworld. During this time there are destructive forces that roam the earth. Each of the twelve rays emanating from its central point symbolize the sun's passage through the twelve months, and possibly the twelve signs of the zodiac. These *rays* are very similar to the rune "sig," meaning victory or sun, reminding us of Sol Invictus. Adele Nozedar writes in the Signs & Symbols Sourcebook that *"the circular shape of the symbol implies protection and magical powers."*

In Hebrew or Greek *gematria* there are numbers applied to each letter allowing for numerical values to be extracted from names, words, sentences, etc. In the Greek alphabet, as well as with Runes, attributes are given to each character. We will look at Greek and then examine the Runes.

Alpha: meaning bull or cattle; mobile wealth.

Beta: the demonic separator from unity.

Gamma: godliness and the sacred.

Delta: the four elements, directions, etc.

Epsilon: *aion* (or the Latin *aeon*); the fifth element.

Zeta: offering or sacrifice.

Eta: love, harmony, and joy.

Theta: the eighth sphere where the fixed stars stood in early cosmology.

Iota: destiny.

Kappa: brings about bad luck, sickness, and death.

Lambda: plant growth, geometry, etc.

Mu: the stars.

Omicron: the sun.

Pi: the sun in its glory surrounded by rays of light.

Rho: fruitfulness and the power of reproduction.

Sigma: Lord of the Dead.

Tau: the human being.

Ypsilon: water and flowing qualities.

Phi: the phallus and male generative principle.

Chi: property.

Psi: heavenly light embodied by Zeus.

Omega: the final character; riches, abundance, success.

α β γ δ ε ϛ η ϑ ι κ λ μ

ο π ρ σ τ υ φ χ ψ ω

The Greek Alphabet, by author.

Of the Runes and their associated meanings, the following list includes a more detailed, especially for divinatory purposes, list of 33 runes. The first 24 are the same as the *Elder Futhark*, minus the fourth rune in this set. This fourth rune appears here as rune 26.

FEOH: the first rune. It shares some similarity with the Greek *Alpha* having a meaning relating to cattle and mobile wealth; it also represents responsibility, stewardship, money, wealth, and success. It is sacred to the god Frey.

UR (URUZ): the second rune represents the Primal Ox, Audhumla, responsible for forming the progenitor of mankind. It signifies a force of creation, perseverance, strength, etc. In divination, it refers to individual success, positive luck, and the common good.

THORN (THUS): the third rune and a symbol of the defensive power of Thor; it is his personal rune, although it has more of a relationship with the Thorn tree and the giant named *Thurs* or *Thurisaz* (Thursday). It is a symbol of fertilization and any changes brought about as suddenly as lightning. *THUS* further relates to positive fortune and good news.

OS: the fourth rune of the 29 and 33 rune rows, replacing the rune ASA of the *Elder Futhark*. This is the rune of Odin, a mouthpiece through which the divine sound is expressed, like the Hindu creative sound *Om*. It represents the meaning of communication and information, and the wisdom of human society.

RAD: the fifth rune relating to the wheel and road; a way forward; to arrive at some destination; transference and transformation.

CEN: the sixth rune and a symbol of the flaming torch. It represents mystery, regeneration by death like the phoenix, and the creative fire by which material is transmuted. It signifies protection and positive sexuality in relation to Freyr and the goddess Freyja.

GYFU: the seventh rune, representing a *gift* or *to give something*, especially to the gods.

WYN: the eighth rune represents joy and the *mystery of harmony* in a world of disharmony.

HÆGL: the ninth rune signifies any processes by which something is accomplished. Often it is used as a talisman of protection placed on doorframes.

NYD (NEED): the tenth rune representants need and necessity.

IS: the eleventh rune. It is the principle of static existence, which is represented specifically by ice because the water has ceased to flow; it has changed form.

GER (JER): the twelfth rune representing the cycles of nature. It is another rune of the god Freyr. As with *CEN*, we find the marriage of Freyr and Freyja again. Freyr is god of the sun and rain and his relationship with Freyja, goddess of fertility, signifies the regenerative properties of nature. Both characters can be related to the Egyptian deities Geb and Nut.

Freyja and Freyr

EOH: the thirteenth rune and a symbol of the Yew tree, which is sacred to the dead.

PEORTH: the fourteenth rune. It represents the force of destiny operating in the world. *Destiny* is not the same as *predetermination*, however, as it is merely that which eventually and inevitably will occur, not something *written in stone* as an inevitable and specific *fate*.

EOLH (EOLX, EOLHSECG): the fifteenth rune and a symbol of the Elk; a rune of protection.

SIGEL: the sixteenth rune associated with the sun and its light in all forms. It is the power of decency throughout the world that counteracts destructive forces. It shares similarities thus with the *Yin Yang, Yab Yum* and *In Yo.* SIGEL is also called SIG, known as a symbol of victory.

TYR: the seventeenth rune is one of positive regulation. It represents success and happiness.

BEORC: the eighteenth rune of mystery and the Birch tree, symbolizing purity.

EH (AIHWS): the nineteenth rune, simply meaning horse. It is associated with that which is linked together as in a horse and its rider, or twins. Astrologically it corresponds with Gemini (the Twins).

MAN: the twentieth rune representing the nature of a what it means to be human in all forms.

LAGU: the twenty-first rune means fluidity, water, and the uncertainty of existence. LAGU is the direct opposite of IS.

ING: the twenty-second rune related to the god Ing, the male counterpart of the earth goddess. It implies potential energy. Ing is said to be an older name for Frey.

ETHEL (ODIL): the twenty-third rune; a symbol of family and personal land. It draws positive energy when placed on a house Gable.

DAG: the twenty-fourth rune and the last of the *Elder Futhark.* It translates as "day" and is a symbol of awakening or illumination. It also acts as a form of protection when placed on doorframes or upon the frames of windows. DAG shares in the virtues of OMEGA.

AC: the twenty-fifth rune. It means "Oak," which is a sacred tree to Thor. The acorn that it produces represents the cosmic egg. Contained therein is the potentiality of all creation and manifestation.

ÆSC: the twenty-sixth rune representing the sacred Ash tree, whereupon Odin was crucified and realized the runes. This rune symbolizes the divine force presently at work in all things.

YR: the twenty-seventh rune has the meaning of a "bow," which also acts as an instrument of divination in relationship to the arrow. It signifies physical defense and pinpoint accuracy of "hitting the target."

IOR (IAR): the twenty-eighth rune is representative of the sea serpent or world serpent known as *Jörmungandr*. The IOR is the embodiment of necessary evil.

EAR: the twenty-ninth rune is a character of dust. It represents the inevitable and unavoidable cessation of all things. EAR is thus related to *destiny* or *fate*.

CWEORTH: the thirtieth rune symbolizing the flames of any ritual fire, like those lit during certain sacred festivals in the *Elder Faith.*

Jörmungandr

CALC: The thirty-first rune with the meaning of an offering cup. It represents that which is attainable but has not been accomplished.

STAN: the thirty-second rune; it represents stone.

GAR: the thirty-third and final of the extended runic row. It represents the spear, also used in divination, but specifically the *Gungnir,* or Ash-handled spear of Odin, which symbolizes the Cosmic Axis-tree Yggdrassill. GAR ends the rune row and thus represents completion, housing the other thirty-two runes in its sphere of influence.

Orthography & Sacred Words

In reciting an *incantation*, especially in Egypt, it was believed that every single word and how it was pronounced had a dramatic effect upon the operation. The "magic" was not merely in *sacred names*. If a word was required to be spoken, then it had significance, as did its *intonation*, or the rising and falling of the voice when speaking. *Intonation* of an *incantation* is only the first stage of using magical phrases. The second stage involves *belief* in what is being spoken and *intention* to bring that thing about. Agrippa writes in his *Occult Philosophy* of the power of speaking:

> "*For hence voices and words have efficacy in magical works: because that in which nature first exerciseth magic efficacy, is the voice of God.*"

Casting a *spell* (incantation) or uttering a *curse* are ideas derived from the actual spelling or words, sometimes written in the format of cursive. *Spelling* is the activity of writing the letters of words and names in a certain order, otherwise known as *orthography*. The writing of letters or symbols in fluidic motion so that they are joined is called *cursive*. Sometimes a powerful word may be extracted from another word, or a name from a name, as is the case of *Messia*, משיה, from *Ismah*, ישמה, and *Michael* from *Malachi*, מלאכי. Some words are considered too sacred and powerful, however, to be uttered by the tongue of man. Just as one cannot investigate the *Face of God*, for it is blinding, HIS name was never to be spoken either. It was instead reduced to the four Hebrew letters we know as YHVH. Writing or speaking the *name* of God, or depicting him with human characteristics, has traditionally been seen as sacrilege and blasphemous. It was seen as an offensive act of *black magic* to reduce the ALL to finite details. Sorcerers casting *dark spells* violate the sacred by writing or speaking words and names out of order or backwards. For example: writing backwards the name *Aphrodite*, goddess of love, was useful in invoking hatred and destruction. Any distorted writing or speaking of magical phrases is believed to invert their power. This is why some recite the *Lord's Prayer* in reverse or sign diabolic contracts in backwards spelling. The most barbarous and unintelligible words are said to have the most influence in the *dark arts*, since they readily call upon the infernal, while beautiful words and sacred names draw upon angelic virtues. Here is what philosopher Alan Watts writes about the power of language and words:

> "*Language in its broadest sense, including words, numbers, signs, and symbols of all kinds, is what peculiarly distinguishes men from animals, and enables us to know that we know. Language is the symbolic echo of direct experience, lending to it resonance that enhances it - as a great cathedral, with its subtle reverberations, lends an other-worldly magnificence to the voice of a choir.*"

Francis Barrett, in <u>The Magus</u>, further explains how "*the virtue of man's words are so great, that, when pronounced with a fervent constancy of the mind, they are able to subvert Nature, to cause earthquakes, storms, and tempests.*" The meaning to be derived here is clearly one of metaphor. Roger Bacon (1214-1294), the English philosopher and scientist, writes here on the power of words in relation to the soul:

> "*We must consider that it has great force; all miracles at the beginning of the world were made by the word. And the peculiar work of the rational soul is the word, in which the soul rejoices. Words have a great virtue when they are pronounced with concentration and deep desire, with the right intention and confidence. For when these four things are joined together, the substance of the rational soul is moved more quickly to act according to its virtue and essence, upon itself and upon exterior things.*"

Israel Regardie further explains in his book <u>The Tree of Life</u> the power of *vibration* and *sound* as they relate to the pronunciation of divine names:

> "It is held in Magic that the vibration of certain god or divinenames conduces to the production of its psychological and spiritual phenomena. 'Why?' asks Blavatsky in her Secret Doctrine. Answering her own question, she states " Because the spoken word has a potency unknown to, unsuspected and disbelieved in, by the modern ' sages.' Because sound and rhythm are closely related to the four elements of the ancients; and because such or another vibration in the air is sure to awaken corresponding powers, union with which produces good or bad results, as the case may be." The legend pertaining to the Hebrew Tetragrammaton is interesting. He who knows the correct pronunciation of YHVH, called the Slzem ha-Mephoresh, the Unpronounceable Name, possesses the means of destroying the universe, his own particular universe, and hurling that individual consciousness into Samadhi. Moreover, the magical theory has it that the vibration set up by the human voice has the power not only of moulding the plastic substance of the Astral Light into variegated shapes and forms depending upon the tone and volume, but also of compelling the attention of meta~hvsical entities and Essences to that mould."

> "The vibration of God-names, then, constitutes one of the most important divisions in a ceremonial invocation. The incenses, perfumes, colours, sigils and lights around the magical circle will assist in evoking the desired idea or spirit from the imagination and to manifest itself in an appropriate garb coherent and tangible to the exorcist. Not alone must there be intention and thought, but there should be the concrete expression of thought in an action or a word which, to the idea, must be as a logos."

Angelical Script

Sometime in the 16th-century two men began working together at the task of obtaining and understanding the language of angels. Dr. John Dee, the mystic and astrologer of Queen Elizabeth I, believed that such a script would be the most powerful tool any magician could possess. He partnered for the work with an alchemist and clairvoyant medium named Edward Kelley. During a *scrying* session with a crystal ball (crystallomancy) Kelley saw a series of blurry letters. Asking for clarification, the angels caused these symbols to temporarily appear on a piece of paper so that Dee could trace their outlines. Commonly called *Enochian Script* today, because it is believed the prophet Enoch was the last person to understand this angelic language, Dee instead called it *Angelical Script* or *Celestial Speech*. The angels told Dee that this alphabet had actually been taught to Adam by God *in the beginning*, and so we derive the name *Adamical Script*. There are twenty-one characters in this alphabet and it is written usually right to left, bringing the symbols closer to the heart. The image below is supposedly taken from Dr. John Dee's diary from May 6, 1583.

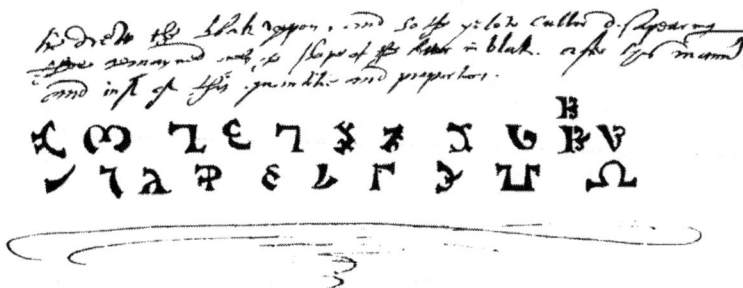

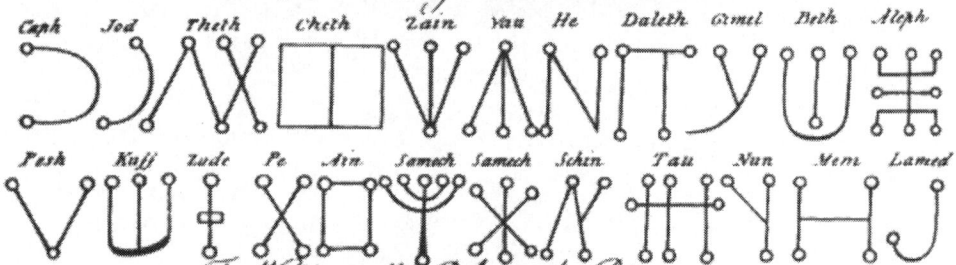

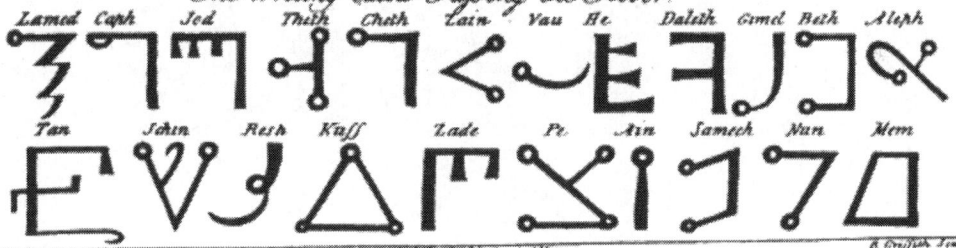

Magical Alphabets from <u>The Magus</u> by Francis Barrett.

Writing down the *mysteries* was authoritatively deemed unlawful with common text and so alphabets were created to conceal these *secrets:* the *alphabet of Theban, Celestial Script,* the *Malachim Alphabet,* and *Passing of the River.* Plato, Pythagoras, and Porphyrius all bound their followers to silence like Harpocrates. This is also the meaning of Matthew 13:10-11 where we read:

> *"And the disciples came, and said unto him, Why speakest thou unto them in parables? He answered and said unto them, Because it is given unto you to know the mysteries of the kingdom of heaven, but to them it is not given."*

The Word Made Myth: Heka, Magical Tools, the Tetrad, Tarot & Kabbalah

"Horrors lurked in the primeval forest, not nymphs and naiads [a water inhabitant]. Terror lived there, with its close attendant, Magic, and its most common defense, Human Sacrifice. Mankind's chief hope of escaping the wrath of whatever divinities were then abroad lay in some magical rite, senseless but powerful, or in some offering made at the cost of pain and grief."

~ Edith Hamilton ~

The Word Made Myth

The word *mythology* is derived from the Greek *mythos*, meaning a narrative theme or plot structure and a "set of beliefs about something." Myth contains words, concepts, and stories reflecting the values and attitudes of a people. At its core, *myth* sustains the vital essence of those people and may therefore reveal far more than any standard historical record. This is not to dismiss historical accounts, but to suggest their equal necessity alongside myth in understanding our past and present: *myth* must be viewed as having some form of historical accuracy. As the famed mythologist Joseph Campbell wrote:

> *"Mythology is not a lie, mythology is poetry, it is metaphorical. It has been well said that mythology is the penultimate truth-- penultimate because the ultimate cannot be put into words. It is beyond words. Beyond images, beyond that bounding rim of the Buddhist Wheel of Becoming. Mythology pitches the mind beyond that rim, to what can be known but not told."*

The ancient city of Troy was once thought to be a mere *legend*; a city besieged and conquered by the Greek army led by King Agamemnon. The battle that captured the city was fought, according to Homer's <u>Iliad</u>, because of the abduction of Helen, Queen of Sparta. Although this may be considered a mostly fictional story, though not entirely, the real city of Troy was found by archeologists on the northwest coast of Turkey, today known by the name Hisarlik. Real people and places can be mythologized, as was certainly the case with Jesus Christ, too, but their existence may still be part of the historical record. Author David Fideler writes in <u>Jesus Christ Sun of God</u> about the word *mythos*:

> "In antiquity, the word mythos had just the opposite meaning and denoted a traditional narrative designed to entertain, to educate, and to transmit the very soul and gnosis of the culture."

The philosopher Alan Watts expands on *myth* in <u>The Book: On the Taboo Against Knowing Who You Are</u>, by explaining what it is and is not:

> "At one extreme of its meaning, 'myth' is fable, falsehood, or superstition. But another, 'myth' is a useful and fruitful image which we make sense of life in somewhat the same way that we can explain electrical forces by comparing them with the behavior of water or air. Yet 'myth', in this second sense, is not to be taken literally, just as electricity is not to be confused with air or water. Thus in using myth one must take care not to confuse image with fact, which would be like climbing up the signpost instead of following the road."

When *myth* is viewed in the above ways it quickly and clearly becomes an incredibly sophisticated form of *magic* and *science* that dates to antiquity. Although few were *learned* in those days, myths still provide us historical evidence that our ancestors were anything but primitive. Through the mythologized characters and concepts ancient man was able to commune directly with the forces of nature and God in ways we can only theorize on today. Mark Booth mentions this in <u>The Secret History of the World</u>, suggesting we imagine ourselves as someone thousands of years ago *"walking through woodland to a sacred grove or a temple, such as Newgrange in Ireland, or Eleusis in Greece,"* or somewhere similar:

> "To such a person the wood and everything in it was alive. Everything was watching him. Unseen spirits whispered in the movements of the trees. A breeze brushing against his cheek was the gesture of a god."

To our ancestors the *divine* was always present. God was always watching through the *Eye of Providence*. Every action and reaction were either in favor or disfavor with *celestial forces* and so the ceremonial practice of magic in all its forms developed around the world. Arthur E. Waite explains in <u>The Book of Black Magic</u> the two dichotomous forms of magic:

> "White Ceremonial Magic is, by the terms of its definition, an attempt to communicate with Good Spirits for a good, or at least an innocent, purpose. Black Magic is the attempt to communicate with Evil Spirits for an evil, or for any, purpose."

> "The most objectionable works are not those which openly announce that they are evil, but those which teach evil under the pretence of excellence."

Heka Magic

Before the *time* of *creation*, there came into existence what the Egyptians called *Heka* or *Hike*. While most are familiar with RA, the supreme deity, Heka was either the *first emanation* of source or a direct companion to the sun god himself. Encyclopedia Britannica says that according to the Egyptians: "…*heka was the primordial force present at the creation of the world, that it could be summoned up during the observance of religious ritual, and that its chief function was the preservation of the natural world order.*" If not the *first emanation*, at the very least Heka accompanied RA in his solar boat as it made its daily journey across the sky like Apollo in his chariot, or the Kami in Japan riding the *heavenly-rock-boat*. Heka is both an attribute of RA, or Re-Atum, and the direct personification of divinity in its first manifestation as *light*. Heka is therefore the foundation and personification of *magical power*, which is usually how the word itself is translated. This power is a *celestial influence* operating through the solar gateway. The Greek *logos* represents *order* from whence we obtain *truth* and *balance*. *Logos* is also purely *Heka*, the protector and sustainer of humanity and the gods of heaven. There is ultimately a direct connection between Heka and the goddess of truth and justice, Ma'at, who strives to bring harmony to all things through wisdom, or Thoth. Heka is also linked to the heart and tongue, from whence we feel and speak the *Word of Creation*. This is accomplished in magic by uttering incantations. According to the World History Encyclopedia:

> "*Heka referred to the deity, the concept, and the practice of magic. Since magic was a significant aspect of medical practice, a physician would invoke Heka in order to practice heka. The universe was created and given form by magical means, and magic sustained both the visible and invisible worlds. Heka was thought to have been present at creation and was the generative power the gods drew upon in order to create life.*"

Magic Wands & Other Tools

The most famous, infamous, comical, and stereotypical emblem of both *magic* and *magick* is, of course, the *wand*. This device, like a ritual *athame* (dagger) used by pagans and wiccans, is a symbolic physical extension of the *body* and *mind*. The wand is akin to a conductor's baton that indicates tempo and rhythm to an orchestra. Wands also play a similar role to the royal *scepter*, an ornamented staff carried by powerful people to denote their connection to God. A scepter or staff symbolizes an *umbilical cord* connecting the *Sky Mother* with her children below. As an extension of the *Sky Father*, these objects are tools that can direct His heavenly graces, i.e., the *Astral Light* of Eliphas Levi. Holding a staff gives one heavenly authority over the world below just as the *globus cruciger* suggests the supremacy of the Church (cross) over all the earth (globe): *Catholic* comes from the Greek *katholikos*, meaning "universal." Other stereotypical instruments are the *chalice*, *sword*, and *pentacle*. Each of these, along with the wand, correspond to a physical or mental quality and one of the four elements: the wand represents the *will* and air; the chalice or cup represents *intuition* and water; the sword represents *mind* and fire; and the pentacle represents the *bodily temple* or earth. Some traditions assign the wand to *mind-fire* and sword to *will-air*. We all use these types of

tools daily without realizing the fact; from cooking utensils to dental hygiene products like a toothbrush, we are exercising our *will* and *mind* in performing magical actions as routine chores.

In the east we find the *athame* in the form of a *phurba*, a triune spike-like-dagger used for creating sacred spaces for ritual ceremonies. Its original use was as a stake to secure the tether of sacrificial animals. A *phurba* can be simple or complexly decorated just like an *athame*.

Phurba

It would require evidence for most to prove the claim that Jesus himself employed the magic wand for his works. From the multiplication of loaves and fishes, to turning water into wine and raising Lazarus from the dead, there are numerous depictions of the Christian savior using a magic wand. As with a wand, staffs are employed for the same reason, usually acting as an umbilical cord to heaven, as is the case with Moses and his direct connection to God. Priests of Dagon, known by different names to the Sumerians, Philistines, and Babylonians, not only wore fish hats identical to the contemporary Pope's *mitre* headdress, but they also carried magic wands like the Pope's staff.

The image on the left is from Santa Sabina Church, Rome, depicting the miracles of Jesus performed with a magic wand. The image on the right is from the Catacomb of St. Callixtus, Rome, depicting Moses striking a rock.

Hollywood Wands

There is no other *wand* more famous today than the one made from the wood of *holly*, i.e., *Hollywood*. Druids, the priestly class of the ancient Celtic culture, saw holly as a magical shrub perfect for making these wands. When we think of Hollywood there is recall to the *silver screen*, which shares a relationship with the storms conjured up by these Druidic magicians. The *movie magic* of *Hollywood* likewise fits into our magical lexicon. The showing of a movie is simply this: *putting on a show*. That show is projected, downloaded, loaded, or streamed as a *broadcast*. This broad *casting* involves the projection of what was *spelled* out in the script.

Movies are a special type of *rite* with selected dialogue and costumes; they are part of a magical formula meant to influence an audience into states of emotion like laughter or fear to make money (currency). If a movie is *screened* in a *theater*, there is a ritual projection or allusion being cast on the *silver screen*, because it is, ultimately, *just a movie*. The dim lighting, seats, unique smells, and our food and beverages are all part of the production. The word *theater* itself comes from the Greek *theatron* and *theasthai*, which means to "behold something," perhaps with *suspended disbelief*; to *believe something that isn't true*. The word *entertain* likewise has a similar meaning. From the Lain *inter* and *tenere*, which means "among" and "to hold," respectively, we get a definition of "entertainment" that means *to be held in a form of perceptual bondage*. If a movie is shown on television, it is known as television broadcasting or *television broad casting*. The *television* is what is told to our *vision* through *programming*, the process of preparing something like a rite or ritual to have influence on its viewers.

The Trident & Tilaka

The trident Ⴈ is a commonly associated with the personification of Satan. It is sacred because it preserves the synthesis of *trinity* within the *monad*, which together forms the holy *tetrad*.

This three-pronged spear in classical mythology is associated with Neptune-Poseidon (Roman-Greek), god of seas, water, and earthquakes. Because of the trident being associated with water it became the alchemical symbol of this element. But it is also a tool of fire since the three-prongs resemble flames. Tridents are therefore representative of thunderbolts and lightning too.

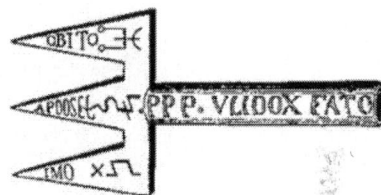

The Trident from Eliphas Levi's Transcendental Magic.

Also called *trisula* त्रिशूल in Sanskrit, the staff gives its possessor the triune powers of nature. It is a symbol of the Hindu God Shiva, representing the threefold qualities of *creation*, whose followers wear a trident-like symbol called *tilaka*. The latter symbol often resembles a tuning fork, with two white lines on either side and a red streak in the middle. When Shiva wielded his staff, it represented the three phases of time: past, present, and future; and the three conceptual worlds: Heaven, Earth, and Hell. It also represents the Three Jewels of the Buddha, the Dharma, and the Sangha. Much like the *mjolni,* a magical hammer belonging to Odin, the *gungnir* is a tool resembling the trident that always strikes its target and then returns like a boomerang. It is also called *Odin's Spear* or *Odin's Javelin*. Odin's son Thor likewise carries the same spear. Paracelsus often combined the *wand* with a *magnetized fork* to create the *trident*. The repetition of names in sets of three were *"united to triangular combinations in magical ceremonies,"* according to Levi in his book Transcendental Magic. He recounts that Paracelsus ascribed to the trident *"all the virtues which Kabbalistic Hebrews attribute to the name of Jehovah and the thaumaturgic properties of the ABRACADABRA,"* that magic triangle of pagan theosophists also used by Alexandrian hierophants.

Magic Circles

The *magic circle* can be seen in popular entertainment today as frequently as it may be found in a text at a specialty occult bookstore. Its purpose is to act as a *barrier* between a ceremonial magician and that which is being conjured. A magician may stand within the circle and conjure a spirit on the outside or they may conjure a spirit within the circle while they stand on the outside. Either way it serves the same protective purpose. These *circles* can be made with salt (a preserver), ash, chalk, grain, etc., or simply drawn with a wand in the air by use of a *visualization* technique. In ceremonial magic there are to be written sacred names and drawn sacred symbols as part of the defensive wall. The *magic circle* also shares a relationship with the *fairy circle* and those *flying saucer impressions* (saucer nests) often referred to as *crop circles*. Stephen Skinner writes in <u>Techniques of Graeco-Egyptian Magic</u> of Assyrian circles utilizing basic elements like water and flour:

> *"In the Assyrian texts, protective circles were drawn on the ground with a mixture of water and flour. These two substances were, respectively, sacred to Ea and Nisaba, water being the 'shining waters of Ea' and the flour forming circle being the 'net of Nisaba, the corn-god'."*

Magic Circle from the *Heptameron*, Peter de Abano, 1655.

Pentacle of Solomon from <u>The Book of Black Magic and Pacts</u>, Arthur E Waite, 1898.

The Sacred Tetrad

Tetrads are a group of four things. When the *Holy Trinity* is combined with the sacred *Monad* a tetrad is formed. When the arms of a *trident* are unfolded into a *cross* there is produced the *solar divisions*. These three arms that become four are likened to the combination of *threefold man* and the *four elements*, which is why the number *seven* is sacred. If the three and four be multiplied the result is an equally sacred number preserving the twelve months and zodiac signs.

Corners of Creation	East	South	West	North
Fixed Zodiac Signs	Aquarius	Leo	Scorpio	Taurus
Parts of Cherubim	Man	Lion	Eagle	Bull
Seasons	Spring	Summer	Autumn	Winter
Ages of Man	Childhood	Youth	Maturity	Age
States of Existence	Birth	Growth	Maturity	Decay
Parts of Man	Spirit	Soul	Mind	Body

Parts of Man (alt)	Spiritual	Emotional	Intellectual	Physical
Enochian Spirits	Hcoma	Bitom	Exarp	Nanta
Worlds of Elements	Aquatic	Infernal	Aerial	Terrestrial
Qualities of Elements	Cold	Heat	Moisture	Dryness
Qualities of Celestials	Agility	Light	Ethereal	Solidity
Rulers of Elements	Tharsis תרשיט	Seraph שרפ	Cherub כרוב	Ariel אריאל
Elementals	Undines	Salamanders	Sylphs (Slyphs)	Gnomes
Rulers of Four Corners	Gabriel גברואל	Michael מיכאל	Raphael רפאל	Uriel אוריאל
Perfect Mixed Bodies	Metals	Animals	Plants	Stones
Kinds of Animals	Swimming	Walking	Flying	Creeping
Horses of Apocalypse	White	Red	Black	Pale
Evangelists	Matthew	Mark	John	Luke
Agents of Alchemy	Mercury	Salt	Sulphur	Azoth
Scientific Elements	Hydrogen	Nitrogen	Carbon	Oxygen
States of Matter	Liquid	Plasma	Solid	Gas
Forms of Divination	Hydromancy	Pyromancy	Geomancy	Aeromancy
Metals	Mercury	Copper	Lead	Gold or Silver
Powers of Soul	Phantasy	Intellect	Reason	Sense
Judiciary Powers	Opinion	Faith	Science	Experience
Moral Virtues	Prudence	Justice	Temperance	Fortitude
Humours	Phlegm	Choler	Blood	Melancholy
Infernal Rivers	Styx	Phlegethon	Cocytus	Acheron
Senses	Taste & Smell	Sight	Hearing	Touch
Elements	Air ריח	Fire אש	Water כוים	Earth עפר
Ichirei Shikon of Shintō	Nigimitama	Sachimitama	Kushimitama	Aramitama
Four Devas of Buddha	Jikokuten	Zōchōten	Kōmokuten	Tamonten
Sacred Hindu Writings	Śruti	Tantra	Purāṇa	Smriti

Tarot Cards & Adda-Nari

Tarot cards are reportedly based on *hieroglyphic science* from Egypt. Although there is no official correlation between these cards and either mainline Jewish belief or the Sepher Yetzirah, some believe there is indeed still a connection. What we call the *magical alphabet* is thought to have been derived from the famous *Book of Thoth*, supposedly divined by French Scholar Court de Gebelin (1728-1784), and preserved today in Tarot cards. Whatever the case, countless decks are as varied as interpretations of their original origin.

The twenty-two letters of the Hebrew alphabet are relatable to the 22 cards of the *Major Arcana* in Tarot. The first letter ALEPH א corresponds to the *Juggler* (magician) card, which also expresses by hand and arm positioning the hermetic axiom: As Above So Below. In Greek we call it Alpha and Omega, and in India and Japan it is of the same nature. The four lettered Hebrew names YHVH (Yahweh) and JHVH (Jehovah) are extracted from the *tetragrammaton*, or *tetrad*, and each of their letters corresponds with one of the four Tarot suits: *wand, cup, sword, pentacle*. Each of these items is further related to the elements and seasons, and the ceremonial tools of practicing magicians.

1) **JHVH** is spelled but never pronounced. The consonants are YOD, HE, VAU, HE.

2) **ADNI** means *Lord* and is pronounced ADONAI.

3) **AHIH** represents *Being* and is pronounced EIELE.

4) **AGLA** is pronounced as written and is said to comprise all the mysteries of Kabbalah in hieroglyphics. The word is formed of the first letters of the benediction: *Atha Gibor Leolam Adonai* (Thou art mighty for ever, O Lord).

In all these examples is proof of *Notarikon*, defined as a system of abbreviation that involves shortening words or writing only one letter of each word, as in the case of YHVH.

Temurah is a way of rearranging letters from words and sentences in the Bible to derive a mystical meaning. One version of this is called *Atbash*.

Of the four suits in Tarot: the *wand* represents YOD, east, air, eagle, Scorpio, and *Azoth*; the *cup* corresponds to HE, west, water, man, Aquarius, and *Mercury*; the *sword* refers to VAU, south, fire, lion, Leo, and *Sulphur*; and the *pentacle* signifies the second HE, north, earth, bull, Taurus, and *Salt*. The eagle, man, lion, and bull are together called *tetramorph*. Hindus know this as *Adda-Nari*, the figure flanked by a bull and tiger and holding wand, sword, cup, and sphere inside a *magic circle*. When Raymond Lully wrote his *Ars Memoria* (Art of Memory), printed in the mid-fifteenth century, he attempted to reconcile the themes present in the Four Gospels by creating a series of images to symbolize the *Four Evangelists* - from whence we derive the animal correspondences above. These correspondences can also be found in the *Cherub of Ezekiel*. Of the *Adda-Nari*, Levi explains:

ADDA-NARI

"This pantheistic image represents Religion or Truth, terrible for the profane and gentle for initiates. It has more than one analogy with the Cherub of Ezekiel. The human figure is placed between a bridled bull and a tiger, thus forming the triangle of Kethar, Geburah, and Gedulah, or Chesed. In the Indian symbol, the four magical signs of the Tarot are found in the four hands of Addha Nari — on the side of the initiate and of mercy are the sceptre and the cup on the side of the profane, represented by the tiger, are the sword and the circle, which latter may become either the ring of a chain or an iron collar."

The *Four Worlds* in Kabbalah are **Atziluth**, the divine world of *YOD*; **Briah**, the archangelic or creative world of *HEH*; **Yetzirah**, the formative world of *VAV*; and **Assiah**, the material world of action and the second *HE*. Akin to these are the *Four Geometries*: Monad, Dyad, Triad, and Tetrad, or the Divine Being, Spirit, Son, and Daughter. Alongside the geometries are the *Four Mathematics*: point, line, superficies, profundity.

Tarot decks come in nearly endless themes and styles today. Their purpose is, to the occultist, the preservation of sacred knowledge in the form of what many interpret as a simple game. But Eliphas Levi explains how Tarot is far more:

> *"But it requires a considerable exercise of reason to make use of an instrument belonging to reason and to science; the poor king, in his childish condition, saw only the playthings of an infant in the artist's pictures and he turned the mysterious Kabbalistic alphabet into a game of cards."*

Modern playing cards, which are often less than one dollar in cost, also conceal the same powerful symbology hiding behind complex pictures in Tarot. Manly Hall writes in The Secret Teachings of All Ages of this fact:

> *"Modern playing cards are the minor trumps of the Tarot, from each suit of which the page, or valet, has been eliminated, leaving 13 cards. Even in its abridged form, however, the modern deck is of profound symbolic importance, for its arrangement is apparently in accord with the divisions of the year."*

The red and black colors of modern cards symbolize the divisions of a year during which the sun is north and then south of the equator. Four suits in the deck equate to the yearly seasons: spring and summer are red; autumn and winter are black. Each suit shares a relationship with the Tarot deck and magical tools: Clubs are wands and air-fire; Hearts are cups and water; Spades are swords fand fire-air; Diamonds are pentacles and earth. Hall continues:

> *"The twelve court cards are the signs of the zodiac arranged in triads of a Father, a Power, and a Mind according to the upper section of the Bembine Table. The ten pip cards of each suit represent the Sephirothic trees existing in each of the four worlds (the suits). The 13 cards of each suit are the 13 lunar months in each year, and the 52 cards of the deck are the 52 weeks in the year…The chessboard consists of 64 squares alternately black and white and symbolizes the floor of the House of the Mysteries."*

The Death Card

Divination by cards, especially Tarot, is a largely misunderstood and comical practice today with just about anyone being able to *play* with the varied oracles. The mass majority are not looking to divine information, however, and instead simply use Tarot for fun, though some take it seriously, or play with the 52 cards in hopes of winning some money at gambling.

To understand the Tarot and divination we must recall what was said earlier about *fate* and *destiny*: it is inevitable that we will die but the location, time, and method of our death is up to *chance;* we still maintain *free will* to choose how we live. This is precisely what a Tarot reading provides. The idea is that one's aura can be "read" by a psychic or from touching the cards themselves before they are drawn, essentially transferring your energy to the deck. Whatever is laid before you are a *fortune* but one that is not only infinite in interpretation, one that may change the very next moment. Tarot should thus be used as a *guidepost* instead of a *stop sign*.

For example: the death card is pulled from the deck, causing fear. But that card must be read alongside the other cards and interpreted in relation to the intent of the reading: general, specific questions, advice, etc. The death card could just as likely signify the end of a tumultuous time in your life as it does physical death. In fact, the card's common *white rose* implies something akin to the purity of resurrection or rebirth, which may apply to your life, a job, or a relationship. On the flip side, someone using Tarot for daily guidance may find ultimately that the cards are merely a visual aid and that any happiness derived is purely personally cultivated. This is the nature of ceremonial magic.

The Devil Card & Baphomet

The Devil Card consists of a creature with the horns of a ram, torso of a man, legs of a goat, and the feet of a dragon perched on a black cube He has wings, an inverted pentagram, and a downward facing torch to illuminate the infernal. His characteristics may remind one of the Greek Pan or Celtic Cernunnos. In either case, he is a god of sexuality, fertility and being *horny*, i.e., he is the "horned god." His image was preceded by the *Horned Shaman,* who holds a serpent in his left hand and ring in the right. Also known as the *Dancing Sorcerer*, this latter character from paintings dates back beyond 10,000 BCE and is said to depict a shaman preparing for a ritual ceremony. He may also be meditating or performing yoga.

Cernunnos-figure on the Gundestrup Cauldron.

Eliphas Levi's *Baphomet* from the book <u>Transcendental Magic</u> is certainly based off these earlier depictions and today has come to be associated with every conspiracy and hint of malevolence anywhere it presents itself in the world. His drawing is something called the *Goat of Mendes* or the *Sabbatic Goat* and it without doubt has been used by satanists.

Baphomet is perhaps feared more than even a swastika, despite its mass gathering of esoteric symbols that lead our attention upward instead of downward like *The Devil* card. Baphomet does indeed mirror the latter card, but key areas are different.

For example, the goat's horns are turned upward ever so slightly, representing the difficulty but necessity of moral works. The flaming torch illuminating the abyss in the card is placed between the two upward horns of Baphomet so that it illuminates the heavens. Whereas the pentagram on the head of *The Devil* points downward like his horns, Baphomet's pentagram points upward and signifies spirit, the fifth point, aligning with the torch and *true light* of heaven between the pillars (upward horns) of the *High Priestess* known as Boaz and Jachin. This is where Christ was crucified and where one can find the *Middle Way* of the Buddha.

The androgynous nature of the goat, further implied by the black and white moons, and black and white caduceus, signifies the alchemical marriage. In case of *The Devil* card, we find the two humans separated from each other, one man and one woman, and chained to the black cube. One could also surmise that Baphomet's wings are far more angelic than the demonic wings of *The Devil*. One final note about the card is that it is the fifteenth, which numerologically equates to six, reminding us of the *Magic Square of Saturn*. Hall interprets this card in the following way:

> *"The fifteenth numbered major trump is called Le Diable, the Devil, and portrays a creature resembling Pan with the horns of a ram or deer, the arms and body of a man, and the legs and feet of a goat or dragon. The figure stands upon a cubic stone, to a ring in the front of which are chained two satyrs. For a scepter this so-called demon carries a lighted torch or candle. The entire figure is symbolic of the magic powers of the astral light, or universal mirror, in which the divine forces are reflected in an inverted, or infernal, state. The demon is winged like a bar, showing that it pertains to the nocturnal, or shadow inferior sphere. The animal natures of man, in the form of a male and a female elemental, are chained to its footstool. The torch is the false light which guides unillumined souls to their own undoing. In the pseudo-Egyptian Tarot appears Typhon – a winged creature composed of a hog, a man, a bat, a crocodile, and a hippopotamus – standing in the midst of its own destructiveness and holding aloft the firebrand of the incendiary. Typhon is created by man's own misdeeds, which, turning upon their maker, destroy him."*

THE DEVIL .

Other Tarot Cards

THE MAGICIAN.

The Magician is the first numbered card in the Major Arcana after *The Fool* and his white rose. In the pseudo-Egyptian Tarot, the magician wears a golden band or uræus around his forehead, reminiscent of the Egyptian serpent headdress poised to strike forth from the *Third Eye* and alter the physical world. The infinity symbol above his head in this case implies the endless cycles of time and the candidate's journey from *The Fool* to his conquering of *The World* in card twenty-two. His tunic is held closed by a girdle in the form of *ouroboros*. The removal of this symbol in the *mysteries* signified the candidate's freedom from illusion.

The square table symbolizes the four-cornered natural world and its elements. Upon it are the magical tools: sword, wand, pentacle, and cup. In one hand he holds a wand to the Heavens, symbolic of the umbilical cord between God and man, and in the other hand a coin, which signifies the tempting nature of reality that diverts our attention from higher truths. The position of his hands, one raised *Above* and the other facing *Below*, are reminiscent of Baphomet, *The Devil* card, and Aleph א in Hebrew. The only magic being performed here is an understanding, for the first time, of the superphysical qualities of nature, and how to apply them in shaping our lives.

The Chariot depicts a victorious warrior in a cart that is usually pulled forward by two sphinxes. These two guardians of secret knowledge are contrasted by black and white, reminding us of the floor in the house of the *mysteries* and the same found in Masonic temples. A *Sphinx* is guardian of the sacred pathway to wisdom, as is the case with *Regulus*, the brightest star in the constellation Leo, the lion. In legend it is Oedipus who is confronted by this creature on his journey from between Thebes and Delphi. The *Sphinx* asks: *what creature walks on four legs in the morning, two legs at noon, and three legs in the evening?* The answer, of course, is a *human*: babies, adults, and the elderly with cane.

A starry canopy held by four columns hangs above the warrior. Pillars sustain the dome of heaven and represent the laws of nature that support society. The chariot is in the form of a cube with the warrior emerging from the center. Here we have an indication of the spirit of man rising from the tomb of materiality like Indra or Osiris. The rider holds a staff in his hand, a symbol of power like the scepter, or the magician's wand, signifying his mastery of illusion and his connection to God. He wears upon his shoulders the magical elements of *Urim* and *Thummim*. Depicted on the chariot itself are a shield offered for protection along with the winged solar disc representing the soul's ascension.

THE CHARIOT.

THE HERMIT.

The Hermit lights a path so that all other preceding cards in the Major Arcana can find their *way*, hence why he looks behind. His beard signifies wisdom and experience. The lantern symbolizes illumination of the dark and the overcoming of ignorance through seclusion and study. He carries it in his *right* hand, the true path of light. Inside of the lantern is a hexagram, a symbol of the unification of both the inferior and superior, the active and passive principles of nature. Whereas a pentagram represents man, the hexagram represents a purified man.

The staff in his left hand indicates that despite his age the journey is not entirely complete. It also represents the *support* that comes through knowledge and wisdom. The overall image represents dedication to a higher authority. Although alone, he is happy and content upon the path of spiritual enlightenment.

His head is thus bowed in humble patience, a great difference from where he began as *The Fool*. Having solved the *riddle of the Sphinx*, he has been granted access to the storehouse of wisdom guarded by that creature.

The High Priestess sits between two pillars marked by a "B" for Boaz and "J" for Jachin, those pillars used in construction of Solomon's Temple. They also signify male (Jachin) and female (Boaz), the columns of the Kabbalistic *Tree of Life*. Her position between said pillars signifies her balancing of opposing forces. Besides Hermes, messenger of the gods, the only one seated in this way can be God Himself. The cross upon her chest implies reverence. It is where the "x marks the spot," an indicator of buried treasure. Below the "x" is spiritual gold, concealed in a scroll containing the wisdom and secrets of the universe. As Mark Booth informed us earlier: *"knowledge of the secret doctrine of the Mystery schools was denoted by the holding of a rolled scroll."*

Her draped veil is that of the Static Isis: *"I, Isis Am All That Has Been, That Is Or Shall Be; No Mortal Man Hath Ever Me Unveiled."* By "no mortal man" is to be understood that a novice is not granted access to the *mysteries*, and that no one has ever been bestowed wisdom. As Hall says, "it is achieved." Her *crown* is a symbol of heavenly authority and her *throne* of earthy power. The crown itself is also composed of the *Triple Goddess*, a symbol representing the three aspects of the feminine: mother, maiden, crone. She stands on the moon, like Mary, Isis, Selene, Luna, Tsukuyomi, Máni, and Coyolxauhqui.

THE HIGH PRIESTESS.

WHEEL of FORTUNE.

The Wheel of Fortune indicates the closing of a cycle to signify *completion*. Whereas *The Hermit* card indicates a solitary life, this card signifies the opposite. It expresses positive and negative experiences, good or bad luck, and the *Yin Yang*, *Yab Yum*, and *In Yo*. The creatures on either side of the wheel itself are perceived to be ascending and descending by its turning.

The card epitomizes the four corners of the world, as exemplified by the *tetramorph*, comprised of the bull, lion, eagle, and angelic being, each examining a book. These are the four constellations of Taurus, Leo, Aquarius, and Scorpio. The same image can be seen in *The World* card, too, which depicts a nude woman draped in the red cloth and holding two wands. The *wheel* is a solar symbol that represents the daily and yearly cycles of the sun on it journey through the heavens. Resting above the wheel is a sphinx wielding a sword, the guardian of *secret teachings* and wisdom, which are personified by the light of the sun. The *Wheel of Fortune* preserves the eight *Holy Days*, and the word TARO is spelled by the points of the solstices and equinoxes. In the very center is *spirit*.

The World is the last of card in the Major Arcana. It represents youth becoming an adult, or the "coming of age." In the center is a young woman surrounded by a vesica piscis, or mandorla, representing the egg, out of which emerges new life. It is the *Osirian Seed*, *Orphic Egg*, and *Egg of Phanes*. Her legs are positioned as to depict the number four, much like *The Hanged Man* card, a symbol of the adversity that must be overcome to attain enlightenment. Four is also the *tetrad* and *tetramorph* that we once again see in each corner of the card. The circular world is surrounded by the zodiac.

The woman is partly nude, but given a reddish cloth draped around her body like a slithering serpent. This cloth is reminiscent of the scarlet robes, symbolic of the fires of life, worn by sacred women in the *Mystery Schools*. The red also represents uprightness and truth. Biblically it is also the *Red Horse* of Revelation, the heat of summer, and the two red suits in a deck of playing cards. The card itself signifies birth, life, and victory, as the youth comes of age ready to go about conquering the world. Laurel leaves are a traditional symbol of victory (*see* Apollo and Delphi), often given to great heroes. They are here surrounding the woman on all sides. Although the card is listed XXI it is really the twenty-second because *The Fool*, or the beginning of our journey, is counted as zero.

THE WORLD.

Sacred Kabbalah & 32 Paths of Wisdom

Sign	Position on Tree	Name of Planet	Greek Deity	Alchemical Metal	Symbolic Quality
♄	3	Saturn	Kronos	Lead	Time and Form
♃	4	Jupiter	Zeus	Tin	Paternal Wisdom
♂	5	Mars	Ares	Iron	Active Energy
☉	6	Sun	Helios	Gold	Harmony and Beauty
♀	7	Venus	Aphrodite	Copper	Emotional Relation
☿	8	Mercury	Hermes	Quicksilver	Reflective Intelligence
☽	9	Moon	Selene	Silver	Patterns of Instinct
⊕	10	Earth	Gaia	All of the Above	All of the Above

Kabbalists divide the universe into four worlds and four trees. *The Sephirothic Tree* has 10 globes arranged in three vertical columns that are connected by 22 channels or paths. These pathways are correlated to the 22 letters of the Hebrew alphabet, and Major Arcana of Tarot, by which through various combinations all laws of the universe are established. When combined these twenty-two paths and the ten globes equal to the sacred number thirty-two, as in the 32nd degree of Freemasonry. According to Kabbalists, all the keys of knowledge are contained in letters and numbers, and by a secret system of arrangement these would reveal the "mysteries of creation."

At the very top the *Tree* is a globe separated by the two aspects of the white and black god, as depicted by the *Great Kabbalistic Symbol of the Zohar*. It is the *Horizon of Eternity* where the worlds of darkness and light were separated at *creation*. The four central spheres are numbered one, six, nine and ten. The spheres on the left are numbered three, five and eight. The spheres on the right are numbered two, four and seven. The top sphere is *The One* and the first sphere to its right, number two, is assigned the position of *Fixed Stars*. The remaining eight are explained in the table above. In the table below are described the ten names of God with their powers and numerations called Sephiroth, along with their respective intelligences.

Name of God	Numeration	Intelligence
Eheia	Cether (essence of deity)	Metatron
Jod	Hochma (wisdom)	Raziel
Tetragrammaton	Elohim Prina (understanding)	Zaphkiel
El	Hesed (clemency)	Zadkiel
Elohim Gibor	Gebusach (judgment)	Camael
Eloha	Tiphereth (beauty)	Raphael
Adonai Sabaoth	Nezah (triumph)	Haniel
Elohim Sabaoth	Hod (honor)	Michael
Sadai	Jesod (foundation)	Gabriel
Adonai Melech	Malchuth (kingdom)	Metatron

REPRESENTATION CONTAINING THE SUM TOTAL OF THE CABALA FOR INSERTION
IN VOL. II, BOOK IV, CONCERNING CABALA OF THE HEBREWS

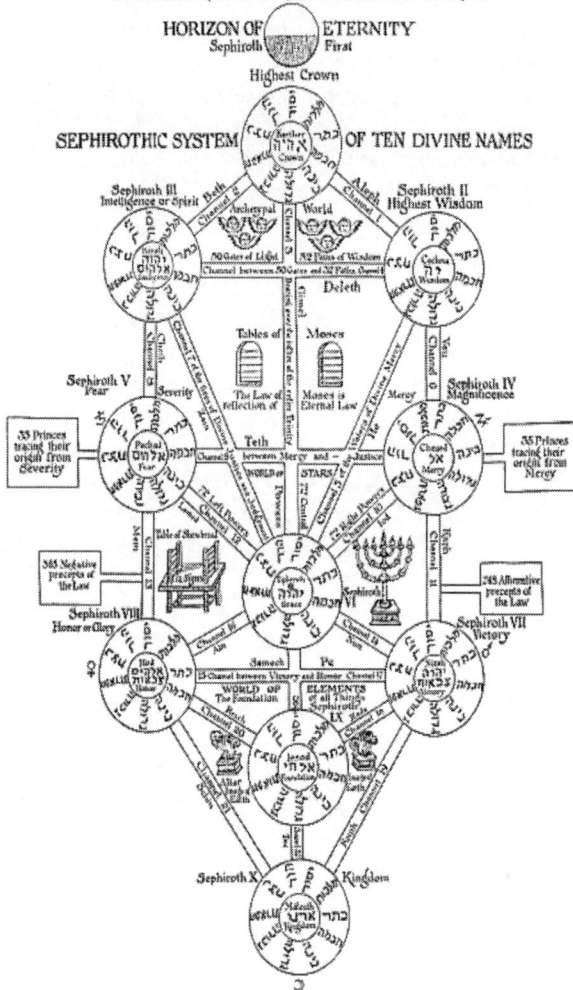

HORIZON OF   ETERNITY
Sephiroth   First
First

Highest Crown

SEPHIROTHIC SYSTEM   OF TEN DIVINE NAMES

KETHER is the power of God, the initial emanation that produced all of existence. Within this *Supreme Crown* there are two principles, one active ad another passive, one male and another female. These are the twin forces of the universe. Below the uppermost sphere of the *Tree of Life* are also an active force and a passive force.

The active force **HOKMAH** is positive and rests behind *movement* and *growth*. Hokmah is "wisdom." Its opposite is **BINAH**, the passive principle remaining *stable* and *unchanging*. Binah is "understanding." The mingling of these forces in the primordial waters brought forth life. Therefore, Hokmah is *Father* of the universe and Binah is the *Mother*.

Beyond the three initial spheres are the trinity of father, mother, and child. Here we find **HESED**, a just and forgiving force, and its opposite, **GEBURAH**, also a symbol of authority, but a destructive force and necessary evil. Hesed is "love" and Geburah is "power." Their equilibrium is **TIFARETH**, traditionally held as a sphere of the solar principle. Tifareth is the child of Hesed and Geburah, representing the urge to survive and the vital energy compelling life to continuously progress forward. Tifareth signifies "beauty."

David Conway explains in <u>Ritual Magic</u> how Tifareth attains adulthood and brings us to the next two spheres, or the third triangle of the *Tree*. Here we find the male **NETSAH**, a force encouraging survival. It urges a continuation of life despite its hardships, and represents passions, instincts, and primeval desires. Netsah is "triumph of endurance." Its opposite force here is the female principle known as **HOD**. This power deals with mental activity while very little of its essence deals with sensory perceptions. Hod is "majesty." Creating equilibrium between the two previous spheres is **YESOD**, which represents "balance."

The final sphere at the root of the Tree is **MALKUTH**, the "kingdom." David Conway explains of this lower sphere: *"Its source, it is true, is lost in the light of the eternal, but we need not despair of reaching that light. We are a part of it. Indeed, being a composite symbol of the universe, the tree can be used to help us draw closer to the fountainhead. We can use it too as our guide to the astral world whenever we choose to leave the sphere of Malkuth; for by recollecting the pattern of the tree we may safely go ahead and explore the astral without any risk of losing our way."*

The *Infinite* or *All* is named *Ain Soph* (ain = *nothing*) in the *Kabbalah*. According to tradition, and as described in <u>The Tree of Life</u> by Israel Regardie, this *infinite potential* is not a *Spirit* or *Will*, but an "underlying cause of both." *Ain Soph* is not a force of *matter* but "that which underlies them." It is their fundamental *Cause*. Regardie provides one of the clearer and more precise descriptions of the *Tree* by breaking down the bulbs of the structure and explaining their relationship with numbers:

> *"It was the view of several Magicians that by the ideas expressed in number was Nature conceived in the bosom of infinite space. From these ideas or universals issued the primordial elements, the immense cycles of time, the cosmic bodies, and all the host of heavenly changes."*

It goes without critical analysis that zero represents the infinite space that gives way to various intelligences and branches of *Sephiroth*, the *spheres of light*. The first emanations initiate *manifestation* and provide balance in the *Pillar of Beneficience*.

The "Cosmic Metaphysical Center" of this emanating "tree" is known as *Kether*, which becomes the first number (1). In the *Zohar* this center is known as *The Concealed One*. It is the central sphere of manifestation, the top of our *Tree*, from whence all branches come out of. It is the *Logos* that we know as *order* and *knowledge*. As the branches grow downward the number (1) splits into duality, the two principles that become permanent throughout all lower spheres. In other words, the androgynous splits into what we refer to as men and women, or precisely speaking, the *father* and *mother*.

Kether, the Crown, flows into the *Pillar of Mercy* where we find *Chokmah*, our number (2). Across the tree through the central pillar is a connection to *Binah*, our number (3), which initiates the *Pillar of Severity* as it flows from the *Crown* through the second sphere. *Chokmah* is "wisdom" and the "father," *Binah* is "understanding" and the "mother." Regardie explains that the four letters of YHVH, or Tetragrammaton, are here associated with the father and mother principles. The former is given the letter "Y" to its name and the latter is given "H." From these two principles comes the child, or *"from consciousness and its vehicle are all things formed."* All of these "things" are what we refer to as the *material world* and they develop outward from the father and mother through the next seven spheres of light on the *Tree*. This is likely one of the main sources, or the source, for the sacredness of the number seven in relation to creation. These first three spheres, (Kether, Chokmah, Binah) are considered unique and "Supernal" in the sense that they have less of a relationship with the material world than the others.

The fourth Sephiroth is known as *Chesed* and means "grace." It flows downward from *Chokmah* on the *Pillar of Mercy* though its number (4).

The fifth Sephiroth is known as *Geburah* and means "might." The fourth and fifth unite in flow to the sixth sphere. This sphere is known as *Tiphareth*, which in Hebrew means "beauty" and "harmony." This *harmony* is the *balance* provided to the former forces. Regardie adds, *"in the human being Tiphareth, the harmonious emanation of the Sun, is the Sephirah of the soul of Man, the center of the microcosmic system, and the luminous intermediary between the brooding spirit above and the body with the instincts below."* Speaking on the Tetragrammaton, the third letter "V" is assigned to this sixth sphere of light. It comprises the second trinity of the *Tree* in that of *Chesed*, *Geburah* and *Tiphareth*. The first, of course, being *Kether*, *Chokmah* and *Binah*. The third triad is comprised first of *Netzach* (7), which means "triumph" or "victory." The next sphere is *Hod* (8), meaning "splendor." Seven is male and eight is female. The third sphere of this third and final trinity is the ninth sphere known as *Yesod*, which is "stability" in "change." It is Lunar in nature and associated with *Astral Light*: all things form here before being crystalized in the final sphere.

The final sphere is *Malkuth,* or "kingdom," the tenth representing finalization and crystallization. It is tangible to the senses and *"all the qualities of the preceding planes."* Regardie refers to this tenth sphere as Bridge, *"the Daughter, and the Virgin of the World."* It is the final letter "H" in Tetragrammaton.

For every virtue of the ten Sephiroth, there are an equal number of vices. The twenty-two paths of the *Tree* are called *Navitoth* and along with the ten emanations form the 32 *Paths of Wisdom.* The *Sephiroth* are receptive and feminine, and the *Navitoth* are assertive and masculine. Between the left *Pillar of Severity* and the right *Pillar of Mercy* is the *Middle Pillar of Mildness* known as *THE WAY.* Chic Cicero and Sandra Tabatha Cicero write in <u>Golden Dawn Magic</u> about the famed Serpent of Wisdom and the Tree:

> *"The Flaming Sword is the descending current of divine energy that facilitates the manifestation of the Universe. It is the Way of Involution of the descent of Spirit into matter. The Serpent of Wisdom, on the other hand, is the counterbalancing ascent of materialized energy. This is the Way of Evolution from matter back to its Divine Source."*

The Inverted Sephiroth Tree, by Robert Fludd.

For a clearer understanding of the esoteric Hebrew writings known as <u>Zohar</u>, we will take an extract from Joseph Campbell's <u>A Hero With A Thousand Faces</u>:

The Zohar (zohar, "light, splendor") is a collection of esoteric Hebrew writing, given to the world about 1305 by a learned Spanish Jew, Moses de Leon. It was claimed that the material had been drawn from secret original;, going back to the teachings of Simeon ben Yohai, a rabbi of Galilee in the second century A.D. Threatened with death by the Romans, Simeon had hidden for twelve years in a cave; ten centuries later his writings had been found there, and these were the sources of the books of the Zohar.

Simeon's teachings were supposed to have been drawn from the hokmah nistarah or hidden wisdom of Moses, i.e., a body of esoteric lore first studied by Moses in Egypt, the land of his birth, then pondered by him during his forty years in the wilderness (where he received special instruction from an angel), and finally incorporated cryptically in the first four books of the Pentateuch, from which it can be extracted by a proper understanding and manipulation of the mystical number-values of the Hebrew alphabet. This lore and the techniques for re-discovering and utilizing it constitute the cabala.

It is said that the teachings of the cabala (qabbalah, "received or traditional lore") were first entrusted by God himself to a special group of angels in Paradise. After Man had been expelled from the Garden, some of these angels communicated the lessons to Adam, thinking to help him back to felicity thereby. From Adam the teaching passed to Noah, and from Noah to Abraham. Abraham let some of it slip from him while he was in Egypt, and that is why this sublime wisdom can now be found in reduced form in the myths and philosophies of the gentiles. Moses first studied it with the priests of Egypt, but the tradition was refreshed in him by the special instructions of his angels.

far Eastern Magic & the Paranormal

Nihon no Mahō - 日本の魔法

The above title translates as *Nihon* (Japan 日本), *no* (possessive の), *Mahō* (magic, sorcery, witchcraft 魔法) – *Japanese Magic*. Little is known in the western world of eastern occult traditions with exception maybe to the <u>I Ching</u>, or *Book of Changes*, and the classic Hindu texts: <u>Bhagavad Gita</u>, <u>Mahabharata</u>, and the <u>Vedas</u>. Perhaps one is familiar with Taoism too. But besides a few animal symbols here and a few monsters there, or healing practices like acupuncture and yoga, ancient eastern magical practices are relatively unknown in the west or completely lost even to the regions of their origin. The "secrets" of Masonry are also believed to have largely been lost. What we call *magic*, even in the west, is also still defined as folklore in general and so it is not always set aside as some metaphysical practice. In fact, whether in the east or west we find that the *supernatural* is ultimately quite *natural*. When acquiring material on such a subject it becomes clear that a western view of magic may be far more corrupted than an eastern view for this reason, because the natural worldview is still far more preserved in the Buddhist east than it is in the Christian west.

Western practices are also more popular due to the spreading of Islam and Christianity, not to mention the power of the United States as it has been exerted around the world. Furthermore, virtually all the greatest "magical minds" that anyone can think of come from the west of Asia, perhaps with exception to the Russian (Ukrainian born) Helena Petrovna Blavatsky or the infamous Grigori Rasputin. There is some manner of semantics involved here, too, because Russia is technically in both Europe and Asia. Something similar can be said of India, a vast region of southern Asia, that is often separated geographically in the magical world into its own region. It is true that much sacred wisdom came from the western Jewish world, as in the Kabbalah, which was extracted from the Egyptian and Mesopotamian *mysteries*, but also from the eastern *mysteries* of India that Levi calls *"the Kabbalah in profanation."* And the same can be said of human history in general, which certainly at its core is likely to have spawned from India and China rather than Africa. Perhaps we should then refer to "eastern magic" in this section as "far eastern magic," since we willingly acknowledge the contributions India has made but specifically focusing on Japan. Regional differences in geography, cultural customs, societal norms, and philosophical world views, are things that largely separate *western magic* from *eastern magic* so far as we are concerned in this section. None of these differences, however, are any better or worse than any other.

Japanese Kuji Magic

The Japanese *do-man* is a magical grid comprised of nine lines drawn one at a time starting with a horizontal stroke, then vertical, and so forth moving right and then down. Each line corresponds to a concept within the sacred Japanese system of *Kuji*, defined as a series of simple mantras. It is broken into four parts that include the nine basic "words of power," the *Kuji In* (mudra) hand gestures corresponding to those nine words, the protective grid known as *Kuji Kiri*, and a tenth symbol known as *Juji*. In numerology, there are also nine forces connected to the numbers one through nine, the very number of gods in the Egyptian Ennead. There is also the *Nine Emperor Gods Festival* celebrated throughout various Asian countries as an honoring of Dou Mu, goddess of the

North Star who holds the registrar of life and death. The nine knots of the *Witches' Ladder* talisman, comprised of red string, are also said to bring protection just as the *Red String of Fate* (*unmei no akai ito*) in Japan ties all things and people together.

The "words of power" are Rin, Pyo, Toh, Sha, Kai, Jin, Retsu, Zai, and Zen. Nine hand gestures accompany them. When applied to the *do-man* pattern they establish a symbolic base for which the tenth symbol can be placed. The *Juji* is an ideogram placed over the grid that holds the intention of the practitioner and what they seek to accomplish. For example, the symbol for dragon (*Ryū* - 龍) can be placed over the *do-man* when seeking protection from water, or the symbol for victory (*Shō* - 勝) can be used when seeking the success.

Any *spell* can be completed with the sound *A-UN*! This is like Amun, Amon-Ra, or AMEN.

Number	Japanese	Pronunciation
1	臨	Rin
2	兵	Pyo
3	闘	Toh
4	者	Sha
5	皆	Kai
6	陣	Jin
7	列	Retsu
8	在	Zai
9	前	Zen

From left to right: *Kuji* "words of power" and the *Kuji Kiri* protection grid, which can be cut into the air or written on the palm or paper.

Credit for these images goes entirely to Antony Cummins and his wonderful book, <u>The Dark Side of Japan</u>, published in 2017 by Amberley Books.

Chinese Ku Magic

There are, of course, darker forms of magic that are just as ancient in this region of the world. The dark magic (*Kokumajutsu*) of *Ku* is considered particularly malicious in Japanese lore, probably because it originates in China. The term "KU" is also like "KUJI." The root of the former means "warehouse" while the latter root of "ku" means "ward" and the entire word "kuji" means "lottery." From the idea of a *warehouse* or *ward* we acquire the notion of *storehouses of energy* or what magicians may refer to as *reservoirs*. Antony Cummins put it simply in <u>The Dark Side of Japan: Ancient Black Magic, Folklore, Ritual</u>, when he wrote, "*Ku magic is very evil.*" Interestingly, the Greek and English "K" is eleven, and thus evil or dark. In more detail, he explains how this magic is practiced, though it should be noted that any *Kokumajutsu* (黒魔術) should be left untouched:

> "*To practice this you are to collect as many venomous creatures as possible and place them all in a pot together. After a while of fighting and feasting only one creature will be left alive; this is the Ku animal. This creature can bring you riches but it can also kill your enemy with ease… This Ku creature is a powerful entity and is difficult to destroy. It is said that through it a magician will gain wealth and power and that any souls that the creature kills will serve the magician and not go on to the afterlife.*"

Hotsuma Tsutaye

In 1966 a man named Yoshinosuke Matsumoto found a rare historical and literary gem in a Tokyo bookstore. What he stumbled over that day is now known, after much translation and research, as the Hotsuma Tsutaye, an epic poem written in a peculiar, and seemingly beyond-ancient, script. The text is fragmented, and it is unknown if the authenticity is completely genuine. However, there are many fascinating components to the stories within that seem to confirm other ancient, or pre-ancient, histories. *Hotsuma Tsutaye* speaks from the *age of the kami*, beings described not as

The *woshite* syllabary, as published in The Sacred Science of Ancient Japan by Avery Morrow.

immaterial spirits, but as semi-immortal nobles who descended from the great north. The script utilized is called *woshite*, which was used in ancient Japan according to parahistorians. The *Hotsuma Tsutaye* was reportedly deposited in the same shrine where the Kujiki-72 was found. It was translated into Classical Chinese by Yūnoshin Ibo and released in 1775, only later to be rediscovered in 1966. In 1992 a man named Takao Ibo found the original Ibo manuscript near his home: he was the descendant of Yūnoshin Ibo. Described in the various versions and interpretations of this ancient writing is something akin to all other occult studies. Man is described as a combination of elements: space, wind, fire, water, and stone. The *Way of Heavenly Being*, or *Ame-naru-Michi*, is described as an understanding of writing and books. The soul is said to be bound to a human body but ultimately it belongs to another world. After death it is released and can either return to its point of origin or inhabit another body. The *Hotsuma Tsutaye* also details a chart used to predict the future. This method of divination is called *futomani*.

The *futomani* divination chart, supposedly used to predict future events in pre-history.

Supernatural Japan & the *Hitsuki Shinji* Manuscript

The Japanese tend to identify themselves as non-religious, even when they practice Shintō as a way of life, despite the fact Buddhism and Christianity are very popular in the country. Since Shintō itself, the indigenous belief of Japan, is not defined as a religion, spiritual practice, or philosophy, it is hard to categorize the practice, except to say that it preserves a piece of the old world largely snuffed out in the west. Belief in the supernatural is famous on these islands and so Shintō has acted as an unofficial container of a far eastern worldview that is rooted in what we would call *natural magic* in the west. The word translates to "True-Way" or "Kami-Way," signifying the presence of the supernatural in *everything* and the importance of honoring nature, ancestors, community, and personal responsibilities. In modern Japan this is certainly not universal, but there is still a strong focus within the country to preserve nature and her supernatural forces that takes on a different feeling than environmentalism in the west. For many living in the western world, where ghosts and monsters may be of interest but are mostly relegated to the

Yuki-onna from the *Hyakkai-Zukan* picture scroll by Sawaki Suushi.

"fringe," the eastern world is still haunted by such specters, even if due only to tradition. This is especially relevant in Japan, where otherworldly forces still inhabit everyday locations. This is not only true in Japan, but for our brief overview of *Nihon no Mahō* it is appropriate to note. What follows is a brief overview of Japan's supernatural terminology.

Monsters are given the generic term *yōkai*, which could refer to *Bakemono, Obake,* or *Kaii Gensho,* all three meaning a *changeling.* Small goblin-like creatures are known as *Kappa* and the *Tengu* are demi-demons appearing like long-nosed goblins, dogs, or sometimes half-human-half-crow entities. *Tengu* are known to steal people and return them in a sort of irrational state of mind, and when this happens it is called *tengu-kakushi* (to be *hidden* by *tengu*). Interestingly, the Greek letter *kappa* is thought to represent bad luck, sickness, and death.

Spirits of the dead are known as *shi-ryo* (死霊), said to only be active at night. *Spirits of the living* are known as *iki-ryo* (生霊). Generally, the Japanese refer to all spirits as *Kami.*

One Japanese vampire is called *Yuki-onna,* a pale, white-skinned woman with raven black hair and blood-red lips. Although the personification of cold and snow, sometimes called *snow woman,* she also shares similarities in myth with *Yamamba* witch and the *Ubume,* a deity associated with childbirth and motherhood. The mother of all demons is *Kishimojin* or *Kishimonji,* who takes either the form of the patron goddess of children and motherhood, or a demon that cannibalizes children with striking similarities to the Mesopotamian and Judaic Lamashtu-Lilith. A common protector of children is the guardian deity *Jizo.* There is also another vampiric creature we would just call a *mosquito.* This monster was *"sentenced to drink blood due to transgressions in a previous life,"* according to Antony Cummins. In other words, the spirit acting through the insect must consume blood, or *life,* for atonement. Another horrifying monster, *jikininki,* is a soul cursed by its corporeal greed to consume men in a fashion reminiscent of the Wendigo.

Possessions in Japan may seem slightly different by western standards where evil demons with wings and sharp teeth take control of the body. In Japan, possession by fox (*kitsune-tsuki*) and dog (*inu-tsuki* or *inu-gami-mouchi*) are common. Possession by fox was once thought so serious that Salem-witch-like hunts and trials were prevalent!

Other malevolent influences may come from the *Goryo* or *Goryi-shin*, spirits of once noble people who now intend to create disease, war, and chaos. The *Yamamba* is a classic mountain demon or hag with supernatural powers. She is like the *Baba Yaga* of Slavic tradition or the Chinese devil *Momo*. Interestingly, the Japanese fox-witch is known as *Tamamo no Maye* or *Tamamo no Mae*, wherein we find the Chinese word *mo*, meaning "do not." This Japanese witch takes the form not of a black cat but of a nine-tailed fox. In some depictions of witches, we find that their fingertips have become darkened. Perhaps her *idle hands have become tools of the Devil*. Black fingertips indeed indicate her pact with infernal forces, but also relate to a Japanese belief that under the fingernails, particularly the thumb, there is a gateway for spirits to enter the body. Perhaps this was a metaphor urging cleanliness. The nine-tailed fox motif is found also in Korea where ghosts are called *gwisin* (*yuryeong*).

One particularly terrifying creature, the *Baku*, is more like Meister Eckhart's devils that *"are really angels setting your spirit free."* It is the *eater of dreams* like the *Sandman*. By putting a picture of the *Baku* (Obaku) on your wall, or writing its name on your pillow, you essentially invoke the power of a *dream catcher*.

Poltergeists are also an issue in Japanese tradition, but simple methods can be used to rid the home of these spirits. One must begin with the heart sutra *gyate gyate haragyate haragyate bochi sowaka* and repeat it one hundred times. Next, a promise must be offered to the dead that their wishes will be granted, and finally the nine "words of power" should be said. Much like the sacred names of *Adonai, Jesus Christ*, and *Tetragrammaton* are used to dispel evil, we can also use the name of the Buddha - *Nembutsu* - to accomplish the same. The Japanese *Bean-throwing Festival* helps to rid homes of malevolent forces by the throwing of roasted soya beans outside while chanting, *"Demons leave – luck, please enter."* These beans are an offering, i.e., the *treat* offered instead of the *trick*. Oftentimes these spirits are simply *yōkai* that have taken possession of everyday objects, or what the Japanese call *tsukumogami*. These fantastical and comical characters are prevalent in nearly all fairytales, folklore, and mythology, with one of the best examples being those animated objects from *Beauty and the Beast*.

Exorcisms were also performed in Japan, usually by a *samurai* and their sword. With a prayer and the cutting of air above an inflicted person's head, the demon was considered exorcised. The process is called *katana-kagi* (sword key) and meant to sever the connection a malevolent spirit has with the human body.

The ritual sacrifice known as *seppuku* is suicide by disembowelment from a sword. To prevent suffering, a *kaishakunin* assisted with the process to make death swift. Samurai women performed the same ritual of *seppuku* by sticking a dagger in their throats. Perhaps the most famous ritual sacrifice involving the self is what we call *hara-kiri*, appropriately pronounced *ha-ra-kee-ree* since the "i" sounds like an "e" in Japanese. Both words mean the same, but the Japanese prefer *seppuku*.

Bad luck and sins could be cleansed away with basic purification techniques using water. One tradition involves a square section of white cloth whereupon a person's name was written in black ink. Four sticks of equal size would then be placed into the ground near a stream and the cloth attached with name facing upward. A ladle was placed next to the setup so that anyone passing by could pour water over the name, eventually washing away the *sins* of that person.

Japanese Talismans (*omamori*) are meant to protect their user from bad dreams, evil spirits, curses, robbery, etc. They can be prepared by using the ideogram for demon 鬼 with additional characters being added for whatever is required or thought necessary: returning a curse, recovering from disease, living longer, attracting women, or obtaining good luck.

Some Japanese myths relate to the Bible: Luke 9 tells of how Jesus multiplied "five loaves of bread and two fish," and Daniel 3 tells of the story of Shadrach, Meshach, and Abednego being put "into the blazing fiery furnace" only to be protected by Christ. Both stories are reminiscent of a necromancer in the east called Saji, who was unharmed by flames and could produce fish from a bowl of clean water.

Certain divinatory practices in Japan include reading a turtle shell crack or observing smoke from a fire. The reading of *chi* within smoke was done by an esoteric tactician called *gunbaisha*. The same could be done with flags blowing in the wind. There is also the practice of placing a bowl of rice on top of a tripod comprised of three bamboo sticks. The words "*kokkuri-sama, kokkuri-sama, please descend, please descend, please descend quickly,*" are then chanted before questions are asked. The tilt of the stand signifies either yes, by lifted leg, or no, by zero movement.

Legend has it that during a 1944 parahistorical meeting in Japan, where branches were used to make divinatory marks in sand, something called the *Sun-Moon Revelation* was obtained. Like a Ouija board, the letters AM, HI, TSU, KU were spelled out when the operators asked who they were speaking with. Tenmei Okamoto eventually traced this name to a shrine near Tokyo. Once there he reportedly began an automatic writing session, which resulted in the *Hitsuki Shinji* manuscript. The spirit of divination was said to have been the Abrahamic God who informed Okamoto that the world was run by dark forces called *Ishiya*. The spirit also revealed an interesting piece of data, not only about Japan, which was forecast to lose World War II, but of the entire spiritual nature of man. It said that many citizens of Japan are loyal to foreign lands, while "*some are children of kami even in foreign lands.*" Perhaps this was an unconscious projection of the *lost heart* of the Japanese people, something that would certainly have been thought in the 1940s. Below is a partial English translation of the revelation, followed by a fragment of the *Hitsuki Shinji* manuscript in its native writing:

Behold! Fuji has driven off clouds of chaos, and all heavens are cleared.

The time has come at last when true God of kingdom of ☉ will show His mighty power. Buddhism, Christianity, and even Islamism shall be united for this sacred mission.

There shall be no need of difficult theories nor logics, neither any hardship of livelihood. God will provide you such a happy and merry world, therefore, seek after the truth with earnestness, purifying your spirit incessantly. However, there lies a tribulation before the Kingdom of God comes. Unless you are purified and cleansed, you shall not be able to preserve yourself through this tribulation. Because this is the tribulation, such as was not since the very beginning of the world to this time, nor shall ever be. And the end of this tribulation shall never be brought unless God's power is revealed.

Everything that shall happen from now on is absolutely beyond the capacity of human conception.

Kingdom consisted of purified souls shall gain real power, however, kingdom of dirty spirit shall not be able dominant anymore.

Cities must be purified and the rustic place must be purifies as well, but the most significant of all is the purification of man.

The *Hitsuki Shinji* manuscript.

Possibly a *kamiyo moji* or *jindai moji*, a Japanese script from the age of Kami, i.e., the *Golden Age.*

Philologist Atsutane Hirata examined numerous ancient scripts from Japan and found many to be forgeries. The one here is dubbed *Ahiru script* and believed to be the most authentic. However, it is admittedly like Korean *Hangul script*, and so skeptics shun its authenticity.

The Book of Changes

The Yijing, known also as Yi-Ching or I-Ching, is one of the *Five Classics*, a set of ancient Chinese texts. Dating to the 12th-century BCE, the material is focused on a divinatory practice used by wizards of the Zhou dynasty (1064-256 BCE). It comprises 64 symbolic hexagrams that reveal an understanding of nature and thus the methods by which to learn of and influence future events. Each hexagram is formed by combining pairs of the eight basic trigrams called *bagua*, a group of three lines that are broken or unbroken to represent *Yin* (female energy) or *Yang* (male energy). The hexagrams were supposedly discovered by China's first mythical emperor Fu Xi, or Fuxi, who derived them from the shell of a tortoise.

A hexagram is built from top to bottom by casting lots. Unbroken lines are phallic, represent *yang*, and are given the number nine. Broken lines are yonic, represent *yin*, and are given the number six. The eight trigrams are further related to one of the following: earth, mountain, water, wind, thunder, fire, lake, and heaven, all qualities that provide necessary context to any interpretation of the oracle. In a painting of Fu Xi, now in the National Museum, Taipei, Taiwan, you can see the first hexagram in the bottom left corner and the mythical tortoise in the bottom right corner.

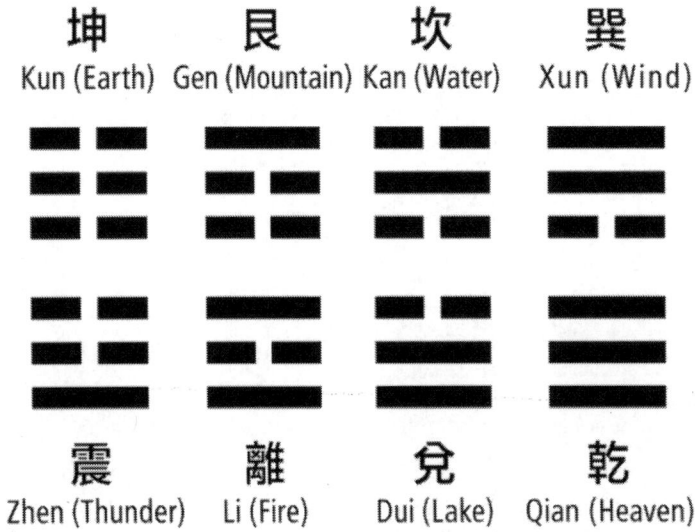

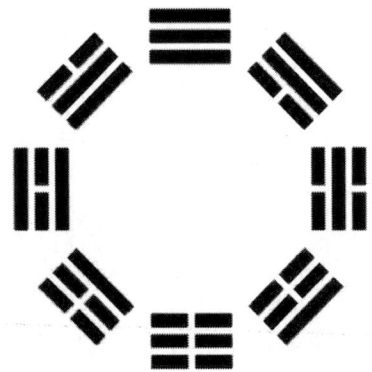

坤   艮   坎   巽
Kun (Earth)   Gen (Mountain)   Kan (Water)   Xun (Wind)

震   離   兌   乾
Zhen (Thunder)   Li (Fire)   Dui (Lake)   Qian (Heaven)

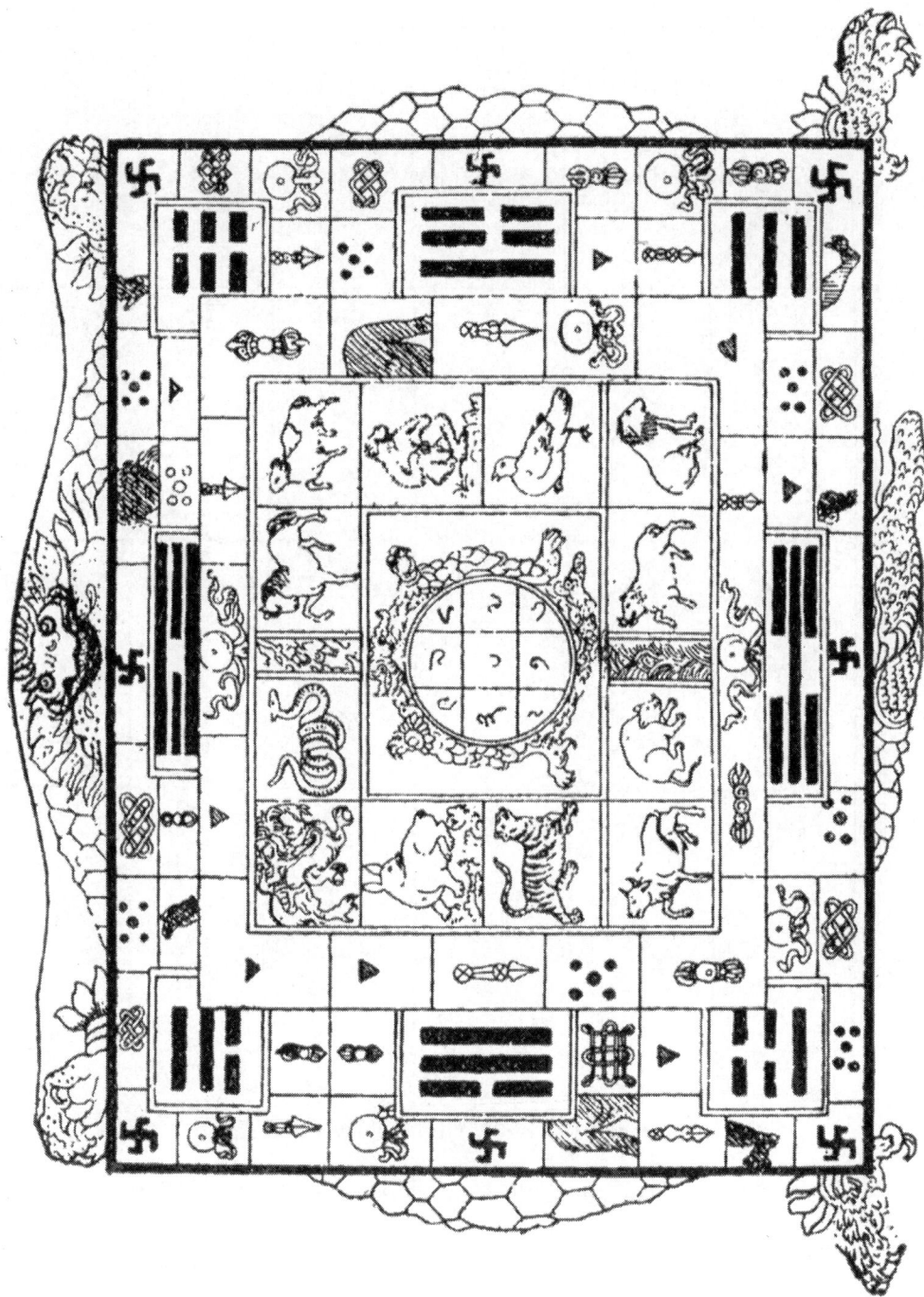

A mystical table from Tibet containing the eight trigrams on top of a large tortoise, accompanied by the twelve Chinese zodiac signs.

星	參	胃	室	牛	心	東角
張	井北	昴	壁	女	尾	亢
巽	鬼	畢	奎西	虛	箕	氐
軫	柳	嘴	婁	危	南斗	房

From the *Book of Ninja*, 1676.

This table shows the twenty-eight lunar mansions according to the Japanese.

These are the 28 positions in the nighttime sky identified by 28 different constellations.

This chart was used to map a lunar month.

With a solar calendar it assisted in structuring the entire year.

Occult Japan: Shintoism & The Kami Way

"…the kami-faith is one that is maintained through the observance of traditional ways rather than by overt propaganda."

- Dr. Sokyo Ono –

Shintō

There are countless religions, faiths, doctrines, dogmas, cults, and the like throughout the world. Some may qualify to be termed "religion" while others "cult.". Often the two overlap each other, though a *cult* is not necessarily a dark and sinister organization. In fact, a *cult* is merely a system of religious veneration directed at a particular figure or object. Likewise, a *doctrine* may be associated with a *religion* or *faith* even if it has no other religious affiliation. As a set of beliefs held and sometimes taught to others, what *doctrine* amounts to is simply *a way of thinking or living*. One could see doctrine, separate from the rigidity of dogma, as a philosophy to be experienced and lived rather than followed.

But these *words* - our attempts to explain and label the spiritual nature of existence - are unsatisfactory in explaining some *philosophies*. Buddhism, for example, is technically a religion and a philosophy but fundamentally it is simply a *state of being*. For our treatment of any spiritual matter,

Common Shintō Shrine

however, we must be willing to walk away from definitions and from the etymology we employ in attempting to define those things we maintain as *belief*. This is not to say that words are in opposition of the divine. On the contrary, words, which are symbols we express in writing and with sound, are the foundational elements of Creation, i.e., the *Word of God*. Attempting to understand the *Word* and all of *Creation* certainly requires grounding in the physical, but most importantly it requires the necessity of looking beyond that into the spiritual.

The Japanese word *kotodama,* or "spirit of the word," is an expression of this idea. We must, therefore, let ourselves be guided by *spirit*, that thing which permeates all the *cosmos*. Shintō (Shintōism) is the domestic "religious system" of Japan. It is known by name throughout much of the world but few, including adherents locally, could provide an absolute definition of its traditions outside of generalities or historical timelines. Shintō is a practice that preserves and maintains the individual, community, and country, through a system of gratitude, duty, and reverence for nature.

Here we have a *doctrine* which is more focused on *tradition* than a *belief* based on *dogmatic faith*. Shintō, in simplistic terms, may sound familiar to many *spiritual* philosophies, as Motohisa Yamakage writes in The Essence of Shinto: *"In Shinto, heaven, earth, and humanity are different manifestation of one life energy."* In other words, we are ONE and the ONE is ALL.

Those unfamiliar with Shintō may find it peculiar, not because of its differences from their own beliefs, or due to its foreign or eastern appeal, but because it has virtually none of the hallmarks of what we would classify as *religion*. In essence, it is the veneration of nature and a practical belief in the existence of Kami (*divine beings* or *lords*). Since *nature* was created by Kami it can be inferred that this is their domain, i.e., in the trees, rocks, waters, mountains, etc. An 18th-century scholar named Motoori Norinaga has provided one of the clearest definitions of kami:

> *"Speaking in general, however, it may be said that kami signifies, in the first place, the deities of heaven and earth that appear in the ancient records and also the shrines where they are worshipped. It is hardly necessary to say that it includes human beings. It also includes such objects as birds, beasts, trees, plants, seas, mountains, and so forth. In ancient usage, anything whatsoever which was outside the ordinary, which possessed superior power or which was awe-inspiring was called kami."*

> *"The kami of the divine age were for the most part human beings of that time and, because the people of that time were all kami, it is called the Age of the Gods (kami)."*

Avery Morrow describes the Kami in his book, The Sacred Science of Ancient Japan, as *"referring to great heroes of the past, to a sort of Greek pantheon living outside our physical world, to a single, cosmic spirit. Kami created the world, but also inhabit it."*

There are Kami of simple tasks, Kami of sacred places, and ancestral Kami, among others. They are believed to permeate in all of nature, from humans and animals to plants, each functioning and operating as part of a chain or hierarchy encompassing the ALL. They are broken into three categories: *amatsukami* (heavenly Kami of *Takamagahara*, adobe of heavenly gods), *kunitsukami* (earthly Kami), and *yaoyorozu no kami* (many other Kami). However, Shintō is not really a polytheistic or monotheistic system, and in fact there really is no *system*.

Kami, no matter in what form or category, are creative expressions of life and honoring them, i.e., nature especially, is a duty. We are obligated by life itself. As with Akhenaten's religious reorganization of Egypt, Shintō is more of a rationale monotheism wherein all Kami are part of a hierarchy under one supreme deity called *Amenominakanushi no okami*. This name may also encourage recall of the Egyptian Amen-RA (although the Kami name is broken up as such: Ame-no-Minakanushi). Either way, Shintō *"is at once polytheistic and monotheistic."*

Practice of Shintō is an *intention* to connect our internal mind and external body with that of the external world. The purpose of worship is *"not to impose a single idea or belief system, but to create a pervasive sense of reverence and awe,"* for the practitioner to more easily *"access the spiritual dimension."* This is done in a manner largely unlike any other religion or spiritual practice, as Motohisa Yamakage explains:

> *"In Shinto, it is important for each person to experience and feel in his or her own way and not to use language to force others to believe in a certain way."*

Likewise, *"It does not matter how one believes in and chooses to describe the divine power or powers, as long as that belief is not used to justify destructive ambition, or to do evil to others."* Occultists may therefore recognize that Shintō shares a closer relationship with Freemasonry than with any religion, since in the former Order it does not matter how one identifies the *Highest Authority,* so long as a belief is maintained in the *Cosmic Mind* – note: not destructive divinity.

Shintō has zero dogma, doctrine, codes, laws, Commandments, guilt, or even *suffering* as is the case in Buddhism. Shintōists see life and humans as inherently *good* while *"misfortune is associated with all that is warped, curved, or crooked, including one's own mind and heart."* This "curved spirit" is called *magatsubi,* the cause of evil deeds, diseases, disasters, misfortunes, etc. As a result, there is no karmic influence in Shintō, and ultimately *"living in the world is a positive experience,"* though *"it is not regarded as the only reality,"* and thus, *"never should the present and power of an 'unseen' world be denied."*

There is a parallel here between this eastern philosophy and the western Neoplatonic view that matter itself is not evil, but becomes evil when pursued as an end. On the other hand, Gnostic sects tend to see matter as inherently evil, a theme found in Buddhism which lives in harmony with Shintō in Japan.

Shintō has neither a Devil nor a deity likened to Satan. But there are Japanese names for these characters. An *Oni* is akin to an ogre, orc, troll, demon, or general devil. In Japanese folklore this *Oni* is a type of *yōkai,* described as a sort of fairy, sprite, demon, or other supernatural entity. The word *akuma* applies to both the Devil as a demon and to the character we know as Satan (Hebrew śāṭān), the accuser or the adversary.

According to Motohisa Yamakage, *evil* is split into two categories: *amatsu tsumi* (moral and social crimes) and *kunitsu tsumi* (lesser crimes). How we choose to act - morally or immorally - and whether we seek *purification,* is ultimately a determining factor in our spiritual development in any religion. In Shintō, however, as with certain practices such as Buddhism, this concept is simplified:

> *"Good or moral behavior is associated with balance of mind, body, and spirit; evil or immoral behavior with imbalance, be it spiritual, intellectual, or physical."*

Shintō likewise has no polarizing, and often confusing non-polarizing, version of heaven or hell: the light and warmth of heaven as opposed to a bright fiery pit; hell is traditionally a dark ice palace. Here the Japanese names are *sora* (sky), *tengoku* (heaven), or *ame* (heaven), for *Heaven,* and *jigoku* for *Hell.* The adobe of the heavenly gods is *Takamagahara.* The word *Yomi* also applies to Hell since it is the Japanese *underworld.* The *hidden world,* or that of spirit, is called *Yukai.*

Sin is another non-factor in Shintō, though there is a word for the concept, *zaiaku,* which can also be translated as *guilt.* But the only *sin* or *guilt* found in Shintō is a result of neglecting the Kami and one's duties: neglecting family and ancestors, neglecting nature, neglecting responsibilities, etc. All the *evil* and *sin* in the world is a result of Kami and therefore Shintō is concerned with harmonizing the *self* with the *natural world,* both of which are inherently *good.*

Ritual cleansing is meant to wash away all *kegare* (uncleanliness, impurity, pollution) and to make a shrine - be it a natural location or home shrine (*kamidana*) – and both body and mind, fit for the presence of Kami. It's the same reason we dress nicely to attend any religious service; we are in the presence of God. Sin, therefore, could be expressed as lacking *kiyome,* a state of cleanliness, clearness, and beauty. Otherwise, filth and confusion breeds ugliness. Sin is likewise seen as *error* and *fault,* i.e., mistakes committed by an immature soul. Such errors can be forgiven easily though. In Shintō the soul-spirit is considered *flawless,* even if humans are guilty of some mistakes.

Since there is no dogma professed in Shintō, there are virtually no sacred texts, as is the case for other religions. The holy books of Shintō are instead designated as historical and mythological (often a superstitious and fragmented history of Japan). The *Kojiki* (Record of Ancient Matters) and the *Nihongi* or *Nihon Shoki* (Chronicles of Japan) are the main foundational books. They focus on the origins of the Imperial Throne, clan lineage, and provide background information on Japanese culture.

Many other religions, particularly those of a large institutional variety, may see Shintō as a sort of barbarian practice akin to paganism. It is important to note that Shintō, however, is rarely even referred to as such in Japan, and is instead a way of life. Some foreigners may see it as soulless or evil. But this would be utterly ludicrous and incomprehensibly ignorant if it were the case. Dr. Sokyo Ono describes in his book Shinto: The Kami Way how, *"The meaning and value of an action"* in Shintō philosophy *"depends on its circumstances, motive, purpose, time, place, etc."* Judgments can only be made if we consider that a *"man's heart must be sincere; his conduct must be courteous and proper"*; and that selfishness must be removed. So, although typical definitions of *good* and *evil* are absent in Shintō, there is no doubt that the practice is still focused exclusively on the positive spiritual development of man alongside nature. In other words, the Kami only react in *evil* or *harsh* ways when we neglect our responsibilities. They are, like traditional western demons (spirits of things, places, actions, etc.) provoked to aggression as a natural response to our *transgressions* or *sins*. In fact, as we learned in a much earlier chapter, many demons are merely there to strip away impurities after death. It bears repeating once more the words of the mystic Meister Eckhart: *"If you fight your death, you'll feel the demons tearing away at your life, but, if you have the right attitude to death, you will be able to see that the devils are really angels setting your spirit free."* In his History of the Devil Paul Carus concludes similarly:

> *"God being All in All, regarded as the ultimate authority for conduct, is neither evil itself or goodness; but nevertheless he is the good, and he is in the evil. God is in growth and decay; he reveals himself in life and in death."*

In the Zend Avesta we read in the epilogue the following verse, which also seems to share a relationship with the inherent nature of change and the purification it brings:

> *Evil exists not,*
> *Only the past.*
> *The past is past;*
> *The present is a moment;*
> *The future is all.*

Some may also see Shintō as "pagan" not only because it is both polytheistic and monotheistic, but because there is no core belief in the danger(s) of materiality. For those unfamiliar with the matter, it suffices to say that Shintō allows for *desire* so long as it serves the Kami – i.e., harmony with what others call nature or God. In other words, material goods are not necessarily seen as *evil*, but their absence does not imply spiritual progress. In fact, this version of *desire serving Kami* is akin to the concept of God's *Divine Plan*. Regardless of the condition of *possession* or *desire*, so long as one is serving the *Kami* then all else is secondary. This obviously in no way implies, suggests, or factually states that Shintō allows for any kind of *evil*. On the contrary, it is absent of what we may call *evil*. To *serve the Kami* means to harmonize with nature and contribute to society by fulfilling your obligations to family, community, country, and your ancestors. Dr. Ono explains the abuse of desire as *"seeking after and using wealth for selfish purposes or in ways that injure others is not in accord with the way of the kami."* If selfishness be the reason of your *desire*, then for all intents and purposes it would be considered *evil*, or *crooked*. These simplified but complex and sophisticated spiritual concepts, and *ways of living*, are not confined to Japan, though they are uniquely observed in this country. In this capacity, Shintōism is an extension and outgrowth of Japanese cultural and social customs.

The Japanese concept of *shikata* is broken into *shi* (serve) and *kata* (form), meaning "way of doing" something. For example: *tabe kata* (way of eating), *kaki kata* (way of writing), *kangae kata* (way of thinking), and *iki kata* (way of living). These *ways* can be associated with the Kami and Shintō in general, which means *True-Way* or *Kami-Way*. To *serve* the *harmony* and *balance* of the *Tao*.

To traditional Japanese there is either a correct *way* of completing a task or no "way" at all. There is no in-between. If you are uncertain or unable, then do not try. The purpose of *kata* is to harmonize the true inner self with the external world. Boye Lafayette De Mente describes in his book Behind the Japanese Bow how individuals must know their *"own honshin (hone-sheen), 'true' or 'right' heart,' then learn and follow the kata to keep in sync with society and the cosmos."* The *kata* is therefore a mundane parallel to the spiritual practice of Shintō. Following the *kata* with a *true heart* (*honshin* or *magokoro*) leads to what De Mente calls *Wa* (haromy), though the appropriate word today would likely be *chōwa* or the *spirit of harmonious partnership* – the referenced book here was published in 1995 and much has changed since then. Harmony is said to be achieved through *kata* and *honshin* (*magokoro*), but specifically in following *bun* and *giri* – life *roles* and *obligations* respectively. Modern word usage may be *gimu* (obligation) and *jinsei no yakuwari* (life role). This harmonious concept was embedded in traditional Japanese education wherein the goal of professional classes was for the *"pupil to become one with the object of his training."* For example, *"the goal of the swordsman was to merge his consciousness with his sword, the painter's with his brush, the potter's with his clay; the garden designer's with the materials of the garden."*

Such adherence to conscious development and arguably what one may call *perfection* is a serious factor in what makes the Japanese who they are, and both their cultural customs and spiritual practices so uniquely alluring and powerful. De Mente adds how the *"wa concept pervades"* their culture [in the 1990s, at least]: *"it appears as wall art in the form of calligraphy. It is a key part of such common words as peace (heiwa), peaceful resolution (wa kai), and peaceful concord (wa go). The original name of the country, Yamato, is written with the characters for 'Great Harmony' (Dai Wa [chōwa])."*

This is what gave the Japanese an edge in *"designing, manufacturing, and packaging products, as well as in promoting and selling them."* Their culture, as with Shintō, puts great emphasis on *"aesthetic excellence, quality, and propriety."* Much of this is still accurate today, not that Japan is the only country where this is true! At one point, this was the American way too!

Shintō at its foundational core encourages the spirit or soul (*reikon*) of an individual to be harmonized with both nature and the divine *holy powers* called Kami. Such harmony must then be maintained. As with so many other practices, traditions, religions, etc., the Shintō maintains another version of the Biblical description of Jesus Christ in John 14:6 which reads: *"I am the way, the truth, and the life."* The word Shintō means *Kami Way*. The word can be broken down into *shin* and *to* (pronounced like toe). *Shin* is a given name relating to *Kami* and *do* or *to* relates to *michi*, which means *way*. The former can also translate into the word *true*. Therefore, Shintō could mean both *Kami-Way* and *True-Way*. The "truth" found in Shintō is *harmony*, just as it is harmonious things which *calm the beast*. Taoism, or Dōkyō, also means *teaching of the way*. Shintō deals with the mystical rules of nature and how the individual can be harmonized with the same, while still allowing for an acceptance of all other faiths. Dr. Sokyo Ono's book explains how Shintō *"is an all-inclusive term embracing the various faiths which are comprehended in the kami-idea."* As mentioned above, we are dealing with a traditional practice that involves adherence to certain ideas, attitudes, and ways (the *kami-way)* of living life and interacting with nature, community, etc.

Shintō has also, as some may assume, changed, and adapted to the times, while still maintaining *The Way*. Despite cultural influences, invasions, and wars, or religious opposition, Shintō has remained fundamentally unchanged at its core, although it has made many concessions and adaptations in the 20th-century. Dr. Ono writes that the purpose of Shintō, as an "all-inclusive term," is to use worship (*sūhai*) "*to unite and harmonize the various kinds of kami.*" Therefore, he says, "*spirit of tolerance and cooperation is an hitherto unnoticed aspect of Shinto.*" The usage of the word *sūhai* here implies not just *worship* but also a deep respect (or *respect wholeheartedly*) for the *divine*, something often lost in other religions concerned exclusively with dogmas and doctrines, or with specific rituals. Shintō may have certain guidelines, but overall, it must be *experienced* and *lived* individually.

If Shintō *teaches* anything it would be that the *world* and *creation* are not in contrast with man; that man is blessed by Kami and that life is inherently good. It also *teaches* what we call *community* and *civilization*. It promotes the individual, public welfare in general, all levels of community, and nature while preserving the core of human society in the form of family, especially if they have passed on. Since our lives are so full of natural and divine blessings it is only appropriate that man, as Dr. Ono writes, "*accept his obligations to society and contribute to the vital development of all things entrusted to him.*"

Sūhai (worship) in Shintō is famously conducted in front of various types of shrines which are traditionally located in sacred, or even just common, locations near or within natural beauty. Such *beauty* can be found in mountains, hills, large rocks, caves, groves, rivers, lakes, the ocean, and so on. Adoration for mountains (*yama*) and rocks is not necessarily unique to Japan but it is famously Japanese. The word *reizan* refers to a "sacred mountain" and the word *shintaizan* denotes a mountain as an object of worship or a "divine body mountain." Famous Japanese Mountains include Fuji, Haku, Tateyama (the Three Sacred Mountains), Haguro, Yudono, Ōmine, Miwa, and Yamagata.

Many Shintō shrines are located on top of mountains or at their base. In numerous cultures it is the mountain where divine inspiration or knowledge is received. Mount Sinai is where Moses (one of many lawgivers) famously received the Ten Commandments and Mount Ararat is the famous location where Noah's Ark came to rest under the protection of God, therefore making it a conduit connecting heaven and earth. The idea of a *conduit* is precisely what *reizan* denotes; sacred locations, particular mountains, but also large rocks, which act as conduits through which man can reach out to commune with the divine. Such images conjure the phrase *As Above, So Below*, suggesting universal uniformity and an outreached arm from heaven willingly assisting those on earth seeking wisdom or guidance. The *iwakura* rock, which is any rock housing kami, is one example of this connection to heaven. The Hittite culture of the ancient near east called these rocks Ḫuwaši.

There are many types of Shintō. Listed below are the different names with brief descriptions of each.:

Shrine: Shintō of the oldest and most prevalent variety, dating from the earliest times. Dr. Ono documents how "*there were shrines even before the dawn of Japanese history.*"

Popular: also known as Folk Shintō, the popular version simply speaks to the ingrained worship of kami, or the *Kami-Way,* in everyday life.

Domestic: Shintō practiced at home.

Sectarian: Shintō as was once nationalized as a state cult.

State: a combination of Imperial Household Shintō and Shrine Shintō.

Imperial Household: practiced at three shrines used by the Imperial Family.

Grand Shrine of Ise: a sacred shrine dedicated to the Sun Goddess Amaterasu (Ama-terasu-ō-mikami).

The last shrine mentioned here is of upmost importance in Shintō. The Grand Shrine of Ise, or the Ise Grand Shrine, is dedicated not only to Amaterasu but to the indigenous people of Japan and their spiritual traditions. Ise Jingū is in fact a shrine complex composed of many shrines with focus on *Naikū* and *Gekū* shrines. Amaterasu and her Ise Grand Shrine can be found to share striking similarities with the Egyptian goddess Isis, as we have pointed out elsewhere in this book.

The simple story of Amaterasu, goddess of the sun, involves her entombment in the earth for three days before being miraculously resurrected. It is strikingly familiar with story of Jesus Christ, and of course relates to the movements of the stars and our sun. But before Amaterasu there was Ame-no-minaka-nushi-no-kami, the *Kami of the Center of Heaven*. Even before this *universal* Kami was the *World-Egg* which separated into *yin* and *yang*, and here is found the influence of Chinese Taoism in Japan. This was a time known as *kamiyo*, or the *Age of Kami* before their descent to earth. Then came the *kami* of birth and growth, known respectively as *Taka-mimusubi-no-mikoto* and *Kami-musubi-no-mikoto*. It was much later that the parental figures of *Izanagi-no-mikoto* and *Izanami-no-mikoto* appeared, giving birth to the *High Plain of Heaven*, the *Great Eight Islands*, and numerous other *Kami*. Their children are Ama-terasu-ō-mikami, Susa-no-o-no-mikoto, and Tsuki-yomi-no-mikoto: otherwise known simply as Amaterasu (goddess of the sun), Susanoo (god of earth), and Tsukuyomi (goddess of the moon).

According to legend, when Izanami and Izanagi first descended from the heavens, they botched creation and had to begin again. As comical as this may seem, it also implies a slight relationship with the Biblical God and his desire to restart mankind with a deluge. Flood myths of this nature persist all over the world to this day, as we learned earlier. Fire was the final Kami born before their more well-known children like Amaterasu. As the final element of creation, the fire burned Izanami's body and sent her to *Yomi*, the underworld of Japan. In classical Persephone fashion, Izanagi ventures to *Yomi* to rescue his wife. But Izanami had eaten food in the underworld and was therefore bound to the *dead*. Izanagi said to his wife, *"The lands that I and thouh made are not yet finished making; so come back!"* Izanami informs her husband to wait while she speaks with the higher powers of Yomi about his proposal. Unable to wait patiently, Izanagi follows his wife and sees her in the inner sanctum covered in maggots. This story is parallel to that of Orpheus and Eurydice in Hades. As a result, Izanami is filled with shame and rage, and chases Izanagi to the surface. Izanagi then goes to purify himself in a body of water, stripping away his clothes in a manner like that of Ishtar and her garb. It is here that Amaterasu and her siblings are born from the water, which was certainly as significant to an island nation as it was to desert dwellers around the Nile.

Amaterasu and Susanoo can further be paralleled to the Egyptian sky goddess Nut and earth god Geb. The usage of "god" and "goddess" here should be considered in relationship with what we already known about Shintō. According to the *Kojiki*, Amaterasu hid in the celestial cave because her brother Susanoo was acting violently in his capacity as the Japanese storm god. This resulted in darkness descending over heaven and earth. In other words, a cataclysm of some sort blocked out the sun for some time. The Kami responded by performing dramas and dancing for the goddess outside her cave, still an integral dance in Shintō today. Eventually she emerged bringing light, warmth, and life back to the world. This drama between heaven and earth further relates to the conflict and balance between light and dark, good and evil (necessary), earthly desire and spiritual strength, etc. or, as Graham Hancock wrote in <u>Underworld</u>, the drama could be a memory of global cataclysmic changes, from earthquakes and storms to a darkening of the sun.

After her entombment like Jesus or Persephone, Amaterasu awakens from her deep sleep like *Sleeping Beauty* - what we call physical life - and restores light and life to the world like Horus, Mithra(s), and Demeter-Ceres upon the return of her daughter. She then merges with her male Kami and becomes *Amateru*, before

Izanami and Izanagi creating the world from the 'Floating Bridge of Heaven', Woodblock Print, 19th Century.

descending to the shrine of *Ise Amaterasu* or *The Grand Shrine of Ise*. Worship of Ama-terasu-ō-mikami is sometimes referred to as *The Way of Ise*.

For his aggressions, Susanoo was banished to the lower world, but by certain redeeming actions his descendant Kami named Izumi (Ōkuni-nushi-no-kami) ruled parts of pre-historic Japan.

A descendant of Amaterasu named Ninigi-no-mikoto eventually lowered from heaven and began ruling Japan. He was provided three sacred objects of authority: a mirror, a string of jewels, and a sword - integral parts of Shintō today that are often found within shrines. The great grandson of Ninigi-no-mikoto later became the first Emperor of Japan. His name was Jimmu.

The historical creation of Japan, including its general mythology, results in the formation of an unseen world parallel to the visible, both a *Hidden Land* (*yukai*) and a *Land of the Dead* called *Yomi* or *Yomi-no-kuni*. This unseen realm is inhabited by Kami that personify nature and are ascribed certain qualities like fertility and growth. They are associated with natural phenomena like wind, rain, lighting, and thunder, and are anthropomorphic expressions of mountains, rocks, trees, water, and so on. In these cases, they are no different than any other mythological god or goddess, hero, or heroine. Kami exist as part of a hierarchal chain of *being*. From the Kami we obtain the beautiful, natural world and life itself. Kami dwell in all natural things and therefore we are each a *child-spirit*, as some refer, of the Kami. This spirit is called *bunrei* and is explained by Motohisa Yamakage as such: *"everything in existence is generated by and transformed from the Ultimate Origin of Life; every (human) being has a full-fledged potential to become Kami; all forms of life are a Child-Spirit of original Kami."*

The Kami are thus honored by expressing *okage*, indebtedness and gratitude. When we seek wisdom and protection from Kami in exchange for *okage* and *offerings* we are forging a connection between the mundane and spiritual. We are also speaking to our inner-self, or inner-Kami.

Amaterasu emerging from the celestial cave or earthly womb, brining light back to Japan.

Utagawa Kunisada, The Goddess Amaterasu Emerging from Earth, woodblock print, 1860.

It is an interesting note that the Japanese word *mori,* which means forest, is sometimes used as a title for Shintō shrines. Although many shrines throughout Japan are no longer located directly within nature, the designation *mori* obviously stems from a time when most shrines were almost exclusively located in the forest or nearby in a similar natural setting. The word *kannabi* likewise refers to the surrounding woods as "shelter of a kami."

Today these sacred woods, *chinju-no-mori,* can still be found near shrines, though this is not always the case. After all, as with most cultures, and in Voodoo, trees are considered to house divinity and provide wisdom in Shintō. With such divinity and consciousness comes *order* and *justice,* or *harmony,* and as Dr. Ono writes, the *"kami function harmoniously in cooperation with one another and rejoice in the evidence of harmony and cooperation in this world."* Motohisa Yamakage adds, *"Trees used for ritual purposes are known as himorogi."* Forests are often chosen for Kami worship because of the powerful influence of trees which act as *yorishiro.* The *yorishiro* is an antenna or conduit for Kami to descend upon and occupy, just like *iwakura. Yori* means "base for dwelling."

Torii

Kami clearly share a relationship, conceptually, with the notion of planetary energies and spirits; they have personalities, a capacity for substance, missions to accomplish, and *"in a sense each is worshipped as the founder or guardian of some definite object or phenomenon."* Even something so simple like the distribution of water (*mizu*) has a Kami aspect. As with national gods, the Kami were also traditionally the guardians of clans (*uji*) or of a particular place (*ujigami*).

The use of shrines is meant to assist the visiting worshiper with universally acceptable methods of contacting the divine, including purification, prayer, and certain settings to transport the senses into a spiritual domain. This begins with the entrance gateway (*torii*), sometimes preceded with stairs, which lead to the path (*sandō*) that can be followed to the main sanctuary (*honden*) of a shrine. Since the *Shintō Shrine* is a divine dwelling place for Kami, a place for them to inhabit while being honored, when one steps onto those grounds, they are in fact leaving the mundane world behind. Although it is not always practical or possible, shrines are typically located in beautiful natural settings for this reason, and always have serene architecture and landscaping techniques - *ascetics*. The purpose of an institutionalized shrine is for ritual service and prayers (paying respects) that reflect the rhythms of daily life. Assistance and protection are sought from Kami in exchange for *offerings* and *okage*, which is a sense of indebtedness and gratitude expressed in paying one's respect at the shrine.

A *torii* is a portal that separates the inside and outside worlds, what we call the *mundane material* and *divine spiritual*. Traditionally they were constructed from wood, but stone, concrete, metal, and even plastic are also used. Some place small *torii* in their gardens for protection. The *torii* is thus a separator of our world from the spirit realm. Of this gateway, profess B. H. Chamberlain writes:

> "*The Koreans erect somewhat similar gateways at the approach of their royal the Chinese p'ai lou, serving to record the vir-tues of male or female worthies, seem related in shape as well as in use and the occurrence of the word turan in Northern India and of the word tori in Central India, to denote gateways of strikingly cognate appearance, gives matter for reflection.*"

Since shrines are a manifestation of the trust placed in the Kami, all the shrine rites and festivals are therefore the highest expressions of that respect. After entering the *torii* and proceeding along a *sandō* adherents reach the purification fountain (*temizuya*) where it is customary to rinse the mouth and hands. Often there is a second *torii* gateway followed by two guardian statues called *komainu*. These statues are usually lion-dogs, male and female, that guard the shrine. Outside of Japan the same imagery can be found in the divine guardianship of secret knowledge by two sphinxes or the protection afforded wisdom by two owls. Beyond the guardians is a separate sacred fence (*tamagaki*) protecting the shrine. Within that fence is the shrine office (*shamusho*), worship hall or oratory (*haiden*), another inner fence, and then finally the main sanctuary (*honden*).

Within the main sanctuary is an inner chamber (holy of holies) and a space in front, usually with a table, to display offerings for the Kami. The inner chamber preserves a symbol representing the body (*shintai*) of the Kami being honored. This *shintai*, which means "divine body" or "god body," is the heart of the entire shrine. If removed from the inner chamber the shrine loses its divinity.

Some authorities note that the Kami do not reside in the shrine itself and instead a guardian spirit protects the Kami's core – *kamizane* – which acts as a *katashiro* (substitute form) for the Kami. Although the *shintai* may not be removed, in other cases it is customary during festivals to symbolically transfer the Kami from the shrine. This is done with a portable Shintō shrine, or palanquin, called *mikoshi*. It is also common for children to have their own small shrine which houses a piece of paper with the name of a particular Kami written thereon.

Typically, there are two doors protecting the inner shrine chamber, preventing damage or theft from occurring. They are kept closed during worship, and a curtain hangs over the chamber even if the doors are opened. Oftentimes a mirror is placed in the center between the offering table and those same doors. Mirrors (*kagami*) traditionally represent purity. Their essence reflects the good and bad with impartiality. They show us the inner self. As Motohisa Yamakage relates, mirrors represent a *"bright, shining, radiant light body, reflecting the spirit of Kami but not representing Kami in a material form."* Dr. Ono also recounts how in the myth of Amaterasu a mirror is placed outside of her celestial cave to *"catch her spirit."* The moon goddess Tsukuyomi may have some part to play in this myth considering that the lunar disk is esoterically known as *the great reflector in the sky*.

Shintō Shrines also house certain simple sacred objects for use in worship, including the *gohei* and *harai-gushi*. The *offering wand* and *purification wand*, respectively, are used for the purposes inferred by their names. Banners and pictures of animals are often present too. An indicator of the presence of a Kami is the item known as *shimenawa*, or sacred rope, which holds up zigzag-cut paper (*shide* or *hakuhei*). Dr. Ono informs us thus:

> *"These ropes are used to symbolically indicate sacred places where kami are believed to dwell or objects offered to the kami."*

Shimenawa are therefore not confined to official Shintō shrines, or smaller shrines. They are often found on trees in general and small ones can be found on *kamidana*. Wherever they are found these sacred ropes are usually accompanied by *shide* to indicate the presence of *Kami*. Motohisa Yamakage explains in detail the purpose of the rope:

> *"This is for attracting and attaching bad vibrations, kegare, and any other negative elements to the rope in order to protect the shrine. Therefore, when changing shimenawa, one experiences powerful unclean influences, such as malicious and poisonous thoughts, on contact with the discarded rope."*

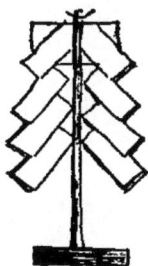 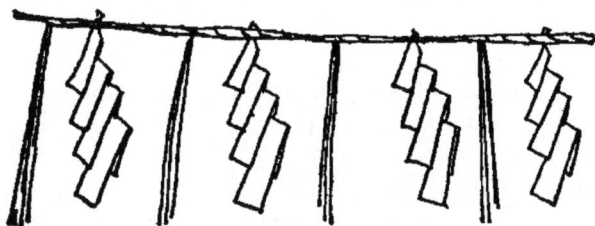 

gohei   *shimenawa*   *harai-gushi*

Shimenawa and *Shide* should be changed at minimal once a year and with every festival, since they are believed to absorb *crooked energy*. Knowing the importance of trees as conduits or vessels for Kami, we must say again that many shrines are typically surrounded by small sacred forests called *chinju-no-mori*. If forests are not plentiful in a particular location it is still common to find at least one tree upon which *shimenawa* and *shide* are placed. The *cleyera japonica (sakaki)* evergreen tree is the most sacred of all trees in Shintō. Its branches are often given as offering to the Kami. In the modern world that tree, or at least the branches of *sakaki*, could be artificial. Avery Morrow writes how although some shrines promote certain beliefs and practices, *"Japanese people do not assume that visiting a shrine implied endorsement of any particular doctrine."* For many Japanese, everything we have discussed is merely a part of life, like being raised Christian and knowing where the churches are but rarely attending even if you still maintain certain values.

Traditionally there are four methods used in honoring the Kami: *purification, offering, prayer*, and the *symbolic feast*.

PURIFICATION (*harai*): a process of ceremonial cleansing whereby evil, pollution, and negative energies are washed away with clean water. Meaning for *harai* stems from *harashiau* which means "clearing away each other." This clearing and purifying restores balance and cleanses by atonement like a baptism. Most water for this purpose, at a shrine or in your bathroom, is called "hand water" (*temizu*), and it is used to rinse the mouth and fingertips. Purification of the entire body by washing is called *misogi* – bathing in water. But purification for a priest (*kannushi*) preparing for a ceremony involves more than just water. Like all the known and obscure *mystery schools* from South America to Africa, and from the Middle East to Asia, abstinence is part of the process for everything from sex and social interaction to food. We learned earlier this was even the case in Voodoo. Dr. Ono informs us of how the Shintō priest is to prepare:

> "*From the evening of the previous day those who are to officiate must prepare themselves spiritually by entering the priests' quarters, if there is one, or by secluding themselves from other people. This is called saikai, literally 'restraint and rules.' They bathe (kessai) frequently, put on clean clothes, take only specific food, and lead a calm and continent life, abstaining from all forbidden acts.*"

The act of washing and purifying is more deeply seen to separate the secular and the sacred. Motohisa Yamakage adds that *Kami* will not descend or maintain a presence if everything and everyone is not cleansed. *Seimei Seichoku* is a combination of four types of purification: clean, bright (happy), right, and straight (honest). Grand Master Yamakage says that "*clean is expressed in Japanese with the Chinese pronunciation sei, bright as mei, right as sei, and straight as choku.*" He explains *Seimei Seichoku* further in <u>The Essence of Shinto</u>:

> **Seimei**: "*clean and happy attitude of inner mind, that is, without impurity together with a bright, happy, or clear mind.*"

> **Seichoku**: "*right action or behavior as well as the social aspect of being, (that is, not committing any sing, crime, or offense) and behaving with honesty, openness, and frankness towards others.*"

The purpose of purification and cleansing in Shintō is obvious, as with any similar religious practice. It is to wash away the unclean, impure, and all forms of pollution, be them physical, mental, emotional, or spiritual. All these defilements are called *kegare*. Although there is no dogma or doctrine in Shintō, the process of *harai* is extremely important so that Kami can be honored in a state of *kiyome*, or being clean, clear, and bright. Any water suffices, for the most part, though areas in which river water empties into the ocean are considered most appropriate, and even sacred. Since river water is considered masculine and ocean water feminine (likely because of the influence of the moon), we find their interaction as a type of symbolic sexual intercourse. Thus, we find that *misogi harai* is twofold: cleaning both the body and mind. *Kegare* can also be cleansed using certain plants which are believed to absorb our faults and errors, since *original sin*, as many call it, does not exist in Shintō. Such *negatives* are called *mononoke*, or vengeful ghosts and low-vibrational energies. Motohisa Yamakage describes three types of *harai* in his writings: purification by words, salt, and fire.

As we saw at the beginning of this chapter, the Japanese call the "spirit of words" *kotodama*. Their word for the "spirit of sound" is *otodama*. When certain words have positive influence, and make someone happy, they are called *kotohogi*, or "celebration words." These are like *blessings*.

In Shintō, as with virtually every culture anywhere and at any time, salt is an extremely powerful purifying and protective substance because it *preserves*. It is used in cleaning, cooking, and as a food preservative, as well as being considered a source of life. Salt is an important offering to Kami and can be found in countless magical practices. Since the elements of human body fluid – sodium, magnesium, potassium, calcium – can be found in ocean water, sea salt in particular, especially for the Japanese, is a critical purifying agent. Just as important as *sound* and *salt is fire* and the *image of man*. In Genesis we read how man was created in *"our image, in our likeness,"* and likewise Kami are said to exist in the *form of man*. This makes since considering that many are believed to have physically lived at one time. Like the elemental salamander, they are said to sometimes manifest by fire. In fact, Kami are the Japanese versions of the European elemental spirits. Purification by fire is called *imibi no harai*. Note that fire is often a substitute for the soul, but in general it provides warmth, light, cooked food, boiled water, and acts as a foundational element of life like salt.

Purification by using an object shaped like a human being is called *katashiro no harai*. The most popular form of the latter is called *hitogata*, usually a paper image of a basic human form. These paper images are usually used to absorb negative energy from an individual before they are burned or tossed into water. This form of spiritual practice is also known as *sympathetic magic*, though this has nothing officially to do with Shintō.

OFFERING (*shinsen*): items or actions (singing and dancing) given or performed for the Kami. If the Kami are not kept happy, then misfortune is said to follow. There are four types of offerings including money, food and drink, materials, and symbolic objects. Money offerings involve placing a coin into an offering box, donating to the shrine, or paying for a specific service. These donations are unlike the *tithe*. For food and drink it is customary to offer fish, rice, seaweed, grain, vegetables, fruits, and rice wine. Physical materials offered range from paper and silk to jewels and weapons. Symbolic objects or offerings range from dancing and wrestling to a sacred branch of *sakaki*. A *tamagushi* (jewel skewer) is an offering made from a *sakaki* branch decorated with strips of paper, straw rope, and other elements. Sacred dances (*kagura*), sacred music modeled after ancient imperial court music (*gagku*), and sacred masked dramas (*noh*) are also offered to the Kami in a more formal manner. Dr. Ono again provides us with a basic overview:

> *"Among the many forms of entertainment provided in shrines are sacred dances (kagura), music, classical dances (bugaku), archery contest, archery on horseback (yabusame), horse racing, and Japanese wrestling (sumo)."*

PRAYER (*norito*): the basis of *norito* can be found in the Japanese concept of *kotodama*. Prayers should be made as offerings and requests should be made for, as was the case for Solomon, *wisdom* and *protection* rather than *material possessions* – the latter, however, are not evil in Shintō so long as they serve Kami. Dr. Ono explains the purpose and intention behind these words and prayers:

> *"As a rule the prayers open with words in praise of the kami make some reference to the origin and possibly the history of the specific rite, festival or occasion being observed; express thanksgiving, report to or petition the kami, as may be appropriate; enumerate the offerings presented; give the status and name of the officiant; and finally add some parting words of respect and awe."*

Although not a prayer by some definitions, concentrated meditations are part of the process for many. This is called *chinkon* - a *Koshinto* meditation which brings awareness to the existence of the *Hidden Land*.

SYMBOLIC FEAST (naorai): this final honorific comes in the form of drinking a sip of rice wine. In some cases, say larger ceremonies, there is more drinking and eating.

The purposes behind these traditions and rites are to commemorate not only the Kami and their offered protections, but daily life in general and major events, whether of the self, community at large, or the entire nation. Adherence to particulars is NOT inherently important in Shintō. Since Shintō promotes the individual, public welfare, community, and nature while preserving the core of human society in the form of family and culture, and since our lives are so full of natural and divine blessings, it is our responsibly to honor the Kami by purifying ourselves and harmonizing with them. As Dr. Ono writes, "*…the evil heart, selfish desire, strife, dispute, hatred and the like have been dissolved, conciliation has been practiced, and a feeling of goodwill, cooperation and affection has been realized among the people."* This is the intention of Shintō or the *Kami-Way*. It is customary that if one is ill, bleeding, or mourning, they should avoid attending a shrine due to impurities. However, home shrines can still be used. But even if you are not experiencing physical impairments, a home shrine is an easy and effective way to honor the Kami. A house shrine is approached in the same manner as any other shrine. Dr. Ono explains the purpose:

> "*To awaken early, wash the face, rinse the mouth, and purify the body and mind by worshiping the kami and the ancestral spirits gives meaning to the day and enables one to begin work with a pure feeling."*

Private shrines are usually housed within a personal garden or inside the house. A *kamidana* is a miniature household altar used to enshrine the kami in the same, albeit smaller, way that a larger shrine functions with its *shintai*. Household shrines incorporate mirrors, lanterns, branches of *sakaki*, and straw rope with paper pendants - *shimenawa* and *shide* - stretched across the top of the altar. Ancestral kami shrines are typically located on a lower shelf below the household version of the larger shrines. They are constructed with a small box that contains the memorial tablets of the family and a mirror. An *ofuda*, or card made of paper or wood wrapped in white paper, is placed inside the home shrine. On the paper is written the name of Kami. Be it a small or large shrine it is also customary to ring a bell to drive away evil and to call attention to the Kami, a practice certainly not confined to Japan. Clapping the hands is another version of this practice. Clapping brings awareness to the spirits and the internal self, as does the bell. Dr. Ono explains here the typical method, although it can be simplified for time, of worshiping the Kami at home:

> "*Having washed the hands, rinsed the mouth, and placed fresh offerings before the kami, the worshiper stands or seats himself on a mat facing the miniature shrine and makes first a slight bow and then two deep bows. Following this whatever comes to mind as a prayer is repeated either audibly or in silence. Two deep bows, two claps with the hands in a raised position at about the level of the chest, a deep bow, and a slight bow and the right is over. Later the special food offerings are removed and served at meal time. Before eating, however, the devout Shintoist closes his eyes, slightly bows his head, and either silently or audibly claps the hand as a token of gratitude to the kami."*

With all that we have considered here it is perhaps most vitally important to remember that Shintō relies on visual and sensory experiences derived from traditional rites and natural phenomena instead of theological dogmas. Thus, as Dr. Ono puts it, *"the kami-faith is one that is maintained through the observance of traditional ways rather than by overt propaganda."* Boye Lafayette De Mente adds:

> *"Shintoism is an animistic belief based on cosmic harmony among gods, spirits, people, and the physical world of nature. It is the indirect, but culturally pervasive, source of many of the attitudes and customs that disguise the Japanese from all other people."*

Such *animistic* beliefs in nature can be found all throughout Japanese folklore and mythology. This is illustrated by *irui-kon*, or a person who marries an animal which has shape-shifted into a human being. We will discuss this tradition in the next chapter.

Salvation in Shintoism is only attained *"in the harmonious development of the world."* This means that anything obstructing creation and life (Kami) is harmful and *evil*. The goal of human life is thus to become like Kami, just as others say it is to follow in the footsteps of Christ. In essence, this means refining one's character by overcoming extremes, purifying the body, mind, and space, engaging in acts of charity or kindness, performing one's duties, and expressing the true self with honesty.

Shintō it seems is the essence of *the secret teachings*. We find further proof of this in the concept of *ichirei shikon*, or one spirit and four souls. The single spirit is *naohinomitama*, a combination of words meaning honest, sun, and spirit. *Naohinomitama* (true self or *shinga*) is the *wakemitama* (child-spirit or *bunrei*) of the *daigenrei* or *Original Spirit* – what some may call God. The four souls are *aramitama* (rough, gross), *nigimitama* (harmony), *sachimitama* (happy), and *kushimitama* (magical, mysterious). The latter four souls correspond to the four elements of earth, water, fire, and air respectively. Shintō therefore shares the philosophy of both Madame Blavatsky's *Theosophy* and Rudolf Steiner's *Anthroposophy* in the concept and belief of physical, etheric, astral, mental, and casual bodies.

When we choose to live in harmony, gratitude, and service, great spiritual strength (*miitsu*) is gained. We are reminded of *Seimei Seichoku,* the four types of purification: cleanliness, brightness, (happiness), rightness (duty), and straightness (honesty).

The concept of a hidden world (*kakuriyo*) mirroring the visible world (*utsushiyo*), and vice versa, is likewise found in Shintō, hence why the mirror (*kagami*) is so important for shrines. It is a gateway to the other side, to the hidden. It is the *Great Kabbalistic Symbol of the Zohar*, where this book began, depicting the reflection of God in the primordial waters.

~

One further note should be added about Ama-terasu-ō-mikami. Amaterasu is a name which translates to *"light of heaven."* This is a more specific meaning than the general interpretation of *sun-goddess*. Although Nihongo 日本語 (Japanese language) is not our focus here, it is still important to recognize its relationship with Shintō. The Japanese have words to describe things that in English we would find difficult to grasp. For example, *gamen* is the "enduring of something unbearable with dignity." Since much of the language of Japan, China, Korea, etc., is conceptually varied, rather than particular like English, many *Kanji* have almost endless meanings.

The kanji for *sun* 日 also means *bright, day, clear,* and even *pure.* Most are aware of the Japanese flag with red sun on a white background. In Old Japanese the word for *red* also meant *bright* and *pure.* The deeper meaning that could possibly be derived here has to do with the same knowledge sets found all over the world, despite how traditionally isolated Japan in particular has been. Even the Jōmon culture, supposedly just hunter-gatherers, are believed to have traversed the oceans and even harvested rice. Their pottery was far more sophisticated than even the later Yayoi people, though the simplicity of the latter should not be taken as less advanced.

If the word for *red*, which today is *aka*, also meant bright and pure, then it shares a direct relationship with Amaterasu, the sun-goddess. The sun is seen as yellow, orange, and red, depending on the time of day, and Japan is known as the *Land of the Rising Sun.* The fact that the sun Kami is female speaks to the preservation of perhaps more ancient and sacred wisdom - *koshikoden* - that has been left unscathed in the far east. What is meant by this is the consideration for red pigment found on the walls of the King's Chamber (Giza) in Egypt, on the walls of Ġgantija on the island of Gozo, and the red walls found in the Hypogeum on Malta. These red-walled chambers represent the *womb* of earth, the goddess, for which we are all born at least once. Even *Adam*, the first man, is Hebrew for *son of the red earth*. The red symbolizes the blood of birth-rebirth and a sort of purification – *blood of the lamb* and being *washed in the blood of Christ*. That red blood is purifying, as is the sun. The red "hats" of the Moai on Rapa Nui (Easter Island) could also be considered solar coronas, just like those depicted behind paintings of Jesus Christ or Egyptian gods like Horus. Upon rebirth into such an awareness we thus become *sons* or *daughters* of God rather than being the same of *man* and *woman*. We thus become more like *suns of God*. That sun is a universal spark inherent in ALL, an *Osirian Seed*. That *spark* is the *soul*, often symbolized by *fire* and a *bright light*. It is an extension of the mundane and spiritual sun – *God* or *Amaterasu*.

Fine Wind, Clear Morning, woodblock by Japanese artist Hokusai (1830-1832).

Mt. Fuji 富士山 (Fugaku) – Mount Fuji, or Fuji-Yama, was termed in the past, *"The Never-dying Mountain."*
Later it obtained a new name from Lafcadio Hearn, *"The Supreme Altar of the Sun."* The goddess of this
powerful natural formation is named Sengen, *"Radiant Blooming as the Flowers of the Trees."*

Amaterasu emerges from her cave to restore light to the world,
by Taiso Yoshitoshi, 1882.

Amaterasu is a goddess of the sun and married to the god of the moon. Each night the sun descends into the western world of shadow and upon each morning rises *reborn* in the east. This daily cycle is also played out similarly each month by the cycles of the moon, and each year by the cycles of the sun as it loses strength and symbolically dies during the winter solstice. After her entombment like Jesus or Persephone, she awakens from her deep sleep like *Sleeping Beauty,* or what we call physical life, and restores light to the world. She then merges with her male *kami* and becomes *Amateru,* before descending once more to the shrine of *Ise Jingu.*

Japanese Creationism

We have saved the Japanese creation story, although alluded to and in essence told in the above parts, for this last section in order for the simplicity of comparison with western myth and religion. *In the beginning* there was no *creation* or *form* as we understand today. Both heaven and earth were fused in the form of a *cosmic egg,* which contained the *white* and *yolk* called *In Yo,* as in *Yin Yang* or *Yab Yum.* These contents respectively represented male and female forces, or those of the positive-active and negative-passive. One force was *heavy* and the other *light,* and when they separated the former sunk to from *earth* while the latter rose to become *heaven.* Between these two realms there formed three kami and then an additional seven generations of kami after them. The seventh generation included Izanagi and Izanami.

Thus far from this story we can see the influence of Daoism, but more importantly the universality of *creation* myths, including the *egg,* polarity, and characters representing the primordial parents – Adam and Eve. The original three kami are the universal *trinity*, or Hindu *Trimurti*, and the *seven generations* are equivalent to the *seven days of creation* and seven divine rays of light often shown emanating from the god Mithra(s), or in the solar disc of Horus or Jesus Christ.

Izanagi and Izanami were standing on a *rainbow bridge* when they thrust a spear into the waters below. What dripped afterward from their spear formed the first island where they later descended. The marriage pillar which they erected to unite themselves is not unlike the *May Day* pole of tradition, or from an above view a symbol of the *monad* and also sperm fertilizing an egg. Their first interaction involved Izanami speaking, which upset Izanagi as the active force. The spoken word of the passive female without consent from the active resulted in a child being born with no structure, i.e., no bones. So the couple placed their first child, *Yebisu* (or Ebisu), in a basket and placed it on the water. He would go on to become god of fishermen and luck. We read in the *Kojiki*, or <u>Record of Ancient Matters</u> (Japan - 712 AD), Chapter 4:11 of the child:

> *"Nevertheless, they commenced procreation and gave to a birth leech-child. They placed this child into a boat made of reeds and floated it away."*

There is similarity to this story on the Polynesian island of Anaa, too, as Paiore, a high Chieftain, once explained: *"The first man was Matata, produced without arms; he died shortly after he had come into being."* And in the Finnish <u>Kalevala</u> is the story of Väinämöinen, the first deity birthed from Ilmater, the air goddess who took up residency in the ocean. He was unable to reach his full potential, however.

Now the ritual was performed again but this time with Izanagi speaking, the result being formation of the Japanese islands. Let us read Genesis 1:7-9 which says: *"And God made the firmament, and divided the waters which were under the firmament from the waters which were above he firmament: and it was so. And God called the firmament Heaven. And the evening and morning were the second day. And God said, Let the waters under the heaven be gathered together unto one place, and let the dry land appear: and it was so."* There can be zero doubt here of the relationship this story - that of Ebisu - has with Isis and Horus, Rhea and Zeus, Osiris and Set, and perhaps most famously with Moses. The first failed attempt at creation mirrors the countless myths already described which tell of the gods deciding to destroy their failure and start again, usually with water. Genesis 6:13 says:

> *"So God said to Noah, 'I am going to put an end to all people, for the earth is filled with violence because of them. I am surely going to destroy both them and the earth."*

Here we see the archetype of Noah's Ark taking the place of the little basket. Just as Ebisu goes to become god of luck and fortune, a protective deity, the God of Genesis makes an everlasting covenant between Himself and "every living creature of all flesh that is on the earth," as per Chapter 9:16, that he will not flood creation again. A rainbow is issued as a sign of peace with heaven - the rainbow is the Bilröst bridge connecting Midgard and Asgard in Norse mythology, and the place where Izanagi and Izanami created Japan. Izanagi and Izanami next give birth to wind, grass, mountains, and the fire god Kagu Tsuchi, whose birth burns and kills his mother. Distraught over his wife, Izanagi attempts to find her in the land of Yomi. His hopes of retrieval are squashed when she informs him: *"I have already eaten of the cooking-furnace of Yomi."* Izanami then tells her husband, *"I pray thee do not look at me."* The parallels here to other myths are likewise fascinating, particularly those of Persephone in the underworld, but also the romance of Cupid and his lover Psyche, who is told by her lover the same thing Izanami spoke to Izanagi.

Izanami and Izanagi stirring the primal sea while standing on a rainbow bridge, from a hanging scroll by Nishikawa Sukenobu, 18th-century Japan.

In seeking purification from his trip to Yomi, which became the baptismal ritual of *misogi* and *temizu*, Izanagi visited a river where he cleansed himself. Taking off his garments birthed new children and washing his face produced a new trinity. These stripped garments are easily related to the same dress of Ishtar and the story of Inanna, not to mention the universal gates or paths of the various underworlds. Other times we know these paths as the planetary spheres. As with the gods, man must pay the price of the underworld too. Coins were dropped inside purses placed around the neck of any deceased, in the old world, so they would be able to cross the River of Three Roads (Sanzu-no-Kawa) or River of Six Roads (Rokudokawa) and pay a toll to Sodzu (Shozuka) Baba.

Washing the left eye produced Amaterasu, washing the right eye produced Tsukuyomi, and washing the nose produced Susanoo. The sun, moon, and forces of nature thus correspond to the body and universal symbolism of the eye: Odin's eye was removed so that he could obtain wisdom (light), just as Horus removed his eye, usually the left, so that his father could illuminate the underworld. This eye is still used as a good luck symbol on fishing boats in Malta, two things directly related to Ebisu. It is no coincidence that the Sovereign Military Order of Malta, or the Knights of Malta, were stationed there and on the nearby island of Gozo. Perhaps the idea of one's nose growing when telling a lie has something to do with the chaotic element represented by Susanoo, and by the destruction lies can cause. There is also the world famous *Hamsa* eye, or Hand of Fatima, which comes from Africa and the Middle East.

Susanoo is so chaotic that his parents decide to send him permanently to Yomi, though his request to see his sister is granted before. At first all is fine in heaven when Susanoo interacts with Amaterasu, but soon he frightens her so badly she seeks shelter in a cave. It is perhaps most obvious that this story is universal since the sun, too, is universal and seeks refuge in the winter months. In Myths and Legends of Japan F. Hadland Davis writes of this story:

"Extremely angry, she determined to leave her adobe; so, gathering her shining robes about her, she crept down the blue sky, entered a cave, fastened it securely, and there dwelt in seclusion. Now the world was in darkness, and the alternation of night and day was unknown."

With assistance from several other gods and goddesses, Uzume, the Heavenly-Alarming-Female, is able to lure the personified sun from her hiding. One of the items used was a mirror made from a fusing of stars, which became a central feature of Shintoism.

Amaterasu's grandson, Ninigi, who we have already read about, found liking to the "Princess who makes Flowers of the Trees Bloom." Ninigi and Ko-no-Hana produce three boys as offspring, including Hoderi (Fire-shine), a great fisherman, and Hoori (Fire-fade), a great hunter, who must share commonality with Herne, Osiris, Nimrod, etc. Davis writes of these two:

"Hoori's son married his aunt, and was the father of four children, one of whom was Kamu-Yamato-Iware- Biko, who is said to have been the first human Emperor of Japan, and is now known as Jimmu Tenno."

Readers will probably recognize that within this story the couples and siblings represent triune forces or dual aspects. For example, the kami of disaster is called Magatsuhi and the kami of un-disaster is called Naobi. Ultimately all things stem form Masubi, the principle of unification equivalent to the concept of angelic guidance or 'God's Divine Plan'. This idea is central to Shintō. The kami - personifications of nature and things - are to be worshiped with offerings and prayers in order for man to maintain a harmonious relationship with these spirits who in turn offer protection and resources.

The ritual purification practice of *harae,* which includes *kagare* (death, disease) and *tsumi* (crime, disrespect), can be equated with the concept of sin and its washing away through baptismal waters and the blood of Christ. There is no need for Ten Commandments here because lying, coveting, disrespect, murder, etc., are already considered pollution that can be cleansed. Disease and sickness in Egypt was likewise cured with waters from the Nile, a symbol of the sweat, urine, saliva, vaginal discharge, tears, and blood of Isis. In the story of Yosoji and his ailing mother, he is told by Kamo Yamakiko to fetch water from Mount Fuji: *"Go fetch this water, and give it to your mother, for this alone will cure her."*

Amaterasu's Shimenawa & Christ's Cross

The mirror used to coax the sun goddess from her underworld dwelling is meant to reflect both the physical and spiritual self. In our story we find it tied to a tree decorated with jewels and surrounded by great merriment from an assortment of gods and goddesses hopeful and joyous of the sun's eminent return. Most will recognize the merriment around a decorated tree as symbolic of the western, and German pagan, Saturnalia and Christmas celebrations. Yet here it is also in the far east centered on a feminine solar deity. Joseph Campbell explains in A The Hero With A Thousand Faces that this female motif is universal, but preserved only in a few places, Japan being one. In archaic times, *"the great maternal divinity of South Arabia is the feminine sun, Ilat,"* and, *"the word in German for the sun (die Sonne) is feminine."* Finnish folklore provides us with the story of *Ilmatar*, the virgin daughter of the air. Her name is similar to the Latin root for the British *mater*, meaning mother.

Amaterasu is enamored with her own reflection in the mirror, seeing within herself the *Supreme Deity*. A visit to most Shintō shrines will offer a glimpse into the self with a variety of *kagami* (mirrors) placed in the center of the shrine, and sometimes off to the side. When one presents an offering, rings the bell, bows twice, claps twice, prays, and bows again, they are paying respect to the enshrined deity, or nature, ancestors, and the self. Amaterasu's reflection in the mirror can be likened to Makroprosopos, the Hebrew God reflecting on Himself. The tales of *vampires* having no reflection probably relates to their lack of a verifiable soul, and thus a glance of the eye into the mirror does not perceive a spirit since the eyes are the *gateway to the soul*. There is another parallel here to the Mexican Quetzalcoatl, who upon fleeing his rival sits under a tree like Buddha and gazes into a mirror like Amaterasu.

As the sun goddess is drawn from the cave by her own reflection, a straw rope called shimenawa was placed at the entrance to prevent her permanent return; to place a limit on her retreat - as each night humans and the sun take rest. Campbell identities this iconic Shintō symbol, placed on trees, rocks, and at shrines, as a representation of *"the graciousness of the miracle of the light's return… the simplistic sign of the resurrection."* Just as Buddha, his temptation, enlightenment, and return to teach is the eastern story of Jesus Christ, the shimenawa is the eastern Christian cross. And as the western God is known as Alpha and Omega, the eastern Goddess preserves the same: she is the beginning of each day in the land of the rising Sun, and the end of each day. In the *shide*, which hangs from shimenawa in zig-zag cut paper, is the holy trinity.

Author at Ishi-no-Hoden megalith with altar box comprising
the *Tomoe* trinity symbol, *shimenawa*, and triune *shide*.

Author photograph of the mirror within Himeji Gokoku-Jinja Shrine.

Author photograph of the floating Torii gate of Itsukushima Shrine on Miyajima Island.

Standing on Holy Ground

There are several Asian countries where removal of shoes before entering homes or certain businesses is customary, most famously in Korea and Japan. The reasoning is simple: cleanliness and respect. Central areas of many Buddhist and Shintō shrines in Japan require the removal of one's shoes before entering into the sanctum. Although removing shoes helps to preserve these sacred, and often ancient, though sometimes rebuilt, structures, it would be disrespectful and unclean to wear shoes inside regardless. In the book of Exodus 3:5 we famously read about Moses and the burning bush, and how the removal of shoes was instructed:

> "'Do not come any closer,' God said. 'Take off your sandals, for the place where you are standing is holy ground'."

Removing shoes is not merely due to preservation, cleanliness, or respect, however. As in the story of Moses, the ground itself is holy, and when one steps through the Torii gates they enter this sacred space before proceeding deeper to the inner sanctum. The shrine or temple is, like with churches, mosques, and synagogues, a representation of the heaven within and without. Usually built in heavily wooded areas, on top of mountains, or on water, the shrine is another world altogether. This threshold is guarded by lions, foxes, and monsters. In the Irish story of Oisin, he is not permitted to touch the earthly ground or he will lose his immortality. A gateway separates these worlds just as a wedding ring insulates a wife or husband, or a vampire must avoid daylight, or a gnome and elf must avoid the same less they turn into stick or stone. There is a shared motif here with the story of Persephone-Proserpina and the eating of food in the underworld. We find also in the children's game of *Floor is Lava* the imaginary separation of worlds.

This is also why Buddhist Temples, Catholic Churches, and in far simpler form Shintō shrines, are decorated so wonderfully and kept so immaculate; they are visual aids for the realm of spirit. Although some Buddhists may be wealthy, the purpose of the temple itself is to act as a physical representation of heaven on earth, not to obtain wealth from donations. For Revelation 21:21 points out about heaven: *"The twelve gates were twelve pearls, each gate made of a single pearl. The great street of the city was of gold, as pure as transparent glass."* In <u>Shinto Gobusho</u> it is explained: *"What pleases the Deity is virtue and sincerity, not any number of material offerings."* Hence the Japanese saying: *"The gods only laugh when men pray to them for wealth."*

Ise Jingu

The vast Ise Jingu shrine is located in Ise, Mie Prefecture, Japan. It occupies an area roughly equivalent to the city of Paris. Thousands of rituals are performed here each year, mainly for prosperity of the Imperial family, an abundant harvest, and for worldwide peace. Also called Kotaijingu (Naiku), Ise Jingu enshrines the sun goddess Amaterasu. The Ujibashi bridge, which crosses the Isuzugawa river into the complex, like the Torii gates on both sides, acts as a gateway to the realm of kami. The bridge is destroyed and rebuilt every 20 years, as is the custom for the main shrine of Ise Jingu. This ensures purity and reminds one of the impermanence of life and the importance of purging oneself. After a new divine palace is constructed at an alternative location, using the same dimensions as the previous one, the sacred apparel, furnishing, and treasures are also remade. The Holy Mirror is then moved to the new sanctuary in a ritual called *Shikinen Sengu*.

Amaterasu is the bringer of light and life, but specifically clothing, shelter, and food, to her people. Her main sanctuary is shrouded with a white veil, reminiscent of the red veil concealing Isis, and the white veils of the western bride (*see* Bride of Christ). The fully developed worship of Amaterasu and her overall story date back officially 2,000 years. Its development surely formed over centuries previous. There is no doubt her story comes from both the universal human language of nature, with vastly older influences. The official history from the Jingu Administration Office says the following:

> "Amaterasu-omikami was originally worshiped in the Imperial Palace by successive Emperors of Japan. However, during the reign of the 10th Emperor Sujin, the Holy Mirror (the symbol of Amaterasu-omikami) was moved from the Imperial Palace. Then, during the reign of the 11th Emperor Suinin, the Emperor ordered his princess, Yamatohime-no-mikoto, to seek the most appropriate place to permantely enshrine and worship Amaterasu-omikami. After searching in many regions, finally the princess received a revelation that Amaterasu-omikami should be enshrined and worshipped eternally in Ise. It is approximately 2,000 years ago. In the era of the 21st Emperor Yuryaku, about 1,500 years ago, Toyo'uke-no-omikami was, in accordance with another revelation from Amaterasu-omikami, summoned from the north of Kyoto prefecture and enshrined in Ise."

Toyo'uke-no-omikami is the provider of companionship and sacred foods for Amaterasu, and enshrined at Toyoukedaijingu (Geku). Jingu, generally called Ise Jing, is comprised of 125 jinja (Shintō shrines), focused on Naiku and Geku.

Shintō is focused on respecting nature, since we all have dominion like Adam over all of creation. This idea of respect and cleanliness is the soul of Buddhism too, and famously the soul of Japan. The white flag with red dot signifies the soulful fire burning in each of us. We must therefore cleanse the vessel of the soul, an element also found in 1 Corinthians ("*your bodies are temples of the Holy Spirit*").

The main sanctuary of Ise Jingu employs a white veil to
conceal the inner sanctum - *credit to Ise city website.*

Shangdi: The Jade Emperor

It is difficult to translate the western conception of *creation* and *creator* into eastern language, just as it is difficult to translate the eastern conception of such things into western language. The word *musubi* is Japanese for "union," "joining," and "ending," which implies a separation and beginning. It could thus translate as the *alpha* and *omega*; birth and death; creator and destroyer; and so on. This is Amaterasu of Japan and Visnu of Inida. After creation, however, there must be maintenance of what has been produced and so in India we find Braham (creator) and Siva (destroyer) balanced by Vishnu (preserver). This is essentially the role played by a supreme deity in Chinese tradition called *Shangdi*. Also known as Yuhuang Shangdi (Yu-huang Shang-ti), Yudi (Yu Ti) or Mr. Heaven (Lao-t'ien ye), his earthly name is the *Jade Emperor*. Shangdi is an overseer like the architect of a building, facilitating but not actually constructing; he is Saturn-Cronus. His relationship with the two latter gods becomes stronger when observing depictions of Shangdi as having long hair, a beard, and distinguished features. He also holds the tablet, a job for Thoth-Hermes-Mercury, and is adorned with a solar crown like Christ.

The Chinese say the world came about when matter (K'i) and movement (Li) joined in union (masubi). This then resulted in the production of metal, wood, earth, fire, and water (*Wuxing*).

Shangdi

Shangdi simply observes and facilitates this creation as an all-seeing eye in the sky where he resides in a beautiful palace situated in the highest part of heaven; he is the sun. Jade is his gemstone because, as in the Bible, it signifies wealth and nobility, along with strength and happiness. Originally worship of the Jade Emperor was nothing more than folk religion and spoken mythology, but that changed when Emperor Shenzong of the Song Dynasty had a vision of this heavenly deity and responded by incorporating him into state-sponsored Chinese religion. This story may remind curious readers of Constantine's vision of the cross in 312 AD.

In the heavens reside Shangdi's family and attendants, which are obviously the stars in the sky. One manager of the palace is Wang the Transcendent Official, who protects mortals from evil. Guarding the gates of heaven, Wang wears armor and holds a heavy staff. The parallel this image has to Saint Peter and his keys is striking – the silver key protects mortals below and the golden key the divine above. There may be some disagreement as to the true nature of Shangdi, especially because his likeness dates back 4,000 years or more, but some very peculiar similarities arise when comparing his story with western religion and myth. Christendom in particular may be frightened by the fact Shangdi forbid the worshiping of false idols, declared all sin an offense against himself, and required sinners to repent with burnt offerings and blood sacrifices of animals. Nothing could save the soul or cleanse away sins like the blood of the man from heaven who took on the sins of all his people. How much this influenced the west and vice versa will probably always remain a mystery.

Occult Japan: Yokai, Kaiju, Yurei

In <u>The Book of Yōkai</u>, Michael Dylan Foster describes *Kami* as "powerful" but *"not necessarily good in the moral sense."* Throughout Japanese history, including pre-history, the spirit of a thing could manifest in two ways: *"it could be angry and rough, and would be known as aratama, or gentle and beneficial, known as a nigitama."* Such powerful spirits, collectively called *yōkai* today, are both *aratama* and *nigitama*. What we call an evil spirit may do something morally right, and what we call a good spirit may do something morally wrong. Thus, as Foster puts it, *"the very thing that threatens human enterprises and society (aratama, yōkai) can be changed into a beneficial and cooperating power (nigitama, kami) in these same enterprises."* This is how we can look at both *Kami* and *Yōkai*. They are distinct, yet similar or sometimes identical.

The *yōkai* of today is a term that refers to what most of us call spirits, phantoms, specters, sprites, fairies, elementals, shapeshifters, demons (*oni*), aliens, monsters (*bakemono* or *obake*) etc. They are energetic personifications of crossroads, bridges, tunnels, of living on the edge of town or between

Hyakkiyagyō by Shinonome Kijin, taken from The Book of Yōkai, 2015.

villages, of the top of mountains, of deep inside forests, or in the depths of the ocean. What we speak of here can also be named *twilight forces*, those 'things' which appear most actively during the *witching hours*, usually 2-4 AM, when night is the darkest and as it begins to give way to morning. These hazy, vague, transitional moments between night and day open a sort of gateway between worlds, much like the shifting changes of earth's seasons. The *witching hours* are a time of phantoms, apparitions, ghosts, and all manner of spooky occurrences. Michael Foster describes how *yūrei* (ghosts) favor the earliest part of these hours, or a time called *ushimitsu*, appearing in *"the third quarter of the hour of the ox, about 2:00-2:30 AM, when night was at its darkest."* The ox is also heavily associated with Japanese demon *Oni*.

Yanagita Kunio (1875-1962), one of Japan's most influential voices on folkloric studies, classifies *bakemono* and *yūrei* slightly differently, stating that the former *"generally appear in set locations"* and haunt a particular place, whereas the latter haunt a particular person. He says *yūrei* tend to arrive before the twilight time whereas *bakemono* prefer the *"dim light of dusk or dawn."*

Call them *bakemono* or *yūrei*, monsters or ghosts, we are essentially talking about the same phenomenon in different forms. Most monsters, ghosts, demons, etc., are more present at night, and in spooky locations where there is uncertainty and often a history of trauma – usually a battlefield or graveyard. In zoological terms we can call these spirits from the otherworld *crepuscular*, something relating to twilight.

Other names for such entities are *mono-no-ke*, an old term referring to general *mysterious* or *suspicious* activities or *things*. Thus, *yōkai* are more than individual monsters, they are also *unexplainable phenomena* in general. They can inhabit and possess everyday objects, or *tsukumogami*, such as a musical instrument or a kitchen utensil.

Foster writes of Heian-period texts that discuss a *"procession of dangerous beings"* which were said to have occasionally passed through the Heian capital, or present-day Kyoto. This *night procession of one hundred oni*, or *hyakkiyagyō*, was a result of the physical and spiritual worlds temporarily intersecting, creating a dangerous and unpredictable situation.

We use terms like *monster* to describe those things which go *bump in the night*. The word *monster* stems from the Latin *monstrum*, meaning a supernatural event or a warning sign or portent from the gods. Western monsters, like eastern *yōkai*, are anthropomorphic and individual, but simplistically help us to generally visualize strange sounds or shadows. As the words *monstrum* and *yōkai* suggest, *a supernatural occurrence* is a *monstrous thing*. The monsters and personalities we derive from such things are part of our attempt at explaining the unexplainable, or at least the temporarily unexplainable. The nighttime is their domain because it is a time of blurry lines, when details are hard to discern, and when our senses are in very vulnerable states, on high alert for danger. Simply being able to identify a noise with a named thing (*bakemono, yūrei, yōkai*) helps to put our minds at ease. Foster describes how all five senses can help to alert us to the domain or object in question, and how we choose to identify that causative agent afterward:

> *"When you feel that this phenomenon (genshō) or event (dekigoto) is caused by an 'undesirable supernatural thing' (nozomashikunai chōshizenteki na mono), you are positing the intervention of a 'yōkai'."*

Japan is also famous for its movie monsters (*kaijū eiga*) like Godzilla (*Gojira*) or Gamera. Rather than being classified as *yōkai*, however, these monstrous creatures are called *kaijū*, a word only somewhat like *yō-kai*. The difference is that *kaijū*, usually translated as "strange beasts," do not appear in legends or folktales like an *Oni*. Godzilla may be scary to a Japanese city, or to the whole world in newer movies, but ultimately, he is a different type of fictional metaphor representing the dangers of nuclear technologies. *Yōkai*, on the other hand, tell of personal stories and experiences. When we decipher their meanings, *"we hear voices of people who lived in the otherworld of the past,"* writes Foster.

Godzilla and other *kaijū* may give dire technological or environmental warnings, but they are not scary in the same way as some *yōkai* because the latter are so personalized and intimate. Gamera, a giant dragon-like turtle, is so alien it is hard to identify with. The same alien qualities are found in Ghidorah. They are entertaining but not *yōkai*-scary.

These *kaijū* are like a snake or centipede in the sense that the former has no legs, and the latter may have too many. This results in a type of non-human-conformity in which we see the snake as evil or the centipede as just a creepy-crawly. Although some may fear them, it is an all-around different fear than if one were faced with their own internal *yōkai*. Perhaps future generations will look back on this text or countless others - not to include the movies, video games, comics, etc. - where these *bakemono, yōkai, yūrei*, and *kaijū*, are described and depicted. Perhaps they will wonder in five hundred years about what Godzilla meant to the 20th and 21st centuries, just as we wonder what the countless *yōkai* meant to ancient and modern Japan. In this way, as Foster contends, *"we project our own voices into the otherworld of the future."*

Let us take this into consideration not only with Godzilla, but also with popular fictions such as *Lord of the Rings* or *Harry Potter*. In both stories there are monstrous spiders with legions of smaller spiders that chase the protagonists. In J. R. R. Tolkien's version, the spider is named *Shelob*. In J. K. Rowling's version, the spider is named *Aragog*. Despite the very European histories, and particularly Norse and Greek mythologies, that highly influenced both former stories, the Japanese have their own version of this terrifying spider too. In Japanese folklore *tsuchigumo* (dirt spider) is an enormous spider surrounded by a progeny of smaller spiders.

The great warrior Raikō beheading the **tsuchigumo**, by 'artist unknown'.

The stories of *Harry Potter* contain another very obscure *yōkai*. Hiding in a third-floor bathroom, and in the third stall, is a spirit called *Toire no Hanako-San,* or "ghostly girl who haunts the school bathroom." In the former stories she is known as *Moaning Myrtle*.

These stories are universal. They draw on a past of both superstation and science, of folklore and mythology, and their inclusion in popular culture guarantees their perpetuation into *the otherworld of the future*.

Just as the Germanic hero Siegfried was able to slay a great dragon, so too was the Japanese god Susanoo. In the myth, we find Susanoo meeting an old couple in distress because a large dragon named *Yamata no Orochi* devours one of their daughters every year. The dragon is described naturally, covered in moss and cypress trees, and the length of eight valleys with the same number of mountain peaks or heads. Susanoo uses eight barrels of wine to drunken each one of dragon's heads. After the monster falls into a drunken sleep, Susanoo cuts him to pieces with his sword. In the process, his sword breaks, but in digging around for the remains he discovers a better sword of legend called *Kusanagi*, something that reminds us also of King Arthur's sword *Excalibur*.

Kappa by Shinonome Kijin, taken from The Book of Yōkai, 2015.

Some great examples of the relationship between science and mythology in *Yōkai* parlance are the water creatures *Kappa* and *Ningyo*, and the land creatures *Oni* and *Yamabiko*.

The ***kappa*** is notorious for drowning horses and cattle by pulling them unsuspectingly into the water. In a darker sense, they are also fond of drowning young children. As Foster explains, they would *"extract their internal organs through their anuses."* Despite their graphic description, a *kappa* is generally no more than a warning for children to be careful swimming in bodies of water or streams. But *kappa* has a playful side, too, and an affinity for cucumbers, probably because of their high water content. In fact, the sushi roll *kappa maki* (cucumber roll) is named in honor of this *yōkai*. They are generally slimy, greenish, and have webbed feet and hands. Sometimes a *kappa* goes by the name *kawatarō*, a title comprised of the Japanese word for river – *kawa*. There is, however, a regional distinction between *kappa* and *kawatarō*. Foster explains:

> *"The shell-bearing, amphibious yōkai was generally found in eastern Japan, from the Kanto (Edo) region to Tohoku. In western Japan, from Kansai to parts of Shikoku and Kyushu, the creature was called a kawatarō (or some variation of this name) and was hairy and walked upright and monkeylike."*

The famous *Tengu* also likes to target children, kidnaping them from their parents; another childhood warning about wandering into the wilderness.

The ***ningyo*** is another famous Japanese cryptid creature that dwells in water. The name itself means half-human, half-fish, or what most would call a *mermaid*. Depictions usually show this *yōkai* with the body of a fish and torso of a human. In the Japandemonium encyclopedia, the authors describe *ningyo* as such:

> *"It has a human face, a fish body, and no legs. From the chest up it is human, and like a fish below."*

It is believed that eating their meat will bring long life and prevent disease. Considering the obvious Japanese reliance on ocean waters, and the general health benefits of some seafood, it would make sense that eating of the *ningyo* would have some type of positive health outcome. Any body of water is life sustaining, but partaking of a supernatural water creature may have even more benefit. Simply looking at a *ningyo* is said to bring good luck, and perhaps this has something to do with the calming powers of the ocean or water itself. Ningyo also stand as omens of impending disasters, like typhoons, tsunamis, and earthquakes. In Edo period depictions, there are *"horns protruding from their otherwise humanlike heads,"* Fosters informs us. This is interesting because the unicorn horn is likewise associated with longevity and health.

Ningyo from the Encyclopedia, Japandemonium Illustrated, 2017.

Unlike the *kappa*, *kawatarō*, or *ningyo*, which tend to inhabit smaller bodies of water, the water spirit ***Gamishiro*** inhabits the ocean. The ***Kudan*** has the body of a cow or bull with a human face. It is believed to prophesize the future and there are many interpretations of why this is the said. Regardless, a *kudan* is thought to bring great luck just like the *ningyo*.

An ***Oni*** is like an ogre, lumbering giant, or troll. Like the Biblical Samson's hair, Oni derive their strength from horns protruding from their head. Michael Foster describes them as *"large, powerful, frightening, humanlike male figures with red, blue, black, or yellow faces, clawed hands, and sharp,*

鬼

Oni by Shinonome Kijin, taken from The Book of Yōkai, 2015

やまびこ
幽谷響

Yamabiko from the Encyclopedia, Japandemonium Illustrated, 2017.

protruding fangs." Carol K. Mack and Dinah Mack describe them as having a *"pink or blue"* body, with a face that is *"basically human but grotesquely flat, with a mouth that runs ear to ear and a third eye."*

Oni are usually carrying an iron staff or some type of club. Since they are always present when disaster strikes, their weapon symbolizes chaos. Carol and Dinah explain how *"despite their great powers, they are so preoccupied with satisfying excessive bodily needs that their intelligence is diminished."* These details and descriptions show that the Oni are like a lumbering giant with a club. Their association with the underworld, *Yomi* in Japan, goes back to their earliest depictions on the *Jigoku-zōshi,* or Buddhist *Hell Scrolls.*

The Oni basically encapsulate everything and anything that is chaotic in the world of humans and nature. They also represent specific directional chaos. Oni are often associated with the north-east, which is where the *kimon* (demon gate) is located. From this direction it is believed misfortune can enter a community or a personal home. The Japandemonium encyclopedia describes this as such:

> *"The direction known as ushitora ['ox-tiger,' northeast] is also called kimon ['gate of oni']. Today, oni are portrayed with the horns of an ox and tiger-skin loincloths. This is a combination of the directions of ox and tiger."*

Although supernatural in origin, the Oni itself is a form which may be taken by wicked men and women, much like *werewolves, Wendigo, Wetiko,* and *Skinwalker.* A person could take the superficial form of a monster but when they act like a demon by committing murder, for example, they become Oni and are dragged of their own will to *Yomi* to be tormented by hell hags. The *Yomotsu-shikome,* or the *hags of Yomi,* are demonic women who chased Izanagi from the underworld after he glimpsed, like Orpheus, on his deceased bride. Foster concludes, *"if Oni are the Other of the human, embodying the fears and dangers of the worldly existence, then their defeat – in narrative and ritual – reflects a symbolic triumph of human order over chaos."*

The **Yamabiko**, or "mountain echo," is thought to be responsible for the returning echo one hears when shouting in the woods or in the mountains. The word itself can mean *echo* and so we are talking about the *spirit of an echo*, transformed into a strange looking little creature that partially resembles a monkey. Other translations of the word, based on kanji, are *spirit of the valley reverberation*.

The **Kodama**, or *Tree Spirit*, is another form of this echoing found in the wilderness. Another spirit of the trees is **Kijimunā**, a trickster *yōkai* like kappa. Some sounds, as in a tree falling, can be attributed to mountain demons like the *tengu*. Within these explanations for natural phenomenon are likewise found reasons to protect nature, to preserve the spirits that comprise the forest, mountains, rivers, etc. In the same way mythical monsters draw tourists to certain locations like Loch Ness in Scotland, *yōkai* do the same for Japan while also pleading for the protection of nature.

The **Yamamba** is a perfectly terrifying example of nature's wrath when not appeased. The word *yamamba* means "mountain old woman" – *yama* alone means mountain. She has a proclivity for kidnapping young women, and particularly young children, from local villages. Her insistence on entering a home, usually with only young children inside, may be metaphoric of nature attempting to reclaim her own innocence in response to the encroachment of man. If appeased, Yamamba can provide good luck and abundance so long as you do not venture too far into her woods. This means you should not take more than you need from nature. It is from the mountains and valleys that we acquire food, water, wood, etc. By balancing what we take with what we give, and paying our respects, we may appease nature and live harmoniously within her fertile womb. Although there is no official relationship between a Yamamba and a *Nurikabe*, or the solid plaster wall, the same metaphor applies.

The **Nurikabe** is supposedly a random wall one bumps into while walking, usually at night on a lonely road. Foster says, *"suddenly a wall appears in front of you, and you cannot go anywhere."* It is likely that this *yōkai* represents the need for our bodies and minds to rest. When we are exhausted and cannot go on working some say they have "hit a wall."

But perhaps you are walking on a dark and lonely road late at night and instead of "hitting a wall" you feel creeped out by strange noises or shadows. This is also *yōkai*. **Zozo-Gami**, or the God of Cowardice, causes fear and shivering: *buru buru*, or shaking and shivering, is the onomatopoeia for this spirit. The verb *zotto suru* means "creeped out"' and so Zozo-Gami is essentially *God of the Creeps*.

The *yamamba* also shares a relationship with another iconic *yōkai* called *ubume*. The **Ubume** is known as the "birthing woman." She is essentially the incarnation of a woman who dies in childbirth, and then later appears at crossroads covered in blood and carrying her baby. Her image represents the timeless concerns over pregnancy and childbirth, while embodying the essence or spirit of motherhood. According to an ancient text called <u>Three Realms</u>:

> *"Because this is the incarnation of a woman who has died in childbirth, she has breasts and likes to steal other people's children, raising them as her own."*

Suffice to saym ancient people, as much as those in the modern world, observed with their senses and then labeled their experiences like scientists. This becomes our folklore, tradition, myth, etc., and since science is the observation and classification of nature, it is also pure science. Names and identities are given to accidents, occurrences, natural phenomena, etc., which are then categorized in a manner likened how we classify the elements today. We call them hydrogen, nitrogen, oxygen, and carbon. In older times they were called water, fire, air, and earth.

If *Yamabiko* is denied existence, then so too is science and our ability to interact with the natural world. If we deny the *Oni* an existence, we are denying the chaos of life itself, a necessary evil leading to moments of what we call coincidence and miracle.

Other notable, and famous, *yōkai* include *inari*, *kitsune*, and *tanuki*. The first of these spirits oversees rice fields and the fertility of those crops: the **Inari** are one of the most revered of all *yōkai* and share that reverence with the *kitsune*, or fox spirit. Most *inari* shrines are protected by statues of guardian foxes, because as F. Hadland Davis writes in <u>Myths and Legends of Japan</u>, *"Inari was* *originally the God of Rice, but in the eleventh century he became associated with the Fox God…"* **Kitsune** are known for making fire by striking the ground with their tail. The *kitsune-no-yomeiri*, or fox wedding, which is a string of lights in the distance, is an example of natural phenomenon deified. Here is the Japanese version of *fairy lights* and upon further investigation we also find that foxes also share a relationship with those tricky creatures known as fairies or goblins – the *little people* – since any reward bestowed by a fox is only partially real, since *"at least one tempting coin is bound to turn very quickly into grass."* This is said of rewards offered by the *little* creatures in general. Whereas the *inari* are protectors of rice fields and harvests, the *kitsune* are far more than guardians, even of something as sacred and necessary as rice. Fox spirits are said to be able to possess or bewitch humans, or *kitsune-tsuki*. There are also thought to be generational human families which employ foxes to do their biddin: *kitsune tsukai*. Davis writes of the Fox in further detail:

> *"They have the power of infinite vision ; they can hear everything and under- stand the secret thoughts of mankind generally, and in addition they possess the power of transformation and of transmutation. The chief attribute of the bad fox is the power to delude human beings, and for this purpose it will take the form of a beautiful woman, and many are the legends told in this connection."*

Humans thought to be possessed by *kitsune*, as with demonic possession in the Catholic faith, will consume all manner of bizarre things and act in an erratic manner. We may simply call this *hysteria*, though with no reference to the word's use in belittling female emotions. The fox spirit is said to enter the body under the fingernails, a European tradition likewise held for witches. A treatise was even written about fox possession in 1885 by a German doctor named Erwin von Bälz (1849-1913). He labelled the phenomena *alopecanthropy*, something essentially akin to *lycanthropy*, or the ability of a human to turn into a wolf or Oni. And regarding shapeshifting, we must address another famous *yōkai*. The **Tanuki** are supernatural tricksters that, like many *yōkai*, are real animals too. In this case, they are badgers or raccoons. They reside somewhere on the line between civilization and nature, and other than having an incredible ability to shapeshift, are symbols of fertility and prosperity. Their ability to change shape is not confined to the immediate body but can extend outward to include the land itself. The 1994 film *Pom Poko* is an excellent depiction of these mysterious creatures.

Some spirits, however, simply embody occurrences that are no more complex than a mysterious scratch or cut. The **Kamaitachi**, or "sickle weasel," is said to be responsible for such a mark. The **Kamikiri**, on the other hand, cuts off a person's hair randomly, usually around the twilight hours.

When thunder booms and lighting strikes, it is the "thunder beast" known as **Raijū**. The **Yanari**, or "sounding house," is of particular interest here too. These little creatures, as they are thought to exist, are the responsible parties for all manner strange sounds heard in the middle of the night around a home. Yanari is, in essence, a *yōkai* for poltergeist activity. Perhaps those strange noises are also caused by common household items which take on a life of their own after one hundred years: *tsukumogami*. Whether these objects become kind or mischievous depended on how they were treated prior to their partial transformation. In Japan it is not a simple *yūrei* (ghosts) that causes such unnatural disturbances, though that word itself is sort of akin to plural *yōkai*.

We call things monsters, cryptids, ghosts, phantoms, specters, demons, aliens, etc., to classify what we might not otherwise understand. In other cases, we anthropomorphize everything from household items to mysterious marks on our bodies, only to identify our surroundings. Call it superstition, myth, folklore, fairy tale, or legend, it is, once again, science. Contemporary sightings of characters like *slender man* are really *yōkai* that have traversed the world and visited every culture, regardless of their Japanese origins. The **Nopperabō** is one of these creatures, having human features but no face. Foster says the areas of the face is *"completely featureless, lacking eyes, nose, mouth, and any kind of expression."* It is a face *"as smooth as an egg."*

Stories of missing children that seem to defy conventional explanation, even in modern times, are identified as *spiriting away* in Japan. For example, a child suddenly disappears from an area where they were playing just moments ago. There is nowhere for the child to run or hide, and no sign of abduction. Some stories tell of parents who literally turn their back for a split second and upon turning back around realize their child is suddenly missing. Then a frantic search begins. After no evidence of abduction, or any evidence of anything, is found, the child usually shows up later in a bizarre place. They are confused and dazed but usually in good health. The is called **Kamikakushi** or being **Spirited Away**.

Yūrei from the encyclopedia, Japandemonium Illustrated, 2017.

Voodoo

"A black religious cult practiced in the Caribbean and the southern US, combining elements of Roman Catholic ritual with traditional African magical and religious rites, and characterized by sorcery and spirit possession."

The Mysteries of Voodoo

There is perhaps no religious practice more reviled or feared than Voodoo, besides Santeria, covens of witches, proud satanists, or other more obscure cults. But contrary to common belief, cultivated by popular culture, ignorance and fear, Voodoo generally shares more in common with Christianity than with Satanism. Originating in the darkest parts of Africa, Voodoo was brought by the slave trade to the West Indies, and then finally to America where it flourished in the south, famously in New Orleans, Louisiana. Based on a belief in extrasensory forces, Voodoo practitioners believe that certain people can harness and utilize these powers. This is essentially what ceremonial *White Magicians* believe. It is also the definition of *religion* in general: *"the belief in and worshipping of a superhuman power or powers."*

Black Rooster

Contrary to the often-confused usage of the word *Hoodoo*, the practice of *Voodoo* is a religion. Hoodoo, on the contrary, is comprised of West African folk traditions that merged with similar practices of the Native Americans and Europeans. Voodoo is also spelled: *Vaudan, Vaudau, Vaudou, Vaudaux, Vodu, Vodun, Voudou, Voudoun,* and *Voudoux.* It may be a surprise to some that nearly three quarters of Voodooists, on average, are women. Although Roman Catholicism is the official religion of Haiti, most Haitians still practice some form of Voodoo. Even though it is associated with cannibalism, human sacrifice, animal sacrifice and blood drinking, many of these attributes are not part of Voodoo today, nor have they been for some time, or ever. This is not to say that Voodoo is always a peaceful practice. It is not, especially among the paranoid, superstitious, and ignorant. However, human and animal sacrifices are as much a part of the three major world religions, such as Christianity, Islam, and Hinduism, not to mention Judaism, as they are in Voodoo. Even the drinking of blood and eating of flesh is ritualized as Eucharist in Christianity with wine and bread. In Leviticus 17:11 we learn how *"it is the blood that makes atonement for one's life."* And in Hebrews 13:11 we read:

> *"The high priest carries the blood of animals into the Most Holy Place as a sing offering, but the bodies are burned outside the camp."*

The goal of citing these two verses is to prove that Voodoo is, in this manner, little different than Christianity, and perhaps this is why the two merged so easily in Haiti. Maybe it was the bloody nature of the Church that attracted Voodooists in the first place!

If we were to examine the practice of *metzitzah b'peh*, when an official sucks the blood away from a circumcised penis, we may label this barbaric or even Satanic, if it weren't for that one word which clearly identifies the ritual as Jewish. Then there is the Catholic *Inquisition* and the ongoing Muslim *Jihad*, though neither of these horrors adequately represents the virtues of these world religions.

The practice of literal human sacrifice may also be a charge against certain heathens, for example, who refused to convert to Christianity, and yet we know that this practice is still very real. The Hindu *Gadhimai festival* in Nepal is held every five years with hundreds of thousands of goats, buffalo, and birds ritually killed in barbaric ways to the goddess of which

L'Kabrit

the event is named. The goal of comparing Voodoo and Hinduism is not to defend the former. Our point is simply that few understand the origins or fringes of their own communities, let alone something so terrifying as the mention of Voodoo!

Great irony also exists in arguments suggesting that the Christian, Muslim, Hindu, and Jew practice rites that are merely misunderstood, and yet Voodoo is the *Devil's Religion*. Although to many Christians and Muslims they may think this of each other and Hinduism.

As for Voodoo, it is documented that even as early as 1861 two black Voodooists in New Orleans had hanged a child over a fireplace to be roasted alive as part of a ritual. Despite what we have learned about the words "virgin" or "kid" in reference to a *baby goat*, literal child sacrifices performed by Voodooists are called *Hornless Goat* or *Goat without Horns*, i.e., an actual human kid. These practices largely originated and were operated in ancient Africa, less in Haiti, and even less in the Southern United States.

A sacrificial goat in Voodoo is referred to as a *cabrit*, and the special black goat is called *L'Kabrit*. Before the goat is killed it is dressed in a red robe and anointed with oil; a *veve*, or sacred symbol, is drawn on its back and then it is killed quickly. All those in attendance, beginning with the priest, will sip the blood of the animal form a wooden bowl.

Similarly, the *black rooster* is a symbol of Satan in Voodoo. Its blood is considered precious, and it is used in blood baptisms or baths. Attendees are sprinkled with some blood first and then each drinks a little as well. Robert W. Pelton documents in <u>The Complete Book of Voodoo</u> the nature of blood consumption, and both animal and human sacrifices:

> *"Blood baths and tasting fresh warm blood, generally animal and preferably the still warm blood of a black cat, were quite commonplace in early American Voodoo ceremonies. And human sacrifices, especially young children, were sometimes accurately reported by the press and writers of that particular period in history."*

Voodoo includes all the same elements as nearly every major religion, cult, and spiritual practice, even reminding us of the ancient *Mystery Schools* of Greece or Egypt. It includes the practice of baptism (*Ablution*), chapels and temples (*Hounfor* or *Tonnelle*), altars (*Pe*), sacred drinks for communion (*Clairin*), *Libation*, tithing (during *Adoration*), crosses, priests (*Houngan*), priestesses (*Mambo*), incenses, oils, dancing, chants, music, speaking in tongues (the language of the *loa* called *Langage*), endings to prayers (amen: *Adobo* or *Reler*), ceremonies, rituals, rites, spirits or saints (*Loa*) - heavily influenced by Christian Saints - and even the *Gran Maite* or *Corps Cadavres,* the one singular God, or the *Supreme Being* and *Creator of the Universe.* Voodooists even have a Virgin Mary in the *loa Aido Ouedo.* Voodooists likewise see the sun as a sacred object and refer to it as *Mystère.*

Goat Without Horns

Of special consideration here is the *ablution* because the overall process involves an early morning ritual bathing of the body. This is only used in Voodoo initiation rites. Prior to bathing, initiates are required to abstain from sexual activity for seven days. Afterwards, sexual activities are encouraged. Washing the body is symbolic of cleansing the soul, by washing the external and internal. Pelton says, *"A 40-day period of absolute seclusion (couche) is necessary for purifying the prospective priest or priestess."* Isaiah 1:16 reminds us of the same:

"Wash you, make you clean; put away the evil of your doings from before mine eyes; ceases to do evil."

The same was true in Voodoo for abstaining from animal flesh and alcohol. In Matthew 25:42 it is further written:

"For I was an hungered, and ye gave me no meat: I was thirsty and ye gave me no drink."

By cleaning and proper preparations, one is made worthy of receiving divine influences from the *Cosmic Mind*, and in Voodoo from the *loas*. The initial stage of initiation is known as *Lavé Tête*, which takes place before the soul cleansing ceremony called *Bruler Zin*. Here is where all future *houngans* (priests) and *mambos* (priestesses) learn the songs, gestures, secret rights, and all other necessary practices of Voodoo. The 40-days of seclusion for *houngans* and *mambos* is common throughout the world and the *mysteries*, and we read that in Luke 4:1-2, which says:

> *"Jesus, full of the Holy Spirit, left the Jordan and was led by the Spirit into the wilderness, where for forty days he was tempted by the devil. He ate nothing during those days, and at the end of them he was hungry."*

Upon reaching initiate status, and becoming possessed in some manner by a spirit, the ritual is called *Danse Vaudou*. In the *Mystery Schools* candidates would likewise commune with the *dead*. When the initiate completes their journey in Voodoo, they are awarded the sacred *ason* and called *Nom Vaillant*. This *ason* is a very sacred ritual rattle, which is the *houngan* or *mambo* emblem of priesthood and high office. It is used for summoning the spirits. The Egyptian Isis holds a similar item called *sistrum*, a musical instrument with metal frame and rods that rattled when shaken. Priestesses of *Ise Jingu*, the sacred shrine in Japan where Amaterasu descended from heaven, also use nearly identical rattles.

Each priest or priestess, *houngan or mambo*, may have followers in a particular cult group. This group is called a *Société*. Here members pledge their faith to a leader. Voodoo priests and priestesses practicing harmonious magic are considered "high-type." Those practicing baneful magic are called "low-type."

In Voodoo there are hundreds of spirits and saints called *loas*. Much like the traditional notion of good versus evil, or white and black, or day and night, *loas* can be helpful, harmful, or both. Pelton explains how certain rites are held to bind the evil *loas* specifically:

> *"Special Voodoo rites are held to bind or restrain the evil loa for a specific number of years. Walking in an open fire and dancing on live coals are part of these restraining rituals. Each loa is an invisible ruler who appears through the possession of a worshipper. Getting a loa to accept a food offering is they key to appeasing him. If the possessed person takes the offering of food, it is believed to be really the loa acting through his or her body. By accepting food, an evil loa is said to have agreed to go away, while a good loa is said to have agreed to assist the possessed person gain his or her desire."*

An *engagement* is a "pact" made between a Voodoo practitioner and a particular *loa*. This "pact" is essentially the same as those made with demons, or between witches and the Devil. To pay respects to a *loa* is quite simple in Voodoo practice. Face the alter and then face *West* while saying *D'abord*; *East* while saying *A table*; *South* while saying *Adonai*; and North while saying *Olande'*. Prayers spoken in all four directions are called *En-Carre*.

Other Voodoo rituals such as *Boucan* involve large bonfires built in honor of the *loa Legba*, one week before New Year's Eve. The fires are then kept burning one week beyond these celebrations. This festival is like the bonfires of *Mabon*, *Samhain*, and *Beltane* especially. But *Boucan* reminds us of the candles lit during *Imbolc*, or the logs burned during *Yule* to illuminate the dark both literally and symbolically, and to provide warmth while warding off all evil influences. The *Bruler Zin* ritual involves three separate fires that are lit to purify the soul.

Wangas, Fetishes (Charms & Talismans) & Voodoo Dolls

In Voodoo there are countless curses, hexes, charms, talismans, etc. Some are used for inflicting harm and others for obtaining protection, health, love, and wealth. These are generally referred to as *wangas*. More specifically, a *wanga* is a *black magic spell* used to place hexes on people. They are most often small cloth effigies in the form of a doll made in black, red, or both. The dolls are then stuffed with things believed to possess the power to bring about the desired magical outcome. In other words, a *Voodoo Doll* functions as a form of sympathetic magic. They can be used to bind, seduce, attract spiritual help and good fortune, cause accidents or bring death. Pelton says the same of *wangas*, they *"can force someone to do a person's bidding, defeat a love rival, seduce one you may be fatally attracted to, cause accidents, or even bring on death, etc."* Their other name is *caprelata*, denoting a curse or evil charm.

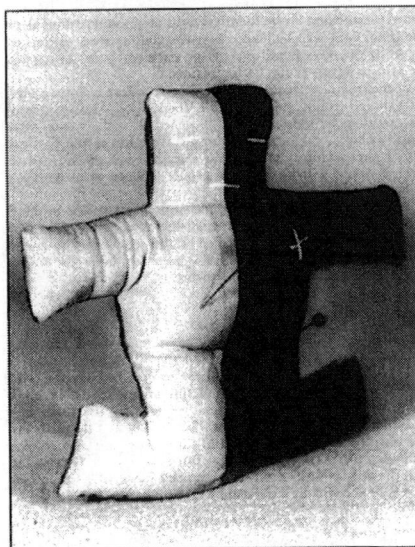

Voodoo Doll

In eastern tradition, particularly in Japan, dolls called *Wara Ningyo* – Straw Curse Dolls – were used to curse opponents with misfortune, suffering, and death. Such a practice dates to at least the 6th-century.

Red flannel is valued for making *wangas* and charms. It is also a common material used in numerous other Voodoo practices. It is believed that the hair of a person or dust from their footprint will make the most powerful *wangas*. Since hair and nails continue to grow after death, they traditionally have been used to summon the dead by necromancers, and thus share a relationship with the impure. In *onychomancy* the fingernails are even used for divination. As has been related by the alchemists Paracelsus, who wrote of the usage of hair in the dark arts:

"Witches give their hair to Satan as a deposit on the contract they make with him."

Kurt Seligmann provides further historical context on the same subject in his book The Mirror of Magic, wherein he writes:

"Cut hair and nails are hidden away by many primitive people; or, deposited in sacred places, they are burned to prevent their falling into the hands of sorcerers who would use them for evil spells against their former owners."

The *Voodoo Doll* is perhaps the best-known element to outsiders of the religion. But not all practitioners use the dolls, and those that do require their service may make dolls that look entirely different than the ones commonly associated with the faith. Pelton written of these famous dolls:

"Voodoo dolls are most commonly used in hexing another individual. It must always be remembered that it is not the doll itself, for it is merely the medium which represents the intended victim. And the doll is the means by which thought transference is successfully transmitted."

The most powerful kind of doll is made by the actual practitioner intending to cast a specific spell on someone. Although these things may be purchased as novelty or otherwise, it is customary to create your own. The same is said of a magician's *athame,* or ritual dagger. The *Voodoo Doll* must be constructed from several items carrying the *vibration(s)* of the intended victim. These should be personal items such as clothing or things like hair and nails. An item of clothing is best for the outside cover of the doll, which should be stuffed with straw or cotton and then with the personal items. Upon stuffing the doll, you should hand stitch the final section while setting your focus on the target with mental concentration.

Contrary to popular belief, a *Voodoo Doll* does not have only the intended purpose of causing *harm.* It can also be used to draw one to your *desires,* though such an act of *love magic(k)* is *dark,* because it likely acts against the *will* of your target. These *Voodoo Love Dolls* are made with black, white, and red or blue. The black side is used for *cursing,* the white for *spiritual help* or *love spells* (if red), and the back for obtaining *spiritual assistance* (if blue). These dolls may also be made from clay, paper, wax, and even butter or dough.

Yet another connection to Catholicism is the Voodoo charm called *Oraison,* made in the form of a Catholic prayer. In fact, many practices in Voodoo require the assistances of the *Book of Psalms* contained in the Bible.

Magical charms meant to guard against poor health, financial ruin, bad luck, and property loss, are called *Gris-Gris.* They are hung over doorways, on the door, buried in the ground, or are sometimes worn.

An *Ouanga* is a special name given to talismans, mascots, or magical charms, and are often used as a love *fetish.* The latter term "fetish" is just another name for talismans, mascots, and magical charms. Fetishes are believed to be the seat or house of a spiritual force, i.e., an inanimate object upon which a spirit is drawn.

Black magic spells called *Gros-Pouin* are already powerful but made even stronger by blood and semen. These ingredients attract certain spirits and are used to feed them in some rituals. Semen is very sacred in Voodoo and one of the most protective devices. Blood is considered an important ingredient in *wangas* (dolls) too. Pelton adds, "they may" also *"be stuffed with dirt from an open grave site, ashes from a ritual fire, leaves believed to possess certain desired magical qualities, and salt."*

Voodoo good-luck charms (*paquets*) are made in a ritual called *Marre Paquet.* The *Paquet* is a bundle of secret ingredients enclosed in a flannel bag. It is a good-luck charm typically made with a blend of powdered roots and herbs, spices, and flowers. When made as an effigy doll it is called a *Paquet Congo.*

Colliers are powerful charms made into a necklace using alligator or numerous other types of animal teeth, shells, and snake vertebrate. Alligator teeth and snake vertebrate are both considered protective charms in Voodoo, along with oxtails, garlic and the teeth, claws, and whiskers of a cat.

Small flannel bags made as a *wanga* to cast an evil hex, or to assist in protection, are called a *Conjure Bag* or *Goofer Bag.* These bags are placed near the door of an *enemy,* inside of their home, or in their yard; someplace they will walk over it. *Goofer Dust* is the dirt from a grave site, also called *Conjure Dust.* The seemingly benign sounding *Conjure Balls,* comprised of a wad of black wax, contain either human hair or human flesh. Pelton says, *"It is considered to be an omen of death when found in the yard or house, and is a most powerful wanga."*

Sex is an important part of hex breaking and is instigated between partners, or in orgies, to please the *loas,* while furthermore most *société* members are polygamists. Homosexuality is also a major part of Voodoo and is typically a necessary component in some communities.

Voodoo Candles, Powders & Incense

Candles are considered an important part of most rituals or ceremonies, and in Voodoo this is no different. Voodooists consider it bad luck to burn two candles on the same table or three in the same room unless a specific spell is being worked, or a special service is being held. It is considered good-luck and protection, although it could be dangerous, to burn a candle at night while one sleeps.

Green and white candles are commonly given out at Voodoo services. Green candles signify money but can also attract success in general. White candles signify purity, protection, and success; Pink candles deal in love or passions; blue candles are used for gambling; brown to get rid of enemies.

Cross Altar Candles are burned as *spiritual purifying agents* to attract spiritual forces for rituals and ceremonies: for Sunday, Lemon Yellow; Monday is White; Tuesday is Crimson Red; Wednesday is Lavender; Thursday is Light Blue; Friday is Nile Green; and Saturday is appropriately Pitch Black, since it is the day of Saturn, as is Sunday the day of the Sun. For *Astral Candles* we find the following:

Capricorn - Red & Gold	**Cancer** - Orange and Nile Green
Aquarius - Yellow & Blue	**Leo** - Pink & Orange
Pisces - Blue & Emerald Green	**Virgo** - Pink & Gold
Aries - Rose Pink & White	**Libra** - Gold & Green
Taurus - Red & Lemon Yellow	**Scorpio** - Yellow & Blue
Gemini - Crimson Red & Green	**Sagittarius** - Red & Orange

Voodoo powders are considered extremely powerful but will lose their strength unless stored in a small and tightly corked bottle. The bottle must then be placed away from direct sunlight. These powders are said to do everything from alleviating confusion and casting a hex, to attracting a mate and breaking a hex. Others are used for protection of the home or to gain greater success in life. *Draw Back Powder* is said to be very good in preventing evil from being done against the user. It prevents a hex from even being cast and reverses the effects of all evil actions. *John the Conqueror Powder* supposedly has a similar nature, helping to eliminate curses and evil spells. Of all the variations of love powders the most powerful is called *Venus Powder*. It will reportedly force others to be drawn to you, especially those of the opposite sex, since you will be irresistible to them. *XXX Cross Powder* is used for darker purposes and is considered the most powerful of all hexing ingredients. It is believed that no matter how powerful a person, they cannot avoid a curse initiated with this powder.

Voodoo oils are used to produce visions and aid in communicating with spirits. They also provide general assistance in ceremonies where participants are anointed on their head and body to induce a state of ecstasy. Secret instructions for making these anointing perfume oils are alleged to have been divinely revealed in the darkest regions of Africa and Haiti. Only a Voodoo priests or priestess is allowed to prepare the oils. Just like Voodoo powders, these holy oils are likewise used for casting or breaking bewitchments, attracting the opposite sex, conjuring spirits, making dreams prophetic, obtaining wealth, or gaining luck while gambling. *Hyssop Oil* is said to make lovers more faithful and to increase financial gains, while attracting new friends. This oil is made from the small bushy aromatic plant of the mint family, which is used in cooking and herbal medicines. It is one of the most used ingredients in magical practices. *Lemon Grass Oil* is a wonderful assistant in becoming more psychic. It is said to aid in the calling of spirits. Another similar oil is *Zorba Perfume Oil*, which specifically helps with clairvoyance, or perceiving future events beyond sensory contact. *Lucky Dog Oil* aids in the practice of gambling, throwing dice or dealing cards. One aid to break hexes and uncross friends is *Myrrh Oil*, while *Musk Perfume Oil* helps one to build confidence, self-reliance, and determination. To wash, cleanse, and purify a room, *Van Van Perfume Oil* is often used. *Venus Perfume Oil* is, of course, the most powerful love oil, making one irresistible to the opposite sex and drawing love towards the user. Special oil called *Zula Zula Perfume Oil* is used for anointing the infamous *Voodoo Doll* and an equally powerful blend, *Yula Perfume Oil*, is used to bring death upon an enemy. *Selaginella oil* is also used as protection against bewitchments.

    Voodoo suffumigations come in a variety of forms, much like powders and oils. They serve the same purposes and functions as any other incense used for magical operations, or religious rites. The smell of incense is said to please Voodoo *loa* or saints, and this is why in other magical practices certain sweet incenses are used to call upon harmonious spirits, while unsavory pungent scents are said to attract harmful spirits. It is another common theme in Voodoo that as incense smoke rises in the air it brings our prayers along to the gods. Other incenses are burned to mask the smell of ritual practices or to ward off evil energies. Since Voodoo is so closely related to Christianity, specifically Catholicism, incense is used as an element in most rituals and ceremonies just as it is in the *censer*. Christianity did not invent suffumigations, but the connection is emphasized due to the nature of the relationship between these two religions. *John the Conqueror Incense* is utilized for removing curses and hexes. It is also considered beneficial when gambling or in court. Two sacred Voodoo incense varieties are *Frankincense*, used to gain favor with good spirits, and *Myrrh*, used to make dreams come true if burned before going to bed. *Sandalwood Incense* is considered good for healing and attracting psychic vibrations. The most powerful love incense is *Venus Incense*, which is considered dangerous since it completely holds the love of anyone desired. Other love aromas include *Fire of Passion, Flaming Power, Red Rose,* and *Devil's Master*. To protect, cleanse, and purify a home, one should use the appropriately named *House Blessing Incense*. For sacred places, *Temple Incense* is useful for purifying the room.

    Voodoo herbs and plants are mixed into a variety of combinations and used in rituals. Like incense, these mixtures are often burned to cover up the obnoxious odors created by roasting sacrificial flesh, and one could also imagine the spilled entrails and blood. *Christians may scoff at this yet continue to eat their sacrificial steaks and burgers [meant to clarify a point!] so long as the entrails and blood remain at a slaughterhouse.*

    Some herbs and roots are mixed with bathwater or cleansing water to purify the body, home, or business. They are chewed and swallowed, or sometimes spit, depending on the nature of the charm or hex. When these roots and herbs are harvested, they should be found on high ground rather than low ground. They should be picked in pairs and with male and female specimens. These herbs, plants, and roots have the same purpose as do Voodoo powders, oils, and suffumigations. *Basil Leaves* are believed to provide women with fertility and men with success, while providing overall protection against hexes. *Bay Leaves* are likewise protective charms against being hexed. One can ward off evil with *Foenugreek Seed*, which can be brewed into tea and used as head wash in Voodoo rituals. If blended with *Goofer Dust* and sprinkled in a room, *Nettle* is believed to relieve a hex. *Fern* has the same protective qualities against bewitchments. For protection while sleeping use *Eucalyptus*. *Valerian Root* is also said to calm nerves if placed in a pillow while sleeping. *Celery Seed* is considered good for casting spells and bringing about better concentration. The commonly used *Hyssop* can be brewed into a tea and used in bathwater for purification before a ritual. To purify the home and bring harmony, use *Lavender*. *Echinacea* is used for stimulating business growth and financial income. For better luck, love charms, wealth, and general positive attributes, *John the Conqueror Root* should be utilized. Mixtures of *Mango Tree Leaves* are often used to help pregnant women in labor. *Rose Buds* are used to aid in bruises and *Rose Hips* are generally used in love spells.

For a complete list of candles, powders, oils, suffumigations, herbs, and plants,
one should consult <u>The Complete Book of Voodoo</u> by Robert W. Pelton.

Sacred & Mystical Voodoo

Some of the most sacred symbols of Voodoo include the palm tree, sugar cane, bananas, basil, rice, black-eyed peas, eggs, and rum. Fireflies are also considered very beneficial because they attract money and love. Although one typically does not think about the "luck of the Irish" when discussing Voodoo, we still find the four-leaf *clover* used as a charm against snakes and other creatures in these rites. It is carried in a red flannel pouch for good luck. In any place this clover is found the same qualities are ascribed to its leaves: faith, hope, love, and luck. A clover is thought to carry luck in the same way that a lion's tooth retains the strength of a lion, or that a horseshoe possesses that animal's swiftness. Often, we find that numbers are considered lucky or unlucky and in Voodoo this is no different, according to Pelton:

> *"Three is believed to be a good number in Voodoo, but five is even more mystically powerful. Seven is said to be one of the best conjuring numbers. Nine is believed to be even better. Four times four is believed to be the most powerful combination for fighting the effects of a wanga or evil spell. Ten is always considered unfortunate."*

Voodooists also use *wands* to heal the sick. A limb cut from a cypress tree over a period of three months becomes a wand. All trees are considered sacred, too, since they are home to certain *loas*. Cypress Root has the same powers. Sacred trees are called *reposoir*, described by Pelton as:

> *"A stone, tree, or other temporary home of a spirit. A circular stone or cement enclosure is often placed around the foot of a sacred tree which is known to house a loa. This too is called a reposoir."*

Voodooists even have their own magic mirrors used for *scrying*. A *Minore* is a magic mirror used for obtaining visions. Such mirrors are made of polished metal and are consecrated during social rites. The *loa* called *Agove Minoire* is a female cemetery spirit symbolized by a phallus carved out of wood, but she may also be represented with a mirror. She guards the graves of the dead. These two elements connect when attempting to invoke a spirit, and so *Agove Minoire* would be helpful in this operation. One method of doing this is visiting a cemetery either at noon or midnight, while being sure to bring a new mirror and a pair of scissors. Upon the striking of twelve, look into the mirror and let the scissors drop to the ground while calling upon the name of a person you wish to commune with. Another method involves breaking a black crow egg into a glass of water. The mixture is then used as an invoking face wash. This is also like *Oomancy*, or divination by egg, the shells of which are commonly used in Voodoo practice. Like the number seven, consuming a snake or bat brain, or eating a live frog or lizard, is said to provide better conjuring skills.

Veves & Loas

A Voodoo *veve* is a mystical sign, symbol, design, or drawing, made on the ground, either inside a room or outside under a covering (*Tonnelle*), for a worship service, ceremony, or rite. They may only be made by a *houngan* or *mambo*. Otherwise, they are considered powerless. A special *veve* called *croisignin* is made in the form of a single cross, yet another sacred symbol of Voodoo, usually used on the altars. Much like Hindu *kolems*, or Navajo sand paintings, each of these symbols attracts *spiritual influences* embodied by the planets.

The veve of Dambhalah and Aida Hwédo, the greatest of all the loas. Dambhalah is also known as Dambhalah Hwédo and is a representation of God the Father. He personifies simultaneous fire and water. Aida Hwédo is Dambhalah's wife and symbolizes God the Mother. She personifies the rainbow and all the waters. As Dambhalah is the biggest of all the fish, Aida Hwédo is the biggest of all *female* fish, often represented by the whale. Their combined symbol is two snakes, intertwined.

Each *veve* represents a single spirit or it can represent a group of spirits. Corn is one of the most common elements used in creating these ritual diagrams. Interestingly, the earth-covered dwellings where Navajo sand paintings are made are called *Hougan*, virtually identical to the name for Voodoo high priests – *Houn'gan*. Robert Pelton explains:

> "Veves are generally made to represent a specific loa or group of loas who are being invoked during Voodoo rituals. They are drawn by pouring ashes, flour, coffee grounds, brick dust, or white corn meal from a bowl. Corn meal is considered to be the most potent ingredients, and is more commonly used than are the others. The finished veve becomes the focal point of the worshippers at every Voodoo ceremony. It must be carefully constructed either before or during the actual service."

Corn is a powerful medium because it symbolizes the pregnancy of the Virgin Mary, known as the *loa* called *Aido Ouedo*. A closely related *loa* to Selene-Luna is *Agove Royo*, who rules the sea. Although this spirit is a man, his talisman is nearly identical to the *Triple Moon* or *Triple Goddess* symbol of Wiccans, showing the waxing, full, and waning moon phases. His shows two stars and a crescent moon instead, though it still implies his control over waters.

In Voodoo tradition these signs embody heavenly forces like any talisman. They are believed to connect with a spirit through the image, and they therefore act as a bridge between the astral world and physical world. With its assistance the *loa* can make direct contact with the physical world using the *veve* as a point of contact. In this way, they are like *consecrated magic circle*. This principle is consistent with the purpose behind specific colors, candles, incenses, oils, etc., of any rite or ritual. The strength of a *veve* comes from the soul it receives during the rite, typically from certain foods, drinks, odors, and actions.

It should also be clear that considering Voodoo was largely practiced by the poor, and thus those who were often illiterate, many words are misspelled from other languages or made up entirely, like the term *oto*, which means automobile.

The following images are extracted from Pelton's, <u>The Complete Book of Voodoo</u>, and presented here with recommendation to read both that book and his <u>Voodoo Secrets from A to Z</u>.

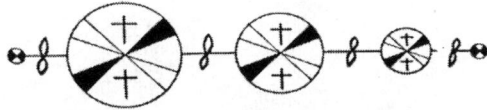

Another veve for blessing the three drums

Veve of the loa Damballa-Wedo

Veve of the loa Pierre-Boucassin

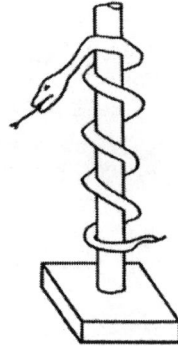

Veve of the loa Aido-Wedo (wife of the loa Damballa-Wedo)

Veve of the loa Assakerly

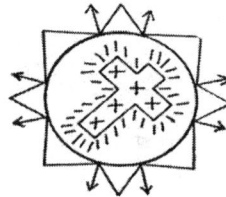

Veve of the loa Agassou

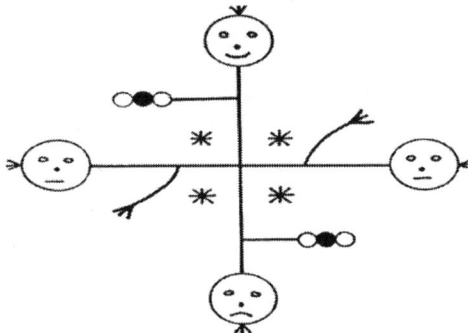

Veve of the loa Kalfu

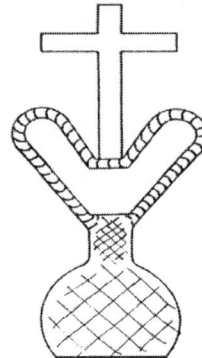

Veve representing death. Drawn when sacrificial offerings are being made in Voodoo rituals.

Veve of the loa Lenguesou

Veve of the loa Brigitte

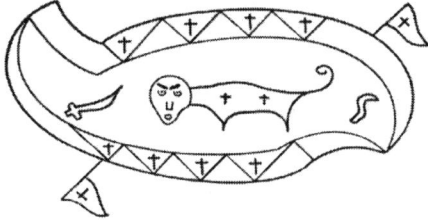
Veve of the loa Moundong

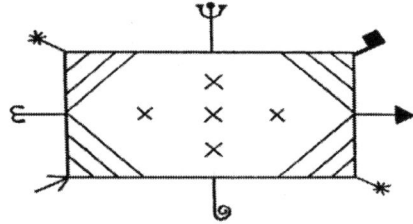
Veve of the loa Agarou-Tonnerre and the loa Danh

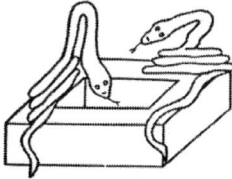
Veve of the loa Ayizan

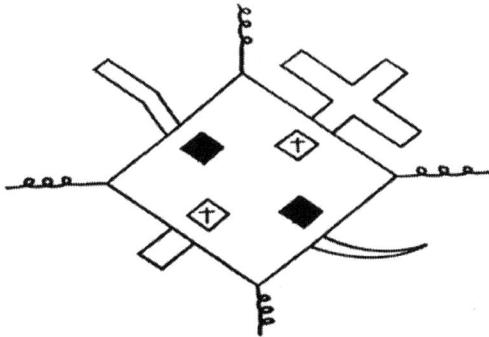
Veve of the loa Azacca

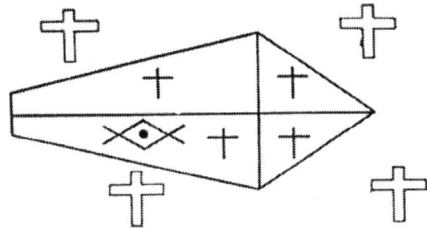
Veve of the loa Ghede

Veve of the loa Grand Bois

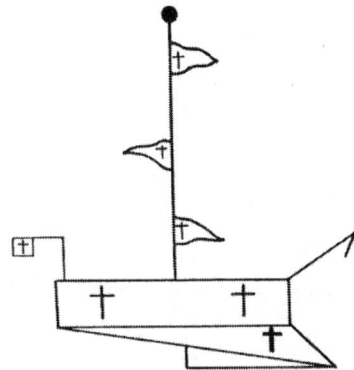
Veve of the loa Immamou

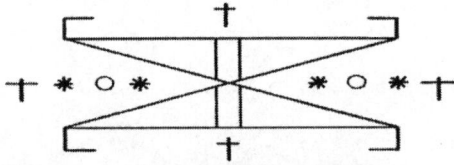

Veve of the loa Ogoun Badagris

The veve of the loa Erzulie, the Venus of the Voodoo pantheon.

Veve of the loa Ogu-Ferraille

The veve of Grand Erzulie. This powerful loa is often syncretized as the Holy Ghost of the Christian Trinity. She shares the dominion of the heart with the loa Legba.

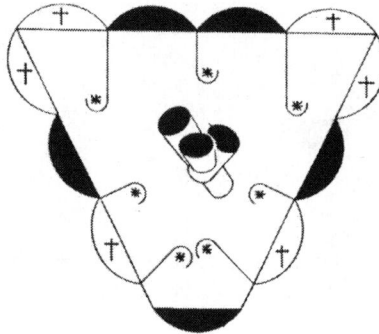

A special mystical veve used for blessing the various Voodoo drums. Fresh banana leaves are carefully laid over this veve and the three different size drums are placed upon the leaves. This procedure is known as a resting period, or a time in which the drums regain their dissipated strength for use in future Voodoo ceremonies and rituals.

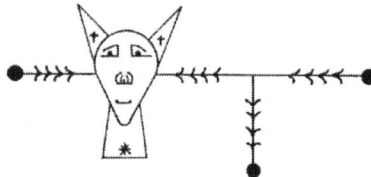

Veve of the loa Ezili-Taureau

Loa Bossu-trois-cornes—protects wearer from all war injuries and accidents.

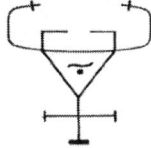

Loa Aizan—protects wearer from all evil spirits.

Loa La-Sirene—aids in the seduction of the opposite sex.

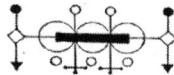

Loa Zaca Tonerre—protects interests of the poor.

Loa Agassou—best known for the power of healing.

Loa Aida-Ouedo—controls one's destiny.

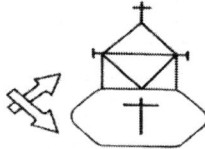

Loa Legba—brings wearer general good fortune.

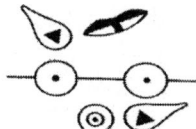

Loa Simi—bestows clairvoyant power on wearer.

Loa Onzoncaire—helps wearer accomplish anything desired.

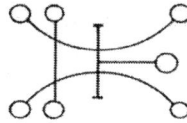

Loa Brise—creates mental anguish and suffering in the lives of others.

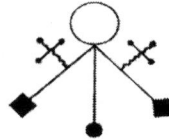

Loa Ibo—helps wearer fulfill all responsibilities.

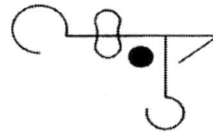

Loa Zaka—helps crop growth when farming.

Loa Gran Bois—clears up all feelings of confusion.

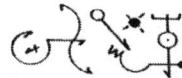

Loa Sobo—protects the wearer during storms.

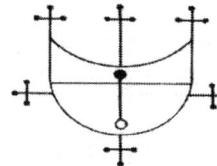

Loa Nago-Piman—heals the wearer and friends.

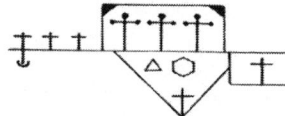

Loa Ogu—protects wearer from any injury.

Loa Pierre-Boucassin—draws the opposite sex to the wearer.

Loa Agoue Royo—protects wearer while on water.

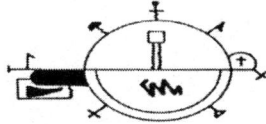

Loa Guede-Ti-Waive—Guarantees justice to the wearer.

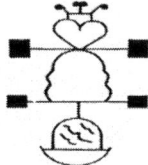

Loa Babako—allows the wearer to practice black magic.

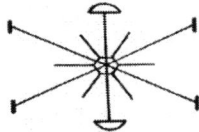

Loa Marinette—protects against all sickness.

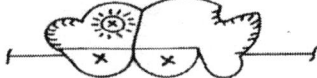

Loa Guede-Nimbo—helpful in all areas of life. A very lucky talisman.

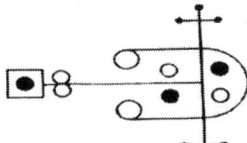

Loa Avrada—assists wearer in childbirth and pregancy.

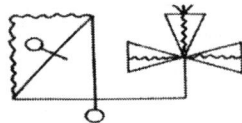

Loa Loco—gives healing power to wearer.

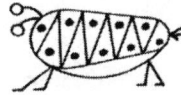

Loa Guede-masaka—protects wearer against poisoning.

Loa Ezili-Freda-Dahomey—leads wearer to sensual pleasures.

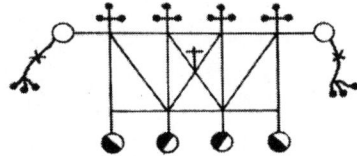

Loa Danh—brings wearer and associates tremendous wealth.

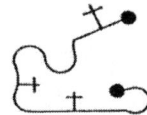

Loa Bakulu-Baka—protects wearer from death hexes.

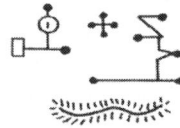

Loa Taureau-Trois-Graines—increases sexual potency.

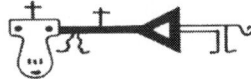

Loa Kalfu—protects traveling people at all times.

Loa Champagne-miotre—inflicts illness and disease on others.

Loa Brigitte—makes one more fertile.

Names of Loas & their Signs

These are the names of certain *loas*, or spirits and saints, in Voodoo practice. They share similarities with other spirits, gods, and goddesses, in much the same way that the Greek and Roman pantheons are identical, and comparable globally.

Agarou Tonnerre: a vicious spirit represented by a bloodless animal or snake.

Agassou: guardian of all customs and traditions. Also, able to heal and cure all ailments.

Agau: can cause earthquakes.

Agove Royo: a spirit of the sea. Protects travelers on waters.

Agwe-Taroyo: a spirit of the sea represented by ships or seashells.

Aida Ouedo: a powerful female spirit and the wife of *Damballa*. She likes red wine and determines man's destiny.

Ayizan: protects against other evil spirits and is repented by a palm leaf.

Azacca: heals with herbs.

Babako: a purely evil spirit.

Baka: a very evil spirit whose services may be purchased with monetary offering.

Bakulu-Baka: a spirit that hides in the woods and drags chains.

Baron Samedi: male ruler of cemeteries. His symbol is a black cross on a tomb.

Brigette: female ruler of cemeteries and partner of Baron Samedi.

Brise: creates mental illness and is represented by thunder and lightning.

Champagne-Miofre: inflicts sickness on the hexed.

Damballa: the most powerful of all Voodoo spirits. His wife is *Aida Ouedo* and his day is Thursday.

Danh: the "heavenly snake" represented by a rainbow. Brings wealth and luck.

Elizi: a spirit of love and sensuality. She is the patron goddess of all love.

Erzile: the mistress of *Damballa*. She likes sacrifices of white pigeons.

Erzulie-Freda-Dahomey: a goddess comparable to the Greek Aphrodite or Roman Venus.

Ghede: ruler of fire and spirit of death.

Grand Bois: a spirit able to reverse bad luck and clear up confusion.

Guede Nimbo: a powerful spirit who will assist in any request.

Guede-Z-Arignee: a spider-spirit that can cause harm or bring great peace of mind.

Ibo: helps one to overcome any problem. Her color is red.

Kalfu: he protects travelers and is the "guardian of crossroads."

La Balainne: a spirit represented by a whale that brings good fortune and financial gain.

La Sirene: protector of children when they are near water. This spirit is a mermaid or naiad.

Legba: helps to find things that are lost.

Loco: the spirit of all vegetation. Heals with leaves and herbs.

Marinette: protects against all illness. Also creates animosity.

Marmette-Pied-Rouge: a protective spirit that will protect a person from being cursed.

Moundong: a spirit that demands sacrificial offerings and blood.

Ogoun Badagris: a spirit who demands human sacrifices. Appeased by baptisms of blood.

Ogu: a warrior spirit.

Ogu-Ferraille: protects one in battle.

Pierre-Boucassin: enjoys sexual exploits and sensual pleasures.

Simi: a water naiad with clairvoyant powers that may be bestowed on children.

Sobo: brings fame and fortune to delivers.

Taureau-Tois-Graines: a spirit of sexual pleasure and promiscuity.

Zaca Tonerre: protector against misfortunes of poor people.

Zaka: a spirit of agriculture. Prefers offerings of avocado and boiled corn. Helps farmers.

Similar in nature to Voodoo *veves*, *Hex Signs* are a combination of cosmic symbols that share a parallel with Kabbalistic elements. Their usage varies from offering *protection* against dark magic and the *evil eye*, to curing sickness. The following images were extracted from Migene González-Wippler's, <u>The Complete Book of Amulets & Talismans</u>.

This hex sign symbolizes the four elements and the four seasons. It represents the earth protected by the sun. It is also a prayer for plenty, fertility and balance in life's sorrows and joys.

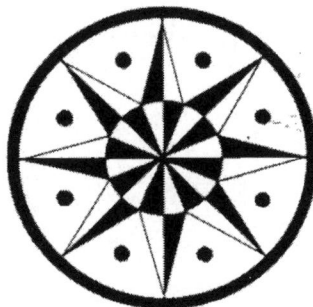

A very popular hex sign, where the entire annual cycle is enclosed by the dual protection of the circle and the eight-rayed star, symbols of life and balance.

One of the earliest versions of the swastika within the protective circle of life.

One of the versions of the hex sign known as the Great and Lesser Seals. It refers to the six steps of creation and protects all things.

A sign for strength and courage. It uses the famous double-headed eagle motif to symbolize watchfulness. The tulips represent fertility.

The Emerald Tablet, Hermeticism & Masonic Symbolism

"The evil serpent of paradise was transformed by the Gnostics into the beneficent Ouroboros. The Ouroboros was changed into the alchemist's dragon, and its body being light and dark found a chemical interpretation."

~ Kurt Seligmann ~

Thrice Great

Hermes Trismegistus is an amalgamation of the Greek Hermes and Egyptian Thoth, the god of writing, medicine, astronomy, and magic. The full name is Greek for Thoth, who the Rosetta Stone calls "the great, the great." To Trismegistus was attributed all learning and wisdom. His "written" works included 36,525 books on the *Principles of Nature*, which correspond to the 365.2422 days in a solar year. Iamblichus, the Neoplatonist philosopher, reduced the number of these books to 20,000 before Clement of Alexandria further reduced them to 42, a highly significant occult number often tied to Kabbalah. Iamblichus writes:

> *"Hermes, the god who presides over language, was formerly very properly considered as common to all priests; and the power who presides over the true science concerning the gods is one and the same in the whole of things. Hence our ancestors dedicated the inventions of their wisdom to this deity, inscribing all their own writings with the name of Hermes."*

Hermes-Thoth was said to have made his books invisible, and as G. R. S. Mead writes, *"unseeable, undefinable."* They shall remain unseen *"for every one whose foot shall tread the plains of this land"* until God fashions garments for the soul. We read something similar in Joshua 1:3, that: *"every place that the sole of your foot shall tread upon, that have I given unto you, as I said unto Moses."* Matthew 7:7 relates further: *"Ask and it will be given to you; seek and you will find; knock and the door will be opened to you. For everyone who asks receives; the one who seeks finds; and to the one who knocks, the door will be opened."* In other words, the "books" are within us, and they can only be obtained by a seeker of truth following the *True Way*. Christians know this from Luke 17: *"the kingdom of God is within you."* These *garments for the soul* are human bodies. Souls must therefore incarnate for the *books* to be *seen*.

It is also said Jesus will enter your heart, associated with the sun, so long you open the door when he knocks. Revelation 3:20 says: *"Here I am! I stand at the door and knock."* Interestingly, there is a direct connection here between Jesus and Hermes-Thoth, also referred to as *Djehuti* or *Tehuti*. The word *tehu* is Egyptian for ibis, and *ti* is the bestowing of that bird's triune powers: one foot in the *mud*, a *body* above water, and the *ability to soar above it all*. These qualities relate to alchemy, astrology, and theurgy. The Egyptian word *tehu* stems from *tekh*, meaning "weight," which was represented by the symbol of a heart. As such, Thoth was known as the *Heart of Ra* along with other *Hermetic* names like *The Lord of the Divine Books* and *Scribe of the Company of the God*.

This *hermetic* tradition is dated, at least, to pre-dynastic Egypt, perhaps even before, with some speculating on its origins during the mythical age of Atlantis. The most significant of *hermetic* texts beyond the *Coptic Hermetic* of Nag Hammadi is the *Corpus Hermeticum*, a collection of Greco-Egyptian writings. They include seventeen treatises and are written as a dialogue between Hermes, Nous, Asclepius, Tat, Ammon, and Agathodaimon. One of the few remaining texts is referred to as *Poimandres*, the *Good Shepard* or *Man-Shepard*, a name given to the character *Nous*, which means "mind" or "evasive." Marlene Bremner explains in her <u>Hermetic Philosophy and Creative Alchemy</u> this *hermetic* history, confirming much of what we have explored thus far. She summarizes the *Definitions of Hermes Trismegistus to Asclepius*, wherein the three cosmological structures of God, Cosmos, and Man are described:

> "God is intelligible, immovable, and invisible good that permeates the visible world. Cosmos is the visible and sensible world, and within the sensible world is Man, the destructible and reasonable world, visible and dependent on the invisible for its being."

Just as we find a triune nature in the *Great Evils* known as ignorance, superstition, and fear, and in the intellectual, spiritual, and material suns, we find that humans have three bodies: *"intelligible (soul), animated (spirit), and material (body),"* according to the *Definitions of Hermes*.

Our mortal and immortal aspects reside within the above and below: within the *above* rational that is *"beyond the influence of the fate spheres, or planetary energies and their attendant daimons,"* and within the *below* world *"driven and shaped by the tyranny of the daimons."*

In another *hermetic* treatise, *Asclepius* (meaning *Perfect Sermon* or *Perfect Discourse*), we are taught by Trismegistus that ALL things are ONE, and within and without each other. Bremner summarizes here:

> "One is All, and All is One; that the Cosmos is One, its Soul is One, and God is One; that the Cosmos consists of the Four Elements – Fire, Water, Earth, and Air; that Heaven rules all bodies; and the Sun and Moon are responsible for all growth and waning."

Hermes is famously known as *Thrice Great* for, among other reason, he knew the wisdom of alchemy, astrology, and theurgy, or the operations of the sun, stars, and gods. This triune knowledge remains *hermetically sealed* from the uninitiated. Adonis, the Greek god of beauty and rebirth, shares a similar name in that of *Thrice-Lamented Adonis*, and the Hindu god Vishnu is said to have measured the world *"thrice setting down his footstep, widely striding."* The universal *Holy Trinity* is obviously applicable here too. *Hermes Trismegistus* literally means *Thrice Great Hermes*.

Smaragdine Tablet

The *Emerald Tablet*, also known as *Smaragdine Table* or *Tabula Smaragdine*, of Hermes-Thoth Trismegistus has been published in so many forms it is difficult to keep track. From full books to sets of commandments, it has become a cornerstone of New Age movements and pseudo-spiritual cults. Its earliest edition comes from the *Leyden Papyrus* discovered in the tomb of an anonymous magician in Thebes, Egypt, in 1828. But the history is richer than such anonymity implies. Bremner explains how the *Emerald Tablet* was originally discovered by Alexander the Great in the tomb of "Hermes" around 331 BCE. Alexander, who had visited the Oracle of Zeus-Ammon (Oracle at Siwa), felt compelled to facilitate a promulgation of the tablet under his pronouncement as "son of Ammon" or "son of Zeus." Said to be made of "green, glass-like material" the *Tabula Smaragdina* was reportedly put on display in Heliopolis, city of the sun. Little is known about what happened to this priceless piece of history, which no doubt has taken on a life and mythos of its own no matter its true origin. Some believe the tablet was hidden within an underground cavern with other "sacred items" in modern turkey (Cappadocia). Bremner explains how it was *"rediscovered by Balinas (born 16 CE), known as Apollonius of Tyana, who brought it to Alexandria, where it was kept in the Great Library after his death in 98 CE."* Perhaps it is concealed within our very nature, like all the books of Hermes-Thoth, and like the Sphinx guarding sacred wisdom, it is to be found in the hidden *Middle Chamber*, which is not a location to found on a map. Continuing on her tablet discourse, Bremner documents that the *"earliest version of the Tabula Smaragdina (Emerald Tablet) is found within an eighth-century text attributed to the Muslim alchemist Jabir ibn Hayyan (ca. 721-815)…"* That text is known as *Book of the Secret of Creation and the Art of Nature*. As an alchemical document, sacred to the enlightened of Europe and the Arab world, its "emerald" quality signifies its relationship to the symbolism of that gemstone, which represents *truth* and *love*. Here is one simplified version of the text:

1) *Truth! Certainty! That which there is no doubt*

2) *That which is above is from that which is below, and that which is below is from that which is above, working the miracles of one.*

3) *As all things were from one.*

4) *Its father is the sun and its mother the Moon*

5) *The Earth carried it in her belly, and the Wind nourished it in her belly, as Earth which shall become fire.*

6) *Feed the Earth from that which is subtle, with the greatest power.*

7) *It ascends from the earth to the heaven and becomes ruler over that which Is above and that which is below.*

8) *And I have already explained the meaning of the whole of this in two of these books of mine.*

Provided here is a lengthier description of what was concealed in the great hermetically sealed work of Hermes-Thoth:

"Tis true, without falsehood, and most real: that which is above is like that which is below, to perpetrate the miracles of One thing. And as all things have been derived from one, by the thought of one, so all things are born from this thing, by adoption. The Sun is its Father, the Moon is its Mother. Wind has carried it in its belly, the Earth is its nurse. Here is the father of every perfection in the world. His strength and power are absolute when changed into earth; thou wilt separate the earth from fire, the subtle from the gross, gently and with care. It ascends from earth to heaven, and descends again to earth to receive the power of the superior and the inferior things. By this means, though wilt have the glory of the world. And because of this, all obscurity will flee from thee. Within this is the power, most powerful of all powers. For it will overcome all subtle things, and penetrate every solid thing. Thus the world was created. From this will be, and will emerge, admirable adaptions of which the means are here. And for this reason, I am called Hermes Trismegistus, having the three parts of the philosophy of the world. What I have said of the Sun's operations is accomplished."

The **Emerald Tablet** from Heinrich Khunrath's <u>Amphitheatrum Sapientiae
Aeternae, Solius Verae</u>, Hannover, 1609.

Manly Hall describes the tablet as introducing Chiram Abiff, "the hero of Masonic legend."
The first two large words on the plate indicate *the secret work,* while the second line of letters
"CHIRAM TELAT MECHASOT" means *"Chiram, the Universal Agent, one in Essence, but three in
aspect."* Hall quotes in his <u>The Lost Keys of Freemasonry</u> a rare, unpublished manuscript on the
masonic and hermitic mysteries of *Chiram* as the *Universal Agent*:

> *The sense of this Emerald Tablet can sufficiently convince us that the author was well acquainted with
> the secret operations of Nature and with the secret work of the philosophers (alchemists and
> Hermetists). He likewise well knew and believed in the true God. It has been believed for several ages
> that Cham, one of the sons of Noah, is the author of this monument of antiquity. A very ancient author,
> whose name is not known, who lived several centuries before Christ, mentions this tablet, and says
> that he had seen it in Egypt, at the court; that it was a precious stone, an emerald, whereon these
> characters were represented in bas-relief, not engraved. He states that it was in his time esteemed over
> two thousand years old, and that the matter of this emerald had once been in a fluidic state like melted
> glass, and had been cast in a mold, and that to this flux the artist had given the hardness of a natural
> and genuine emerald, by (alchemical) art.*

The Canaanites were called the Phoenicians by the Greeks, who have told us that they had Hermes for one of their kings. There is a definite relation between Chiram and Hermes. Chiram is a word composed of three words, denoting the Universal Spirit, the essence whereof the whole creation does consist, and the object of Chaldean, Egyptian, and genuine natural philosophy, according to its inner principles or properties. The three Hebrew words *Chamah, Rusch,* and *Majim,* mean respectively Fire, Air, and Water, while their initial consonants, *Ch, R, M,* give us *Chiram,* that invisible essence which is the father of earth, fire, air and water; because, although immaterial in its own invis ible nature as the unmoved and electrical fire, when moved it becomes light and visible; and when collected and agitated, becomes heat and visible and tangible fire; and when associated with humidity it becomes material. The word *Chiram* has been metamorphosed into Hermes and also into Herman, and the translators of the Bible have made Chiram by changing Chet into He; both of these Hebrew word signs being very similar.

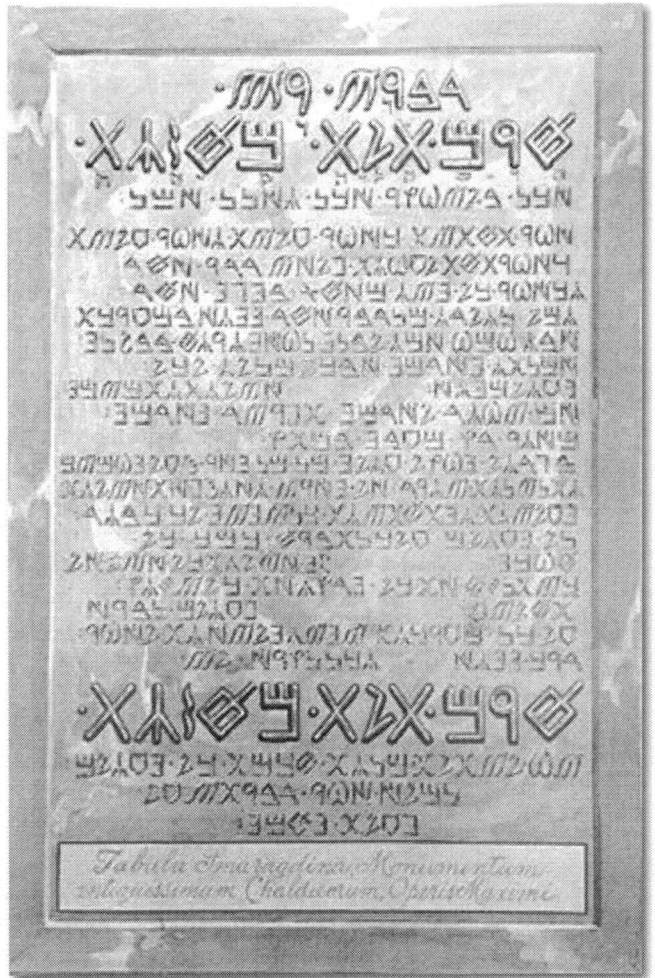

The Emerald Tablet of Hermes, from Manly Hall's <u>The Lost Keys of Freemasonry</u>.

In the word Hermaphrodite, (a word invented by the old philosophers), we find Hermes changed to Hern, signifying Chiram, or the Universal Agent, and Aphrodite, the passive principle of humidity, who is also called Venus, and is said to have been produced and generated by the sea.

We also read that Hiram (Chiram), or the Universal Agent, assisted King Solomon to build the temple. No doubt as Solomon possessed wisdom, he understood what to do with the corporealized Universal Agent. The Talmud of the Jews says that King Solomon built the temple by the assistance of Shamir. Now this word signifies the sun, which is perpetually collecting the omnipresent, surrounding, electrical fire, or Spiritus Mundi, and sending it to us in the planets, in a visible manner called light. This electrical flame, corporealized and regenerated into the Stone of the Philosophers, enabled King Solomon to produce the immense quantities of gold and silver used to build and decorate his temple.

As translated by John Everard, the hermetic text <u>Divine Pymander</u> provides us with an introduction by Hargrave Jennings on the more historically accepted legend of Hermes:

> *"In a treatise attributed to Albertus Magnus, we are told that the tomb of Hermes was discovered by Alexander the Great in a cave near Hebron. In this was found a slab of emerald, which had been taken, from the hands of the dead Hermes, by 'Sarah, the wife of Abraham,' and which had inscribed upon it, in Phoenician characters, the precepts of the great master concerning the art of making gold. This inscription consisted of thirteen sentences, and is to be found in numerous alchemical works."*

Alchemy in Genesis

Aristotle said of the of the *mystery* traditions: *"The initiates had not to learn, but to experience."* Therefore, their understanding was derived from dedication and study rather than a parlor trick. And so, as Hall famously said: *"wisdom is not bestowed, it is achieved."* We may then add that with proper preparation, study, and learned experience, a magician may *"have the glory of the world."*

Zosimos (Zosimus), a Greek historian, maintained that knowledge of metals, stones, scents, colors, etc., dated to the early days of Genesis, as we also alluded to earlier regarding animals and astrology. As per the tablet, these corresponding things *"receive the power of the superior and the inferior things."* Zosimus speaks of an early master of alchemy known as Chemes, author of <u>Chema</u>, a book supposedly used to provide teaching lessons to the daughters of man. The word-name "Chemes" comes from many sources including the Greek word for chemistry, or *chemeia*, meaning "cast together." From Latin we get *alchymicus*, meaning "alchimia" or "alchemy." The word *chemical* is derived from the French *chimique*, which is also rooted in *alchemy*. In fact, just as astronomy is derived from astrology, chemistry is derived from alchemy – especially from the work of Arab physician and alchemist Al-Razr. The term is also rooted in the Arabic *Al* and Greek *Khemia*, a word used to describe the black land of Egypt – thus, *Al-Khemia*, the Black Art. Part of the history of this practice involves correspondences and mixtures of stones and metals. What we can discern from the name Chemes, therefore, is that this was certainly not a real person, and the persona is more akin to Hermes Trismegistus, a composite character. When Zosimus informs us that <u>Chema</u> was used to teach the *daughters of man*, we are to finally understand a greatly misunderstood Biblical passage. Genesis 6:2 has been interpreted to mean everything from extraterrestrial aliens to angelic rape, while its true meaning is openly concealed. The "sons of God" are emanations of the *Celestial Mind*, and the "daughters of men" are those female personas of the Universal Mother, i.e., the Greek goddess Sofia, goddess of wisdom, or who the Kabbalists call *Ain Sof*, the *infinite*. When the "sons" took the "daughters" as "wives" we are to understand that they engaged in a cosmic *hieros gamos*, or sacred alchemical marriage. The children born from this spiritual intercourse, those "men of renown," are the "sons of man," also called the "sons of God," or "suns of God." These are the sons and daughters of the *widow* Isis and comprise the greatest intellectuals throughout human history. In other words, God shed his graces on man through the angels, those powerful celestial forces like Hermes-Thoth, that taught him the alchemical *mysteries*. We read in Genesis 6:1-2 a reminder of this: *"And it came to pass, when men began to multiply on the face of the earth, and daughters were born unto them, that the sons of God saw the daughters of men that they were fair; and they took them wives of all which they chose."* Olivier Dufault writes also in his book <u>Early Greek Alchemy, Patronage and Innovation in Late Antiquity</u>: *"Contemporary papyri (from Nag Hammadi) as well as Gnostic and Hermetic literature suggest that processes meant to change the color of textiles, stones and metals served as a metaphor for the transformation of the self in the third century…"*

Back to Egypt

There is one interesting hermetic manuscript produced by a priestess named Isis, addressing Horus, her son, and declaring that her knowledge also came from *Anael*, first of the angels and prophets. This is also how Enoch acquired his wisdom. From these names, which are obviously symbolic, Kurt Seligmann wrote:

> *"Everything relating to alchemy, however, leads us back constantly to Egypt."*

Ouroboros (One is All), from Cleopatra's Chrysopeia.

Another alchemy pseudonym was Mary the Jewess, a Greek, who was identified by Zosimus with Miriam, the sister of Moses. Another was named Cleopatra, who titled her book Chrysopeia (Gold Making). Zosimus dedicated his own book to Imhotep, a high priest at Heliopolis and the supposed architect of stepped pyramids. In Cleopatra's Chrysopeia we find the serpent consuming its own tail surrounding the axiom: *One is All*. Here we are reminded of the Kybalion and one of the seven hermetic principles called *mentalism*: all Creation is expressed from the All. The usage of an ouroboros as an alchemical symbol is derived partly from a Gnostic sect known as the Ophites. Their name comes from the Greek word *ophis*, which appropriately means "serpent." Ophites worshiped the serpent, holding a different interpretation of its role in the Garden. Their belief maintained how the serpent directed man towards knowledge that could be used as a weapon against Iadalbaoth, the false god. Most Gnostic sects agreed that creation was not the work of the highest God but instead that of the *demiourgos* or *demiurge*. Also called Iadalbaoth, he was created in error by Sophia, who sent a serpent to encourage man to eat from the *Tree of Knowledge* where this *demiurge* had placed a *restriction*. The wisdom acquired from a bite of the sacred apple, i.e., *realization*, allowed man to wage a battle with his material creator. In realizing their nudity, Adam and Eve recognized *birth*, when the soul descends into flesh and is nailed to the spinal cross. Genesis 3:7 explains just that: *"Then the eyes of both of them were opened, and they realized they were naked."*

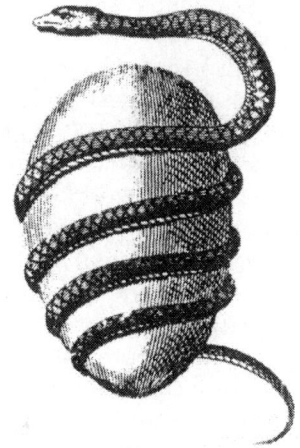

Orphic Egg, from Jacob Bryant's An Analysis of Ancient Mythology.

The serpent can be seen in the opposing forces of *caduceus*, which very well may represent the building blocks of life. The Greeks personified DNA and *creation* as the god Phanes, who was surrounded by the zodiac and with serpents wrapped around his body inside the *Cosmic Egg*. This is ouroboros and the *Orphic Egg*. It features prominent in Egyptian, Buddhist, Polynesian, and Indian mythology, among others. The Chandogya Upanishad explains genesis as such: *"In the beginning this world was merely non-being. It was existent. It developed. It turned into an egg. It lay for the period of a year. It was split asunder. One of the two eggshell parts became silver, one gold. That which was of silver is the earth. That which was of gold is the sky."* These are the silver and gold ages and the keys of St. Peter. Just as mRNA carries messages in the body, Hermes-Mercury, with his staff and writing utensil, carries those messages between heaven and earth. Hermes Trismegistus carries the same staff.

Solve Et Coagula & Prima Materia

True *alchemy* is the transmutation of man as preserved in the metaphors and allegories of metal. Mediaeval and Renaissance alchemists taught that children were far more able to transmute lead into gold than adults, because the child maintains a certain form of innocence. Adults find it increasingly difficult to obtain the *Philosopher's Stone* until one day, later in life, and close to death, they realize the childlike meaning of life once more. And lo and behold, there in their mind was the "stone" the entire time! As with death all things must break down to be reborn like a phoenix. This is the meaning of *solve et coagula*, meaning "to dissolve and coagulate." Elements must be broken down and mixed for transformation to occur, a fact that makes cooking an act of magic and alchemy.

Alchemical philosophers say the *prima materia*, or primitive formless base of all things, needed for this work can be found in all the corners of the world, but it is trampled by the profane. Paracelsus writes of this material how *"the poor have more of it than the rich. The good part of it people discard, and the bad part they retain. It is visible and invisible, children play with it…"* There are many interpretations of this but one of the simplest is *soul* itself, reminding us of the books of Hermes-Thoth which are hidden *"for every one whose foot shall tread the plains of this land."*

Hermes Trismegistus in all his wisdom.

Homunculus & Putrefaction

Abraham Lambsprinck, author of <u>The Treatise of the Philosopher's Stone</u> (*On the Philosopher' Stone*), summarized with one word the allegory of how chemically treated mercury changes color: *putrefaction*. In alchemy the first state is *decay*; the dragon, or mercury, must be killed. From this *putrefaction* certain magical beings, as relates Paracelsus, are then generated. A *homunculus*, or "little man," is a child created through the process of shutting certain alchemic, or *spagyric*, substances in a glass vessel and allowing them to putrefy for forty days in horse manure. After this period, it is written that a living being will begin stirring in the container. It will be like a man, but transparent and without a body. We are to feed him the "arcanum" of human blood for forty weeks while he remains in the artificial womb. At the end of such an operation a living child is said to emerge, but smaller than those generated through physical sexual intercourse. This no doubt is another seemingly absurd story concealing a deeper spiritual reality. The putrefaction is the death that comes in old age. The horse manure is the body and all those pollutions which cause it to decay.

The "arcanum" of human blood fed to the *homunculus* for forty weeks while it remains in the artificial womb is likened to the "arcana," or the *mysteries*, which feed that *little child inside us*. The body itself is the vessel. Not only is *"the kingdom of god… within you,"* but so is the *Philosopher's Stone* and *homunculus!*

The forty days of concealment and forty weeks of feeding relate to several things: there were forty days between Christ's crucifixion and his ascension into the heavens; the probation period in the *mysteries*, the same for Voodoo leaders, was forty days; and as we read in Matthew 4 of Jesus being tempted:

> *Then Jesus was led by the Spirit into the wilderness to be tempted by the devil. After fasting forty days and forty nights, he was hungry. The tempter came to him and said, 'If you are the Son of God, tell these stones to become bread.' Jesus answered, 'It is written: 'Man shall not live on bread alone, but on every word that comes from the mouth of God'.*

> *Then the devil took him to the holy city and had him stand on the highest point of the temple. 'If you are the Son of God', he said, 'throw yourself down. For it is written: 'He will command his angels concerning you, and they will lift you up in their hands, so that you will not strike your foot against a stone'.*

> *Jesus answered him, 'It is also written: Do not put the Lord your God to the test'.*

> *Again, the devil took him to a very high mountain and showed him all the kingdoms of the world and their splendor. 'All this I will give you,' he said, 'if you will bow down and worship me'.*

> *Jesus said to him, 'Away from me, Satan! For it is written: 'Worship the Lord your God, and serve him only'.*

> *Then the devil left him, and angels came and attended him.*

Alkalizing Alchemical Salt

Accompanying the famous stone was also an all-dissolvent liquid, the *alkahest*, mentioned first by Paracelsus, who wrote:

> *"There is also the spirit alkahest, which acts very efficiently upon the liver; it sustains, fortifies, and preserves form the diseases within its reach… Those who want to use such medicine must know how the alkahest is prepared."*

The Belgian doctor Jean Baptiste Van Helmont, who helped the alkahest gain more popular consideration, expanded on this reference. He called it a wonder medicine, adding:

> *"It is a salt, most blessed and most perfect of all salts; the secret of its preparation is beyond human comprehension and God alone can reveal it to the chosen."*

Adepts of alchemy tended towards the *alkahest* being an anagram. Johann Rudolf Glauber, who discovered sodium sulphate, or Glauber salt, thus used the word *alkali*. This is a chemical compound that neutralizes acids. We know today that salt itself is the most important component in alkalizing the body. Proper salt intake regulates pH balance and water content. Turning our attention to the world of medicine in the 20th-century, we find the work of Dr. Otto Warburg. He won the 1931 Nobel Prize in Physiology for the discovery (rediscovery?) that diseases such as cancer were contributed to, or even caused by, weakened cell respiration due to a lack of oxygen in cells. He wrote, "*...every single person who has cancer has a pH that is too acidic.*" Adding, "*...there is no disease whose prime cause is better known so that today ignorance is no longer an excuse.*" Dr. Otto Warburg may have coined the term *homeostasis*, meaning *balance*, but the concept of living a balanced lifestyle is one of the oldest philosophies associated with *the secret teachings* of the philosophers. It involves a balancing of mind and body in thoughts, actions, and emotions. *Mystery Schools* typically required abstinence from alcohol, certain foods like meat, coitus, and even social interactions in general for a period of time. They demanded piety, seclusion, dedication, and secrecy.

Hippocrates (460-375 BCE) and the ancient Greeks thought health to be a state of harmonious balance while disease was the result of disharmony. Aristotle (384-322 BCE) also believed health was based on balance. Another Greek philosopher named Epicurus (341-270 BCE) wrote about psychological stress and suggested that a person's quality of life was improved by coping with emotional stressors. Eastern philosophers from India also came to similar conclusions about balance and health as early as 120 AD. In a general medical text called Caraka from India, health was said to be the result of a balancing of bodily elements known as *dhatus*, along with a happy mental state called *prasana*. Caraka is close to the Sanskrit *cakra*, or what we call *chakra*, meaning wheel or circle. If the energy flowing through these wheels is heavy or stuck it is said that sickness results.

Making the Fixed Volatile

How can such perfection of body-mind-soul-spirit be obtained? Adepts answer: "*Make the fixed volatile – unite the fugitive female with the fixed male.*" The "fixed" is *mercury* and *male*. The "volatile" is *evaporating mercury* and *female*. Mixing the "volatile" female, or "fugitive," with the "fixed male" produces *perfection*. The result of this *hieros gamos* is the *Universal Androgyne* that we have met throughout this work as Adam-Eve, Rebis and Baphomet. As Elphias Levi wrote: "*Generation is in fact a work of the human androgyne; in their division man and woman remain sterile.*"

Woodcut of a winged sun hovering above a sepulchre filled with water, from Rosary of the Philosophers, Frankfurt, 1550.

The Unicorn Elixir

Occult author Abraham Lambsprinck here describes the *unicorn* and *deer* within the forest home of the *hermetic dragon*. The unicorn represent *spirit*, the deer is *soul*, and the forest is *body*:

> *The sages say truly*
> *That two animals are in the forest;*
> *One glorious, beautiful, and swift,*
> *A great and strong deer;*
> *The other a unicorn.*
> *They are concealed in the forest,*
> *But happy ill be the man*
> *Who shall capture them.*

The *Philosopher's Stone* and *unicorn* share a few similarities, primarily that they can only be obtained by the humble, worthy, and pure of heart.

The Alchemical Allegory of Body (forest), Spirit (unicorn), and Soul (deer), from
Abraham Lambsprinck's book, <u>On the Philosophers' Stone</u>.

The Hero & the Dragon

The Sages claim that lives in the Woods, A Dragon whose skin is of complete blackness. But if someone cuts off its head, It instantly loses its darkness. And becomes, in a whole, as white as snow.

If you wish to understand this shady spot,
Note that, in disappearing that black color,
Which name is said to be "Crow's Head ",
It appears, readily, its all-white color,
And the thing is called "the Beheaded".

In disappearing that Dark Cloud,
The Wise One rejoice in their heart,
And conceal the fact carefully,
So that no food comes to know

However, they reveal it to their peers and brothers, And write them telling the good news. Only to those who rely on the divine favor, Only to them we reveal the secret of things.

The Alchemical Allegory of the Hero and the Dragon,
from Abraham Lambsprinck's book, <u>On the Philosophers' Stone</u>.

Alchemical Allegory of Putrefaction from Basil Valentine's book <u>Azoth</u>. This woodcut shows the warm and cold winds with the sun, moon, and planets overhead. The body raises its head to heaven as the black raven removes the flesh from its bones. The soul and mind, seen above as white birds, have left the body with a final breath. This imagery reminds us of the Egyptian KA, BA, and AKH, of which the BA, or the mobility of the soul after death, is symbolized by a bird.

The Homunculus or *Little Man*. His manufacture is a magical art that involving putrefaction of select alchemic substances iin a vessel, itself put in horse manure for forty days, until a transparent body takes form. After being fed with blood for forty weeks further, a small child emerges requiring great care. This is not to be taken literally.

Hermes-Thoth standing on the back of Typhon, symbolizing *universal wisdom* mastering or slaying the *beast-dragon*, which is indicative of ignorance, perversion, deceit, desire, and death. Typhon is the devourer of souls, like the "eater of the dead", symbolic of the physical world, which consumes the spiritual nature of mankind. Hermes is seen carrying a caduceus staff with entwined serpents and a winged disc at the top. This is the staff of Mercury and emblematic of the movements of the sun and possibly literal DNA. Hermes is also to be identified with the Grand Masonic Master CHiram Abiff and the mercury of the alchemists. In his right hand is the *Emerald Tablet* inscribed with the raised letters of the total sum of philosophy. Above Hermes is an ibis with curved bill. The Egyptians depicted Thoth with the body of a man and the head of this bird. The dog perhaps plays reference to the animal nature of man present on *The Fool* tarot card. Or it represents Anubis and the other various dog or jackal creatures that are present in the underworld myths from various cultures. In Egypt, that dog is Anubis. In Welsh myth, the Annwn also has its hounds of hell. The Greek Hecate and her black guide dogs can be found at crossroads. There is also Cerberus and the hounds of Hades.

From Manly Hall's <u>The Secret Teachings of All Ages.</u>

Apollonius of Tyana & Lamia

Apollonius of Tyana was an ancient Greek Pythagorean Philosopher. Upon returning from a trip to India, goes one story, he ventured through Greece, stopping in Athens, Ephesus, and Corinth, where, according to his biographer, another philosopher named Philostratus, he met a vampire. This story is derived from the *Life of Apollonius of Tyana*, a text composed of eight books written in ancient Greek.

A youthful student named Menippus, who possessed only a cloak, followed Apollonius on his journey. A rumor had circulated from friends that there was a very wealthy and beautiful woman desperate to make him her husband, despite their social ranks. She was a Phoenician and Menippus was elated to hear of her love and to make her his wife, for he loved her deeply too.

He invited his master to be a guest of honor at the wedding breakfast, but Apollonius held reservations, citing intuitive impending danger for his disciple. Apollonius agreed to attend despite this and announced that he was, only for this special occasion, to break his habit of abstinence from expensive meal

Alchemist carrying the lantern of the hermit,
by Michael Majer, 1687.

The alchemists is in pursuit of *nature*, here personified as a woman. In following her tracks, he is on a path to perfection of the soul.

and drink. Arriving at the wealthy bride's home he sent to make her acquaintance, but in looking her over, turned to his disciple inquiring as to whom owned the numerous silver and gold containers and decorations in the banquet hall. Menippus insured they belonged to the woman, *"for this is all I possess,"* he said, referring to his cloak. In response, Apollonius said, *"All this adornment is not reality but semblance, and thy fine and dainty bride is not a mortal but a vampire, a Lamia."*

These creatures were mythical monsters with the body of a serpent and head of a woman, or the body of a woman and head of a serpent. Apollonius went on to explain how *"these beings are devoted to the delights of Aphrodite, but still more to devouring human flesh."* In other words, they are like a succubus. The wealthy bride protested in a diatribe against philosophers and then demanded Apollonius leave her home, for he was now unwelcome. But the master instead grabbed a silver goblet from the table and felt for its weight, determining that it was virtually weightless like a feather. The goblet then vanished along with the plates and other vessels. So too did the servants and cooks fall to dust when Apollonius spoke a certain imprecation (curse), and then the house likewise vanished. In anguish, the vampire begged for relief and was forced to confess her plan to fatten and

devour Menippus, for *"it was her habit to feed upon young and beautiful bodies, because their blood is pure and strong."*

We shall extract from this story meaning pertaining to our study of all matters mundane, occult, and arcane. For the promise of various riches or worldly love and happiness are as weightless as the silver goblets and rich vessels adorning the tables at the wedding breakfast. The beautiful structures of *matter* are but illusions like Lamia's house. Let us not be subdued by these sirens seeking to devour our flesh by *delusions of grandeur*. We must slay the alchemical dragon and then we will find the *stone* of the philosopher where it has been hidden in the most perfect and secure location.

~ LONG HAS THOU DWELT IN DARKNESS, QUIT THE NIGHT AND SEEK THE DAY! ~

Apollonius of Tyana with his disciple Menippus. He exposed the youth's beautiful and wealthy bride as a flesh-eating vampire, or Lamia. Published in <u>The Mirror of Magic.</u>

Masonic Symbolism

Freemasonry refers to a fraternal organization that adheres to no religion but still requires its members to maintain belief in a *Supreme Authority*. Masons call this power GAOTU: or Grand Architect of the Universe. Also known as the Craft, masons employ certain symbols to conceal a *hidden truth*, or the *key of the master mason*, also found in various religious texts like the Bible. Understanding of these symbols and stories may change and compound as one climbs the ladder of degrees. Many masonic legends are allegorical, the foundational account being of Chiram Abiff, who is often confused with Hiram of Tyre, the man king Solomon fetched to assist in the building of his temple. But Hiram of Tyre was indeed a mason, and thus, as 1 Kings 7:14 says, he was "a widow's son." As for Chiram Abiff, or Hiram of Abif, he is associated with Hermes Trismegistus, making him a composite character. Of all the symbolic elements of masonry there are some more famous than others, including the degrees themselves, pillars, hoodwinks, the square and compass, the apron, and the coffin. Some believe the *first major lodge* dates to 1717 when four London Lodges merged and declared themselves a Grand Lodge. The Order, however, is much older, at least by the Biblical account just mentioned, even if this were the first official Grand Lodge in the modern world. Freemasons, a term referring to contracted stone masons, i.e., those *free* to find employment, may use the phrases, codes, and symbols of stone masons, especially the hand gestures and rough ashlar, but the true masonic fraternity is one of symbolism. This is especially true so far as these masonic symbols relate to the mind, body, and community.

~

The first Master Mason was said to be, according to Genesis 4:22, *"Tubal-Cain, who forged all kinds of tools out of bronze and iron."* We recall here also what Helena Blavatsky said of the prophet Enoch, who *"fearing that the real and precious secrets would be lost, concealed before the Deluge in the bowels of the Earth"* the foundational elements of masonry. Despite the correlations made between masonry and various groups, secret societies, priestly classes, etc., of antiquity, the word itself is derived from *maçonner*, meaning "to make" or "to build."

There are two forms of masonry: esoteric and exoteric. The esoteric tradition is comprised of ritualistic work designed for the initiated only. The exoteric tradition is what has been deemed suitable of the uninitiated public. Albert G. Mackey confirms this in his book The History of Freemasonry:

> *"The historical statement relates to the Institution as we look at it from an exoteric or public point of view; the traditional refers only to its esoteric or secret character."*

The All-Seeing Eye is not only the one Horus gave to his father Osiris, or the one Odin removed to obtain wisdom, but also the sun which gives us light to see, and all the stars above, and thus "the eyes" mentioned in Proverbs 15:3, which reads:

> *"The eyes of the Lord are everywhere, keeping watch on the wicked and the good."*

The altar was used in various religions of antiquity by priests and commoners to honor God. From the works of Albert G. Mackey, as preserved in various Masonic Bibles, including the A. J. Holman edition, we learn the purpose of the masonic altar: *"to pass around the Altar in the course of the sun, that is to say, from the east, by way of the south, to the west, singing hymns of praise to Deity as part of their worship."*

COMPASSES, PLACED IN A LODGE OF ENTERED APPRENTICES, "BOTH POINTS COVERED BY THE SQUARE."

COMPASSES PLACED IN A LODGE OF FELLOW CRAFT MASONS, "ONE POINT ELEVATED ABOVE THE SQUARE."

COMPASSES, PLACED IN A LODGE OF MASTER MASONS, "BOTH POINTS ELEVATED ABOVE THE SQUARE."

Each degree, inducing the first three, is a successive step in the advancement toward reaching the sublime.

The Blue Lodge represents the first three degrees of masonry: Entered Apprentice, Fellowcraft, Master. Blue symbolizes truth. Referencing the same Masonic Bible, *"It is an emblem of universal friendship and benevolence; and instructs us that, in the mind of a Mason, those virtues should be as expansive as the blue arch of Heaven itself."* We also read in 2 Corinthians 5:11 the following:

> *"For we know that if the earthly tent we live in is destroyed, we have a building from God, an eternal house in heaven* [the blue sky], *not built by human hands."*

The cable-tow is a symbol of the candidate's pledge, or oath, that he submits himself to the service of the Craft.

The hoodwink symbolizes secrecy and silence, just ss Harpocrates demands. From this shroud of darkness, the *mysteries* are concealed from profane eyes, those mortal men who hath never "unveiled" Isis. Those who have done so are immortal *children of the widow*, i.e., masonic brothers like Hiram of Tyre.

The lambskin apron, like the white gloves, repents innocence and purity. This fact is derived from 1 Peter 1:18-19, which says:

> *"For you know that it was not with perishable things such as silver or gold that you were redeemed from the empty way of life handed down to you from your ancestors, but with the precious blood of Christ, a lamb without blemish or defect."*

A MASTER MASON'S APRON.

The square, compass, level, and trowel: the *square* represents morality and "squared" thoughts, emotions, and actions; the *compass* traces the temples of mind, body, and nature; the *level* is a symbol of equality and order, the forces holding all things together; the *trowel* is, as Malcom Duncan writes in his book <u>Ritual of Freemasonry</u>:

> *"The trowel is an instrument made use of by operative masons to spread the cement which unites a building into one common mass; but we, as Free and Accepted Masons are taught to make use of it for the more noble and glorious purpose of spreading the cement of brotherly love and affection; that cement which unites us into one sacred band, or society of friends and brothers, among whom no contention should ever exist, but that noble contention, or rather emulation, of who best can work and best agree."*

TROWEL.

The coffin and spade are symbols of *memento mori* of both our own mortality and that of Chiram Abiff, the Grand Master. The spade digs the grave and the coffin holds our earthly vessel.

COFFIN, GRAVE, AND ACACIA.   SPADE.

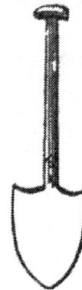

The masonic pillars are Boaz and Jachin. The name Boaz refers to the left-hand pillar of King Solomon's Temple, which represents "strength." The name Jachin is derived from *Jah*, meaning "Jehovah," and *iachin*, meaning "establish." The god Jahbulon, who many are allowed to mistake for wickedness, is the God of Psalm 68:4, which says:

> *"Sing unto God, sing praises to his name: extol him that rideth upon the heavens by his name Jah, and rejoice before him."*

Jah has the same meaning here of Jehovah, but *bulon* or *bulan* means either "hart," which is a deer, or the false idol Baal. Deer are symbols of the soul, so the word could translate to *Jehovah's Soul*, or the *Soul of the World*. Otherwise, it may be correct to assume the name refers to Baal, but Jehovah-Baal would indicate something like the image of Zohar in mystical Judaism, i.e., the reflective white and black God.

Jacob's Ladder is explained by Albert G. Mackey and the Masonic Bible as being that "symbol of progress" with "*its three principle mounds representing Faith, Hope and charity, presenting us with the means of advancing from earth to heaven, from death to life - from mortal to Immortal. Hence its foodie placed on the ground-floor of the Lodge, which is typical of the world, and its top rests on the covering of the Lodge, which is symbolic of heaven.*"

The perfect ashlar is a stone that is truly square. It symbolizes the mind of man, particularly "*at the close of life, after a well-regulate career of piety and virtue, which can only be tried by the square of God's Word, and the compasses of an approving conscience.*"

PERFECT ASHLER.

ROUGH ASHLER.

The Middle Chamber is the resting place of truth and order, like Christ crucified between two thieves, or the twin pillars of Solomon's Temple. The Masonic Bible says that it can be "*reached by ascending that symbolic winding stairway of life, where the symbol only of the Word can be given, where the truth is to be reached by approximation only, and yet where we are to learn that truth will consist of a perfect knowledge of the G.A.O.T.U.,*" i.e., the Grand Architect of the Universe.

The Grand Architect is often symbolized by "geometry" and the "G" even though the original symbol of eternity is Yod, a Hebrew word meaning "arm" or "hand." Its numerical value is ten and so it therefore represents completion and order. The Greek version is the letter Tau, a cross directly associated with Yahweh.

Resurrection is one of the hallmark masonic beliefs. Belief in God and of resurrection to a future life is the cornerstone of the Order. From resurrection we acquire the symbol of the bodily temple. A John 11:25-26 says:

> "*Jesus said to her, 'I am the resurrection and the life. The one who believes in me will live, even though they die; and whoever lives by believing in me will never die. Do you believe this?'*"

The Temple of the Body is an extension of Solomon's Temple, which, according to our same Masonic Bible source, is not a literal structure:

> "*Masonic teachings are not intended to convey an historical fact concerning the erection of a building, but ever to keep in sight, the beauty of that Temple as a symbol of the life in which he should live as a man and Mason.*"

In Joseph Campbell's <u>The Hero With a Thousand Faces</u> he discuss the Navaho mud hut and how its characteristics correspond to the microcosm of man and macrocosm of the universe:

> "*The hogan, or mud hut, of the Navahos of New Mexico and Arizona, is constructed on the plan of the Navaho image of the cosmos. The entrance faces east. The eight sides represent the four direc- tions and the points between. Every beam and joist corresponds to an element in the great hogan of the all-embracing earth and sky. And since the soul of man itself is regarded as identical in form with the universe, the mud hut is a representation of the basic harmony of man and world, and a reminder of the hidden life-way of perfection.*"

John 2:19

"Jesus answered them, 'Destroy this temple, and I will raise it again in three days'."

1 Corinthians 6:19

"Do you not know that your bodies are temples of the Holy Spirit, who is in you, whom you have received from God? You are not your own; you were bought at a price. Therefore honor God with your bodies."

THE THREE RUFFIANS:
THOUGHT——DESIRE——ACTION

These three murderers—perverted thought, uncurbed emotions, and destructive actions—slay the spirit of life in man, and bring down the Temple of Creation in ruins about their own heads. In the Ancient Mysteries woman symbolized the emotional nature of man, typifying emotional excess as one of the slayers of universal energy.

This plate is taken from Hall's book <u>The Lost Keys of Freemasonry</u>, 1923.

For more information on masonry, consult these three books: <u>Duncan's Ritual of Freemasonry</u> by Malcolm Duncan, <u>The History of Freemasonry</u> by Albert Mackey, and <u>The Lost Keys of Freemasonry</u> by Manly Hall.

The Grand Rosicrucian Alchemical Formula by Augustus Knapp incorporates many of the fundamental elements of alchemy and magic into a single image. In the above artwork is expressed the glory of the Godhead and the invisible, or superior, world. The heavenly sphere portrays a diagram of the radiating threefold sun, expressed as the intellectual, spiritual, and physical sun. In the central portion of the upper half circle there are a host of angelic beings surrounding the *Holy Trinity* of a lamb (Son), dove (Holy Ghost), and the Father (God). The glory of God, and the invisible world, is concealed from the *mundane* by the descending dome of the starry heavens, which is itself obscured by clouds. This is the location of many eyes watching over mankind, i.e., stars. The *invisible world* is cut off from the *inferior world* by a line and a half circle encapsulating several astrological and alchemical symbols. Included are five birds, their planetary associations, and their metals, from left to right: crow (Saturn, lead), swan (Jupiter, tin), cock (Mars, Iron), pelican (Venus, copper), and the Phoenix (Mercury, quicksilver).

Above and *below* this section are thinner half circles with various additional elements. Immediately above is a section comprising five signs of the zodiac. In color the circles emanate outward from white to violet, red, orange, yellow and green. In black and white they are read from the inside out. The inner white triangle includes the figure of solar mercury; the violet circle says, *"Four kinds of fire are requisite for the work"*; in the red circle, *"Elementary salt, earthly salt, and central salt"*; the orange, *"Combustible sulphur, fixed sulphur, and volatile, or ethereal, sulphur"*; the yellow, *"The mercury of the sages, corporeal mercury, and common, or visible, mercury"*; and in the green circle, *"The solar year, the stellar year, and the year of winds."*

The *inferior world* is separated into a *nocturnal* scene and a *diurnal* scene. In contrast with each other, one is representative of darkness, water, and the moon, and the other of light, fire and the sun. Although separate, these scenes symbolize the unification of darkness and light, male and female, anima and animus,; the unification of diversity expressed symbolically by the double-headed lion in the center of the image. For although different scenes represent darkness and light, they are part of the same production; although man and woman have different bodies like the lion, they share the same head of a universal androgyny like the *Rebis*. They are primordial parents known as Adam and Eve. Both are attached to the *superior world* by golden chains as also depicted in the Tarot.

In the daytime scene is depicted a rampaging lion, a phoenix above two elemental globes, a burning fire, and a man with symbols of the heavens over his breasts with a star over his regenerative organ. The rampaging lion is spirit, and the bird is a phoenix, which is emblematic of the fire that it is engulfed in at death, only to be regenerated from its own ashes. Below its wings are globes with images of fire and air. The man also stands as a symbol of fire, the active force in contrast with the passive of water. His regenerative nature is covered by a hexagram, a symbol of hermeticism. Below his feet is a burning fire and in his right hand is the sun partly held by the lion. Solar influence is the driving force of creation in all aspects. It is often called *Astral Light*.

In the nocturnal scene is a deer with 12 stars upon its head, an eagle above two elemental globes, a river, and a woman with heavenly symbols over her breasts, and moon over her regenerative organ. The stars express principles of the nocturnal state, those eyes from heaven watching over mankind. The deer symbolizes intuition and soul. Along with the moon and female, the stars on its antlers come from the Egyptian Isis or the Greek Europa, daughter of Phoenix, who was adorned with a crown of the same number of stars. Under the wings of the eagle are two elemental globes with symbols of water and earth. The female stands as a symbol of fluidity, the passive force in contrast with the active of fire. Her regenerative nature is covered by a moon, which is directly related to water and controls the same. Below the woman is a stream of water and in her left hand a full, waxing, and waning moon partly held also by the deer. In the other hand of the deer is a trifoliate leaf symbolic of the threefold division of all things in the natural world. The woman holds grapes in her right hand identical to the grapes covering the right breast of the static Isis.

Upon the hill in the center of the image are trees displaying various alchemical symbols. The alchemical philosopher stands in the central foreground of the hill upon the double-bodied lion, much like the *Rebis*, signifying his accomplishment in unifying diverse forces like the caduceus. He is Hermes Trismegistus . His robes are separated into light and dark and display an array of stars that represent the luminous state of this adept. In each hand are maces of illuminated intellect used to destroy the illusions of darkness and light by uniting the two in harmonious balance.

In Conclusion

"We do not particularly care whether Rip van Winkle, Kamar al-Zaman, or Jesus Christ ever actually lived. Their stories are what concern us: and these stories are so widely distributed over the world – attached to various heroes in various lands – that the question of whether this or that local carrier of the universal theme may or may not have been a historical, living man can be of only secondary moment. The stressing of this historical element will lead to confusion; it will simply obfuscate the picture message… The race and stature of the figure symbolizing the immanent and transcendent Universal is of historical, not semantic, moment; so also the sex… Symbols are only the vehicles of communication; they must not be mistaken for the final term, the tenor, of their reference. No matter how attractive or impressive they may seem, they remain but convenient means, accommodated to the understanding. Hence the personality or personalities of God – whether represented in trinitarian, dualistic, or Unitarian terms, in polytheistic, monotheistic, or henotheistic terms, pictorially or verbally, as documented fact or as apocalyptic vision – no one should attempt to read or interpret as the final thing… Wherever the poetry of myth is interpreted as biography, history, or science, it is killed. The living images become only remote facts of a distant time or sky. Furthermore, it is never difficult to demonstrate that as science and history mythology is absurd. When a civilization begins to reinterpret its mythology in this way, the life goes out of it, temples become museums, and the link between the two perspectives is dissolved."

~ Joseph Campbell ~

"The science [of magic] was driven into hiding to escape the impassioned assaults of blind desire; it clothed itself with new hieroglyphics, falsified its intentions, denied its hopes. Then it was that the jargon of alchemy was created, an impenetrable illusion for the vulgar in their greed of gold, a living language only for the true disciple of Hermes."

~ Eliphas Levi (Alphonse Louis Constant) ~

Bibliography

J. E. Cirlot, A Dictionary of Symbols, 1971

J.C. Cooper, An Illustrated Enclyclopaedia of Traditional Symbols, 1987

Adele Nozedar, The Illustrated Signs & Symbols Sourcebook, 2008

Arthur Cotterell & Rachel Storm, The Ultimate Encyclopedia of Mythology, 1999

Helena Petrovna Blavatsky, The Secret Doctrine, 1999 (from 1888 edition)

Eliphas Levi, translated by A. E. Waite, The History of Magic, 1913

Eliphas Levi, translated by A. E. Waite, Transcendental Magic: Its Doctrine and Ritual, 1958

M. A. Atwood, A Suggestive Inquiry into Hermetic Mystery, 1850

William J. Fielding, Strange Superstitions and Magical Practices, 1945

Magus Incognito, The Secret Doctrine of the Rosicrucians, 1967

Louis Jacolliot, translated by William L. Felt, Occult Science in India and among the Ancients, 1971

Graham Hancock, Fingerprints of the Gods, 1995

Graham Hancock, Underworld, 2002

Manly Palmer Hall, The Secret Teachings of All Ages, 1928

Manly Palmer Hall, Lectures on Ancient Philosophy, 1984

Manly Palmer Hall, Words to the Wise, 1964

Manly Palmer Hall, The Secret Destiny of America, 1944

Manly Palmer Hall, The Lost Keys of Freemasonry, 1923

Manly Palmer Hall, Freemasonry of the Ancient Egyptians, 1937

Manly Palmer Hall, Masonic Orders of Fraternity, 1950

Alan Watts, Beyond Theology: The Art of Godmanship, 1964

Alan Watts, The Book, 1967

Francis Barrett, The Magus, 1967 (from 1801 edition)

Jonathan Black, The Secret History of the World, 2008

Jonathan Black, The Sacred History, 2013

Edith Hamilton, Mythology: Timeless Tales of Gods and Heroes, 1942

David Fideler, Jesus Christ: Sun of God, 1993

Pennick, Nigel, Secret Games of the Gods: Ancient Ritual Systems in Board Games, 1989

Lisa Peschel, A Practical Guide to the Runes, 1989

David Conway, Ritual Magic: An Occult Primer, 1978

Louisa Rhine, Hidden Channels of the Mind, 1961

Margaret Cheney, Tesla: A Man out of Time, 2001

G. R. S. Mead, Pistis Sophia, 2005 (from 1851 & 1895 editions)

Janet and Stewart Farrar, A Witches' Bible: The Complete Witches' Handbook, 1981

Willis Barnstone and Marvin Meyer, The Gnostic Bible, 2003

Christopher Knight and Robert Lomas, The Hiram Key, 1996

D. M. Murdock, The Christ Conspiracy: The Greatest Story ever Sold, 1999

Freddy Silva, The Lost Art of Resurrection, 2014

(Edited & Translated by) Peterson, Joseph, Grimorium Verum, 2006
[Originally published by Alibeck the Egyptian in 1517]

(Edited by) Warwick, Tarl, The Greater Key of Solomon, 2015
[Original manuscript from 1750]

(Edited by) Warwick, Tarl, The Grimoire of Pope Honorius, 2015
[Original manuscript from 1760]

(Edited by) Warwick, Tarl, The Grand Grimoire, 2016
[First edition published by Mathers, Samuel in 1914]

Three Initiates, The Kybalion, 2012
[Original publication date unknown]

Seligmann, Kurt, The Mirror of Magic, 2018 [Originally published 1948]

(Edited and Annotated by) Tyson, Donald,
Three Books of Occult Philosophy: The Foundation Book of Western Occultism, 2017 Edition

Robert W. Pelton, Voodoo Secrets From A to Z, 1973

Robert W. Pelton, The Complete Book of Voodoo, 2002

Paul Carus, The Devil and the Idea of Evil, 1899

William Bramley, The Gods of Eden, 1989

Joseph Campbell, The Hero With a Thousand Faces, 1949

Christian Rätsch and Claudia Müller-Ebeling,
Pagan Christmas: The Plants, Spirits, and Rituals at the Origins of Yuletide, 2003

Antony Cummins, The Dark Side of Japan, 2017, Amberley Books

Marlene Bremner, Hermetic Philosophy and Creative Alchemy, 2022, Simon & Schuster

Ono, Sokyo, and Woodward, William, Shinto The Kami Way, 1962, Tuttle Publishing

Yamakage, Motohisa, The Essence of Shinto: Japan's Spiritual Heart, 2012, Kodansha US Publishing

Morrow, Avery, The Sacred Science of Ancient Japan, 2014, Bear & Company Publishing

Cotterell, Arthur, and Storm, Rachel, The Ultimate Encyclopedia of Mythology, 2010, Hermes House Publishing

Foster, Michael, The Book of Yōkai, 2015, University of California Press

Alt, Matt, and Yoda, Hiroko, Japandemonium Illustrated: The Yokai Encyclopedias of Toriyama Sekien, 2016, Dover Publications

H.P. Blavatsky, Isis Unveiled, Vol. II. Theology, 1998, Theosophical University Press

Day, David, An Encyclopedia of Tolkien, 2019, Printers Row Publishing Group, Octopus Publishing Group

Strassman, M.D., Rick, DMT: The Spirit Molecule, 2001, Park Street Press

Ryan Gable is a veteran radio personality and producer for his weeknight show *The Secret Teachings*. His broadcast focuses on the synchronicity and objective analysis of para-politics, pop-conspiracy, para-history and history, the occult (occulture), the paranormal, symbolism, health, anthropology, theology, and etymology. He attempts to use this knowledge to analyze both historical and contemporary events with objective reasoning. Spending much of his life on air, and having written several books,

Ryan has also been a guest on dozens of other radio shows and podcasts, and has had his broadcast aired on a variety of networks - from WPRK and CBS to Dark Matter Radio, LNM, the FringeFM, and Ground Zero Radio. He was a frequent guest on the *Kev Baker Show* until Kev's passing and is now a frequent guest on *Ground Zero* with Clyde Lewis. Despite this success, all achieved with near-zero capital, his broadcast has also been removed from various networks over the years for his refusal to censor content. He has also been banned from attending some conferences for speaking on subjects considered too controversial or for exposing con artists within the industry.

Ryan and *The Secret Teachings* are not aligned with any specific ideology so that they may stay fluid with information as it is unveiled. He holds himself to the same standards and recommendations suggested on air or in his writings, in relation to food or study. This involves an approach to *kaizen*, or the method of always improving. He focuses on critical thinking and objectivity as keys to understanding, utilizing, and appreciating *The Secret Teachings of All Ages*.

His other books are:

Garden of Hallucinations, The Technological Elixir, Liberty Shrugged, Food Philosophy

You can find more information on his website or by email:

www.TheSecretTeachings.info

rdgable@yahoo.com - or - tstradio@protonmail.com

Notes

Made in the USA
Las Vegas, NV
31 January 2025